T0189007

Lecture Notes in Computer Science 13629

Founding Editors

Gerhard Goos
Karlsruhe Institute of Technology, Karlsruhe, Germany

Juris Hartmanis
Cornell University, Ithaca, NY, USA

Editorial Board Members

Elisa Bertino
Purdue University, West Lafayette, IN, USA

Wen Gao
Peking University, Beijing, China

Bernhard Steffen
TU Dortmund University, Dortmund, Germany

Moti Yung
Columbia University, New York, NY, USA

More information about this series at https://link.springer.com/bookseries/558

Sankalp Khanna · Jian Cao · Quan Bai ·
Guandong Xu (Eds.)

PRICAI 2022: Trends in Artificial Intelligence

19th Pacific Rim International Conference on Artificial Intelligence
PRICAI 2022, Shanghai, China, November 10–13, 2022
Proceedings, Part I

 Springer

Editors
Sankalp Khanna 🔟
CSIRO Australian e-Health Research Centre
Brisbane, QLD, Australia

Quan Bai 🔟
University of Tasmania
Hobart, TAS, Australia

Jian Cao 🔟
Shanghai Jiao Tong University
Shanghai, China

Guandong Xu 🔟
University of Technology Sydney
Sydney, NSW, Australia

ISSN 0302-9743   ISSN 1611-3349 (electronic)
Lecture Notes in Computer Science
ISBN 978-3-031-20861-4   ISBN 978-3-031-20862-1 (eBook)
https://doi.org/10.1007/978-3-031-20862-1

© The Editor(s) (if applicable) and The Author(s), under exclusive license
to Springer Nature Switzerland AG 2022
This work is subject to copyright. All rights are reserved by the Publisher, whether the whole or part of the material is concerned, specifically the rights of translation, reprinting, reuse of illustrations, recitation, broadcasting, reproduction on microfilms or in any other physical way, and transmission or information storage and retrieval, electronic adaptation, computer software, or by similar or dissimilar methodology now known or hereafter developed.
The use of general descriptive names, registered names, trademarks, service marks, etc. in this publication does not imply, even in the absence of a specific statement, that such names are exempt from the relevant protective laws and regulations and therefore free for general use.
The publisher, the authors, and the editors are safe to assume that the advice and information in this book are believed to be true and accurate at the date of publication. Neither the publisher nor the authors or the editors give a warranty, expressed or implied, with respect to the material contained herein or for any errors or omissions that may have been made. The publisher remains neutral with regard to jurisdictional claims in published maps and institutional affiliations.

This Springer imprint is published by the registered company Springer Nature Switzerland AG
The registered company address is: Gewerbestrasse 11, 6330 Cham, Switzerland

Preface

These three-volume proceedings contain the papers presented at the 19th Pacific Rim International Conference on Artificial Intelligence (PRICAI 2022), held as a hybrid conference with both physical and online options during November 10–13, 2022, in Shanghai, China.

PRICAI, which was inaugurated in Tokyo in 1990, started out as a biennial international conference concentrating on artificial intelligence (AI) theories, technologies, and applications in the areas of social and economic importance for Pacific Rim countries. It provides a common forum for researchers and practitioners in various branches of AI to exchange new ideas and share experience and expertise. Since then, the conference has grown, both in participation and scope, to be a premier international AI event for all major Pacific Rim nations as well as countries from all around the world. In 2018, the PRICAI Steering Committee decided to hold PRICAI on an annual basis starting from 2019.

This year, we received an overwhelming number of valid submissions to the main track (403 submissions), the special track (18 submissions), and the industry track (11 submissions). This number was impressive considering the continuing COVID-19 pandemic situation around the globe. All submissions were reviewed and evaluated with the same highest quality standard through a double-blind review process.

Each paper received at least two reviews, with over 90% receiving three or more. During the review process, discussions among the Program Committee (PC) members in charge were carried out before recommendations were made, and, when necessary, additional reviews were sourced. Finally, the conference and program co-chairs read the reviews and comments and made a final calibration for differences among individual reviewer scores in light of the overall decisions. The entire Program Committee (including PC members, external reviewers, and co-chairs) expended tremendous effort to ensure fairness and consistency in the paper selection process.

Eventually, we accepted 91 regular papers and 39 short papers for oral presentation. This gives a regular paper acceptance rate of 21% and an overall acceptance rate of 30%.

The technical program consisted of three workshops and the main conference program. The workshops included the "Principle and practice of data and Knowledge Acquisition Workshop (PKAW 2022)," the "Decoding Models of Human Emotion Using Brain Signals Workshop", and the "The 1st International Workshop on Democracy and AI (DemocrAI2022)". The main program included an industry track and a special track on "Strong and General AI."

All regular and short papers were orally presented over four days in parallel and in topical program sessions. We were honored to have keynote presentations by four distinguished researchers in the field of AI whose contributions have crossed discipline boundaries: Toby Walsh (University of New South Wales, Australia), Qing Li (Hong Kong Polytechnic University, China), Jie Lu (University of Technology Sydney, Australia), and Yu Zheng (JD Technology, China). We were grateful to them for sharing their insights on their latest research with us.

The success of PRICAI 2022 would not be possible without the effort and support of numerous people from all over the world. First, we would like to thank the authors, PC members, and external reviewers for their time and efforts spent in making PRICAI 2022 a successful and enjoyable conference. We are also thankful to various fellow members of the conference committee, without whose support and hard work PRICAI 2021 could not have been successful:

- Advisory Board: Abdul Sattar, Beyong Kang, Takayuki Ito, Zhihua Zhou, Chengqi Zhang, and Fenrong Liu
- Special Track Chairs: Ji Zhang and Biao Wang
- Industry Chair: Hengshu Zhu
- Workshop Chairs: Ryuta Arisaka and Zehong Cao
- Tutorial Chairs: Weiwei Yuan and Rafik Hadfi
- Finance Chair: Shiyou Qian
- Local/Virtual Organizing Chairs: Shiyou Qian and Nengjun Zhu
- Publicity Chairs: Yi Yang and Mukesh Prasad
- Sponsorship Chairs: Dengji Zhao and Xiangfeng Luo
- Webmaster: Shiqing Wu

We gratefully acknowledge the organizational support of several institutions including the University of Tasmania (Australia), the University of Technology Sydney (Australia), Shanghai Jiao Tong University (China), CSIRO (Australia), Griffith University (Australia), Kyoto University (Japan), ShanghaiTech University (China), the University of South Australia (Australia), Nanjing University of Aeronautics and Astronautics (China), Shanghai University (China), Hefei University of Technology (China), the University of Southern Queensland (Australia), and the Shanghai Computer Society (China). Finally, we thank the team at Springer for their assistance in publishing the PRICAI 2022 proceedings as three volumes of its Lecture Notes in Artificial Intelligence series.

November 2022

Sankalp Khanna
Jian Cao
Quan Bai
Guandong Xu

Organization

PRICAI Steering Committee

Steering Committee

Hideyuki Nakashima (Chair)	Future University Hakodate, Japan
Zhi-Hua Zhou (Vice-chair)	Nanjing University, China
Abdul Sattar (Treasurer)	Griffith University, Australia
Sankalp Khanna (Secretary)	CSIRO Australian e-Health Research Centre, Australia
Quan Bai	University of Tasmania, Australia
Tru Hoang Cao	Ho Chi Minh City University of Technology, Vietnam
Xin Geng	Southeast University, China
Guido Governatori	Singapore Management University, Singapore
Takayuki Ito	Kyoto University, Japan
Fenrong Liu	Tsinghua University, China
Byeong Ho Kang	University of Tasmania, Australia
M. G. M. Khan	University of the South Pacific, Fiji
Dickson Lukose	Monash University, Australia
Abhaya Nayak	Macquarie University, Australia
Seong-Bae Park	Kyung Hee University, South Korea
Duc Nghia Pham	MIMOS Berhad, Malaysia
Alok Sharma	RIKEN, Japan, and University of the South Pacific, Fiji
Thanaruk Theeramunkong	Thammasat University, Thailand

Honorary Members

Randy Goebel	University of Alberta, Canada
Tu-Bao Ho	Japan Advanced Institute of Science and Technology, Japan
Mitsuru Ishizuka	University of Tokyo, Japan
Hiroshi Motoda	Osaka University, Japan
Geoff Webb	Monash University, Australia
Albert Yeap	Auckland University of Technology, New Zealand
Byoung-Tak Zhang	Seoul National University, South Korea
Chengqi Zhang	University of Technology Sydney, Australia

Conference Organizing Committee

General Chairs

Guandong Xu   University of Technology Sydney, Australia
Quan Bai   University of Tasmania, Australia

Program Chairs

Sankalp Khanna   CSIRO Australian e-Health Research Centre,
                                       Australia
Jian Cao   Shanghai Jiao Tong University, China

Special Track Chairs

Ji Zhang   University of Southern Queensland, Australia
Biao Wang   Zhejiang Lab, China

Industry Chair

Hengshu Zhu   Baidu Inc., China

Workshop Chairs

Ryuta Arisaka   Kyoto University, Japan
Zehong Cao   University of South Australia, Australia

Tutorial Chairs

Weiwei Yuan   Nanjing University of Aeronautics and
                                       Astronautics, China
Rafik Hadfi   Kyoto University, Japan

Local and Virtual Conference Chairs

Shiyou Qian   Shanghai Jiao Tong University, China
Nengjun Zhu   Shanghai University, China

Finance Chair

Shiyou Qian   Shanghai Jiao Tong University, China

Sponsorship Chairs

Dengji Zhao   ShanghaiTech University, China
Xiangfeng Luo   Shanghai University, China

Publicity Chairs

Yi Yang   Hefei University of Technology, China
Mukesh Prasad   University of Technology Sydney, Australia

Webmaster

Shiqing Wu   University of Tasmania, Australia

Advisory Board

Abdul Sattar   Griffith University, Australia
Byeong Kang   University of Tasmania, Australia
Takayuki Ito   Kyoto University, Japan
Zhihua Zhou   Nanjing University, China
Chengqi Zhang   University of Technology Sydney, Australia
Fenrong Liu   Tsinghua University, China

Program Committee

Eriko Aiba   University of Electro-Communications, China
Abdullah Alsuhaibani   University of Technology Sydney, Australia
Patricia Anthony   Lincoln University, New Zealand
Mohammad Arshi Saloot   MIMOS Berhad, Malaysia
Mohamed Jaward Bah   Zhejiang Lab, China
Quan Bai   University of Tasmania, Australia
Chutima Beokhaimook   Rangsit University, Thailand
Ateet Bhalla   Independent Technology Consultant, India
Chih How Bong   Universiti Malaysia Sarawak, Malaysia
Poonpong Boonbrahm   Walailak University, Thailand
Aida Brankovic   CSIRO Australian e-Health Research Centre,
                                Australia
Xiongcai Cai   University of New South Wales, Australia
Jian Cao   Shanghai Jiao Tong University, China
Jimmy Cao   University of South Australia, Australia
Tru Cao   University of Texas Health Science Center at
                                Houston, USA
Hutchatai Chanlekha   Kasetsart University, Thailand
Siqi Chen   Tianjin University, China
Songcan Chen   Nanjing University of Aeronautics and
                                Astronautics, China
Tony Chen   University of Adelaide, Australia
Wu Chen   Southwest University, China
Yakun Chen   University of Technology Sydney, Australia

Yingke Chen	Sichuan University, China
Wai Khuen Cheng	Universiti Tunku Abdul Rahman, Malaysia
Yihang Cheng	Tianjin University, China
Boonthida Chiraratanasopha	Yala Rajabhat University, Thailand
Dan Corbett	University of Sydney, Australia
Zhihong Cui	Shandong University, China
Célia da Costa Pereira	Université Côte d'Azur, France
Jirapun Daengdej	Assumption University, Thailand
Abdollah Dehzangi	Rutgers University, USA
Clare Dixon	University of Manchester, UK
Zheng Dong	Baidu Inc., China
Shyamala Doraisamy	Universiti Putra Malaysia, Malaysia
Tri Duong	University of Technology Sydney, Australia
Shanshan Feng	Shandong Normal University, China
Somchart Fugkeaw	Thammasat University, Thailand
Katsuhide Fujita	Tokyo University of Agriculture and Technology, Japan
Naoki Fukuta	Shizuoka University, China
Marcus Gallagher	University of Queensland, Australia
Dragan Gamberger	Rudjer Boskovic Institute, Croatia
Xiaoying Gao	Victoria University of Wellington, New Zealand
Xin Geng	Southeast University, China
Manolis Gergatsoulis	Ionian University, Greece
Alban Grastien	Australian National University, Australia
Charles Gretton	Australian National University, Australia
Jie Gui	University of Michigan, USA
Fikret Gurgen	Boğaziçi University, Turkey
Rafik Hadfi	Kyoto University, Japan
Songqiao Han	Shanghai University of Finance and Economics, China
Bavly Hanna	University of Technology Sydney, Australia
David Hason Rudd	University of Technology Sydney, Australia
Hamed Hassanzadeh	CSIRO Australian e-Health Research Centre, Australia
Tessai Hayama	Nagaoka University of Technology, Japan
Linlin Hou	Zhejiang Lab, China
Juhua Hu	University of Washington, USA
Liang Hu	University of Technology Sydney, Australia
Jiwei Huang	China University of Petroleum, Beijing, China
Xiaodi Huang	Charles Sturt University, Australia
Nguyen Duy Hung	Thammasat University, Thailand
Huan Huo	University of Technology Sydney, Australia

Van Nam Huynh	Japan Advanced Institute of Science and Technology (JAIST), Japan
Masashi Inoue	Tohoku Institute of Technology, Japan
Md Rafiqul Islam	University of Technology Sydney, Australia
Takayuki Ito	Kyoto University, Japan
Sanjay Jain	National University of Singapore, Singapore
Guifei Jiang	Nankai University, China
Ting Jiang	Zhejiang Lab, China
Yichuan Jiang	Southeast University, China
Nattagit Jiteurtragool	King Mongkut's University of Technology North Bangkok, Thailand
Hideaki Kanai	Japan Advanced Institute of Science and Technology (JAIST), Japan
Ryo Kanamori	Nagoya University, Japan
Natsuda Kaothanthong	Thammasat University, Thailand
Jessada Karnjana	National Electronics and Computer Technology Center, Thailand
C. Maria Keet	University of Cape Town, South Africa
Gabriele Kern-Isberner	Technische Universitaet Dortmund, Germany
Nor Khalid	Auckland University of Technology, New Zealand
Sankalp Khanna	CSIRO Australian e-Health Research Centre, Australia
Nichnan Kittiphattanabawon	Walailak University, Thailand
Sébastien Konieczny	CRIL - CNRS, France
Alfred Krzywicki	University of Adelaide, Australia
Li Kuang	Central South University, China
Young-Bin Kwon	Chung-Ang University, South Korea
Ho-Pun Lam	Data61, CSIRO, Australia
Nasith Laosen	Phuket Rajabhat University, Thailand
Siddique Latif	University of Southern Queensland, Australia
Roberto Legaspi	KDDI Research, Inc., Japan
Gang Li	Deakin University, Australia
Guangliang Li	Ocean University of China, China
Qian Li	Chinese Academy of Sciences, China
Tianrui Li	Southwest Jiaotong University, China
Weihua Li	Auckland University of Technology, New Zealand
Yicong Li	University of Technology Sydney, Australia
Zihao Li	University of Technology Sydney, Australia
Chanjuan Liu	Dalian University of Technology, China
Guanfeng Liu	Macquarie University, Australia
Hao Liu	HKUST(GZ), China
Kangzheng Liu	Huazhong University of Science and Technology, China

Tun Lu	Fudan University, China
Dickson Lukose	GCS Agile Pty. Ltd., Australia
Xiangfeng Luo	Shanghai University, China
Haiping Ma	Anhui University, China
Michael Maher	Reasoning Research Institute, Australia
Xinjun Mao	National University of Defense Technology, China
Eric Martin	University of New South Wales, Australia
Sanparith Marukatat	NECTEC, Thailand
Michael Mayo	University of Waikato, New Zealand
Qingxin Meng	Nottingham University Business School, China
Nor Liyana Mohd Shuib	Universiti Malaya, Malaysia
M. A. Hakim Newton	University of Newcastle, Australia
Phi Le Nguyen	Hanoi University of Science and Technology, Vietnam
Kouzou Ohara	Aoyama Gakuin University, Japan
Mehmet Orgun	Macquarie University, Australia
Maurice Pagnucco	University of New South Wales, Australia
Songwen Pei	University of Shanghai for Science and Technology, China
Laurent Perrussel	IRIT, Université de Toulouse, France
Bernhard Pfahringer	University of Waikato, New Zealand
Jantima Polpinij	Mahasarakham University, Thailand
Thadpong Pongthawornkamol	Kasikorn Business-Technology Group, Thailand
Mukesh Prasad	University of Technology, Sydney, Australia
Shiyou Qian	Shanghai Jiao Tong University, China
Chuan Qin	Baidu, China
Joel Quinqueton	LIRMM, France
Teeradaj Racharak	Japan Advanced Institute of Science and Technology, Japan
Jessica Rahman	Australian National University, Australia
Farid Razzak	New York University, USA
Fenghui Ren	University of Wollongong, Australia
Mark Reynolds	University of Western Australia, Australia
Vahid Riahi	CSIRO Australian e-Health Research Centre, Australia
Kazumi Saito	University of Shizuoka, Japan
Chiaki Sakama	Wakayama University, Japan
Nicolas Schwind	National Institute of Advanced Industrial Science and Technology (AIST), Japan
Lin Shang	Nanjing University, China
Alok Sharma	RIKEN, Japan

Dazhong Shen	University of Science and Technology of China, China
Chenwei Shi	Tsinghua University, China
Kaize Shi	University of Technology Sydney, Australia
Zhenwei Shi	Beihang University, China
Soo-Yong Shin	Sungkyunkwan University, South Korea
Yanfeng Shu	CSIRO, Australia
Chattrakul Sombattheera	Mahasarakham University, Thailand
Insu Song	James Cook University, Australia
Markus Stumptner	University of South Australia, Australia
Xing Su	Beijing University of Technology, China
Xin Sun	Catholic University of Lublin, Poland
Ying Sun	The Hong Kong University of Science and Technology (Guangzhou), China
Boontawee Suntisrivaraporn	DTAC, Thailand
Thepchai Supnithi	NECTEC, Thailand
David Taniar	Monash University, Australia
Xiaohui Tao	University of Southern Queensland, Australia
Yanyun Tao	Soochow University, China
Mingfei Teng	Rutgers University, USA
Michael Thielscher	University of New South Wales, Australia
Satoshi Tojo	Japan Advanced Institute of Science and Technology (JAIST), Japan
Shikui Tu	Shanghai Jiao Tong University, China
Miroslav Velev	Aries Design Automation, USA
Muriel Visani	Hanoi University of Science and Technology, Vietnam, and La Rochelle University, France
Nhi N. Y. Vo	Royal Melbourne Institute of Technology University, Vietnam
Biao Wang	Zhejiang Lab, China
Chao Wang	Guangzhou HKUST Fok Ying Tung Research Institute, China
Hao Wang	Nanyang Technological University, Singapore
Xiangmeng Wang	University of Technology, Sydney, Australia
Xinxhi Wang	Shanghai University, China
Zhen Wang	Zhejiang Lab, China
Xiao Wei	Shanghai University, China
Paul Weng	UM-SJTU Joint Institute, China
Yang Wenli	University of Tasmania, Australia
Wayne Wobcke	University of New South Wales, Australia
Sartra Wongthanavasu	Khon Kaen University, Thailand
Brendon J. Woodford	University of Otago, New Zealand

Hongyue Wu	Zhejiang University, China
Ou Wu	Tianjin University, China
Shiqing Wu	University of Technology Sydney, Australia
Xing Wu	Shanghai University, China
Xiaoyu Xia	University of Southern Queensland, Australia
Kaibo Xie	University of Amsterdam, The Netherlands
Dawei Xu	University of Technology Sydney, Australia
Guandong Xu	University of Technology Sydney, Australia
Ming Xu	Xi'an Jiaotong-Liverpool University, China
Shuxiang Xu	University of Tasmania, Australia
Zenghui Xu	Zhejiang Lab, China
Hui Xue	Southeast University, China
Kong Yan	Nanjing University of Information, Science and Technology, China
Bo Yang	University of Science and Technology of China, China
Chao Yang	University of Technology, Sydney, Australia
Haoran Yang	University of Technology Sydney, Australia
Wencheng Yang	University of Southern Queensland, Australia
Yang Yang	Nanjing University of Science and Technology, China
Yi Yang	Hefei University of Technology, China
Roland Yap	National University of Singapore, Singapore
Kenichi Yoshida	University of Tsukuba, Japan
Dianer Yu	University of Technology Sydney, Australia
Hang Yu	Shanghai University, China
Ting Yu	Zhejiang Lab, China
Weiwei Yuan	Nanjing University of Aeronautics and Astronautics, China
Takaya Yuizono	Japan Advanced Institute of Science and Technology (JAIST), Japan
Du Zhang	California State University, USA
Haijun Zhang	Harbin Institute of Technology Shenzhen Graduate School, China
Ji Zhang	University of Southern Queensland, Australia
Le Zhang	University of Science and Technology of China, China
Min-Ling Zhang	Southeast University, China
Qi Zhang	University of Science and Technology of China, China
Shichao Zhang	Guangxi Normal University, China
Wen Zhang	Beijing University of Technology, China
Xiaobo Zhang	Southwest Jiaotong University, China

Xuyun Zhang	Macquarie University, Australia
Yang Zhang	Zhejiang Lab, China
Zili Zhang	Deakin University, Australia
Dengji Zhao	ShanghaiTech University, China
Hongke Zhao	Tianjin University, China
Ruilin Zhao	Huazhong University of Science and Technology, China
Sirui Zhao	Southwest University of Science and Technology, China
Yanchang Zhao	CSIRO, Australia
Shuigeng Zhou	Fudan University, China
Chen Zhu	Baidu Talent Intelligence Center, China
Guohun Zhu	University of Queensland, Australia
Hengshu Zhu	Baidu Inc., China
Nengjun Zhu	Shanghai University, China
Xingquan Zhu	Florida Atlantic University, USA
Guobing Zou	Shanghai University, China

Additional Reviewers

Agyemang, Brighter	Haiyang, Xia	Li, Renjie
Arisaka, Ryuta	Han, Aiyang	Li, Ruijun
Bea, Khean Thye	Hang, Jun-Yi	Li, Shu
Burgess, Doug	He, Yifan	Lin, Shuxia
Cao, Zehong	He, Zhengqi	Liu, Xiaxue
Chalothorn, Tawunrat	Hu, Jianshu	Liu, Yuxin
Chandra, Abel	Hu, Liang	Ma, Zhongchen
Chandra, Rohitash	Hu, Mengting	Malysiak, Kevin
Chen, Siqi	Hu, Yuxuan	Mayer, Wolfgang
Clifton, Marshall	Ishikawa, Yuichi	Meng, Qiang
Colley, Rachael	Jia, Binbin	Mezza, Stefano
Dawoud, Ahmed	Jiang, Shan	Mi, Yuxi
Delobelle, Jérôme	Jiang, Yunpeng	Miao, Ran
Dinh, Thi Ha Ly	Jiang, Zhaohui	Ming, Zuheng
Duan, Jiaang	Khan, Naimat Ullah	Mittelmann, Munyque
Duchatelle, Théo	Kliangkhlao, Mallika	Muhammod, Rafsanjani
Effendy, Suhendry	Konishi, Tatsuya	Ngo, Courtney
Everaere, Patricia	Kumar, Shiu	Nguyen, Mau Toan
Feng, Shanshan	Lai, Zhong Yuan	Nguyen, Minh Hieu
Feng, Xuening	Le, Van An	Nguyen, Trong-Tung
Gao, Jianqi	Leow, Steven	Nguyen, Trung Thanh
Gao, Shang	Li, Jinpeng	Niu, Hao
Gao, Yi	Li, Li	Parker, Timothy
Geng, Chuanxing	Li, Pengbo	Pereira, Gean

Pho, Ngoc Dang Khoa
Pino Perez, Ramon
Polpinij, Jantima
Qian, Junqi
Raboanary, Toky Hajatiana
Rashid, Mahmood
Ren, Yixin
Riahi, Vahid
Rosenberg, Manou
Sahoh, Bukhoree
Selway, Matt
Sharma, Ronesh
Shi, Jingli
Shi, Kaize
Song, Baobao
Song, Zhihao
Sun, Qisong
Sun, Ruoxi
Takeda, Naoto
Tan, Hongwei
Tang, Huaying

Tang, Wei
Tao, Yanyun
Thao Nguyen, Truong
Tran, Kim Dung
Vo, Chau
Wang, Deng-Bao
Wang, Guodong
Wang, Hui
Wang, Mengyan
Wang, Xinyu
Wang, Zirui
Wanyana, Tezira
Wardah, Wafaa
Wu, Yao
Xia, Dawen
Xia, Yewei
Xiangru, Yu
Xie, Kaibo
Xu, Rongxin
Yang, Bo
Yang, Yang

Yang, Yikun
Yang, Zhichao
Yao, Naimeng
Ye, Tangwei
Yi, Fan
Yin, Ze
Yu, Guanbao
Yu, Yongxin
Yuan, Weiwei
Zang, Hao
Zhang, Chris
Zhang, Jiaqiang
Zhang, Qingyong
Zhang, Sixiao
Zhang, Tianyi
Zhang, Yao
Zhang, Yi-Fan
Zhao, Jianing
Zhou, Wei

Contents – Part I

Data Mining and Knowledge Discovery

Contents – Part II

Natural Language Processing

Neural Networks and Deep Learning

Contents – Part III

Strong General AI

Vision and Perception

AI Foundations/Decision Theory

Fair Allocation with Special Externalities

Shaily Mishra$^{(\boxtimes)}$, Manisha Padala, and Sujit Gujar

Machine Learning Lab, International Institute of Information Technology,
Hyderabad, India
{shaily.mishra,manisha.padala}@research.iiit.ac.in,
sujit.gujar@iiit.ac.in

Abstract. Most of the existing algorithms for fair division do not consider externalities. Under externalities, the utility of an agent depends not only on its allocation but also on other agents' allocation. An agent has a positive (negative) value for the assigned goods (chores). This work studies a special case of externality which we refer to as 2-D. In 2-D, an agent receives a positive or negative value for unassigned items independent of who receives them. We propose a simple valuation transformation and show that we can adapt existing algorithms using it to retain some of the fairness and efficiency notions in 2-D. However, proportionality doesn't extend in 2-D. We redefine PROP and its relaxation and show that we can adapt existing algorithms. Further, we prove that maximin share (MMS) may not have any multiplicative approximation in this setting. Studying this domain is a stepping stone towards full externalities where ensuring fairness is much more challenging.

Keywords: Resource allocation · Fairness · Externalities

1 Introduction

We consider the problem of allocating m *indivisible* items fairly among n agents who report their valuations for the items. These scenarios often arise in the division of inheritance among family members, divorce settlements and distribution of tasks among workers [12, 33, 38–40]. Economists have proposed many fairness and efficiency notions widely applicable in such real-world settings. Researchers also explore the computational aspects of some widely accepted fairness notions [9, 15, 18, 21, 36]. Such endeavours have led to web-based applications like Spliddit, The Fair Proposals System, Coursematch, etc. However, most approaches do not consider agents with *externalities*, which we believe is restrictive.

In the absence of externality, the utility corresponding to an unallocated item is zero. Externality implies that the agent's utility depends not only on their bundle but also on the bundles allocated to other agents. Such a scenario is relatively common, mainly in allocating necessary commodities. For example, the COVID-19 pandemic resulted in a sudden and steep requirement for life-supporting resources like hospital beds, ventilators, and vaccines. There has been

ⓒ The Author(s), under exclusive license to Springer Nature Switzerland AG 2022
S. Khanna et al. (Eds.): PRICAI 2022, LNCS 13629, pp. 3–16, 2022.
https://doi.org/10.1007/978-3-031-20862-1_1

4 S. Mishra et al.

a heavy disparity in handling resources across the globe. Even though there was a decrease in GDP worldwide, low-income countries suffered more than high-income countries. We can categorize externality into positive and negative; i.e., if it affects the agent positively, we refer to it as a positive externality and vice versa. Getting a vaccination affects an agent positively. The agent values it positively, possibly less, even if others get vaccinated instead of it. However, not receiving a ventilator results in negative utility for the patient and family. While there has been an increase in demand for pharmaceuticals, we see a steep decrease in travel. Such a complex valuation structure is modeled via externalities.

Generally with externalities, the utility of not receiving an item depends on which other agent receives it. That is, each agent's valuation for an item is an n-dimensional vector. The jth component corresponds to the value an agent obtains if the item is allocated to agent j. In this work, we consider a special case of externalities in which the agents incur a cost/benefit for not receiving an item. Yet, the cost/benefit is *independent* of which other agent receives the item. This setting is referred to as 2-D, i.e., value v for receiving an item and v' otherwise. When there are only two agents, the 2-D domain is equivalent to the domain with general externalities. We refer to the agent valuations without externalities as 1-D. For the 2-D domain, we consider both goods/chores with positive/negative externality for the following fairness notions.

Fairness Notions. Envy-freeness (EF) is the most common fairness notion. It ensures that no agent has higher utility for other agent's allocation [20]. Consider 1-D setting with two agents - $\{1, 2\}$ and two goods - $\{g_1, g_2\}$; agent 1 values g_1 at 6 and g_2 at 5, while agent 2 values g_1 at 5 and g_2 at 6. Allocating g_1 and g_2 to agent 1 and 2, respectively, is EF. However, if agent 1 receives a utility of -1 and -100 for not receiving g_1 and g_2. And agent 2 receives a utility of -100 and -1 for not receiving g_1 and g_2; this allocation is no longer EF.

Externalities introduce complexity, so much that the definition of proportionality cannot be adapted to the 2-D domain. Proportionality (PROP) ensures that every agent receives at least $1/n$ of its complete bundle value [39]. In the above example, each agent should receive goods worth at least $11/2$. Guaranteeing this amount is impossible in 2-D, as it does not consider the dis-utility of not receiving goods. Moreover, it is known that EF implies PROP in the presence of additive valuations. However, in the case of 2-D, it need not be true, i.e., assigning g_2 to agent 1 and g_1 to agent 2 is EF but not PROP.

We consider a relaxation of PROP, the maximin share (MMS) allocation. Imagine asking an agent to divide the items into n bundles and take the minimum valued bundle. The agent would divide the bundles to maximize the minimum utility, i.e., the MMS share of the agent. An MMS allocation guarantees every agent its MMS share. Even for 1-D valuations, MMS allocation may not exist; hence researchers find multiplicative approximation α-MMS. An α-MMS allocation guarantees at least α fraction of MMS to every agent. [25] provides an algorithm that guarantees $3/4 + 1/12n$-MMS for goods and authors in [27] guarantees $11/9$-MMS for chores. In contrast, we prove that for 2-D valuation, it is impossible to guarantee multiplicative approximation to MMS. Thus, in order to guarantee existence results, we propose relaxed multiplicative approximation and also explore additive approximations of MMS guarantees.

In general, it is challenging to ensure fairness in the settings with full externality, hence the special case of 2-D proves promising. Moreover, in real-world applications, the 2-D valuations helps model various situations (e.g., COVID-19 resource allocation mentioned above). Studying 2-D domain is especially significant for α-MMS. We prove that there cannot exist any multiplicative approximation for MMS in 2-D. Therefore, we define Shifted α-MMS that always exists in 2-D. In summary our approach and contributions are as follows,

Our Approach. There is extensive literature available for fair allocations, and we primarily focus on leveraging existing algorithms to 2-D. We demonstrate in Sect. 3 that existing algorithms cannot directly be applied to 2-D. Towards guaranteeing fairness notion in 2-D, we propose a property preserving transformation $\mathfrak{T}$ that converts 2-D valuations to 1-D; i.e., an allocation that satisfies a property in 2-D also satisfies it in transformed 1-D and vice-versa.

Contributions.

1. We demonstrate in Sect. 3 that studying fair allocation with externalities is non-trivial and propose $\mathfrak{T}$ to retain fairness notions such as EF, MMS, and its additive relaxations and efficiency notions such as MUW and PO (Theorem 1). Thus, we can adapt the existing algorithms for the same.
2. We introduce PROP-E for general valuations for full externalities (Sect. 2) and derive relation with existing PROP extensions (Sect. 4).
3. We prove that α-MMS may not exist in 2-D (Theorem 2). We propose Shifted α-MMS, a novel way of approximating MMS in 2-D (Sect. 5.3).

Related Work

While fair resource division has an extremely rich literature, externalities is less explored. Velez [41] extended EF in externalities. [13] generalized PROP and EF for divisible goods with positive externalities. Seddighin et al. [37] proposed average-share, an extension of PROP, and studied MMS for goods with positive externalities. Authors in [6] explored EF1/EFX for the specific setting of two and three agents and provided PROP extension. For two agents, their setting is equivalent to 2-D, hence existing algorithms [4,15,35] suffice. Beyond two agents, the setting is more general and they proved the non-existence of EFX for three agents. In contrast, EFX always exists for three agents in our setting.

Envy-freeness up to one item (EF1) [14,32] and Envy-freeness up to any item(EFX) [15] are prominent relaxation of EF. EF may not exist for indivisible items. We consider two prominent relaxations of EF, Envy-freeness up to one item (EF1) [14,32] and Envy-freeness up to any item(EFX) [15]. We have poly-time algorithms to find EF1 in general monotone valuations for goods [32] and chores [11]. For additive valuations, EF1 can be found using Round Robin [15] in goods or chores, and Double Round Robin [2] in combination.

[35] present an algorithm to find EFX allocation under identical general valuations for goods. [16] proved that an EFX allocation exists for three agents. Researchers have also studied fair division in presence of strategic agents, i.e., designing truthful mechanisms [8,10,34]. A great deal of research has been done on mechanism design [22,23]. PROP1 and PROPX are popular relaxation of PROP. For additive valuations, EF1 implies PROP1, and EFX implies PROPX. Unfortunately, in paper [4], the authors showed the PROPX for goods may not always exists. [31] explored (weighted) PROPX and showed it exists in polynomial time. MMS do not always exist [29,36]. The papers [1,7,24,36] showed that 2/3-MMS for goods always exists. Paper [25,26] showed that 3/4-MMS for goods always exists. Authors in [25] provides an algorithm that guarantees $3/4 + 1/12n$-MMS for goods. Authors in [5] presented a polynomial-time algorithm for 2-MMS for chores. The algorithm presented in [7] gives 4/3-MMS for chores. Authors in [27] showed that 11/9-MMS for chores always exists. [28] explored α−MMS for a combination of goods and chores. In [15] showed that MNW is EF1 and PO for indivisible goods and [9] gave a pseudo-polynomial time algorithm. [2] presented algorithm to find EF1 and PO for two agents. [4] presented an algorithm to find PROP1 and fPO for combination. [3] proposed a pseudo-polynomial time algorithm for finding utilitarian maximizing among EF1 or PROP1 in goods.

2   Preliminaries

We consider a resource allocation problem $(N, M, \mathcal{V})$ for determining an allocation A of $M = [m]$ indivisible items among $N = [n]$ interested agents, $m, n \in \mathbb{N}$. We only allow complete allocation and no two agents can receive the same item. That is, $A = (A_1, \ldots, A_n)$, s.t., $\forall i, j \in N, i \neq j; A_i \cap A_j = \emptyset$ and $\bigcup_i A_i = M$. A_{-i} denotes the set $M \setminus A_i$.

2-D Valuations. The valuation function is denoted by $\mathcal{V} = \{V_1, V_2, \ldots, V_n\}$; $\forall i \in N, V_i : 2^M \to \mathbb{R}^2, \forall S \subseteq M, V_i(S) = (v_i(S), v_i'(S))$, where $v_i(S)$ denotes the value for receiving bundle S and $v_i'(S)$ for not receiving S. The value of an agent i for item k in 2-D is (v_{ik}, v_{ik}'). If k is a good (chore), then $v_{ik} \geq 0$ $(v_{ik} \leq 0)$. For positive (negative) externality $v_{ik}' \geq 0$ $(v_{ik}' \leq 0)$.

The utility an agent $i \in N$ obtains for a bundle $S \subseteq M$ is, $u_i(S) = v_i(S) + v_i'(M \setminus S)$ Also, $u_i(\emptyset) = 0 + v_i'(M)$ and utilities in 2-D are not normalized[1]. When agents have additive valuations, $u_i(S) = \sum_{k \in S} v_{ik} + \sum_{k \notin S} v_{ik}'$. We assume monotonicity of utility for goods, i.e., $\forall S \subseteq T \subseteq M, u_i(S) \leq u_i(T)$ and anti-monotonicity of utility for chores, i.e., $u_i(S) \geq u_i(T)$. We use the term *full externalities* to represent complete externalities, i.e., each agent has n-dimensional vector for its valuation for an item. We next define fairness and efficiency notions.

---

[1] Utility is normalized when $u_i(\emptyset) = 0, \forall i$.

Definition 1 (Envy-free (EF) and relaxations [2,14,15,20,41]**).** *For the items (chores or goods) an allocation A that satisfies* $\forall i, j \in N,$[2]

$$u_i(A_i) \geq u_i(A_j) \text{ is EF}$$

$$\left. \begin{array}{l} v_{ik} < 0, u_i(A_i \setminus \{k\}) \geq u_i(A_j); \forall k \in A_i \\ v_{ik} > 0, u_i(A_i) \geq u_i(A_j \setminus \{k\}); \forall k \in A_j \end{array} \right\} \text{ is EFX}$$

$$u_i(A_i \setminus \{k\}) \geq u_i(A_j \setminus \{k\}); \exists k \in \{A_i \cup A_j\} \text{ is EF1}$$

Definition 2 (Proportionality (PROP) [39]**).** *An allocation A is said to be proportional, if* $\forall i \in N$, $u_i(A_i) \geq \frac{1}{n} \cdot u_i(M)$.

For 2-D, achieving PROP is impossible as discussed in Sect. 1. To capture proportional under externalities, we introduce *Proportionality with externality* (PROP-E). Informally, while PROP guarantees $1/n$ share of the entire bundle, PROP-E guarantees $1/n$ share of the sum of utilities for all bundles. Note that, PROP-E is not limited to 2-D and applies to a full externalities. Formally,

Definition 3 (Proportionality with externality (PROP-E)). *An allocation A satisfies PROP-E if,* $\forall i \in N$,$u_i(A_i) \geq \frac{1}{n} \cdot \sum_{j \in N} u_i(A_j)$

Definition 4 (PROP-E relaxations). *An allocation A* $\forall i, \forall j \in N$, *satisfies PROPX-E if it is PROP-E up to any item, i.e.,*

$$\left. \begin{array}{l} v_{ik} > 0, u_i(A_i \cup \{k\}) \geq \frac{1}{n} \sum_{j \in N} u_i(A_j); \forall \ k \in \{M \setminus A_i\} \\ v_{ik} < 0, u_i(A_i \setminus \{k\}) \geq \frac{1}{n} \sum_{j \in N} u_i(A_j); \forall \ k \in A_i \end{array} \right\}$$

Next,A satisfies PROP1-E if it is PROP-E up to an item, i.e.,

$$\left. \begin{array}{l} u_i(A_i \cup \{k\}) \geq \frac{1}{n} \sum_{j \in N} u_i(A_j); \exists \ k \in \{M \setminus A_i\} \ or, \\ u_i(A_i \setminus \{k\}) \geq \frac{1}{n} \sum_{j \in N} u_i(A_j); \exists \ k \in A_i \end{array} \right\}$$

Finally, we state the definition of MMS and its multiplicative approximation.

Definition 5 (Maxmin Share MMS [14]**).** *An allocation A is said to be MMS if* $\forall i \in N$, $u_i(A_i) \geq \mu_i$, *where*

$$\mu_i = \max_{(A_1, A_2, \dots, A_n) \in \prod_n (M)} \min_{j \in N} u_i(A_j)$$

An allocation A is said to be α-MMS if it guarantees $u_i(A_i) \geq \alpha \cdot \mu_i$ *for* $\mu_i \geq 0$ *and* $u_i(A_i) \geq \frac{1}{\alpha} \cdot \mu_i$ *when* $\mu_i \leq 0$, *where* $\alpha \in (0,1]$.

Definition 6 (Pareto-Optimal (PO)). *An allocation A is PO if* $\nexists A'$ *s.t.,* $\forall i \in N$, $u_i(A_i') \geq u_i(A_i)$ *and* $\exists i \in N$, $u_i(A_i') > u_i(A_i)$.

We also consider efficiency notions like Maximum Utilitarian Welfare (MUW), that maximizes the sum of agent utilities. Maximum Nash Welfare (MNW) maximizes the product of agent utilities and Maximum Egalitarian Welfare (MEW) maximizes the minimum agent utility.

In the next section, we define a transformation from 2-D to 1-D that plays a major role in adaptation of existing algorithms for ensuring desirable properties.

---

[2] Beyond 2-D, one must include the concept of swapping bundles in EF [6,41].

3   Reduction from 2-D to 1-D

We define a transformation $\mathfrak{T} : \mathcal{V} \to \mathcal{W}$, where $\mathcal{V}$ is the valuations in 2-D, i.e., $\mathcal{V} = \{V_1, V_2, \ldots, V_n\}$ and $\mathcal{W}$ is the valuations in 1-D, i.e., $\mathcal{W} = \{w_1, w_2, \ldots, w_n\}$.

Definition 7 (Transformation $\mathfrak{T}$).   *Given a resource allocation problem $(N, M, \mathcal{V})$ we obtain the corresponding 1-D valuations denoted by $\mathcal{W} = \mathfrak{T}(\mathcal{V}(\cdot))$ as follows,*

$$\forall i \in N, w_i(A_i) = \mathfrak{T}(V_i(A_i)) = v_i(A_i) + v_i'(A_{-i}) - v_i'(M) \qquad (1)$$

When valuations are additive, we obtain $w_i(A_i) = v_i(A_i) - v_i'(A_i)$. An agent's utility in 2-D is $u_i(A_i)$ and the corresponding utility in 1-D is $w_i(A_i)$.

Lemma 1. *For goods (chores), under monotonicity (anti-monotonicity) of $\mathcal{V}$, $\mathcal{W} = \mathfrak{T}(\mathcal{V}(\cdot))$ is normalized, monotonic (anti-monotonic), and non-negative (negative).*

Proof. We assume monotonicity of utility for goods in 2-D. Therefore, $\forall S \subseteq M, w_i(S)$ is also monotone. And $w_i(\emptyset) = v_i(\emptyset) + v_i'(M) - v_i'(M) = 0$ is normalized. Since $w_i(\cdot)$ is monotone and normalized, it is non negative for goods. Similarly we can prove that $w_i(\cdot)$ is normalized, anti-monotonic and non-negative for chores.

Theorem 1. *An allocation A is $\mathfrak{F}$-Fair and $\mathfrak{E}$-Efficient in $\mathcal{V}$ iff A is $\mathfrak{F}$-Fair and $\mathfrak{E}$-Efficient in the transformed 1-D, $\mathcal{W}$, where $\mathfrak{F} \in \{EF, EF1, EFX, PROP\text{-}E, PROP1\text{-}E, PROPX\text{-}E, MMS\}$ and $\mathfrak{E} \in \{PO, MUW\}$.*

Proof Sketch. We first consider $\mathfrak{F} = $ EF. Let allocation A be EF in $\mathcal{W}$ then,

$$\forall i, \ \forall j, \ w_i(A_i) \geq w_i(A_j)$$
$$v_i(A_i) + v_i'(A_{-i}) - v_i'(M) \geq v_i(A_j) + v_i'(A_{-j}) - v_i'(M)$$
$$u_i(A_i) \geq u_i(A_j)$$

We can proof the rest in a similar manner.
From Lemma 1 and Theorem 1, we obtain the following.

Corollary 1. *To determine $\{EF, EF1, EFX, MMS\}$ fairness and $\{PO, MUW\}$ efficiency, we can apply existing algorithms to the transformed $\mathcal{W} = \mathfrak{T}(V(\cdot))$ for general valuations.*

Existing algorithms cannot be directly applied. Modified *leximin* algorithm gives PROP1 and PO for chores for 3 or 4 agents in [17], but it is not PROP1-E (or PROP1) and PO in 2-D when applied on utilities. The following example demonstrates the same,

Example 1. Consider 3 agents $\{1, 2, 3\}$ and 4 chores $\{c_1, c_2, c_3, c_4\}$ with positive externality. The 2-D valuation profile is as follows, $V_{1c_1} = (-30, 1)$, $V_{1c_2} = (-20, 1)$, $V_{1c_3} = (-30, 1)$, $V_{1c_4} = (-30, 1)$, $V_{3c_1} = (-1, 40)$, $V_{3c_2} = (-1, 40)$, $V_{3c_3} = (-1, 40)$, and $V_{3c_4} = (-1, 40)$. The valuation profile of agent 2 is identical to agent 1. Allocation $\{\emptyset, \emptyset, (c_1, c_2, c_3, c_4)\}$ is leximin allocation, which is not PROP1-E. However, allocation $\{c_3, (c_2, c_4), (c_1)\}$ is leximin on transformed valuations; it is PROP1 and PO in $\mathcal{W}$ and it is PROP1-E and PO in $\mathcal{V}$.

For chores, the authors in [31] showed that any PROPX allocation ensures 2-MMS for symmetric agents. This result also doesn't extend to 2-D. For e.g., consider two agents $\{1, 2\}$ having additive identical valuations for six chores $\{c_1, c_2, c_3, c_4, c_5, c_6\}$, given as $V_{1_{c1}} = (-9, 1)$, $V_{1_{c2}} = (-11, 1)$, $V_{1_{c3}} = (-12, 1)$, $V_{1_{c4}} = (-13, 1)$, $V_{1_{c5}} = (-9, 1)$, and $V_{1_{c6}} = (-1, 38)$. Allocation $A = \{(c_1, c_2, c_3, c_4, c_5), (c_6)\}$ is PROPX-E, but is not 2-MMS in $\mathcal{V}$. Further, adapting certain fairness or efficiency criteria to 2-D is not straightforward. E.g., MNW cannot be defined in 2-D because agents can have positive or negative utilities. Hence MNW implies EF1 and PO doesn't extend to 2-D. The authors proved that MNW allocation gives at least $\frac{2}{1+\sqrt{4n-3}}$-MMS value to each agent in [15], which doesn't imply for 2-D. Similarly, we show that approximation to MMS, α-MMS, does not exist in the presence of externalities (Sect. 5).

4   Proportionality in 2-D

We remark that PROP (Definition 2) is too strict in 2-D. As a result, we introduce PROP-E and its additive relaxations in Definitions 3 and 4 for general valuations.

Proposition 1. *For additive 2-D, we can adapt the existing algorithms of PROP and its relaxations to 2-D using $\mathfrak{T}$.*

Proof. In the absence of externalities, for additive valuations, PROP-E is equivalent to PROP. From Theorem 1, we know that $\mathfrak{T}$ retains PROP-E and its relaxations, and hence all existing algorithms of 1-D is applicable using $\mathfrak{T}$.

It is known that EF $\implies$ PROP for sub-additive valuation in 1-D. In the case of PROP-E, $\forall i, j \in N$, $u_i(A_i) \geq u_i(A_j) \implies u_i(A_i) \geq \frac{1}{n} \cdot \sum_{j=1}^{n} u_i(A_j)$.

Corollary 2. *EF $\implies$ PROP-E for arbitrary valuations with full externalities.*

We now compare PROP-E with existing PROP extensions for capturing externalities. We consider two definitions stated in literature from [37] (Average Share) and [6] (General Fair Share). Note that both these definitions are applicable when agents have additive valuations, while PROP-E applies for any general arbitrary valuations. In [6], the authors proved that Average Share $\implies$ General Fair Share, i.e., if an allocation guarantees all agents their average share value, it also guarantees general fair share value. With that, we state the definition of Average Share (in 2-D) and compare it with PROP-E.

Definition 8 (Average Share [37]). *In $\mathcal{V}$, the average value of item k for agent i, denoted by $avg[v_{ik}] = \frac{1}{n} \cdot [v_{ik} + (n-1)v'_{ik}]$. The average share of agent i, $\overline{v_i(M)} = \sum_{k \in M} avg[v_{ik}]$. An allocation A is said to ensure average share if $\forall i, u_i(A_i) \geq \overline{v_i(M)}$.*

Proposition 2. *PROP-E is equivalent to Average Share in 2-D, for additive valuations.*

Proof Sketch. $\forall i \in N$,

$$u_i(A_i) \geq \frac{1}{n} \cdot \sum_{j \in N} u_i(A_j) = \frac{1}{n} \cdot \sum_{j \in N} v_i(A_j) - v_i'(M \setminus A_j)$$

$$= \frac{1}{n} \cdot \sum_{k \in M} v_{ik} - \frac{1}{n} \cdot \sum_{k \in M} (n-1)v_{ik}'$$

Next, we briefly state the relation of EF, PROP-E, and Average Share beyond 2-D and omit the details due to space constraints.

Remark 1. In case of full externality, EF $\not\Rightarrow$ Average Share [6].

Proposition 3. *Beyond 2-D, PROP-E $\not\Rightarrow$ Average Share and Average Share $\not\Rightarrow$ PROP-E.*

To conclude this section, we state that for the special case of 2-D externalities with additive valuations, we can adapt existing algorithms to 2-D, and further analysis is required for the general setting.

We now provide analysis of MMS for 2-D valuations in the next section.

5   Approximate MMS in 2-D

From Theorem 1, we showed that transformation $\mathfrak{T}$ retains MMS property, i.e., an allocation A guarantees MMS in 1-D *iff* A guarantees MMS in 2-D. We draw attention to the point that,

$$\mu_i = \mu_i^{\mathcal{W}} + v_i'(M) \tag{2}$$

where $\mu_i^{\mathcal{W}}$ and μ_i are the MMS value of agent i in 1-D and 2-D, respectively. [30] proved that MMS allocation may not exist even for additive valuations, but α-MMS always exists in 1-D. The current best approximation results on MMS allocation are $3/4 + 1/(12n)$-MMS for goods [25] and $11/9$-MMS for chores [27] for additive valuations. We are interested in finding multiplicative approximation to MMS in 2-D. Note that we only study α-MMS for complete goods or chores in 2-D, as [28] proved the non-existence of α-MMS for combination of goods and chores in 1-D. From Eq. 5 for $\alpha \in (0,1]$, if μ_i is positive, we consider α-MMS, and if it is negative, then $1/\alpha$-MMS.

We categorize externalities in two ways for better analysis 1) Correlated Externality 2) Inverse Externality. In the correlated setting, we study goods with positive externality and chores with negative externality. And in the inverse externality, we study goods with negative externality and chores with positive externality. Next, we investigate α-MMS guarantees for correlated externality.

5.1 α-MMS for Correlated Externality

Proposition 4. *For correlated externality, if an allocation A is α-MMS in $\mathcal{W}$, A is α-MMS in $\mathcal{V}$, but need not vice versa.*

Proof. **Part-1.** Let A be α-MMS in $\mathcal{W}$,

$$\forall i \in N, w_i(A_i) \geq \alpha\mu_i^{\mathcal{W}} \quad \implies \quad u_i(A_i) - v_i'(M) \geq -\alpha v_i'(M) + \alpha\mu_i \qquad \text{for goods}$$

$$\forall i \in N, w_i(A_i) \geq \frac{1}{\alpha}\mu_i^{\mathcal{W}} \quad \implies \quad u_i(A_i) - v_i'(M) \geq -\frac{1}{\alpha}v_i'(M) + \frac{1}{\alpha}\mu_i \quad \text{for chores}$$

For goods with positive externalities, $\mu_i > 0$, $\alpha \in (0,1]$, and $\forall S \subseteq M, v_i'(S) \geq 0$. We derive $v_i'(M) \geq \alpha v_i'(M)$, and hence we can say $u_i(A_i) \geq \alpha\mu_i$. For chores with negative externalities, $\mu_i < 0$, $1/\alpha \geq 1$, and $\forall S \subseteq M, v'(S) \leq 0$. Similarly to the previous point, we derive $v'(M) \geq \frac{1}{\alpha}v'(M)$ and thus $u_i(A_i) \geq \frac{1}{\alpha}\mu_i$.
Part-2. We now prove A is α-MMS in $\mathcal{V}$ but not in $\mathcal{W}$.

Example. Consider $N = \{1,2\}$ both have additive identical valuations for goods $\{g_1, g_2, g_3, g_4, g_5, g_6\}$, $V_{ig_1} = (0.5, 0.1)$, $V_{ig_2} = (0.5, 0.1)$, $V_{ig_3} = (0.3, 0.1)$, $V_{ig_4} = (0.5, 0.1)$, $V_{ig_5} = (0.5, 0.1)$, and $V_{ig_6} = (0.5, 0.1)$. After transformation, we get $\mu_i^{\mathcal{W}} = 1$ and in 2-D $\mu_i = 1.6$. Allocation, $A = \{\{g_1\}, \{g_2, g_3, g_4, g_5, g_6\}\}$ is $1/2$-MMS in $\mathcal{V}$, but not in $\mathcal{W}$. Similarly, it is easy to verify the same for chores.

Corollary 3. *We can adapt the existing α-MMS algorithms using $\mathfrak{T}$ for correlated externality for general valuations.*

Corollary 4. *For correlated 2-D externality, we can always obtain $3/4 + 1/(12n)$-MMS for goods and $11/9$-MMS for chores for additive.*

5.2 α-MMS for Inverse Externality

Motivated by the example given in [30] for non-existence of MMS allocation for 1-D valuations, we adapted it to construct the following instance in 2-D to prove the impossibility of α-MMS in 2-D. We show that for any $\alpha \in (0,1]$, an α-MMS or $1/\alpha$-MMS allocation may not exist for inverse externality in this section. We construct an instance V^g such that α-MMS exists in V^g only if MMS allocation exists in $W = \mathfrak{T}(V^g)$. Note that W is exactly the instance of the example in [30]. Hence the contradiction.

Non-existence of α-MMS in Goods. Consider the following example.

Example 2. We consider a problem of allocating 12 goods among three agents, and represent valuation profile as V^g. The valuation profile V^g is equivalent to $10^3 \times V$ given in Table 1. We set $\epsilon_1 = 10^{-4}$ and $\epsilon_2 = 10^{-3}$. We transform these valuations in 1-D using $\mathfrak{T}$, and the valuation profile $\mathfrak{T}(V^g)$ is the same as the instance in [30] that proves the non-existence of MMS for goods. Note that $\forall i, v_i'(M) = -4055000 + 10^3\epsilon_1$ The MMS value of every agent in $\mathfrak{T}(V^g)$ is 4055000 and from Eq. 2, the MMS value of every agent in V^g is $10^3\epsilon_1$.

Table 1. Additive 2-D valuation profile (V)

Item	Agent 1 (v_1, v_1')	Agent 2 (v_2, v_2')	Agent 3 (v_3, v_3')
k_1	$(3\epsilon_2, -1017+3\epsilon_1-3\epsilon_2)$	$(3\epsilon_2, -1017+3\epsilon_1-3\epsilon_2)$	$(3\epsilon_2, -1017+3\epsilon_1-3\epsilon_2)$
k_2	$(2\epsilon_1, -1025+2\epsilon_1+\epsilon_2)$	$(2\epsilon_1, -1025+2\epsilon_1+\epsilon_2)$	$(1025 - \epsilon_1, -\epsilon_1)$
k_3	$(2\epsilon_1, -1012+2\epsilon_1+\epsilon_2)$	$(1012 - \epsilon_1, -\epsilon_1)$	$(2\epsilon_1, -1012+2\epsilon_1+\epsilon_2)$
k_4	$(2\epsilon_1, -1001+2\epsilon_1+\epsilon_2)$	$(1001 - \epsilon_1, -\epsilon_1)$	$(1001 - \epsilon_1, -\epsilon_1)$
k_5	$(1002 - \epsilon_1, -\epsilon_1)$	$(2\epsilon_1, -1002+2\epsilon_1+\epsilon_2)$	$(1002 - \epsilon_1, -\epsilon_1)$
k_6	$(1022 - \epsilon_1, -\epsilon_1)$	$(1022 - \epsilon_1, -\epsilon_1)$	$(1022 - \epsilon_1, -\epsilon_1)$
k_7	$(1003 - \epsilon_1, -\epsilon_1)$	$(1003 - \epsilon_1, -\epsilon_1)$	$(2\epsilon_1, -1003+2\epsilon_1+\epsilon_2)$
k_8	$(1028 - \epsilon_1, -\epsilon_1)$	$(1028 - \epsilon_1, -\epsilon_1)$	$(1028 - \epsilon_1, -\epsilon_1)$
k_9	$(1011 - \epsilon_1, -\epsilon_1)$	$(2\epsilon_1, -1011+2\epsilon_1+\epsilon_2)$	$(1011 - \epsilon_1, -\epsilon_1)$
k_{10}	$(1000 - \epsilon_1, -\epsilon_1)$	$(1000 - \epsilon_1, -\epsilon_1)$	$(1000 - \epsilon_1, -\epsilon_1)$
k_{11}	$(1021 - \epsilon_1, -\epsilon_1)$	$(1021 - \epsilon_1, -\epsilon_1)$	$(1021 - \epsilon_1, -\epsilon_1)$
k_{12}	$(1023 - \epsilon_1, -\epsilon_1)$	$(1023 - \epsilon_1, -\epsilon_1)$	$(2\epsilon_1, -1023+2\epsilon_1+\epsilon_2)$

Recall that $\mathfrak{T}$ retains MMS property (Theorem 1) and thus we can say that MMS allocation doesn't exist in V^g.

Lemma 2. *There is no α-MMS allocation for the valuation profile V^g of Example 2 for any $\alpha \in [0, 1]$.*

Proof. An allocation A is α-MMS for $\alpha \geq 0$ iff $\forall i, u_i(A_i) \geq \alpha\mu_i \geq 0$ when $\mu_i > 0$. Note that the transformed valuations $w_i(A_i) = \mathfrak{T}(V_i^g(A_i))$. From Eq. 1, $u_i(A_i) \geq 0$, iff $w_i(A_i) \geq -v_i'(M)$, which gives us $w_i(A_i) \geq 4055000 - 0.1$. For this to be true, we need $w_i(A_i) \geq 4055000$ since $\mathfrak{T}(V^g)$ has all integral values. We know that such an allocation doesn't exist [30]. Hence for any $\alpha \in [0, 1]$, α-MMS does not exist for V^g.

Non-existence of $1/\alpha$-MMS in Chores. Consider the following example.

Example 3. We consider a problem of allocating 12 chores among three agents. The valuation profile V^c is equivalent to $-10^3 V$ given in Table 1. We set $\epsilon_2 = -10^{-3}$. We transform these valuations in 1-D, and $\mathfrak{T}(V^c)$ is the same as the instance in [5] that proves the non-existence of MMS for chores. Note that $v_i'(M) = 4055000 - 10^3\epsilon_1$. The MMS value of every agent in $\mathfrak{T}(V^c)$ and V^c is -4055000 and $-10^3\epsilon_1$, respectively.

Lemma 3. *There is no $1/\alpha$-MMS allocation for the valuation profile V^c of Example 3 with $\epsilon_1 \in (0, 10^{-4}]$ for any $\alpha > 0$.*

Proof. An allocation A is $1/\alpha$-MMS for $\alpha > 0$ iff $\forall i, u_i(A_i) \geq \frac{1}{\alpha}\mu_i$ when $\mu_i < 0$. We set $\epsilon_1 \leq 10^{-4}$ in V^c. When $\alpha \geq 10^3\epsilon_1$ $\forall i$ then $u_i(A_i) \geq -1$. From Eq. 1, $u_i(A_i) \geq -1$ iff $w_i(A_i) \geq -4055001 + 10^3\epsilon_1$. Note that $0 < 10^3\epsilon_1 \leq 0.1$ and since $w_i(A_i)$ has only integral values, we need $\forall i, w_i(A_i) \geq -4055000$. Such A does not exist [5]. As ϵ_1 decreases, $1/\epsilon_1$ increases, and even though approximation guarantees weakens, it still does not exist for V^c.

From Lemma 2 and 3 we conclude the following theorem,

Theorem 2. *There may not exist α-MMS for any $\alpha \in [0,1]$ for $\mu_i > 0$ or $1/\alpha$-MMS allocation for any $\alpha \in (0,1]$ for $\mu_i < 0$ in the presence of externalities.*

Interestingly, in 1-D, α-MMS's non-existence is known for α value close to 1 [19,30], while in 2-D, it need not exist even for $\alpha = 0$. It follows because α-MMS could not lead to any relaxation in the presence of inverse externalities. Consider the situation of goods having negative externalities, where MMS share μ_i comprises of the positive value from the assigned bundle A_i and negative value from the unassigned bundles A_{-i}. We re-write μ_i as follows, $\mu_i = \mu_i^+ + \mu_i^-$ where μ_i^+ corresponds to utility from assigned goods/unassigned chores and μ_i^- corresponds to utility from unassigned goods/assigned chores. When $\mu_i \geq 0$, applying $\alpha\mu_i$ is not only relaxing positive value $\alpha\mu_i^+$, but also requires $\alpha\mu_i^-$ which is stricter than μ_i^- since $\mu_i^- < 0$. Hence, the impossibility of α-MMS in 2-D. Similar argument holds for chores. Next, we explore MMS relaxation such that it exists in 2-D.

5.3 Re-defining Approximate MMS

In this section, we define *Shifted α-MMS* that guarantees a fraction of MMS share shifted by certain value, such that it always exist in 2-D. We also considered intuitive ways of approximating MMS in 2-D. These ways are based on relaxing the positive value obtained from MMS allocation μ^+ and the negative value μ^-, $\mu = \mu^+ + \mu^-$. In other words, we look for allocations that guarantee $\alpha\mu^+$ and $(1+\alpha)$ or $1/\alpha$ of μ^-. Unfortunately, such approximations may not always exist. We skip the details due to space constraints.

Definition 9 (Shifted α-MMS). *An allocation A guarantees shifted α-MMS if $\forall i \in N, \alpha \in (0,1]$*

$$\left. \begin{array}{l} u_i(A_i) \geq \alpha\mu_i + (1-\alpha)v_i'(M) \\[6pt] u_i(A_i) \geq \frac{1}{\alpha}\mu_i + \frac{\alpha-1}{\alpha}v_i'(M) \end{array} \right\} \qquad \begin{array}{l} \textit{for goods} \\[6pt] \textit{for chores} \end{array}$$

Proposition 5 *An allocation A is α-MMS in $\mathcal{W}$ iff A is shifted α-MMS in $\mathcal{V}$.*

Proof For goods, if allocation A is shifted α-MMS, $\forall i, u_i(A_i) \geq \alpha\mu_i + (1-\alpha)v_i'(M)$. Applying $\mathfrak{T}$, we get $w_i(A_i) + v_i'(M) \geq \alpha\mu_i^{\mathcal{W}} + \alpha v_i'(M) + (1-\alpha)v_i'(M)$ which gives $w_i(A_i) \geq \alpha\mu_i^{\mathcal{W}}$. For chores, if A is shifted $1/\alpha$-MMS, $\forall i, u_i(A_i) \geq \frac{1}{\alpha}\mu_i + \frac{(\alpha-1)}{\alpha}v_i'(M)$, which gives $w_i(A_i) \geq \frac{1}{\alpha}\mu_i^{\mathcal{W}}$. Similarly we can prove vice versa.

Corollary 5. *We can adapt all the existing algorithms for α-MMS in $\mathcal{W}$ to get shifted α-MMS in $\mathcal{V}$.*

We use $\mathfrak{T}$ and apply the existing algorithms and obtain the corresponding shifted multiplicative approximations. In the next section, we examine the additive relaxation of MMS since a multiplicative approximation need not exist in the presence of externalities.

Additive Relaxation of MMS

Definition 10 (MMS relaxations). *An allocation A that satisfies,* $\forall i, j \in N,$

$$\left. \begin{array}{l} \forall \, k \in \{M \setminus A_i\}, v_{ik} > 0, u_i(A_i \cup \{k\}) \geq \mu_i \\ \forall \, k \in A_i, v_{ik} < 0, u_i(A_i \setminus \{k\}) \geq \mu_i \end{array} \right\} \quad \text{MMSX, MMS upto any item}$$

(3)

$$\left. \begin{array}{l} \exists \, k \in \{M \setminus A_i\}, u_i(A_i \cup \{k\}) \geq \mu_i, \ or, \\ \exists \, k \in A_i, u_i(A_i \setminus \{k\}) \geq \mu_i \end{array} \right\} \quad \text{MMS1, MMS upto an item}$$

(4)

Proposition 6. *From Lemma 1 and Theorem 1, we conclude that MMS1 and MMSX are preserved after transformation.*

EF1 is a stronger fairness notion than MMS1 and can be computed in polynomial time. On the other hand, PROPX might not exist for goods [4]. Since PROPX implies MMSX, it is interesting to settle the existence of MMSX for goods. Note that MMSX and Shifted α-MMS are not related. It is interesting to study these relaxations further, even in full externalities.

6 Conclusion

In this paper, we conducted a study on indivisible item allocation with special externalities – 2-D externalities. We proposed a simple yet compelling transformation from 2-D to 1-D to employ existing algorithms to ensure many fairness and efficiency notions. We can adapt existing fair division algorithms via the transformation in such settings. We proposed proportionality extension in the presence of externalities and studied its relation with other fairness notions. For MMS fairness, we proved the impossibility of multiplicative approximation of MMS in 2-D, and we proposed Shifted α-MMS instead. There are many exciting questions here which we leave for future works. (i) It might be impossible to have fairness-preserving valuation transformation for general externalities. However, what are some interesting domains where such transformations exist? (ii) What are interesting approximations to MMS in 2-D as well as in general externalities?

References

1. Amanatidis, G., Markakis, E., Nikzad, A., Saberi, A.: Approximation algorithms for computing maximin share allocations. ACM Trans. Algor. (TALG) **13**(4), 1–28 (2017)
2. Aziz, H., Caragiannis, I., Igarashi, A.: Fair allocation of combinations of indivisible goods and chores. CoRR abs/1807.10684 (2018). http://arxiv.org/abs/1807.10684
3. Aziz, H., Huang, X., Mattei, N., Segal-Halevi, E.: Computing fair utilitarian allocations of indivisible goods. CoRR abs/2012.03979 (2020), https://arxiv.org/abs/2012.03979

4. Aziz, H., Moulin, H., Sandomirskiy, F.: A polynomial-time algorithm for computing a pareto optimal and almost proportional allocation. Oper. Res. Lett. **48**(5), 573–578 (2020)
5. Aziz, H., Rauchecker, G., Schryen, G., Walsh, T.: Algorithms for max-min share fair allocation of indivisible chores, pp. 335–341. AAAI 2017, AAAI Press (2017)
6. Aziz, H., Suksompong, W., Sun, Z., Walsh, T.: Fairness concepts for indivisible items with externalities (2021)
7. Barman, S., Biswas, A., Krishnamurthy, S., Narahari, Y.: Groupwise maximin fair allocation of indivisible goods. In: Proceedings of the AAAI Conference on Artificial Intelligence, vol. 32 (2018)
8. Barman, S., Ghalme, G., Jain, S., Kulkarni, P., Narang, S.: Fair division of indivisible goods among strategic agents. In: Proceedings of the 18th International Conference on Autonomous Agents and MultiAgent Systems, pp. 1811–1813. AAMAS 2019, International Foundation for Autonomous Agents and Multiagent Systems, Richland, SC (2019)
9. Barman, S., Krishnamurthy, S.K., Vaish, R.: Finding fair and efficient allocations. In: Proceedings of the 2018 ACM Conference on Economics and Computation, pp. 557–574 (2018)
10. Bei, X., Huzhang, G., Suksompong, W.: Truthful fair division without free disposal. Soc. Choice Welf. **55**(3), 523–545 (2020). https://doi.org/10.1007/s00355-020-01256-0
11. Bhaskar, U., Sricharan, A.R., Vaish, R.: On approximate envy-freeness for indivisible chores and mixed resources. CoRR abs/2012.06788 (2020). https://arxiv.org/abs/2012.06788
12. Brams, S.J., Brams, S.J., Taylor, A.D.: Fair Division: From Cake-Cutting to Dispute Resolution. Cambridge University Press, Cambridge (1996)
13. Brânzei, S., Procaccia, A., Zhang, J.: Externalities in cake cutting. In: Twenty-Third International Joint Conference on Artificial Intelligence (2013)
14. Budish, E.: The combinatorial assignment problem: approximate competitive equilibrium from equal incomes. J. Political Econ. **119**(6), 1061–1103 (2011)
15. Caragiannis, I., Kurokawa, D., Moulin, H., Procaccia, A.D., Shah, N., Wang, J.: The unreasonable fairness of maximum nash welfare. ACM Trans. Econ. Comput. (TEAC) **7**(3), 1–32 (2019)
16. Chaudhury, B.R., Garg, J., Mehlhorn, K.: EFX exists for three agents. In: Proceedings of the 21st ACM Conference on Economics and Computation, pp. 1–19 (2020)
17. Chen, X., Liu, Z.: The fairness of leximin in allocation of indivisible chores. arXiv preprint arXiv:2005.04864 (2020)
18. de Keijzer, B., Bouveret, S., Klos, T., Zhang, Y.: On the complexity of efficiency and envy-freeness in fair division of indivisible goods with additive preferences. In: Rossi, F., Tsoukias, A. (eds.) ADT 2009. LNCS (LNAI), vol. 5783, pp. 98–110. Springer, Heidelberg (2009). https://doi.org/10.1007/978-3-642-04428-1_9
19. Feige, U., Sapir, A., Tauber, L.: A tight negative example for mms fair allocations. arXiv preprint arXiv:2104.04977 (2021)
20. Foley, D.K.: Resource allocation and the public sector. Yale University (1966)
21. Freeman, R., Sikdar, S., Vaish, R., Xia, L.: Equitable allocations of indivisible goods. In: IJCAI (2019)
22. Garg, D., Narahari, Y., Gujar, S.: Foundations of mechanism design: a tutorial part 2-advanced concepts and results. Sadhana **33**(2), 131–174 (2008)
23. Garg, D., Narahari, Y., Gujar, S.: Foundations of mechanism design: a tutorial part 1-key concepts and classical results. Sadhana **33**(2), 83–130 (2008)

24. Garg, J., McGlaughlin, P., Taki, S.: Approximating maximin share allocations. Open Access Series in Informatics 69 (2019)
25. Garg, J., Taki, S.: An improved approximation algorithm for maximin shares. Artif. Intell., 103547 (2021)
26. Ghodsi, M., HajiAghayi, M., Seddighin, M., Seddighin, S., Yami, H.: Fair allocation of indivisible goods: improvements and generalizations. In: Proceedings of the 2018 ACM Conference on Economics and Computation, pp. 539–556 (2018)
27. Huang, X., Lu, P.: An algorithmic framework for approximating maximin share allocation of chores. In: Proceedings of the 22nd ACM Conference on Economics and Computation, pp. 630–631 (2021)
28. Kulkarni, R., Mehta, R., Taki, S.: Indivisible mixed manna: on the computability of MMS+ PO allocations. In: Proceedings of the 22nd ACM Conference on Economics and Computation, pp. 683–684 (2021)
29. Kurokawa, D., Procaccia, A.D., Wang, J.: When can the maximin share guarantee be guaranteed? In: Thirtieth AAAI Conference on Artificial Intelligence (2016)
30. Kurokawa, D., Procaccia, A.D., Wang, J.: Fair enough: guaranteeing approximate maximin shares. J. ACM (JACM) 65(2), 1–27 (2018)
31. Li, B., Li, Y., Wu, X.: Almost (weighted) proportional allocations for indivisible chores. arXiv preprint arXiv:2103.11849 (2021)
32. Lipton, R.J., Markakis, E., Mossel, E., Saberi, A.: On approximately fair allocations of indivisible goods. In: Proceedings of the 5th ACM Conference on Electronic Commerce, pp. 125–131 (2004)
33. Moulin, H.: Fair Division and Collective Welfare. MIT Press, Cambridge (2004)
34. Padala, M., Gujar, S.: Mechanism design without money for fair allocations (2021)
35. Plaut, B., Roughgarden, T.: Almost envy-freeness with general valuations. SIAM J. Discret. Math. 34(2), 1039–1068 (2020)
36. Procaccia, A.D., Wang, J.: Fair enough: guaranteeing approximate maximin shares. In: Proceedings of the Fifteenth ACM Conference on Economics and Computation, pp. 675–692 (2014)
37. Seddighin, M., Saleh, H., Ghodsi, M.: Externalities and fairness. In: The World Wide Web Conference, pp. 538–548 (2019)
38. Segal-Halevi, E.: Cake-cutting with different entitlements: how many cuts are needed? J. Math. Anal. Appl. 480(1), 123382 (2019)
39. Steihaus, H.: The problem of fair division. Econometrica 16, 101–104 (1948)
40. Su, F.E.: Cake-cutting algorithms: be fair if you can by Jack Robertson and William Webb. Am. Math. Monthly 107(2), 185–188 (2000)
41. Velez, R.A.: Fairness and externalities. Theor. Econ. 11(1), 381–410 (2016)

Robust Weighted Partial Maximum Satisfiability Problem: Challenge to Σ_2^P-Complete Problem

Tomoya Sugahara[1]([✉]), Kaito Yamashita[1], Nathanaël Barrot[2][ID],
Miyuki Koshimura[1][ID], and Makoto Yokoo[1][ID]

[1] Kyushu University, Fukuoka, Japan
sugaharat@agent.inf.kyushu-u.ac.jp
[2] EPF, Graduate School of Engineering, Cachan, France

Abstract. This paper introduces a new problem called the Robust Maximum Satisfiability problem (R-MaxSAT), as well as its extension called the Robust weighted Partial MaxSAT (R-PMaxSAT). In R-MaxSAT (or R-PMaxSAT), a problem solver called defender hopes to maximize the number of satisfied clauses (or the sum of their weights) as the standard MaxSAT/partial MaxSAT problem, although she must ensure that the obtained solution is robust (In this paper, we use the pronoun "she" for the defender and "he" for the attacker). We assume an adversary called the attacker will flip some variables after the defender selects a solution. R-PMaxSAT can formalize the robust Clique Partitioning Problem (robust CPP), where CPP has many real-life applications. We first demonstrate that the decision version of R-MaxSAT is Σ_2^P-complete. Then, we develop two algorithms to solve R-PMaxSAT, by utilizing a state-of-the-art SAT solver or a Quantified Boolean Formula (QBF) solver as a subroutine. Our experimental results show that we can obtain optimal solutions within a reasonable amount of time for randomly generated R-MaxSAT instances with 30 variables and 150 clauses (within 40 s) and R-PMaxSAT instances based on CPP benchmark problems with 60 vertices (within 500 s).

Keywords: MaxSAT · Clique Partition Problem · Robust solution

1 Introduction

In the past few decades, research on the Boolean Satisfiability problem (SAT) has significantly progressed. In particular, various practical SAT solvers have evolved that can solve real-life problem instances reasonably well [1,7,10]. SAT solvers have now become invaluable tools in artificial intelligence, circuit design, and automatic theorem proving. At the same time, various extensions of the standard SAT have been proposed, such as Satisfiability Modulo Theories (SMT) [4], and the Maximum Satisfiability problem (MaxSAT) [2,23,25]. SMT enriches a standard Conjunctive Normal Form (CNF) formula with some background

© The Author(s), under exclusive license to Springer Nature Switzerland AG 2022
S. Khanna et al. (Eds.): PRICAI 2022, LNCS 13629, pp. 17–31, 2022.
https://doi.org/10.1007/978-3-031-20862-1_2

theories, such as the theory of real numbers, the theory of finite trees, and so on. MaxSAT maximizes the number of satisfied clauses instead of checking the satisfiability of the given clauses.

In this paper, we introduce yet another SAT extension called the *Robust Maximum Satisfiability problem* (R-MaxSAT). In R-MaxSAT, the problem solver, which we call the *defender*, hopes to maximize the number of satisfied clauses (like standard MaxSAT), although it must ensure that the obtained solution is robust against the attack of an adversary, called the *attacker*. After the defender selects a solution (i.e., an assignment of all variables), the attacker can flip a fixed number of variables to minimize the number of satisfied clauses.

Our R-MaxSAT model is inspired by a vast amount of literature on security games [29] developed over the last decade. A typical security game is the Stackelberg type, where the defender commits to a mixed (randomized) strategy, and then the attacker chooses his best response given a mixed strategy. Previous studies assume the attacker needs to solve relatively easy problems, many of which are solvable in polynomial time. In our model, the defender commits to a pure strategy, but the attacker needs to solve an NP-hard optimization problem. The decision version of the defender's problem becomes Σ_2^P-complete, which is one level higher than NP-complete problems in the polynomial hierarchy [28].

The Quantified Boolean Formula problem (QBF) allows universal or existential quantifiers to bind the Boolean variables [6,8,14]. Ignatiev *et al.* [18] propose an optimization extension of QBF called the quantified MaxSAT (QMaxSAT). Let us consider a two-level QBF instance $\exists X \forall Y \phi$, where ϕ is a formula represented in CNF and X and Y are sets of variables. If we assume that the existentially quantified variables are assigned by the defender, and the universally quantified variables are assigned by the attacker, this problem has the same structure as R-MaxSAT. However, one fundamental difference is that the variables the attacker can modify in R-MaxSAT are not predefined, as in QBF/QMaxSAT. Actually, a QBF instance with the above structure is equivalent to a standard SAT instance with ϕ', where ϕ' is obtained by simply removing all occurrences of literals containing variables in Y, and its complexity is NP-complete. Research on super-models/solutions [12,13] also considers robust solutions, where a solution must be repaired after the attack. R-MaxSAT's goal is different from that of a super-solution; it simply maximizes the satisfied clauses after the attack without any repairs.

The basic formalization of R-MaxSAT has several limitations in modeling real-life applications. We propose a further extended model called the Robust weighted Partial MaxSAT (R-PMaxSAT) that introduces hard clauses and the attacker's decision/auxiliary variables.[1] We show that R-PMaxSAT can formalize the robust Clique Partitioning Problem (robust CPP), where CPP has many real-life applications. Next, we show that the decision version of R-MaxSAT is Σ_2^P-complete. Then, we develop two algorithms to solve R-PMaxSAT, by utilizing the state-of-the-art SAT/QBF solvers as a subroutine.

---

[1] These variables can overlap with the defender's decision/auxiliary variables.

The rest of the paper is organized as follows. In Sect. 2, we first introduce the model of R-MaxSAT and discuss its limitation. Then, we introduce R-PMaxSAT as an extension of R-MaxSAT. We also introduce the robust CPP as a possible application of R-PMaxSAT. Next, in Sect. 3, we show that the complexity of the decision version of R-MaxSAT is Σ_2^P-complete. Then, in Sect. 4, we introduce two new algorithms for solving R-PMaxSAT, which utilizes state-of-the-art SAT/QBF solvers as a subroutine. In Sect. 5, we compare the performance of these algorithms using randomly generated instances and robust CPP instances. Finally, Sect. 6 concludes this paper.

2 Model

A Boolean Satisfiability problem (SAT) instance is represented as a propositional formula in a Conjunctive Normal Form (CNF). A CNF formula is a conjunction ($\wedge$) of clauses. A clause is a disjunction ($\vee$) of literals. A literal is either a variable or its negation ($\neg$). We regard a clause as the set of the literals in it, and a CNF formula as a set of clauses.

Let Σ denote a set of clauses, and let $X = vars(\Sigma)$ denote the set of variables in Σ. Assignment τ of variables $X' \subseteq X$ maps $X' \mapsto \{0,1\}$. Let $T(X')$ denote all possible assignments to X'. Assignment τ is extended to literals, clauses, and sets of clauses. For all $x \in X$, $\tau(\neg x) = 1$ (or 0) iff $\tau(x) = 0$ (or 1). For clause α, $\tau(\alpha) = 1$ (or 0) iff $\tau(\ell) = 1$ for some $\ell \in \alpha$ (or otherwise). For set of clauses Σ, $\tau(\Sigma) = 1$ (or 0) iff $\tau(\alpha) = 1$ for all $\alpha \in \Sigma$ (or otherwise). Clause α is *satisfied* (or *falsified*) by τ iff $\tau(\alpha) = 1$ (or 0). Let $s(\tau)$ denote the number of clauses satisfied by τ.

The definition of the Maximum Satisfiability problem (MaxSAT) is given as follows.

MaxSAT Problem:
Input: An instance $\langle X, \Sigma \rangle$ of the Maximum Satisfiability problem.
Goal: Find $\tau^* = \arg\max_{\tau' \in T(X)} s(\tau')$.

An instance of the Robust Maximum Satisfiability problem (R-MaxSAT) is defined by tuple $\langle X, \Sigma, m \rangle$, where $m \in \mathbb{N}$ is the maximum number of variables the attacker can flip.

For subsets of variables X' and X'', $\tau' \in T(X')$, $\tau'' \in T(X'')$, and $Y \subseteq X' \cap X''$, let $d(\tau', \tau'', Y)$ denote the number of disagreements between τ' and τ'' for variables in Y, i.e., $|\{y \in Y \mid \tau'(y) \neq \tau''(y)\}|$. Furthermore, let $s_{-m}(\tau)$ denote the minimum number of satisfied clauses after the attacker flipped at most m variables:

$$s_{-m}(\tau) = \min_{\tau' \in T(X), d(\tau,\tau',X) \leq m} s(\tau').$$

The definition of the R-MaxSAT problem is given as follows.

R-MaxSAT Problem:
Input: An instance $\langle X, \Sigma, m \rangle$ of the Robust Maximum Satisfiability problem.
Goal: Find $\tau^* = \arg\max_{\tau' \in T(X)} s_{-m}(\tau')$.

The decision version of this problem asks for given threshold value $\theta \in \mathbb{N}$, whether τ exists s.t. $s_{-m}(\tau) \geq \theta$ holds.

To model real-life applications, the R-MaxSAT formalization has the following limitations.

Hard clauses: When we model a problem as a SAT instance, some clauses may represent physical/mathematical laws, which govern not only the defender but also the attacker. Furthermore, some rules/constraints might exist concerning how the attacker can modify variable values. Such rules/clauses must be obeyed/satisfied by the attacker.

Auxiliary variables: In a SAT formalization, some variables are directly related to the choice/decision making of the problem solver, and other variables are auxiliary, e.g., they are introduced to represent some constraints as CNF. The values of such variables are automatically determined by the value assignment of other variables and hard clauses. Thus, limiting the number of variables that the attacker can flip only makes sense for decision variables; the values of such auxiliary variables must be set appropriately based on the change of the decision variables.

To overcome these limitations, we extend the R-MaxSAT formalization based on the weighted Partial MaxSAT problem (PMaxSAT). PMaxSAT is an extension of MaxSAT, where some clauses are declared to be *soft*, and the rest are declared to be *hard*. The goal is to find an assignment that satisfies all the hard clauses and maximizes the weighted sum of the satisfied soft clauses. Let Σ_H denote the set of hard clauses, and let Σ_S denote the set of soft clauses. Each soft clause $\alpha \in \Sigma_S$ is associated with its weight $w(\alpha) \in \mathbb{N}$. Let $w(\tau)$ denote the weighted sum of the soft clauses satisfied by τ, i.e., $\sum_{\alpha \in \Sigma_S, \tau(\alpha)=1} w(\alpha)$. The definition of the PMaxSAT problem is given as follows, where $X = vars(\Sigma_H) \cup vars(\Sigma_S)$ denotes the set of variables in Σ_H or Σ_S.

PMaxSAT Problem:

Input: An instance $\langle X, \Sigma_H, \Sigma_S, w \rangle$ of the Partial Maximum Satisfiability problem.

Goal: Find $\tau^* = \arg\max_{\tau' \in T(X), \tau'(\Sigma_H)=1} w(\tau')$.

In the Robust weighted Partial Maximum Satisfiability problem (R-PMaxSAT), which is a strict generalization of R-MaxSAT, we consider two sets of hard clauses: Σ_{H_D} is the set of hard clauses that the defender must satisfy, and Σ_{H_A} is the set of hard clauses that the attacker must satisfy. We assume Σ_{H_D} and Σ_{H_A} can overlap. Let X denote all the variables, i.e., $vars(\Sigma_{H_D}) \cup vars(\Sigma_{H_A}) \cup vars(\Sigma_S)$. Furthermore, we assume the set of decision variables for the attacker is explicitly specified as well as the auxiliary variables related to him. More specifically, two sets of variables Y and Z are specified, where $Y \subseteq Z \subseteq vars(\Sigma_{H_A}) \cup vars(\Sigma_S)$ holds. The attacker can flip at most m variables in Y, and he can flip any number of variables in $Z \setminus Y$. For $\tau \in T(X)$ and $\tau_Z \in T(Z)$, let $\tau|\tau_Z$ denote the assignment based on τ, where the assignment of variables in Z is replaced by τ_Z.

Let $w_{-m}(\tau)$ denote the minimum value of the weighted sum of the satisfied clauses in Σ_S after the attacker modified the assignment of Z:

$$w_{-m}(\tau) = \min_{\tau_Z \in T(Z), d(\tau, \tau_Z, Y) \leq m, \tau | \tau_Z(\Sigma_{H_A}) = 1} w(\tau | \tau_Z).$$

The definition of the R-PMaxSAT problem is given as follows.

R-PMaxSAT Problem:

Input: An instance $\langle X, Y, Z, \Sigma_{H_D}, \Sigma_{H_A}, \Sigma_S, w, m \rangle$ of the Robust weighted Partial Maximum Satisfiability problem.

Goal: Find $\tau^* = \arg\max_{\tau' \in T(X), \tau'(\Sigma_{H_D}) = 1} w_{-m}(\tau')$.

Let us illustrate how a real-life application can be formalized as R-PMaxSAT. First, we introduce the Clique Partition Problem (CPP) [17,24]. A CPP instance is a complete edge-weighted undirected graph $G = (V, E, c)$ where V is a set of vertices, E is a set of edges, and c is a weight function $c : E \mapsto \mathbb{Z}$ (note that a weight value can be negative). For simplicity, we denote $c_{i,j} = c(\{i, j\})$. $A \subseteq E$ is *clique partitioning* if partition $\{V_1, V_2, \ldots, V_p\}$ of V exists such that $A = \bigcup_{\ell=1}^{p} \{\{i, j\} \in E \mid i, j \in V_\ell\}$. We call each V_ℓ a *cluster* $(\ell = 1, \ldots, p)$. The goal of CPP is to find clique partitioning A to maximize the sum of weights $\sum_{\{i,j\} \in A} c_{i,j}$. CPP can formalize various application domains, for example: (i) correlation clustering [3,5], where each vertex represents an item (e.g., a document), an edge weight represents the similarity between two documents, and the goal is to cluster the documents into topics, (ii) coalition structure generation [27], where each vertex represents an agent, an edge weight represents the positive/negative synergy between two agents, and the goal is to find a grouping of agents s.t. their total productivity is maximized. CPP can also formalize group technology [16], community detection [11], and so on.

Next, let us introduce the robust CPP, where the attacker can remove at most m vertices (as well as its adjacent edges) after the defender chooses clique partitioning. For the coalition structure generation problem, we assume that the attacker can prevent at most m agents from joining coalitions.[2] For correlation clustering of documents, we can assume that the original data include at most m faked documents created by the attacker, and we optimize the solution quality in the worst case.

We can formalize a CPP instance as PMaxSAT. For each $(i, j) \in P$ ($= \{(i, j) \mid 1 \leq i < j \leq |V|\}$), we introduce variable $x_{i,j}$, which equals 1 if $i, j \in V$ are in the same cluster and 0 otherwise. Hard/soft clauses are given as follows.

Hard clauses Σ_H:

$$\neg x_{i,j} \vee \neg x_{j,k} \vee x_{i,k} \ \forall (i, j, k) \in T,$$
$$\neg x_{i,j} \vee x_{j,k} \vee \neg x_{i,k} \ \forall (i, j, k) \in T,$$
$$x_{i,j} \vee \neg x_{j,k} \vee \neg x_{i,k} \ \forall (i, j, k) \in T.$$

---

[2] A similar problem is considered in [26], while they assume a coalition's value is given as a black-box function called a *characteristic function*.

Defender's hard clauses Σ_{H_D}

$$\neg x_{i,j} \vee \neg x_{j,k} \vee x_{i,k} \; \forall (i,j,k) \in T,$$
$$\neg x_{i,j} \vee x_{j,k} \vee \neg x_{i,k} \; \forall (i,j,k) \in T,$$
$$x_{i,j} \vee \neg x_{j,k} \vee \neg x_{i,k} \; \forall (i,j,k) \in T,$$
$$\neg z_{i,j} \vee x_{i,j} \qquad \forall (i,j) \in P, c_{i,j} > 0,$$
$$\neg x_{i,j} \vee z_{i,j} \qquad \forall (i,j) \in P, c_{i,j} < 0,$$
$$v_i \qquad\qquad\quad \forall i \in V.$$

Attacker's hard clauses Σ_{H_A}

$$\neg x_{i,j} \vee \neg v_i \vee \neg v_j \vee z_{i,j} \; \forall (i,j) \in P,$$
$$\neg z_{i,j} \vee x_{i,j} \qquad\qquad \forall (i,j) \in P,$$
$$\neg z_{i,j} \vee v_i \qquad\qquad\quad \forall (i,j) \in P,$$
$$\neg z_{i,j} \vee v_j \qquad\qquad\quad \forall (i,j) \in P.$$

Soft clauses Σ_S

$$z_{i,j} \text{ with weight } c_{i,j} \qquad \forall (i,j) \in P, c_{i,j} > 0,$$
$$\neg z_{i,j} \text{ with weight } - c_{i,j} \; \forall (i,j) \in P, c_{i,j} < 0.$$

Attacker's decision variables Y

$$v_i \quad \forall i \in V.$$

Attackers auxiliary variables $Z \setminus Y$

$$z_{i,j} \quad \forall (i,j) \in P.$$

Fig. 1. Robust CPP instance formalized as R-PMaxSAT

Soft clauses Σ_S:

$$x_{i,j} \text{ with weight } c_{i,j} \qquad \forall (i,j) \in P, c_{i,j} > 0,$$
$$\neg x_{i,j} \text{ with weight } - c_{i,j} \; \forall (i,j) \in P, c_{i,j} < 0.$$

Here $T = \{(i,j,k) \mid 1 \leq i < j < k \leq |V|\}$. These hard clauses are called *transitivity constraints*, which enforce that if i and j, as well as j and k are in the same cluster, then i and k are also in the same cluster, etc. To handle edge $x_{i,j}$ with negative weight $c_{i,j}$, we assume $-c_{i,j}$ is obtained if $x_{i,j}$ is not selected.

Figure 1 illustrates how a robust CPP instance can be formalized as R-PMaxSAT. Variable v_i represents whether vertex i is present ($v_i = 1$) or absent ($v_i = 0$) due to an attack. The attacker can remove at most m vertices. $z_{i,j}$ is an auxiliary variable, which represents $v_i \wedge v_j \wedge x_{i,j}$. If $z_{i,j} = 1$, the associated weight $c_{i,j}$ is counted. The defender hopes to make $z_{i,j}$ to 1 (or to 0) as much as possible if $c_{i,j}$ is positive (or negative). The defender's hard clauses ensure that she can set $z_{i,j} = 1$ (or $z_{i,j} = 0$) only if $x_{i,j} = 1$ (or $x_{i,j} = 0$). The attacker's goal is contrary. His hard clauses ensure that (i) he can flip $z_{i,j}$ from 1 to 0 only when either $v_i = 0$ or $v_j = 0$ holds, (ii) he cannot flip $z_{i,j}$ from 0 to 1, and (iii) if he makes vertex i (or j) absent, the weights of all edges related to i (or j) are not counted.

3 Complexity of R-MaxSAT Problem

In this section, we examine the complexity of the decision version of R-MaxSAT. First, we introduce the following verification problem called R-MaxSAT-Verif. For $X' \subseteq X$ and $\tau \in T(X)$, let $\tau_{\overline{X'}}$ denote the assignment obtained from τ by flipping the variables in X'.

R-MaxSAT-Verif:
Input: A Robust Maximum Satisfiability instance $\langle X, \Sigma, m \rangle$, threshold value $\theta \in \mathbb{N}$, and assignment τ of X.
Question: Does $X' \subseteq X$, $|X'| \leq m$ exist such that assignment $\tau_{\overline{X'}}$ satisfies at most θ clauses?

Our proof utilizes a Σ_2^P-complete problem called CO-MINMAXCLIQUE, which is a complement of MINMAXCLIQUE [22]. These problems are based on the well-known MAXCLIQUE problem.

---

co-MinMaxClique:
Input: Graph $G = (V, E)$, two sets I and J that partition V into $\{V_{i,j} \mid i \in I, j \in J\}$, and integer k.
Question: Does function $t : I \rightarrow J$ exist such that subgraph $G[\cup_{i \in I} V_{i,t(i)}]$ does not contain a clique of size k?

Intuitively, V is partitioned into $|I| \cdot |J|$ subsets $V_{i,j}$, and for each function $t : I \rightarrow J$, we consider a MAXCLIQUE problem in subgraph $G[\cup_{i \in I} V_{i,t(i)}]$. Problem CO-MINMAXCLIQUE remains Σ_2^P-complete when $J = \{0, 1\}$.

We start by showing that R-MaxSAT-Verif is NP-complete.

Theorem 1. *Problem R-MaxSAT-Verif is NP-complete.*

Proof. First, R-MaxSAT-Verif is trivially in NP, since given a solution X', we can compute the number of clauses satisfied by assignment $\tau_{\overline{X'}}$ in polynomial time. We show that R-MaxSAT-Verif is NP-hard by reduction from MAXCLIQUE.

Given graph $G = (V, E)$ and integer k, we construct an instance of R-MaxSAT-Verif:

- For each $v \in V$, we create variable $x_v \in X$.
- For each $e = \{v, w\} \in E$, we create clause $\sigma_e : \neg x_v \vee \neg x_w$ in Σ.
- Finally, we set $m = k$, $\theta = |\Sigma| - k(k-1)/2$, and τ such that all variables are false.

($\Rightarrow$) Assume that a clique of size k exists in G, denoted by V'. Consider $X' = \{x_v \in X \mid v \in V'\}$. Since V' is a clique, for all $x_v, x_w \in X'$, clause $\sigma_{\{v,w\}}$ belongs to Σ and is false under assignment $\tau_{\overline{X'}}$. Hence, assignment $\tau_{\overline{X'}}$ satisfies at most $\theta = |\Sigma| - k(k-1)/2$.

($\Leftarrow$) Assume there exists $X' \subseteq X$, $|X'| \leq k$ such that at least $k(k-1)/2$ clauses are not satisfied under $\tau_{\overline{X'}}$. By the definition of τ, clause $\sigma_{\{v,w\}}$ is false under $\tau_{\overline{X'}}$ if and only if both $x_v, x_w \in X'$. This implies that $|X'| = k$ and for all $x_v, x_w \in X'$, clause $\sigma_{\{v,w\}}$ belongs to Σ. Hence, for all $v, w \in V$ such that $x_v, x_w \in X'$, edge $\{v, w\}$ belongs to E and thus $V' = \{v \in V \mid x_v \in X'\}$ is a clique of size k.

We can now show that R-MaxSAT is Σ_2^P-complete.

Theorem 2. *The decision version of R-MaxSAT is Σ_2^P-complete.*

Proof. First, R-MaxSAT is in Σ_2^P by Theorem 1. R-MaxSAT is proved Σ_2^P-hard by reduction from co-MINMAXCLIQUE.

Given graph $G = (V, E)$, set I that partitions V into $\{V_{i,j} \mid i \in I, j \in \{0, 1\}\}$, and integer k, we construct an instance of R-MaxSAT. Partition sets X and Σ: $X = X^V \cup Z \cup Y$ and $\Sigma = \Sigma^E \cup \Sigma^Z \cup \Sigma^Y$.

- For each $v \in V$, we create variable $x_v \in X^V$.
- For each $i \in I$, we create two variables $z_{i0}, z_{i1} \in Z$.
- We create a set of k dummy variables $Y = (y_i)_{i \in [1, \ldots, k]}$.
- For each $e = \{v, w\} \in E$, with $v \in V_{i,j}$ and $w \in V_{i',j'}$, we create clause $\sigma_e : \neg x_v \vee \neg x_w \vee \neg z_{ij} \vee \neg z_{i'j'}$ in Σ^E.
- For each $i \in I$, we create two clauses $\sigma_{i1}^z : z_{i0} \vee z_{i1} \vee y_1$ and $\sigma_{i2}^z : \neg z_{i0} \vee \neg z_{i1} \vee y_1$ in Σ^Z.
- For each $i \in [1, \ldots, k-1]$ and $j \in [i+1, \ldots, k]$, except for arbitrary pair (i, j), we create clause $\sigma_{ij}^y : y_i \vee y_j$ in Σ^Y.
  Notice that $|\Sigma^E| = |E|$, $|\Sigma^Z| = 2 \cdot |I|$, and $|\Sigma^Y| = k(k-1)/2 - 1$.
- We set $m = k$ and $\theta = |\Sigma| - k(k-1)/2 + 1$, where $|\Sigma| = |\Sigma^E| + |\Sigma^Z| + |\Sigma^Y| = |E| + 2 \cdot |I| + k(k-1)/2 - 1$.

($\Rightarrow$) Assume that there exists function $t^* : I \mapsto \{0, 1\}$ such that no clique of size k exists in the subgraph induced by $\bigcup_{i \in I} V_{i t^*(i)}$. Consider assignment τ^*: for all $v \in V$, variable x_v is false; for all $i \in I$, $z_{i t^*(i)}$ is true and $z_{i(1-t^*(i))}$ is false; and for all $i \in [1, \ldots, k]$, y_i is true.

Toward a contradiction, assume that there exists $X' \subseteq X$, $|X'| \leq k$, such that at least $k(k-1)/2$ clauses are not satisfied in $\tau_{\overline{X'}}^*$. Denote $h_1 = |X' \cap X^V|$, $h_2 = |X' \cap Z|$, and $h_3 = |X' \cap Y|$. Note that in τ^*, all clauses are satisfied. Moreover, by construction of τ^*, the only way that $k(k-1)/2$ clauses are not satisfied in $\tau_{\overline{X'}}^*$ is when $h_1 = k$, $h_2 = h_3 = 0$ and for all $x_v, x_w \in X'$, (i) clause $\sigma_{\{v,w\}}$ belongs to Σ and (ii) $\sigma_{\{v,w\}}$ is not satisfied under $\tau_{\overline{X'}}^*$. For all $x_v, x_w \in X'$, condition (i) implies that edge $\{v, w\}$ belongs to E and condition (ii) implies that nodes v and w belong to $\bigcup_{i \in I} V_{i, t^*(i)}$.

Thus, $V' = \{v \in V : x_v \in X'\}$ is a clique of size k in the subgraph induced by $\bigcup_{i \in I} V_{i, t^*(i)}$, which is a contradiction.

($\Leftarrow$) Assume assignment τ^* exists such that for all $X' \subseteq X$, $|X'| \leq k$, at most $k(k-1)/2 - 1$ clauses are not satisfied by $\tau^*_{\overline{X'}}$.

First, we show that each $y_i \in Y$ is true in τ^*. Assume that $y_i \in Y$ exists and is false in τ^*. Let $Y^* = \{y_i \in Y : y_i \text{ is true in } \tau^*\}$. By setting $Y^* \subseteq X'$, the $k(k-1)/2 - 1$ clauses in Σ^Y are not satisfied by assignment $\tau^*_{\overline{X'}}$. Then if z_{10} and z_{11} are both true/false in τ^*, we set $X' = Y^*$; otherwise, we set $X' = Y^* \cup \{z_{10}\}$. In both cases, one additional clause (σ^z_{11} or σ^z_{12}) is false in $\tau^*_{\overline{X'}}$, which is a contradiction.

We now show that for all $i \in I$, exactly one variable from $\{z_{i0}, z_{i1}\}$ is true. Assume that $i' \in I$ exists such that variables $z_{i'0}$ and $z_{i'1}$ are both true/false in τ^*. By setting $X' = Y$, the $k(k-1)/2 - 1$ clauses in Σ^Y are not satisfied and at least one additional clause ($\sigma^z_{i'1}$ or $\sigma^z_{i'2}$) is not satisfied by assignment $\tau^*_{\overline{X'}}$, which is a contradiction.

Hence, we can define function $t^* : I \mapsto \{0,1\}$ such that $t^*(i) = 0$ if z_{i0} is true, and $t^*(i) = 1$ if z_{i1} is true.

Finally, toward a contradiction, assume that a clique of size k exists in subgraph $G[\bigcup_{i \in I} V_{i,t^*(i)}]$. Let V^* denote such a clique and consider $X' = \{x_v \in X^V \mid v \in V^* \text{ and } x_v \text{ is false in } \tau^*\}$. Then all $x_v \in X^V$ such that $v \in V^*$ are true in $\tau^*_{\overline{X'}}$. Since V^* is a clique, for all $v, w \in V^*$, clause $\sigma_{\{v,w\}}$ belongs to Σ^E and is not satisfied in $\tau^*_{\overline{X'}}$. Hence, at least $k(k-1)/2$ clauses from Σ^E are not satisfied by assignment $\tau^*_{\overline{X'}}$, which is a contradiction.

4 R-PMaxSAT Algorithms

4.1 Iterative Best Response (IBR) Algorithm

The outline of our newly developed Iterative Best Response (IBR) algorithm is as follows. IBR first chooses an optimal solution of defender τ assuming there is no attack. Then, it calculates the best attack τ_Z against τ and revises τ s.t. it is optimal against τ_Z. Next, it revises τ_Z, so that it is the best attack against the revised τ. It keeps all the attacks examined so far and revises the defender's best preparation. IBR can be considered as an optimization version of *Counter Example Guided Abstraction Refinement (CEGAR)* for 2-level QBF [9,21].

Algorithm 1 shows the details of IBR. Here, Δ is the set of attacks examined so far (which is initialized to an empty set at line 2). At line 4, we select assignment τ that maximizes $w_{-\Delta}(\tau)$, where $w_{-\Delta}(\tau)$ denotes $\min_{\tau_Z \in \Delta, \tau | \tau_Z(\Sigma_{H_A})=1} w(\tau | \tau_Z)$. That is, τ is the defender's best assignment, assuming the possible attacks are limited to Δ (here, we consider only *valid* attacks s.t. attacker's hard clauses are satisfied). If $w_{-\Delta}(\tau) < ub$, we update ub to $w_{-\Delta}(\tau)$ (line 6). At line 8, we select the attacker's best attack against τ. Here, for $\tau \in T(X)$, *best-attack(τ)* is defined:

$$\arg \min_{\tau_Z \in T(Z), d(\tau, \tau_Z, Y) \leq m, \tau | \tau_Z(\Sigma_{H_A})=1} w(\tau | \tau_Z).$$

If $w(\tau | \tau_Z) \geq lb$ holds, we update lb and *best-assignment* to $w(\tau | \tau_Z)$ and τ (line 10). At line 12, τ_Z is added to Δ.

Algorithm 1: Iterative best response (IBR)

Input: $\Sigma_{H_D}, \Sigma_{H_A}, \Sigma_S, X, Y, Z, w, m$

Output: lower bound lb, upper bound ub, and a defender's optimal assignment τ^*

1: $(lb, ub, best\text{-}assignment) \leftarrow (0, \max_{\tau' \in T(X), \tau'(\Sigma_{H_D})=1} w(\tau'), \emptyset)$

2: $\Delta \leftarrow \emptyset$ // a set of attacks examined so far

3: **while** *true* **do**

4:    $\tau \leftarrow \arg\max_{\tau' \in T(X), \tau'(\Sigma_{H_D})=1} w_{-\Delta}(\tau')$

5:    **if** $w_{-\Delta}(\tau) < ub$ **then**

6:       $ub \leftarrow w_{-\Delta}(\tau)$

7:    **end if**

8:    $\tau_Z \leftarrow best\text{-}attack(\tau)$

9:    **if** $w(\tau|\tau_Z) \geq lb$ **then**

10:       $(lb, best\text{-}assignment) \leftarrow (w(\tau|\tau_Z), \tau)$

11:    **end if**

12:    $\Delta \leftarrow \Delta \cup \{\tau_Z\}$

13:    **if** $lb = ub$ **then**

14:       **return** $(lb, ub, best\text{-}assignment)$

15:    **end if**

16: **end while**

At line 4, τ is obtained as follows. Let $\Sigma(\tau_Z)$ denote a set of clauses Σ, where the variables in Z are instantiated as τ_Z. Furthermore, let $W(\Sigma, \theta)$ denote a formula representing the fact that the weighted sum of satisfied clauses in Σ is at least θ (where each $\alpha \in \Sigma$ is associated with its weight). First, we set $\theta = ub$ and check whether there exists τ s.t. for each $\tau_Z \in \Delta$, $\neg\Sigma_{H_A}(\tau_Z) \vee (\Sigma_{H_D}(\tau_Z) \wedge W(\Sigma_S(\tau_Z), \theta))$ is satisfiable by using a SAT-solver. If so, τ maximizes $w_{-\Delta}(\tau)$. Otherwise, we decrease θ one by one until the above condition is satisfied.

Next, let us describe how to obtain $best\text{-}attack(\tau)$ at line 8. Let Y' and Z' ($Y' \subseteq Z'$) denote copies of the variables of Y and Z. Also, let $\widehat{\Sigma}$ denote a set of clauses Σ, where each variable in Z is replaced by the corresponding variable in Z'. Furthermore, let $D(Y, Y', m)$ denote a formula representing the fact that the number of disagreements between Y and Y' is at most m, and let $\tau_{X \backslash Z}$ denote the assignment of variables $X \backslash Z$ based on τ, i.e., $\tau_{X \backslash Z}(x) = \tau(x)$ holds for all $x \in X \backslash Z$. Using these notations, $\tau_Z = best\text{-}attack(\tau)$ is given as a solution of the following minimization problem:

Hard clauses: $\widehat{\Sigma}_{H_A}(\tau_{X \backslash Z}) \cup D(Y, Y', m)$,

Soft clauses: $\widehat{\Sigma}_S(\tau_{X \backslash Z})$.

In our experiment, we translated the above minimization problem to a PMaxSAT instance. Regarding the termination of IBR, lb and ub will eventually meet; in the worst case, Δ contains all possible attacks. IBR is an anytime algorithm; it can be interrupted at any time, i.e., the following theorem holds.

Theorem 3. *During the execution of IBR, $lb \leq w_{-m}(\tau^*) \leq ub$ holds. Thus, when IBR is interrupted during its execution, the absolute difference between the optimal value and the value of the obtained solution is bounded by $ub - lb$.*

Proof. Since lb is equal to $w(\tau|\tau_Z) = w_{-m}(\tau)$ for one particular assignment τ, $lb = w_{-m}(\tau) \leq \max_{\tau'} w_{-m}(\tau') = w_{-m}(\tau^*)$ holds. Also, ub is equal to $w_{-\Delta}(\tau)$, where τ is the best assignment for one particular Δ. By definition, $w_{-m}(\tau^*) \leq w_{-\Delta}(\tau^*)$ holds, since $w_{-m}(\cdot)$ considers all possible attacks while $w_{-\Delta}(\cdot)$ only considers attacks in Δ. Also, $w_{-\Delta}(\tau^*) \leq w_{-\Delta}(\tau)$ holds since τ is the best assignment against Δ. Thus, $w_{-m}(\tau^*) \leq ub$ holds.

4.2   Ascending Linear Search in QBF (ALSQ) Algorithm

The decision version of an R-PMaxSAT instance with threshold value $\theta \in \mathbb{N}$ asks whether there exists τ s.t. $w_{-m}(\tau) \geq \theta$ holds. It can be translated into a QBF formula:

$$\exists X \forall Z'[\Sigma_{H_D} \wedge \widehat{\Sigma}_{H_D} \wedge \{(\widehat{\Sigma}_{H_A} \wedge D(Y, Y', m)) \rightarrow W(\widehat{\Sigma}_S, \theta)\}].$$

Using the above translation technique, we can construct another algorithm for solving an R-PMaxSAT instance. We set lb (initialized to 0) and solve the corresponding QBF with $\theta = lb$ using a QBF solver. This formula is an instance of 2-level QBF, whose complexity is Σ_2^P-complete [8]. If the QBF formula is satisfiable, then we continue to increment the value of lb by one until the QBF formula becomes unsatisfiable. We call this algorithm the Ascending Linear Search in QBF (ALSQ). A similar algorithm, called the Quantified Linear Search UNSAT-SAT (QLSUS), is presented in [18].

Algorithm 2: Ascending linear search in QBF (ALSQ)

Input: $\Sigma_{H_D}, \Sigma_{H_A}, \Sigma_S, X, Y, Z, w, m$
Output: lower bound lb, upper bound ub, and a defender's optimal assignment τ^*
1: $(lb, ub, \text{best-assignment}) \leftarrow (0, \max_{\tau' \in T(X), \tau'(\Sigma_{H_D})=1} w(\tau'), \emptyset)$
2: **for** $lb = 1$ **to** ub **do**
3:      $(flag, \tau) \leftarrow \text{QBF}(lb)$
4:      **if** $flag = false$ **then**
5:          **return** $(lb, lb, \text{best-assignment})$
6:      **end if**
7:      $(lb, \text{best-assignment}) \leftarrow (lb + 1, \tau)$
8: **end for**

Algorithm 2 shows the outline of ALSQ. Here $\text{QBF}(\theta)$ denotes the call of a QBF solver for the above QBF formula with threshold θ, which returns *true* (or *false*) when the QBF is satisfiable (or unsatisfiable) as well as τ (the assignment of X) when the QBF is satisfiable. Unlike IBR, this algorithm cannot obtain/update ub. Thus, we use $\max_{\tau' \in T(X), \tau'(\Sigma_{H_D})=1} w(\tau')$ as ub if the algorithm is interrupted during its execution.

We have examined a seemingly more sophisticated search method, e.g., a binary search, but its performance degraded significantly. This is because the call of $\text{QBF}(\theta)$ for an unsatisfiable instance is much more expensive compared to a call for a satisfiable instance.

Table 1. Experimental data of random instances ($n = 30$)

	ALSQ			IBR		
	lb	ub	time [s]	lb	ub	time [s]
$\ell = 50$	46.0	46.0	5.53	46.0	46.0	1.01
$\ell = 75$	69.0	69.0	530.73	69.0	69.0	2.28
$\ell = 100$	91.8	99.4	538.22	92.1	92.1	8.16
$\ell = 125$	114.4	125.0	>3600	114.7	114.7	20.61
$\ell = 150$	136.6	150.0	>3600	137.5	137.5	36.28

Table 2. Experimental data of R-CPP instances

	ALSQ			IBR		
	lb	ub	time [s]	lb	ub	time [s]
$p = 12$	25	25	2.04	25	25	0.02
$p = 18$	66	66	13.51	66	66	0.05
$p = 28$	89	160	>3600	95	95	25.84
$p = 38$	297	336	>3600	299	299	3.60
$p = 42$	355	432	>3600	369	369	99.29
$p = 59$	571	688	>3600	593	593	461.90
$p = 64$	837	960	>3600	866	871	>3600

5 Experimental Evaluation

We experimentally evaluated the performance of our proposed algorithms with both random R-MaxSAT and R-PMaxSAT instances based on CPP benchmark problems. We ran our tests on the following hardware/software: an Intel Core i7-6700X CPU 4.00-GHz processor with 32-GB RAM, Windows 10 Education 64 bit, and a Python toolkit, PySAT [19,20]. We used a SAT solver called CaDiCaL [7] for IBR, and a QBF solver called QuAbS [30] for ALSQ. We also used pseudo-Boolean and cardinality encodings provided by PySAT with the default settings to generate formulas $W(\Sigma, \theta)$ and $D(Y, Y', m)$ described in Sect. 4.

5.1 Random Instances

The experiments were based on synthetic 3-SAT instances, which we randomly generated with n variables with ℓ clauses. We set the number of variables n to 30 and the number of clauses ℓ to [50, 150]. We set the maximum number of attacked variables m to $n/10$. Table 1 shows the execution time, as well as lb/ub. Each data is an average of 10 problem instances. We set the time limit to 3600 s. For all the problem instances, IBR obtained an optimal solution. In Table 1, ">3600" means that ALSQ fails to terminate for all 10 instances. When $\ell = 100$ (the shaded cell), ALSQ can solve just one instance in 538 s.

For the largest problem instances (where $\ell = 150$), IBR's running time to obtain an optimal solution was less than 40 s. For these problem instances, we ran ALSQ without a time limit; it did not terminate even after 24 h. ALSQ requires a very long time in the last execution of line 3 in Algorithm 2, where its return value is *false*, i.e., the given QBF formula is unsatisfiable.

5.2   Robust CPP Instances

We created robust CPP instances from CPP instances for group technology [24], which were generated from manufacturing cell formation datasets on http://mauricio.resende.info/data. The number of vertices p is $12, 18, 28, 38, 42, 59$, or 64. A detailed description of the datasets can be found in [15].

We set the maximum number of attacked variables m to $\lceil \frac{p}{10} \rceil$, and the time limit to 3600 s. After the translation, the obtained R-PMaxSAT instance has $O(p^2)$ variables, $O(p^3)$ hard clauses, and $O(p^2)$ soft clauses.

Table 2 shows the upper/lower bounds and the execution times obtained by these algorithms. Clearly, IBR is more efficient than ALSQ. IBR obtained an optimal solution for all cases except $p = 64$, while ALSQ failed to obtain an optimal solution within the time limit where $p \geq 28$. The obtained lower/upper bounds, in particular, the upper bounds, are rather far from optimal values. When $p = 64$, both algorithms cannot obtain an optimal solution within the time limit, while IBR obtains better lower/upper bounds compared to ALSQ.

IBR solves many NP-complete problem instances, while ALSQ solves fewer Σ_2^P-complete problem instances. Our evaluation results imply that the former approach seems more promising. We do not have a clear answer yet why this is the case, but one possible reason is that IBR can utilize the information of ub obtained during the search process.

6   Conclusions

We introduced new variations of MaxSAT called R-MaxSAT and R-PMaxSAT, where the goal is to find a robust solution against an adversary's attack. We proved that the decision version of R-MaxSAT is Σ_2^P-complete. We then introduced two algorithms for solving R-PMaxSAT: IBR/ALSQ, which utilize state-of-the-art SAT/QBF solvers. Experimental evaluations showed that IBR is much faster than ALSQ and can obtain optimal solutions within a reasonable amount of time for fairly large problem instances. Our immediate future works include examining how to model other application domains as R-PMaxSAT and extending/improving IBR, e.g., introducing an abstraction method similar to CEGAR such that Δ becomes compact and we can solve related optimization problems more efficiently.

Acknowledgements. This work is supported by JSPS KAKENHI Grant Numbers JP19H04175, JP20H00609, and JP22K19813.

References

1. Audemard, G., Simon, L.: Predicting learnt clauses quality in modern SAT solvers. In: Proceedings of the 21st International Joint Conference on Artificial Intelligence (IJCAI-2009), pp. 399–404 (2009)
2. Bacchus, F., Järvisalo, M., Martins, R.: Maximum satisfiability. In: Handbook of Satisfiability, Second Edition, pp. 929–991. IOS Press (2021)
3. Bansal, N., Blum, A., Chawla, S.: Correlation clustering. Mach. Learn. **56**(1–3), 89–113 (2004)
4. Barrett, C., Sebastiani, R., Seshia, S.A., Tinelli, C.: Satisfiability modulo theories. In: Handbook of Satisfiability, Second Edition, pp. 1267–1329. IOS Press (2021)
5. Berg, J., Järvisalo, M.: Cost-optimal constrained correlation clustering via weighted partial maximum satisfiability. Artif. Intell. **244**, 110–142 (2017)
6. Beyersdorff, O., Janota, M., Lonsing, F., Seidl, M.: Quantified Boolean formulas. In: Handbook of Satisfiability, Second Edition, pp. 1177–1221. IOS Press (2021)
7. Biere, A., Fazekas, K., Fleury, M., Heisinger, M.: CaDiCaL, Kissat, Paracooba, Plingeling and Treengeling entering the SAT Competition 2020. In: Proceedings of SAT Competition 2020: Solver and Benchmark Descriptions, vol. B-2020-1, pp. 51–53. Department of Computer Science, University of Helsinki (2020)
8. Büning, H.K., Bubeck, U.: Theory of quantified Boolean formulas. In: Handbook of Satisfiability, Second Edition, pp. 1131–1156. IOS Press (2021)
9. Clarke, E., Grumberg, O., Jha, S., Lu, Y., Veith, H.: Counterexample-guided abstraction refinement. In: Emerson, E.A., Sistla, A.P. (eds.) CAV 2000. LNCS, vol. 1855, pp. 154–169. Springer, Heidelberg (2000). https://doi.org/10.1007/10722167_15
10. Eén, N., Sörensson, N.: An extensible SAT-solver. In: Giunchiglia, E., Tacchella, A. (eds.) SAT 2003. LNCS, vol. 2919, pp. 502–518. Springer, Heidelberg (2004). https://doi.org/10.1007/978-3-540-24605-3_37
11. Fortunato, S.: Community detection in graphs. Phys. Rep. **486**, 75–174 (2010)
12. Genc, B., Siala, M., O'Sullivan, B., Simonin, G.: Robust stable marriage. In: Proceedings of the 31st AAAI Conference on Artificial Intelligence (AAAI-2017), pp. 4925–4926 (2017)
13. Ginsberg, M.L., Parkes, A.J., Roy, A.: Supermodels and robustness. In: Proceedings of the 15th National Conference on Artificial Intelligence (AAAI-1998), pp. 334–339 (1998)
14. Giunchiglia, E., Marin, P., Narizzano, M.: Reasoning with quantified Boolean formulas. In: Handbook of Satisfiability, Second Edition, pp. 1157–1176. IOS Press (2021)
15. Gonçalves, J.F., Resende, M.G.: An evolutionary algorithm for manufacturing cell formation. Comput. Industr. Eng. **47**(2–3), 247–273 (2004)
16. Groover, M.P.: Automation, Production Systems, and Computer-Integrated Manufacturing. Third Edition, Pearson (2008)
17. Grötschel, M., Wakabayashi, Y.: A cutting plane algorithm for a clustering problem. Math. Program. **45**(1–3), 59–96 (1989)
18. Ignatiev, A., Janota, M., Marques-Silva, J.: Quantified maximum satisfiability. Constraints **21**(2), 277–302 (2016)
19. Ignatiev, A., Morgado, A., Marques-Silva, J.: PySAT: a Python toolkit for prototyping with SAT oracles. In: Proceedings of the 24th International Conference on Theory and Applications of Satisfiability Testing (SAT-2018), pp. 428–437 (2018)

20. Ignatiev, A., Morgado, A., Marques-Silva, J.: RC2: an efficient MaxSAT solver. J. Satisf. Boolean Model. Comput. **11**(1), 53–64 (2019)
21. Janota, M., Klieber, W., Marques-Silva, J., Clarke, E.M.: Solving QBF with counterexample guided refinement. Artif. Intell. **234**, 1–25 (2016)
22. Ko, K.I., Lin, C.L.: On the complexity of Min-Max optimization problems and their approximation. In: Minimax and Applications, pp. 219–239. Springer (1995). https://doi.org/10.1007/978-1-4613-3557-3_15
23. Li, C.M., Manyà, F.: MaxSAT, hard and soft constraints. In: Handbook of Satisfiability, Second Edition, pp. 903–927. IOS Press (2021)
24. Miyauchi, A., Sonobe, T., Sukegawa, N.: Exact clustering via integer programming and maximum satisfiability. In: Proceedings of the 32nd AAAI Conference on Artificial Intelligence (AAAI-18), pp. 1387–1394 (2018)
25. Morgado, A., Heras, F., Liffiton, M.H., Planes, J., Marques-Silva, J.: Iterative and core-guided MaxSAT solving: A survey and assessment. Constraints **18**(4), 478–534 (2013)
26. Okimoto, T., Schwind, N., Demirović, E., Inoue, K., Marquis, P.: Robust coalition structure generation. In: Miller, T., Oren, N., Sakurai, Y., Noda, I., Savarimuthu, B.T.R., Cao Son, T. (eds.) PRIMA 2018. LNCS (LNAI), vol. 11224, pp. 140–157. Springer, Cham (2018). https://doi.org/10.1007/978-3-030-03098-8_9
27. Rahwan, T., Michalak, T.P., Wooldridge, M.J., Jennings, N.R.: Coalition structure generation: a survey. Artif. Intell. **229**, 139–174 (2015)
28. Stockmeyer, L.J.: The polynomial-time hierarchy. Theor. Comput. Sci. **3**(1), 1–22 (1976)
29. Tambe, M.: Security and Game Theory: Algorithms, Deployed Systems, Lessons Learned. Cambridge University Press, Cambridge (2011)
30. Tentrup, L.: CAQE and QuAbS: abstraction based QBF solvers. J. Satisf. Boolean Model. Comput. **11**(1), 155–210 (2019)

Epistemic Logic via Distance and Similarity

Xiaolong Liang[1] and Yì N. Wáng[2]([✉]) [iD]

[1] School of Philosophy and Sociology, Shanxi University, Taiyuan 030006, China
[2] Department of Philosophy (Zhuhai), Sun Yat-sen University, Zhuhai 519082, China
ynw@xixilogic.org

Abstract. A weighted graph extends a standard Kripke frame for modal logic with a weight on each of its edges. Distance and similarity measures can be imposed so that the edges stand for the dissimilairty/similarity relation between nodes (in particular, we focus on the distance and similarity metrics introduced in [5]). Models based on these types of weighted graphs give a simple and flexible way of formally interpreting knowledge. We study proof systems and computational complexity of the resulting logics, partially by correspondence to normal modal logics interpreted in Kripke semantics.

1 Introduction

Epistemic logic [11] is a classical discipline of modal logic that has been successful especially by interpretation using Kprike semantics [6,8,15]. There have been studies in a vast variety of topics in this area, e.g., those about modeling *group knowledge* (such as common and distributed knowledge), modeling *knowability* [1,2] and modeling *knows-how* [18]. In recent years there has been a strand that builds a relationship to weighted models for modal logic [10,13]. For example, [16] introduces a logic of confidence that uses a type of weighted models in which the weight between two nodes (possible worlds) stands for the distance between them, and a formula $\Box_a^c \varphi$ expresses that "agent a knows φ under the degree c of uncertainty" in the sense that φ is true in all possible worlds that are of distance $\leq c$ from the actual world (too dissimilar for the agent treat them the same). [7] extends this to similarity models where $\Box_a^r$ expresses that "agent a knows with capability r that φ is the case" in the sense that φ is true in all possible worlds that are similar to the actual world in a degree $\geq r$ (too similar for the agent to discern between).

In this paper we study epistemic logic interpreted over weighted models, with some considerations in particular that make this work different from existing literature. First of all, distance/dissimilarity and similarity are notions closely related to each other, and we are interested in comparing the ways in which we interpret knowledge using either of the notions. Second, we borrow the characterizations of distance and similarity metrics from the area of data mining

Supported by the National Social Science Fund of China (Grant No. 20&ZD047).

© The Author(s), under exclusive license to Springer Nature Switzerland AG 2022
S. Khanna et al. (Eds.): PRICAI 2022, LNCS 13629, pp. 32–45, 2022.
https://doi.org/10.1007/978-3-031-20862-1_3

(see, e.g., [17]), but we are interested in more sophisticated characterizations of distance and similarity rather than the basic ones. In particular, we adopt the notion of a similarity metric introduced in [5] where five conditions are required for the real-valued similarity measures. Finally, we choose to use the standard epistemic language where only sentences like $K_a\varphi$ which reads "agent a knows φ" – without an explicit degree of epistemic uncertainty/ability appearing in the sentence – are allowed for expressing knowledge. This gives us a good perspective of comparing the formal interpretations of knowledge using standard Kripke models and weighted models.

While a duality result can be expected between the basic logics interpreted via distance and similarity (called ELD⁻ and ELS⁻, respectively), the distance and similarity models we will work on (which give us the logics ELD and ELS) lead us to more properties as will be explained in later sections. Interesting results also include a complexity result – weighted models do not increase computational complexity for the model and satisfiability checking problems.

The structure of the paper is as follows. In the next section we introduce the basic concepts of graphs, models and the epistemic language. In Sect. 3 four different epistemic logics interpreted in distance and similarity models are introduced. Then we work on sound and complete aximotizations for these logics (Sect. 4) and the computation complexity of the model and satisfiability checking problems (Sect. 5). We conclude and discuss in Sect. 6.

2   Preliminaries

In this section we introduce the models and the language of the logics that will be introduced later.

We shall make use of a type of weighted graphs, in which weights are real numbers, for the purpose of modeling epistemic abilities. A **weighted graph** (for this purpose) is defined formally as a pair (W, E) where:

– W is a nonempty set of states, and
– The edge function $E : W \times W \to \mathbb{R}$ assigns to every pair of states a real number, standing for the degree of (dis)similarity between the states.

We now introduce two special types of weighted graphs which will be the bases for the epistemic logics to be introduced.

Definition 1 (distance graphs). *A pair (W, E) is called a* distance graph *if it is a weighted graph such that the following hold for all states $s, t, u \in W$:*

1. *$E(s,t) \geq 0$ (non-negativity),*
2. *$E(s,t) = E(t,s)$ (symmetry),*
3. *$E(s,u) \leq E(s,t) + E(t,u)$ (triangle inequality), and*
4. *$E(s,t) = 0$ if and only if $s = t$ (identity of indiscernibles).*

The four conditions on the edge function in the above definition are standard for forming a *distance metric* over the weights.

Unlike classical literature on similarity measures (say, those defined in [17, Section 2.4.4] for similarities between data objects[1]), we are interested in a more sophisticated definition of similarity metric introduced in [5], where five conditions on the weights are enforced and explained in detail. We adopt these conditions and introduce the following definition of similarity graphs.

Definition 2 (similarity graphs). *A pair* (W, E) *is called a* similarity graph *if it is a weighted graph such that the following hold for all states* $s, t, u \in W$:

1. $E(s,t) = E(t,s)$,
2. $E(s,s) \geq 0$,
3. $E(s,s) \geq E(s,t)$,
4. $E(s,t) + E(t,u) \leq E(s,u) + E(t,t)$, *and*
5. $E(s,s) = E(t,t) = E(s,t)$ *if and only if* $s = t$.

We assume Ag to be a finite nonempty set of agents and Prop a countable set of propositional atoms.

Definition 3 (models). *A* model *is a quadruple* (W, E, C, ν) *such that:*

- (W, E) *is a weighted graph,*
- $C : Ag \to \mathbb{R}$ *assigns to every agent a degree of its epistemic ability, and*
- $\nu : W \to \wp(Prop)$ *is a valuation assigning to every state a set of propositional atoms that are true in it.*

A model (W, E, C, ν) *is called a* distance model *(resp.* similarity model*) if* (W, E) *forms a distance graph (resp. similarity graph).*

We shall work on the standard formal language of epistemic logic.

Definition 4 (language). *The formulas of the default language is given inductively as follows:*

$$\varphi :: = p \mid \neg\varphi \mid (\varphi \to \varphi) \mid K_a\varphi$$

where $p \in Prop$ *and* $a \in Ag$. *Other boolean connectives, such as conjunction* $(\wedge)$, *disjunction* $(\vee)$, *equivalence* $(\leftrightarrow)$ *and falsum* $(\bot)$ *are treated as defined operators in a usual way.* $K_a\varphi$ *is intended to stand for "agent* a *knows* φ*".*

3   Logics

We introduce four logics in this section: ELD (Epistemic Logic via Distance) and its generalization ELD⁻, and ELS (Epistemic Logic via Similarity) and its generalization ELS⁻.

---

[1] A weighted epistemic logic over similarities defined as such is studied in [7].

3.1   Epistemic Logic via Distance (ELD)

We can understand the knowledge of an agent as a kind of certainty or confidence based on the agent's epistemic abilities, in the sense that φ is known as long as it is true in all possible worlds that are less different than that the agent is capable to see. This interpretation is very similar to that introduced in the logic of confidence [16], though we use a different language by which the exact degree of confidence cannot be spoken out.

The logic we introduce here in accordance with the above understanding of knowledge is called ELD, with its formal semantics given below.

Definition 5. *Given a distance model $M = (W, E, C, \nu)$, a state $s \in W$ and a formula φ, we say φ is true (or* satisfied*) at s of M, denoted $M, s \models^d \varphi$, if the following recursive conditions are met:*

$$M, s \models^d p \qquad\quad \Longleftrightarrow p \in \nu(s)$$
$$M, s \models^d \neg\psi \qquad\quad \Longleftrightarrow not\ M, s \models^d \psi$$
$$M, s \models^d (\psi \to \chi) \Longleftrightarrow if\ M, s \models^d \psi\ then\ M, s \models^d \chi$$
$$M, s \models^d K_a\psi \qquad \Longleftrightarrow for\ all\ t \in W,\ if\ C(a) \geq E(s,t)\ then\ M, t \models^d \psi.$$

We often write "$M, s \models \varphi$" instead of "$M, s \models^d \varphi$" (i.e., omitting the superscript ^{d}) where there is no confusion from the context.

In the formal interpretation of $K_a\psi$ in the above definition, there is a condition "$C(a) \geq E(s,t)$" which intuitively expresses that agent a is not capable of discerning between the states s and t. So the formula $K_a\psi$ says that "ψ is true in all states that a is uncertain of (to the best of its ability)". Here $C(a)$ expresses the least distance that agent a is able to figure out.

In Definition 5, if we do not restrict ourselves to distance models, but rather any models are considered, we achieve a more general satisfaction relation, and the resulting more general – hence weaker – epistemic logic is denoted ELD$^-$.

We say a formula φ is $ELD-valid$ (resp. $ELD^- - valid$), if $M, s \models^d \varphi$ for all states s of all *distance models* (resp. *models*).

Example 1. Each state of a distance model can be treated as a set. In this example, states s_1, s_2, s_3, s_4 are sets of numbers. $s_1 = \{n \in \mathbb{N} \mid 2 \leq n \leq 98\}$; $s_2 = \{n \in \mathbb{N} \mid 1 \leq n \leq 50\}$; $s_3 = s_1 \setminus \{25\}$ and $s_4 = s_2 \setminus \{25\}$. The distance function d between two sets A and B is defined to be $d(A, B) = |A \setminus B| + |B \setminus A|$. The pair $(\{s_1, s_2, s_3, s_4\}, d)$ forms a distance graph, as the reader may check. Let the agents a, b and c are such that their degrees of epistemic abilities are $C(a) = 96$, $C(b) = 0.5$, $C(c) = 49$, respectively. Consider the propositional atoms $p_1 - p_4$, where p_1 says "there are more than 49 elements", p_2 says "the number of elements is a multiple of ten", p_3 says "the number of elements is odd" and p_4 says "there is a gap in the numbers". Figure 1 illustrates a distance model based on the above setting, as well as some facts about the truth of several formulas in the model.

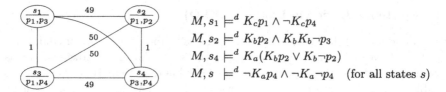

$$M, s_1 \models^d K_c p_1 \wedge \neg K_c p_4$$
$$M, s_2 \models^d K_b p_2 \wedge K_b K_b \neg p_3$$
$$M, s_4 \models^d K_a (K_b p_2 \vee K_b \neg p_2)$$
$$M, s \models^d \neg K_a p_4 \wedge \neg K_a \neg p_4 \quad \text{(for all states } s)$$

Fig. 1. Illustration of a distance model for Example 1. A node stands for a set, and the label of a line between two nodes stands for the distance between them. Propositional atoms (among p_1–p_4) are put in a node/set meaning that they are true for that set. We omit the self loops since $E(s, s) = 0$ for any state s in a distance model.

Lemma 1. *Given formulas φ and ψ, agents $a, b, c_1, \ldots, c_m, d_1, \ldots, d_n$, the following hold:*

1. $K_{c_1} \cdots K_{c_m} (K_b \varphi \to K_a \varphi) \vee K_{d_1} \cdots K_{d_n} (K_a \psi \to K_b \psi)$ *is valid in ELD$^-$;*
2. $\neg K_a \bot \to (K_a \varphi \to \varphi)$ *is valid in ELD;*
3. $\neg \varphi \to K_a \neg K_a \varphi$ *is valid in ELD;*
4. $K_{c_1} \cdots K_{c_m} K_a \bot \vee K_{d_1} \cdots K_{d_n} \neg K_a \bot$ *is valid in ELD.* ☐

3.2 Epistemic Logic via Similarity (ELS)

On the other hand, we can also understand an agent's knowledge via the notion of similarity. An agent's certainty or confidence of a formula φ is now treated as that φ is true in all possible worlds that are more alike than that the agent is capable to discern between.

The formal semantics of the language is given as follows.

Definition 6. *Given a similarity model $M = (W, E, C, \nu)$, a state $s \in W$ and a formula φ, we say φ is true (or satisfied) at state s of M, denoted $M, s \models^s \varphi$ (the superscript ^{s} is often omitted when it is clear in the context), if the following recursive conditions hold:*

$$M, s \models^s p \qquad \Longleftrightarrow p \in \nu(s)$$
$$M, s \models^s \neg \psi \qquad \Longleftrightarrow \text{not } M, s \models^s \psi$$
$$M, s \models^s (\psi \to \chi) \Longleftrightarrow \text{if } M, s \models^s \psi \text{ then } M, s \models^s \chi$$
$$M, s \models^s K_a \psi \qquad \Longleftrightarrow \text{for all } t \in W, \text{ if } C(a) \leq E(s, t) \text{ then } M, t \models^s \psi.$$

In the above definition, the condition "$C(a) \leq E(s,t)$" intuitively expresses that agent a is not capable of discerning between the states s and t. So the formula $K_a \psi$ says that "ψ is true in all states that a is uncertain of (to the best of its ability)". By this type of interpretation, unlike in ELD, $C(a)$ stands for the highest degree of similarity that agent a is able to discern between two states.

The epistemic logic interpreted in the above way (Definition 6) is called ELS, and its generalization to the interpretation by the class of all models is called ELS$^-$. We say a formula φ is *ELS − valid* (resp. *ELS$^-$ − valid*), if $M, s \models^s \varphi$ for all states s of all *similarity models* (resp. *models*).

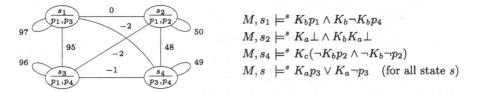

$$M, s_1 \models^s K_b p_1 \wedge K_b \neg K_b p_4$$
$$M, s_2 \models^s K_a \bot \wedge K_b K_a \bot$$
$$M, s_4 \models^s K_c (\neg K_b p_2 \wedge \neg K_b \neg p_2)$$
$$M, s \;\; \models^s K_a p_3 \vee K_a \neg p_3 \quad \text{(for all state } s)$$

Fig. 2. Illustration of a similarity model for Example 2.

Example 2. We treat states s_1–s_4 the same as in Example 1. A similarity function s is such that $s(A, B) = |A \cap B| - |A \setminus B| - |B \setminus A|$ which is known to make a similarity metric [5]. Using the same setting as in Example 1, we can reach a similarity model and some results of satisfaction illustrated in Fig. 2.

Lemma 2. *Given formulas φ and ψ, agents $a, b, c_1, \ldots, c_m, d_1, \ldots, d_n$,*

1. $K_{c_1} \cdots K_{c_m}(K_b\varphi \to K_a\varphi) \vee K_{d_1} \cdots K_{d_n}(K_a\psi \to K_b\psi)$ *is valid in* ELS$^-$;
2. $\neg K_a \bot \to (K_a\varphi \to \varphi)$ *is valid in* ELS;
3. $\neg\varphi \to K_a \neg K_a \varphi$ *is valid in* ELS. $\qquad\qquad\qquad\qquad\qquad\qquad\square$

4 Axiomatic Systems

We now axiomatize the logics introduced in the previous section. We first focus on the axiomatizations for the epistemic logics via distance, and then move on to those via similarity.

4.1 Axiomatizations for ELD and ELD$^-$

The axiomatization **KS** is consisted of all the axioms and rules of the axiomatization **K** for classical modal logic together with an extra axiom (S). The axiomatization **KStBz** consists of three more axioms (t) (B) and (z). See Fig. 3.

We now show that **KS** is sound and complete for the logic ELD$^-$, and **KStBz** is a sound and complete axiomatization for ELD. Soundness follows from Lemma 1, with the validity of the classical axioms and rules (PC), (K), (MP) and (N) easily verifiable. Here we focus on the completeness.

Theorem 1 (KS completeness). **KS** *is strongly complete w.r.t.* ELD$^-$. *I.e., for any set Φ of formulas, if Φ is* **KS**-*consistent, then Φ is* ELD$^-$-*satisfiable.*

Proof. Let Φ be a **KS**-consistent set of formulas. We first look at this from viewpoint the classical Kripke semantics for modal logic. Since **KS** is a normal system, it is strongly complete with respect to its canonical model [3, Theorem 4.22]. A canonical model for **KS** is a tuple $M = (W, R, V)$ such that (i) W is the set of all maximal **KS**-consistent sets of formulas, (ii) $R : Ag \to \wp(W \times W)$ is such that for each agent a, $(\Gamma, \Delta) \in R(a)$ iff for all formulas φ, $K_a\varphi \in \Gamma$ implies

---

KS consists of the following axioms and rules:

(PC)   instances of propositional tautologies

(K) $K_a(\varphi \to \psi) \to (K_a\varphi \to K_a\psi)$

(MP)   from φ and $\varphi \to \psi$, infer ψ

(N)   from φ infer $K_a\varphi$

(S) $K_{c_1} \cdots K_{c_m}(K_b\varphi \to K_a\varphi) \vee K_{d_1} \cdots K_{d_n}(K_a\psi \to K_b\psi)$

KStBz contains the following axioms in addition:

(t) $\neg K_a\bot \to (K_a\varphi \to \varphi)$

(B) $\neg\varphi \to K_a\neg K_a\varphi$

(z) $K_{c_1} \cdots K_{c_m} K_a\bot \vee K_{d_1} \cdots K_{d_n} \neg K_a\bot$

Fig. 3. The axiomatizations **KS** and **KStBz**, where φ and ψ are formulas and $a, b, c_1, \ldots, c_m, d_1, \ldots, d_n$ are agents.

$\varphi \in \Delta$, and (iii) $\mathsf{V} : \mathsf{Prop} \to \wp(\mathsf{W})$ is such that for all propositional atoms p, $\mathsf{V}(p) = \{\Gamma \in \mathsf{W} \mid p \in \Gamma\}$. So there must be a $\Gamma \in \mathsf{W}$ such that Φ is true (in the classical sense) in (M, Γ).

Now we build a genuine model for Φ out of M. Let $\Phi^+ \supseteq \Phi$ be a maximal consistent set, and $\mathsf{M}' = (\mathsf{W}', \mathsf{R}', \mathsf{V}')$ be the submodel of M that is point generated by Φ^+ (namely to keep all the canonical states that are reachable from Φ^+; cf. [3, Definition 2.5]). We claim that M' has the following property for all $a, b \in \mathsf{Ag}$:

$$\text{Either } \forall \Gamma \in \mathsf{W}'[\mathsf{R}'(a)(\Gamma) \subseteq \mathsf{R}'(b)(\Gamma)] \text{ or } \forall \Gamma \in \mathsf{W}'[\mathsf{R}'(b)(\Gamma) \subseteq \mathsf{R}'(a)(\Gamma)] \quad (\dagger)$$

where $\mathsf{R}'(a)(\Gamma) = \{\Gamma' \mid (\Gamma, \Gamma') \in \mathsf{R}'(a)\}$ and similarly for $\mathsf{R}'(b)(\Gamma)$.

Define a binary relation $\preceq$ on Ag such that for any $a, b \in \mathsf{Ag}$, $a \preceq b$ iff $\forall \Gamma \in \mathsf{W}'[\mathsf{R}'(a)(\Gamma) \subseteq \mathsf{R}'(b)(\Gamma)]$. The property $(\dagger)$ of M' guarantees that for any $a, b \in \mathsf{Ag}$, either $a \preceq b$ or $b \preceq a$. By the transitivity of $\subseteq$, we can verify that $\preceq$ is also transitive. In fact $\preceq$ is linear order on Ag. Therefore, there must be a numbering $f : \mathsf{Ag} \to \mathbb{Z}^+$ that assigns a positive integer to every agent a and $f(a) \leq f(b)$ whenever $a \preceq b$. Let $l = \sup\{f(a) + 1 \mid a \in Ag\}$.

Now we translate $\mathsf{M}' = (\mathsf{W}', \mathsf{R}', \mathsf{V}')$ to a model $M = (\mathsf{W}', E, C, \nu)$ such that:

- For all $\Gamma, \Delta \in \mathsf{W}'$, $E(\Gamma, \Delta) = \inf(\{f(b) \mid b \in \mathsf{Ag} \text{ and } (\Gamma, \Delta) \in \mathsf{R}'(b)\} \cup \{l\})$;
- For all $a \in \mathsf{Ag}$, $C(a) = f(a)$, and
- For all $\Gamma \in \mathsf{W}'$, $\nu(\Gamma) = \{p \in \mathsf{Prop} \mid p \in \Gamma\}$.

and we show that for any φ and $\Gamma \in \mathsf{W}'$, $M, \Gamma \models^d \varphi$ iff φ is true in (M', Γ).

By induction on φ. The atomic and boolean cases are easy to verify. Here we only show the case for the knowledge operator:

$$M, \Gamma \models^d K_a\psi \Longleftrightarrow \text{for all } \Delta \in \mathsf{W}', \text{ if } C(a) \geq E(\Gamma, \Delta) \text{ then } M, \Delta \models^d \psi$$
$$\Longleftrightarrow \text{for all } \Delta \in \mathsf{W}', \text{ if } C(a) \geq E(\Gamma, \Delta) \text{ then } \psi \text{ is true in } (\mathsf{M}', \Delta)$$
$$\Longleftrightarrow \text{for all } t \in \mathsf{W}', \text{ if } (\Gamma, \Delta) \in \mathsf{R}'(a) \text{ then } \psi \text{ is true in } (\mathsf{M}', \Delta)$$
$$\Longleftrightarrow K_a\psi \text{ is true in } (\mathsf{M}', \Gamma)$$

where the equivalence between the second line to the third can be argued as follows. Suppose $(\Gamma, \Delta) \in \mathsf{R}'(a)$. We have $C(a) = f(a) \geq \inf(\{f(b) \mid b \in \mathsf{Ag}$ and $(\Gamma, \Delta) \in \mathsf{R}'(b)\} \cup \{l\}) = E(\Gamma, \Delta)$. For the other direction, suppose $C(a) \geq E(\Gamma, \Delta)$, we have $f(a) \geq \inf(\{f(b) \mid b \in \mathsf{Ag}$ and $(\Gamma, \Delta) \in \mathsf{R}'(b)\} \cup \{l\})$, then there exists $b \in \mathsf{Ag}$ such that $(\Gamma, \Delta) \in \mathsf{R}'(b)$ and $f(a) \geq f(b)$. So we have $b \preceq a$, and $\forall \Gamma \in \mathsf{W}'[\mathsf{R}'(b)(\Gamma) \subseteq \mathsf{R}'(a)(\Gamma)]$, hence $(\Gamma, \Delta) \in \mathsf{R}'(a)$.

We conclude that $M, \Phi^+ \models^d \Phi$, which entails that Φ is ELD$^-$ satisfiable. $\square$

Theorem 2 (KStBz completeness). **KStBz** *is strongly complete w.r.t. ELD. I.e., for any set Φ of formulas, if Φ is* **KStBz**-*consistent, Φ is ELD-satisfiable.*

Proof. Let Φ be a **KStBz**-consistent set of formulas. Extend it to a maximal consistent set Φ^+. We achieve a model M' just as in the proof of Theorem 1 (replacing the **KS** with **KStBz** of course). We define the binary relation $\preceq$ and numbering f and the number l in the same way.

Let $k = \inf(\{f(a) \mid a \in \mathsf{Ag}$ and $(\Phi^+, \Phi^+) \in \mathsf{R}'(a)\} \cup \{l\})$. Define $g : \mathbb{R} \to \mathbb{R}$ such that $g(x) = arctan(2(x - k))$. The model $M = (\mathsf{W}', E, C, \nu)$ is given as follows:

- For all $\Gamma, \Delta \in \mathsf{W}'$, $E(\Gamma, \Delta) =$

$$\begin{cases} \inf(\{g(f(b) + 0.5) \mid b \in \mathsf{Ag} \text{ and } (\Gamma, \Delta) \in \mathsf{R}'(b)\} \cup \{g(l + 0.5)\}), & \text{if } \Gamma \neq \Delta, \\ \inf(\{g(f(b)) \mid b \in \mathsf{Ag} \text{ and } (\Gamma, \Delta) \in \mathsf{R}'(b)\} \cup \{g(l)\}), & \text{if } \Gamma = \Delta. \end{cases}$$

- For all $a \in \mathsf{Ag}$, $C(a) = g(f(a) + 0.5)$, and
- For all $\Gamma \in \mathsf{W}'$, $\nu(\Gamma) = \{p \in \mathsf{Prop} \mid p \in \Gamma\}$.

To show by induction that for any φ and $\Gamma \in \mathsf{W}'$, $M, \Gamma \models^d \varphi$ iff φ is true in (M', Γ), the key step to achieve $(\Gamma, \Delta) \in \mathsf{R}'(a) \iff C(a) \geq E(\Gamma, \Delta)$ for any $\Gamma, \Delta \in \mathsf{W}'$. Since the values of the numbering f are all integers, and g is monotonically increasing, we can verify that $g(f(a) + 0.5) \geq g(f(b)) \iff g(f(a) + 0.5) \geq g(f(b) + 0.5) \iff b \preceq a$ for any $a, b \in \mathsf{Ag}$. So we can get this by a similar proof of this key step to that for Theorem 1.

What remains to show is that M is indeed a distance model, namely the four conditions in Definition 1 hold.

- Symmetry. with the existence of the axiom (B), it is easy to see that the submodel M' of the canonical Kripke model is symmetric. The definition of the edge function E preserves the symmetry.
- Non-negativity and identity of indiscernibles. Key steps are as follows:

$$\begin{aligned} E(\Gamma, \Gamma) &= \inf(\{g(f(b)) \mid b \in \mathsf{Ag} \text{ and } (\Gamma, \Gamma) \in \mathsf{R}'(b)\} \cup \{g(l)\}) \\ &= \inf(\{arctan(2(f(b) - k)) \mid b \in \mathsf{Ag} \text{ and } (\Gamma, \Gamma) \in \mathsf{R}'(b)\} \cup \{g(l)\}) \\ &= arctan(2(\inf(\{f(b) \mid b \in \mathsf{Ag} \text{ and } (\Gamma, \Gamma) \in \mathsf{R}'(b)\} \cup \{l\}) - k)) \\ &= arctan(2(\inf(\{f(b) \mid b \in \mathsf{Ag} \text{ and } (\Phi^+, \Phi^+) \in \mathsf{R}'(b)\} \cup \{l\}) - k)) \\ &= arctan(2(k - k)) = 0; \end{aligned}$$

$E(\Gamma, \Delta)$
$= \inf(\{g(f(b) + 0.5) \mid b \in \text{Ag and } (\Gamma, \Delta) \in \text{R}'(b)\} \cup \{g(l + 0.5)\})$
$= \inf(\{\arctan(2(f(b) + 0.5 - k)) \mid b \in \text{Ag and } (\Gamma, \Delta) \in \text{R}'(b)\} \cup \{g(l + 0.5)\})$
$= \arctan(1 + 2(\inf(\{f(b) \mid b \in \text{Ag and } (\Gamma, \Delta) \in \text{R}'(b)\} \cup \{l\}) - k))$
$\geq \arctan(1 + 2(\inf(\{f(b) \mid b \in \text{Ag and } (\Gamma, \Gamma) \in \text{R}'(b)\} \cup \{l\}) - k))$
$= \arctan(1 + 2(k - k)) \quad = \quad \frac{\pi}{4} > 0 \qquad (\text{for } \Gamma \neq \Delta).$

– Triangle inequality. By the calculation above, for any $\Gamma, \Delta, \Theta \in \text{W}'$, if $\Gamma = \Delta$ or $\Delta = \Theta$, we have $E(\Gamma, \Theta) \leq E(\Gamma, \Theta) + 0 = E(\Gamma, \Theta) + E(\Delta, \Delta) = E(\Gamma, \Delta) + E(\Delta, \Theta)$. If $\Gamma \neq \Delta$ and $\Delta \neq \Theta$, we have $E(\Gamma, \Delta) \geq \frac{\pi}{4}$ and $E(\Delta, \Theta) \geq \frac{\pi}{4}$, so $E(\Gamma, \Theta) \leq \frac{\pi}{2} \leq E(\Gamma, \Delta) + E(\Delta, \Theta)$.   □

4.2   Axiomatizations for ELS and ELS⁻

In this section we study the axiomatizations for ELS and ELS⁻. We show that the axiomatic system **KS** is sound and complete for ELS⁻, and **KStB** is sound and complete for ELS, where the axiomatization **KStB** contains all the axioms and rules of **KStBz** but the axiom (z).

Soundness follows from Lemma 2, with the validity of the classical axioms and rules easily verifiable. We focus on the completeness here.

First we show a lemma about the duality of $\models^d$ and $\models^s$.

Lemma 3 (duality). *Let $M = (W, E, C, \nu)$ and $M' = (W', E', C', \nu')$ be two models. Suppose $W = W'$, $\nu = \nu'$ and for any $a \in \text{Ag}$ and $s, t \in W$, $C(a) \geq E(s, t)$ iff $C'(a) \leq E'(s, t)$. Then, for all $s \in W$ and all formulas φ, $M, s \models^d \varphi$ iff $M', s \models^s \varphi$.*   □

Theorem 3. **KS** *is a strongly complete axiomatization for ELS⁻. Namely, for any set Φ of formulas, if Φ is **KS**-consistent, then Φ is ELS⁻-satisfiable.*

Proof. Since **KS** is a strongly complete with respect to ELD⁻. It suffice to show that for any set Φ of formulas, Φ is ELS⁻-satisfiable iff Φ is ELD⁻-satisfiable. Suppose Φ is ELD⁻-satisfiable, then there is a model $M = (W, E, C, \nu)$ and $s \in W$ such that $M, s \models^d \Phi$. Let $M' = (W, E', C', \nu)$ be such that $C'(a) = -C(a)$ for all $a \in \text{Ag}$ and $E'(s, t) = -E(s, t)$ for all $s, t \in W$. By Lemma 3 we have $M', s \models^s \Phi$, so Φ is ELS⁻-satisfiable. The other direction can be shown similarly.

Theorem 4. **KStB** *is strongly complete with respect to ELS. Namely, for any set Φ of formulas, if Φ is **KStB**-consistent, then Φ is ELS-satisfiable.*

Proof. A proof can be given in a similar way to that of Theorem 2 (but let $f(a) \geq f(b)$ whenever $a \preceq b$). We omit all the details here except for the definition of a translation of the pointed generated submodel $M' = (W', R', V')$ of the canonical Kripke model; that gives us the model $M = (W', E, C, \nu)$ such that

– For all $\Gamma, \Delta \in \text{W}'$,
$$E(\Gamma, \Delta) = \begin{cases} \sup(\{4^{f(b)} \mid b \in \text{Ag and } (\Gamma, \Delta) \in \text{R}'(b)\} \cup \{1\}), & \text{if } \Gamma \neq \Delta, \\ \sup(\{4^{f(b)+0.5} \mid b \in \text{Ag and } (\Gamma, \Gamma) \in \text{R}'(b)\} \cup \{2\}), & \text{if } \Gamma = \Delta. \end{cases}$$
– For all $a \in \text{Ag}$, $C(a) = 4^{f(a)}$, and
– For all $\Gamma \in \text{W}'$, $\nu(\Gamma) = \{p \in \text{Prop} \mid p \in \Gamma\}$.   □

5   Computational Complexity

We study the complexity results of model and satisfiability checking problems of the four logics introduced in this paper. As a quick summary, the model checking problem for each of the logics is in polynomial time, and the satisfiability problem for each of them is PSPACE complete. Now we proceed with the details.

5.1   Model Checking

Given a (distance, similarity) model M, a state s of M and a formula φ, the model checking problem is to decide whether "$M, s \models \varphi$" (here the satisfaction relation "$\models$" can be "$\models^d$" or "$\models^s$" depending on the logic) is true or not.

We can introduce a polynomial-time algorithm that is similar to that introduced in [14] for the model checking problem for ELD^-. In particular, Algorithm 1 computes the *truth set* of a given formula φ in a given model M (i.e., the set $\{s \in W \mid M, s \models \varphi\}$), and the model checking problem is then reducible to the membership checking of the truth set. As the reader may check, the function $Val(M, \varphi)$ terminates in time polynomial in the size of the input, and the time consumption for the membership checking of the truth set is linear to its size – these in total lead to a polynomial-time algorithm for model checking in ELD^-.

Model checking in ELS^- is very similar to that in ELD^-: if we replace "$C(a) \geq E(t, u)$" in line 10 by "$C(a) \leq E(t, u)$", we obtain an algorithm for computing the truth set of a formula in ELS^-. So the model checking problem for ELS^- is also in P.

Algorithm 1. Computing the truth set of a formula in ELD^-

Require: $M = (W, E, C, \nu)$ is a model, and φ is a formula
 1: **function** $Val(M, \varphi)$
 2:     **if** $\varphi = p$ **then return** $\{s \in W \mid p \in \nu(s)\}$
 3:     **else if** $\varphi = \neg\psi$ **then return** $W \setminus Val(M, \psi)$
 4:     **else if** $\varphi = \psi \to \chi$ **then return** $(W \setminus Val(M, \psi)) \cup Val(M, \chi)$
 5:     **else if** $\varphi = K_a\psi$ **then**
 6:         initialize $tmpVal = \emptyset$
 7:         **for all** $t \in W$ **do**
 8:             initialize $n = true$
 9:             **for all** $u \in W$ **do**
10:                 **if** $C(a) \geq E(t, u)$ **and** $u \notin Val(M, \psi)$ **then** $n \leftarrow false$
11:                 **end if**
12:             **end for**
13:             **if** $n = true$ **then** $tmpVal \leftarrow tmpVal \cup \{t\}$
14:             **end if**
15:         **end for**
16:         **return** $tmpVal$ ▷ $\{t \in W \mid \forall u \in W : C(a) \geq E(t, u) \Rightarrow u \in Val(M, \psi)\}$
17:     **end if**
18: **end function**

Both distance and similarity models are special types of models, so the model checking problem for ELD and ELS is, respectively, a subproblem of that for ELD⁻ and ELS⁻, and both problems are in P as a result.

Theorem 5. *The model checking problems for all the four logics are in P.*   □

5.2   Satisfiability Checking

Given a formula φ, the satisfiability problem is to decide whether there is a (distance, similarity) model M and a state s such that $M, s \models \varphi$. We show that the satisfiability problem for the four logics are all PSPACE complete.

To get the lower bound of the satisfiability problem, we first show two lemmas. We assume acquaintance of the modal logics K and KTB (a.k.a. B) interpreted by the Kripke semantics, and their axiomatizations **K** and **KTB**.[2]

Lemma 4. *Given an agent a, for any formula φ such that there is no other agent occurring in it, if $\vdash_{\mathbf{KTB}} \varphi$, then $\vdash_{\mathbf{KtB}} (\neg K_a \bot \to \varphi)$.*   □

Lemma 5. *Given an agent a, for any formula φ such that there is no other agent occurring in it, the following hold:*

1. *φ is K satisfiable $\iff$ φ is ELD⁻ satisfiable $\iff$ φ is ELS⁻ satisfiable;*
2. *φ is KTB satisfiable $\iff$ $\varphi \wedge \neg K_a \bot$ is ELD satisfiable $\iff$ $\varphi \wedge \neg K_a \bot$ is ELS satisfiable.*

Proof. 1. Suppose φ is satisfied in a state s of a Kripke model $N = (W, R, V)$. Let $M = (W, E, C, \nu)$ be a model such that:

– For all $t, u \in W$, $E(t, u) = \begin{cases} 0, & \text{if } (t, u) \in R(a) \\ 1, & \text{if } (t, u) \notin R(a) \end{cases}$
– $C(a) = 0.5$, and
– For all $t \in W$, $\nu(t) = \{p \in \mathsf{Prop} \mid t \in V(p)\}$.

By the above, for any $t, u \in W$, $C(a) \geq E(t, u)$ iff $(t, u) \in R(a)$, so by induction on ψ we can show that for any formula ψ and $t \in W$, $M, t \models^d \psi$ iff ψ is true in (N, t). Thus, φ is ELD⁻ satisfiable.

If φ is not K satisfiable, then by the completeness of **K** with respect to K, we have that φ is inconsistent in **K**, hence also inconsistent in **KS**. By the soundness of **KS** with respect to ELD⁻, we get that φ is not ELD⁻ satisfiable.

The equivalence to the satisfiability in ELS⁻ follows from Lemma 3 (if we swap the weights 0 and 1 in the model).

2. Suppose φ is KTB satisfiable, then there is a Kripke KTB model $N = (W, R, V)$ and state $s \in W$ such that φ is satisfied in (N, s). Let $M = (W, E, C, \nu)$ be a model such that:

---

[2] The axiomatic system **K** is **KS** without the axiom (S); see Fig. 3 for details. By adding the axiom schemes (B) and (T), i.e., $K_a \varphi \to \varphi$ for the latter, to the system **K**, we get the axiomatic system **KTB**.

- For all $t, u \in W$, $E(t, u) = \begin{cases} 0.5, & \text{if } (t, u) \in R(a) \text{ and } t \neq u \\ 0, & \text{if } t = u \\ 1, & \text{otherwise} \end{cases}$
- $C(a) = \max(\{-0.5\} \cup \{E(t, u) \mid (t, u) \in R(a)\})$, and
- For all $t \in W$, $\nu(t) = \{p \in \mathsf{Prop} \mid t \in V(p)\}$.

One can verify that M is indeed a distance model. We can show that for any formula ψ and $t \in W$, $M, t \models^d \psi$ iff ψ is true in (N, t). Thus we have proved that if φ is KTB satisfiable then it is also ELD satisfiable. Suppose φ is KTB satisfiable, since every model of KTB is reflexive, then $\varphi \wedge \neg K_a\bot$ is KTB satisfiable, so $\varphi \wedge \neg K_a\bot$ is ELD satisfiable.

If φ is not KTB satisfiable, then $\neg\varphi$ is valid in KTB. By the completeness of **KTB** we have $\vdash_{\mathbf{KTB}} \neg\varphi$. By Lemma 4 we have $\vdash_{\mathbf{KtB}} \neg K_a\bot \rightarrow \neg\varphi$, and so $\vdash_{\mathbf{KStBz}} \neg K_a\bot \rightarrow \neg\varphi$. By the completeness of **KStBz** with respect to ELD, we have $\varphi \wedge \neg K_a\bot$ is not ELD$^-$ satisfiable.

The equivalence to the satisfiability in ELS follows from Lemma 3 (we can replace all the weights x in M with $1 - x$, and $C(a)$ with $1 - C(a)$ to get a similarity model; in fact this similarity metric was mentioned in [5]).   □

It is known that the satisfiability problem for the uni-modal logic K is PSPACE complete [12], and that for the uni-modal logic KTB is also PSPACE complete [4]. We can achieve the PSPACE hardness of our logics by polynomial-time reduction from the satisfiability problems for these logics.

Theorem 6. *The satisfiability problems for these logics are PSPACE hard.*

Proof. By Lemma 5, uni-modal K satisfiability problem can be reduced to that for ELD$^-$ and ELS$^-$. The reductions can be made in polynomial time (see the proof of that lemma). So the satisfiable problem for ELD$^-$ and ELS$^-$ are both PSPACE hard, since that for K is known to be so [12].

Given a formula φ, by Lemma 5, to compute whether φ is (uni-modal) KTB satisfiable can be reduced in polynomial time to compute whether $\varphi \wedge \neg K_a\bot$ (here a is the only agent appears in φ) is ELD/ELS satisfiable. Since the former is known to be PSPACE complete [4], the satisfiable problems for ELD and ELS are both PSPACE hard.   □

Theorem 7. *The satisfiability problems for all the four logics are in PSPACE.*

Proof. Using a similar method as in the proof of Theorem 2, we can verify that a formula φ is ELD satisfiable iff φ is satisfiable in a Kripke frame $F = (W, R)$ with the following properties:

(1) F is a point generated subframe (such as the fundamental frame of M');
(2) $\forall a, b \in \mathsf{Ag}$, either $\forall s \in W[R(a)(s) \subseteq R(b)(s)]$ or $\forall s \in W[R(b)(s) \subseteq R(a)(s)]$;
(3) For any $s, t \in W$ and $a \in \mathsf{Ag}$, $(s, t) \in R(a)$ implies $(s, s) \in R(a)$;
(4) For any $s, t \in W$ and $a \in \mathsf{Ag}$, $(s, t) \in R(a)$ implies $(t, s) \in R(a)$;
(5) For any $s, t \in W$ and $a \in \mathsf{Ag}$, $(s, s) \in R(a)$ implies $(t, t) \in R(a)$.

From the proofs of Theorems 1 and 4, we conclude that: (i) φ is ELD$^-$/ELS$^-$ satisfiable iff φ is satisfiable in a frame satisfying the conditions (1–2), and (ii) φ is ELS satisfiable iff φ is satisfiable in a frame satisfying the conditions (1–4).

We use the tableau method from [9] to show the theorem. An *ELD tableau* is a K tableau (cf. [9]) that in addition satisfies the following conditions (which corresponds to the above conditions (2–5) respectively):

- If $(s,t) \in R(a) \setminus R(b)$, then for any u, v, $(u,v) \in R(b)$ implies $(u,v) \in R(a)$;
- If $(s,t) \in R(a)$, then $(s,s) \in R(a)$;
- If $(s,t) \in R(a)$, then $(t,s) \in R(a)$;
- If $(s,s) \in R(a)$, then for all t, $(t,t) \in R(a)$.

During the process we need to make sure that the constructed tableau satisfies the above conditions. The last two are easy to be enforced:

- Whenever (s,t) is added to $R(a)$, also add (s,s) and (t,s) to $R(a)$;
- Whenever (s,s) is added to $R(a)$, also add (t,t) for all existing nodes t.

The first condition is slightly involved. When (s,t) is added to $R(a)$ and $R(a) = R(b)$, it is not certain whether we should add (s,t) to $R(b)$. We do the construction for all possible cases one by one. For each linear order $\preceq$ on agents appearing in φ, we make sure to add (s,t) to $R(b)$ whenever (s,t) is added to $R(a)$ and $a \preceq b$. The construction uses polynomial space, and we carry this on for all linear orders. φ is satisfiable iff one of constructions returns "φ is satisfiable". We need to mark the recently examined linear order, and total space cost is still polynomial. An *ELD$^-$/ELS$^-$ tableau* only need to enforce the first tableau condition, and an *ELS tableau* needs to meet the first three.   □

6   Conclusion

We studied epistemic logics interpreted over distance and similarity models, leading to four different – yet closely related – logics. We axiomatized the logics and achieved the computational complexity results of the model and satisfiability checking problems for them. We found interesting links between these logics from both proof-theoretical and computational aspects. We have presented a quite thorough picture of this work. Via the notions of distance and similarity, weighted models give us the flexibility of capturing scenarios more meticulously. Yet we do not get overloaded. One of the most interesting results is that the resulting logics are simple. Not only that the complexity results do not go higher than standard epistemic logics, but the axiomatizations are also arguably easy to comprehend. This may show an advantage of adopting weighted model in epistemic logic. As we have mentioned in the very beginning, topics such as group knowledge, dynamics of knowability, knows-how modeling have attracted much attention in the area of epistemic logic. For future work we are interested in examining these topics on top of our framework.

References

1. Ågotnes, T., Balbiani, P., van Ditmarsch, H., Seban, P.: Group announcement logic. J. Appl. Logic **8**(1), 62–81 (2010)
2. Balbiani, P., Baltag, A., van Ditmarsch, H., Herzig, A., Hoshi, T., de Lima, T.: Knowable' as 'known after an announcement. Rev. Symbol. Logic **1**(3), 305–334 (2008)
3. Blackburn, P., De Rijke, M., Venema, Y.: Modal Logic, Cambridge Tracts in Theoretical Computer Science, vol. 53. Cambridge University Press, Cambridge (2001)
4. Chen, C.C., Lin, I.P.: The computational complexity of the satisfiability of modal Horn clauses for modal propositional logics. Theor. Comput. Sci. **129**, 95–121 (1994)
5. Chen, S., Ma, B., Zhang, K.: On the similarity metric and the distance metric. Theor. Comput. Sci. **410**(24–25), 2365–2376 (2009)
6. van Ditmarsch, H., van der Hoek, W., Kooi, B.: Dynamic Epistemic Logic, Synthese Library, vol. 337. Springer, Netherlands (2007). https://doi.org/10.1007/978-1-4020-5839-4
7. Dong, H., Li, X., Wáng, Y.N.: Weighted modal logic in epistemic and deontic contexts. In: Ghosh, S., Icard, T. (eds.) LORI 2021. LNCS, vol. 13039, pp. 73–87. Springer, Cham (2021). https://doi.org/10.1007/978-3-030-88708-7_6
8. Fagin, R., Halpern, J.Y., Moses, Y., Vardi, M.Y.: Reasoning About Knowledge. The MIT Press, Cambridge (1995)
9. Halpern, J.Y., Moses, Y.: A guide to completeness and complexity for modal logics of knowledge and belief. Artif. Intell. **54**(3), 319–379 (1992)
10. Hansen, M., Larsen, K.G., Mardare, R., Pedersen, M.R.: Reasoning about bounds in weighted transition systems. LMCS **14**, 1–32 (2018)
11. Hintikka, J.: Knowledge and Belief: An Introduction to the Logic of Two Notions. Cornell University Press, Ithaca, New York (1962)
12. Ladner, R.E.: The computational complexity of provability in systems of modal propositional logic. SIAM J. Comput. **6**(3), 467–480 (1977)
13. Larsen, K.G., Mardare, R.: Complete proof systems for weighted modal logic. Theor. Comput. Sci. **546**(12), 164–175 (2014)
14. Liang, X., Wáng, Y.N.: Epistemic logics over weighted graphs. In: Liao, B., Markovich, R., Wáng, Y.N. (eds.) Second International Workshop on Logics for New-Generation Artificial Intelligence (2022)
15. Meyer, J.J.C., van der Hoek, W.: Epistemic Logic for AI and Computer Science. Cambridge University Press, Cambridge (1995)
16. Naumov, P., Tao, J.: Logic of confidence. Synthese **192**(6), 1821–1838 (2015). https://doi.org/10.1007/s11229-014-0655-3
17. Tan, P.N., Steinbach, M., Kumar, V.: Introduction to data mining. Pearson (2005)
18. Wang, Y.: A logic of goal-directed knowing how. Synthese **195**(10), 4419–4439 (2018)

Abstract Argumentation Goes Quantum: An Encoding to QUBO Problems

Marco Baioletti$^{(\boxtimes)}$ (iD) and Francesco Santini$^{(\boxtimes)}$ (iD)

Department of Mathematics and Computer Science, Università degli Studi di
Perugia, Perugia, Italy
{marco.baioletti,francesco.santini}@unipg.it

Abstract. We present an encoding of some NP-Complete problems in
Abstract Argumentation to *Quadratic Unconstrained Binary Optimization* (*QUBO*) problems. A solution for a QUBO problem corresponds to
minimize a quadratic function over binary variables (0/1), whose coefficients can be represented by a symmetric square matrix. Being this
problem NP-Complete as well, there exist approximate solvers: from
the *D-Wave Ocean SDK* we test a *simulated annealing* algorithm and a
real *quantum annelaer* provided by the *Leap^{TM} Quantum Cloud Service*.
Hence, we propose a new encoding for *Abstract Argumentation* problems,
which will benefit from the future development of quantum computation.

Keywords: Abstract argumentation · Computational model ·
Quadratic unconstrained binary optimization · Simulated annealing

1 Introduction

Computational Argumentation is an interdisciplinary field that brings together
philosophy, AI, linguistics, psychology, and a variety of different application
fields. An *Abstract Argumentation Framework* (*AF* for short) [12] is one of
the formalisms used in Argumentation: it can be represented as a simple pair
$\mathscr{F} = (\mathsf{A}, \rightarrow)$, composed of respectively a set of arguments and an attack relationship between them. Such a simple representation can be condensed into a
directed graph with nodes (arguments) and directed edges (attacks). Despite the
simplicity of the model, several problems in Abstract Argumentation are hard to
solve [14,22], and this consequently stimulated the design and implementation
of solvers in order to tackle such a complexity.

A *Quadratic Unconstrained Binary Optimization* problem (*QUBO*),[1] is a
mathematical formulation that encompass a wide range of critical *Combinatorial*

F. Santini—The author is a member of INdAM - GNCS. The author has been partially
supported by project "BLOCKCHAIN4FOODCHAIN" funded by "Ricerca di Base
2020" (Univeristy of Perugia), Project "DopUP - REGIONE UMBRIA PSR 2014–
2020".

[1] Different names and abbreviations may be found in the literature, as for example
Unconstrained Binary Quadratic Programming (*UBPQ*) [21], or *Quadratic Pseudo-
Boolean* optimization (*QPBO*) [1].

© The Author(s), under exclusive license to Springer Nature Switzerland AG 2022
S. Khanna et al. (Eds.): PRICAI 2022, LNCS 13629, pp. 46–60, 2022.
https://doi.org/10.1007/978-3-031-20862-1_4

Optimization problems: QUBO has been surveyed in [1, 21], and the first work dates back to 1960 [20]. A solution for a QUBO problem simply corresponds to minimize a quadratic function over binary variables (0/1), whose coefficients can be represented with a symmetric square matrix. QUBO problems are NP-Complete: therefore, a vast literature is dedicated to approximate solvers based on heuristics or meta-heuristics, such as *simulated annealing* approaches (*SA*), *tabu-serch*, *genetic algorithms* or *evolutionary computing* [21]. There exist also exact methods that are capable of solving QUBO problems with 100–500 variables [21]. Also *quantum* annealers and Fujitsu's *digital annealers*[2] can be used to find global minima by using quantum *fluctuations*. QUBO models are at the heart of experimentation with quantum computers built by D-Wave Systems.[3]

QUBO has been intensively investigated and is used to characterize and solve a wide range of optimization problems: for example, it encompasses SAT Problems, Constraint Satisfaction Problems, Maximum Cut Problems, Graph Coloring Problems, Maximum Clique Problems, General 0/1 Programming Problems and many more [18]. There exist QUBO embeddings also for Support Vector Machines, Clustering algorithms, Markov Random Fields and Probabilistic Reasoning [2, 23].

In this paper, we propose an encoding to QUBO of some hard problems in Abstract Argumentation, such as the credulous acceptance of a given argument and the existence of a non-empty extension. We focus on these problems because for some semantics in Abstract Argumentation they are NP-Complete, exactly as the solution of QUBO problems. We then use a SA algorithm to compute a solution to these problems: SA is a meta-heuristic to approximate global optimization in a large search space for an optimization problem. Hence, our solver is approximate as other proposals participating in the recent ICCMA21 competition (see Sect. 3): for this reason, we compare our accuracy with the best approximate solver of the competition if we consider the complete semantics (i.e., Harper++),[4] as we do in our tests in this paper. We finally show how to solve a small problem by using a real quantum annealer provided by the *Leap^{TM} Quantum Cloud Service*. Future (expected) improvements of quantum-computing platforms will lead to better capabilities for solving our model.

The paper is structured as follows: in Sect. 2 we report the introductory notions about Abstract Argumentation and QUBO. Section 3 reports some of the most related work, while Sect. 4 presents the QUBO encoding of some NP-Complete problems in Abstract Argumentation. Section 5 presents an empirical validation of the model by executing tests and comparing the results against *i)* an exact and *ii)* an approximate solver. This section also introduces how to use real quantum annealers. Finally, Sect. 6 wraps up the paper with final thoughts and future work.

---

[2] Fujitsu's digital annealer: https://bit.ly/3ySnkrq.

[3] D-Wave webiste: https://www.dwavesys.com.

[4] Results of ICCMA21, slide 18/26: http://argumentationcompetition.org/2021/downloads/iccma_results_ijcai.pdf.

2 Background

2.1 Abstract Argumentation Problems

An *Abstract Argumentation Framework* (AF, for short) [12] is a tuple $\mathscr{F} = (A, \rightarrow)$ where A is a set of arguments and $\rightarrow$ is a relation $\rightarrow \subseteq A \times A$. For two arguments $a, b \in A$ the relation $a \rightarrow b$ means that argument a *attacks* argument b. An argument $a \in A$ is *defended* by $S \subseteq A$ (in $\mathscr{F}$) if for each $b \in A$ such that $b \rightarrow a$ there is some $c \in S$ such that $c \rightarrow b$. A set $E \subseteq A$ is *conflict-free* (**cf** in $\mathscr{F}$) if and only if there are no $a, b \in E$ with $a \rightarrow b$. E is *admissible* (**ad** in $\mathscr{F}$) if and only if it is **cf** and each $a \in E$ is defended by E. Finally, the range of E in $\mathscr{F}$, i.e., $E_{\mathscr{F}}^{+}$, collects the same E and the set of arguments attacked by E: $E_{\mathscr{F}}^{+} = E \cup \{a \in A \mid \exists b \in E : b \rightarrow a\}$. A directed graph can straightforwardly represent an AF: an example with five arguments is given in Fig. 1 (e.g., both arguments a and c attacks b, but not vice-versa).

The *collective acceptability* of arguments depends on the definition of different *semantics*. Four of them are proposed by Dung in his seminal paper [12], namely the complete (**co**), preferred (**pr**), stable (**st**), and grounded (**gr**) semantics.

Semantics determine sets of jointly acceptable arguments, called *extensions*, by mapping each $\mathscr{F} = (A, \rightarrow)$ to a set $\sigma(\mathscr{F}) \subseteq 2^A$, where 2^A is the power set of A, and σ parametrically stands for any of the considered semantics. The extensions under complete, preferred, stable, semi-stable, stage, grounded, and ideal semantics are defined as follows. Given $\mathscr{F} = (A, \rightarrow)$ and a set $E \subseteq A$,

- $E \in \mathbf{co}(\mathscr{F})$ iff E is admissible in $\mathscr{F}$ and if $a \in A$ is defended by E in $\mathscr{F}$ then $a \in E$,
- $E \in \mathbf{pr}(\mathscr{F})$ iff $E \in \mathbf{co}(\mathscr{F})$ and there is no $E' \in \mathbf{co}(\mathscr{F})$ s.t. $E' \supset E$,
- $E \in \mathbf{sst}(\mathscr{F})$ iff $E \in \mathbf{co}(\mathscr{F})$ and there is no $E' \in \mathbf{co}(\mathscr{F})$ s.t. $E_{\mathscr{F}}'^{+} \supset E_{\mathscr{F}}^{+}$,
- $E \in \mathbf{st}(\mathscr{F})$ iff $E \in \mathbf{co}(\mathscr{F})$ and $E_{\mathscr{F}}^{+} = A$,
- $E \in \mathbf{stg}(\mathscr{F})$ iff E is conflict-free in $\mathscr{F}$ and there is no E' that is conflict-free in $\mathscr{F}$ s.t. $E_{\mathscr{F}}'^{+} \supset E_{\mathscr{F}}^{+}$,
- $E \in \mathbf{gr}(\mathscr{F})$ iff $E \in \mathbf{co}(\mathscr{F})$ and there is no $E' \in \mathbf{co}(\mathscr{F})$ s.t. $E' \subset E$,
- $E \in \mathbf{id}(\mathscr{F})$ if and only if E is admissible, $E \subseteq \bigcap \mathbf{pr}(\mathscr{F})$ and there is no admissible $E' \subseteq \bigcap \mathbf{pr}(\mathscr{F})$ s.t. $E' \supset E$.

For a more detailed view on these semantics please refer to [3]. Note that both grounded and ideal extensions are uniquely determined [12,13]. Thus, they are also called *single-status* semantics. The other semantics introduced are *multi-status* semantics, where several extensions may exist. The stable semantics is the only case where $\mathbf{st}(\mathscr{F})$ might be empty, while the other semantics always return one extension at least.

As an example, if we consider the framework $\mathscr{F}$ in Fig. 1 we have that $\mathbf{co}(\mathscr{F}) = \{\{a\}, \{a, d\}, \{a, c, e\}\}$, $\mathbf{pr}(\mathscr{F})$ and $\mathbf{st}(\mathscr{F}) = \{\{a, d\}, \{a, c, e\}\}$, and $\mathbf{gr}(\mathscr{F}) = \{\{a\}\}$.

We now report below the definition of seven well-known problems in Abstract Argumentation, where the first six are decisional (yes/no answer):

- Credulous acceptance **DC**-σ: given $\mathscr{F} = (A, \rightarrow)$ and an argument $a \in A$, is a contained in some $E \in \sigma(\mathscr{F})$?

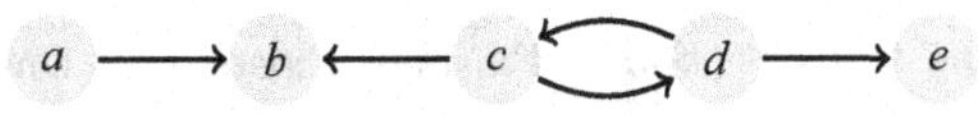

Fig. 1. An example of an AF represented as a directed graph.

- Skeptical acceptance **DS**-σ: given $\mathscr{F} = (\mathsf{A}, \rightarrow)$ and an argument $a \in \mathsf{A}$, is a contained in all $E \in \sigma(\mathscr{F})$?
- Verification of an extension **Ver**-σ: given $\mathscr{F} = (\mathsf{A}, \rightarrow)$ and a set of arguments $E \subseteq \mathsf{A}$, is $E \in \sigma(\mathscr{F})$?
- Existence of an extension **Exists**-σ: given $\mathscr{F} = (\mathsf{A}, \rightarrow)$, is $\sigma(\mathscr{F}) \neq \varnothing$?
- Existence of non-empty extension **Exists**-$\sigma^{\neg\varnothing}$: given $\mathscr{F} = (\mathsf{A}, \rightarrow)$, does there exist $E \neq \varnothing$ such that $E \in \sigma(\mathscr{F})$?
- Uniqueness of the solution **Unique**-σ: given $\mathscr{F} = (\mathsf{A}, \rightarrow)$, is $\sigma(\mathscr{F}) = \{E\}$?
- Enumeration of extensions **Enum**-σ: given $\mathscr{F} = (\mathsf{A}, \rightarrow)$, return all $E \in \sigma(\mathscr{F})$.

For example, **DC-co** for the AF in Fig. 1 returns "YES" for argument c and "NO" for argument b; **DS-co** returns "YES" for argument a only; **Exists-st**$^{\neg\varnothing}$ returns "YES".

Table 1 summarises the complexity classes the aforementioned problems [14, 22]. As we can see, most of the problems need efficient solvers. As a reminder, intractable complexity classes are $NP, coNP, DP \subseteq \Theta_2^p \subseteq \Sigma_2^P, \Pi_2^P \subseteq D_2^p$, while all the other classes in Table 1 are tractable: $L \subseteq P$. The nOP class (not contained in the class $OutputP$) means that the enumeration problem is not solvable in polynomial time in the size of the input and the output. Class $DelayP$ means that the extensions can be enumerated with a delay which is polynomial in the size of the input, while $DelayP_P$ also requires the use of polynomial space. $DelayP$ and $DelayP_P$ are tractable while nOP is intractable [22].

2.2 QUBO

Quadratic Unconstrained Binary Optimization (in short, QUBO) is an important form of optimization problems which has recently gained a great popularity because of fast solvers and dedicated computing devices, such as quantum and digital annealers. Hence, several optimization problems, in a large range of application domains, have been formulated as QUBO problems, in order to be solved by these new methods [18,19].

A QUBO problem is defined in terms of n binary variables $x_1, \ldots, x_n$ and a $n \times n$ upper triangular matrix and consists in minimizing the function

$$f(x) = \sum_{i=1}^{n} Q_{i,i} x_i + \sum_{i<j}^{n} Q_{i,j} x_i x_j$$

Table 1. The complexity of some problems in Abstract Argumentation [14,22].

	Ver-σ	DC-σ	DS-σ	Exists-σ	Exists-$\sigma^{\neg\varnothing}$	Unique-σ	Enum-σ
Conflict-free	in L	in L	triv.	triv.	in L	in L	DelayP$_P$
Admissible	in L	NP-c	triv.	triv.	NP-c	coNP-c	nOP
Complete	in L	NP-c	P-c	triv.	NP-c	coNP-c	nOP
Preferred	coNP-c	NP-c	$\prod_2^P$-c	triv.	NP-c	coNP-c	nOP
Semi-stable	coNP-c	$\sum_2^P$-c	$\prod_2^P$-c	triv.	NP-c	in Θ_2^p	nOP
Stable	in L	NP-c	coNP-c	NP-c	NP-c	DP-c	nOP
Stage	coNP-c	$\sum_2^P$-c	$\prod_2^P$-c	triv.	in L	in Θ_2^p	nOP
Grounded	P-c	P-c	P-c	triv.	P-c	triv.	DelayP
Ideal	Θ_2^p	Θ_2^p	Θ_2^p	triv.	Θ_2^p	triv.	nOP

The diagonal terms $Q_{i,i}$ are the linear coefficients and the non-zero off-diagonal terms $Q_{i,j}$ are the quadratic coefficients. This can be expressed more concisely as

$$\min_{x\in\{0,1\}^n} x^T Q x$$

where x^T denotes the transpose of the vector x.

The formulation of a discrete constrained optimization problem as QUBO requires the following steps (i) find a binary representation for the solutions (ii) define a penalization function, which penalizes unfeasible solutions (i.e., violating a constraint).

3   Related Work

In the literature we can find large plethora of general computational techniques and practical implementations for solving problems related to formal argumentation in AI. It is possible to distinguish between *i)* approaches to Abstract Argumentation frameworks, *ii)* approaches to structured argumentation frameworks (such as *ASPIC+* and *Defeasible Logic Programming*), *iii)* other alternatives, such as semi-formal systems for visualizing argumentation processes or web-based argument exchange, as stated in [4, Ch. 14] and [10]. In this section we focus on *i*, which in turn differentiates between *reduction-based* and *direct* approaches, which are the two types of solver implementations for Abstract AFs. The former reduces the considered problem into a different formalism in order to take advantage of existing solvers from that formalism. The latter consists in designing ad-hoc algorithms to directly solve the problem.

The *International Competition on Computational Models of Argumentation* (*ICCMA* for short)[5] is the reference biennial-competition dedicated to Abstract

---

[5] ICCMA Website: http://argumentationcompetition.org.

Argumentation, whose objectives are to provide a forum for the empirical comparison of solvers, with the purpose to highlight challenges to the community, to propose new directions for research, and to provide a core of common benchmark instances and a representation formalism that can aid in the comparison and evaluation of solvers.

We point the interested reader to the survey of participants and results achieved in ICCMA15 [25], ICCMA17 [17], and ICCMA19 [5]. ICCMA21 saw the participation of nine solvers, and it confirmed a third class of solvers besides reduction-based and direct techniques: approximate approaches. An exploratory track dedicated to such algorithms was included for the first time: the decision problems **DC**-σ and **DS**-σ were considered for six different semantics, such as $\sigma \in \{\mathbf{co}, \mathbf{pr}, \mathbf{st}, \mathbf{sst}, \mathbf{stg}, \mathbf{id}\}$ (**DC-id** is equivalent to **DS-id**). Solvers were evaluated with respect to their accuracy, i.e. the ratio of instances that were correctly solved. The main motivation behind approximate solutions was their (potential) faster execution than exact solvers: for this reason, the timeout was reduced to 60 s, instead of the 600 s allowed in ICCMA21 for exact solvers.

Two approximate tools participated in ICCMA21; one is Harper++ by M. Thimm:[6] such a solver first computes the grounded extension of an input framework and then use that to approximate the results of **DC**-σ and **DS**-σ tasks with $\sigma \in \{\mathbf{co}, \mathbf{st}, \mathbf{pr}, \mathbf{sst}, \mathbf{stg}, \mathbf{id}\}$. A positive answer to **DS-gr** implies a positive answer to **DC** and **DS** for the other semantics. On the contrary, if an argument is attacked by an argument contained in the grounded extension, then the answer to **DC** and **DS** is negative. According to [11], sceptical reasoning with any semantics generally overlaps with reasoning with the grounded semantics on many practical cases of AFs.

AFGCN, by Lars Malmqvist, competed in ICCMA21 as well. It exploits a Graph Convolutional Network [26] to compute approximate solutions to **DC**-σ and **DS**-σ tasks with $\sigma \in \{\mathbf{co}, \mathbf{st}, \mathbf{pr}, \mathbf{sst}, \mathbf{stg}, \mathbf{id}\}$, exactly as Harper++. The model is trained by using a randomized training process using a dataset of AFs from previous ICCMA competitions in order to maximize generalization from the input AFs. In addition, to speed up calculation and somewhat improve accuracy, the solver uses the pre-computed grounded extension as an input feature to the neural network.

4   Encoding

In this section we encode some of the Abstract Argumentation problems and semantics presented in Sect. 2. We focus only on some of the NP-Complete combinations presented in Table 1 because solving QUBO is NP-Complete as well. More specifically, the encoded problems are **DC**-σ and **Exists**-$\sigma^{\neg\varnothing}$, while the considered semantics is **co**.

Without loss of generality, we assign to each argument an index, hence A = $\{a_1, \ldots, a_n\}$, where n is the number of arguments. The encoding of problems in

---

[6] GitHub repository of Harper++: https://github.com/aig-hagen/taas-harper.

Abstract Argumentation uses a set of n binary variables $x_1, \ldots, x_n$ to represent a set E of arguments. The meaning is that the argument $a_i \in E$ if and only if $x_i = 1$. We denote by $\underline{x}$ the tuple $(x_1, \ldots, x_n)$ and by $\mathbf{x} \in \{0,1\}^n$ a vector of possible values for $x_1, \ldots, x_n$.

Each semantics σ will be associated to a quadratic penalty function P_σ such that P_σ assumes its minimum value at $\mathbf{x}$ if and only if the corresponding set $E = \{a_i \in A : x_i = 1\}$ is an extension valid for σ.

Each step in the encoding process will be explained with an example applied to the AF shown in Fig. 1, where the arguments are numbered as $a_1 = a, a_2 = b, a_3 = c, a_4 = d$, and $a_5 = e$.

Most of the argumentation semantics require admissible sets. Therefore, we define a penalty function P_{ad} which enforces this property. P_{ad} is the sum of four terms and contains new additional variables. The first term forces the set E to be **conflict-free**:

$$P_{cf} = \sum_{i \to j \text{ or } j \to i} x_i x_j$$

In fact, the value of P_{cf} corresponds to the number of self attacks in E and its value is 0 if and only if E is conflict-free.

The term P_{cf} for the example is

$$P_{cf} = x_1 x_2 + x_3 x_2 + x_3 x_4 + x_4 x_5.$$

The constraints to model the notion of **defense** are more complicated: we use a first set of additional variables $t_1, \ldots, t_n$, denoting which arguments are attacked by E: $t_i = 1$ if and only if a_i is attacked by some argument of E. The variables $d_1, \ldots, d_n$ of the second set denote which arguments are defended by E: $d_i = 1$ if and only if a_i is defended (from all the possible attacks) by some arguments of E.

For each argument a_i, the penalty function P_t^i forces t_i to be 1 if and only if a_i is attacked by E, i.e., $t_i = \bigvee_{j \to i} x_j$.

Let h_i be the number of attackers of a_i and let $i_1, \ldots, i_{h_i}$ be their indices. If $h_i = 0$, then t_i is simply 0, while if $h_i = 1$, then $t_i = x_{i_1}$: in these cases, we set $P_t^i = 0$. If $h_i = 2$, then $P_t^i = OR(t_i, x[i_1], x[i_2])$, where

$$OR(Z, X, Y) = Z + X + Y + XY - 2Z(X + Y)$$

is the way of expressing as a quadratic function the constraint that the binary variable Z is the disjunction of the binary variables X and Y, as shown in [24]. Finally, if $h_i > 2$

$$P_t^i = OR(t_i, x[i_1], \alpha_i^1) + OR(\alpha_i^1, x[i_2], \alpha_i^2) + \ldots$$
$$+ OR(\alpha_i^{h_i-3}, x[i_{h_i-2}], \alpha_i^{h_i-2}) + OR(\alpha_i^{h_i-2}, x[i_{h_i-1}], x[i_{h_i}]),$$

where $\alpha_i^1, \ldots, \alpha_i^{h_i-2}$ are $h_i - 2$ auxiliary binary variables.

The variables t_i associated to the example are $t_1 = 0, t_2, t_3 = x_4, t_4 = x_3, t_5 = x_4$ where t_2 is constrained by the term $P_t^2 = OR(t_2, x_1, x_3)$. No other term P_t^i is needed and consequently no auxiliary variable is used.

The other penalty function P_d^i forces d_i to be 1 if and only if a_i is defended by E, i.e., $d_i = \bigwedge_{j \to i} t_j$. If $h_i = 0$, then d_i is simply 1, while if $h_i = 1$, then $d_i = t_{i_1}$: in these cases, $P_d^i = 0$. If $h_i = 2$, then $P_d^i = AND(d_i, t[i_1], t[i_2])$, where

$$AND(Z, X, Y) = 3Z + XY - 2Z(X + Y)$$

is the way of expressing the conjunction $Z = X$ and Y as a quadratic function [24].

Otherwise, if $h_i > 2$ then

$$P_d^i = AND(d_i, t[i_1], \delta_i^1) + AND(\delta_i^1, t[i_2], \delta_i^2) + \dots$$
$$+ AND(\delta_i^{h_i-3}, t[i_{h_i-2}], \delta_i^{h_i-2}) + AND(\delta_i^{h_i-2}, t[i_{h_i-1}], t[i_{h_i}])$$

where $\delta_i^1, \dots, \delta_i^{h_i-2}$ are new $h_i - 2$ auxiliary binary variables.

The variables d_i associated to the example are $d_1 = 1, d_2 = 0, d_3 = x_3, d_4 = x_4, d_5 = x_3$ and no term P_d^i is needed. Note that $d_2 = 0$ because a attacks b but it is not attacked by any argument.

The number of auxiliary variables needed for this encoding is hence $N = 2n + 2\sum_{i=1}^n \max(h_i - 2, 0)$, excluding the n variables $x_1, \dots, x_n$. Note that, if $h = \max h_i$, then $N = O(nh)$.

The final term

$$P_{def} = \sum_{i=1}^n x_i(1 - d_i)$$

forces each argument in E to be defended by E.

The term P_{def} for the example is

$$P_{def} = x_2 + x_3(1 - x_3) + x_4(1 - x_4) + x_5(1 - x_3)$$

which can be simplified as $P_{def} = x_2 + x_5(1 - x_3)$ because for any binary variable b the term $b(1 - b)$ is always 0.

Summing up, the penalty function for **admissible** sets is

$$P_{ad} = P_{cf} + \sum_{i=1}^n P_t^i + \sum_{i=1}^n P_d^i + P_{def}.$$

In the example the penalty function is

$$P_{ad} = x_1 x_2 + x_3 x_2 + x_3 x_4 + x_4 x_5 + OR(t_2, x_1, x_3) + x_2 + x_5(1 - x_3)$$

However, the term $OR(t_2, x_1, x_3)$ can be neglected because t_2 does not appear elsewhere.

It is easy to prove that the minimum value of P_{ad} is 0 and the related values for $\underline{x}$ correspond to admissible sets.

Considering the **complete** semantics, we simply need to add an additional term to P_{ad} which forces all the arguments defended by E to be elements of E:

$$P_{co} = P_{ad} + \sum_{i=1}^n (1 - x_i)d_i$$

The additional term for the complete semantics corresponding to the example is

$$(1 - x_1) + (1 - x_3)x_3 + (1 - x_4)x_4 + (1 - x_5)x_3$$

which reduces to $(1 - x_1) + (1 - x_5)x_3$. *Hence,*

$$P_{co} = x_1x_2 + x_3x_2 + x_3x_4 + x_4x_5 + x_2 + x_5(1 - x_3) + (1 - x_1) + (1 - x_5)x_3.$$

To express that E is not empty (task **Exists**$^{\neg\varnothing}$) in a given semantics σ, it is enough to add the following term to the corresponding penalty function P_σ:

$$P_{ne} = (1 - x_1)(1 - \xi_1) + OR(\xi_1, x_2, \xi_2) + \cdots + OR(\xi_{n-3}, x_{n-2}, \xi_{n-2}) + OR(\xi_{n-2}, x_{n-1}, x_n)$$

where $\xi_1, \ldots, \xi_{n-2}$ are new $n - 2$ auxiliary variables. This additional term corresponds to the constraint $\bigvee_{i=1}^{n} x_i = 1$. Hence, the minimum value of $P_\sigma + P_{ne}$ is 0 if and only if there exists a not empty extension.

The additional term to express the non-emptiness in the example is

$$(1 - x_1)(1 - \xi_1) + OR(\xi_1, x_2, \xi_2) + OR(\xi_2, x_3, \xi_3) + OR(\xi_3, x_4, x_5).$$

To express that a given argument a_i must appear in E (i.e., the **DC** task) it is sufficient to replace x_i with 1 and propagate this setting on all the encoding, obtaining thus a simplified quadratic function, with a reduced number of binary variables. It is easy to see that the minimum value of this function is 0 if and only if a_i is credulously accepted.

Suppose that we want to solve the **DC** *task for the argument* a_3 *in the example for the complete semantics. Hence, we replace* x_3 *with 1 in the corresponding* P_{co} *thus oobtaining the simplified penalty function*

$$x_1x_2 + x_2 + x_4 + x_4x_5 + x_2 + (1 - x_1) + (1 - x_5).$$

5   Implementation and Tests

The Ocean SDK includes a suite of open source Python tools[7] for solving hard problems with local solvers, such as SA algorithms, but also quantum annealers by using the Leap^{TM} Quantum Cloud Service.[8]

The software stack implements the computations needed to transform an arbitrarily posed problem to a form suitable for a quantum solver. First the problem needs to be encoded as an expression H representing the constraints among variables, by using the encoding shown in Sect. 4; then the expression needs to be compiled (*model* = *H.compile()*) in order to obtain the QUBO matrix. Finally, the model can be directly solved by using local or quantum annealers.

---

[7] D-Wave Ocean SDK: https://github.com/dwavesystems/dwave-ocean-sdk.
[8] Leap^{TM} Cloud Quantum: https://cloud.dwavesys.com/leap/login/?next=/leap/.

5.1 Tests and Comparison

The tests in this section have the primary goal to prove the correctness of the encoding: we compared all the results with *ConArg* [6,8], a reduction-based (exact) solver using *Constraint Programming*, which has been also used to validate the results in ICCMA19. Moreover, to have a first comparison with a different approximate solver we run the same problems with Harper++, an approximate solver by M. Thimm (see the related work in Sect. 3). This solver was chosen because it ranked at the first position in the **co** track at ICCMA21, and for this reason it represents the best baseline to test **DC-co**.

All the tests in this section were performed on a 2 GHz Quad-Core Intel Core i5 with 16 GB of RAM. We set a timeout of 60 s, as applied in ICCMA21 when considering approximate solvers. Moreover, all the tests in this section were executed locally by using the SA algorithm provided by the Ocean SDK package in the Python *SimulatedAnnealingSampler* class. We set the *number of reads* parameter of the algorithm to *nArguments* × 2 (*nArguments* is the number of arguments in the considered instance): each read is generated by one run of the SA algorithm. We set *number of sweeps* used in annealing to min(*nArguments* × 50, 1000). In case no solution with energy 0 is found after a run, the initial random *seed* is changed and a successive iteration of SA is executed, until a zero-energy solution is found or the timeout is met, with an upper limit of 100 iterations for each AF.

In Table 2 we detail the results on 104 *"Small"* instances that are part of the benchmark selected in ICCMA19.[9] The 104 instances have from 5 to 191 arguments (median 28.5) and from 8 to 8192 attacks (median 296). We test the credulous acceptance of the same argument used in ICCMA19, and we focus on the complete semantics: we test **DC-co**. The columns of Table 2 respectively show the instance name, the number of arguments in the considered AF instance (*#nArgs*), the number of executed iterations of the SA algorithm (*#iter*), the answer provided by the solver ("YES" the argument is credulously accepted, "NO" it is not) and the time taken in seconds, respectively for the QUBO encoding and Harper++: *rQUBO/tQUBO* and *rHarp/tHarp*.

To summarize Table 2, SA provided the right answer 85/104 times, while Harper++ always proved to be correct (104/104) when compared to ConArg. SA reached the timeout 19 times; the frameworks on which SA timed-out have 103, 49, 95, 99, 30, 48, 85, 47, 191, 191, 95, 95, 71, 85, 99, 103, 99, 43, and

---

[9] The original *"Small"* benchmark included 108 instances: in our tests we use 104 instances because we discarded 4 AFs with more than 200 arguments, which we considered as too large for these tests w.r.t. the other instances, which have a median of 28.5 arguments.

96 arguments. About successful instances instead, the average number of SA iterations is 2.96, with a median of 1.0, and a maximum number of 37 iterations. The median times to create a QUBO expression, compile it, and solve it with SA are respectively 0.017, 0.058, and 0.203 s.

Therefore, with these tests we empirically validate the encoding provided in Sect. 4 (no wrong answer was returned), and we show that, even if Harper++ always performs better in terms of time, SA proves to be quite fast most of the times, even if on some instances it fails to provide a positive answer before the timeout.

The second round of tests concerns the accuracy of SA in case of "NO" answers, compared to Harper++. As it is possible to see from Table 2, all the tests were performed on pairs of $\langle AF, argument \rangle$ in which the argument is credulously accepted. Since from internal tests we noticed that all the possible arguments in those AFs are always credulously accepted, we were forced to completely change the benchmark: we now use 100 frameworks with 80 arguments each, generated as *Erdős-Rényi (ER)* graphs [15]. Such AFs were used in previous works [7] as a dataset to compare different solvers.

In the ER model, a graph is constructed by randomly connecting n nodes. Each edge is included in the graph with probability p independent from any other edge. Clearly, as p increases from 0 to 1, the model becomes more and more likely to include graphs with more edges. In this dataset $p = c \cdot log(n)/n$ (with n the number of nodes and c empirically set to 2.5), ensuring the connectedness of such graphs. The ER model has been also used as part of the benchmark in the ICCMA competitions, since ICCMA17. On these 100 frameworks we first randomly selected one argument each that is not credulously accepted. We did this by using ConArg, being an exact solver. On this new benchmark, SA returns 100/100 timeouts (still set to 60 s), while Harper++ returns 4/100 correct ("NO") answers and 96/100 incorrect ("YES") answers.

We finally switched to a third benchmark by selecting one credulously accepted argument for each ER graph; because of this, we discarded 10 frameworks for which it was not possible to find such an argument. By using the same parameters as the previous experiment, SA provided the correct ("YES") answer for 64/90 and 26 timeouts, while Harper++ answered 90/90 correct answers. Considering successful instances, SA has an average number of iterations of 3.15, with a median of 2.0 and a maximum number of 25. If we consider our timeouts as "NO", SA has an overall accuracy of 84% on the ER dataset, while Harper++ has an accuracy of 49%.

We noticed a general tendency of Harper++ to return a positive answer, while clearly SA returns "NO" not only if there is no solution, but also in case the timeout is reached.

Table 2. The correctness and performance in time (seconds) of QArg and Harper++, measured on "Small" instances from the ICCMA19 benchmark (**DC-co** task). **TOUT** stands for "timeout".

instance	#nArgs	#iter	rQUBO	rHarper	tQUBO	tHarper	instance	nArgs	#iter	rQarg	rHrper	tQarg	tHarper
Small-result-b87	24	4	YES	YES	0.732	0.005	Small-result-b21	23	1	YES	YES	0.192	0.017
Small-result-b93	103	2	TOUT	YES	–	0.019	Small-result-b20	23	2	YES	YES	0.344	0.022
Small-result-b44	27	1	YES	YES	0.242	0.011	Small-result-b34	8	1	YES	YES	0.036	0.020
Small-result-b50	51	1	YES	YES	2.214	0.010	Small-result-b22	47	1	YES	YES	1.883	0.021
Small-result-b78	25	3	YES	YES	1.230	0.010	Small-result-b36	19	1	YES	YES	0.127	0.018
Small-result-b79	25	15	YES	YES	6.180	0.011	Small-result-b37	17	2	YES	YES	0.224	0.019
Small-result-b51	49	28	TOUT	YES	–	0.018	Small-result-b23	47	1	YES	YES	1.771	0.018
Small-result-b6	95	3	TOUT	YES	–	0.018	Small-result-b12	30	2	YES	YES	0.861	0.016
Small-result-b45	25	1	YES	YES	0.240	0.012	Small-result-b13	6	1	YES	YES	0.012	0.016
Small-result-b92	99	2	TOUT	YES	–	0.017	Small-result-b11	14	1	YES	YES	0.053	0.018
Small-result-b86	24	1	YES	YES	0.139	0.013	Small-result-b39	17	1	YES	YES	0.063	0.018
Small-result-b90	85	1	YES	YES	6.941	0.013	Small-result-b38	14	3	YES	YES	0.185	0.015
Small-result-b84	12	1	YES	YES	0.038	0.013	Small-result-b10	6	1	YES	YES	0.009	0.014
Small-result-b53	49	1	YES	YES	1.976	0.014	Small-result-b14	13	2	YES	YES	0.135	0.023
Small-result-b47	22	3	YES	YES	0.676	0.014	Small-result-b15	30	1	YES	YES	1.230	0.024
Small-result-b4	23	1	YES	YES	0.186	0.013	Small-result-b29	16	1	YES	YES	0.045	0.024
Small-result-b5	47	1	YES	YES	1.693	0.016	Small-result-b17	14	1	YES	YES	0.095	0.026
Small-result-b46	24	1	YES	YES	0.250	0.013	Small-result-b16	6	1	YES	YES	0.015	0.020
Small-result-b52	48	24	TOUT	YES	–	0.018	Small-result-b107	78	1	YES	YES	9.379	0.019
Small-result-b85	24	4	YES	YES	0.640	0.015	Small-result-b65	71	14	TOUT	YES	–	0.026
Small-result-b91	99	2	YES	YES	56.193	0.019	Small-result-b71	26	2	YES	YES	0.740	0.028
Small-result-b108	78	1	YES	YES	10.581	0.019	Small-result-b59	67	1	YES	YES	1.991	0.022
Small-result-b95	85	6	TOUT	YES	–	0.019	Small-result-b58	8	1	YES	YES	0.016	0.020
Small-result-b81	22	1	YES	YES	0.236	0.017	Small-result-b70	25	8	YES	YES	3.604	0.018
Small-result-b56	46	1	YES	YES	1.960	0.013	Small-result-b64	32	1	YES	YES	1.039	0.016
Small-result-b42	13	1	YES	YES	0.028	0.011	Small-result-b106	78	1	YES	YES	7.270	0.020
Small-result-b43	12	1	YES	YES	0.024	0.010	Small-result-b104	78	1	YES	YES	8.133	0.026
Small-result-b57	8	1	YES	YES	0.008	0.010	Small-result-b99	96	1	YES	YES	15.142	0.020
Small-result-b80	25	1	YES	YES	0.447	0.011	Small-result-b72	25	1	YES	YES	0.432	0.019
Small-result-b94	85	1	YES	YES	10.988	0.014	Small-result-b66	67	1	YES	YES	2.083	0.019
Small-result-b82	25	2	YES	YES	0.771	0.014	Small-result-b67	25	1	YES	YES	0.422	0.019
Small-result-b96	85	1	YES	YES	9.776	0.015	Small-result-b73	64	10	YES	YES	4.626	0.015
Small-result-b69	25	5	YES	YES	1.890	0.014	Small-result-b98	85	3	TOUT	YES	–	0.022
Small-result-b41	6	1	YES	YES	0.008	0.013	Small-result-b105	78	1	YES	YES	8.492	0.018
Small-result-b2	5	1	YES	YES	0.004	0.010	Small-result-b101	99	1	YES	YES	30.632	0.024
Small-result-b55	45	2	YES	YES	4.668	0.015	Small-result-b88	99	6	TOUT	YES	–	0.022
Small-result-b54	47	35	TOUT	YES	–	0.018	Small-result-b8	8	1	YES	YES	0.019	0.017
Small-result-b3	11	1	YES	YES	0.028	0.014	Small-result-b77	25	5	YES	YES	2.123	0.019
Small-result-b40	15	2	YES	YES	0.146	0.012	Small-result-b63	32	4	YES	YES	4.136	0.018
Small-result-b68	25	4	YES	YES	1.746	0.012	Small-result-b62	32	1	YES	YES	1.109	0.017
Small-result-b97	85	4	YES	YES	53.101	0.018	Small-result-b76	43	1	YES	YES	1.971	0.018
Small-result-b83	12	1	YES	YES	0.035	0.014	Small-result-b9	16	1	YES	YES	0.027	0.015
Small-result-b27	191	1	TOUT	YES	–	0.010	Small-result-b89	103	5	TOUT	YES	–	0.020
Small-result-b33	9	1	YES	YES	0.072	0.010	Small-result-b100	78	1	YES	YES	5.461	0.022
Small-result-b26	191	1	TOUT	YES	–	0.012	Small-result-b102	99	2	TOUT	YES	–	0.023
Small-result-b30	16	1	YES	YES	0.070	0.011	Small-result-b48	23	37	YES	YES	7.033	0.019
Small-result-b24	95	3	TOUT	YES	–	0.028	Small-result-b60	32	8	YES	YES	6.558	0.015
Small-result-b18	30	100	TOUT	YES	–	0.018	Small-result-b74	64	13	YES	YES	5.709	0.016
Small-result-b19	11	1	YES	YES	0.028	0.017	Small-result-b75	43	43	TOUT	YES	–	0.022
Small-result-b25	95	3	TOUT	YES	–	0.021	Small-result-b61	32	2	YES	YES	1.792	0.017
Small-result-b31	16	1	YES	YES	0.043	0.014	Small-result-b49	55	1	YES	2	2.173	0.018
Small-result-b35	7	1	YES	YES	0.013	0.017	Small-result-b103	96	4	TOUT	–	–	0.022

5.2 Execution on the Leap™ Quantum Cloud Service

To use a D-Wave machine to solve a given problem, the logical graph representing the corresponding QUBO or Ising model must be embedded into the physical graph of D-Wave's hardware. In Listing 1.1 we present the Python code to translate the model into QUBO and then execute it in the Leap^{TM} Quantum Cloud Service; *MYSOLVER* = *"Advantage_system6.1"*, while the API key is generated for each use to access the service and monitor the consumption of resource.

```
1  def dwave_sol(model):
2    qubo, qubo_offset = model.to_qubo()
3    sampler_kwargs = {"num_reads": 50, "annealing_time": 50, "
        num_spin_reversal_transforms": 4, "auto_scale": True, "
        chain_strength": 2.0, "chain_break_fraction": True}
4    dw_sampler = DWaveSampler(endpoint="https://cloud.dwavesys.com/sapi
        ", token=MYTOKEN, solver=MYSOLVER)
5    sampler = EmbeddingComposite(dw_sampler)
6    sampleset = sampler.sample_qubo(qubo)
7    decoded_samples = model.decode_sampleset(sampleset)
8    best_sample = min(decoded_samples, key=lambda x: x.energy)
9    return best_sample
```

Listing 1.1. The Python code to execute the QUBO model in the Leap^{TM} Quantum Cloud Service.

This function returns the solution with the best (i.e., lowest) energy (*best_sample*). In case the requested problem is the existence of a non-empty complete extension, which is an NP-Complete problem (see Table 1), the result if we create the model of the framework in Fig. 1 is a zero-energy solution. If we print the labels of zero-energy variables in *best_sample* we can also directly obtain the arguments of the returned non-empty complete extension, e.g., $\{a, c, e\}$. The parameters at line 3 guide the mapping of the model to the architecture of D-Wave's quantum hardware: they need further exploration in order to optimize the execution of the quantum annealer, as suggested in Sect. 6.

6 Conclusions and Future Work

This paper presents the first approximate computational-approach to well-known Abstract Argumentation problems by using a QUBO encoding and a solver based on simulated/quantum annealing. Approximate methods are not totally new to the Argumentation community (e.g., in ICCMA21, see Sect. 3), but indeed the use of quantum machines is so. After presenting the QUBO encoding for some of the NP-Complete problems in Abstract Argumentation, we have validated it by empirically proving its correctness with tests. Moreover, we have compared the accuracy and performance against a different approximate solver, i.e., Harper++. Clearly the goal is to exploit the future development and availability of quantum machines to fully take advantage of the presented encoding in terms of time performance.

The future work that appears in front of us follows many different paths, as the paper is seminal with respect to the topic. First, we need to define a QUBO encoding of further semantics for which related taska are NP-Complete. Then, we would like to better study ad-hoc SA algorithms with respect to Abstract Argumentation problems: we believe performance can be further improved with "simple" non-quantum annealers.

In addition, the optimization behind mapping QUBO models derived from an Argumentation problem to the architecture of quantum machines is still unexplored and challenging: several parameters need further investigation to better exploit the hardware and the connections among qubits, which are limited on D-Wave's architectures.

Finally, we will extend the QUBO encoding to weighted problems in Argumentation [9][16, Chapter 6], with the purpose to represent weights (or probabilities) associated with arguments or attacks: this is allowed by the use of linear or quadratic coefficients that encode a weight in the expression modelling the problem.

References

1. Anthony, M., Boros, E., Crama, Y., Gruber, A.: Quadratic reformulations of non-linear binary optimization problems. Math. Program. **162**(1–2), 115–144 (2017)
2. Baioletti, M.: Probabilistic reasoning as quadratic unconstrained binary optimization. In: Fieldsend, J.E., Wagner, M. (eds.) GECCO 2022: Genetic and Evolutionary Computation Conference, Companion Volume, Boston, Massachusetts, USA, 9–13 July 2022, pp. 2177–2181. ACM (2022). https://doi.org/10.1145/3520304.3534005
3. Baroni, P., Caminada, M., Giacomin, M.: An introduction to argumentation semantics. Knowl. Eng. Rev. **26**(4), 365–410 (2011)
4. Baroni, P., Gabbay, D., Giacomin, M., van der Torre, L.: Handbook of Formal Argumentation. College Publications, London (2018)
5. Bistarelli, S., Kotthoff, L., Santini, F., Taticchi, C.: A first overview of ICCMA 2019. In: Advances in Argumentation in Artificial Intelligence (AIxIA 2020). CEUR Workshop Proceedings, vol. 2777, pp. 90–102. CEUR-WS.org (2020)
6. Bistarelli, S., Rossi, F., Santini, F.: ConArg: a tool for classical and weighted argumentation. In: Computational Models of Argument - Proceedings of COMMA. Frontiers in Artificial Intelligence and Applications, vol. 287, pp. 463–464. IOS Press (2016)
7. Bistarelli, S., Rossi, F., Santini, F.: Not only size, but also shape counts: abstract argumentation solvers are benchmark-sensitive. J. Log. Comput. **28**(1), 85–117 (2018)
8. Bistarelli, S., Rossi, F., Santini, F.: ConArgLib: an argumentation library with support to search strategies and parallel search. J. Exp. Theor. Artif. Intell. **33**(6), 891–918 (2021)
9. Bistarelli, S., Santini, F.: Weighted argumentation. FLAP **8**(6), 1589–1622 (2021)
10. Cerutti, F., Gaggl, S.A., Thimm, M., Wallner, J.: Foundations of implementations for formal argumentation. IfCoLog J. Log. their Appl. **4**(8), 2623–2705 (2017)
11. Cerutti, F., Thimm, M., Vallati, M.: An experimental analysis on the similarity of argumentation semantics. Argument Comput. **11**(3), 269–304 (2020)
12. Dung, P.M.: On the acceptability of arguments and its fundamental role in non-monotonic reasoning, logic programming and n-person games. Artif. Intell. **77**(2), 321–358 (1995)
13. Dung, P.M., Mancarella, P., Toni, F.: Computing ideal sceptical argumentation. Artif. Intell. **171**(10–15), 642–674 (2007)
14. Dvořák, W., Dunne, P.E.: Computational problems in formal argumentation and their complexity. FLAP **4**(8) (2017)

15. Erdős, P., Rényi, A.: On the evolution of random graphs. Bull. Inst. Int. Statist **38**(4), 343–347 (1961)
16. Gabbay, D., Giacomin, M., Simari, G.: Handbook of Formal Argumentation, vol. 2. no. v. 2. College Publications, London (2021)
17. Gaggl, S.A., Linsbichler, T., Maratea, M., Woltran, S.: Design and results of the second international competition on computational models of argumentation. Artif. Intell. **279**, 103193 (2020)
18. Glover, F.W., Kochenberger, G.A., Du, Y.: Quantum bridge analytics I: a tutorial on formulating and using QUBO models. 4OR **17**(4), 335–371 (2019)
19. Glover, F.W., Kochenberger, G.A., Ma, M., Du, Y.: Quantum bridge analytics II: QUBO-Plus, network optimization and combinatorial chaining for asset exchange. 4OR **18**(4), 387–417 (2020)
20. Hammer, P., Rudeanu, S.: Hammer, P., Rudeanu, S.: Boolean Methods in Operations Research and Related Areas, ökonometrie und unternehmensforschung/Econometrics and Operations Research, vol. 1007, p. 978. Springer, Berlin (1968)
21. Kochenberger, G., et al.: The unconstrained binary quadratic programming problem: a survey. J. Comb. Optim. **28**(1), 58–81 (2014). https://doi.org/10.1007/s10878-014-9734-0
22. Kröll, M., Pichler, R., Woltran, S.: On the complexity of enumerating the extensions of abstract argumentation frameworks. In: Proceedings of the Twenty-Sixth International Joint Conference on Artificial Intelligence, IJCAI, pp. 1145–1152. ijcai.org (2017)
23. Mücke, S., Piatkowski, N., Morik, K.: Learning bit by bit: extracting the essence of machine learning. In: Proceedings of the Conference on "Lernen, Wissen, Daten, Analysen". CEUR Workshop Proceedings, vol. 2454, pp. 144–155. CEUR-WS.org (2019)
24. Rosenberg, I.: Reduction of bivalent maximization to the quadratic case. Cahiers du Centre d'Etudes de Recherche Opérationnelle **17**, 71–74 (1975)
25. Thimm, M., Villata, S.: The first international competition on computational models of argumentation: results and analysis. Artif. Intell. **252**, 267–294 (2017)
26. Wu, Z., Pan, S., Chen, F., Long, G., Zhang, C., Yu, P.S.: A comprehensive survey on graph neural networks. IEEE Trans. Neural Networks Learn. Syst. **32**(1), 4–24 (2021)

Diversification of Parallel Search of Portfolio SAT Solver by Search Similarity Index

Yoichiro Iida[1]([✉]), Tomohiro Sonobe[2], and Mary Inaba[1]

[1] Graduate School of Information Science and Technology, The University of Tokyo, Tokyo, Japan
yoichiro-iida@g.ecc.u-tokyo.ac.jp, mary@is.s.u-tokyo.ac.jp
[2] National Institute of Informatics, Tokyo, Japan
tomohiro_sonobe@nii.ac.jp

Abstract. Parallelization is essential for the acceleration of SAT solvers, and for this purpose, the portfolio approach is a key technique. As the diversity of search is an important factor that affects the performance of portfolio-type parallel SAT solvers, several methods have been proposed to diversify their searches. This paper proposes the use of the Search Similarity Index (SSI)—a metric that quantifies the degree of diversity by measuring the similarity between searches performed by parallel workers—to develop a method to change the solver's activity when the value of SSI indicates that the searches of parallel workers are similar. The implementation of SSI and the proposed method increases the diversity between parallel workers by preventing the performance of similar searches. Experimental results indicate that the proposed metric significantly contributes to the acceleration of solver performance, with the number of solved benchmark instances increasing by +4.3% in the case of 32 parallel workers compared to the state-of-the-art portfolio parallel solver. The result implies that similar searching of the portfolio-type parallel SAT solver degrades its performance and that increasing the degree of search diversity can improve their performance.

Keywords: Parallel SAT solver · Portfolio approach · Diversification

1 Introduction

The propositional satisfiability problem (SAT problem) is one of the most fundamental problems in computer science. SAT solvers, which are used to solve the SAT problem, have been applied to several real-world problems [8,11,19] Such solvers search a set of Boolean value assignments to variables that satisfy the problem, called a solution, or a proof of "unsatisfiability". Many methods have been proposed to accelerate SAT solvers, including ones based on parallelization. The divide-and-conquer and portfolio [7] approaches are the two primary methods to achieve parallelization. In the parallel category of recent annual SAT

© The Author(s), under exclusive license to Springer Nature Switzerland AG 2022
S. Khanna et al. (Eds.): PRICAI 2022, LNCS 13629, pp. 61–74, 2022.
https://doi.org/10.1007/978-3-031-20862-1_5

competitions [16], portfolio-type parallel solvers have exhibited relatively better results than divide-and-conquer-type ones. Unlike divide-and-conquer type parallelization, which divides the problem into sub-problems and each of which is assigned to parallel workers, portfolio solvers do not divide the problem. Instead, every worker in the portfolio-type parallel solvers searches for a solution to the same problem and attempts to search in different ways. The searches performed by workers are considered to be competitive because the first result obtained by a worker is adopted as the result of the solver. Hence, if each worker in a portfolio-type solver searches in the same way, the benefits of parallelization are not obtained. Therefore, diversity of search, i.e., different searches performed by different workers, is essential for the performance of portfolio-type parallel solvers. Although various diversification methods have improved solver performance, few studies have quantitatively evaluated whether they achieve the desired search diversity. This study hypothesizes that the performance of SAT solvers can be improved by ensuring search diversity based on its quantitative evaluation.

Upon the consideration of the precise parameters of "search diversity" required by portfolio-type parallel solvers, the simplest method is to divide the search space into a set of sub-spaces, and to search each sub-space uniformly, e.g., with the same probability. However, the practical searches for the SAT problems related to real-world problems are not uniform. SAT solvers utilize depth-first and intensive search algorithms to select the assignments that are most likely to yield a solution based on heuristic techniques. Incorporating such a biased search algorithm has improved the performance of SAT solvers. Similarly, the searches for practical parallel solvers are also biased. This study advocates that the measurement of the similarity between the searches of different workers represents the measurement of search diversity of the parallel solvers. When searches between workers are similar, the diversity is low, and vice versa. Reducing the degree of similarity between searches increases the diversity and improves the performance of parallel solvers.

This paper proposes the Search Similarity Index (SSI)—a metric that quantifies the degree of similarity between searches performed by parallel workers—to develop a method to change the solver's activity when the value of SSI indicates that the searches of parallel workers are similar. In this context, the search is defined as the solver's activity of assigning Boolean values to variables, which is primarily characterized by two parameters regarding the variables—the polarity of Boolean values (True or False) and the selection order of variables while assigning Boolean values. SSI compares these two parameters corresponding to parallel workers and calculates their similarity. In addition, this study proposes a method to enhance search diversity based on SSI. When the SSI value indicates higher similarity than a threshold, the activity of the solver is appropriately changed to avoid similar searches. This study implements SSI and the aforementioned method on P-MCOMSPS [18], the state-of-the-art parallel SAT solver, and conducts experiments to assess the performance improvement induced by the proposed method.

The remainder of this paper is structured as follows: Sect. 2 introduces techniques related to SAT solvers, Sect. 3 introduces the design of SSI and defines a method based on such to enhance search diversity, Sect. 4 describes the experimental verification of the proposed method. Finally, Sect. 5 summarizes this paper and outlines prospective directions for future research.

2   Preliminaries

2.1   The SAT Problem and SAT Solvers

The satisfiability problem (SAT problem) is a fundamental research topic in computational science, and it was in this context that NP-completeness was first demonstrated. It is formulated as a propositional logic formula (henceforth referred to as an instance) in which Boolean variables are combined using logical operators. The problem is usually presented in the conjunctive normal form, in which variables are combined into clauses using disjunctions, which are, in turn, combined using conjunctions. It considers the existence of a set of assignments of Boolean values to variables that satisfy the instance, i.e., evaluate it as True. Assignments that satisfy an instance are called solutions.

SAT solvers are applications used to solve SAT problems and are also applied to real-world industrial problems. Thus, the study of SAT solvers is highly important. Operationally, SAT solvers conduct searches to derive solutions. A search is a repetitive procedure comprising the assignment of Boolean values to variables and subsequent verification of whether or not the assignment satisfies the instance. SAT solvers continue the search until they derive a solution (called satisfiable state or SAT) or they prove that there is no assignment that satisfies the instance (unsatisfiable, UNSAT). Usually, solvers are constrained by a few criteria, such as a time limit to finish their search. In case this constraint is not satisfied, e.g., runtime exceeds the limit, the UNKNOWN state is returned as the output. The entire set of assignment combination is called the whole search space. A search space is a subset of the whole search space where some Boolean variables exhibit fixed or assigned.

2.2   Techniques Employed by SAT Solvers

To solve real-world SAT problems, SAT solvers are primarily Conflict-Driven Clause Learning (CDCL) solvers based on the Davis-Putnam-Logemann-Loveland (DPLL) algorithm [2], which consists of three phases—*decision, propagation,* and *conflict and backtrack.* In the decision phase, a variable is selected, and a Boolean value is assigned to it as an assumption. The variable and its polarity (True or False) of the Boolean value are usually selected by heuristic methods. In the propagation phase, the solver assigns Boolean values to other variables whose polarities are uniquely determined as logical consequences of the decision. If it detects a logical inconsistency (called conflict) during the propagation, it moves to the conflict and backtrack phase. Otherwise, it repeats the decision and propagation phases until an SAT or UNSAT state is identified. In the conflict and backtrack phase, the solver cancels the previous decision, analyzes the root cause of the conflict, and derives a new clause (called a learnt clause [1]) to avoid the same conflict in future searches. Subsequently, it returns to the decision phase and initiates another assumption. Restart [3] is a type of backtracking operation, which cancels all decisions and initiates another assumption from scratch.

Variable state independent decaying sum (VSIDS) [13], learning rate based branching heuristic (LRB) [10], and phase-saving [14] are the major heuristic techniques used during the decision phases. VSIDS and LRB are used to select variables during the decision phase. Both heuristics manage the sequence of variables and the variable with the highest score is selected for the assignment. The phase-saving technique determines the polarities of Boolean values assigned to the variables. In addition to these methods, several techniques have contributed to the acceleration of SAT solvers. Two-watch literals [13] and trail saving techniques [6] reduce the time required during the propagation phase.

2.3 Parallelization

Parallelization is a key technique for the acceleration of SAT solvers, of which the divide-and-conquer and the portfolio are two primary approaches. The divide-and-conquer approach divides an instance into sub-instances. This is usually accomplished by selecting some of the instance's Boolean variables and assigning either true or false values to them. Therefore, each sub-instance exhibits an independent search space. The solver assigns each sub-instance to a parallel worker, ensuring that there are no overlapping searches among the workers.

Conversely, all workers of a portfolio-type parallel solver search the same instance in different ways without division into sub-instances, and the result of the fastest worker is adopted as the output of the entire solver. Little difference in searches among workers, i.e., similar assignments, results in little difference in the duration to complete their searches, making it difficult to derive the benefits of parallelization to improve performance. Therefore, search diversity is essential to optimize the performance of the portfolio approach. Several methods have been proposed to this end. ppfolio [15] executes multiple excelled solvers in the past SAT competitions, assigning these solvers as its parallel workers where each performs the search individually. As each solver is developed based on different methods, parameters, etc., their searches can also be expected to be reasonably different. ManySAT [5] utilizes a single solver, but it is parallelized using different configurations. For example, it imposes different rules on the heuristic decision method, such as the polarity selection of Boolean values. Block Branching [17] changes the priority of variable selection, i.e., it groups variables into certain sets based on the connections between the variables in the instance, and each parallel worker selects a distinct group of variables during the decision phase. This technique forces workers to focus the decision on sets of variables with strong connections to resolve.

2.4   Related Works: Measurement of Distances Between Solvers

Some studies have attempted to measure distances between pairs of searches, especially between parallel workers. Guo and Lagniez [4] proposed the calculation of the distance between parallel workers using the information of actual assignment of Boolean values. To this end, they counted the number of variables with identical polarity in both workers and deemed them to be similar if the ratio of this number to the number of all variables was high. However, their study focused only on polarity, and their objective was to improve the polarity selection heuristic. Thus, they did not consider the sequence of variable assumptions. This study hypothesizes that the priority of variables is also an important factor as the search duration is significantly dependent on the sequence.

Moon and Inaba [12] also attempted to define similarity based on Boolean values. First, they divided the variables into a few groups. Variables in the same clauses of instance were regarded as connected, and strongly connected variables were categorized into the same group. The authors calculated the percentage of Boolean values in each group and if the ranges of percentages corresponding to two workers were similar, the searches performed by those workers were regarded to be similar. This study also uses only polarity but did not consider the sequence of variable assumptions.

Kanbara and Nabeshima [9] used the information of shared learnt clauses among parallel workers to define similarity. They measured the degree of overlap and usage ratios of the learnt clauses between workers. If the overlap exceeded a certain threshold, one of the workers' activity was altered randomly by the inversion of the polarity of variables.

3   Methods: Search Similarity Index (SSI)

This section introduces the definition of the Search Similarity Index (SSI). SSI is a metric that quantifies the similarity between searches. Given a set of N parallel workers as $W = \{w_1, w_2, ..., w_N\}$, the state of the search $State_{w_i^k}$ can be modeled with *learnt clauses*, *search history*, and *search direction*. w_i^k denotes the i-th parallel worker at k-th step of the search, e.g., the number of decisions, conflicts, and restarts, where $k \in \mathbb{N}$. *learnt clauses* are the learnt clauses in the solver's database at w_i^k. *search history* denotes the assignment of Boolean value to variables by decisions and propagations by the k-th step, and *search direction* denotes the assignment plan of Boolean value to the unassigned variables from k-th step.

This study defines the similarity of search to be represented by the similarity between *search directions* and we utilize neither *learnt clauses* nor *search history* for the reasons below. Regarding learnt clauses, their size increases fast, and comparing them between workers is expensive. In addition, learnt clauses include noise—useless clauses to find solutions or UNSAT proof. Therefore, it is essential to extract good clauses to represent the search appropriately but difficult to identify the good clauses for the worker. For *search history*, this information can be ignored because we utilize the similarity that is obtained at the restart and before any decisions made after the restart. Using SSI at restart enables accurate simulation of subsequent searches sufficiently and saves enough resources in order to manage *search history* information.

3.1 Definition of Current Search Direction (CSD)

In the DPLL algorithm, assignment is performed during the decision phase and the plan of assignment is managed in a table of decisions commonly maintained by SAT solvers. The assignment procedure can be decomposed into two subprocesses—determination of the *"polarity"* of Boolean value and the determination of the variable to which it is assigned. The latter subprocess can be restated as the order of variables in terms of assignment (henceforth referred to as *"priority"*). This study denotes the information of *search direction* at current step as the *Current Search Direction* (CSD). The CSDs of two parallel workers are compared to calculate the similarity of search and the value of the SSI. $CSD_{w_i^k}$ is the CSD at the k-th step (in this paper k-th restart) of the i-th parallel worker. $CSD_{w_i^k}$ comprises $polarity_{w_i^k}(v)$ and $priority_{w_i^k}(v)$ s.t. $v \in V$ (the whole variables).

First, $polarity(v)$ is defined as the Boolean value assigned to v. In most polarity decision methods, such as the phase-saving method, subsequent assignments are stored in a table in the method. The value of $polarity_{w_i^k}(v)$ is a Boolean value of variable v in the table at the k-th step.

$$polarity_{w_i^k}(v) := \{True, False \mid v \in V\} \tag{1}$$

Second, for the variable selection in the decision, all variables are sorted by their scores (e.g., VSIDS score). The order of the variable selection is represented by the $priority(v)$. If all variables in two searches exhibit identical polarities in the same order, then the two searches are identical. We define $priority(v)$ as having a value between 0 and 1. The order of the first variable v_{first} is 1, i.e., the v_{first} is firstly selected for decision before any assignment is conducted; thus, the value of $priority_{w_i^k}(v_{first})$ is close to 0. The order of the last variable v_{last} in the selection sequence is $|V_{w_i^k}|$; thus the value of $priority_{w_i^k}(v_{last})$ is 1.

$$priority_{w_i^k}(v) := \frac{order\ of\ variable\ v}{|V_{w_i^k}|} \tag{2}$$

Note that $|V_{w_i^k}|$ stands for the set of effective variables in the i-th worker at the k-th step. In practice, variables near the end of the selection sequence are rarely selected for decision. Therefore, this study establishes a score threshold to reduce the computational load of SSI. Variables with scores less than the threshold are excluded from CSD and others are included in $V_{w_i^k}$. In the case of VSIDS, the threshold is taken as 1.0.

3.2   Definition of Search Similarity Index (SSI)

SSI represents the similarity between two searches, where each search is represented by a CSD. In this paper, the two searches correspond to those performed by two parallel workers. SSI is defined as the weighted sum of the similarity of each variable corresponding to the two workers. When the two CSDs—polarities and priorities of all variables—are similar, their searches are considered to be similar. The similarity between a variable's polarities is denoted by *PolaritySimilarity* and that between its priorities by *PrioritySimilarity*. *PolaritySimilarity* between w_i^k and w_j^l is defined as follows:

$$PolaritySimilarity_{w_i^k, w_j^l}(v) := \begin{cases} 1 & \text{if } polarity_{w_i^k}(v) = polarity_{w_j^l}(v) \\ 0 & \text{otherwise} \end{cases} \tag{3}$$

Regarding the priority, by the definition of *PrioritySimilarity*, a variable with similar priorities in two CSDs is considered to exhibit high similarity—higher agreements between the priorities in the two CSDs correspond to higher degrees of similarity. Further, it takes values between zero and one, with identical priorities corresponding to one, and completely opposite priorities corresponding to zero. *PrioritySimilarity*$_{w_i^k, w_j^l}(v)$ is defined as follows.

$$PrioritySimilarity_{w_i^k, w_j^l}(v) := 1 - \left| priority_{w_i^k}(v) - priority_{w_j^l}(v) \right| \tag{4}$$

The similarity of a variable *similarity*$_{w_i^k, w_j^l}(v)$ is defined by the multiplication of *PolaritySimilarity* and *PrioritySimilarity*.

$$similarity_{w_i^k, w_j^l}(v) := PrioritySimilarity_{w_i^k, w_j^l}(v) \times PolaritySimilarity_{w_i^k, w_j^l}(v) \tag{5}$$

A weight factor for the similarity of each variable is the *importance*(v). Higher *importance* scores are assigned to variables with higher *priorities* because higher-priority variables are selected at earlier decision points than lower-priority ones. In general, variables selected at earlier decision points affect the search more than those selected at later points. Virtually, the degree of similarity between important variables significantly influences the process of determining the degree of similarity between the searches. The *importance*(v) is defined as follows: C denotes a constant representing the slope to the importance of variables; in this paper, the value of C is set at 0.1.

$$importance_{w_i^k, w_j^l}(v) := 2^{-priority_{w_i^k} \times C} + 2^{-priority_{w_j^l} \times C} \tag{6}$$

To use SSI as a similarity metric, its value is normalized to lie between zero and one—zero represents zero similarity, whereas one represents identical searches. Since both *PolaritySimilarity* and *PrioritySimilarity* lie between zero to one, the maximum value of the multiplication of *importance* and *similarity* is equal to the sum of the *importance* of all variables. Thus, we normalize SSI by the division of the sum of *importance*. The Algorithm 1 presents the overall steps of SSI calculation.

$$SSI_{w_i^k, w_j^l} := \frac{\sum_v (similarity_{w_i^k, w_j^l}(v) \times importance_{w_i^k, w_j^l}(v))}{\sum_v (importance_{w_i^k, w_j^l}(v))} \quad (7)$$

Algorithm 1. Calculation of Search Similarity Index between w_i^k and w_j^l

---

Require: $CSD_{w_i^k}, CSD_{w_j^l}$
1: **for** $v \in variables$ **do**
2:     Get *PolaritySimilarity(v)* by (3)
3:     Get *PrioritySimilarity(v)* by (4)
4:     *similarity(v)* = *PrioritySimilarity(v)* × *PolaritySimilarity(v)* by (5)
5:     Calculate *importance(v)* by (6)
6: **end for**
7: $SSI_{w_i^k, w_j^l} = \sum_v (similarity(v) \times importance(v)) / \sum_v importance(v)$

3.3 Method to Change Solver's Activity

This subsection discusses the procedure to change a solver's activity when the value of SSI indicates that the searches of parallel workers are similar.

A typical distribution of SSI values of an instance is depicted in Fig. 1 as an example. Preliminary experiments were conducted using the parallel solver, P-MCOMSPS, in its default configuration on 400 instances from the SAT competition 2021. Every SSI value was rounded up to three decimal places. The example illustrates the bell-shaped curve of the SSI value distribution. The other instances also exhibit similar shapes; only the position of the peak of the distribution depends on the instance.

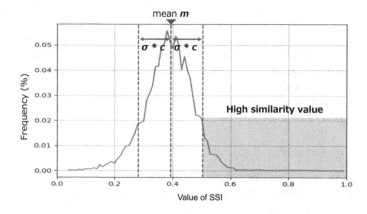

Fig. 1. Distribution of SSI values in the case of instance '20-100-frag12-0_sat.cnf' and the criterion to judge the degree of similarity

Next, a criterion is defined to judge whether or not the obtained SSI value indicates similarity based on the shape of the SSI distribution. Higher SSI values correspond to searches that are similar to a greater degree. SSI values satisfying the defined criterion are adjudged to be highly similar; otherwise, standard or low similarity is assumed. We assume the SSI follows a Gaussian distribution due to its bell-shaped curve. This study uses the upper probability of statistics, i.e., $threshold := m + \sigma \times c$ where m and σ are the mean and the standard deviation of the distribution of SSI values, respectively. The value of constant c was set to two in this study based on the results of preliminary experiments. Each parallel worker obtains the CSDs of other workers at restart. The worker calculates SSI values between its latest CSD and the shared CSD from each of the other workers. For example, in an eight-workers environment, each worker derives seven SSI values at every restart. A certain number of recent SSI values are stored—in this paper, the most recent 1000 SSI values are used for this purpose—and the mean and standard deviation are calculated from the data. If at least one of the SSI values at the restart exceeds the threshold, the search is adjudged to be similar. Subsequently, the activity of the solver is altered.

Finally, we introduces a function to alter the activity of the solver, which is achieved by changing the decision priority by assigning higher priority to low-priority variables. During variable selection in the decision phase, the variables are arranged in terms of their scores. A certain percentage of variables are selected from the bottom of the queue—in this paper, it is considered to be the bottom 10%. Then, incremental scores are added to push them to the top of the queue to be selected preferentially.

4   Experiments

In this study, we experimentally assessed the impact of the proposed method—the search diversification using SSI in parallel SAT solvers. Experiments were conducted on a computer with an AMD Threadripper Pro 3995WX processor and 512 GB (128 GB 4 slots, DDR4-3200 MHz) RAM. The benchmark instance sets from the SAT Race 2019 and SAT competition 2020 and 2021 were used. A total of 1200 instances were selected—400 instances of the main track benchmark per year. The base solver used was P-MCOMSPS [18], a state-of-the-art parallel solver as of 2021 and winner of the parallel track category of the SAT competition 2021 that utilizes a decision variable scoring table and a Boolean polarity table. These tables are not unique to P-MCOMSPS; they are common in almost all CDCL SAT solvers. The necessary functions were implemented onto the base solver. P-MCOMSPS uses a master/worker structure, and its component types are named the sharer and worker, respectively. Each worker submits its CSD to the sharer at restart, after which the sharer distributes them to the workers during the import or export of the learnt clauses. For other configurations, the default configuration of P-MCOMSPS was used. This study compared the performance of the base solver with that of the solver equipped with the proposed method. The performance was then evaluated in terms of the number of instances solved within a time limit—1200 s on a wall clock—and the PAR-2 score, defined as the total time required to solve all instances with a penalty (an additional 1200 s) for each unsolved instance.

Table 1 summarizes the results where the first column lists the number of parallel workers employed by the solver, and the second column presents the method used. "Base" denotes the base solver, P-MCOMSPS, and "the proposed method" denotes the solver equipped with the proposed method. The next three columns present the number of instances identified as SAT, UNSAT, and their sum, i.e., SAT+UNSAT, respectively. The final column presents the PAR-2 score rounded off to the nearest thousand. Figure 2 shows the same result in a cactus-plot.

Table 1. Experimental result of the performances comparison between the base solver and the solver equipped with the proposed method corresponding to 8, 16, 32, and 48 parallel workers respectively

# of workers	Method	SAT	UNSAT	Total	PAR-2 (K)
8	Base	214	265	479	1892
	Proposal	232	269	501	1839
16	Base	241	286	527	1779
	Proposal	266	288	554	1709
32	Base	250	293	543	1736
	Proposal	295	300	595	1630
48	Base	274	319	593	1606
	Proposal	279	305	584	1634

The results indicate that the proposed method is superior to the base solver corresponding to the cases involving 8, 16, and 32 parallel workers. Greater improvement is observed in cases involving more parallel workers—the number of solved instances increased by +21, +27, and +52 corresponding to 8-, 16-, and 32-worker environments, respectively. The results indicate that the proposed method is more effective, corresponding to a larger number of parallel workers. This is attributed to the higher possibility of similar searches that can occur between more parallel workers than between fewer. Thus, the proposed method, which is aimed at avoiding similar searches, is more effective in the case of more parallel workers. Similarly, the PAR-2 score improved by 53,038, 69,540, and 106,750 compared to those of the base solver corresponding to 8, 16, and 32 parallel workers, respectively.

The results also indicate that most of the improvements correspond to SAT instances, which is consistent with intuition. A satisfiable instance sometimes has many solutions, and these solutions are distributed in the whole search space. The proposed method distributes the searches for diversification, and this helps our solver to encounter at least one of the solutions with a higher probability than

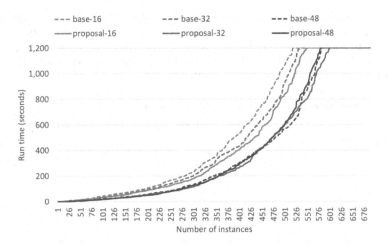

Fig. 2. Experimental result of the performances comparison in the Cactus-plot corresponding to 16, 32, and 48 parallel workers' cases. The vertical axis represents the search runtime with a 1200-s time limit. Horizontal axis represents the number of instances that are sorted according to their runtime. 500 instances which were unsolved by any solvers within the time limit are excluded for visibility

the base solver. On the other hand, UNSAT proof is achieved by the resolution of an empty clause, and it is said to require good learning. Diversification of the search by our method necessarily does not contribute to it.

Conversely, in the case of 48 parallel workers, the performance deteriorates. We assume that this is due to the computational load due to the increase in parallel workers. We conducted an additional experiment with 48 parallel workers and the same benchmarks as the above experiments. A time-tracking function was added to measure the duration spent by the proposed method. Table 2 represents the ratio of duration to the total runtime of the worker and sharer, respectively. In the case of workers, we observed that the proposed method spent an average of 18% of its runtime on tasks such as calculating SSI and assembling CSD from tables. Computational load for unsolved instances was about twice that for solved instances: 23% and 12%, respectively. Furthermore, 35% of the runtime was spent in the instances which were unsolved by our proposal solver but solved by the base solver. In the same way, for the sharer, 28% of total runtime was spent for the proposed method, 35% in unsolved instances, and 47% in instances unsolved by the proposed method but solved by the base. This implies that the computational load affects the proposed method's performance. The complexity of SSI calculations is proportional to the number of variables and parallel workers. Therefore, performance deteriorates with 48 workers compared to 32 workers. Corresponding to 32 workers, the performance improvement affected by the proposed method exceeded the effect of increased time consumption owing to the proposed method; however, corresponding to 48 workers, the effect was reversed.

Table 2. The percentage of the average time consumption in workers and sharer respectively, spent for the proposed method in the total runtime in the 48 parallel worker's environment. Solved indicates that of the instances which the solver found SAT or UNSAT result. Unsolved indicates that of UNKNOWN instances, which the solver reaches its time limit before finding a result.

	Solved by proposal	Unsolved by proposal			Total
		Solved by base	Unsolved by base	Subtotal	
Worker	12%	35%	21%	23%	18%
Sharer	19%	47%	32%	35%	28%

5 Concluding Remarks

This paper proposed the Search Similarity Index (SSI) and developed a method to enhance the search diversify of solvers. Experimental results confirmed that the proposed method improves the performance of the parallel SAT solver, with the number of solved instances increasing by +1.8%, +2.3%, and +4.3% in the case of 8, 16, and 32 parallel workers, respectively, compared to the current state-of-the-art solver. The results indicate that similar searches in portfolio solvers lose their parallel efficiency, and the performance improvement achieved by increasing their degree of diversification is significant. Conversely, the performance is observed to deteriorate with 48 parallel workers due to increased time consumption by the proposed method. The approach of managing the diversification of search is presumed to be beneficial to the other methods of sequential SAT solvers, e.g., restart and decision.

There is still scope for future research. First, reducing the computational load is essential for further performance improvement in environments with more than 48 workers. Further investigations about the computational load are required by the types of instances, e.g., satisfiability (SAT or UNSAT) of the instance, variable clause ratio, and the graph structure of the instance. Second, the method of changing solver activity when the diversity is low can be improved. Third, the application of our proposed method to other portfolio solvers or using other parameter settings has room for improving performance. In addition, it is expected that SSI can be utilized for other purposes. For instance, as SSI measures the degree of diversity, it can be used to evaluate existing portfolio diversification methods and improve them by combining them dynamically or selectively choosing parameters. In addition to portfolio-type parallel solvers, the restart and decision methods can be improved as they are also essential to control the diversity of the search.

Acknowledgments. We thank the anonymous reviewers for their helpful suggestions and comments to aid the publication of this paper.

References

1. Bayardo, R.J., Schrag, R.C.: Using CSP look-back techniques to solve real-world SAT instances. In: Proceedings of the 14th National Conference on Artificial Intelligence and 9th Conference on Innovative Applications of Artificial Intelligence, pp. 203–208. AAAI Press, Palo Alto (1997). https://doi.org/10.5555/1867406.1867438
2. Davis, M., Logemann, G., Loveland, D.: A machine program for theorem-proving. Commun. ACM **5**(7), 394–397 (1962). https://doi.org/10.1145/368273.368557
3. Gomes, C.P., Selman, B., Kautz, H.: Boosting combinatorial search through randomization. In: Proceedings of the 15th National Conference on Artificial Intelligence and 10th Conference on Innovative Applications of Artificial Intelligence, pp. 431–437. AAAI Press, Palo Alto (1998). https://doi.org/10.5555/295240.295710
4. Guo, L., Lagniez, J.M.: Dynamic polarity adjustment in a parallel SAT solver. In: Proceedings of the 23rd IEEE International Conference on Tools with Artificial Intelligence, pp. 67–73. IEEE Press, New York (2011). https://doi.org/10.1109/ICTAI.2011.19
5. Hamadi, Y., Jabbour, S., Sais, L.: ManySAT: a parallel SAT solver. J. Satisfiability Boolean Model. Comput. **6**(4), 245–262 (2009). https://doi.org/10.3233/SAT190070
6. Hickey, R., Bacchus, F.: Trail saving on backtrack. In: Pulina, L., Seidl, M. (eds.) SAT 2020. LNCS, vol. 12178, pp. 46–61. Springer, Cham (2020). https://doi.org/10.1007/978-3-030-51825-7_4
7. Huberman, B.A., Lukose, R.M., Hogg, T.: An economics approach to hard computational problems. Science **275**(5296), 51–54 (1997). https://doi.org/10.1126/science.275.5296.51
8. Heule, M.J.H., Kullmann, O., Marek, V.W.: Solving and verifying the Boolean Pythagorean triples problem via cube-and-conquer. In: Creignou, N., Le Berre, D. (eds.) SAT 2016. LNCS, vol. 9710, pp. 228–245. Springer, Cham (2016). https://doi.org/10.1007/978-3-319-40970-2_15
9. Kanbara, K., Nabeshima, H.: An adaptive search strategy for portfolio parallel SAT solvers. In: Proceedings of the 109th Japan Special Interest Group on Fundamental Problems in Artificial Intelligence, pp. 16–19. The Japanese Society for Artificial Intelligence, Tokyo (2019). https://doi.org/10.11517/jsaifpai.109.0_04
10. Liang, J., Ganesh, V., Poupart, P., Czarnecki, K.: Exponential recency weighted average branching heuristic for SAT solvers. In: Proceedings of the 30th AAAI Conference on Artificial Intelligence, pp. 3434–3440. AAAI Press, Palo Alto (2016). https://doi.org/10.1609/aaai.v30i1.10439
11. Narodytska, N., Kasiviswanathan, S., Ryzhyk, L., Sagiv, M., Walsh, T.: Verifying properties of binarized deep neural networks. In: Proceedings of the 32th AAAI Conference on Artificial Intelligence, pp. 6615–6624. AAAI Press, Palo Alto (2018). https://doi.org/10.1609/aaai.v32i1.12206
12. Moon, S., Inaba, M.: Dynamic strategy to diversify search using a history map in parallel solving. In: Festa, P., Sellmann, M., Vanschoren, J. (eds.) LION 2016. LNCS, vol. 10079, pp. 260–266. Springer, Cham (2016). https://doi.org/10.1007/978-3-319-50349-3_21
13. Moskewicz, M.W., Madigan, C.F., Zhao, Y., Zhang, L., Malik, S.: Chaff: engineering an efficient SAT solver. In: Proceedings of the 38th Design Automation Conference, pp. 530–535. Association for Computing Machinery, USA (2002). https://doi.org/10.1145/378239.379017

14. Pipatsrisawat, K., Darwiche, A.: A lightweight component caching scheme for satisfiability solvers. In: Marques-Silva, J., Sakallah, K.A. (eds.) SAT 2007. LNCS, vol. 4501, pp. 294–299. Springer, Heidelberg (2007). https://doi.org/10.1007/978-3-540-72788-0_28
15. ppfolio solver. https://www.cril.univ-artois.fr/~roussel/ppfolio/. Accessed 02 Sept 2022
16. The international SAT Competition Web Page. http://www.satcompetition.org/. Accessed 02 Sept 2022
17. Sonobe, T., Inaba, M.: Portfolio with block branching for parallel SAT solvers. In: Nicosia, G., Pardalos, P. (eds.) Learning and Intelligent OptimizationLearning and Intelligent Optimization. LNCS, vol. 7997, pp. 247–252. Springer, Heidelberg (2013). https://doi.org/10.1007/978-3-642-44973-4_25
18. Painless solver. https://www.lrde.epita.fr/wiki/Painless. Accessed 02 Sept 2022
19. Vizel, Y., Weissenbacher, G., Malik, S.: Boolean satisfiability solvers and their applications in model checking. Proc. IEEE **103**(11), 2021–2035 (2015). https://doi.org/10.1109/JPROC.2015.2455034

Dagster: Parallel Structured Search with Case Studies

Mark Alexander Burgess$^{(\boxtimes)}$, Charles Gretton, Josh Milthorpe, Luke Croak,
Thomas Willingham, and Alwen Tiu

Australian National University, Canberra, Australia
mark.burgess@anu.edu.au

Abstract. We describe DAGSTER, a system that implements a new
approach to scheduling interdependent (Boolean) SAT search activities in high-performance computing (HPC) environments. This system
allows practitioners to solve challenging problems by efficiently distributing search effort across computing cores in a customizable way. Our
solver takes as input a set of disjunctive clauses (i.e., DIMACS CNF)
and a labelled directed acyclic graph (DAG) structure describing how
the clauses are decomposed into a set of interrelated search problems.
Component problems are solved using standard systematic backtracking search, which may optionally be coupled to (stochastic dynamic)
local search and/or clause-strengthening processes. We show the performance of DAGSTER in combinatorial case study examples, particularly
the model counting of Costas arrays, and in finding solutions to large
Pentomino tiling problems. We also use DAGSTER to exhibit a novel
workflow for Bounded Model Checking of network protocols where we
perform independent searches at different problem fidelities, in parallel.
Low fidelity solutions trigger further independent searches for refined
solutions in higher fidelity models.

Keywords: SAT · High-performance computing · Decomposition

1 Introduction

We present a tool for solving problems by scheduling search activities on distributed and high-performance computing (HPC) systems. Our tool, DAGSTER,
can solve large and/or challenging problems by distributing search effort across
processing elements. Our design aims to minimize synchronization and communication effects and efficiently use local memory hierarchies. DAGSTER takes
as input a set of clauses in conjunctive normal form (CNF) and a graphical
structure. The CNF gives the available constraints/clauses, and the graphical
structure is used to represent how those constraints are grouped into interdependent subproblems, which together form a distinct SAT problem to be solved.
DAGSTER uses available processing elements (e.g., CPU cores) to solve subproblems in parallel, such that the answer to the underlying problem is derived via

© The Author(s), under exclusive license to Springer Nature Switzerland AG 2022
S. Khanna et al. (Eds.): PRICAI 2022, LNCS 13629, pp. 75–89, 2022.
https://doi.org/10.1007/978-3-031-20862-1_6

the combination of subproblem solutions. DAGSTER search tasks can be made to enumerate satisfying assignments; thus, the tool directly supports solving both decision (SAT) problems and counting (#SAT) problems.

2 Related Work

A range of sound and complete frameworks and systems have been developed for solving SAT problems by distributing the computation performed by (a systematic) search. Portfolio approaches run multiple algorithms on the same formula, often in parallel, and typically have a mechanism for sharing learnt clauses. A wide range of architectures have been proposed, showcased in tools such as SATZILLA [38][1], PLINGELING [4], HORDESAT and its cloud-ready counterpart [3,35], the multi-core SYRUP and its hybrid counterpart D-SYRUP [1].

Divide-and-conquer and cube-and-conquer approaches contrast against portfolio approaches because they do not work on the same formula in parallel; rather, they break the search space into disjoint subspaces by resolving with an array of partial assignments. These approaches use parallel computation by distributing what would otherwise be a monolithic proof exercise to a pool of independent search processes working on disjoint problems. There is a communications trade-off between solving all subproblems independently in parallel and having them solve interdependently, with learnt clause communication between them. Conquering approaches are exhibited in systems such as DPLL-TD [22], PMSAT [21], TLINGELING [5], and PARACOOBA [24]. Search space breaking can be static, or dynamic - such as featured in the top-down cube-and-conquer model counter DMC [30]. Additionally, there exist intermediary solvers, such as the PAINLESS framework by Le Frioux et al. [19], which employ a range of parallel solver architectures, seamlessly mixing portfolio and conquering ideas.

Hamadi and Wintersteiger [23] provide a characterization of challenges to derive benefit using parallel computing in the SAT context. Our contributions are aligned with Challenges C3, and C6 - specifically: (C3) developing new parallel processing techniques that leverage SAT problem decompositional structure, and (C6) deriving new encodings of SAT problems specific for parallel computation. For C3 and C6, we considered that the scientist, engineer, or AI tool[2], in formulating a problem in propositional logic, would have explicit succinct represented knowledge about how to decompose the problem for distributed search. Thus, we are left to develop a flexible way for that knowledge to be represented for scheduling the specified interdependent search activities. As with many conquering systems, we support distributing search for subproblems in HPC environments, but unlike existing conquering tools, we have left the problem of determining the decomposition and the relationship between subproblems to the domain expert. The case studies presented in this paper are representative of the motivating problems we

---

[1] A serial portfolio with 'pre-solving' and 'solving' stages amenable to parallel/distributed computing.

[2] For example, in AI planning, automatic problem decomposition is available using factoring techniques [9], and also using obligation approaches in [8].

have developed, which can be tackled using SAT-based search in HPC environments. Finally, regarding portfolio techniques, although our tool supports invoking multiple solver processes—of the same type and otherwise—on the same input formula, our focus is not on the portfolio effect.

3   System Description

DAGSTER[3] takes as input a CNF formula and a labelled graphical structure as a directed acyclic graph (DAG). Each node of the DAG represents a subset of the clauses of the original formula, and finding solutions to these subsets of clauses constitutes a subproblem (see Fig. 1). Nodes are connected by edges labelled with a subset of shared variables present in the clauses of both nodes. The directed nature of the graph means that the variable valuations in satisfying solutions found for each node are passed along the edges to constrain the solutions of subsequent node(s). Given an edge between nodes, each satisfying assignment found by the destination node must be consistent with the shared variable valuations emitted as solutions to the source node/s.

DAGSTER uses a Master-Worker architecture, coded in C++ using MPI [31] to conduct the solution process. The master process is responsible for issuing and processing the work to and from the worker processes, where each worker solves its issued subproblems using a complete SAT solver. DAGSTER currently supports using both: *(i)* the lightweight CDCL procedure based on TINISAT [26,27], and *(ii)* MINISAT [17]. A worker process executes the CDCL solving procedure until it finds a satisfying assignment, or proves unsatisfiability. The worker reports each satisfying assignment to the master and adds its negation as a "no-good" constraint to produce a further-constrained subproblem for further generating distinct solutions. This process continues until the worker finds UNSAT, at which point the subproblem is complete. The master uses the shared variable assignments from each subproblem solution to seed computation on further nodes in the DAG.

We designed DAGSTER to be modular and agnostic about the underlying CDCL solver. However, along with a CDCL solver, each worker may also be configured to collaborate with one or more helper processes, to form a worker group. Helper processes may include: a *strengthener* performing concurrent clause strengthening [37] to accelerate search; and/or many *stochastic local search* (SLS) processes, which use the GNOVELTY+ dynamic local search algorithm [33] to find satisfying solutions to the subproblem. The SLS processes may also suggest which variables/values that CDCL worker should assign next; in this way the SLS functions to find solutions and also functions as a variable selection heuristic mechanism. We note that SLS has been investigated in the context of systematic search previously, such as in the context of rephasing heuristics [7,12], for completing promising partial assignments and for frequency based search guidance in [12].

---

[3] Sourcecode: Zenodo [11], and GitHub, https://github.com/ANU-HPC/dagster.

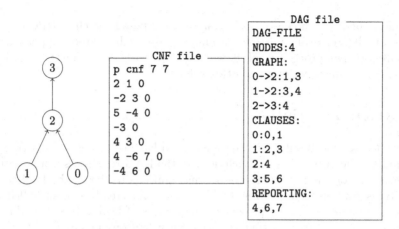

Fig. 1. Example DAGSTER inputs. The graph (left) is described in the "DAG file" (right). The "CLAUSES" block in that file identifies subproblems at graph nodes, by a list of indexes of clauses in the "CNF file" (centre). The "GRAPH" block indicates what variables are shared over a directed arc between nodes/subproblems. "REPORTING" identifies variables of interest in resulting solution/s

The DAGSTER architecture can be understood as an interaction between the master process and a collection of worker groups, as illustrated in Fig. 2. DAGSTER supports different modes of operation depending on what helper processes are in each worker group: CDCL only (mode 'C'), CDCL + local search (mode 'CL'), CDCL + strengthener (mode 'CS'), and CDCL + strengthener + local search (mode 'CSL').

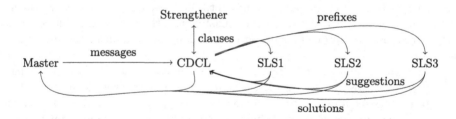

Fig. 2. Relationship and messages between the master and worker groups.

For modes where there are local search processes interracting with CDCL modules, such as shown in Fig. 2, the variable suggestions given to the CDCL search by the various SLSs are based on variables the SLS has most recently flipped. If a variable is flipped frequently, it will likely be early in a queue of suggestions for the CDCL to select. Additionally, each SLS is assigned to work at a given depth and point in the CDCL's search tree by a prefix of partial assignments, which the CDCL issues to the SLS. This dynamic is illustrated in Fig. 3, where a trace of the CDCL search is depicted, showing the prefix of partial

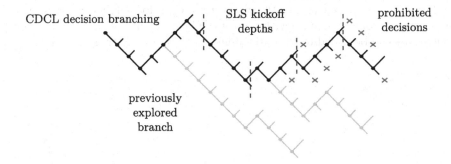

Fig. 3. Illustration of worker backtracking search with SLS suggestion processes set to work constrained from partial assignments at various depths in the search branch (blue dashed lines), shown are previously explored branches (gray) and prohibited decisions arising from conflicts (red crosses). (Color figure online)

assignments (at various depths) given to the SLS processes to constrain their searches. In this way, the CDCL communicates with a series of SLS processes that work at various points in the search near where the CDCL search is working, to find solutions and return the most appropriate variable suggestions to the CDCL search.

4 Case Study: Costas Arrays

In our first case study we consider the Costas array model counting problem, where we evaluate the performance of DAGSTER's different operational modes.

A Costas array is a set of n points in an $n \times n$ array such that each column and row contains exactly one point, and each of the $n(n-1)/2$ displacement vectors between the points are distinct. An example of a Costas array is shown in Fig. 4a. Using search to solve for Costas arrays is known to be challenging, and searching processes have been conducted at least up to size $n = 29$ [15,16]. However, whether arrays exist at $n \in \{32, 33\}$ are open problems. As a number of Costas array subclasses of those sizes have been eliminated [10], it is conjectured (but not confirmed) that Costas arrays of those sizes do not exist [34].

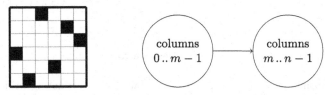

(a) An example Costas array   (b) A DAG decomposing Costas problem into two parts.

Fig. 4. Costas array problem example and suggested decomposition method of first solving the first m columns.

For each size n, we can directly synthesize a CNF formula whose models are in one-to-one correspondence with the set of Costas arrays of size n. Lex-leader constraints can be added to break the dihedral group symmetries (reflection and

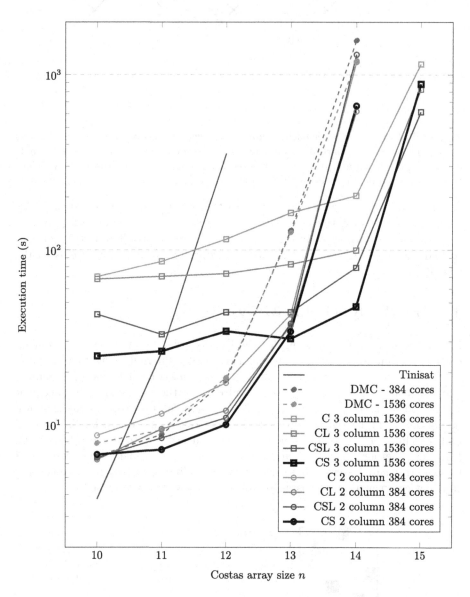

Fig. 5. Runtime performance of DAGSTER against model counting with TINISAT and DMC on Costas problems with different number of columns in the decomposition and processor cores. C = CDCL only; CL = CDCL + local search; CS = CDCL + strengthener; CSL = CDCL + strengthener + local search; DAGSTER running with TINISAT CDCL processes

rotation) [36]. For the purpose of using SAT-search to count unique arrays for values of n using DAGSTER, we employ a simple DAG structure (see Fig. 4b, showing two connected nodes) where the first node is the placing of the first m columns of the Costas array, and the second part is the placement of the remainder.

The performance of DAGSTER at solving Costas problems for different sized Costas arrays n, and for different numbers of columns m solved in the first node, for different numbers of computing cores and DAGSTER modes, is given in Fig. 5. In our evaluations here, the CDCL workers are instances of TINISAT processes. We compare DAGSTER against the distributed model counter DMC [30], and against the performance of model counting by repeatedly calling TINISAT. Figure 5 demonstrates the benefits of helper processes with clause strengthening and/or local search, by presenting runtimes for configuration modes: C, CL, CS, and CSL, with one SLS and/or Strengthener process per worker group.

Examining the time it takes systems to enumerate Costas arrays, for smaller and easier Costas problems (of size $n \leq 12$), we can see that the parallel overhead of using DAGSTER is the primary determinant of the solution time. DAGSTER systems perform worse compared to TINISAT, which has minimal overhead; this overhead is most pronounced with the more granular decompositions that include more columns (e.g. for Costas-10, 3-column is worse than 2-column). However, for larger and harder Costas problems ($n > 12$), DAGSTER consistently outperforms TINISAT - the CDCL procedure which DAGSTER workers are employing here; as well as outperforming the DMC model counter. Additionally, for large problems, having one local search (modes denoted with 'L') and/or clause strengthening process (modes denoted with 'S') per worker group complements workers and yielding improved runtime performance.

A compelling feature of DAGSTER is that it allows easy experimentation regarding the decomposition employed. In our results thus far, we have only considered decompositions into contiguous blocks of columns (where the first node/subproblem has the first m columns, and the second node has the remainder), but we can also consider decompositions with interleaved columns. There are also many configurable DAGSTER settings, related to restarting policy and variable selection heuristics. With workers using the VSIDS heuristic [32] and DAGSTER's geometric restart policy, in Table 1 we see how changing the index of the columns and the allocated/type-of computing resources in a bi-level decomposition can affect the runtime performance.

5   Case Study: Pentominoes

In this second case study we considered larger problems—i.e., with many more clauses—exhibiting clear compositional structure, with unique solutions, to evaluate DAGSTER comparing it to a wide range of approaches.

Particularly, we considered pentomino tiling problems where different tiling regions correspond to different subproblems. The problems are to fill a grid area with pentominoes such that no pentomino crosses a bolded wall and no two

Table 1. DAGSTER runtime in seconds using bi-level Costas decompositions with "Columns" determined in the first DAG node. Evaluation also considers strengtheners (S) - i.e. modes C and CS (w/ TINISAT processes), number of computing "Cores", and array "Size (n)".

Size (n)	Cores	Columns	S	Runtimes	Size (n)	Cores	Columns	S	Runtimes
9	48	{4}		5.527	13	48	{2,4,6}		8.427
10	2	{2,4}		1.356	13	48	{2,4,6}	✓	10.242
10	48	{2,4}		5.191	14	2	{5,7,9}		524.414
11	2	{2,4}		4.155	14	384	{5,7,9}		16.562
11	48	{2,4}		5.642	14	383	{5,7,9}	✓	12.118
12	48	{2,4}		21.234	15	384	{5,7,9,11}		118.133
12	48	{2,4}		7.267	15	383	{5,7,9,11}	✓	86.125
12	48	{2,4}	✓	7.419	16	528	{5,7,9,11}		275.127
13	2	{2,4,6}		91.22	16	527	{5,7,9,11}	✓	235.25

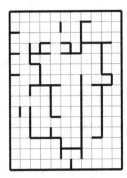

(a) Pentomino puzzle featured on Youtube channel *Cracking the Cryptic*

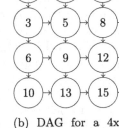

(b) DAG for a 4x4 pentomino superproblem - Decomposition A

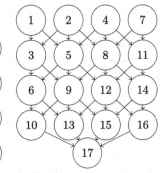

(c) DAG for a 4x4 pentomino superproblem - Decomposition B

Fig. 6. An example Pentomino puzzle, and two DAG arrangements for solving a cascaded grid of connected sub-problems (youtube.com/watch?v=S2aN-s3hG6Y)

pentominoes of the same shape (counting reflections/rotations) touch each other. An example problem is shown in Fig. 6a. We created a program to randomly generate hard 15×15 pentomino subproblems by: 1) randomly fill a 15×15 grid with pentominoes, 2) outlining those pentominoes with walls, and 3) iteratively remove a random wall segment so that the puzzle is still uniquely solvable, until no further removals are possible.

We use our program to generate large pentomino superproblems, by cascading 15×15 compatible subproblems side-by-side in a grid pattern. In this way, the grid of pentomino problems constitutes a larger superproblem with logically distinct parts, where each subproblem is only constrained by its immediate neighbours. As every pentomino subproblem is uniquely solvable, the larger pentomino superproblem is also uniquely solvable.

We considered two DAG structures (A and B, in Figs. 6b and 6c) as process schemata for solving pentomino superproblems: (A) from the top left diagonally through to the bottom right, and (B) solving the subproblems in parallel by rows, and a final verification node.

We measured the performance of DAGSTER (with TINISAT and MINISAT workers, and both decompositions) against a range of solvers, including TIN-ISAT, LINGELING and MINISAT baselines, and some parallel baselines including PAINLESS-MCOMSPS [19], PARACOOBA [24], DMC [30] and D-SYRUP [1] (note that, with the exception of DMC, these solvers are not configured as model counting tools, and thus not reasonably used in the Costas results in Sect. 4). The results for different sized pentomino problems are shown in Fig. 7 where we see a range of different performances, with DAGSTER (Decomposition B using MIN-ISAT workers) outperforming other solvers. DAGSTER demonstrates a speedup due to parallelization by solving a larger structured problem with coupled subproblems and the runtime performance depends on the decomposition and the number and type of CDCL workers used.

The coupling between subproblems creates leverage which DAGSTER exploits to provide the witnessed speedup, and the structure and arrangement of the solving process between the subproblem elements (between Decompositions A and B) can create a large difference in the resulting performance.

6   Case Study: Bounded Model Checking with Abstraction Invariants

In our third case study we show that the workload for software model checking can be reduced via an abstraction hierarchy that is amenable to distributed search using DAGSTER. We show how DAGSTER can be used with existing tools to interrogate the functioning of finite-state-machines and circuits, and in particular to verify that particular error states of such machine cannot be reached. Our checking processes will be based on search performed by SAT reasoning, as exemplified in [6]. A survey of approaches to model checking software systems is in [2], and we note a wide range of systems exist in this setting, including CBMC [13,29], F-SOFT [28], ESBMC [14], LLBMC [18], and ESBMC [20]. In our case study, we shall be using CBMC as a basis for generating structured SAT queries for DAGSTER.

Our case study considers the wireless security protocol for communication with an implantable low-power medical device described in [25]. *Alwen Tiu* determined *a priori*, and by manual inspection, that this protocol has a potential issue. The protocol is based on encrypted communication using a 32-bit secret key K, shared between an implantable medical device (IMD) and a base-station (BASE). The IMD has a 32-bit serial number S that uniquely identifies it among other devices. Both the IMD and BASE have a 32-bit message counter, A for the device, and B for BASE, with both counters initially set at zero. Messages

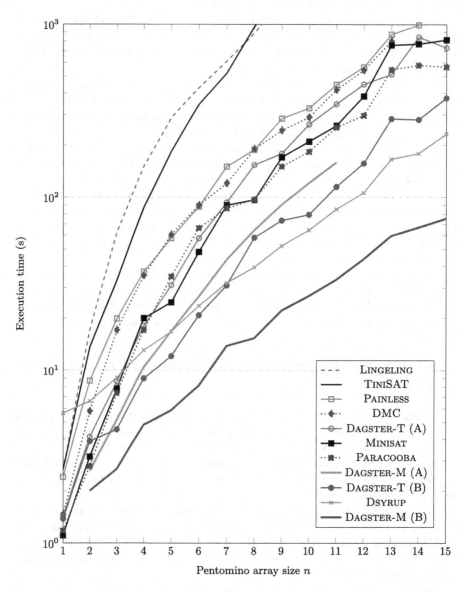

Fig. 7. Runtime model counting performance (medians across 86 samples) of DAGSTER (w/ decompositions A and B, w/ TINISAT (T) and MINISAT (M) cores) against TIN-ISAT, LINGELING, MINISAT, PAINLESS-MCOMSPS, PARACOOBA, DMC and DSYRUP solvers, for $n \times n$ superproblem arrays of 15×15 pentomino subproblems. All parallel algorithms use 17 cores.

communicated are 64-bits. We use notation $X\|Y$ to denote bit string concatenation, and $\mathsf{Split}(A)$ to denote splitting a bit string A into two halves, and $\mathsf{Interleave}(A, B)$ to denote the result of interleaving A and B bit strings. We also write $\{A\}_K$ to denote the bit string A encrypted with K. For a message transmitted from the BASE to the IMD, and be accepted (i.e., not "dropped"), the following is required:

1. BASE has a 64-bit message X (larger messages chunked/padded into 64 bits)
2. BASE adds one to its message counter B
3. BASE produces a message $M_1, M_2 = \mathsf{Split}(\mathsf{Interleave}(X, S\|B))$
4. BASE sends the message $\{M_1\}_K\|\{M_2\}_K$ to IMD
5. IMD receives $\{M_1\}_K\|\{M_2\}_K$ and decrypts each part with K, then joins and de-interleaves to find X, S, B
6. IMD checks compatible S, dropping the message if S is not recognised. It then checks message counter B against its own counter A. If $B > A$ it accepts the message and sets A to be equal to B, otherwise it drops the message

Examining this protocol, we note there is an issue, particularly, an adversary can witnesses a message $\{M_1\}_K\|\{M_2\}_K$ from the BASE to the IMD, and subsequently send a message $\{M_1\}_K\|\{M_1\}_K$ to the IMD. This message from the adversary will then cause the IMD's message counter A to be incremented to S, potentially causing the IMD to cease accepting legitimate messages from the BASE, and thereby causing catastrophic failure. This error state in the protocol is subject to model checking, which can be done using DAGSTER.

We approach model checking this protocol compositionally, using DAGSTER, by appealing to a notion of process abstraction. Specifically, intending to proceed with CBMC, we faithfully describe the protocol in the C programming language. State variables describing the evolution of the protocol–e.g., whether an attacker or BASE is sending a message at timestep i—are of a fixed type. Variables encoding protocol registers, such as A, B, X, etc., being of a range of types, depending on where we are in an abstraction hierarchy. State variables of a fixed type we call *abstraction invariant* (AI). Our abstraction hierarchy then considers the other variables at a range of fidelities, with 8-bit registers modelling protocol instructions at the highest level of abstraction (lowest fidelity) and 64-bit registers at the lowest level (highest fidelity). We see that the protocol is much easier to model check, in practice, at a high abstraction level, and so our approach takes assignments to AI variables from satisfying assignments to highly abstract models, and uses those to inform search at lower levels of abstraction. A simulated run of the bidirectional communication from between the base-station (BASE) and the medical-device (IMD) is described in C, multiple-times, with variables having different fidelities in different representations. Such models are passed to the CBMC software to generate corresponding SAT instance problems with annotations for AI variables' bit values.[4]

We augment those formulae and annotations, by graphically representing the identity relationship of the AI variables between those different fidelity SAT

---

[4] https://github.com/ThomWillingham/bmc-summer2122.

models of the protocol. Using the graphical structure DAGSTER automates the search workflow, solving the lower fidelity problem/s and then carrying across the AI variable values as constraints to the higher fidelity models (as indicated in the DAG shown in Fig. 8). Here, we document the observed improvement in performance of this process, over running the higher fidelity models directly in a SAT solver. Our results are in Fig. 9, where we can see that solving the 64 bit model using AI solutions from lower fidelity models results in a improvement in search performance. Particularly, we can see that using AI variable information saves an order of magnitude on the number of conflicts encountered as well as a reduction of ∼5 times fewer variable assignments. In this way AI information can be used to accelerate bounded model checking. The results presented here were achieved using DAGSTER in mode C, with one CDCL TINISAT process.

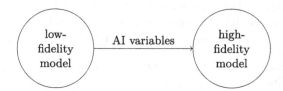

Fig. 8. A DAG for the IMD case study, with AI variables being communicated from low fidelity models to higher fidelity models

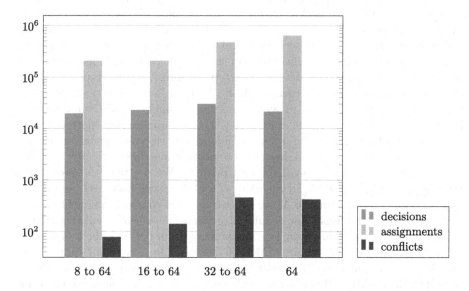

Fig. 9. DAGSTER performance measurements of IMD model checking with communication of AI valuations between searches at different fidelities; specifically between 8/16/32 bit and the 64 bit, with a monolithic 64 bit run plotted for comparison.

7   Conclusions and Future Work

We have outlined our new tool, DAGSTER, summarising some capabilities using three case studies: Costas arrays, Pentomino tiling problems, and also bounded model checking of an implantable medical device. DAGSTER operates by solving large and/or hard problems via a user-provided decomposition, according to a DAG which delineates different subproblems, and dictates the order in which they are to be solved together. DAGSTER has other features which are not presented in this paper. We plan to continue working on DAGSTER, implementing subproblem scheduling and allocation algorithms to further enhance DAGSTER's utilization of HPC resources, and adding snapshotting and incrementality features.

Acknowledgements. Contributions to the Dagster project were made by Eamon Barrett—specifically, functionality related to decision diagrams—and Marshall Clifton—specifically, the clause strengthening subsystem—during their undergraduate studies at the Australian National University. This research was undertaken with the assistance of resources from the National Computational Infrastructure (NCI Australia), an NCRIS enabled capability supported by the Australian Government.

References

1. Audemard, G., Lagniez, J.-M., Szczepanski, N., Tabary, S.: A distributed version of SYRUP. In: Gaspers, S., Walsh, T. (eds.) SAT 2017. LNCS, vol. 10491, pp. 215–232. Springer, Cham (2017). https://doi.org/10.1007/978-3-319-66263-3_14
2. Baldoni, R., Coppa, E., D'Elia, D.C., Demetrescu, C., Finocchi, I.: A survey of symbolic execution techniques. ACM Comput. Surv. **51**(3), 1–39 (2018)
3. Balyo, T., Sanders, P., Sinz, C.: HordeSat: a massively parallel portfolio SAT solver. In: Theory and Applications of Satisfiability Testing - SAT 2015 (2015)
4. Biere, A.: Lingeling, Plingeling, PicoSAT and PrecoSAT at SAT Race 2010. FMV Technical Report 10/1, Johannes Kepler University, Linz, Austria (2010)
5. Biere, A.: Splatz, Lingeling, PLingeling, Treengeling, YalSAT. In: Proceedings of the SAT Competition, pp. 44–45 (2016)
6. Biere, A., Cimatti, A., Clarke, E.M., Strichman, O., Zhu, Y.: Bounded model checking. Adv. Comput. **58**, 117–148 (2003)
7. Biere, A., Fleury, M.: Chasing target phases. In: 11th Workshop on Pragmatics of SAT (POS 2020) (2020)
8. Bradley, A.R.: SAT-based model checking without unrolling. In: Jhala, R., Schmidt, D. (eds.) VMCAI 2011. LNCS, vol. 6538, pp. 70–87. Springer, Heidelberg (2011). https://doi.org/10.1007/978-3-642-18275-4_7
9. Brafman, R.I., Domshlak, C.: Factored planning: how, when, and when not. In: 21st National Conference on Artificial Intelligence and 18th Innovative Applications of Artificial Intelligence Conference, pp. 809–814. AAAI Press (2006)
10. Brown, C.P., Cenkl, M., Games, R.A., Rushanan, J.J., Moreno, O., Pei, P.: New enumeration results for Costas arrays. In: IEEE International Symposium on Information Theory (1993)
11. Burgess, M.A.: Dagster - parallel structured search - source code (2022). https://doi.org/10.5281/zenodo.7016083

12. Cai, S., Zhang, X.: Deep cooperation of CDCL and local search for SAT. In: Li, C.-M., Manyà, F. (eds.) SAT 2021. LNCS, vol. 12831, pp. 64–81. Springer, Cham (2021). https://doi.org/10.1007/978-3-030-80223-3_6
13. Clarke, E., Kroening, D., Lerda, F.: A tool for checking ANSI-C programs. In: Jensen, K., Podelski, A. (eds.) TACAS 2004. LNCS, vol. 2988, pp. 168–176. Springer, Heidelberg (2004). https://doi.org/10.1007/978-3-540-24730-2_15
14. Cordeiro, L.C., Fischer, B., Marques-Silva, J.: SMT-based bounded model checking for embedded ANSI-C software. IEEE Trans. Software Eng. 38(4), 957–974 (2012)
15. Drakakis, K., Iorio, F., Rickard, S., Walsh, J.: Results of the enumeration of Costas arrays of order 29. Adv. Math. Commun. 5(3), 547–553 (2011)
16. Drakakis, K., et al.: Results of the enumeration of Costas arrays of order 27. IEEE Trans. Inf. Theory 54(10), 4684–4687 (2008)
17. Eén, N., Sörensson, N.: An extensible SAT-solver. In: Giunchiglia, E., Tacchella, A. (eds.) SAT 2003. LNCS, vol. 2919, pp. 502–518. Springer, Heidelberg (2004). https://doi.org/10.1007/978-3-540-24605-3_37
18. Falke, S., Merz, F., Sinz, C.: The bounded model checker LLBMC. In: ASE, pp. 706–709. IEEE (2013)
19. Frioux, L.L., Baarir, S., Sopena, J., Kordon, F.: PaInleSS: a framework for parallel SAT solving. In: Theory and Applications of Satisfiability Testing - SAT 2017 (2017)
20. Gadelha, M.R., Menezes, R.S., Cordeiro, L.C.: ESBMC 6.1: automated test case generation using bounded model checking. Int. J. Softw. Tools Technol. Transf. 23(6), 857–861 (2021)
21. Gil, L., Flores, P.F., Silveira, L.M.: PMSat: a parallel version of MiniSAT. J. Satisfiability Boolean Model. Comput. 6(1–3), 71–98 (2009)
22. Habet, D., Paris, L., Terrioux, C.: A tree decomposition based approach to solve structured SAT instances. In: 2009 21st IEEE International Conference on Tools with Artificial Intelligence, pp. 115–122. IEEE Computer Society (2009)
23. Hamadi, Y., Wintersteiger, C.: Seven challenges in parallel SAT solving. In: AAAI Conference on Artificial Intelligence (2012)
24. Heisinger, M., Fleury, M., Biere, A.: Distributed cube and conquer with Paracooba. In: Pulina, L., Seidl, M. (eds.) SAT 2020. LNCS, vol. 12178, pp. 114–122. Springer, Cham (2020). https://doi.org/10.1007/978-3-030-51825-7_9
25. Hosseini-Khayat, S.: A lightweight security protocol for ultra-low power ASIC implementation for wireless implantable medical devices. In: 2011 5th International Symposium on Medical Information and Communication Technology, pp. 6–9 (2011)
26. Huang, J.: A case for simple SAT solvers. In: Bessière, C. (ed.) CP 2007. LNCS, vol. 4741, pp. 839–846. Springer, Heidelberg (2007). https://doi.org/10.1007/978-3-540-74970-7_62
27. Huang, J.: The effect of restarts on the efficiency of clause learning. In: 20th International Joint Conference on Artificial Intelligence (IJCAI), pp. 2318–2323 (2007)
28. Ivancic, F., Yang, Z., Ganai, M.K., Gupta, A., Ashar, P.: Efficient SAT-based bounded model checking for software verification. Theoret. Comput. Sci. 404(3), 256–274 (2008)
29. Kroening, D., Tautschnig, M.: CBMC – C bounded model checker. In: Ábrahám, E., Havelund, K. (eds.) TACAS 2014. LNCS, vol. 8413, pp. 389–391. Springer, Heidelberg (2014). https://doi.org/10.1007/978-3-642-54862-8_26
30. Lagniez, J., Marquis, P., Szczepanski, N.: DMC: a distributed model counter. In: Lang, J. (ed.) Proceedings of the Twenty-Seventh International Joint Conference

on Artificial Intelligence, IJCAI 2018, Stockholm, Sweden, 13–19 July 2018, pp. 1331–1338. ijcai.org (2018)

31. Message Passing Interface Forum: MPI: A Message-Passing Interface Standard Version 3.1, June 2015

32. Moskewicz, M.W., Madigan, C.F., Zhao, Y., Zhang, L., Malik, S.: Chaff: engineering an efficient SAT solver. In: Proceedings of the 38th Design Automation Conference, DAC 2001, Las Vegas, NV, USA, 18–22 June 2001, pp. 530–535. ACM (2001)

33. Pham, D.N., Thornton, J., Gretton, C., Sattar, A.: Combining adaptive and dynamic local search for satisfiability. J. Satisfiability Boolean Model. Comput. **4**(2–4), 149–172 (2008)

34. Russo, J.C., Erickson, K.G., Beard, J.K.: Costas array search technique that maximizes backtrack and symmetry exploitation. In: 44th Annual Conference on Information Sciences and Systems (CISS), pp. 1–8. IEEE (2010)

35. Schreiber, D., Sanders, P.: Scalable SAT solving in the cloud. In: Theory and Applications of Satisfiability Testing - SAT 2021 (2021)

36. Walsh, T.: General symmetry breaking constraints. In: Benhamou, F. (ed.) CP 2006. LNCS, vol. 4204, pp. 650–664. Springer, Heidelberg (2006). https://doi.org/10.1007/11889205_46

37. Wieringa, S., Heljanko, K.: Concurrent clause strengthening. In: Theory and Applications of Satisfiability Testing - SAT 2013 (2013)

38. Xu, L., Hutter, F., Hoos, H.H., Leyton-Brown, K.: SATzilla: portfolio-based algorithm selection for SAT. J. Artif. Intell. Res. **32**, 565–606 (2008)

Faster Optimistic Online Mirror Descent for Extensive-Form Games

Huacong Jiang, Weiming Liu, and Bin Li[(✉)]

University of Science and Technology of China, Hefei, China
{jw091006,weiming}@mail.ustc.edu.cn, binli@ustc.edu.cn

Abstract. Online Mirror Descent (OMD) is a kind of regret minimization algorithms for Online Convex Optimization (OCO). Recently, they are applied to solve Extensive-Form Games (EFGs) for approximating Nash equilibrium. Especially, optimistic variants of OMD are developed, which have a better theoretical convergence rate compared to common regret minimization algorithms, e.g., Counterfactual Regret Minimization (CFR), for EFGs. However, despite the theoretical advantage, existing OMD and their optimistic variants have been shown to converge to a Nash equilibrium slower than the state-of-the-art (SOTA) CFR variants in practice. The reason for the inferior performance may be that they usually use constant regularizers whose parameters have to be chosen at the beginning. Inspired by the adaptive nature of CFRs, in this paper, an adaptive method is presented to speed up the optimistic variants of OMD. Based on this method, Adaptive Optimistic OMD (Ada-OOMD) for EFGs is proposed. In this algorithm, the regularizers can adapt to real-time regrets, thus the algorithm may converge faster in practice. Experimental results show that Ada-OOMD is at least two orders of magnitude faster than existing optimistic OMD algorithms. In some extensive-form games, such as Kuhn poker and Goofspiel, the convergence speed of Ada-OOMD even exceeds the SOTA CFRs. https://github.com/github-jhc/ada-oomd

Keywords: Adaptive optimistic online mirror descent ·
Extensive-form games · Nash equilibrium · Counterfactual regret
minimization

1 Introduction

An imperfect information game is one in which only partial or no information about the opponent is known by each player. It can be used to model many realistic problems, such as negotiation, auctions, physical security, and so on. Among these games, there is a broad class of games, characterized by sequential interaction and stochastic outcomes, which can be modeled as extensive-form games

---

The work is supported by the National Natural Science Foundation of China under Grants No. U19B2044 and No. 61836011.

© The Author(s), under exclusive license to Springer Nature Switzerland AG 2022
S. Khanna et al. (Eds.): PRICAI 2022, LNCS 13629, pp. 90–103, 2022.
https://doi.org/10.1007/978-3-031-20862-1_7

(EFGs). In an EFG, multiple players can make multiple moves sequentially. At the end of the game, each player will receive a payoff (a loss). In common settings, the goal for each player is to maximize its expected payoff (minimize its expected loss) by carefully tweaking its strategy for making moves. One of the possible strategy solutions is known as Nash equilibrium [1], especially for two-player zero-sum games. Nash equilibrium is a profile of strategies that no player can improve his expected payoff by unilaterally deviating to a different strategy. It is known that the complexity of finding an exact Nash equilibrium in a game is (PPAD) hard [2], therefore, people usually use iterative algorithms to approximate a Nash equilibrium. In this paper, we mainly focus on regret minimization algorithms, exactly, Online Mirror Descent (OMD) algorithm.

By using the dilated distance-generating function, one can apply OMD, and their optimistic variants to approximate Nash equilibrium of extensive-form games. Although these online optimization algorithms have better theoretical convergence guarantee, they converge slower than the SOTA CFRs [3] in practice. CFR is a kind of efficient algorithm for finding Nash equilibrium, an agent trained with this algorithm once beat the top human players in the field of Heads-Up Limit Hold'em poker. The inconsistency between theory and practice shows that there is still a large room for improvement in the convergence speed of OMD algorithms in solving two-player zero-sum extensive-form games.

In previous works, such as [20], they usually use constant regularizers whose parameters have to be chosen at the beginning, which may limit the convergence speed of the algorithm. In order to reduce the limitation of fixed parameters on the convergence speed. Inspired by the adaptive nature of CFRs, by using the dilated Euclidean distance-generation function, we propose an adaptive method to speed up the convergence speed of the optimistic variants of OMD, resulting a new algorithm, Adaptive Optimistic OMD (Ada-OOMD) for EFGs. We theoretically prove that this new algorithm is convergent and give a specific theoretical minimum convergence rate of $O(T^{-0.5})$. We also experiment with six extensive-form games, and the experimental results verify that our algorithm has greatly improved the convergence speed compared with the fixed regularization function. In some games, such as Kuhn poker and Goofspiel, the adaptive optimistic OMD even has a faster convergence speed than CFR+.

2   Related Work

Extensive-form games (EFGs) are an important class of games in game theory and artificial intelligence which can model imperfect information and sequential interactions. EFGs are typically solved by finding or approximating a Nash equilibrium. A great successful application of calculating Nash equilibrium is poker, such as Kuhn poker, Leduc poker, and Heads-Up Limit Hold'em poker. Among them, Texas hold'em has always been a very challenging problem due to its large number of nodes, until [4] computed a near-optimal Nash equilibrium for Heads-Up Limit Hold'em poker, and [5] beat top human specialist professionals. The core of solving this large-scale game is to quickly calculate its

Nash equilibrium. There are many game-solving algorithms, such as, abstraction [6,7], endgame solving [8,9], depth-limited sub-game solving [10], fictitious play [11], and CFRs. Counterfactual Regret Minimization (CFR) [3,12] has been the most popular method in computing Nash equilibrium, which minimizes the total regrets of the players, by minimizing the counterfactual regrets of each decision point. In recent years, there are many variants of CFR, such as Discounted CFR [13], Deep CFR [14], and predictive CFR [15].

Online optimization algorithms have been shown to have appealing theoretical properties. Online Mirror Descent (OMD) [17] in Online Convex Optimization (OCO) [18] have been applied to EFGs. In this paper, we only consider two-player zero-sum imperfect information games, so at each time step t, these first-order methods receive some loss vector l^t (inner product of the opponent's strategy and payoff matrix), and must then recommend a strategy from some convex set based on the series of past strategies and losses. However, the theoretical convergence rate of these algorithms is $O(T^{-0.5})$. A recent series of papers [19] showed that by adding the estimate of the next loss faced, the rate of convergence to Nash equilibrium increases. [20] proposes the dilated Euclidean DGF, which applies the l_2 norm as a DGF at each information set. They show the first explicit bounds on the strong-convexity parameter for the dilated Euclidean DGF when applied to the strategy space of an EFG, the algorithm converges to Nash equilibrium at the improved rate $O(T^{-1})$.

In this work, we propose an adaptive method to speed up the optimistic Online Mirror Descent algorithms suitable for extensive-form games. The method can change the regularization function of each information set in real-time, so as to accelerate the convergence speed of the algorithm. In some games, the convergence speed of Ada-OOMD is even much faster than CFR+.

3   Notation and Background

Two-player zero-sum extensive-form games with perfect recall, exactly, every player will not forget the previous historical information, can be described as a sequence of decision-making processes, in which two players make decisions, in turn. The problem of computing its Nash equilibrium can be formulated as a bilinear saddle-point problem (BSPP) [22],

$$\min_{x \in \mathcal{X}} \max_{y \in \mathcal{Y}} x^\top \mathbf{A} y = \max_{y \in \mathcal{Y}} \min_{x \in \mathcal{X}} y^\top \mathbf{A} x. \tag{1}$$

In the EFG literature, this is known as the sequence-form formulation [23], where x and y represent the strategy vectors of player one and player two respectively, and matrix $\mathbf{A}$ represents the loss matrix for player one, which is also the payoff matrix for player two, $\mathcal{X}$ and $\mathcal{Y}$ are the players' sequence-form strategy spaces, which are convex polytopes. A best response BR(y) of player one is a strategy that $BR(\boldsymbol{y}) = \text{argmin}_{\boldsymbol{x}' \in \mathcal{X}} \boldsymbol{x}'^\top \mathbf{A} \boldsymbol{y}$, exactly, when player two adopts strategy $\boldsymbol{y}$, the strategy that player one adopts to minimize the loss is the best response strategy. A Nash equilibrium $(\boldsymbol{x}^*, \boldsymbol{y}^*)$ is a strategy profile that every player plays a best response. For any strategy profile $(\boldsymbol{x}, \boldsymbol{y})$, the distance to a Nash equilibrium is measured by the *exploitability* which is defined as $\epsilon(\boldsymbol{x}, \boldsymbol{y}) = \max_{\boldsymbol{y}' \in \mathcal{Y}} \boldsymbol{x}^\top \mathbf{A} \boldsymbol{y}' - \min_{\boldsymbol{x}' \in \mathcal{X}} \boldsymbol{x}'^\top \mathbf{A} \boldsymbol{y}$. In solving two-player zero-sum extensive-form games, the average strategy of CFRs and OMD algorithms converge to Nash equilibrium as the number of iterations increases, so, when measuring the quality of the strategy, what we need to calculate is the distance between the average strategy profile and Nash equilibrium:

$$\epsilon(\overline{\boldsymbol{x}}, \overline{\boldsymbol{y}}) = \frac{R_{\mathcal{X}}^T + R_{\mathcal{Y}}^T}{T}, \tag{2}$$

where $\overline{\boldsymbol{x}}$ and $\overline{\boldsymbol{y}}$ are the average strategy of the two players during minimization, and $R_{\mathcal{X}}^T$ and $R_{\mathcal{Y}}^T$ are the total regrets of the two players, defined as $R_{\mathcal{X}}^T = \max_{\boldsymbol{x}' \in \mathcal{X}} \sum_{t=1}^T (\langle \boldsymbol{l}^t, \boldsymbol{x}^t \rangle - \langle \boldsymbol{l}^t, \boldsymbol{x}' \rangle)$, where $\boldsymbol{l}^t = \mathbf{A} \boldsymbol{y}^t$ is determined by the loss matrix and the strategy of the opponent. Formula (2) shows that the average strategy is a $(R_{\mathcal{X}}^T + R_{\mathcal{Y}}^T)/T$ Nash equilibrium, therefore, as long as the player's cumulative regret grows sub-linearly, the *exploitability* of average strategies converges to zero. For example, if both $R_{\mathcal{X}}^T$ and $R_{\mathcal{Y}}^T$ are bounded by $O(T^{0.5})$, then $\epsilon(\overline{\boldsymbol{x}}, \overline{\boldsymbol{y}})$ will convergence to zero at a rate of $O(T^{-0.5})$.

3.1 Treeplex

Two-player zero-sum extensive-form games can be represented as a sequential decision process, so, we can assume that each player has a set of decision points denoted by $\mathcal{J}$ and a set of observation points denoted by $\mathcal{K}$ which is also the opponent's decision points. In this subsection, we adopt some definitions similar to [20,24]. For each decision node $j \in \mathcal{J}$, the actions that can be taken at the current node constitute the action set A_j of size n_j. Given a specific action $a \in A_j$, the set of possible observation points that the player may next face is denoted by $K_{j,a}$, at each observation point, the opponent makes a decision, and the player receives a signal $s \in S_k$, after observing the signal, the player reaches another decision point $j' \in \mathcal{J}$, so the set of all the next decision nodes represented as $C_{j,a}$, which can be thought as representing all of the different decision points that the player may arrive after taking action a, if no more actions are taken after j, a, it can be an empty set. For all other convex sets and action choices j', a', we assume that $C_{j,a} \cap C_{j',a'} = \emptyset$ which is equivalent to the perfect-recall assumption in extensive-form games. If $j' \in C_{j,a}$, we call that j' is the child decision point of j, written as $p(j') = j$. Moreover, define $C_{\downarrow j} = \{j\} \cup \{j' \in \mathcal{J} | p(j') \in C_{\downarrow j}\}$ as the set of all descending decision points of j (including j). To simplify the analysis, we can assume that the root node, denoted as o, is a decision point. Otherwise, we can always add a virtual root node with only one action pointing to the root node, as a result, we have $C_{\downarrow o} = \mathcal{J}$. In order to visualize the tree structure of the player's action space, in Fig. 1, we use Kuhn poker as an example. Kuhn poker consists of a three-card deck: king, queen, and jack. Figure 1 has shown the action space of the first player. Combining the diagram with the relevant definitions for treeplex we can get: $\mathcal{J} = \{0, 1, 2, 3, 4, 5, 6\}$; $n_0 = 1$; $n_j = 2$ for all $j \in \mathcal{J} \backslash \{0\}$; $A_0 = \{start\}$, $A_1 = A_2 = A_3 = \{check, raise\}$, $A_4 = A_5 = A_6 = \{fold, call\}$; $\mathcal{C}_{0,start} = \{1, 2, 3\}$; $\mathcal{C}_{1,check} = \{4\}$; $\mathcal{C}_{2,raise} = \emptyset$.

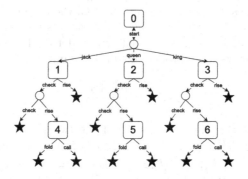

Fig. 1. player's sequential action space in the game of Kuhn poker, ★ represents the end of the decision process, ○ denotes an observation point, and □ represents decision points.

3.2 Sequence Form

Let $l = Ay = (l_{j_0}, ..., l_{j_{|\mathcal{J}|}})$ be the loss vector and let $x = (\hat{x}_{j_0}, ..., \hat{x}_{j_{|\mathcal{J}|}})$ be the strategy vector, where $\{j_0, ..., j_{|\mathcal{J}|}\} = \mathcal{J}$. The expected loss $\sum_{j \in \mathcal{J}} \pi_j \langle l_j, \hat{x}_j \rangle$ is non-linear in the strategy x. This non-linearity is due to π_j, which is the probability of reaching each decision node j and is computed as the probability product of all actions taken on the path from the root to node j. We now introduce a well-known alternative representation of the strategy that preserves linearity which is called the *sequence form* [23]. In the sequence form representation, for a common decision point $j \in \mathcal{J}$, its simplex strategy space is scaled by the decision variable associated with the last action in the path from the root of the process to j. In this formulation, the value of any action represents the probability product of the entire sequence of actions from the root to that action. This causes each item in the expected loss to be weighted only by the sequence ending with the corresponding action. The sequence form has been used to instantiate many methods for computing Nash equilibrium of zero-sum EFGs, such as linear programming [18] and first-order methods [3,16,18]. Formally, based on the characteristics of the tree structure, the sequence-form representation $\mathcal{X}$ of a sequential decision process can be obtained recursively. At every observation point $k \in \mathcal{K}$, $\mathcal{X}_k = \mathcal{X}_{j_1} \times \mathcal{X}_{j_2} \times \cdots \mathcal{X}_{j_{n_k}}$, where $\{j_1, j_2, \cdots, j_{n_k}\} = \mathcal{C}_k$, the set of feasible decision points at observation point k. At every decision point $j \in \mathcal{J}$,

$$\mathcal{X}_j = \{(\hat{x}_j, \hat{x}_{ja_1} x_{k_1} \ldots, \hat{x}_{ja_{n_j}} x_{k_{n_j}}) :$$
$$\hat{x}_j \in \Delta^{n_j}, x_{k_1} \in \mathcal{X}_{k_1}, \ldots, x_{k_{n_j}} \in \mathcal{X}_{k_{n_j}}\}, \tag{3}$$

where $\{k_1, \ldots, k_{n_j}\} = C_j$, the set of feasible observation points at decision point j, and $\left(\hat{x}_{ja_1}, \ldots, \hat{x}_{ja_{n_j}}\right) = \hat{x}_j \in \Delta^{n_j}$ is the probability distribution of actions at decision node j. Denote the strategy in space $\mathcal{X}_j$ as $x_j \in \mathcal{X}_j$, the whole sequence-form strategy space is $\mathcal{X} = \mathcal{X}_o$. Sometimes, we may have to "slice" (i.e., select some adjacent elements from a vector to form a new vector) a sub-vector related to a decision point j from a vector $z \in \mathbb{R}^{\Sigma n_j}$ (z can be a strategy $x \in \mathcal{X}$ or a loss vector $l \in \mathbb{R}^{\Sigma n_j}$). We use $[z]_j$ to represent the n_j entries related to j, and $[z]_{ja}$ to represent the entry corresponding to action a in $[z]_j$. Besides, let $[z]_{\downarrow j}$ denote the entries related to $C_{\downarrow j}$. Let x_{p_j} be the variable that scales x_j, i.e., $x_{p_j} = \pi_{p_j}$. If decision point j does not have parent decision point, we simply set $x_{p_j} = 1$. So, there is a simple mapping between a sequence-form strategy and the local decision: $\hat{x}_j = [x_j]_j = [x]_j / x_{p_j}$ for each $j \in \mathcal{J}$. Then, the expected loss for the whole process is $\langle l, x \rangle$, where l satisfies $[l]_j = l_j$. In the rest of the paper, we use normal symbols, e.g., x and l, to represent the variables related to the sequence-form strategy space, and use symbols with hats, e.g., $\hat{x}_j$ and $\hat{l}_j$, to represent the variables related to local decision points.

3.3   Dilate Euclidean Distance Generate Function

Because the player's strategy has a sequential form, for the regularization function that computes the next strategy, a particular type of distance-generate function which is suitable for sequential decision-making problems is needed. [25] has proposed dilated DGF, which is defined as $d^t(x) = \sum_{j \in \mathcal{J}} x_{p_j} \varphi_j^{t-1}(\hat{x}_j)$, where $\hat{x}_j = \frac{x_j}{x_{p_j}} \in \Delta^{n_j}$, $\varphi_j^{t-1} : \mathbb{R}^{n_j} \to \mathbb{R}$ is any strongly convex function suitable for Δ^{n_j}.

Definition 1. *A directionally differentiable function $f: \mathcal{X} \mapsto \mathbb{R}$ is η-strongly convex with respect to norm $\| \cdot \|$, if and only if:*

$$f(x) - f(y) - \langle \nabla f(y), x - y \rangle \geq \frac{\eta}{2} \|x - y\|^2. \tag{4}$$

In this paper, the local dilated DGFs we used for simplexes is the Euclidean DGF, defined as $\varphi_j^t(b) = \frac{1}{2}\beta_j^t\|b\|_2^2$, which is β_j^t-strongly convex with respect to the l_2 norm, where b is a vector in the n-dimensional simplex Δ^n. The coefficients in front of our regularization function are not fixed, exactly, we let $d^t(x) = \sum_{j \in \mathcal{J}} x_{p_j} \beta_j^{t-1} \|\hat{x}_j^t\|^2$, where β_j^{t-1} is an adaptive parameters.

3.4   Counterfactual Regret Minimization

CFR and its variants are a classical algorithm in two-player zero-sum games with imperfect information, it has been proven that the exploitability of the average strategies of the players is bounded by $O(T^{-0.5})$ after T iterations. [15,24] have pointed out that under certain conditions, CFR algorithm is equivalent to OMD algorithm. Inspired by this, we introduce the related concepts of CFR algorithm into our algorithm setting. Given a sequence-form strategy $\boldsymbol{x}^t \in \mathcal{X}$ and a loss vector $\boldsymbol{l}^t \in \mathbb{R}^{\sum n_j}$, CFR constructs a kind of local loss $\hat{l}_j^t$ for every $j \in \mathcal{J}$, with

$$\hat{l}_j^t = \langle \hat{\boldsymbol{l}}_j^t, \hat{\boldsymbol{x}}_j \rangle, \quad where \quad [\hat{\boldsymbol{l}}_j^t]_a = [\boldsymbol{l}^t]_{ja} + \sum_{j' \in \mathcal{C}_{ja}} \hat{l}_{j'}^t, \tag{5}$$

$[\hat{l}_j^t]$ is called the counterfactual loss, so the instantaneous counterfactual regret is defined as $\hat{\boldsymbol{r}}_j^t = \hat{l}_j^t \boldsymbol{e} - \hat{\boldsymbol{l}}_j^t$, where $\boldsymbol{e}$ is a vector that is all 1. A more straightforward explanation for $\hat{\boldsymbol{r}}_j^t$ is that when the current loss is $\boldsymbol{l}^t$, the virtual regret value that the player obtained when taking strategy $\boldsymbol{x}^t$ at decision point j.

3.5   Regret Minimization Algorithms

One's ability to learn and make decisions rests heavily on the availability of feedback. Indeed, a player may improve himself when he can reflect on the outcomes of his own taken actions. In many environments, feedback is readily available, and many online convex optimization algorithms [25] are proposed based on it, such as regret minimization algorithms. In regret minimization algorithms, the decision maker is constantly making decisions $\boldsymbol{x}^1, \boldsymbol{x}^2, \cdots, \boldsymbol{x}^t \in \mathcal{X}$ without knowing the environment, $\mathcal{X}$ is a convex compact set. After a decision $\boldsymbol{x}^t$ is made at time t, the environment feeds back a linear loss $\boldsymbol{x}^t \mapsto \langle \boldsymbol{l}^t, \boldsymbol{x}^t \rangle$ to the decision maker, where $\boldsymbol{l}^t \in \mathbb{R}^{\sum n_j}$. Summarizing, when it comes to the next iteration, the decision maker can use past strategies $\boldsymbol{x}^1, \boldsymbol{x}^2, \ldots, \boldsymbol{x}^t$ and corresponding losses $\boldsymbol{l}^1, \boldsymbol{l}^2, \ldots, \boldsymbol{l}^t$ to develop strategies $\boldsymbol{x}^{t+1}$ for the next step to increase payoff.

In the process of interaction with the unknown environment, the difference between the loss of the current strategy and the loss of the best strategy is defined as the regret value, the quality metric for a regret minimizer is its cumulative regret, and the cumulative regret up to time T is:

$$R^T := \sum_{t=1}^{T} \langle \boldsymbol{l}^t, \boldsymbol{x}^t \rangle - \min_{\hat{\boldsymbol{x}} \in \mathcal{X}} \sum_{t=1}^{T} \langle \boldsymbol{l}^t, \hat{\boldsymbol{x}} \rangle. \tag{6}$$

If the cumulative regret grows sublinearly in T, then we say the regret minimizer is "good". Now, we present a classical regret minimization algorithm, The online mirror descent (OMD) algorithm:

$$\boldsymbol{x}^{t+1} = \operatorname*{argmin}_{\boldsymbol{x} \in \mathcal{X}} \{ \langle \boldsymbol{l}^t, \boldsymbol{x} \rangle + \frac{1}{\eta} \mathcal{B}_d(\boldsymbol{x} \| \boldsymbol{x}^t) \}, \tag{7}$$

where $\mathcal{B}_d(\boldsymbol{x} \| \boldsymbol{x}^t) := d(\boldsymbol{x}) - d(\boldsymbol{x}') - \langle \nabla d(\boldsymbol{x}'), \boldsymbol{x} - \boldsymbol{x}' \rangle$ is defined as Bregman divergence constructed by dilated DGF $d(\boldsymbol{x})$. When calculating the strategy of the next round, the prediction of the loss function at the next moment $\boldsymbol{m}^{t+1}$ was added to the optimization function, thus obtaining the optimistic variant of the regret minimization algorithm. Now, we present a optimistic variant of classical regret minimization algorithms, Optimistic Online Mirror Descent

(OOMD) algorithm and its policy update form:

$$x^{t+1} = \underset{x \in \mathcal{X}}{\operatorname{argmin}}\{\langle m^{t+1}, x \rangle + \frac{1}{\eta}\mathcal{B}_d(x\|z^t)\},$$

$$z^{t+1} = \underset{z \in \mathcal{X}}{\operatorname{argmin}}\{\langle l^{t+1}, z \rangle + \frac{1}{\eta}\mathcal{B}_d(z\|z^t)\}. \tag{8}$$

Pay attention to that x^{t+1} is selected before observing loss l^{t+1} while z^{t+1} is selected after.

4   Adaptive Methods and Analysis

One can see that the regularization function of the above optimization algorithm is fixed when updating the strategy. However, the regularization function with fixed constant limits the convergence speed of the algorithm. As mentioned earlier, inspired by the adaptive nature of the CFRs algorithms, we propose an adaptive method and apply it to the OOMD algorithm to make the regularization function change in real-time with the accumulated regret, and obtain a new algorithm Ada-OOMD. In this section, we will give the specific form of the algorithm and prove that our algorithm converges to a Nash equilibrium at a speed of $O(T^{-0.5})$. The proof details of all theorems and corollaries in this section can be found in the appendix.[1]

4.1   Adaptive Regularization Function

This subsection presents the application of our adaptive method to the OOMD algorithm. The specific flow of the algorithm is as follows.

Algorithm 1. Adaptive Optimistic Online Mirror Descent

Input: $z^0 = 0$
1: **for** iteration $t = 0$ to T **do**
2:    **if** t=0 **then**
3:       $m^{t+1} \leftarrow 0.$
4:    **else**
5:       $m^{t+1} \leftarrow \text{Estimate}(l^1, \dots, l^t, x^1, \dots, x^t).$
6:    **end if**
7:    $x^{t+1} \leftarrow \text{Update}(m^{t+1}, z^t).$
8:    $l^{t+1} \leftarrow \text{Obverseloss}(x^{t+1}).$
9:    $z^{t+1} \leftarrow \text{Intermediate-variable}(l^{t+1}, z^t).$
10: **end for**

Take a list of regularization functions $q^0, q^1, \cdots, q^t$, satisfy $q^0(x) = \sum_{j \in \mathcal{J}} \frac{1}{2\eta} x_{p_j} \beta_j^0 \|\hat{x}_j\|^2$, and $\sum_{i=0}^{t} q^i(x) = \sum_{j \in \mathcal{J}} \frac{1}{2\eta} x_{p_j} \beta_j^t \|\hat{x}_j\|^2$, then policy x^{t+1}

---

[1] https://tinyurl.com/5yj7ndnz.

and intermediate variable z^{t+1} are obtained by the following equations.

$$\begin{aligned}
\boldsymbol{x}^t &= \underset{\boldsymbol{x} \in \mathcal{X}}{\arg\min} \left\{ \langle \boldsymbol{m}^t, \boldsymbol{x} \rangle + q^t(\boldsymbol{x}) + \mathcal{B}_{q^{0:t-1}}(\boldsymbol{x} \| \boldsymbol{z}^t) \right\}, \\
\boldsymbol{z}^{t+1} &= \underset{\boldsymbol{x} \in \mathcal{X}}{\arg\min} \left\{ \langle \boldsymbol{l}^t, \boldsymbol{x} \rangle + q^t(\boldsymbol{x}) + \mathcal{B}_{q^{0:t-1}}(\boldsymbol{x} \| \boldsymbol{z}^t) \right\},
\end{aligned} \tag{9}$$

where $q^{0:t-1} = \sum_{i=0}^{t-1} q^i$. In the process of iteration, the parameter β_j^t is constantly changing, and we'll talk more about it in later chapters. For example, in Sect. 4.2, it can be seen that the cumulative regret upper bound of the algorithm is related to β_j^t, so, by setting β_j^t to some specific value, the algorithm can be proved to be convergent.

4.2   Convergence Analysis

In the process of deriving the upper bound on regret for the Ada-OOMD algorithm, we decompose the accumulated regret into the following three parts.

$$\sum_{t=1}^{T} \langle \boldsymbol{l}^t, \boldsymbol{x}^t - \boldsymbol{x}' \rangle = \sum_{t=1}^{T} \langle \boldsymbol{m}^t, \boldsymbol{x}^t - \boldsymbol{z}^{t+1} \rangle + \sum_{t=1}^{T} \langle \boldsymbol{l}^t, \boldsymbol{z}^{t+1} - \boldsymbol{x}' \rangle + \sum_{t=1}^{T} \langle \boldsymbol{l}^t - \boldsymbol{m}^t, \boldsymbol{x}^t - \boldsymbol{z}^{t+1} \rangle. \tag{10}$$

Calculating the upper bound on the regret value of each part separately, we get the following theorem.

Theorem 1. *For Ada-OOMD, if $q^{0:t}, t \geq 0$ is strongly convex and differentiable in $\mathcal{X}$, then,*

$$\begin{aligned}
\sum_{t=1}^{T} \langle \boldsymbol{l}^t, \boldsymbol{x}^t - \boldsymbol{x}' \rangle \leq & \, q^{0:T}(\boldsymbol{x}') - \sum_{t=0}^{T} q^t(\boldsymbol{x}^t) + \langle \boldsymbol{l}^t - \boldsymbol{m}^t, \boldsymbol{x}^t - \boldsymbol{z}^{t+1} \rangle \\
& - \sum_{t=1}^{T} \left(\mathcal{B}_{q^{0:t-1}}(\boldsymbol{x}^t \| \boldsymbol{z}^t) + \mathcal{B}_{q^{0:t}}(\boldsymbol{z}^{t+1} \| \boldsymbol{x}^t) \right).
\end{aligned} \tag{11}$$

As defined earlier, by bring the definition $\sum_{i=0}^{t} q^i(\boldsymbol{x}) = \sum_{j \in \mathcal{J}} \frac{1}{2\eta} x_{p_j} \beta_j^t \|\hat{\boldsymbol{x}}_j\|^2$ into Theorem 1, one can get a more explicit upper bound on regret as follows.

Theorem 2. *For Ada-OOMD, if $\beta_j^t \geq \beta_j^{t-1} > 0, \forall j \in \mathcal{J}, t > 0$, then,*

$$\sum_{t=1}^{T} \langle \boldsymbol{l}^t, \boldsymbol{x}^t - \boldsymbol{x}' \rangle \leq \frac{1}{2} \sum_{j \in \mathcal{J}} \left(\frac{\beta_j^T}{\eta} + \sum_{t=1}^{T} \frac{\eta \|\hat{\boldsymbol{r}}_j^t - \hat{\boldsymbol{r}}_j'^t\|_2^2}{\beta_j^t} \right), \tag{12}$$

where $\hat{\boldsymbol{r}}'^t$ is instantaneous counterfactual regret when loss vector is $\boldsymbol{m}^t$ and current strategy is $\boldsymbol{x}'$.

Corollary 1. *If $\beta_j^t = \sqrt{\sum_{k=1}^{t} \|\hat{\boldsymbol{r}}_j^k - \hat{\boldsymbol{r}}_j'^k\|_2^2}$ and $\beta_j^t \geq \beta_j^{t-1} > 0, \forall j \in \mathcal{J}, t > 0$, then, the total regret of T iterations of Ada-OOMD is*

$$\sum_{t=1}^{T} \langle \boldsymbol{l}^t, \boldsymbol{x}^t - \boldsymbol{x}' \rangle \leq \frac{1}{2} \left(2\eta + \frac{1}{\eta} \right) \sum_{j \in \mathcal{J}} \sqrt{\sum_{t=1}^{T} \|\hat{\boldsymbol{r}}_j^t - \hat{\boldsymbol{r}}_j'^t\|_2^2}. \tag{13}$$

According to the lemma 1 of [27], we can get that,

$$\sum_{t=1}^{T} \|\hat{r}_j^t\|^2 \le \overline{y}_j^T |A_j| U^2 \, T, \tag{14}$$

where $\overline{y}_j^T$ denotes the opponent's average strategy at decision point j in the T-th iteration, U is the range of the current player's revenue, and $|A_j|$ is the number of available actions at node j. So, if we set $\beta_j^t = \sqrt{\sum_{k=1}^{t} \|\hat{r}_j^k - \hat{r}_j'^k\|_2^2}$, then $R^T(x') = O(T^{0.5})$ for any strategy x', therefore, the theoretical convergence rate of our method is $O(T^{-0.5})$. As we mentioned earlier, although the theoretical convergence rate of CFR+ is $O(T^{-0.5})$, its actual convergence rate can reach $O(T^{-1})$ in practice. Similarly, though the theoretical convergence rate of our method is $O(T^{-0.5})$, the experimental results show that our method is much faster than fixed parameters which is proposed in [20] with a convergence rate of $O(T^{-1})$, what's more, in some games, the convergence rate of our method is even faster than CFR+.

4.3   Dilated Distance Generating Function and Local Minimization

The update applied at each iteration of several OCO algorithms which run on the sequence-form polytope of $\mathcal{X}$ can be described as an instantiation of a prox mapping, exactly, our algorithm can be described as follow:

$$Prox(m^{t+1}, z^t) = \underset{x \in \mathcal{X}}{\mathrm{argmin}} \left\{ \langle m^{t+1}, x \rangle + q^t(x) + \mathcal{B}_{q^{0:t-1}}(x \| z^t) \right\}. \tag{15}$$

A prox mapping on a treeplex constructed from a dilated DGF can be decomposed into local prox mappings at each decision point, therefore, we can solve the minimization problem through the method of Prox mapping to get the strategy of the next iteration recursively, we give an example below for the recursive updating rule. Let $q_j^{0:t}(x_j) = \sum_{j' \in C_{\downarrow j}} x_{p_{j'}} / x_{p_j} q_{j'}^{0:t}(\hat{x}_{j'})$ be a regularizer defined in the space of $\mathcal{X}_j$. Note that $q_j^{0:t}(x_j)$ is equivalent to $q^{0:t}(x)$ under the assumption that $x_{p_j} = 1$. Let $F^{t+1}(x) = \langle m^{t+1}, x \rangle + q^t(x) + \mathcal{B}_{q^{0:t-1}}(x \| z^t)$, then the next strategy is computed by $x^{t+1} = \mathrm{argmin}_{x \in X} F^{t+1}(x)$, and $F_j^{t+1}(x_j) = \langle [m^{t+1}]_{\downarrow j}, x_j \rangle + q_j^{0:t}(x_j) + \mathcal{B}_{q_j^{0:t-1}}(x_j \| z_j^t)$ accordingly. Then, $F(x) = F_o(x_o)$, and we have $q^{0:t}(x) = q_o^{0:t}(x_o)$. Based on these and [24], we can get the calculation expression of the next iteration strategy:

$$\hat{x}_j^{t+1} = \frac{\eta}{\beta_j^t} [\alpha_j^t e - [m^{t+1}]_j - \frac{\beta_j^{t-1}}{\eta} \hat{z}_j^t]^+, \tag{16}$$

where $\alpha_j^t \in \mathbb{R}$ satisfies $\|\hat{x}_j^{t+1}\|_1 = 1$, i.e., α_j^t fulfills $\| [\alpha_j^t e - [m^{t+1}]_j - \frac{\beta_j^{t-1}}{\eta} \hat{z}_j^t]^+ \|_1 = \beta_j^t$. The policy update formula mainly leverages the linearity of the loss in the strategy space and the recursive property of the dilated DGF.

5   Experiment Results and Analysis

From the theoretical analysis in the previous section, we can find that the theoretical convergence rate of the Ada-OOMD algorithm is $O(T^{-0.5})$. Compared to the OOMD algorithm which has a fixed regularization function, our algorithm has similar adaptive properties to the CFR algorithm. Next, we will test the performance of our algorithms on different games.

5.1   Experimental Setup

We experimentally evaluate the performance of adaptive optimistic regret minimization methods instantiated with dilated distance-generating functions. A total of six games were used to test the algorithm's performance, such as, Kuhn poker, Leduc poker, Liars-dice, Goofspiel and its variants. According to the results given by Corollary 1 above, in the experiment, it's better to set $\beta_j^t = \sqrt{\sum_{k=1}^t \|\hat{r}_j^k - \hat{r}_j'^k\|_2^2}$. However, $\sqrt{\sum_{k=1}^t \|\hat{r}_j^k - \hat{r}_j'^k\|_2^2}$ is complicated to calculate, and as mentioned before, the l_2-norm of the cumulative counterfactual regret of each decision point is bounded by $U\sqrt{\bar{y}_j^t|A_j|t}$ [27], so, we set $\beta_j^t = U\sqrt{\bar{y}_j^t|A_j|t}$ instead, and this parameter setting can still ensure that the algorithm has a convergence speed of $O(T^{-0.5})$. From the expression we can see that β_j^t is related to the average strategy of the opponent, however, the calculation method of the average strategy is not unique. In this paper, we tried three methods separately. *Uniform Averaging (UA)*, i.e., $\overline{y}^T = \frac{1}{T}\sum_{t=1}^T y^t$, *Linear Averaging (LA)*, i.e., $\overline{y}^T = \frac{2}{T(T+1)}\sum_{t=1}^T ty^t$ and *Square average (SA)*, i.e., $\overline{y}^T = \frac{6}{T(T+1)(2T+1)}\sum_{t=1}^T t^2 y^t$. We found the calculation method of linear average (LA) has a faster convergence speed than other settings. Therefore, we use this parameter setting to experiment on the six games mentioned earlier. As for the learning rate η, it's a hyper-parameter, in different games, the setting of hyper-parameter η is different, for example, in Kuhn poker, we set $\eta = 2$, in Leduc poker, we set $\eta = 200$, and so on. The experimental results will be shown in the next section.

5.2   Experimental Results

The experimental results of OOMD, Ada-OOMD, CFR, and CFRPLUS are reported below, all the algorithms tested here use alternating updating, which is a standard method widely used in CFRs [12].

From the experimental results, we can see that our method does accelerate the convergence speed than that of the fixed parameters in all test games. Figure 2 shows the performance of the Ada-OOMD algorithm on Goofspiel-5, leduc poker and liars-dice. One can see that the convergence speed of the Ada-OOMD algorithm is at least two orders of magnitude faster than that of the fixed-parameter OOMD algorithm. Although it is still not as good as the CFR+

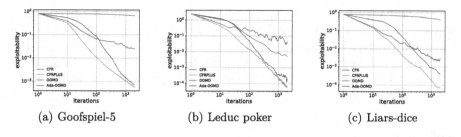

(a) Goofspiel-5	(b) Leduc poker	(c) Liars-dice

Fig. 2. Performance curve of each algorithm in the game. The x-axis is the number of iterations. The y-axis is the Exploitability. Our adaptive algorithm surpasses the algorithm of the fixed regularization function and is closer to the CFRPLUS algorithm.

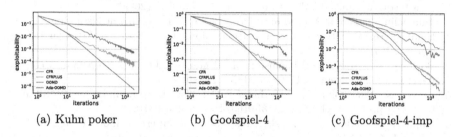

(a) Kuhn poker	(b) Goofspiel-4	(c) Goofspiel-4-imp

Fig. 3. Performance curve of each algorithm in the game. The x-axis is the number of iterations. The y-axis is the Exploitability. Our adaptive algorithm outperforms algorithms with fixed regularization functions and even the CFRPLUS algorithm.

algorithm, it is very close. In Fig. 3, One can see that the convergence speed of the Ada-OOMD algorithm is not only at least two orders of magnitude faster than that of the fixed-parameter OOMD algorithm, but even exceeds the CFR+ algorithm. We have reason to believe that the online optimization algorithm has great potential in solving two-player zero-sum extensive-form games. One can continue to improve its theoretical and practical convergence speed in future research, and solve imperfect information games better and faster.

6 Conclusions

We propose an adaptive method, and apply it to the optimistic variants of OMD that accelerates the convergence to Nash equilibrium in two-player zero-sum extensive-form games. In this method, the regularization function is changed in real-time according to the accumulated regret. We have proved that this adaptive approach is convergent on the optimistic variants of OMD, and give a specific minimum convergence rate $O(T^{-0.5})$. Although our method does not theoretically give a better upper bound on regret value than $O(T^{-1})$, its actual experimental convergence speed is faster than the optimistic online convex optimization algorithms with fixed parameter, which has the convergence rate of $O(T^{-1})$ in theory. In addition, our method has the same theoretical convergence rate as SOTA CFRs, and in experiments, we find that our adaptive method converges close to CFR+ in some games, and in other games, such as Kuhn poker and Goofspiel, our method outperforms it, which is encouraging. Later, the proof method can be further adjusted to obtain a better theoretical bound, and the performance of the algorithm can be further improved by setting better adaptive parameters.

References

1. Nash, J.: Non-cooperative games. Ann. Math., 286–295 (1951)
2. Daskalakis, C., Goldberg, P.W., Papadimitriou, C.H.: The complexity of computing a nash equilibrium. SIAM J. Comput. **39**(1), 195–259 (2009)
3. Tammelin, O., Burch, N., Johanson, M., Bowling, M.: Solving heads-up limit Texas Hold'em. In: Twenty-Fourth International Joint Conference on Artificial Intelligence (2015)
4. Bowling, M., Burch, N., Johanson, M., Tammelin, O.: Heads-up limit Hold'em poker is solved. Science **347**(6218), 145–149 (2015)
5. Brown, N., Sandholm, T.: Superhuman AI for heads-up no-limit poker: Libratus beats top professionals. Science **359**(6374), 418–424 (2018)
6. Gilpin, A., Sandholm, T.: Lossless abstraction of imperfect information games. J. ACM (JACM) **54**(5), 25-es (2007)
7. Brown, N., Ganzfried, S., Sandholm, T.: Hierarchical abstraction, distributed equilibrium computation, and post-processing, with application to a champion no-limit Texas Hold'em agent. In: Workshops at the Twenty-Ninth AAAI Conference on Artificial Intelligence (2015)
8. Ganzfried, S., Sandholm, T.: Endgame solving in large imperfect-information games. In: Workshops at the Twenty-Ninth AAAI Conference on Artificial Intelligence (2015)
9. Moravcik, M., Schmid, M., Ha, K., Hladik, M., Gaukrodger, S.: Refining subgames in large imperfect information games. In: Proceedings of the AAAI Conference on Artificial Intelligence, vol. 30 (2016)
10. Brown, N., Sandholm, T.: Superhuman AI for multiplayer poker. Science **365**(6456), 885–890 (2019)
11. Heinrich, J., Silver, D.: Deep reinforcement learning from self-play in imperfect-information games. arXiv preprint arXiv:1603.01121 (2016)
12. Zinkevich, M., Johanson, M., Bowling, M., Piccione, C.: Regret minimization in games with incomplete information. In: Advances in Neural Information Processing Systems, vol. 20 (2007)
13. Brown, N., Sandholm, T.: Solving imperfect-information games via discounted regret minimization. In: Proceedings of the AAAI Conference on Artificial Intelligence, vol. 33, pp. 1829–1836 (2019)
14. Liu, W., Li, B., Togelius, J.: Model-free neural counterfactual regret minimization with bootstrap learning. IEEE Trans. Games, 1 (2022)
15. Farina, G., Kroer, C., Sandholm, T.: Faster game solving via predictive blackwell approachability: connecting regret matching and mirror descent. arXiv preprint arXiv:2007.14358 (2020)
16. Abernethy, J.D., Hazan, E., Rakhlin, A.: Competing in the dark: an efficient algorithm for bandit linear optimization (2009)

17. Beck, A., Teboulle, M.: Mirror descent and nonlinear projected subgradient methods for convex optimization. Oper. Res. Lett. **31**(3), 167–175 (2003)
18. Hazan, E., et al.: Introduction to online convex optimization. Found. Trends® Opt. **2**(3–4), 157–325 (2016)
19. Syrgkanis, V., Agarwal, A., Luo, H., Schapire, R.E.: Fast convergence of regularized learning in games. In: Advances in Neural Information Processing Systems, vol. 28 (2015)
20. Farina, G., Kroer, C., Sandholm, T.: Optimistic regret minimization for extensive-form games via dilated distance-generating functions. In: Advances in Neural Information Processing Systems, vol. 32 (2019)
21. Lee, C.-W., Kroer, C., Luo, H.: Last-iterate convergence in extensive-form games. In: Advances in Neural Information Processing Systems, vol. 34 (2021)
22. Kroer, C., Waugh, K., Kılınç-Karzan, F., Sandholm, T.: Faster algorithms for extensive-form game solving via improved smoothing functions. Math. Program. **179**(1), 385–417 (2020)
23. Koller, D., Megiddo, N., Von Stengel, B.: Efficient computation of equilibria for extensive two-person games. Games Econom. Behav. **14**(2), 247–259 (1996)
24. Liu, W., Jiang, H., Li, B., Li, H.: Equivalence analysis between counterfactual regret minimization and online mirror descent. arXiv preprint arXiv:2110.04961 (2021)
25. Zinkevich, M.: Online convex programming and generalized infinitesimal gradient ascent. In: Proceedings of the 20th International Conference on Machine Learning (ICML-2003), pp. 928–936 (2003)
26. Joulani, P., György, A., Szepesvári, C.: A modular analysis of adaptive (non-) convex optimization: optimism, composite objectives, variance reduction, and variational bounds. Theoret. Comput. Sci. **808**, 108–138 (2020)
27. Brown, N., Sandholm, T.: Strategy-based warm starting for regret minimization in games. In: Proceedings of the AAAI Conference on Artificial Intelligence, vol. 30 (2016)
28. Orabona, F.: A modern introduction to online learning. arXiv preprint arXiv:1912.13213 (2019)

Generalized 3-Valued Belief States
in Conformant Planning

Saurabh Fadnis(✉) ⓘ and Jussi Rintanen ⓘ

Department of Computer Science, Aalto University, Espoo, Finland
saurabh.fadnis@aalto.fi

Abstract. The high complexity of planning with partial observability has motivated to find compact representations of belief state (sets of states) that reduce their size exponentially, including the 3-valued literal-based approximations by Baral et al. and tag-based approximations by Palacios and Geffner.

We present a generalization of 3-valued literal-based approximations, and an algorithm that analyzes a succinctly represented planning problem to derive a set of formulas the truth of which accurately represents any reachable belief state. This set is not limited to literals and can contain arbitrary formulas. We demonstrate that a factored representation of belief states based on this analysis enables fully automated reduction of conformant planning problems to classical planning, bypassing some of the limitations of earlier approaches.

1 Introduction

In comparison to classical planning, which has a single known initial state and deterministic actions and thus a completely predictable and observable future, more general forms of planning with multiple initial states and incomplete observability require considering sets of possible current states, leading to the notion of *belief states*. In this setting, the knowledge state of an agent is initially incomplete, consisting of multiple states (and not just one), and each action maps the current belief state to a new one, consisting of the new possible current states. This is the reason why limited observability increases the complexity by an exponential in comparison to the fully observable case.

Earlier works have used propositional logic and related NP-complete languages for compact belief space representations in planning under partial observability [2,19] and full observability [7]. The representations of state sets in these works use sets of *literals*, that is propositional variables and negated propositional variables, which is equivalent to 3-valued valuations in which a state variable can have the value *true*, *false*, or *unknown*. Sets of literals cannot represent arbitrary state sets. For example, the set $\{01, 10, 11\}$ is not representable as a set of literals, and, more generally, any set with *dependencies* between state variables, which is the typical case, cannot be.

Our goal is to provide a method for determining cases in which all relevant state sets can indeed be accurately represented as sets of literals, and when

© The Author(s), under exclusive license to Springer Nature Switzerland AG 2022
S. Khanna et al. (Eds.): PRICAI 2022, LNCS 13629, pp. 104–117, 2022.
https://doi.org/10.1007/978-3-031-20862-1_8

this is not possible, to determine which type of more general representation is sufficient. Our representation is with sets $T = \{\phi_1, \ldots, \phi_n\}$ of propositional formulas so that any belief state B (state set) is characterized by some $R \subseteq T$ as $B = \{v | v \models \bigwedge R\}$. The component formulas $\phi_1, \ldots, \phi_n$ could be limited to *clauses*, but also unlimited propositional formulas can be used instead. The 3-valued representations [2, 19] can be viewed as a special case, as we could choose the set T to consist of literals x and $\neg x$ for all state variables x.

Hence, belief states can be represented as vectors $(b_1, \ldots, b_n)$, indicating which of the formulas in $T = \{\phi_1, \ldots, \phi_n\}$ hold in the belief state. As this is a bit-vector, different actions are mappings from bit-vectors to bit-vectors, and it is straightforward to turn the conformant planning problem to a standard state-space search problem, solvable for example by classical planners.

The plan of this work is as follows. We will first introduce planning without observability (often known as *conformant planning*), and a novel representation of belief states in terms of subsets of a fixed set of formulas (that we call a *base*). We show how actions can be understood as mappings from valuations of the base to valuations to the base, and we give an algorithm for identifying a base for an arbitrary conformant planning problem. Then we propose a reduction from conformant planning to classical planning, in which each formula in the base is identified with a state variable in classical planning. Both finding a base and deriving the classical planning problem involve worst-case exponential operations, but we show that simple approximation schemes still allow solving many hard conformant planning problems efficiently. We conclude the paper by discussing possible extensions of our work.

2   Preliminaries

Define a problem instance in conformant planning as a tuple $\langle X, I, A, G \rangle$ where

- X is a finite set of *state variables*,
- I is a formula for the *initial states*,
- A is a finite set of formulas over $X \cup \{x' | x \in X\}$ representing *actions*, and
- G is a formula for the *goal states*.

The action representation is the one well known from OBDD and SAT-based planning methods [5], in which the relation between a state and its possible successor states is represented as arbitrary Boolean functions over the state variables $X = \{x_1, \ldots, x_n\}$ and the *next state variables* $X' = \{x'_1, \ldots, x'_n\}$. This is a general representation, to which deterministic and non-deterministic variants of PDDL can be translated.

In Sect. 5.1 we will also use a representation of actions close to standard modelling languages, in which actions are pairs (p, e) where p is a formula and e (the *effect*) is a set of rules $\phi \triangleright l$, where the literals in l are made true conditional on the formula ϕ being true. If $\phi = \top$, then the literals become true unconditionally (which is the case in the simplest so-called STRIPS actions.)

Example 1 (Sorting Networks). Consider a sorting network problem, in which the initial belief state is the set of all possible states over the state variables x_1, x_2, x_3, and the three actions are $(\top, (x_1 \wedge \neg x_2) \triangleright (\neg x_1; x_2))$, $(\top, (x_2 \wedge \neg x_3) \triangleright (\neg x_2; x_3))$, and $(\top, (x_1 \wedge \neg x_3) \triangleright (\neg x_1; x_3))$, or equivalently, $\Phi_{12} = (x_1' \leftrightarrow (x_1 \wedge x_2)) \wedge (x_2' \leftrightarrow (x_1 \vee x_2)) \wedge (x_3' \leftrightarrow x_3)$, $\Phi_{23} = (x_1' \leftrightarrow x_1) \wedge (x_2' \leftrightarrow (x_2 \wedge x_3)) \wedge (x_3' \leftrightarrow (x_2 \vee x_3))$. and $\Phi_{13} = (x_1' \leftrightarrow (x_1 \wedge x_3)) \wedge (x_2' \leftrightarrow x_2) \wedge (x_3' \leftrightarrow (x_1 \vee x_3))$. The actions swap the values of two state variables if they are not in increasing order.

Since the initial state is not known and the actions just reorder the unknown values of the state variables, the value of no state variable ever becomes known. The only known thing is the orderings of some state variables.

3   Theory

Given actions and a formula for the initial belief state, our objective is to identify $T = \{\phi_1, \ldots, \phi_n\}$ so that every reachable belief state can be represented as a conjunction of some $R \subseteq T$. We call such a set T a *base*. When a literal-based approximation [2] is sufficient, T is a set of literals. More generally, T consists of arbitrary formulas. For example, we will see that the 3-input sorting network problem can be represented in terms of $T = \{x_1 \rightarrow x_2, x_1 \rightarrow x_3, x_2 \rightarrow x_3\}$.

Definition 1. *Let X be the set of state variables. Then* a transition relation formula *is any formula over $X \cup X'$, where X' consists of "primed" versions x' of state variables $x \in X$ which represent the values of x in the successor state.*

Definition 2. *A* transition relation formula Φ *is* deterministic *iff there is a logically equivalent formula $\Phi_d = \chi \wedge \bigwedge_{x \in X} x' \leftrightarrow \phi_x$ where χ is a propositional formula over X and each $\phi_x, x \in X$ is a propositional formula over X.*

As is known from BDD-based reachability [5], a formula representing the successors of a given set of states with respect to a transition relation, when the latter two are represented as formulas, can be obtained by using the existential abstraction operation $\exists$ and renaming of variables in X' to the corresponding ones in X, expressed as $[X/X']$.

Definition 3 (Successors). *Given a transition relation formula Φ and a formula ϕ, the* successor *of ϕ w.r.t. Φ (denoted by $succ_\Phi(\phi)$) is $(\exists X.(\phi \wedge \Phi))[X/X']$. For sequences $\Phi_1, \ldots, \Phi_m$ we define $succ_{\Phi_1; \ldots; \Phi_m}(\phi) = succ_{\Phi_m}(\cdots succ_{\Phi_1}(\phi) \cdots)$.*

If the number of formulas in the base T is n, then it would seem that we would have to consider all 2^n different subsets when looking at the possible successor belief states with respect to a given action. We can, however, incompletely and with a complexity reduction from 2^n to n, analyze possible successor belief states for every member of T separately.

Theorem 1. $succ_\Phi(\alpha \wedge \beta) \models succ_\Phi(\alpha) \wedge succ_\Phi(\beta)$ *for any transition relation Φ.*

Proof. We apply the following sequence of equivalences and consequences to each of the variables in X in $\exists X.(\alpha \wedge \beta \wedge \Phi)$, starting from the innermost one, and resulting in $\exists X.(\alpha \wedge \Phi) \wedge \exists X.(\beta \wedge \Phi)$.

$$
\begin{aligned}
\exists x.(\alpha \wedge \beta \wedge \Phi) &\equiv (\alpha \wedge \beta \wedge \Phi)[\top/x] \vee (\alpha \wedge \beta \wedge \Phi)[\bot/x] \\
&\equiv (\alpha[\top/x] \wedge \beta[\top/x] \wedge \Phi[\top/x]) \vee (\alpha[\bot/x] \wedge \beta[\bot/x] \wedge \Phi[\bot/x]) \\
&\models ((\alpha[\top/x] \wedge \Phi[\top/x]) \vee (\alpha[\bot/x] \wedge \Phi[\bot/x])) \\
&\quad \wedge ((\beta[\top/x] \wedge \Phi[\top/x]) \vee (\beta[\bot/x] \wedge \Phi[\bot/x])) \\
&\equiv (\exists x.(\alpha \wedge \Phi)) \wedge (\exists x.(\beta \wedge \Phi))
\end{aligned}
$$

So considering every base formula separately gives *correct* information about successor belief states. But not all information is obtained this way, as the converse of the logical consequence in Theorem 1 does not hold.

Example 2. Consider ϕ_1 that represents the set $\{s_1\}$ and ϕ_2 that represents the set $\{s_2\}$, and Φ that represents the transition relation $\{(s_1, s_3), (s_2, s_3)\}$. Since $\phi_1 \wedge \phi_2 \equiv \bot$, also $\text{succ}_\Phi(\phi_1 \wedge \phi_2) \equiv \bot$. But $\text{succ}_\Phi(\phi_1) \wedge \text{succ}_\Phi(\phi_2)$ represents s_3.

A relation R is *injective* if for all z, whenever xRz and yRz, $x = y$. This means that an action and a successor state determine the predecessor state uniquely. For injective relations the image of conjunction coincides with the conjunction of the images.

Lemma 1. *Let Φ be a transition relation formula that represents an injective relation. Then $\text{succ}_\Phi(\phi \wedge \phi') \equiv \text{succ}_\Phi(\phi) \wedge \text{succ}_\Phi(\phi')$,*

Many actions in standard benchmark problems for classical planning are injective as required in Lemma 1, when restricted to the part of the state space reachable from the initial states, but partially observable problems typically are not. Hence an important problem is the identification of actions and formulas ϕ_1 and ϕ_2 that satisfy $\text{succ}_\Phi(\phi \wedge \phi') \equiv \text{succ}_\Phi(\phi) \wedge \text{succ}_\Phi(\phi')$ even without the action being injective. This is critical for being able to analyze problems efficiently without having to look at all possible combinations of component beliefs.

Nevertheless, in many interesting problems, reasoning about actions is possible even without exhaustive analysis of all combinations of component beliefs.

Example 3. Consider Sorting Networks with three inputs. The shortest plan does compare&swaps for the input pairs $(1, 3)$, $(1, 2)$ and $(2, 3)$, generating the belief states $(x_3 \rightarrow x_1)$, $(x_2 \rightarrow x_1) \wedge (x_3 \rightarrow x_1)$, and $(x_2 \rightarrow x_1) \wedge (x_3 \rightarrow x_1) \wedge (x_3 \rightarrow x_2)$.

Example 4. Consider Sorting Networks with four inputs. The shortest plan consists of compare&swap operations for the input pairs $(1, 3), (2, 4), (1, 2), (3, 4)$ and $(2, 3)$. The first two actions produce the belief state $(x_3 \rightarrow x_1) \wedge (x_4 \rightarrow x_2)$. After that, the third action, swapping 1 and 2, turns the belief state to

$$(x_3 \rightarrow x_1) \wedge (x_2 \rightarrow x_1) \wedge (x_4 \rightarrow x_1) \wedge ((x_3 \wedge x_4) \rightarrow x_2)$$

that contains $((x_3 \wedge x_4) \rightarrow x_2)$. This implication is only obtained as the image of $(x_3 \rightarrow x_1) \wedge (x_4 \rightarrow x_2)$, and is not obtained from any one $x_i \rightarrow x_j$ alone.

More generally, for the sorting network problems, swap actions create new beliefs from complex combinations of prior beliefs.

While relatively good plans can be found with these implications $x_i \rightarrow x_j$ as the beliefs in a conjunctive belief representation, also for larger numbers of inputs, the smallest plans require increasingly complex beliefs. For example, the sorting network with 20 inputs that has the smallest number of layers has $(x_3 \wedge x_7 \wedge x_{10} \wedge x_{11}) \rightarrow (x_8 \vee x_9 \vee x_{12})$ as one of the intermediate beliefs.

Below we list the maximum clause lengths encountered in the best known (smallest number of layers) sorting networks for up to 20 inputs. Here n is the number of inputs and s is the length of the longest clause in the CNF beliefs.

n	s	n	s	n	s	n	s	n	s	n	s	n	s	n	s	n	s
3	2	4	3	5	3	6	3	7	3	8	3	9	4	10	4	11	4
12	5	13	6	14	5	15	6	16	5	17	5	18	6	19	6	20	7

Many other problems have a far simpler belief space, and it is often enough to look at the components of beliefs one at a time.

Example 5. Consider a rectangular grid, where a robot's position in the East-West direction is indicated by state variables $x_0, \ldots, x_9$, and the location in the North-South direction by state variables $y_0, \ldots, y_9$. The "move north" action is

$$\bigwedge_{i=0}^{9} (x_i' \leftrightarrow x_i) \wedge \bigwedge_{j=1}^{8} (y_j' \leftrightarrow y_{j-1}) \wedge (y_9' \leftrightarrow (y_9 \vee y_8)) \wedge \neg y_0'$$

with movement at the north wall having no effect. Moves to the other three cardinal directions are analogous. There is a unique initial location for the robot.

$$(\bigvee_{i=0}^{9} x_i) \wedge (\bigvee_{i=0}^{9} y_i) \wedge \bigwedge_{i=0}^{8} \bigwedge_{j=i+1}^{9} \neg(x_i \wedge x_j) \bigwedge_{i=0}^{8} \bigwedge_{j=i+1}^{9} \neg(y_i \wedge y_j)$$

The beliefs in this problem are the conjuncts of the formula for the initial belief state, as well as all sub-intervals of $[0, 9]$ for positions on both X and the Y axes.

$$\{\bigvee_{i=j}^{k} x_i | 0 \leq j \leq k \leq 9\} \cup \{\bigvee_{i=j}^{k} y_i | 0 \leq j \leq k \leq 9\}$$

Reasoning about location can be done independently for X and Y coordinates, one formula at a time.

4   Algorithm for Identifying a Base

We give an algorithm for finding a base T for a conformant planning problem.

1. We start from the initial state description $\phi_1 \wedge \cdots \wedge \phi_n$, where the minimal conjuncts $\phi_1, \ldots, \phi_n$ are taken to be the tentative base T.
2. Pick some action a and a consistent subset $P \subseteq T$, and do the following.
   a) Compute $\sigma = \text{succ}_{\Phi_a}(\bigwedge_{\phi \in P} \phi)$.
   b) Make the minimal conjuncts of σ explicit as $\sigma = \psi_1 \wedge \cdots \wedge \psi_m$.
   c) Add $\psi_1, \cdots, \psi_m$ to T, while eliminating duplicates modulo equivalence.
3. Repeat the previous step until T does not change.

Here we need the *existential abstraction* operation and the *logical equivalence* test. In our implementation – which is discussed later – we have used Ordered Binary Decision Diagrams (OBDD) [4]. Other representations of Boolean functions could be used instead, with different trade-offs between efficiency and size.

The mapping of images σ to conjuncts determines the formulas in the base. The most general solution is to take the conjuncts to be all the *prime implicates* of σ, that is, the minimal clauses logically entailed by σ, but as we will see, something far simpler often works very well in practice.

The number of subsets P of T is exponential in $|T|$, and therefore this computation is in general not feasible. This is exactly as expected, as not all parts of a reduction from the EXPSPACE-complete conformant planning [8,12] to the PSPACE-complete classical planning [6] can be polynomial time.

However, it turns out that it is often sufficient to limit to subsets $P \subseteq T$ of small cardinality. Often $|P| \leq 1$ is sufficient, so only the empty set and all 1-element subsets of T need to be considered.

The next theorem shows that the general form of our base construction is sufficient to identify a conjunctive decompositions of the belief space in the sense that no matter which action sequence is taken starting in the initial belief state, any reachable belief state can be represented as a conjunction of some subset of formulas in the base.

Theorem 2. *For a formula I and a sequence $\Phi_1, \ldots, \Phi_m$ of transition relation formulas, $\text{succ}_{\Phi_1, \ldots, \Phi_m}(I) \equiv \bigwedge B$ for some $B \subseteq T$.*

Proof. The proof is by induction on the length of the action sequence m, with the claim of the theorem as the induction hypothesis.

Base case $m = 0$: The initial value of T is the conjuncts of the initial state formula, exactly corresponding to the only belief state reachable by not taking any action at all. Hence $\text{succ}_\epsilon(I)$ for the empty sequence ϵ is representable in terms of T.

Inductive case $i \geq 1$: By the induction hypothesis, $\text{succ}_{\Phi_1; \cdots; \Phi_{i-1}}(I) \equiv \bigwedge B$ for some $B \subseteq T$. The algorithm goes through all actions, including one with transition relation formula Φ_i, and through all subsets of T, including B. Hence it will compute $\sigma = \text{succ}_{\bigwedge B}(\Phi_i)$, and the conjuncts of σ, however they are identified, will be included in T. Hence $\text{succ}_{\Phi_1; \cdots; \Phi_i}(I) \equiv \bigwedge B$ for some $B \subseteq T$.

Interestingly, the proof shows that – from the completeness point of view – it is not important how the formula σ is split into conjuncts at step (2b) of the algorithm for finding a base. Essentially, splitting σ to a single conjunct as

$\sigma = \phi_1$ would simply mean that we enumerate all possible beliefs (formulas) reachable from the initial belief state. In this light, Theorem 2 is not surprising.

The important thing in the algorithm – from the scalability point of view – is the splitting of σ to small conjuncts, so that not every belief state needs to be generated explicitly. Instead, the space of all belief states is conjunctively decomposed to smaller formulas, contained in T, so that any belief state can be represented by some subset $B \subseteq T$. The base T may therefore be exponentially smaller than the set of all belief states reachable from the initial belief state.

Finally, we point out that the algorithm does in general not determine reachability of belief states exactly: actions are considered in belief states (conjunctions of subsets of T) that are not actually reachable from the initial belief state. Hence T may contain formulas that could never be true in a reachable state. This is an obvious source of inefficiency. We comment more on this in Sect. 6.1.

5   Reduction from Conformant to Classical Planning

We will represent the conformant planning problem as a full-information classical planning problem, with each formula $\phi \in T$ represented by a single state variable x_ϕ. When solving the full-information planning problem, a state s represents the belief state that corresponds to the formula $\bigwedge \{\phi \in T | s \models x_\phi\}$. The set of state variables in the classical planning problem is $X_T = \{x_\phi | \phi \in T\}$.

Additionally, we define the actions, the initial state, and the goal formula.

For every action a of the original (conformant) problem, we define a new action a' that changes the belief state encoded with the state variables in X_T in a way that corresponds to how a changes the belief state.

5.1   Effects

We define $\mathrm{causes}_a^{\phi_1,\dots,\phi_n}(\phi)$ as holding if ϕ is one of the conjuncts in $\mathrm{succ}_{\Phi_a}(\phi_1 \wedge \cdots \wedge \phi_n)$. We define $\mathrm{minCauses}_a^{\phi_1,\dots,\phi_n}(\phi)$ as holding if

- ϕ is one of the conjuncts in $\mathrm{succ}_{\Phi_a}(\phi_1 \wedge \cdots \wedge \phi_n)$, and
- ϕ is not a conjunct of $\mathrm{succ}_{\Phi_a}(\phi_{i_1} \wedge \cdots \wedge \phi_{i_j})$ for any $\{i_1, \dots, i_j\} \subset \{1, \dots, n\}$.

We iterate over all subsets $\{\phi_1, \dots, \phi_n\}$ of T and all $\phi \in T$, and add the following effects to the action we are constructing.

- If $\mathrm{minCauses}_a^{\phi_1,\dots,\phi_n}(\phi)$ and $\phi_i \not\models \phi$ for all $i \in \{1, \dots, n\}$ then a' has effect $x_{\phi_1} \wedge \cdots \wedge x_{\phi_n} \triangleright x_\phi$.
- If not $\mathrm{causes}_a^\phi(\phi)$, then a' has effect $(x_\phi \wedge C) \triangleright \neg x_\phi$ where C is the conjunction of all $\neg(\phi_{i_1} \wedge \cdots \wedge \phi_{i_k})$ such that $\mathrm{minCauses}_a^{\phi_{i_1},\dots,\phi_{i_k}}(\phi)$.[1]

---

[1] The left-hand side of this conditional effect can be simplified by replacing all occurrences of ϕ by $\top$, as the effect does something only if ϕ is true when the action is taken. This modification is is needed to maximize Graphplan-style [3] parallelism.

Again, this computation takes exponential time in the cardinality of T. And, similarly to the computation of a base, this computation can be limited to "small" subsets S of T. For the sorting network problems, for example, classical planning instances that have non-optimal solutions can be produced with $|S| \leq 2$, but for higher number of inputs larger sets S are needed to find optimal solutions.

5.2 Preconditions

An action can be taken only if its precondition must be true. For this we need all *minimal consistent subsets* of T from which the precondition follows.

Definition 4. *A set $D \subseteq T$ is relevant for a formula χ, if D is consistent, $D \models \chi$, and there is no D' such that $D \subset D'$, D' is consistent, $D' \models \chi$.*

Let $a = \langle \chi, E \rangle$ be an action. Let P be all the sets $D \subseteq T$ relevant for χ. Now the precondition of a' is $\bigvee_{p \in P}(\bigwedge\{x_\phi | \phi \in p\})$.

Clearly, for actions a with the trivial precondition $\top$, the precondition of a' is similarly $\top$. More generally, there may be an exponential number of relevant subsets $D \subseteq T$, so there is no guarantee that this computation is always feasible.

Relevant subsets of T for χ are closely related to *minimal unsatisfiable sets* (MUS) [1,10]: a relevant subset for ϕ is a MUS of $T \cup \{\neg\phi\}$ that contains $\neg\phi$.

Lemma 2. *Assume $\neg\phi \notin P$. Then $P \subseteq T$ is a relevant set for ϕ if and only if $P \cup \{\neg\phi\}$ is a minimal unsatisfiable set of $T \cup \{\neg\phi\}$.*

Proof. Since $P \cup \{\neg\phi\}$ is unsatisfiable, $P \models \phi$. Since $P \cup \{\neg\phi\}$ is minimal unsatisfiable, we have $P_0 \cup \{\neg\phi\}$ satisfiable and hence $P_0 \not\models \phi$ for all $P_0 \subset P$. Since $P \cup \{\neg\phi\}$ is minimal unsatisfiable, P is satisfiable. Hence by the definition of relevance, P is a relevant set for ϕ.

The computation of minimal inconsistent subsets is expensive, and as before, can be limited to "small" subsets.

5.3 Goals

The goal formula is computed similarly to the preconditions as a disjunction of conjunctions of minimal consistent subsets of T that logically entail the original goal formula G. For goals of the form $G = \gamma_1 \wedge \cdots \wedge \gamma_n$ we can determine the entailing subsets of T separately for each γ_i.

6 Implementation

We have implemented all steps for translating conformant planning to classical planning. The logical operations could be implemented with any class of formulas that can represent any Boolean function, but we chose to use ordered binary decision diagrams OBDDs for three reasons: simplicity, logical simplifications provided by OBDDs canonicity, and constant time equivalence tests.

In our reduction from conformant planning to classical planning there are the three exponential components, which we have approximated by not going through all subsets of formulas, but instead only all "small" subsets of cardinality $\leq n$ for some small n. These three parameters, which limits the cardinalities of these subsets, are used in

1. identifying the base (Sect. 4),
2. synthesizing the effects of actions (Sect. 5.1), and
3. synthesizing the formulas for the preconditions and the goal (Sect. 5.2).

When we use the values 1, 2 and 1 for these three parameters, respectively, we indicate this as the configuration $(1, 2, 1)$.

We first experimented with Sorting Networks, due to their difficulty for existing planners. They are parameterized by the number i of inputs, have i state variables, and yield a base of quadratic size with configuration $(1, 2, 1)$, and a base of cubic size with $(2, 2, 1)$. With $(1, 2, 1)$ we can find non-optimal and not very good solutions until 20 inputs, and better non-optimal solutions not quite as far. This problem is not solvable with the $(1, 1, 1)$ configuration.

Many other benchmark problems are harder than sorting networks in terms of having a far higher number of state variables. However, in many cases this is balanced by them being solvable (even optimally) with the easiest $(1, 1, 1)$ configuration. The number of base formulas is in many cases several hundreds or thousands, and brute force generation of the base in configuration $(2, 1, 1)$ as well as synthesis of actions in configuration $(1, 2, 1)$ become infeasible.

An important part of future work is to utilize structural properties of the problem instances to perform these computations far more efficiently, without having to blindly go through all or most N-element subsets of the base.

6.1   Use of Invariants to Reduce the Base

The use of *invariants*, formulas that hold in all reachable states of a transition system, is common in planning methods that work with partial state representation. In the algorithm in Sect. 4, invariants help ignore those formulas that are never true in any reachable state, or that are true in all reachable states. This leads to a smaller base. We use a basic algorithm for finding 2-literal invariant clauses [13]. For instance, the formulas $\neg(x_i \land x_j)$ in Example 5 are part of every belief state, and therefore the possibility of them being false can be ignored.

7   Experiments

We have done experiments with a collection of standard benchmark problems. Of special interest is Sorting Networks, with complex belief space and complex interactions between beliefs. Results are given in Table 1. We list runtimes, the numbers of actions as well as the number of state variables in the original conformant and in the classical instances. The latter number equals the number of

Table 1. Results for SORTNET. C: *Configuration*; X: *variables in the problem*; Xc: *variables in the translated problem*; A: *actions*; MpC: *Madagascar runtime* ; FF: *FF runtime* ; PG: T_0 *runtime with FF*; OOM: *out of memory*

Instance	C	X	Xc	A	MpC	FF	PG
sort4	(2,2,1)	4	17	6	0.00	0.00	0.07
sort5	(2,2,1)	5	68	10	0.12	0.02	0.53
sort6	(2,2,1)	6	239	15	7.64	2.57	5.73
sort7	(2,2,1)	7	790	21	3006.24	OOM	21.26
sort6	(1,2,1)	6	15	15	0.01	0.00	5.73
sort7	(1,2,1)	7	21	21	0.02	0.00	21.26
sort8	(1,2,1)	8	28	28	0.06	0.00	$0.21(K_0)$
sort9	(1,2,1)	9	36	36	0.12	0.00	$0.38(K_0)$
sort10	(1,2,1)	10	45	45	0.26	0.00	$0.73(K_0)$
sort15	(1,2,1)	15	105	105	2.47	0.04	$15.92(K_0)$
sort18	(1,2,1)	18	153	153	7.94	0.17	$121.71(K_0)$

formulas in the base. Palacios & Geffner's [11] T_0 planner uses the K_1 translation by default, but in cases where it does not yield any solutions, we have switched to the K_0 translation, as indicated in the table. We have used the FF [9] and Madagascar [14] planners to solve our PDDL instances. Madagascar constructs *parallel* plans, and an optimality criterion for sorting networks is the number of *layers* of the sorting network, with each layer containing one or more compare&swap actions so that each input is only sorted by at most one of the actions. However, it turned out that although pairs of compare&swaps like on $(1,3)$ and on $(2,4)$ do not interfere when the state variables are the input values, the actions after our translation do interfere, as they impact and depend on the same beliefs $x_i \to x_j$, and hence Madagascar cannot benefit from the parallelism.

All sorting network problems are solvable with the configuration $(1,2,1)$, by looking at the joint images of *pairs* of beliefs of the form $x_i \to x_j$, but this is insufficient to find optimal solutions (see Example 4). The generation of the PDDL in these cases is fast, less than 10 s even for large instances. On these problems we are quite competitive with T_0. As pointed out earlier, optimal solutions e.g. with 20 inputs seem to require the configuration $(7,7,1)$, which leads to quite large PDDL representations.

With the configuration $(2,2,1)$ also formulas $x_i \wedge x_j \to x_k$ are included in the base, and this allows (in principle) optimal solutions to be found until at least 8 inputs, as discussed earlier. While our experiments did not use optimal planners, the configuration $(2,2,1)$ still allows us to find better sub-optimal plans than what can be found with configuration $(1,2,1)$. But, as the number of formulas in the base is cubic in the number of inputs, and not quadratic, the PDDL translation is far bigger, and the planners do not scale up as far as with the

Table 2. Runtimes of a number of benchmark problems

Instance	X	Xc	A	MpC	FF	PG
corners-square-p40	80	1722	4	1.69	0.30	0.53
corners-square-p84	168	7310	4	51.67	5.60	11.71
corners-square-p100	200	10302	4	115.85	11.32	25.14
corners-square-p120	240	14762	4	283.96	27.06	57.05
corners-square-p140	280	29375	4	1492.39	159.50	90.33
corners-square-p200	400	40602	4	3285.06	380.47	485.10
corners-cube-p27	81	1218	6	0.70	0.13	3.80
corners-cube-p52	156	4293	6	13.11	2.31	147.62
corners-cube-p55	165	4788	6	17.37	2.71	226.28
corners-cube-p60	180	5673	6	27.00	4.82	366.48
corners-cube-p75	225	8778	6	75.20	15.01	1463.35
square-center-p24	48	1200	4	0.53	0.11	0.15
square-center-p92	184	17112	4	320.81	80.09	8.99
cube-center-p19	57	1140	6	0.47	0.09	0.15
cube-center-p63	189	12096	6	137.50	25.35	6.33
cube-center-p67	201	13668	6	193.58	38.12	8.01

$(1, 2, 1)$ configuration. Also, the runtimes for generating the PDDL grows very quickly with the increasing number of inputs.

For the rest of the benchmark problems the situation is quite different, as the configuration $(1, 1, 1)$ is always sufficient. The scalability of our approach is only limited by the size of the base, as we only have to look at each formula in the base in isolation at each stage of the translation process. Data on a collection of standard benchmarks similar to that used by Palacios and Geffner [11] are given in Tables 2 and 3. Our runtimes in comparison to Palacios & Geffner's T_0 [11] are in some cases comparable, and in many cases clearly behind, for example in *ring*, *safe* and *blocksworld*. For the latter two producing the PDDL is slow due to high number of actions and a large base. Notice that the listed runtimes do not include the generation of the PDDL. This time is often substantial. For example, bomb100-100 took 636.9 s (10100 actions), bomb20-20 took 0.65 s (420 actions), while Sortnet with 9 inputs and configuration $(1,2,1)$ took 0.24 s (36 actions). The time is dominated by image computation, which we believe can be substantially sped up, especially when actions are simple. Planner by To et al. [18] is often comparable to that of Palacios and Geffner, but in many cases scale up further in the benchmark series.

8   Related Work

Baral, Kreinovich and Trejo [2] investigate 3-valued belief state representations, in which state variables are *true*, *false*, or *unknown*. This form of incompleteness is equivalent to representing belief states as sets (conjunctions) of literals. Baral et al. demonstrate how many types of interesting problems are efficiently solvable with this type of representation, and that the complexity is substantially reduced, down to PSPACE, which is the same as with classical planning.

Table 3. Results from a number of benchmark problems

Instance	X	Xc	A	MpC	FF	PG
comm-p10	69	314	59	0.11	0.00	0.05
comm-p15	99	454	84	0.26	0.00	0.05
comm-p20	245	1130	208	11.94	0.02	0.16
bomb20-20	40	60	420	0.00	0.00	0.05
bomb100-5	105	110	505	0.06	0.00	0.21
bomb100-60	160	220	6060	0.12	0.05	1.04
bomb100-100	200	300	10100	0.24	1.39	2.40
coins-p10	34	200	40	0.41	0.00	0.1
coins-p12	76	1866	88	10340.96	0.09	0.1
coins-p16	86	2020	110	TO	0.19	0.09
coins-p18	86	2020	110	TO	0.18	0.06
coins-p20	86	2020	110	TO	0.17	0.07
uts-p1	5	41	4	0.00	0.00	0.01
uts-p2	9	892	16	2.65	0.10	0.01
uts-p3	13	11354	36	5004.71	104.45	0.03
logistics-p2-2-2	20	48	30	0.00	0.00	0.02
logistics-p4-3-3	69	201	156	0.03	0.00	0.03
uts-l01	5	41	4	0.00	0.00	0.01
uts-l02	9	882	10	1.52	0.08	0.02
safe-p5	6	78	5	0.00	0.00	0.00
safe-p10	11	2102	10	29.09	0.70	0.01

Palacios and Geffner [11] propose an approach to conformant planning that is based on dependencies of state variable values on the initial values of some other state variables. Their literals KL/t could be viewed as implications $t \rightarrow KL$, and the *merges*, inferring KL from $\bigwedge_{t \in T} KL/t \rightarrow KL$ as, as a form of logical deduction, analysis by cases. Their planner can in general solve more of the standard benchmark problems on conformant planning than ours, but our planner outperforms it with the sorting network problems, because Palacios and Geffner's method leads to exponentially large classical planning problems in this case. Further, Palacios&Geffner limit to deterministic actions, whereas our work covers arbitrary actions, including non-deterministic ones.

To et al. [15] used DNF as a belief state representation, then turned to prime implicates [16] and CNF [17], demonstrating different trade-offs. In these works, belief states are sets of formulas, not valuations of propositional variables like in our work, and no reduction to the classical planning problem is considered.

9   Conclusion

We have investigated the representation of belief states as vectors of truth values. This representation attempts to lower the complexity of belief space planning by replacing the combinatorially far harder notion of formulas by much easier states. We have shown our methods to be useful even when strict limits are imposed on how thoroughly an approximate belief space representation is created. These limits risk losing completeness. An important topic for further research is obtaining completeness guarantees even under these size limits. Future work also includes generalizing the results to *partial observability*. Observations help increase the accuracy of the beliefs. In this case we would expect to be able to similarly often achieve an exponential complexity reduction.

References

1. Bailey, J., Stuckey, P.J.: Discovery of minimal unsatisfiable subsets of constraints using hitting set dualization. In: Hermenegildo, M.V., Cabeza, D. (eds.) PADL 2005. LNCS, vol. 3350, pp. 174–186. Springer, Heidelberg (2005). https://doi.org/10.1007/978-3-540-30557-6_14
2. Baral, C., Kreinovich, V., Trejo, R.: Computational complexity of planning and approximate planning in the presence of incompleteness. Artif. Intell. **122**(1), 241–267 (2000)
3. Blum, A.L., Furst, M.L.: Fast planning through planning graph analysis. Artif. Intell. **90**(1–2), 281–300 (1997)
4. Bryant, R.E.: Symbolic Boolean manipulation with ordered binary decision diagrams. ACM Comput. Surv. **24**(3), 293–318 (1992)
5. Burch, J.R., Clarke, E.M., Long, D.E., MacMillan, K.L., Dill, D.L.: Symbolic model checking for sequential circuit verification. IEEE Trans. Comput. Aided Des. Integr. Circuits Syst. **13**(4), 401–424 (1994)
6. Bylander, T.: The computational complexity of propositional STRIPS planning. Artif. Intell. **69**(1–2), 165–204 (1994)
7. Geffner, T., Geffner, H.: Compact policies for non-deterministic fully observable planning as sat. In: ICAPS 2018. Proceedings of the Twenty-Eighth International Conference on Automated Planning and Scheduling, pp. 88–96. AAAI Press (2018)
8. Haslum, P., Jonsson, P.: Some results on the complexity of planning with incomplete information. In: Biundo, S., Fox, M. (eds.) ECP 1999. LNCS (LNAI), vol. 1809, pp. 308–318. Springer, Heidelberg (2000). https://doi.org/10.1007/10720246_24
9. Hoffmann, J., Nebel, B.: The FF planning system: fast plan generation through heuristic search. J. Artif. Intell. Res. **14**, 253–302 (2001)
10. Liffiton, M.H., Sakallah, K.A.: On finding all minimally unsatisfiable subformulas. In: Bacchus, F., Walsh, T. (eds.) SAT 2005. LNCS, vol. 3569, pp. 173–186. Springer, Heidelberg (2005). https://doi.org/10.1007/11499107_13

11. Palacios, H., Geffner, H.: Compiling uncertainty away in conformant planning problems with bounded width. J. Artif. Intell. Res. **35**, 623–675 (2009)
12. Rintanen, J.: Complexity of planning with partial observability. In: ICAPS 2004. Proceedings of the Fourteenth International Conference on Automated Planning and Scheduling, pp. 345–354. AAAI Press (2004)
13. Rintanen, J.: Regression for classical and nondeterministic planning. In: ECAI 2008. Proceedings of the 18th European Conference on Artificial Intelligence, pp. 568–571. IOS Press (2008)
14. Rintanen, J.: Planning as satisfiability: heuristics. Artif. Intell. **193**, 45–86 (2012)
15. To, S., Pontelli, E., Son, T.: A conformant planner with explicit disjunctive representation of belief states. In: Proceedings of the 19th International Conference on Automated Planning and Scheduling, pp. 305–312. AAAI Press (2009)
16. To, S., Son, T., Pontelli, E.: On the use of prime implicates in conformant planning. In: Proceedings of the AAAI Conference on Artificial Intelligence, pp. 1205–1210. AAAI Press (2010)
17. To, S.T., Son, T.C., Pontelli, E.: A new approach to conformant planning using CNF. In: Proceedings of the 20th International Conference on Automated Planning and Scheduling, pp. 169–176. AAAI Press (2010)
18. To, S.T., Son, T.C., Pontelli, E.: A generic approach to planning in the presence of incomplete information: theory and implementation. Artif. Intell. **227**, 1–51 (2015)
19. Tu, P.H., Son, T.C., Baral, C.: Reasoning and planning with sensing actions, incomplete information, and static causal laws using answer set programming. Theory Pract. Logic Program. **7**, 1–74 (2006)

Clustering-Based Network Inference with Submodular Maximization

Lulu Kong[1], Chao Gao[1,2($\boxtimes$)], and Shuang Peng[1]

[1] College of Computer and Information Science, SouthWest University, Chongqing 400715, China
[2] College of Artificial Intelligence, Optics, and Electronics (iOPEN), Northwestern Polytechnical University, Xi'an 710072, China
cgao@nwpu.edu.cn

Abstract. To infer the underlying diffusion network, most existing approaches are almost based on an initial potential edge set constructed according to the observed data (i.e., the infection times of nodes) to infer the diffusion edges. Nevertheless, there are relatively few studies that combine the infection times and infection statuses of nodes to preprocess the edge set so as to improve the accuracy and efficiency of network inference. To bridge the gap, this paper proposes a two-stage inference algorithm, namely, *Clustering-based Network Inference with Submodular Maximization* (CNISM). In the first stage, based on a well-designed metric that fuses the infection times and infection statuses of nodes, we firstly fast infer effective candidate edges from the initial candidate edge set by clustering, then capture the cluster structures of nodes according to the effective candidate edges, which is helpful for the inference of subsequent algorithm. In the second stage, the cluster structures of nodes are integrated into MulTree, which is a submodular maximization algorithm based on multiple trees, to infer the topology of the diffusion network. Experimental results on both synthetic and real-world networks show that compared with the comparative algorithms, our framework is generally superior to them in terms of inference accuracy with a low computational cost.

Keywords: Diffusion network inference · Cluster structure · Submodular maximization

1 Introduction

Nowadays, the diffusion of information and propagation of diseases are becoming more and more ubiquitous and prompt on the information networks and social networks. Meanwhile, the dynamics of propagation process over the network have attracted extensive attention in many areas, such as viral marketing [6], influence maximization [13], propagation source localization [2] and so on. However, the underlying network over which the diffusions and propagations spread is always unobserved and unavailable in reality. Therefore, the diffusion network inference is of great importance for characterizing the propagation process.

© The Author(s), under exclusive license to Springer Nature Switzerland AG 2022
S. Khanna et al. (Eds.): PRICAI 2022, LNCS 13629, pp. 118–131, 2022.
https://doi.org/10.1007/978-3-031-20862-1_9

To infer the structure of the latent diffusion network, the main premise is that we can observe many different contagions (information, disease) spreading over the network. The spreading of a contagion will leave a trace, called a cascade. Generally, the details of diffusion process are difficult to observe, but the infection times of nodes can be easily acquired [8]. For example, we can note when fellow around is talking about a popular topic, but we do not know who told him/her about it in information diffusion.

Most existing methods are mainly divided into two categories, one is to infer the edges of the diffusion network (such as NetInf [8], MulTree [9]), the other is to infer not only the edges but also edge weights (such as ConNIe [18], NetRate [7]). Among them, the main idea of the first type is to establish the likelihood of observed data from the view that the contagion spreads as a directed tree through the network, then solve it by greedy algorithm. While the second type takes the conditional propagation probabilities or transmission rates between nodes as variables to establish the occurrence likelihood of cascades, then solve it by convex optimization. Although these methods can work well on small scale network datasets, their performance on slightly larger network datasets can be further improved. One of the reasons is that they usually only consider the infection times of nodes, and rarely combine the infection times with the infection statuses of the nodes for efficient inference. In addition, although individual literature (such as Dani [19]) jointly takes the information contained in the infection times and infection statuses of nodes into consideration, they can only infer the edges according to the ranking of specific metric of their design that lacks further judgment on the inferred edges, so it is difficult to ensure the accuracy of network inference.

To address the above problems, we make the first attempt to propose a *clustering fast inference model* based on a well-designed metric to preprocess the initial candidate edges. Specifically, we first design the clustering fast inference model to infer the effective candidate edges from all initial candidate edges, and further capture the cluster structures of nodes according to the effective candidate edges. Next, the cluster structures of nodes are input into a submodular maximization inference method to infer the topology of the diffusion network.

The contributions of this paper are summarized as follows.

- We investigate a relatively little-studied but important issue, i.e., how to preprocess all initial candidate edges by combining the infection times and infection statuses of nodes.
- We propose a novel two-stage inference framework CNISM to capture the cluster structures of nodes by preprocessing the initial candidate edges, and incorporate the cluster structures of nodes into a submodular function that is equivalent to the network inference problem.
- We design a novel computation way to calculate the transmission likelihood of each candidate edge in the first stage of the proposed method, which is first normalized inside the cascade and then normalized outside the cascade.
- We perform extensive experiments on both synthetic and real-world datasets, showing the effectiveness of the proposed framework.

2 Related Work

The inference of diffusion network is an inverse problem of propagation, i.e., the structure of a latent diffusion network supporting the diffusion process is inferred according to the partial observation results generated by the diffusion process. Existing methods of network inference can be classified into two main groups:

Inferring the Edges of Diffusion Network. The earlier classical methods are based on submodular maximization. Assuming that the contagion propagates as a directed tree, they built the observed cascades' likelihood, the logarithm of which has submodular property. Considering the most probable directed propagation tree of each cascade, i.e., the most possible way in which a diffusion process spreading over the network can create the cascade, NetInf [8] was proposed. MulTree [9] was developed to achieve higher accuracy by considering all possible directed propagation trees of each cascade. Later, many methods related to network structure property emerged [11,19,20]. To address the data scarcity issue in real-world, MCM [11] built a hierarchical graphical model, where all the diffusion networks share the same network prior, for effective network inference. Dani [19] was proposed to infer the network by preserving the community structure feature of the original network as much as possible. Further, considering that observed cascades are incomplete, NIIC [4] used a Monte-Carlo simulation method to complete the incomplete cascades.

Inferring the Edges and Edge Weights of Diffusion Network. The earlier classical methods are based on the convex optimization in that the log-likelihood of observed cascades to be maximized is a convex function. Assuming that the transmission probability between nodes is heterogeneous in a network, Con-NIe [18] inferred the conditional propagation probability between nodes. Taking transmission rates between nodes as variables, NetRate [7] built the likelihood of observed data according to the survival analysis theory. Due to the high computational complexity of this method, as far as we know, CENI [12] captured the cluster structures of nodes by the clustering embedding method for the first time before the formal inference step, which improves the efficiency of this method.

In conclusion, due to the high computational complexity of the second group, most existing methods belong to the first group. However, most works in the first group only consider the infection times of nodes, and few works study the influence of the combination of the infection times and infection statuses of nodes. In this work, inspired by CENI [12], we develop a general clustering fast inference model to preprocess the initial potential edges according to a well-designed metric that fuses the infection times and infection statuses of nodes.

3 Methodology

3.1 Problem Formulation

Problem Statement. Given a latent directed diffusion network $G^* = (V, E)$, where $V = \{v_1, v_2, \ldots, v_n\}$ denotes the set of nodes, E refers the set of edges, e.g., $(v_i, v_j) \in E$ indicates that the contagion once spread along this edge (v_i, v_j). Now, we only know the node set V and a set of information cascades observed over it, denoted by $C = \{c_1, c_2, \ldots, c_m\}$, where $c_r = \{(v_1, t_1^r), (v_2, t_2^r), \ldots, (v_n, t_n^r)\}$ is the r-th cascade, (v_j, t_j^r) means that the r-th cascade infected node v_j at time t_j^r, and $0 < t_j^r < +\infty$. If the r-th cascade did not infect node v_j, then $t_j^r = +\infty$. Therefore, our aim is to infer the edge set E of the unobserved directed network G^* according to the observed data C, and we refer to the reconstucted or inferred diffusion network as $\hat{G}$.

Model Formulation. (1) *Cluster structures of nodes.* For each node in the network, we assume that there is an associated subset of nodes, which contains potential parent members that are very likely to infect this node. We denote these subsets by $CS = \{CS_1, CS_2, \ldots, CS_N\}$, where CS_j is the set of cluster members associated with the node v_j. (2) *Propagation model.* In this article, we use a variant of the independent cascade model [14] to simulate the spreading process of information. In this model, each node can only be infected by one parent node, and each infected node has only one chance to independently infect its uninfected neighbor nodes with transmission probability β. Now, considering that node v_i gets infected at time t_i and successfully infects node v_j at time t_j $(t_i < t_j)$, then we assume that their infection time difference (i.e., $\Delta t = t_j - t_i$) follows a pairwise transmission likelihood $f(t_j | t_i; \alpha_{ij})$, where α_{ij} represents the contagion transmission rate from node v_i to node v_j. Although in some scenarios it may be possible to estimate a non-parametric likelihood empirically, for the sake of simplicity, we consider three well-known parametric models (i.e., transmission time distributions) as in the previous literature [7–9,18](as shown in Table 1).

Table 1. Pairwise transmission likelihood.

Model	Transmission likelihood $f(t_j\|t_i; \alpha_{ij})$	Applicable scenarios
Exponential (Exp)	$\begin{cases} \alpha_{ij} \cdot e^{-\alpha_{ij}(t_j - t_i)} & \text{if } t_i < t_j \\ 0 & \text{otherwise} \end{cases}$	Information diffusion between users
Power-law (Pow)	$\begin{cases} \frac{\alpha_{ij}}{\delta} \cdot \left(\frac{t_j - t_i}{\delta}\right)^{-1 - \alpha_{ij}} & \text{if } t_i + \delta < t_j \\ 0 & \text{otherwise} \end{cases}$	Information diffusion between users
Rayleigh (Ray)	$\begin{cases} \alpha_{ij}(t_j - t_i) e^{-\frac{1}{2}\alpha_{ij}(t_j - t_i)^2} & \text{if } t_i < t_j \\ 0 & \text{otherwise} \end{cases}$	Diseases propagation among people

3.2 Proposed Method: CNISM

To accurately and efficiently infer the topology of an underlying slightly larger scale diffusion network, we develop a novel two-stage method, Clustering-based Network Inference with Submodular Maximization (CNISM). Figure 1 shows the whole framework of our method.

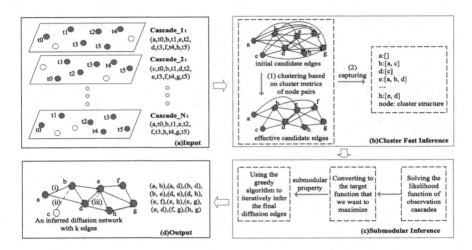

Fig. 1. An overview of the proposed approach. (a) the observed cascades. Two key inference models, i.e., (b) the clustering fast inference model: (1) fast inferring the effective candidate edges by clustering, (2) capturing the cluster structures of nodes, and (c) the submodular maximization inference model based on multiple trees. (d) the inferred edges: (i) the black solid edge indicates the correct inferred edge, (ii) the black dashed edge indicates the true edge that has not been inferred, (iii) the red solid edge indicates the incorrect inferred edge. (Color figure online)

Clustering Fast Inference Based on Final Normalized Transmission Likelihood and Infection Mutual Information

Definition 1. Candidate edge. If the infection time of node v_i is less than the infection time of node v_j in any cascades, there might exist a directed edge going from node v_i point to node v_j, i.e., called a candidate edge or potential edge.

In the first stage, we aim to capture the cluster structures of nodes from all possible candidate edges. Firstly, constructing an initial candidate edge set $E\text{-}initial = \{(v_i, v_j) | \forall c_r \in C, t_i^r < t_j^r\}$. Secondly, building a cluster metric that incorporates the infection times and infection statuses of nodes to identify the cluster members of each node. According to the above, when we know the infection times of nodes, the transmission likelihood $f(t_j | t_i; \alpha_{ij})$ can quantify the transmission possibility between nodes to a certain extent. However, we find that this computation way only considers the infection time difference between two nodes, and does not address the influence of other infected nodes.

For example, in Fig. 2 the infection time of node v_i is less than that of the node v_j in these three cascades, so there is a directed candidate edge going from node v_i to node v_j, so does $(v_i \rightarrow v_k)$ and $(v_k \rightarrow v_j)$. Among them, the infection time differences between node v_i and node v_j are 4, 6 and 4, respectively. According to Table 1, the transmission likelihood of candidate edge (v_i, v_j) in the $r1\text{-}th$ cascade is larger than that in the $r2\text{-}th$ cascade and is equal to that in the $r3\text{-}th$ cascade. Moreover, in the $r3\text{-}th$ cascade, there is another node v_k whose infection time is greater than that of node v_i, and their time difference($=2$) is less than the time difference($=4$) of candidate edge (v_i, v_j). Thus, in the $r3$-th cascade, the transmission likelihood of candidate edge (v_i, v_k) is greater than that of candidate edge (v_i, v_j). Therefore, we can see that the role candidate edge (v_i, v_j) play in the $r1$-th cascade should be different from that in the $r3$-th cascade, and its contribution in the $r1$-th cascade is greater.

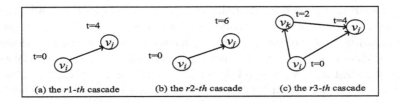

Fig. 2. An example of candidate edges of three cascades.

To recognize the different roles of candidate edges in different cascades, we design a new way to calculate the transmission likelihood of candidate edges, i.e., normalized transmission likelihood. The normalized transmission likelihood $fn_{c_r}(v_i, v_j)$ of candidate edge (v_i, v_j) in the r-th cascade is shown in Eq. (1).

$$fn_{c_r}(v_i, v_j) = \frac{f(t_j^r | t_i^r; \alpha_{ij})}{f_{c_r}(v_i, *)} \tag{1}$$

$$f_{c_r}(v_i, *) = \sum_{(v_l, t_l^r) \in c_r : t_i^r < t_l^r} f(t_l^r | t_i^r; \alpha_{il}) \tag{2}$$

where $f_{c_r}(v_i, *)$ is the sum of the transmission likelihood of all candidate edges starting from node v_i in the r-th cascade. Thus, the total transmission likelihood $fs(v_i, v_j)$ of each candidate edge (v_i, v_j) is calculated as:

$$fs(v_i, v_j) = \sum_{c_r \in C} fn_{c_r}(v_i, v_j) \tag{3}$$

Because the sum of the transmission possibilities that a node infects all its neighbors is 1, we normalized the total propagation likelihood of each potential edge again. Therefore, the final normalized propagation likelihood $fn(v_i, v_j)$ of each potential edge (v_i, v_j) is shown in Eq. (4).

$$fn(v_i, v_j) = \frac{fs(v_i, v_j)}{fs(v_i, *)} \tag{4}$$

where $fs(v_i, *)$ is the sum of the total transmission likelihoods of all candidate edges starting from node v_i. Moreover, due to most existing studies only consider the infection times of nodes, and few studies consider the influence of infection statuses of nodes, we utilize mutual information (MI) to quantify the correlation between two infection status variables. It is calculated by such an Eq. (5):

$$MI(X_i, X_j) = \sum_{X_i} \sum_{X_j} P(X_i, X_j) log \frac{P(X_i, X_j)}{P(X_i)P(X_j)} \tag{5}$$

where $X_i(X_i \in \{0,1\})$ and $X_j(X_j \in \{0,1\})$ are infection status variables of node v_i and node v_j respectively, and $X_i = 0$ means that node v_i is not infected, $X_i = 1$ means that node v_i is infected, so does X_j. It can be seen that all infection status combinations of the two nodes are considered in Eq. (5). A higher MI value indicates that variable X_i and X_j have a greater correlation. However, the correlation evaluated by MI is not equivalent to the positive correlation of infections (when $X_i \cup X_j = 1$ and $X_i \cap X_j = 0$). Because a higher MI value can also indicate variable X_i and X_j have a greater negative correlation. Therefore, we use a modified MI as in literature [10], called infection MI, to measure the infection correlation. The corresponding infection MI can be given as Eq. (6):

$$IMI(X_i, X_j) = MI(X_i = 1, X_j = 1) + MI(X_i = 0, X_j = 0) \\ - |MI(X_i = 1, X_j = 0)| - |MI(X_i = 0, X_j = 1)| \tag{6}$$

To sum up, we use the multiplication principle to fuse the final normalized transmission likelihood derived from the infection times of nodes and infection MI derived from the infection statuses of nodes as the cluster metric of any candidate edges (v_i, v_j) (as shown in Eq. (7)). Obviously, the larger the cluster metric value is, the more likely the corresponding potential edge is to be an effective candidate edge.

$$Cluster\text{-}Metric(v_i, v_j) = fn(v_i, v_j) \cdot IMI(X_i, X_j) \tag{7}$$

Finally, clustering the cluster metric $Cluster\text{-}Metric(v_i, v_j)$ of each candidate edge (v_i, v_j) to fast infer the cluster structures of nodes. Specifically, after performing the 2-means algorithm on all these values, the average value of the class with smaller clustering metric value is selected as the threshold τ, then the candidate edges whose cluster metric value is greater than or equal to the threshold τ are inferred as the effective candidate edges and are retained. At last, we capture the cluster structure of each node v_j as follows:

$$CS_j = \{v_i | (v_i, v_j) \in E\text{-}initial \cap Cluster\text{-}Metric(v_i, v_j) \geq \tau\} \tag{8}$$

Submodular Maximization Inference Based on Multiple Trees. In the second stage, we aim to further accurately and efficiently infer the diffusion edges with the help of the cluster structures of nodes. Firstly, we should solve the likelihood of observed data. Assuming that the observed cascades are conditionally independent for the given network G^*, thus the joint likelihood $f(c_1, c_2, \ldots, c_m | G^*)$ of a set C of cascades occurring in the network G^* is calculated as:

$$f(c_1, c_2, \ldots, c_m | G^*) = \prod_{c_r \in C} f(c_r | G^*) \tag{9}$$

where $f(c_r|G^*)$ is the likelihood of the r-th cascade propagated over the network G^*. By considering all possible directed propagation trees of each cascade, $f(c_r|G^*)$ can be expressed as:

$$f(c_r|G^*) = \sum_{T \in T_{c_r}(G^*)} f(c_r|T)P(T|G^*) \tag{10}$$

where $T_{c_r}(G^*)$ is the set of all possible propagation trees of the r-th cascade given the network G^*, $P(T|G^*)$ is the probability of a tree in the given network G^*. Similar to the MulTree [9], we assume that the prior propagation probability on each edge of the tree are the same, then $f(c_r|G^*)$ can be simplified into:

$$f(c_r|G^*) \propto \sum_{T \in T_{c_r}(G^*)} \prod_{(v_i,v_j) \in E_T} f(t_j^r|t_i^r; \alpha_{ij}) \tag{11}$$

where E_T is the set of possible candidate edges in the tree T. According to Kirchhoff's matrix tree theorem for directed weighted graphs [21], a directed weighted graph consisting of all possible propagation trees derived by a cascade corresponds to a Laplacian matrix, and the right side of Eq. (11) is equal to the product of the diagonal elements of the matrix after removing the row and column where the root node is located. Thus, Eq. (11) can reformulate as:

$$f(c_r|G^*) \propto \prod_{(v_j,t_j^r) \in c_r} \sum_{(v_i,t_i^r) \in c_r : t_i^r < t_j^r} f(t_j^r|t_i^r; \alpha_{ij}) \tag{12}$$

Secondly, considering the role of external source o, i.e., assuming that every node u can get infected by the external source o with an arbitrarily small probability ε, and we maximize the logarithm of Eq. (9) to acquire the $\hat{G}$:

$$\hat{G} = \arg \max_{|G^*| \leq k} F_C(c_1, c_2, \ldots, c_m|G^*) = \arg \max_{|G^*| \leq k} \sum_{c_r \in C} log\left(\varepsilon^{-1} f(c_r|G^*)\right) \tag{13}$$

where the maximization is over all directed networks G^* of at most k edges.

In MulTree [9], although the diffusion network inference problem defined by Eq. (13) is NP-hard, the Eq. (13) is a submodular function. At this point, we integrate the cluster structures of nodes obtained in the previous section into this submodular function, that is, the cluster structures of nodes are concretely integrated into the propagation likelihood function of each cascade $f(c_r|G^*)$, thus Eq. (12) can further reformulate as:

$$f(c_r|G^*) \propto \prod_{(v_j,t_j^r) \in c_r} \sum_{(v_i,t_i^r) \in c_r : t_i^r < t_j^r \cap (v_i \in CS_j)} f(t_j^r|t_i^r; \alpha_{ij}) \tag{14}$$

We see that the addition of the cluster structures of nodes can reduce the number of subitems in the sum part of Eq. (14), i.e., can cut down the number of propagation trees considered for some cascades, thus reducing the overall running time of the algorithm. In addition, adding the cluster structures of nodes does not affect the overall structure of the whole formula, so when the Eq. (13) contains the cluster structures of nodes, it still has submodular property. Likewise, we can still optimize it by using the greedy algorithm to find a near-optimal solution, that means, at iteration i we choose the edge e_i:

$$e_i = \arg\max_{e \in G^* \setminus G^*_{i-1}} \left(F_C(G^*_{i-1} \cup \{e\}) - F_C(G^*_{i-1}) \right) \qquad (15)$$

Finally, the proposed two-stage inference algorithm also stops once it has selected k edges, and returns the near-optimal solution $\hat{G} = \{e_1, e_2, \ldots, e_k\}$.

4 Experimental Evaluation

4.1 Experimental Setup

Datasets. For synthetic networks, we use the well-known model of social network, called the Kronecker graph model [15], to generate three different slightly larger scale Kronecker networks: a random network [5] (parameter matrix [0.5,0.5;0.5,0.5]), a hierarchical network [3] ([0.9,0.1;0.1,0.9]) and a core-periphery network [16] ([0.9,0.5;0.5,0.3]). For real networks, we adopt two directed real-world networks, i.e., polblogs [1], which is a political blogosphere network, and adolescent health [17], which is a friendship network. Some basic statistics of the five network datasets are summarized in Table 2.

Table 2. Statistics of Datasets.

	Network	$|V|$	$|E|$
G_1	Kronecker random network	2048	8189
G_2	Kronecker hierarchical network	2048	6545
G_3	Kronecker core-periphery network	2048	8182
G_4	Polblogs	1490	19025
G_5	Adolescent health	2539	12969

For cascades data C, the generated details are described as follows: we first set the transmission rates of the edges in the network by drawing samples from $\alpha_{ij} \sim U(0.5, 1.5)$ (for adolescent health network, the transmission rates of the edges are set to edge weights, which come from the dataset itself), the prior probability of transmission $\beta = 0.3$, then simulate and record a relatively small set of information cascades spreading over each network by using the propagation model mentioned in Model Formulation section and the three different transmission time models shown in Table 1. Specifically, we record 200 cascades for each network to accommodate the reality of less observational data.

Performance Criteria. To evaluate the accuracy of the CNISM algorithm on the inference of diffusion network topologies, we report the F-score of its inferred directed edges, which can be calculated as

$$F\text{-}score = \frac{2 \cdot Precision \cdot Recall}{Precision + Recall} \quad (16)$$

$$Recall = \frac{N_{TP}}{N_{TP} + N_{FN}}, Precision = \frac{N_{TP}}{N_{TP} + N_{FP}} \quad (17)$$

where N_{TP} denotes the number of correct edges in the inferred network, i.e., the edges in the real network that are inferred correctly by the algorithm; N_{FP} denotes the number of incorrect edges in the inferred network, i.e., the edges in the inferred network that are not in the real network; and N_{FN} denotes the number of true edges in the real network that are not inferred by the algorithm.

Baseline Algorithms. To demonstrate the effectiveness of our proposed method, three kinds of competitive baselines are adopted for comparison. The first kind includes two classic high-performance algorithms based on submodular maximization: NetInf [8] and MulTree [9], which need to specify the number of edges k to be inferred. The second one is NetRate [7], the state-of-the-art method based on convex optimization. The third one is the Dani [19] algorithm based on edges ranking, which is relatively close to our first stage in spirit. We use the publicly available source codes of NetInf [8] and NetRate [7] algorithms, while MulTree [9], Dani [19] and our method are implemented in Python.

4.2 Experimental Results on Synthetic Networks

Due to our proposed method also belongs to the algorithm based on submodular maximization, we set the number of edges k to be inferred as 8500, 7000 and 8500 for the first three artificial networks in Table 2, respectively.

From Tables 3 and 4, we can observe that (1) in most combinations of the three synthetic networks and the three transmission time models, our method almost achieves the highest accuracy compared with other methods, especially

Table 3. The F-score comparison of five algorithms on the synthetic networks.

Network	Transmission time model	NetInf [8]	MulTree [9]	NetRate [7]	Dani [19]	CNISM
G_1	Exp	0.573106	0.576068	0.185185	0.512793	**0.587692**
	Pow	0.556567	0.555216	0.001654	0.348613	**0.568638**
	Ray	0.668385	0.670741	0.003025	0.263407	**0.677572**
G_2	Exp	0.234341	0.242304	0.152710	0.239646	**0.244371**
	Pow	0.196541	0.199631	0.002376	**0.215873**	0.198154
	Ray	0.232901	0.236102	0.102478	0.220746	**0.238464**
G_3	Exp	0.484264	0.483515	0.077180	0.227191	**0.485314**
	Pow	**0.425154**	0.419014	0.020116	0.199257	0.38017
	Ray	0.504766	0.536147	0.002418	0.110059	**0.537705**

Table 4. The running time comparison of five algorithms on the synthetic networks.

Network	Transmission time model	NetInf [8]	MulTree [9]	NetRate [7]	Dani [19]	CNISM
G_1	Exp	$1440\,m\,23\,s$	$419\,m\,0\,s$	$506\,m\,3\,s$	$\mathbf{1\,m\,20\,s}$	$\underline{155\,m\,28\,s}$
	Pow	$1105\,m\,0\,s$	$406\,m\,6\,s$	$458\,m\,52\,s$	$\mathbf{1\,m\,6\,s}$	$\underline{58\,m\,10\,s}$
	Ray	$1804\,m\,0\,s$	$367\,m\,45\,s$	$478\,m\,33\,s$	$\mathbf{1\,m\,8\,s}$	$\underline{135\,m\,58\,s}$
G_2	Exp	$\underline{1\,m\,30\,s}$	$5\,m\,51\,s$	$116\,m\,34\,s$	$\mathbf{0\,m\,1\,s}$	$1\,m\,30\,s$
	Pow	$\underline{0\,m\,21\,s}$	$3\,m\,30\,s$	$135\,m\,39\,s$	$\mathbf{0\,m\,1\,s}$	$0\,m\,29\,s$
	Ray	$3\,m\,28\,s$	$5\,m\,22\,s$	$117\,m\,8\,s$	$\mathbf{0\,m\,2\,s}$	$\underline{1\,m\,59\,s}$
G_3	Exp	$500\,m\,10\,s$	$727\,m\,25\,s$	$504\,m\,35\,s$	$\mathbf{3\,m\,15\,s}$	$\underline{354\,m\,17\,s}$
	Pow	$237\,m\,0\,s$	$745\,m\,48\,s$	$515\,m\,46\,s$	$\mathbf{3\,m\,13\,s}$	$\underline{177\,m\,18\,s}$
	Ray	$391\,m\,0\,s$	$749\,m\,11\,s$	$478\,m\,46\,s$	$\mathbf{3\,m\,12\,s}$	$\underline{370\,m\,42\,s}$

when the transmission time model follows the Exponential distribution or the Rayleigh distribution. (2) the running time (m is minute, s is second) of Dani [19] is the lowest in this three synthetic networks, while our method is the second lowest. The reason is that the Dani [19] algorithm only infers the edges by ranking the metrics related to the edges. In addition, our running time is reduced by 50.52% at least ('G3 and Ray') and 86.19% at most ('G2 and Pow'), compared with the original algorithm MulTree [9]. The above confirms that the preprocessing of the initial candidate edge set and the fusion of the cluster structures of nodes do reduce the number of propagation trees to be considered, especially those that are highly unlikely or have a lower likelihood, thus improvements can be observed.

Further, the results also show that almost all methods have low accuracy on the network with hierarchical structure compared with the random network and the core-periphery network, and the highest F-score is only around 24.4%.

4.3   Experimental Results on Real-World Networks

For the last two real-world networks in Table 2, we set the number of edges k to be inferred as 20000 and 13000, respectively.

Tables 5 and 6 illustrate the F-score and running time of each algortihm on the last two real-world networks respectively, from which we can observe that

Table 5. The F-score comparison of five algorithms on real-world networks.

Network	Transmission time model	NetInf [8]	MulTree [9]	NetRate [7]	Dani [19]	CNISM
G_4	Exp	0.187064	0.243895	0.014757	0.183831	**0.245330**
	Pow	0.152675	0.154567	0.020476	**0.165279**	0.138885
	Ray	0.203823	0.226163	0.014815	0.147393	**0.227239**
G_5	Exp	0.539510	0.547268	0.007473	0.461627	**0.561901**
	Pow	**0.401571**	0.390388	0.004579	0.253456	0.37745
	Ray	0.601433	**0.602333**	0.003865	0.297894	0.596557

Table 6. The running time comparison of four algorithms on the real-world networks.

Network	Transmission time model	NetInf [8]	MulTree [9]	NetRate [7]	Dani [19]	CNISM
G_4	Exp	63 m 0 s	681 m 1 s	175 m 2 s	1 m 42 s	460 m 35 s
	Pow	45 m 22 s	633 m 20 s	225 m 12 s	1 m 40 s	256 m 30 s
	Ray	72 m 0 s	562 m 34 s	195 m 36 s	1 m 41 s	385 m 31 s
G_5	Exp	1875 m 0 s	865 m 21 s	864 m 26 s	3 m 6 s	321 m 4 s
	Pow	1137 m 0 s	895 m 37 s	686 m 58 s	3 m 17 s	200 m 4 s
	Ray	1595 m 0 s	698 m 43 s	841 m 40 s	3 m 3 s	313m50 s

(1) with the same number of cascades, our method achieves a higher accuracy in most combinations of the two real-world networks and the three transmission time models. (2) Dani [19] still executes the fastest. In particular, on the G_4 network, NetInf [8] is the second-fastest, while on the G_5 network, our method is the second-fastest, and our total running time on these two networks is the second-lowest (ours: 1937m34s, NetRate [7]: 2988m54s, MulTree [9]: 4336m36s, NetInf [8]:4787m22s), so our method is the second-fastest on the whole. Moreover, our running time is reduced by 31.47% at least ('G4 and Ray') and 77.66% at most ('G5 and Pow'), compared with the original algorithm MulTree [9].

5 Conclusion

This paper proposed a two-stage inference algorithm for the problem of reconstructing diffusion network topology and proved the effectiveness of the method in both synthetic and real-world network experiments. In the first stage, we preprocessed all initial candidate edges by combining the infection times and infection statuses of nodes and captured the cluster structures of nodes, which can improve the accuracy and efficiency of the final network inference. In the second stage, the cluster structures of nodes were integrated into the submodular maximization network inference algorithm based on multiple propagation trees of the cascade to infer the final diffusion edges. In the future, we plan to combine more characteristics into the first stage to capture the cluster structures of nodes more accurately, such as node degree and betweenness centrality.

Acknowledgements. This work was supported by the Key Program for International Science and Technology Cooperation Projects of China (No. 2022YFE0112300), National Natural Science Foundation of China (No. 61976181), Key Technology Research and Development Program of Science and Technology-Scientific and Technological Innovation Team of Shaanxi Province (No. 2020TD–013).

References

1. Adamic, L.A., Glance, N.: The political blogosphere and the 2004 us election: divided they blog. In: Proceedings of the 3rd International Workshop on Link Discovery, pp. 36–43 (2005)
2. Cheng, L., Li, X., Han, Z., Luo, T., Ma, L., Zhu, P.: Path-based multi-sources localization in multiplex networks. Chaos Solitons Fractals **159**, 112139 (2022)
3. Clauset, A., Moore, C., Newman, M.E.: Hierarchical structure and the prediction of missing links in networks. Nature **453**(7191), 98–101 (2008)
4. Dou, P., Song, G., Zhao, T.: Network topology inference from incomplete observation data. Sci. China Inf. Sci. **61**(2), 028102–1 (2018)
5. Erdos, P., Rényi, A., et al.: On the evolution of random graphs. Publ. Math. Inst. Hung. Acad. Sci **5**(1), 17–60 (1960)
6. Fan, C., Zeng, L., Sun, Y., Liu, Y.Y.: Finding key players in complex networks through deep reinforcement learning. Nat. Mach. Intell. **2**(6), 317–324 (2020)
7. Gomez-Rodriguez, M., Balduzzi, D., Schölkopf, B.: Uncovering the temporal dynamics of diffusion networks. In: Proceedings of the 28th International Conference on Machine Learning, pp. 561–568 (2011)
8. Gomez-Rodriguez, M., Leskovec, J., Krause, A.: Inferring networks of diffusion and influence. In: Proceedings of the 16th ACM SIGKDD International Conference on Knowledge Discovery and Data Mining, pp. 1019–1028 (2010)
9. Gomez-Rodriguez, M., Schölkopf, B.: Submodular inference of diffusion networks from multiple trees. In: Proceedings of the 29th International Conference on International Conference on Machine Learning, pp. 1587–1594 (2012)
10. Han, K., Tian, Y., Zhang, Y., Han, L., Huang, H., Gao, Y.: Statistical estimation of diffusion network topologies. In: Proceedings of the 36th International Conference on Data Engineering, pp. 625–636 (2020)
11. He, X., Liu, Y.: Not enough data? joint inferring multiple diffusion networks via network generation priors. In: Proceedings of the 10th ACM International Conference on Web Search and Data Mining, pp. 465–474 (2017)
12. Hu, Q., Xie, S., Lin, S., Wang, S., Yu, P.: Ceni: a hybrid framework for efficiently inferring information networks. In: Proceedings of the 9th International AAAI Conference on Web and Social Media, pp. 618–621 (2015)
13. Karampourniotis, P.D., Szymanski, B.K., Korniss, G.: Influence maximization for fixed heterogeneous thresholds. Sci. Rep. **9**(1), 1–12 (2019)
14. Kempe, D., Kleinberg, J., Tardos, É.: Maximizing the spread of influence through a social network. In: Proceedings of the 9th ACM SIGKDD International Conference on Knowledge Discovery and Data Mining, pp. 137–146 (2003)
15. Leskovec, J., Chakrabarti, D., Kleinberg, J., Faloutsos, C., Ghahramani, Z.: Kronecker graphs: an approach to modeling networks. J. Mach. Learn. Res. **11**(2), 985–1042 (2010)
16. Leskovec, J., Lang, K.J., Dasgupta, A., Mahoney, M.W.: Statistical properties of community structure in large social and information networks. In: Proceedings of the 17th International Conference on World Wide Web, pp. 695–704 (2008)
17. Moody, J.: Peer influence groups: identifying dense clusters in large networks. Social Netw. **23**(4), 261–283 (2001)
18. Myers, S., Leskovec, J.: On the convexity of latent social network inference. In: Proceedings of the 23rd International Conference on Neural Information Processing Systems, pp. 1741–1749 (2010)

19. Ramezani, M., Rabiee, H.R., Tahani, M., Rajabi, A.: Dani: a fast diffusion aware network inference algorithm. arXiv preprint arXiv:1706.00941 (2017)
20. Tan, Q., Liu, Y., Liu, J.: Motif-aware diffusion network inference. Int. J. Data Sci. Anal. **9**(4), 375–387 (2020)
21. Tutte, W.: The dissection of equilateral triangles into equilateral triangles. In: Proceedings of the Cambridge Philosophical Society, pp. 463–482 (1948)

Applications of AI

A LiDAR Based Control Solution to Achieve High Precision in Autonomous Parking

Xin Xu[1,3], Yu Dong[3], and Fan Zhu[2,4(✉)]

[1] Intelligence Research Department, Hozon Auto Ltd., Shanghai, China
xinme@live.com
[2] ECARX Ltd., Shanghai, China
fan.zhu@ecarxgroup.com
[3] Intelligent Driving Group, Baidu Ltd., Beijing, China
[4] Intelligent Driving Group, Baidu USA Ltd., California, USA

Abstract. Autonomous driving has been quite promising in recent years. While autonomous driving vehicles certainly have a bright future, we have to admit that it is still challenging in complex interactive scenarios. On the other hand, while humans are good at interactive tasks, they are often less competent for tasks with strict precision demands. In this paper, we introduced a real-world, industrial scenario in which autonomous driving system provides a solution to a parking task that human drivers are not capable. This task required ego vehicle to keep a strict lateral distance (*i.e.* $3\sigma \leq 5$ cm) to a reference. To address this challenge, we redesigned the control module from Baidu Apollo open-source autonomous driving system. A specific ($3\sigma \leq 2$ cm) Error Feedback System was first built to enhance the original localization module. Then we investigated the control module thoroughly and added an extra real-time calibration algorithm to guarantee precision. After all those efforts, the results are encouraging, showing that a lateral precision with $3\sigma \leq 5$ cm has been achieved, better than any specially trained and highly experienced human test drivers and original Apollo solution.

Keywords: Autonomous driving · High precision parking · Localization · Control

1 Introduction

In the past a few years, autonomous driving has been intensively studied and discussed. The community has seen tremendous progress made on perception [6, 7,14,22,25], prediction [4,8,20,23,26], simulation [5,9,10,13], etc. Interestingly, there are relatively less literature focused on control in autonomous driving, although it is a very mature topic developed over one hundred years. One reason is that control is usually designed to track planned trajectory, and unfortunately there are plenty unsolved problems in planning [19]. That said, control module

© The Author(s), under exclusive license to Springer Nature Switzerland AG 2022
S. Khanna et al. (Eds.): PRICAI 2022, LNCS 13629, pp. 135–147, 2022.
https://doi.org/10.1007/978-3-031-20862-1_10

can indeed contribute to autonomous driving on its own. In 2020, researchers showed that a control module with longitudinal calibration algorithm improves tracking ability considerably [28]. In this paper, we introduce a redesigned control module, based on an open-source autonomous driving platform (Baidu Apollo [1]), with improved lateral control algorithms at a level of lateral precision down to 5 cm (cm). That is, the ego vehicle is able to keep a lateral distance within ± 5cm, with respect to a reference.

Generally, a system's precision depends on various factors, such as localization, HD (High-Definition) map, control, sensor, actuator, system delay, and even weather and road surface, not to mention that different factors often interact. Hence, it would be very difficult to inspect all factors individually and thoroughly. To address this issue, in this paper, we roughly split factors into two groups, namely controllable factors and uncontrollable factors. Controllable factors mainly include software parts, i.e., localization, HD map, control, system delay, whereas uncontrollable factors include factors such as actuator, sensor, weather, and road condition. Of course, with more resources one could transfer uncontrollable factors into controllable ones, for example, to build a new actuator and/or a new sensor. Nevertheless, we aimed to provide a solution that best suits most autonomous platforms with an affordable cost and minimum modifications. As a result, this paper will focus on software part, and we will show that the lateral precision was indeed improved significantly with modified software, with other conditions remained the same (same sensor, same vehicle, same weather condition, same road, etc.). Further, we divided controllable parts into external and internal factors from a control module's perspective. External factors are signals sent to control module, such as localization, HD map, and system delay. Internal factors are signals processed within control module, such as steering-wheel offset (a vehicle's intrinsic property), heading offset caused by IMU (Inertial measurement unit) mounting error. Based on this concept, this paper will show how we addressed external and internal factors individually and integrated them to eventually achieve an extra high lateral precision.

Taken altogether, in this paper we present an algorithmic architecture that integrates existing work with Baidu Apollo autonomous driving system [1] to solve a real-world problem. Yet, we show that the results were far better than human drivers, bringing the community an example that autonomous driving system outperforms human drivers in real-world, industrial scenarios.

2   Method

2.1   Workflow

Figure 1 shows the architecture of this solution. The architecture can be elaborated from two aspects. First, the external factors, *i.e.*, HD map, localization, and system delay. Figure 1 shows that HD map only provides final heading state, *i.e.*, the heading state the ego vehicle should achieve upon full stop, and localization only provides real time heading feedback. Neither the HD map tells the system where the reference is, nor the localization module tells the system how

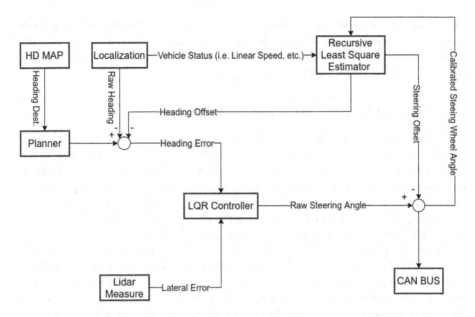

Fig. 1. This figure shows the workflow of proposed method. Every Block represents a function module, whereas arrow lines connecting blocks represent signals.

far away it is from that reference. Some may wonder why not build references into HD map and then use localization module in the most common way [11,12]. The reasons are less intuitive, one can think of that during map collection there is only GNSS-based localization available, which is easily affected by the quality of GNSS signals and the distance between ego vehicle and base station. Furthermore, errors on LiDAR put another burden on map production in terms of accuracy and precision. Thus, HD map's precision and accuracy are affected by both localization and LiDAR performance, and localization performance (with HD map), in turn, is affected by map's accuracy and precision. An example can be seen in a paper published by Apollo localization team in 2018 [24], in which the team showed the best performance of the Apollo localization (with point-cloud HD map) was lateral RMS (root mean square error) around 4cm, with 3σ around 30cm. Obviously, current localization and HD map technology are likely not fully ready for a system with precision within $3\sigma \le 5cm$. It is therefore that this paper only used HD map as a heading reference, instead of a reference with an absolute position. Correspondingly, localization module in this paper only measured ego vehicle's heading, instead of its absolute position. Notice that the system needs heading feedback as an input (see Fig. 1), and we did not find a better of providing heading estimation other than localization module. Simultaneously, lateral error between ego vehicle and its targeting reference was estimated by LiDAR directly, which not only increased precision (only 1–2 cm measurement error) but also reduced system delay (reduced around 100 ms), see later sections for details. Reduction on time delay played an important role in maintaining precision, since a vehicle running at 10 km/h can travel around 3 cm every 100 ms. As to the internal factors, *i.e.*, the steering wheel offset and heading offset, this paper used RLS (recursive least square estimator) [18] to estimate them in a real-time fashion.

2.2   External Factors: Error Feedback System

In order to achieve an end-to-end precision of $3\sigma \leq 5$cm, the error feedback should be even more precise, *e.g.* $3\sigma \leq 2$cm. In this paper, the key was to use LiDAR to do the measurement on lateral error. LiDAR is a piece of standard equipment used in almost all Level-4 autonomous driving vehicles for perception and localization [16]. The LiDAR we used has the capacity of 1 to 2cm precision (according to Hesai Pander40P LiDAR specs [2]), way better than that of a typical localization and/or HD map solution [17,24,27]. The reason we did not use HD map based on this LiDAR is that errors in map production does not only come from LiDAR but also localization during data collection. That is, a LiDAR with 1 to 2cm precision leads to a HD map with larger error. On the other hand, heading feedback still came from localization and HD map modules, because a single LiDAR is simply not capable of providing heading estimation. One may wonder whether the relatively less precise heading estimation (from localization) would affect the overall performance. In fact, since we improved the lateral precision by an order of a magnitude (*i.e.* from $1\sigma \leq 10$cm in localization (with HD map) to $3\sigma \leq 2$cm), the overall precision should benefit significantly just from this. Through direct LiDAR measurement, we also reduced system delay around 100ms, since there was no other modules processing between LiDAR and control algorithm. By contrast, previously lateral error was successively processed by HD map, localization, and planner, resulting to a time delay when eventually passed to control module. Although a compensation to such delay is possible, error was still unnecessarily introduced.

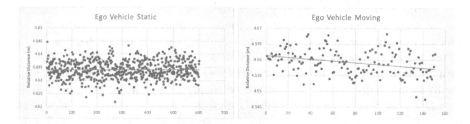

Fig. 2. This figure illustrates distance measurement relative to a reference from LiDAR, with ego vehicle either static (left) or moving parallel to that reference (right). Note that data mainly clustered in a zone about 1cm wide (see vertical axis). The orange line represents the estimated line using Least Square. With the vehicle static, std. of the lateral error is 0.34 cm. With the vehicle moving (as parallel to the reference as possible and as less steering as possible, manual driving), std. of that is 0.42 cm (Color figure online)

Field tests on lateral error feedback from LiDAR, with ego vehicle either static or moving, proved the measurement was sufficiently precise (*i.e.* $3\sigma \leq$ 2cm), see Fig. 2. We should mention that Fig. 2 only shows the standard deviation of this LiDAR was indeed around 1cm during either static or moving, it by no means verify the accuracy of its measurement. In practice, it would require a device with 10 times more precise than the origin one to verify the measurement of the origin one. In this case, if one doubts the ground truth of the lateral error measured by this LiDAR, one should acquire a device with 1 to 2 mm precision to do the verification. In this paper, we took the official manual provided by Hesai as a guarantee and verified its standard deviation.

2.3   Internal Factors: Control Algorithm, Modeling, and Simulation

The control algorithm (Linear-Quadratic Regulator, [15]) was designed under the assumption that ego vehicle often drives at a low to medium speed (*i.e.* 0 to 40 KM/H). This assumption is valid due to that for parking scenarios the ego vehicle often spends a large amount of time cruising at low speed and eventually reach to a stop. Figure 3 illustrates the kinematics model under such assumption, which can be described mathematically as below,

$$\begin{cases} x_{k+1} = x_k + v_k \cdot cos(\psi_k) \cdot \Delta t, \\ y_{k+1} = y_k + v_k \cdot sin(\psi_k) \cdot \Delta t, \\ \psi_{k+1} = \psi_k + v_k \cdot \frac{tan(\delta_k)}{L} \cdot \Delta t \end{cases} \qquad (1)$$

where (x, y), ψ, v, δ, and L refers to the position, heading, linear speed, front-wheel angle, and the wheelbase of the ego vehicle, respectively. Position and heading was obtained in a way described in the section of Error Feedback System (also see Fig. 1), while linear speed was provided directly by IMU. The front-wheel angle, on the other hand, maps to the steering wheel angle through a

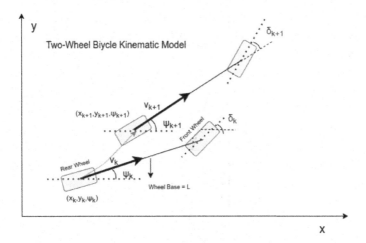

Fig. 3. Kinematics model of the control algorithm

transfer function below.

$$G(s) = \frac{1}{\tau s + 1} \qquad (2)$$

The time constant τ in Eq. (2) was fine-tuned in simulation and field tests, and was set to 0.1668 as a result.

With this model, one can build a decent LQR controller but not the precise one as this paper purposed. The reason is that there are some subtle gaps between the model and the actual vehicle, although in most cases they are ignorable. This model implies that one can get variables such as front-wheel angle and heading estimation ideally, which is incorrect due to errors such as steering-wheel offset and IMU mounting issue. Those errors are only negligible when they are small and extra precision is not desired. A steering-wheel offset may be caused by installation problem in factory, while heading offset in this case is from an askew mounted IMU. Figure 5 presents an example, showing how an askew mounted IMU influences the heading feedback. Note that position O represents the desired mounting point, while O' (x_{offset}, y_{offset}) represents the actual mounting point. h_o is the resulting heading offset.

In order to calibrate those offsets, the follow equations were deduced from the kinematic model (1) and Fig. 4.

$$\begin{cases} tan(\delta + \delta_o) = \frac{L \cdot \omega}{v_1}, \\ v_1 = v_2 \cdot cos(h - h_o) - \omega \cdot y_{offset} \\ v_2 \cdot sin(h - h_o) = \omega \cdot x_{offset}, \end{cases} \qquad (3)$$

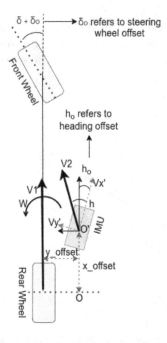

Fig. 4. Heading offset due to incorrect mounting of IMU

where δ_o represents the steering-wheel offset, and h_o, y_{offset}, and x_{offset} represent the heading error, lateral error, and longitudinal error, respectively, due to incorrect mounting of IMU. It should be emphasized that the calculation of v_1 adds complication on offset estimation. In principle, v_1 is the linear speed of the ego vehicle while v_2 is the linear speed read from IMU. If the IMU is perfectly mounted or the vehicle goes perfectly straight (with no yaw rate at all), the two values match. In reality, however, v_1 is not observable and one can only estimate it from v_2. Now, both h_o and y_{offset} are involved in calculating v_1 from v_2, but we are only estimating h_o, which means we should acquire y_{offset} from somewhere else. Of course, one solution is to estimate y_{offset} as well, but it would make the estimation non-linear and hence difficult to solve online in a real-time manner using RLS. Therefore, we set y_{offset} to 0.2 m via carefully checking the mounting point and CAD (computer-aided design) model of the ego vehicle. Some may wonder whether a (reasonable) guess on y_{offset}, instead of a mathematical estimation, affects the precision or not. It can be proven that, for a typical mounting error with h_o at 0.01 rad and y_{offset} at 0.2m, the difference between v_1 and v_2 is less than 1% on $\omega \leq 0.05\,\text{rad/s}$ and $v_2 \geq 1\text{m/s}$, further leading to a calibration error on steering-wheel offset less than 0.01%. From this calculation, it is clear that even with y_{offset} set to zero, the calibration error is negligible, not to mention a reasonable measurement on y_{offset}. Notice that it is not recommended to estimate x_{offset} and/or h_o from the CAD model too, because too many rough estimations rapidly increase the risk of breaking the system's precision. We should always precisely estimate as many variables as possible. Further, it can be proven that a (un-calibrated) h_o at 1 degree will lead to an lateral offset between front wheel and rear wheel around 7 cm. One should always estimate h_o as accurate as possible. As to estimate h_o and δ_o, Eq. 3 can be transformed to

$$\begin{cases} \frac{L \cdot \omega}{v_1} - tan(\delta) = (1 + \frac{L \cdot \omega}{v_1}) \cdot tan(\delta_o), \\ atan(\frac{vy'}{vx'}) = \frac{\omega \cdot x_{offset}}{v_2} + h_o, \end{cases} \tag{4}$$

where v'_x and v'_y refer to linear speed along x-axis and y-axis, respectively, of the IMU body frame. Obviously, this is a standard form of a least square problem:

$$y = \phi \cdot \theta \tag{5}$$

where

$$\begin{cases} y = [\frac{L \cdot \omega}{v_1} - tan(\delta), atan(\frac{v'_y}{v'_x})]^T, \\ \theta = [tan(\delta_o), x_{offset}, h_o]^T, \\ \phi = \begin{bmatrix} (1 + \frac{L \cdot \omega}{v_1}) & 0 & 0 \\ 0 & \frac{\omega}{v_2} & 1 \end{bmatrix} \end{cases} \tag{6}$$

Directly, we can get estimations from the standard least square form, which is set to minimize the following loss function:

$$V(\hat{\theta}, n) = \frac{1}{2} \cdot \sum_{i=1}^{n} (y(i) - \phi^T(i) \cdot \hat{\theta})^2$$

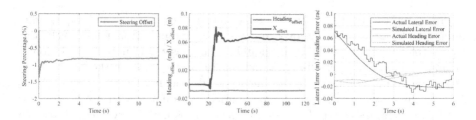

Fig. 5. Calibration process and simulation process

Nevertheless, during driving we need to update estimations every frame as new data keep coming in. Fortunately, we can indeed use least square in a recursive form (Recursive Least Square, RLS for short). Through RLS, one can get estimations, *i.e.* $\hat{\theta}$, in the following form:

$$\hat{\theta}(k) = \hat{\theta}(k-1) + L(k) \cdot [y(k) - \phi^T(k) \cdot \hat{\theta}(k-1)] \tag{7}$$

where

$$L(k) = P(k-1) \cdot \phi(k) \cdot [1 + \phi^T(k) \cdot P(k-1) \cdot \phi(k)]^{-1} \tag{8}$$

and

$$P(k) = P(k-1) \cdot [1 - L(k) \cdot \phi^T(k)] \tag{9}$$

An initial value of $P(0)$ is needed to get RLS started. In fact, $P(0)$ is related to the confidence of the initial guess of $\hat{\theta}(0)$. One can simply set $P(0)$ to a large value (such as 1e6) and initial guess of $\hat{\theta}(0)$ to zero to get RLS started. Figures 5 (a) and (b) show calibration results for steering and heading offset, respectively. Figure 5 (c) presents a simulation result, in which one can see that the models built in this section (*i.e.* simulated lateral/heading error) matches reasonably well with the actual vehicle data (*i.e.* actual lateral/heading error).

3   Result

3.1   Apparatus and Testing Scenario

For the field tests, we used an electronic vehicle with a dimension of 5 m (length) * 2 m (width) * 2.2 m (height) with a drive-by-wire system, and an X86 computer running Apollo autonomous driving system with an architecture shown in Fig. 1, and multiple sensors that are designed for Level 4 autonomous driving systems. The Error Feedback System uses an existing Hesai Pandar40P LiDAR [2] equipped on top of the vehicle. Other sensors are mainly used by other parts (such as the perception module) of the Apollo system [1]. Figure 6 illustrates the testing scenario. As described in previous sections, this paper focuses on lateral precision (with respect to a reference). We hence tested the system through a typical bus-stop scenario. Note that it is a real-world, everyday bus platform built years ago, with no additional design except the grey board (the red rectangle in Fig. 6). The board was added by the testing team to provide a flat and

Fig. 6. Landmark example (Color figure online)

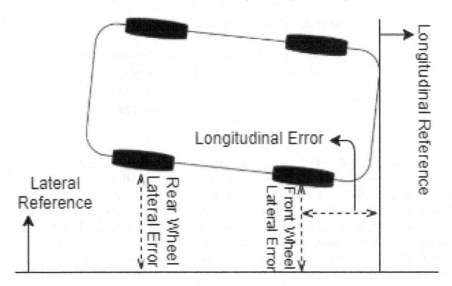

Fig. 7. Measurement method

smooth surface for the LiDAR. The board was approximately 14.6 m long, 0.6 m wide, and in parallel with the road. During driving, the 12th ray from the top LiDAR, which is horizontal according to the Pandar40P manual, was used to measure the lateral distance between the ego vehicle and the board.

3.2   Experiment and Measurement

As long as the ego vehicle was close to the bus stop, *i.e.* LiDAR detects the board, the proposed method would be triggered (Fig. 1). The system then continually adjusted its steering wheel according to the lateral and heading error feedback (see Method Section). For convenience, we used the existing (not drawn by the

Table 1. Precision of proposed control module

| | Longitudinal error (cm) | Lateral error (cm) | | | Heading error (rad) |
		Front	Rear	LiDAR	
Mean	0.2	−0.7	1.7	0.3	0.0061
STD	10.1	0.7	0.9	0.9	0.0013

Table 2. Precision of human drivers

| | Longitudinal error (cm) | Lateral error (cm) | | | Heading error (rad) |
		Front	Rear	LiDAR	
Mean	N/A	−0.5	−0.3	N/A	0.0005
STD	N/A	4.2	4.0	N/A	0.0005

Table 3. Precision of original control module

| | Longitudinal error (cm) | Lateral error (cm) | | | Heading error (rad) |
		Front	Rear	LiDAR	
Mean	N/A	−3.7	−4.0	N/A	−0.0007
STD	N/A	3.1	3.9	N/A	0.0072

testing team), middle, long, white, solid lane line in Fig. 6 as the reference for the control module. That means, the lateral error from LiDAR was first subtracted by a constant offset, *i.e.* the lateral distance between the board and that lane line, before it was fed into the control module. Consequently, the ego vehicle drove towards the lane line, rather than crashing with the board. The lateral and heading errors were then measured with respect to the lane line. Figure 7 shows how results were measured. We first recorded the lateral error (with respect to the lane line) from LiDAR after the ego vehicle fully stopped. We also measured the lateral error of front and rear wheels through an L-ruler (Fig. 7), hence small human error on measurement, *i.e.* ± 0.5cm, is expected. The longitudinal error was measured with respect to a horizontal line drawn by the testing team. Heading error was calculated in a way that:

$$Heading_{error} = \arctan(\frac{Lat\_error_{back} - Lat\_error_{front}}{wheelbase}) \tag{10}$$

Experiments were primarily carried out under standard condition, in which all of below should be satisfied:

- Half load.
- Typical weather with no rain or snow or fog.
- Typical city road with dry and cement surface.

3.3   Results

We expected lateral and heading error to be around zero with small means and standard deviations (std. for short). The lateral error measured by LiDAR was set to align with that of the rear wheel, which means those two values should match in principle. That said, one should consider that both measurement, *i.e.* LiDAR and L-ruler, have accuracy around 1 to 2 cm. Forty consecutive trials were carried out with the proposed method under standard conditions. Table 1 shows the mean and std. for both lateral error and heading error. Both the front wheel and rear wheel were in the zone of the target ± 5 cm. The std. of lateral error is even less than 1 cm. The lateral error measured by LiDAR is close to that by L-ruler, given the measurement accuracy. Heading error is about 0.006 rad with std. around 0.001 rad. The results suggest that the control module was able to provide an end-to-end lateral precision well within $3\sigma \leq 5$ cm. Interestingly, the results also imply that a steady heading error has occurred. The front-wheel was always biased to one side (in this case, right to the target) while the rear wheel biased to the opposite, leading to a 0.006 rad heading error. It is possible the performance on heading correction was limited by the capacity of localization module, and/or the system delay occurred in passing heading error from HD map, localization, and planner, to control module (see Fig 1). Another possibility, on the contrary, is that lateral error and heading error was fed into control directly, other than passing to a planning module beforehand. A planning module can help the control module achieve better precision. For example, a planning module can calculate a trajectory that best describes how to eliminate heading error and lateral error simultaneously upon the ego vehicle fully stops. For this, one can refer to literature related to planning and model predicted control [3, 21].

By comparison, we inspected whether human drivers can reach the same level of control precision with the same test vehicle in the same testing scenario. Four test drivers were involved, all of whom were specially trained for this task. They all spent 2 to 3 years in autonomous driving test and around 1 year on this specific test vehicle. The drivers were provided a full 360-degree view, thanks to the cameras mounted all around the test vehicle. To help drivers perform at their best, we relaxed the requirement on longitudinal precision. Hence drivers only needed to focus on the lateral control, as the longitudinal target was not set for them. Thus, human drivers had an advantage over the proposed automated control module in this test. An overall of thirty trials has been conducted with them. Results (Table 2) show that the lateral error (cm) is around -0.5 ± 4.2 (mean ± std.) for front wheel, and -0.3 ± 4.0 for rear wheel. The heading error (rad) is around 0.0005 ± 0.0005. To conclude, with intensive training and help from the 360-degree surrounding view, human drivers were able to maintain a sound accuracy but not precision. Finally, we also conducted fifteen trials using the original Apollo solution (LQR controller) for comparison. Table 3 shows that the original control module (with original localization module) performed even worse than the human drivers, with -3.7 ± 3.1 for the front wheel, -4.0 ± 3.9 for the rear wheel, and -0.0007 ± 0.0072 for heading.

4   Conclusion

In this study, we integrated both localization and LiDAR techniques to achieve a precise Error Feedback System. We also implemented a lateral calibration algorithm that is able to calibrate a vehicle's steering wheel offset and heading offset in a few seconds. A simulation was built on top of this control module to fine-tune parameters. The results show that, through combining all those techniques, the lateral precision of the control module reaches a new level. A small lateral error (cm) around -0.7 ± 0.7 (front wheel) and 1.7 ± 0.9 (rear wheel), has been achieved, which outperforms existing autonomous driving solutions and experienced human drivers.

Acknowledgements. The vast majority of this paper was performed in Baidu/Baidu USA. The authors acknowledge the resources, i.e. the Apollo Open Source team, the Quality Assurance team, the Safety team, and the Operation team, etc., provided by Intelligent Driving Group, Baidu/Baidu USA.

References

1. https://github.com/apolloauto/apollo
2. https://www.hesaitech.com/en/pandar40p
3. Afram, A., Janabi-Sharifi, F.: Theory and applications of HVAC control systems - a review of model predictive control (mpc). Building and Environment **72**, 343–355 (2014)
4. Alahi, A., Goel, K., Ramanathan, V., Robicquet, A., Savarese, S.: Social LSTM: human trajectory prediction in crowded spaces. In: 2016 IEEE Conference on Computer Vision and Pattern Recognition (CVPR) (2016)
5. Benekohal, R.F., Treiterer, J.: CARSIM: car-following model for simulation of traffic in normal and stop-and-go conditions (1988)
6. Casser, V., Pirk, S., Mahjourian, R., Angelova, A.: Unsupervised monocular depth and ego-motion learning with structure and semantics. In: International Workshop on Visual Odometry Computer Vision Applications Based on Location Clues (2019)
7. Chen, C., Seff, A., Kornhauser, A., Xiao, J.: DeepDriving: learning affordance for direct perception in autonomous driving (2015)
8. Deo, N., Rangesh, A., Trivedi, M.M.: How would surround vehicles move? a unified framework for maneuver classification and motion prediction. IEEE Transactions on Intelligent Vehicles, pp. 129–140 (2018)
9. Dong, Y., Hu, Z., Uchimura, K., Murayama, N.: Driver inattention monitoring system for intelligent vehicles: a review. IEEE Trans. Intell. Transp. Syst. **12**(2), 596–614 (2011)
10. Dosovitskiy, A., Ros, G., Codevilla, F., López, A.M., Koltun, V.: CARLA: an open urban driving simulator. CoRR abs/1711.03938 (2017). http://arxiv.org/abs/1711.03938
11. Durrant-Whyte, H., Bailey, T.: Simultaneous localization and mapping: Part I. IEEE Robot. Autom. Mag. **13**(2), 99–110 (2006)
12. Durrantwhyte, H.F., Bailey, T.: Simultaneous localization and mapping (slam): part II. IEEE Robot. Autom. Mag. **13**(2), 99–110 (2006)

13. Geoffrey, U.: David, Crundall, Peter, Chapman: driving simulator validation with hazard perception - sciencedirect. Transport. Res. F: Traffic Psychol. Behav. **14**(6), 435–446 (2011)
14. Gordon, A., Li, H., Jonschkowski, R., Angelova, A.: Depth from videos in the wild: unsupervised monocular depth learning from unknown cameras. In: 2019 IEEE/CVF International Conference on Computer Vision (ICCV) (2019)
15. Kwakernaak, H., Sivan, R., Tyreus, B.: Linear optimal control system. J. Dyn. Syst. Measur. Control **96**, 373 (1974). https://doi.org/10.1115/1.3426828
16. Levinson, J., et al.: Towards fully autonomous driving: systems and algorithms (2011)
17. Lu, W., Zhou, Y., Wan, G., Hou, S., Song, S.: L3 -net: towards learning based lidar localization for autonomous driving. In: 2019 IEEE/CVF Conference on Computer Vision and Pattern Recognition (CVPR) (2019)
18. Narayanan, K., Harne, R.L., Yuji, F., Pietron, G.M., Wang, K.W.: Methods in vehicle mass and road grade estimation. SAE Int. J. Passenger Cars Mech. Syst. **7**(3), 981–991 (2014)
19. Paden, B., Čáp, M., Yong, S.Z., Yershov, D., Frazzoli, E.: A survey of motion planning and control techniques for self-driving urban vehicles. IEEE Trans. Intell. Veh. **1**(1), 33–55 (2016)
20. Pan, J., et al.: Lane attention: predicting vehicles moving trajectories by learning their attention over lanes. arXiv preprint arXiv:1909.13377 (2019)
21. Pannocchia, G., Rawlings, J.B.: Disturbance models for offset-free MPC control. AIChE J. **49**(2), 426–437 (2010)
22. Sun, P., et al.: Scalability in perception for autonomous driving: Waymo open dataset (2019)
23. Vemula, A., Muelling, K., Oh, J.: Social attention: modeling attention in human crowds. In: 2018 IEEE International Conference on Robotics and Automation (ICRA) (2018)
24. Wan, G., et al.: Robust and precise vehicle localization based on multi-sensor fusion in diverse city scenes. In: 2018 IEEE International Conference on Robotics and Automation (ICRA), pp. 4670–4677 (2018). https://doi.org/10.1109/ICRA.2018.8461224
25. Xie, S., Gu, J., Guo, D., Qi, C.R., Guibas, L.J., Litany, O.: PointContrast: unsupervised Pre-training for 3D Point Cloud Understanding (2020)
26. Xu, K., Xiao, X., Miao, J., Luo, Q.: Data driven prediction architecture for autonomous driving and its application on apollo platform. arXiv preprint arXiv:2006.06715 (2020)
27. Zhou, Y., et al.: DA4AD: end-to-end deep attention-based visual localization for autonomous driving (2020)
28. Zhu, F., Xu, X., Ma, L., Guo, D., Cui, X., Kong, Q.: Autonomous driving vehicle control auto-calibration system: An industry-level, data-driven and learning-based vehicle longitudinal dynamic calibrating algorithm. In: 2020 IEEE Intelligent Vehicles Symposium (IV), pp. 391–397 (2020). https://doi.org/10.1109/IV47402.2020.9304778

Multi-view Heterogeneous Temporal Graph Neural Network for "Click Farming" Detection

Zequan Xu[1], Qihang Sun[2], Shaofeng Hu[2], Jiguang Qiu[3], Chen Lin[1], and Hui Li[1(✉)]

[1] School of Informatics, Xiamen University, Xiamen, China
xuzequan@stu.xmu.edu.cn, {chenlin,hui}@xmu.edu.cn
[2] Tencent, Guangzhou, China
{aaronqhsun,hugohu}@tencent.com
[3] Xiamen Meiya Pico Information Co., Ltd., Xiamen, China
qiujg@300188.cn

Abstract. Multi-purpose Messaging Mobile App (MMMA) combines several functionalities in a single APP to provide integrated service that brings tremendous convenience to users. Therefore, MMMAs become more and more popular. However, the prevalence of MMMAs also makes them a hotbed for cybercrime. Among them, "Click Farming" fraud requires special attention, as it causes substantial pecuniary losses and is challenging to detect. In this paper, we describe Multi-view Heterogeneous Temporal Graph Neural Network (MHT-GNN), a framework for detecting "Click Farming" fraudsters in a popular MMMA called WeChat. We first adopt a Heterogeneous Temporal Graph (HTG) to model spatial, heterogeneous and temporal information contained in MM-MA data. We then extract two different types of user history sequences as two "views" of user behavior patterns from HTG. MHT-GNN contains a pretraining phase and a detection phase. The main components in MHT-GNN include Inductive Heterogeneous GNN Encoder, Temporal Snapshot Sequence Encoder, and User Relation Sequence Encoder. The first encoder aims to capture spatial information and the heterogeneity in each snapshot of HTG. The later two encoders are designed to incorporate temporal information to better reveal user's behavior patterns and MHT-GNN leverages them to capture the two different views of user history behavior data. We conduct experiments on a real-world, million-scale dynamic graph extracted from WeChat. Experimental results demonstrate the effectiveness of MHT-GNN: it significantly exceeds existing detection methods, and it is able to block "Click Farming" fraud activities.

Keywords: Click farming detection · Multi-purpose messaging mobile app · Graph based anomaly detection · Graph neural network

© The Author(s), under exclusive license to Springer Nature Switzerland AG 2022
S. Khanna et al. (Eds.): PRICAI 2022, LNCS 13629, pp. 148–160, 2022.
https://doi.org/10.1007/978-3-031-20862-1_11

1 Introduction

Smart phones have become an essential tool in our everyday life and they provide different functionalities (e.g., socializing, online games, online shopping and mobile payment) via installed apps. Nowadays, one single app is no longer limited to one application scenario. Several functionalities can be assembled in one app to provide integrated service that helps users handle their daily demands. Such apps are often referred to as Multi-purpose Messaging Mobile Apps (MMMAs). WeChat, with over a billion users, is a representative app in this category. Users can easily chat with their friends using texts, voice messages or voice/video calls provided by WeChat. Moreover, the digital payment service of WeChat has revolutionized people's daily life: we can simply use QR code to replace wallet and transfer money, which is more convenient and safer.

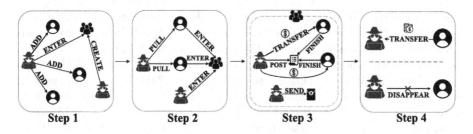

Fig. 1. An illustration of "Click Farming" in WeChat.

The great convenience brought by MMMAs attracts more and more users. On the other hand, the prevalence of MMMAs like WeChat makes them a hotbed for cybercrime [19]. This paper studies the detection task of "Click Farming" in WeChat: a type of deception that recently emerges. As depicted in Fig. 1, in "Click Farming" frauds, fraudsters first use illegally acquired personal information (e.g., phone number) and send "add friend" requests to victims (i.e., ADD in Fig. 1 - Step 1). Additionally, certain chat groups are created where cybercriminals enter and disguise as normal users (i.e., ENTER and CREATE in Fig. 1 - Step 1). Then, fraudsters will invite victims (i.e., PULL in Fig. 1 - Step 2) to join these groups (i.e., ENTER in Fig. 1 - Step 2) by using high reward as bait. After that, group members are encouraged to complete some tasks (i.e., FINISH in Fig. 1 - Step 3) posted in the group (i.e., POST in Fig. 1 - Step 3). Typical tasks include buying a number of products or topping up online shopping cards. The first a few tasks are easy. Victims do not need to pay too much (i.e., TRANSFER in Fig. 1 - Step 3) and fraudsters pay the commission as promised to gain the trust of victims. With victims' guard down, fraudsters raise the request of new tasks and ask victims to pay much more money. Victims may see that other group members (they are conspirators) complete new tasks and get reward. Hence, they decide to pay the money to complete new tasks. However, after victims transfer money, fraudsters disappear and do not response anymore (i.e., DISAPPEAR in Fig. 1- Step 4).

Due to the pecuniary losses that "Click Farming" frauds cause, the "Click Farming" fraudsters detection task (the CFD task) requests our attention. The social nature of WeChat makes it a natural choice to model WeChat user relationships as a user-user interaction graph. This way, the CFD task is closely related to Graph-based Anomaly Detection (GBAD) [1]. However, the CFD task in WeChat has unique properties and therefore is more challenging. The data of WeChat is *dynamic* and *diverse*. A fraudster may appear to be normal in each individual snapshot. But he/she becomes suspicious when considering all his/her different behaviors at each snapshot together.

In the literature, only few works [17,21] study the GBAD task in the dynamic setting. But they cannot handle both dynamics and diversity of WeChat data well. Particularly, all previous works leverage *only one* view of dynamic data (e.g., viewing states of a node in different snapshots of the dynamic graph as a sequence [21]), which is not sufficient to model the dynamic and diverse user behaviors in the CFD task. We propose a framework Multi-View Heterogeneous Temporal Graph Neural Network (MHT-GNN) for the CFD task in WeChat. We extract two types of user history sequences from our designed Heterogeneous Temporal Graph (HTG) as two "views". Then, MHT-GNN captures both temporal dependencies (dynamics) and behavior patterns (diversity) from user history sequences and the HTG through multi-view learning and graph representation learning. To our best knowledge, we are the first to study the "Click Farming" detection problem in MMMAs. The contributions of this work can be summarized as follows:

- We analyze and design features used in the CFD task of WeChat. We further propose a Heterogeneous Temporal Graph to model diverse MMMA data.
- We adopt an Inductive Heterogeneous graph encoder to capture spatial dependencies and heterogeneity in WeChat. It provides better representation learning for the WeChat graph compared to other GNN-based methods and it can generalize to unseen nodes.
- We construct two types of user history sequences for each node as two "views" of the dynamic data. We further design two encoders to encode two views to capture the temporal dependencies and behavior patterns, which helps generate better node representations in the CFD task.
- We conduct evaluations on a million-scale real-world graph extracted from the CFD task in WeChat. Results show that MHT-GNN exceeds existing methods by a large margin.

2   Related Work

2.1   Graph-Based Anomaly Detection (GBAD)

Anomaly detection identifies the abnormal patterns that deviate from the majorities [8]. Graph-based Anomaly Detection (GBAD) extends it to the graph data. Earlier methods for GBAD are mainly based on handcrafted feature engineering [6]. Recent works are mostly inspired by the deep learning techniques. DOMINANT [4] leverages the graph embeddings from GCN to reconstruct the original adjacent matrix for anomaly detection. ALARM [12] further employs multiple attributed views to describe different perspectives of the objects for anomalies detection. Different from previous methods that jointly learn the node representation and the classifier, DCI [18], inspired by the recent advances of self-supervised learning, decouples these two phases for node representation learning.

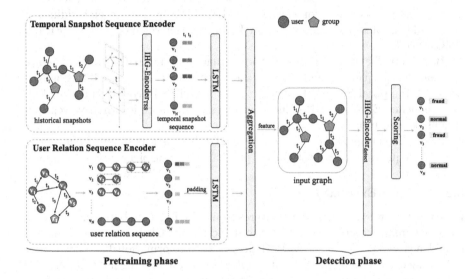

Fig. 2. Overview of MHT-GNN.

2.2 Anomaly Detection in Dynamic Graphs

Anomaly detection in dynamic graphs attracts increasing interest since many real-world networks can be generally represented in the form of dynamic graphs. Earlier methods such as CAD [15] detect node relationships responsible for abnormal changes in graph structure by tacking a measure that combines information regarding changes in both graph structure and edge weights. StreamSpot [10] is a clustering based approach that introduces a new similarity function for heterogeneous graph comparison. Another branch of approaches employs deep learning. [21] first utilizes temporal GCN and attention mechanism to model short-term and long-term patterns. Then a GRU network is introduced to process such patterns and encode temporal features. NetWalk [20] adopts a random walk based encoder to learn the network representations and employs a clustering-based anomaly detector to score the abnormality of each edge. StrGNN [2] extracts the h-hop enclosing subgraph of edges and labels each node to identify its corresponding role in the subgraph. Then it leverages GCN and GRU to capture the spatial and temporal information for anomaly detection.

3   Our Framework MHT-GNN

3.1   Overview

Figure 2 provides an overview of MHT-GNN. It consists of two phases: pretraining and detection. We first extract node features (Sect. 3.2) and construct a Heterogeneous Temporal Graph (Sect. 3.3) for WeChat data. Then, in the pretraining phase (Sect. 3.4), we construct two types of history sequence for each node in the constructed graph, namely temporal snapshot sequence and user relation sequence. These two types of sequences can be regarded as two "views" of user history sequence for each user. MHT-GNN generates embeddings for each node in each snapshot using an Inductive Heterogeneous GNN Encoder (IHG-Encoder).

Based on the graph representations generated by IHG-Encoder, temporal snapshot sequences and user relation sequences are passed through our designed Temporal Snapshot Sequence Encoder (TSS-Encoder) and User Relation Sequence Encoder (URS-Encoder) to generate more informative representations, respectively.

In the detection phase (Sect. 3.5), MHT-GNN uses pretrained encoders to generate sequence representations for predicting the suspicious score of a user.

3.2   Feature Extraction

For each user, we pre-extract six features from WeChat data based on the knowledge of human experts. Note that the detection of "Click Farming" fraudsters should not violate users' privacy. Hence, private information like chat content (text, video or speech) in WeChat is unaccessible. The data used for the CFD task is chosen through a strict investigation process in order to protect users' privacy.

3.3   Graph Construction

To capture the diverse behavior patterns in the WeChat graph, we construct a heterogeneous graph [14] capable of modeling heterogeneous spatial dependencies among different types of node entities and relations. Among different nodes and behaviors in WeChat, we consider two key node types (i.e., users and chat groups) and three important relation types: "join a group" (ENTER), "invite someone to join a group" (PULL) and "become WeChat friends" (ADD). The heterogeneous graph not only depicts the graph structure of WeChat graph, but also provides a higher-level abstraction of the user association. For example, a pattern of $fraudulent\ user \xrightarrow{\text{PULL}} normal\ user \xrightarrow{\text{ENTER}} group \xleftarrow{\text{ENTER}} fraudulent\ user$ in the heterogeneous graph can characterize a "Click Farming" fraud case: a fraudster invites a victim to join a chat group and another fraudster is also a member of this group.

Based on the above designed heterogeneous graph, we propose to further consider temporal dependencies (i.g., evolving user states and behaviors) and build a *Heterogeneous Temporal Graph* (HTG) for the CFD task:

Definition 1. *Heterogeneous Temporal Graph (HTG). We model a HTG as a graph stream consists of discrete snapshots. Let the latest timestamp be T. A graph stream can be denoted as $\mathbb{G} = \{\mathcal{G}^t\}_{t=1}^T$, where each $\mathcal{G}^t = (\mathcal{V}^t, \mathcal{E}^t)$ is a heterogeneous graph at timestamp t. We use $n^t = |\mathcal{V}^t|$ and $m^t = |\mathcal{E}^t|$ to denote the number of nodes and edges at timestamp t, respectively.*

HTG is the combination of several basic heterogeneous graphs from different time points. And each basic heterogeneous graph of the HTG is a snapshot of the HTG at the corresponding time point.

3.4   Pretraining Phase

Inductive Heterogeneous GNN Encoder (IHG-Encoder). We adopt an IHG-Encoder as the backbone of MHT-GNN for encoding graph data.

In the following, we only consider one snapshot of the WeChat graph to illustrate IHG-Encoder. We first project the raw user features $\mathbf{p}_v \in \mathbb{R}^6$ of a user u to a feature space and utilize projected features as the initial user node embedding for u. For the initial embeddings of a group node g, we aggregate all its members' initial embeddings:

$$\mathbf{h}_v^{(0)} = \mathbf{W_h}\mathbf{p}_v, \quad \mathbf{h}_g^{(0)} = \text{mean}(\{\mathbf{h}_{v'}, \forall v' \in N_g\}) \qquad (1)$$

where $\mathbf{h}_v^{(0)}$ and $\mathbf{h}_g^{(0)}$ are initial embeddings for the user node v and the group node g, respectively. N_g denotes users in g, and $\mathbf{W_h}$ is a learnable matrix.

The messaging passing mechanism in IHG-Encoder is *relation-wise*. Representations of neighboring nodes connected to a user u by the same relation r are aggregated by three different pooling methods. Results are concatenated and passed to a single-layer feedforward neural network:

$$\mathbf{x}_{N_i^r}^{(k+1)} = \text{mean}(\mathbf{h}_{r,j_1}^{(k)}, \ldots, \mathbf{h}_{r,j_*}^{(k)}) \qquad \mathbf{h}_{N_i^r}^{(k+1)} = \mathbf{x}_{N_i^r}^{(k+1)} \oplus \mathbf{y}_{N_i^r}^{(k+1)} \oplus \mathbf{z}_{N_i^r}^{(k+1)}$$

$$\mathbf{y}_{N_i^r}^{(k+1)} = \text{max}(\mathbf{h}_{r,j_1}^{(k)}, \ldots, \mathbf{h}_{r,j_*}^{(k)}) \qquad \mathbf{m}_{N_i^r}^{(k+1)} = \mathbf{W}_r\mathbf{h}_{N_i^r}^{(k+1)} + \mathbf{b}_r \qquad (2)$$

$$\mathbf{z}_{N_i^r}^{(k+1)} = \text{sum}(\mathbf{h}_{r,j_1}^{(k)}, \ldots, \mathbf{h}_{r,j_*}^{(k)})$$

where the superscript (k) indicates the k-th iteration, $\oplus$ is the concatenation operation, N_i^r denotes the relation-r-based neighbors of node i and $j_* \in N_i^r$. $\mathbf{h}_{r,j_*}^{(k)}$ is the representation of node j_* for relation r, and $\mathbf{h}_{r,j_*}^{(0)}$ is equivalent to $\mathbf{h}_{j_*}^{(0)}$. mean$(\cdot)$, max$(\cdot)$ and sum$(\cdot)$ are average pooling, max pooling and sum pooling, respectively. W_r and b_r are learnable weights for relation type r.

IHG-Encoder adds a self-connection to each node so that the original node attributes extracted based on human knowledge can be retained in message passing:

$$\mathbf{s}_{r,i}^{(k+1)} = \mathbf{W}_{r,s}\mathbf{h}_{r,i}^{(0)} + \mathbf{b}_{r,s}, \qquad \mathbf{g}_{r,i}^{(k+1)} = \text{RELU}(\mathbf{m}_{N_i^r}^{(k+1)} \oplus \mathbf{s}_{r,i}^{(k+1)}) \qquad (3)$$

where $\mathbf{W}_{r,s}$ and $\mathbf{b}_{r,s}$ are learnable parameters and RELU$(\cdot)$ is the Rectified Linear Unit. The acquired $\mathbf{g}_{r,i}$ is then passed to a feedforward neural network with an L_2 normalization:

$$\mathbf{q}_{r,i}^{(k+1)} = \text{RELU}(\mathbf{W}_{r,q}\mathbf{g}_{r,i}^{(k+1)} + \mathbf{b}_{r,q}), \qquad \mathbf{h}_{r,i}^{(k+1)} = \mathbf{q}_{r,i}^{(k+1)} \Big/ \left\|\mathbf{q}_{r,i}^{(k+1)}\right\| \qquad (4)$$

where $\mathbf{W}_{r,q}$ and $\mathbf{b}_{r,q}$ are learnable weights, and $\mathbf{h}_{r,i}$ indicates the final generated representation of i w.r.t. the relation r.

The output representations of node i for all relations will go through an inter-relation aggregation module and the result is the representation for node i:

$$\mathbf{h}_i^{(k+1)} = \text{AGG}(\{\mathbf{h}_{r,i}^{(k+1)}, \forall r \in R\}) \qquad (5)$$

where AGG is the aggregation function and we adopt mean pooling. IHG-Encoder stacks two of the above GNN layers (i.e., Eqs. 2, 3, 4 and 5) to generate the final representation of node i. Note that some user nodes may only exist in certain view of the constructed heterogeneous graph, e.g., a user only has ADD actions in the considered time period. For other views the users are absent, their corresponding passing messages will be set to zero.

IHG-Encoder can be optimized with a standard binary cross entropy loss over labeled nodes. IHG-Encoder does not maintain node embeddings which are bounded by specific nodes. Instead, learnable weights $\mathbf{W}$ and $\mathbf{b}$ are updated during optimization. In detection, the trained model can be used to produce representations for *new* nodes based on their structural and raw attribute information. Hence, IHG-Encoder is indeed inductive (i.e., the trained model can be used over unseen nodes), which is essential for representation learning in WeChat as new users emerge every day. MHT-GNN, which uses IHG-Encoder as its backbone, is therefore also able to generate representations for unseen nodes.

Temporal Snapshot Sequence Encoder (TSS-Encoder). We observed that, in "Click Farming", a fraudster's fraud actions may spread across multiple timestamps. A fraudster Alice adds many potential victims as friends at time t_1. Alice spends a few days using high reward as bait to convince them to join a "Click Farming" group. Then, at time t_2, Alice will invite baited users to the group. Alice may continue to be active in the group performing actions like sending bonus packages for encouragement at time t_3. On the contrary, a normal user Bob typically does not have so many behaviors within a relatedly short time window. Hence, we concatenate the presentations of a user in different snapshots as its *temporal snapshot sequence* to capture temporal patterns in the HTG.

Given a series of historical snapshots $\{\mathcal{G}^t\}_{t=1}^T$ as inputs, we apply IHG-Encoder over each snapshot to obtain the representations for all the nodes in each snapshot. By doing so, we collect a sequence of representations for each user u at different time steps. Specifically, for each node u, we define its temporal snapshot sequence as $\text{seq}_u^{temp} = [\mathbf{h}_u^1, \mathbf{h}_u^2, \dots, \mathbf{h}_u^T]$. Note that the WeChat graph can easily scale to millions or even tens of millions due to its massive users. We can utilize an efficient database (e.g., a key-value pair database) to store previous feature representations generated by IHG-Encoder for each user. When checking a user's anomalousness in current timestamp t, we can easily retrieve his/her historical representations from the database and construct the temporal snapshot sequence in a blink. Only the current representations requires the generation of the IHG-Encoder.

Next, we aggregate the retrieved temporal snapshot sequence to a representation that captures user behavior patterns. We adopt the Long Short-Term Memory (LSTM) as TSS-Encoder to model the input sequence seq_u^{temp} and capture the dynamic of user activities. LSTM fits perfectly in this scenario for the reason that it recognizes temporal dependencies. Each layer of the LSTM computes the following transformations:

$$\mathbf{f}_t = \sigma(\mathbf{W}_f[\mathbf{h}_{t-1}, \mathbf{e}_t] + \mathbf{b}_f), \qquad \mathbf{c}_t = \mathbf{f}_t \odot \mathbf{c}_{t-1} + \mathbf{i}_t \odot \tilde{\mathbf{c}}_t$$
$$\mathbf{i}_t = \sigma(\mathbf{W}_i[\mathbf{h}_{t-1}, \mathbf{e}_t] + \mathbf{b}_i), \qquad \mathbf{o}_t = \sigma(\mathbf{W}_o[\mathbf{h}_{t-1}, \mathbf{e}_t] + \mathbf{b}_o) \qquad (6)$$
$$\tilde{\mathbf{c}}_t = \tanh(\mathbf{W}_c[\mathbf{h}_{t-1}, \mathbf{e}_t] + \mathbf{b}_c), \quad \mathbf{h}_t = \mathbf{o}_t \odot \tanh(\mathbf{c}_t)$$

where t is the time step, $\mathbf{h}_t$, $\mathbf{c}_t$, $\mathbf{e}_t$ are hidden state, cell state and previous layer hidden state at time t, respectively. $\mathbf{f}_t$, $\mathbf{i}_t$, $\mathbf{o}_t$ are respectively the forget gate, input gate and output gate, and $\odot$ indicates the Hadamard product.

The last hidden state output by TSS-Encoder is used as the representation $\mathbf{h}_{\text{seq}_u^{temp}}$ of temporal snapshot sequences for a user u.

User Relation Sequence Encoder (URS-Encoder). In social networks, a user's *direct* actions explicitly reveal his/her characteristics. In the HTG, a user's direct actions manifest in edges between itself and its 1-hop out-neighbors. Observed from the "Click Farming" fraud example we discussed in Fig. 1, we can conclude that this type of fraud typically involves several direct actions (e.g., ADD and PULL) of fraudsters appearing in different stages of "Click Farming" frauds (i.e., searching, gain trust and deceive). Hence, we believe it is beneficial to consider a special type of sequence called *user relation sequence*. Such sequences are composed of edges in all the 1-hop neighboring subgraphs of a user node from different snapshot and these edges are sorted in chronological order.

Given a node v and its 1-hop out-degree neighboring node set $N_v = [u_1, \ldots, u_m]$ associated with corresponding edge set $E_v = \{(v, u_1, t_1), \ldots, (v, u_m, t_m)\}$ where $|N_v| = m$ and a tuple (v, u_i, t_i) indicates that there is an edge from v to u_i at time step t_i, we sort N_v in a chronological manner and sample nodes from each time step to form a user relation sequence $\{u_1, u_2, \ldots, u_T\}_v$ for user v. For any two nodes u_i and u_j in the sequence with $i < j$, their associated edges (v, u_i, t_i) and (v, u_j, t_j) satisfy that $t_i < t_j$. An example is provided in the bottom left of Fig. 2.

When constructing user relation sequences, some issues require extra attention and we handle them as follows:

– The number of 1-hop neighbors is uneven across the graph, meaning that some users are relatively active in the recorded time period while some are not. Active users have much more user relation sequences than inactive users, which may lead to model bias. Therefore, we sample up to a predefined maximum number of sequences for each user to avoid model bias as well as speed up model training.

- For users with few or no out-degree neighbors during the recorded time period, we take the sub-sequence from other users as sequences. For instance, node v_2 in the bottom left of Fig. 2 has no out-degree neighbors. But v_2 exists in the out-degree neighborhood of v_1. Hence, we extract the sub-sequence from v_1 that starts with v_2 as the user relation sequence for v_2.

User relation sequence describes a user's behavior over time, which remedies the limitation of temporal snapshot sequence that solely contains the hidden state of the same user over time. Given the user relation sequence of node u: $\mathrm{seq}_u^{rel} = [v_1^{(u)}, v_2^{(u)}, \ldots, v_T^{(u)}]$, where $v_t^{(u)}$ ($1 \leq t \leq T$) denotes the user/group node with which u interacts at t-th time step, we first generate initial embeddings for nodes in the sequence using the same projection shown in Eq. 1. Then, similar to TSS-Encoder, the embeddings sequence $[\mathbf{h}_{v_1^{(u)}}, \mathbf{h}_{v_2^{(u)}}, \ldots, \mathbf{h}_{v_T^{(u)}}]$ is fed into URS-Encoder composed of a LSTM to produce the representation $\mathbf{h}_{\mathrm{seq}_u^{rel}}$ of the user relation sequences for the user u.

Optimization of Pretraining Phase. We train TSS-Encoder, URS-Encoder and IHG-Encoder$_{\mathrm{detect}}$ independently on the training data with limited labels using binary cross-entropy loss and Adam optimizer. IHG-Encoder$_{\mathrm{detect}}$ adopts the same encoder design as IHG-Encoder. As shown in Fig. 2, IHG-Encoder$_{\mathrm{detect}}$ is later used in the detection phase. During training, each of TSS-Encoder, URS-Encoder and IHG-Encoder$_{\mathrm{detect}}$ is connected to its own score module, which is a linear mapping layer followed by a sigmoid function, for predicting suspicious scores. If the predicted score of an input node is larger than 0.5, it is labeled as a "Click Farming" fraudster.

3.5   Detection Phase

During the detection phase, for a user node v, we generated temporal snapshot sequence representation $\mathbf{h}_{\mathrm{seq}_v^{temp}}$ and user relation sequence representation $\mathbf{h}_{\mathrm{seq}_v^{rel}}$ using pretrained TSS-Encoder and URS-Encoder. Then, $\mathbf{h}_{\mathrm{seq}_v^{temp}}$, $\mathbf{h}_{\mathrm{seq}_v^{rel}}$ and initial representation $\mathbf{h}_v^{(0)}$ are concatenated and the result is fed into IHG-Encoder$_{\mathrm{detect}}$ followed by its scoring module to estimate the suspicious score of v. If the output value for v is larger than 0.5, v will be predicted as a "Click Farming" fraudster.

4   Experiments

4.1   Experiment Setting

Data. We extract a 14 day-period dataset from WeChat and construct a million-scale HTG as defined in Sect. 3.3. The graph contains nearly 4.6 million user nodes and 190 thousand WeChat chat group nodes. The number of edges are approximately 15 million covering three relations: ADD, PULL and ENTER. We use one day as the interval between two timestamps. Thus, for a 14 days observation period we derive 14 separate graph snapshots. We set the maximum number of sampled user relation sequence for each user to be 10. 85,000 user nodes are manually labeled by human experts: 25,000 are fraudsters and 60,000 are normal users. The labels for other 4.5 million user nodes are unknown. We randomly divide the labeled users by a ratio of 8:1:1 for training, validation and testing.

Baseline. We compare MHT-GNN with several competitive baselines:

- **Non-GNN classification methods.** XGBoost [3] and MLP. XGBoost is a gradient boosting algorithm that shows promising results in numerous prediction tasks and MLP is a feedfoward neural network with three hidden layers to predict the suspicious score of a node. The two methods only relies on data attributes for prediction.
- **Homogeneous graph based methods.** Graph Convolutional Network (GCN) [5] averages neighbor's embeddings with a linear projection, and Graph Attention Network (GAT) [16] utilizes attention mechanism to aggregate information of neighbors.
- **Heterogeneous graph based methods.** Relational Graph Convolutional Network (RGCN) [13] designs different linear projections for different types of relations for information aggregation, and Simple Heterogeneous Graph Neural Network (Simple-HGN) [7] enhances GAT with the redesign of three techniques: learnable edge-type embedding, residual connections, and L_2 normalization on the output embeddings.
- **Temporal graph anomaly detection method.** AddGraph [21] is an dynamic graph anomaly detection method. It leverages a GCN module to capture spatial information, and employs a GRU-attention module to extract short- and long- term dynamic evolving patterns. Furthermore, we modify the base graph encoder of AddGraph from GCN to RGCN in order to model the heterogeneous information and name this variant as AddGraph-H.

To verify the contribution of each component in MHT-GNN, we design several versions of MHT-GNN as follows:

- IHG-Encoder: It only contains the inductive heterogeneous GNN encoder.
- MHT-GNN-T: It is a variant of MHT-GNN that removes URS Encoder.
- MHT-GNN-R: It is a variant of MHT-GNN that removes TSS Encoder.

We adopt the same score module design (i.e., a linear mapping layer followed by a sigmoid function) as MHT-GNN for baselines without a score module. All methods adopt Adam optimizer if possible. We set initial learning rate to be 0.001 and use 128 as the dimension of representations. We use a batch size of 256. All methods will terminate optimization when they converge.

Evaluation Metrics. We use five widely adopted evaluation metrics:

- **AUC**: It signifies the probability that the positive sample's score is higher than the negative sample's score.
- **KS**: It is a measure of the degree of separation between the positive and negative distributions [11].
- **Precision, Recall and F1-score**: Precision is a measure of how many positive predictions are correct while Recall measures how many positive cases the classifier correctly predicted over all the positive cases in the data. F1-score is the harmonic mean of Precision and Recall.

Table 1. Overall detection performance.

Method	AUC	KS	Precision	Recall	F1-score
XGBoost	0.7452	0.3385	0.5783	0.3224	0.4140
MLP	0.7248	0.3375	0.5809	0.3287	0.4193
GCN	0.7946	0.4560	0.6488	0.4670	0.5431
GAT	0.8060	0.4801	0.6443	0.4869	0.5547
RGCN	0.8483	0.5308	0.7063	0.5373	0.6097
Simple-HGN	0.8498	0.5452	0.6972	0.5556	0.6183
IHG-Encoder	0.8623	0.5642	0.6907	0.5990	0.6415
AddGraph	0.8239	0.4949	0.6505	0.5716	0.6085
AddGraph-H	0.8416	0.5499	0.6467	0.6078	0.6251
MHT-GNN	**0.8969**	**0.6397**	**0.7297**	**0.6943**	**0.7115**

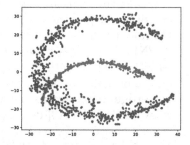

Table 3. t-SNE Projection of User Node Representations Generated by MHT-GNN: (1) Red Nodes: Fraudsters. (2) Blue Nodes: Normal users. (Color figure online)

Table 2. Results of ablation study.

Method	AUC	KS	Precision	Recall	F1-score
IHG-Encoder	0.8623	0.5642	0.6907	0.5990	0.6415
MHT-GNN-R	0.8853	0.6169	0.7222	0.6853	0.7031
MHT-GNN-T	0.8856	0.6239	0.7300	0.6622	0.6944
MHT-GNN	**0.8969**	**0.6397**	**0.7297**	**0.6943**	**0.7115**

Overall Detection Results. Table 1 presents the overall results of each method. The best performance are denoted in bold. From the results, we can see:

1. GNN-based approaches GCN and GAT generally exceed non-GNN methods XGBoost and MLP, indicating the spatial dependencies depicted by graph structure in WeChat contain rich information that can improve model performance in the CFD task.
2. Both dynamic and heterogeneous graph based models could achieve satisfactory results, and heterogeneous graph based methods generally outperform homogeneous graph based approaches. This observation shows that temporal dependencies and multi-relation information help model a user's behavior pattern better and boost the detection accuracy.

3. IHG-Encoder significantly outperforms other GNN-based methods. This observation has supported our decision of using IHG-Encoder as the backbone of MHT-GNN.
4. MHT-GNN achieves much better performance than other baselines including state-of-the-art dynamic graph anomaly detection methods AddGraph and its multi-relation version AddGraph-H. MHT-GNN consistently outperforms all baselines on all measures. The results demonstrate the superiority of MHT-GNN over existing methods for the CFD task.

Ablation Study. Table 2 lists the results of different variations of MHT-GNN. From Table 2, we can observe that:

1. The incorporation of either TSS Encoder or URS Encoder brings performance gain, as both MHT-GNN-T and MHT-GNN-R outperform IHG-Encoder.
2. The complete MHT-GNN shows the best result, indicating that modeling two views of historical data in HTG together can remedy the limitation of capturing only one view.

Overall, we can conclude that each module in MHT-GNN indeed contributes to the superior performance of MHT-GNN over existing detection methods in the CFD task of WeChat.

Visualization of Representation. To investigate the qualities of node representations generated by MHT-GNN, we adopt t-SNE [9] to project representations of nodes in the test set into a 2-dimensional space. The projection result is visualized in Fig. 3. From the result, we can see that representations of fraudsters and normal users have a clear distinction, showing that MHT-GNN is able to produce high-quality representations for the CFD task of WeChat.

5 Conclusion

In this paper, we illustrate MHT-GNN for the CFD task in WeChat. MHT-GNN can capture dynamics and diversity of MMMA data through multi-view learning and graph representation learning. Experiments on a real-world graph extracted from the CFD task in WeChat demonstrate the effectiveness of MHT-GNN. In the future, we will introduce attention mechanism for both intra-relation and inter-relation aggregation to adaptively assign weights for modeling the importance of information and further improve detection results. We also plan to enhance the interpretability of detection results so that fewer normal users will be wrongly labeled as fraudsters.

Acknowledgements. This work was supported by the National Natural Science Foundation of China (No. 62002303, 42171456), the Natural Science Foundation of Fujian Province of China (No. 2020J05001), the China Fundamental Research Funds for the Central Universities (No. 20720210098), and 2021 Tencent WeChat Rhino-Bird Focused Research Program.

References

1. Akoglu, L., Tong, H., Koutra, D.: Graph based anomaly detection and description: a survey. Data Min. Knowl. Discov. **29**(3), 626–688 (2015)
2. Cai, L., et al.: Structural temporal graph neural networks for anomaly detection in dynamic graphs. In: CIKM, pp. 3747–3756 (2021)
3. Chen, T., Guestrin, C.: XGBoost: a scalable tree boosting system. In: KDD, pp. 785–794 (2016)
4. Ding, K., Li, J., Bhanushali, R., Liu, H.: Deep anomaly detection on attributed networks. In: SDM, pp. 594–602 (2019)
5. Kipf, T.N., Welling, M.: Semi-supervised classification with graph convolutional networks. In: ICLR (2017)
6. Li, N., Sun, H., Chipman, K.C., George, J., Yan, X.: A probabilistic approach to uncovering attributed graph anomalies. In: SDM, pp. 82–90 (2014)
7. Lv, Q., et al.: Are we really making much progress?: Revisiting, benchmarking and refining heterogeneous graph neural networks. In: KDD, pp. 1150–1160 (2021)
8. Ma, X., et al.: A comprehensive survey on graph anomaly detection with deep learning. IEEE Transactions on Knowledge and Data Engineering (2021)
9. van der Maaten, L., Hinton, G.: Visualizing data using t-SNE. J. Mach. Learn. Res. **9**, 2579–2605 (2008)
10. Manzoor, E.A., Milajerdi, S.M., Akoglu, L.: Fast memory-efficient anomaly detection in streaming heterogeneous graphs. In: KDD, pp. 1035–1044 (2016)
11. Massey, F.J.: The kolmogorov-smirnov test for goodness of fit. J. Am. Stat. Assoc. **46**(253), 68–78 (1951)
12. Peng, Z., Luo, M., Li, J., Xue, L., Zheng, Q.: A deep multi-view framework for anomaly detection on attributed networks. IEEE Transactions on Knowledge and Data Engineering (2020)
13. Schlichtkrull, M.S., Kipf, T.N., Bloem, P., van den Berg, R., Titov, I., Welling, M.: Modeling relational data with graph convolutional networks. In: Gangemi, A., et al. (eds.) ESWC, pp. 593–607 (2018)
14. Shi, C., Li, Y., Zhang, J., Sun, Y., Yu, P.S.: A survey of heterogeneous information network analysis. IEEE Trans. Knowl. Data Eng. **29**(1), 17–37 (2017)
15. Sricharan, K., Das, K.: Localizing anomalous changes in time-evolving graphs. In: SIGMOD, pp. 1347–1358. ACM (2014)
16. Velickovic, P., Cucurull, G., Casanova, A., Romero, A., Liò, P., Bengio, Y.: Graph attention networks. In: ICLR (2018)
17. Wang, L., et al.: TCL: transformer-based dynamic graph modelling via contrastive learning. arXiv Preprint (2021). https://arxiv.org/abs/2105.07944
18. Wang, Y., Zhang, J., Guo, S., Yin, H., Li, C., Chen, H.: Decoupling representation learning and classification for GNN-based anomaly detection. In: SIGIR, pp. 1239–1248 (2021)
19. Xu, Z., et al.: Efficiently answering k-hop reachability queries in large dynamic graphs for fraud feature extraction. In: MDM, pp. 238–245 (2022)
20. Yu, W., Cheng, W., Aggarwal, C.C., Zhang, K., Chen, H., Wang, W.: NetWalk: a flexible deep embedding approach for anomaly detection in dynamic networks. In: KDD, pp. 2672–2681 (2018)
21. Zheng, L., Li, Z., Li, J., Li, Z., Gao, J.: AddGraph: anomaly detection in dynamic graph using attention-based temporal GCN. In: IJCAI, pp. 4419–4425 (2019)

Deep Forest with Sparse Topological Feature Extraction and Hash Mapping for Brain Network Classification

Junwei Li[1,2(✉)] and Junzhong Ji[1,2]

[1] Faculty of Information Technology, Beijing University of Technology, Beijing, China
liw@emails.bjut.edu.cn
[2] Artificial Intelligence Institute, Beijing Municipal Key Laboratory of Multimedia and Intelligent Software Technology, Beijing, China

Abstract. As a novel non-neural network style deep learning method, the deep forest can perform effective feature learning without relying on a large amount of training data, thus brings us some opportunities to accurately classify brain networks (BNs) on limited fMRI data. Currently, preliminary attempts to use deep forest to classify BNs are already emerging. However, these studies simply adopted the sliding windows to scan the inputted BNs and failed to consider the inherent sparsity of BNs, which makes them susceptible to those redundant edges in BNs with little weight. In this paper, we propose a deep forest framework with sparse topological feature extraction and hash mapping (DF-STFEHM) for BN classification. Specifically, we first design an extremely random forest guided by a weighted random walk (ERF-WRW) to extract sparse topological features from BNs, where the random walk strategy is used to capture their topological structures and the weighted strategy is used to reduce the influence of redundant edges with little weight. Then, we map these sparse topological features into a compact hashing space by a kernel hashing, which can better preserve topological similarities of brain networks in the hashing space. Finally, the obtained hash codes are fed into the casForest to perform deeper feature learning and classification. Experimental results on ABIDE I and ADHD-200 datasets show that the DF-STFEHM outperforms several state-of-the-art methods on classification performance and accurately identifies abnormal brain regions.

Keywords: Brain network classification · Deep forest · Sparse topological feature · Kernel hashing · Random walk

1 Introduction

The human brain is currently the most complex system known. It performs various complex cognitive tasks through interactions and coordination between distributed brain regions [11]. Currently, a lot of studies have shown that when a person suffers from a neuropsychiatric disorder like autism spectrum disorder

© The Author(s), under exclusive license to Springer Nature Switzerland AG 2022
S. Khanna et al. (Eds.): PRICAI 2022, LNCS 13629, pp. 161–174, 2022.
https://doi.org/10.1007/978-3-031-20862-1_12

(ASD), many interactions between these brain regions will be affected to a certain extent [19]. Advances in functional magnetic resonance imaging (fMRI) enabled us to map these patterns of functional interactions in a non-invasive way, and further construct functional brain network (BN) of the whole brain [7]. Therefore, more and more researchers are trying to diagnose neuropsychiatric disorders by classifying the BNs [26].

At present, there are a large amount of machine learning (ML) methods have been employed to classify the BNs. Among them, the early researches were mainly based on traditional ML methods. E.g., Jie et al. [11] employed the multi-kernel support vector machine (SVM) on brain networks for diagnose of Alzheimer' disease. Zhu et al. [31] adopted the weighted least absolute shrinkage and selection operator (LASSO) to boost the classification performance of multiple international BN data sites. Gareth et al. [2] used random forest (RF) to perform robust classification of preterm and term-born neonates. In addition to these traditional ML methods, deep neural network (NN) methods, which achieved great success in many fields in recent years, have also been successfully applied to brain network classification. For example, Kawahara et al. [12] proposed a BrainNetCNN framework which is the first convolutional neural network (CNN) framework designed for BNs. On this basis, Ji et al. [10] proposed another CNN framework with a CKEW kernel (CNN-CKEW) to extract hierarchical topological features for BNs. Similarly, the graph convolutional neural network (GCNN) [14, 16], deep belief network (DBN) [9], graph variational auto-encoder [3], and other methods are also used for brain network classification. Due to their excellent layer-wise feature extraction ability and high-dimensional data processing capacity, these methods can generally achieve better performance than that of the traditional ML-based methods. However, these NN-style methods usually need massive training samples to determine their numerous parameters, and the datasets encountered in neuroimaging are often high-dimensional but small sample-size. Such contradiction between the demand of massive training samples and the objective reality of small-scale brain networks, seriously limits the further applications of these NN methods in brain network classification.

As a newly developed non-NN style deep learning (DL) method, the deep forest (DF) [30] performs layer-wise feature learning and classification by constructing cascade forest (casForest) structure. Moreover, as the number of its cascade layers is automatically determined according to available training samples, the deep forest performs well on many small-scale datasets, providing us with new opportunity for accurately classifying BNs on limited fMRI data. Currently, preliminary attempts to use deep forest to classify BNs are already emerging. For example, Li et al. [13] proposed a deep forest framework with cross-shaped window scanning mechanism (DF-CWSM) for the diagnosis of ASD and achieved better performance than a lot of NN methods. It designed a cross-shaped window scanning mechanism to extract node-level and edge-level topological features respectively, and then input these local topological features into the casForest for layer-wise feature learning and classification. Shao et al. [22] proposed a revised deep forest model which can accurately identify patients with attention deficit hyperactivity disorder (ADHD) from healthy controls. Specifically, it adopted the 1-D and 3-D sliding windows to extract spatial adjacent relationships from the original inputs, and further used casForest to carry out layer-wise feature learning. All excellent performance of these researches proves the effectiveness of the DF method in the field of brain network classification. However, the sliding window scanning mechanisms adopted by these methods treats all features in BNs equally and fails to consider the inherent sparsity of BNs, which makes them susceptible to those redundant edges in BNs with little weight.

In this paper, we propose a deep forest framework with sparse topological feature extraction and hash mapping (DF-STFEHM) for brain network classification. Specifically, we first design an extremely random forest guided by a weighted random walk (ERF-WRW) to extract sparse topological features from BNs, where the random walk strategy is used to capture the topological structures and the weighted strategy is used to reduce the influence of redundant edges with little weight. Then, we design a novel kernel to measure the similarities of the extracted topological features, and map these features into a compact hashing space by a kernel hashing. Finally, the obtained hash codes are fed into the casForest to perform deeper feature learning and classification. Experimental results on ABIDE I and ADHD-200 datasets show that the DF-STFEHM outperforms several state-of-the-art methods on classification performance and accurately identifies abnormal brain regions.

The main contributions of this paper are summarized as follows:

- To take the inherent sparsity of brain networks into account in the classification procedure of our DF-STFEHM framework, this paper proposes an extremely random forest guided by a weighted random walk (ERF-WRW), which combines the weighted walk procedure on BNs (graphs) and the top-down decision making procedure of decision trees to effectively extract sparse topological features from BNs.
- To represent these sparse topological features extracted by ERF-WRW in a more compact way, the paper designs a novel kernel to measure the similarity of these features and employs a kernel hashing to map them into a compact hashing space.
- Systematic experiments on two datasets have been conducted to verify the effectiveness of the proposed DF-STFEHM. Experimental results show that the proposed framework can achieve competitive classification performance.

2   Related Work

2.1   Random Walk-Based Graph Embedding Methods

Graph embedding (or node embedding) is a technique of converting the high-dimensional sparse graphs into low-dimensional, dense vector spaces. Its main task is to encode nodes or edges to lower dimensional vector representations and preserve network structure properties. Motivated by the "word2vec" method [17] to learn word representations by leveraging the contextual information of words in sentences, perozzi *et al.* [20] proposed the first random walk-based graph embedding method, i.e., DeepWalk. It treats the local topological context information obtained from truncated random walks as the equivalent of sentences and learn latent representations for nodes in graph. In the years that followed, various variations of DeepWalk such as Node2Vec [6], Role2Vec [1], and biased random walk graph embedding [29], were proposed. These methods generally follow a similar flow [25]: Firstly, as shown in Fig. 1, the random walk methods are applied to generate a set of node context. For example, w_{v_0} in the figure represents a random walk starting from node v_0. Secondly, each obtained node context information w_{v_i} is embed to low-dimensional vectors (r_i) by an encoder (e.g., SkipGram). Generally, these learned node embedding vectors can be readily and efficiently used for different downstream tasks, such as link prediction, node classification, and community detection.

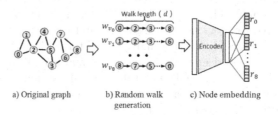

a) Original graph   b) Random walk   c) Node embedding
                              generation

Fig. 1. Schematic diagram of random walk-based graph embedding methods.

2.2 Learning to Hashing

The core idea of hashing learning method is to compress high-dimensional data vector into compact binary code, so as to retrieve and store high-dimensional samples more efficiently [23]. According to the different design ideas of the hash function, hashing methods can be divided into data-independence methods and data-dependence methods. The data-independent hashing method is also called Local Sensitive Hash (LSH), which uses random projections to construct random hash functions. While the data-dependent hashing method (also called learning to hashing) to learn a specific hash function according to a given training sample set. The kernel hashing [8] used in this paper is a kind of data-dependent hashing, which can create efficient hash codes for large scale data of general formats with any kernel function, including kernels on vectors, graphs, sequences, sets and so on.

2.3 Extremely Random Forest

Extremely random forest (ERF) [5], also known as extremely randomized trees, is a classical tree-based ensemble learning method that builds multiple unpruned decision trees according to a top-down procedure and combines their results through a voting process. There are two main characteristics of the decision trees in ERF: a) Each tree in ERF is grown on the whole learning samples. b) The splitting attribute and cut-point of each tree node are randomly selected.

3   Deep Forest with Sparse Topological Feature Extraction and Hash Mapping

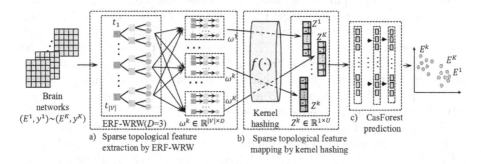

a) Sparse topological feature extraction by ERF-WRW

b) Sparse topological feature mapping by kernel hashing

Fig. 2. The overall framework of our proposed DF-STFEHM.

3.1   Overview of DF-STFEHM

In order to classify BNs more effectively by considering their sparsity, this paper propose a deep forest framework with sparse topological feature extraction and hash mapping (DF-STFEHM). It mainly contains three modules: sparse topological feature extraction by ERF-WRW, sparse topological feature mapping by kernel hashing, and casForest prediction. Suppose $G = (V, E)$ represents a brain network. V is the node set of G, where v_i is the ith node (brain region) in it. $E \in \mathbb{R}^{|V| \times |V|}$ is the adjacency matrix of G, where each edge $e_{i,j}$ represents the connection strength between v_i and v_j. Let $S^G = \{(G^k, y^k)|y^k \in \{0, 1\}, k = 1, 2, ..., K\}$ represent a BN dataset, G^k is the kth sample in it, y^k is the label of G^k. Considering that the brain regions of BN are pre-defined and fixed, the G^k can also be simply represented by E^k, i.e., $S^G = \{(E^k, y^k)|k = 1, 2, ..., K\}$. As shown in Fig. 2, the learning samples S^G are first inputted into the ERF-WRW to train $|V|$ decision trees, in which the growing procedure of the ith tree t_i is guided by the weighted random walk procedure starting from node v_i. D is the depth of the decision trees in ERF-WRW. Accordingly, a topological feature matrix $\omega^k \in \mathbb{R}^{|V| \times D}$ can be obtained for each E^k. Then, ω^k is mapped into a compact hashing space by a kernel hashing. Let Z^k denote the hash code of ω^k, samples with high similar topological features will have similar hash codes in the hashing space. Finally, the obtained hash codes are used to train the casForest and produce the predicted results.

3.2   Sparse Topological Feature Extraction by ERF-WRW

In this algorithm, we first propose an extremely random forest guided by a weighted random walk (ERF-WRW) to extract sparse topological features from the brain networks. Compared with the classical ERF algorithm, the modifications of our ERF-WRW is mainly reflected in the generation of splitting attribute and the output of forest. Here are some details:

a) Instead of selecting splitting attributes and cut-points at random, the ERF-WRW chooses splitting attributes for its tree nodes according to the guidance of a weighted random walk procedure. Specifically, suppose that $T(E)$ denotes a ERF-WRW forest with $|V|$ decision trees. It adopts the adjacency matrix of brain network as input. $t_i(E)$ denotes the ith tree in T, D denotes the maximum depth of the decision trees in $T(E)$. For the sake of understanding, we assume that each tree in $T(E)$ can be represented as a full binary decision tree of depth D. To distinguish, BN nodes (i.e., v_i) represent the nodes in brain network, and tree nodes represent the nodes in ERF-WRW trees. The splitting attribute for a given tree node ϕ is determined by the following procedure:

Firstly, it generates a set of candidate splitting attributes for ϕ. Let $S^\phi = \{(E^{k'}, y^{k'})|k' = 1, 2, ..., K', 1 < K' \leq K\}$ correspond to the local learning samples of ϕ, the candidate splitting attribute set $\varphi(\phi)$ can be obtained by

$$\varphi(\phi) = \{e_{b,l}|Parent(\phi) = e_{a,b}, 0 \leq l < |V|, v_l \in \mathcal{N}(v_b)\} \qquad (1)$$

where $Parent(\phi)$ is a function of ϕ that returns the split attribute of its parent node. When ϕ is the root node of t_i, it returns $e_{i,i}$. $\mathcal{N}(v_b)$ denotes the neighbours of node v_b in BNs. That is to say $\varphi(\phi)$ is a set of adjacent edges of $Parent(\phi)$.

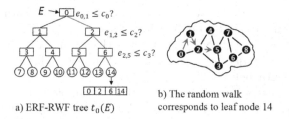

a) ERF-RWF tree $t_0(E)$ b) The random walk corresponds to leaf node 14

Fig. 3. An example of ERF-WRW tree $t_0(E)$ and the walk path corresponding to leaf 14.

Secondly, it selects an attribute from the candidate set $\varphi(\phi)$ as the splitting attribute through weighted random sampling and randomly generate a corresponding cut-point for splitting. Let $p^\phi(e_{b,l})$ denote the probability of $e_{b,l} \in \varphi(\phi)$ being selected as the splitting attribute, it can be calculated by

$$p^\phi(e_{b,l}) = \frac{1}{K'} \cdot \sum_{k'=1}^{K'} \frac{e_{b,l}^{k'}}{\sum_{v_m^{k'} \in \mathcal{N}(v_b^{k'})} e_{b,m}^{k'}} \qquad (2)$$

As $\forall e_{b,l} \in \varphi(\phi)$ is a adjacent edge of $Parent(\phi)$, each decision path in $t_i(E)$ can be regarded as a weighted random walk procedure on G starting from BN node v_i. Figure 3 shows an example of ERF-WRW tree t_0 and the walk path corresponding to leaf node 14. Here, the process of selecting a splitting attribute $e_{b,l}$ from $\varphi(\phi)$ can be regarded as a random walk (single step) from v_b to its neighbor node v_l, and $p^\phi(e_{b,l})$ can be regarded as the transition probability.

Based on the above splitting attribute selecting procedure, t_i can be constructed by a top-down inductive splitting procedure. The detail construction procedure of ERF-WRW trees is summarized in Algorithm 1.

Algorithm 1. Construction procedure of ERF-WRW tree (ERF-WRW-TREE).

Input: Local training data S', initially $S' = S^\phi$. Maximum depth of ERF-WRW tree D and current depth d, initially $d = 1$. Minimum samples for splitting a node M_{min}.
Output: The root node of the decision tree.

1: **if** $d < D$ and $len(S') \geq M_{min}$ **then**
2:     Construct a internal node ϕ
3:     Generate the candidate set $\varphi(\phi)$ for ϕ according to Eq. 1.
4:     Calculate the probability $p^\phi(e_{b,l})$ of each attribute in $\varphi(\phi)$ according to Eq. 2.
5:     Randomly select a attribute from $\varphi(\phi)$ as the splitting attribute according to the selected probabilities $p^\phi(e_{b,l})$.
6:     Randomly generate a cut-point for the splitting attribute.
7:     Split the learning set S' into two sub learning set (S'_1 and S'_2) according to the splitting attribute and cut-point.
8:     Construct the left and the right subtree of ϕ according to algorithm 1, i.e., ERF-WRW-TREE($S'_1, d+1, D, M_{min}$) and ERF-WRW-TREE($S'_2, d+1, D, M_{min}$).
9: **else**
10:    Construct a leaf node τ.
11: **end if**
12: **Return** the constructed node ϕ or τ.

---

b) Since each decision path in ERF-WRW can be regarded as a weighted random walk procedure on brain networks, the ERF-WRW encodes all the prediction decision paths to represent the sparse topological features of BNs. Specifically, the ERF-WRW $T(E)$ takes the adjacency matrix of a BN as input, and sends this data to each root node of trees in it. Once the data traverse down to the leaf nodes for all trees, the ERF-WRW will return a $|V| \times D$ dimensional local topological feature matrix for E. Let $\omega = T(E) \in \mathbb{R}^{|V| \times D}$ denote the out put of ERF-WRW. $\omega_i \in \mathbb{R}^{1 \times D}$ is the output of $t_i(E)$, where the dth element of ω_i denote the index of dth tree node on the prediction decision path of $t_i(E)$. As shown in Fig. 3, suppose that a given BN E^k is inputted t_0, and E^k is traversed down to leaf node 14, ω_0^k will be [0, 2, 6, 14]. The ERF-WRW can output such an sparse topological feature matrix ω for each brain network.

3.3 Sparse Topological Feature Mapping by Kernel Hashing

In order to represent these sparse topological features extracted by ERF-WRW in a more compact way, we adopt the optimized kernel hashing algorithm [8] to map ω into a compact hashing space. Suppose $Z \in \mathbb{R}^{1 \times U}$ denotes a U-dim hash code, where the uth element of Z is generate by a hashing function $f_u(\omega)$. For a given ω^k, a hash code Z^k can be obtained, where Z_u^k is its uth element. The efficient hash codes can be obtained by the following optimization problem:

$$\min_{A,\beta} \frac{1}{2} \sum_{k_1,k_2=1}^{K} \Psi(\omega^{k_1}, \omega^{k_2}) \|Z^{k_1} - Z^{k_2}\|^2 + \lambda \sum_{u=1}^{U} \|Q_u\|^2$$

$$s.t. \quad \sum_{k=1}^{K} Z^k = 0$$

$$\frac{1}{K} \sum_{k=1}^{K} Z^k (Z^k)^T = I \tag{3}$$

$$Z^k \in \{-1, 1\}^U$$

$$Z_u^k = f_u(\omega^k) = sign(Q_u^T \cdot \xi(\omega^k) - \beta_u)$$

$$Q_u = \sum_{n=1}^{N} A_{n,u} \xi(\omega^n)$$

$$k = 1, \cdots, K, u = 1, \cdots, U, n = 1, \cdots, N, 1 \leq N \leq K$$

Here are U hash functions $\{f_u(\omega), u = 1, \cdots, U\}$ in total, each of which is for one hash bit. Each function $f_u(\omega) = sign(Q_u^T \cdot \xi(\omega) - \beta_u)$ is represented in the kernel form, as in most kernel learning method, where Q_u is the hyperplane vector in the kernel space, ξ is the function for embedding samples to the kernel space and usually is not computable. β is a $U \times 1$ vector, where β_u is the uth element in β representing threshold scalar. Since it is infeasible to define the hyperplane vector Q_u directly in the kernel space, we represent Q_u as a linear combination of landmarks in the kernel space with combination weights denoted as $A_{n,u}$. $\{\omega^n, n = 1, \cdots, N, 1 \leq N \leq K\}$ are landmark samples, which is a subset randomly chosen from the original samples, i.e., $\{\omega^k, k = 1, \cdots, K\}$. The term $\sum_{u=1}^{U} \|Q_u\|^2$ is utilized to a regularized term to control the smoothness of the kernel function $\Psi(\omega^{k_1}, \omega^{k_2})$. Given two samples ω^{k_1} and ω^{k_2}, the kernel function $\Psi(\omega^{k_1}, \omega^{k_2})$ denotes the similarity of these two samples. It can be calculated by

$$\Psi(\omega^{k_1}, \omega^{k_2}) = \sum_{i=1}^{|V|} \psi(\omega_i^{k_1}, \omega_i^{k_2}) \tag{4}$$

where $\psi(\omega_i^{k_1}, \omega_i^{k_2})$ is the similarity of the output of t_i for ω^{k_1} and ω^{k_2}, i.e.,

$$\psi(\omega_i^{k_1}, \omega_i^{k_2}) = \frac{1}{2^{D - \eta(\omega_i^{k_1}, \omega_i^{k_2})}} \tag{5}$$

$\eta(\omega_i^{k_1}, \omega_i^{k_2})$ is the index of the last same element of $\omega_i^{k_1}$ and $\omega_i^{k_2}$. For example, if $\omega_0^{k_1} = [0, 2, 6, 13]$ and $\omega_0^{k_2} = [0, 2, 6, 14]$, $\eta(\omega_0^{k_1}, \omega_0^{k_2}) = 3$. That is to say, as shown in Fig. 3, samples E^{k_1} and E^{k_2} reach the leaf 13 and leaf 14 of t_0, respectively. The last same element of their decision path is node 6, and $2^{D-\eta(\omega_i^{k_1},\omega_i^{k_2})}$ is the number of leaf nodes under node 6.

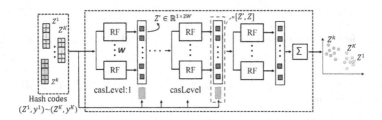

Fig. 4. The schematic diagram of casForest

3.4 CasForest Prediction

CasForest classify the inputted hash codes by automatically extracting high-level features from them. As shown in Fig. 4, the casForest is a multi-layer structure composed of ensembles of decision forests. Suppose there are W forests (extremely random forest or random forest) in each layer, the concatenation of the prediction possibilities of these forests can be considered as augmented feature vector, i.e., $Z' \in \mathbb{R}^{1 \times |y| \cdot W}$. The forests in the 1st layer are trained on $\{(Z^k, y^k), k = 1, \cdots, K\}$ and output the augmented feature vectors to the 2nd layer. For the forests in the 2nd layer, they are trained on the concatenation of Z and Z', i.e., $\{([Z'^k, Z^k], y^k), k = 1, \cdots, K\}$. In a similar fashion, the layer expanding will automatically terminate if there is no significant improvement in accuracy, and the results of the last layer are averaged to make a final prediction.

4 Experiments

4.1 Datasets and Experimental Settings

In this study, we adopted the ABIDE I [4] and ADHD-200 [18] datasets to validate the classification ability of our proposed algorithm. Specifically, there are 1112 subjects with 539 ASD patients and 573 typical controls in ABIDE I, and 876 subjects with 362 ADHD patients and 514 typically controls in ADHD-200. After removing the subjects with erroneous time-series or missing data, 1096 and 850 subjects are retained. Firstly, we adopt the DPARSF to preprocess the raw rs-fMRI images. Then, we parcele the whole brain into 90 regions of interest (ROIs) according to the automated anatomical labeling (AAL) template [24], and extract the mean time-series of each ROI. Finally, the Pearson correlations between each pair of ROIs are calculated to generate the functional connectivity network for each subject. All experiments in this paper are validated by the 5-fold cross-validation. The performances of all methods are evaluated by

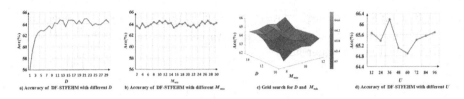

Fig. 5. The feature extraction capability of DF-STFEGHM with different parameters.

computing the classification accuracy, precision, recall and f1 on 10 times independent experiments.

Parameters for ERF-WRW: There are two parameter for ERF-WRW, the maximum depth of decision tree in ERF-WRW D and the minimum sample size for splitting a tree node of decision trees M_{min}. Firstly, we fixed the value of M_{min} at 2 to verify the feature extraction capability of ERF-WRW with different D. As shown in Fig. 5a), when D is small, the accuracy of DF-STFEHM increases rapidly with its increase. And when D reaches 10, it gradually stabilizes. Then, we fixed the value of D at 10 and varied M_{min} from 2 to 30. As shown in Fig. 5b), with the constant change of M_{min}, the accuracy of DF-STFEHM fluctuates slightly. Finally, we applied the grid search to determine the optimal values of D and M_{min}. As shown in Fig. 5c), the corresponding accuracy achieved the highest value when $D = 15$ and $M_{min} = 12$.

Parameters for Optimized Kernel Hashing: There are three parameters in the optimized kernel hashing algorithm [8], i.e., the length of hash codes U, the number of landmark samples N and λ. For N and λ, we use the values recommended in [8], i.e., $\lambda = 0$ and $N = 200$. Moreover, we tested the classification performance of DF-STFEGHM with different U. As shown in Fig. 5d), DF-STFEGHM obtained the hightest accuracy when $U = 36$.

Parameters for casForest: For the casForest, we use the standard cascade structure described in [30], where each cascade layer contains two random forests and two extremely random forests, and each forest contains 500 decision trees.

4.2   Classification Performance of DF-STFEHM

To evaluate our proposed BN classification algorithm DF-STFEHM, we compare it with some typical algorithms, including the traditional ML methods SVM and RF; the NN style methods BrainnetCNN [12], GCNN [16], CNN-CKEW [10], DBN [9], and E-HI-GCN [14]; and non-NN style methods DF [30] and DF-CWSM [13]. Parameters for the comparison methods are selected according to the corresponding references. Classification results of all methods on the two datasets are summarized in Table 1. We can see that our algorithm achieved the highest accuracy and recall rate on the two datasets. Especially in ADHD-200, the DF-STFEHM was almost 1% percent more accurate than other comparison algorithms. The recall rates of DF-STFEHM are at least 5% higher than that

Table 1. Comparison results of different methods

Datasets	Methods	Acc(std)(%)	Pre(std)(%)	Rec(std)(%)	F1(std)
ABIDE I	SVM	63.42	62.34	62.38	0.6236
	RF	63.87	64.74	54.59	0.5923
	BrainnetCNN	65.36(0.48)	64.35(1.36)	67.60(1.78)	0.6593(0.27)
	GCNN	64.00(0.51)	65.41(1.0)	67.41(0.83)	0.6650(0.45)
	CNN-CKEW	67.61(0.39)	65.74(0.48)	63.27(0.68)	0.6448(0.33)
	DBN	67.24(0.75)	**73.10(0.69)**	62.50(0.45)	0.6738(0.59)
	E-HI-GCN	67.64(0.13)	69.51(0.21)	71.76(0.25)	**0.7061(0.94)**
	DF	66.09(0.38)	63.31(0.58)	71.80(0.73)	0.6706(0.11)
	DF-CWSM	66.25(0.14)	63.57(0.78)	71.10(0.27)	0.6709(0.12)
	DF-STFEHM	**68.35(0.4)**	64.06(0.34)	**78.1(0.11)**	0.7039(0.22)
ADHD-200	SVM	60.4	59.1	70.1	0.6413
	RF	62.68	59.58	61.86	0.576
	BrainnetCNN	63.4(0.36)	61.68(0.54)	78.8(0.89)	0.6919(0.35)
	GCNN	67.08(0.56)	73.08(0.93)	74.66(0.95)	**0.7386(0.49)**
	CNN-CKEW	65.9(0.43)	68.02(0.82)	74.3(0.56)	0.7102(0.37)
	DBN	66.03(0.23)	**79.28(0.87)**	53.37(0.72)	0.6379(0.056)
	E-HI-GCN	65.14(0.59)	65.76(0.72)	68.54(0.13)	0.6712(0.56)
	DF	63.16(0.70)	60.32(1.13)	63.13(0.08)	0.5675(0.13)
	DF-CWSM	66.97(0.54)	66.97(0.63)	72.3(0.55)	0.6779(0.57)
	DF-STFEHM	**67.89(0.35)**	62.59(0.47)	**82.86(0.28)**	0.7131(0.53)

of other comparison algorithms. As the precision and recall are a pair of contradictory measures, the precision of DF-STFEHM is inferior to that of the other models. The precision reflects the probability that a predicted patient actually has a brain disease, and the recall represents the probability that a patient can be identified. For disease diagnosis, the cost of misdiagnosing a normal person as a patient is much lower than that of missing a patient. Moreover, its f1 (the comprehensive measure of precision and recall) values are only slightly below the highest values achieved by E-HI-GCN and GCNN. Therefore, our algorithm still performs better than the other comparing algorithms.

4.3 Important Brain Regions

In this section, we investigate the importance of brain regions associated with ASD and ADHD by analysing the feature importance of casForest. The experiment result is shown in Fig. 6, which is consistent with the conclusions of some previous studies. Specifically, authors in reference [28] found lower entropy of PreCG, SMG, and MOG in ASD group than that of typical control. Especially, PreCG is related to motor functions, the reduced ApEu in it may be contribute to the motor function impairments in ASD patients. The reduced entropy in MOG may result in the loss of visual information processing function. Authors in [15] found that the connectivity of SFGdor decreased in ASD group, where SFGdor.L is correlated with the two core symptoms of autism Repetitive Behavior and Communication. SFGdor.R is correlated with the severity of ASD's clinical core symptoms. Results in reference [27] pointed that ASD patients selectively showed enhanced Hilbert weight frequency in PCUN and SFGdor. Reference [21] found abnormal connection between PreCG.L, MFG.L, SFGdor.L, and MOG.L in both ASD and ADHD patients. In a word, our algorithm can not only accurately classify brain networks but also identify abnormal brain regions.

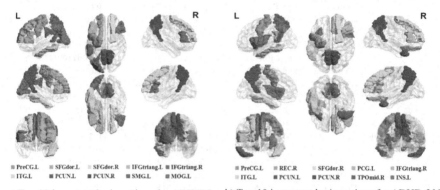

a) Top 10 important brain regions for ABIDE I   b) Top 10 important brain regions for ADHD-200

Fig. 6. Top 10 important brain regions for classification.

5   Conclusions

Deep forest is a novel and effective non-NN style DL method that brings us new hope in accurately classifying BNs on small-scale fMRI datasets. One of the most challenging issues is how to use domain knowledge of BNs to improve the performance for existing DF-based BN classification methods. In this paper, a deep forest framework with sparse topological feature extraction and hash mapping (DF-STFEHM) is proposed for BN classification. Main innovation of DF-STFEHM is that we make full use of the inherent sparsity of BNs and design an extremely random forest guided by a weighted random walk (ERF-WRW), which effectively extracts sparse topological features from BNs. Experimental results on ABIDE I and ADHD-200 have validated the superiority of DF-STFEHM. In future work, we will continue to explore how to utilize other domain knowledge to improve the accuracy of deep forest on brain network classification.

Acknowledgements. This work was supported in part by R&D Program of Beijing Municipal Education Commission (KZ202210005009).

References

1. Ahmed, N., et al.: Role-based graph embeddings. IEEE Trans. Knowl. Data Eng. (2020)
2. Ball, G., et al.: Machine-learning to characterise neonatal functional connectivity in the preterm brain. Neuroimage **124**, 267–275 (2016)
3. Behrouzi, T., Hatzinakos, D.: Graph variational auto-encoder for deriving EEG-based graph embedding. Pattern Recogn. **121**, 108202 (2022)
4. Di Martino, A., et al.: The autism brain imaging data exchange: towards a large-scale evaluation of the intrinsic brain architecture in autism. Mol. Psychiatry **19**(6), 659–667 (2014)
5. Geurts, P., Ernst, D., Wehenkel, L.: Extremely randomized trees. Mach. Learn. **63**(1), 3–42 (2006)
6. Grover, A., Leskovec, J.: node2vec: scalable feature learning for networks. In: Proceedings of the 22nd ACM SIGKDD International Conference on Knowledge Discovery and Data Mining, pp. 855–864 (2016)
7. Guerra-Carrillo, B., Mackey, A.P., Bunge, S.A.: Resting-state fmri: a window into human brain plasticity. Neuroscientist **20**(5), 522–533 (2014)
8. He, J., Liu, W., Chang, S.F.: Scalable similarity search with optimized kernel hashing. In: Proceedings of the 16th ACM SIGKDD International Conference on Knowledge Discovery and Data Mining, pp. 1129–1138 (2010)
9. Huang, Z.A., Zhu, Z., Yau, C.H., Tan, K.C.: Identifying autism spectrum disorder from resting-state fmri using deep belief network. IEEE Trans. Neural Networks Learn. Syst. **32**(7), 2847–2861 (2020)
10. Ji, J., Xing, X., Yao, Y., Li, J., Zhang, X.: Convolutional kernels with an element-wise weighting mechanism for identifying abnormal brain connectivity patterns. Pattern Recogn. **109**, 107570 (2021)
11. Jie, B., Liu, M., Zhang, D., Shen, D.: Sub-network kernels for measuring similarity of brain connectivity networks in disease diagnosis. IEEE Trans. Image Process. **27**(5), 2340–2353 (2018)
12. Kawahara, J., et al.: Brainnetcnn: convolutional neural networks for brain networks; towards predicting neurodevelopment. Neuroimage **146**, 1038–1049 (2017)
13. Li, J., Ji, J., Liang, Y., Zhang, X., Wang, Z.: Deep forest with cross-shaped window scanning mechanism to extract topological features. In: 2019 IEEE International Conference on Bioinformatics and Biomedicine (BIBM), pp. 688–691. IEEE (2019)
14. Li, L., et al.: Te-hi-gcn: an ensemble of transfer hierarchical graph convolutional networks for disorder diagnosis. Neuroinformatics, pp. 1–23 (2021)
15. Lluis, Borràs-Ferrís, Úrsula, Pérez-Ramírez, David, Moratal: Link-level functional connectivity neuroalterations in autism spectrum disorder: a developmental resting-state fmri study. Diagnostics (Basel, Switzerland) (2019)
16. Marzullo, A., Kocevar, G., Stamile, C., Durand-Dubief, F., Terracina, G., Calimeri, F., Sappey-Marinier, D.: Classification of multiple sclerosis clinical profiles via graph convolutional neural networks. Front. Neurosci. **13**, 594 (2019)
17. Mikolov, T., Chen, K., Corrado, G., Dean, J.: Efficient estimation of word representations in vector space. arXiv preprint arXiv:1301.3781 (2013)
18. Milham, M.P., Fair, D., Mennes, M., Mostofsky, S.H., et al.: The adhd-200 consortium: a model to advance the translational potential of neuroimaging in clinical neuroscience. Front. Syst. Neurosci. **6**, 62 (2012)
19. Nicholson, A.A., et al.: Classifying heterogeneous presentations of ptsd via the default mode, central executive, and salience networks with machine learning. NeuroImage Clinical **27**, 102262 (2020)

20. Perozzi, B., Al-Rfou, R., Skiena, S.: Deepwalk: Online learning of social representations. In: Proceedings of the 20th ACM SIGKDD International Conference on Knowledge Discovery and Data Mining, pp. 701–710 (2014)
21. Qian, L., Li, Y., Wang, Y., Wang, Y., Cheng, X., Li, C., Cui, X., Jiao, G., Ke, X.: Shared and distinct topologically structural connectivity patterns in autism spectrum disorder and attention-deficit/hyperactivity disorder. Frontiers in Neuroscience 15 (2021)
22. Shao, L., Zhang, D., Du, H., Fu, D.: Deep forest in adhd data classification. IEEE Access **7**, 137913–137919 (2019)
23. Torralba, A., Fergus, R., Weiss, Y.: Small codes and large image databases for recognition. In: 2008 IEEE Conference on Computer Vision and Pattern Recognition, pp. 1–8. IEEE (2008)
24. Tzourio-Mazoyer, N., et al.: Automated anatomical labeling of activations in spm using a macroscopic anatomical parcellation of the mni mri single-subject brain. Neuroimage **15**(1), 273–289 (2002)
25. Xu, M.: Understanding graph embedding methods and their applications. SIAM Rev. **63**(4), 825–853 (2021)
26. Zeng, K., et al.: Disrupted brain network in children with autism spectrum disorder. Sci. Rep. **7**(1), 1–12 (2017)
27. Zhang, H., Li, R., Wen, X., Li, Q., Wu, X.: Altered time-frequency feature in default mode network of autism based on improved hilbert-huang transform. IEEE J. Biomed. Health Inform. **25**(2), 485–492 (2020)
28. Zhang, L., Wang, X.H., Li, L.: Diagnosing autism spectrum disorder using brain entropy: a fast entropy method. Comput. Methods Programs Biomed. **190**, 105240 (2020)
29. Zhou, Y., Wu, C., Tan, L.: Biased random walk with restart for link prediction with graph embedding method. Physica A **570**, 125783 (2021)
30. Zhou, Z.H., Feng, J.: Deep forest: towards an alternative to deep neural networks. In: Proceedings of the 26th International Joint Conference on Artificial Intelligence, IJCAI 2017, pp. 3553–3559 (2017)
31. Zhu, D., et al.: Classification of major depressive disorder via multi-site weighted LASSO model. In: Descoteaux, M., Maier-Hein, L., Franz, A., Jannin, P., Collins, D.L., Duchesne, S. (eds.) MICCAI 2017. LNCS, vol. 10435, pp. 159–167. Springer, Cham (2017). https://doi.org/10.1007/978-3-319-66179-7_19

COVID-19 Forecasting Based on Local Mean Decomposition and Temporal Convolutional Network

Lulu Sun[1], Zhouming Liu[1], Choujun Zhan[1,2], and Hu Min[1(✉)]

[1] School of Electrical and Computer Engineering, Nanfang College Guangzhou,
Guangzhou 510970, China
{sunll,minh}@nfu.edu.cn, zchoujun2@gmail.com
[2] School of Computing, South China Normal University, Guangzhou 510641, China

Abstract. Since the outbreak of coronavirus disease 2019 (COVID-19) has resulted in a dramatic loss of human life and economic disruption worldwide from early 2020, numerous studies focusing on COVID-19 forecasting were presented to yield accurate predicting results. However, most existing methods could not provide satisfying forecasting performance due to tons of assumptions, poor capability to learn appropriate parameters, etc. Therefore, in this paper, we combine a traditional time series decomposition: local mean decomposition (LMD) with temporal convolutional network (TCN) as a general framework to overcome these shortcomings. Based on the particular architecture, it can solve weekly new confirmed cases forecasting problem perfectly. Extensive experiments show that the proposed model significantly outperforms lots of state-of-the-art forecasting methods, and achieves desirable performance in terms of root mean squared log error (RMSLE), mean absolute percentage error (MAPE), Pearson correlation (PCORR), and coefficient of determination (R^2). To be specific, it could reach 0.9739, 0.8908, and 0.7461 on R^2 when horizon is 1, 2, and 3 respectively, which proves the effectiveness and robustness of our LMD-TCN model.

Keywords: COVID-19 forecasting · Local mean decomposition · Temporal convolutional network

1 Introduction

The coronavirus disease 2019 (COVID-19) pandemic has brought about a devastating effect on human life, public health, daily working and social economy. Until 23 June 2022, there have been 539,893,858 confirmed cases of COVID-19 globally, including 6,324,112 deaths, reported to WHO[1]. As a consequence, timely and accurate COVID-19 forecasting methods play a significant role in instructing the authorities to implement containment measures. In the last 20 years, machine learning, especially deep learning based models have shown tremendous success

---

[1] https://covid19.who.int.

© The Author(s), under exclusive license to Springer Nature Switzerland AG 2022
S. Khanna et al. (Eds.): PRICAI 2022, LNCS 13629, pp. 175–187, 2022.
https://doi.org/10.1007/978-3-031-20862-1_13

in lots of application areas, including computer vision, natural language processing, time series, medicine, games, robots, and education. Throughout all the methods involving COVID-19 forecasting, we could classify them into two types: machine-learning and non-machine-learning based methods.

Machine-Learning Based Models. Machine learning (ML) based algorithms usually learn from historical data or information, build mathematical models, and make predictions. On one hand, classic ML models including support vector machine (SVM) [24], Bayesian analysis [29], k-nearest neighbor (KNN) classifier [22], and XGBoost classifier [20] have been applied widely in COVID-19 forecasting. On the other hand, recent popular deep learning (DL) techniques, like multiple layer perceptron (MLP) [21], recurrent neural network (RNN) [12], gated recurrent unit (GRU) [11], long short-term memory (LSTM) [14,32,33] and transformer [27] make a positive contribution to this field as well. Nevertheless, the accuracy of predicted output depends upon the amount of data, the structure of models, and the training skills. Hence, there is still much chance to explore competitive methods with the intention of providing reliable and repeatable results.

Non-machine-Learning Based Models. Generally, traditional studies focus on propagation dynamics and statistical analyses. The former algorithm contains susceptible-infected-recovered (SIR) model [13], susceptible-infected-dead-recovered (SIDR) model [4], susceptible-exposed-infected-recovered (SEIR) model [3] and so forth. This kind of methods are usually based on tons of assumptions, such as infection rate, average latent time, recovery rate, and death rate, which is hard to determine with regard to the complexity of COVID-19. The latter statistical methods pay attention to calculate short-term predictions from investigating time series of historical data. A typical of this class is autoregressive integrated moving average (ARIMA) [8], which has been utilized to forecast the spread of COVID-19 in many countries [2]. Unfortunately, the predicting performance of ARIMA needs to be improved, due to the powerlessness of learning non-linear patterns from historical time series.

In fact, COVID-19 series is considered as a nonlinear and nonstationary time series. A beneficial skill to analyze such signals is conducting effective decomposition in advance. Local mean decomposition (LMD) has been introduced to decompose signals since 2005. By the LMD process, any signal with nonlinear tendency and oscillation can be decomposed into a finite and often small number of product functions (PFs) and a residue. PFs have simpler frequency components and stronger correlations, thus are easier and more accurate to forecast. In addition, given that temporal convolutional network (TCN) [5] could outperform canonical recurrent networks across a wide range of situations, we hope to adopt such a TCN architecture in this paper.

Inspired by the above analyses, we propose a hybrid LMD based neural network paradigm for COVID-19 forecasting. Our main contributions could be summarized as follows:

1) We firstly introduce LMD technique to deal with COVID-19 forecasting, which helps to produce accurate results and handle the problem of overfitting when training neural networks.
2) We put forward an LMD-TCN framework for predicting weekly new confirmed cases in the field of COVID-19, combing LMD with the specific TCN architecture to generate a better prediction. It can simultaneously provide accurate predicting results from short-term to long-term.
3) We conduct a comprehensive comparison among existing state-of-the-art models to evaluate their forecasting performances. The results show that our hybrid model outperforms any individual model, and achieves desirable performance in terms of all evaluation metrics.

2   Related Work

2.1   Local Mean Decomposition (LMD)

The local mean decomposition (LMD), developed by the author [25] in 2005, aims to demodulate amplitude and frequency modulated signals. It could decompose original signals into a small set of product functions (PFs) and a residue. A PF is the product of an amplitude envelope signal and a frequency-modulated (FM). Accordingly, we could also derive a time-varying instantaneous frequency. The algorithm of LMD for decomposing the signal $x(t)$ into PFs can be broadly described as follows:

(i): Given the original signal $x(t)$, identify all the extrema points n_i, and next calculate the i th mean value m_i of each two successive extrema n_i and n_{i+1} using the following formula:

$$m_i = \frac{n_i + n_{i+1}}{2}. \tag{1}$$

Plot these local means as straight lines extending between successive extrema, and then use moving average to form a smoothly varying continuous local mean function $m_{11}(t)$.

(ii): The local envelope estimate function $a_{11}(t)$ could be calculated, and then local magnitude of each half-wave oscillation could be obtained by

$$a_i = \frac{|n_i - n_{i+1}|}{2}. \tag{2}$$

Similarly, make up a smoothly varying continuous envelope function $a_{11}(t)$ by smoothing the local means.

(iii): Subtract the local mean function $m_{11}(t)$ from the original data $x(t)$,

$$h_{11}(t) = x(t) - m_{11}(t). \tag{3}$$

$h_{11}(t)$ is then amplitude demodulated by dividing it by $a_{11}(t)$,

$$s_{11}(t) = \frac{h_{11}(t)}{a_{11}(t)}. \tag{4}$$

Calculate the envelope function $a_{12}(t)$ of $s_{11}(t)$, which should satisfy $a_{12}(t) = 1$. If not, think of $s_{11}(t)$ as a new signal and iterate the above steps until envelope function $a_{1(n+1)}(t)$ of the $s_{1n}(t)$ satisfies $a_{1(n+1)}(t) = 1$.

(iv): Calculate the corresponding envelope by

$$a_1(t) = a_{11}(t)a_{12}(t)..a_{1n}(t) = \prod_{q=1}^{n} a_{1q}(t), \tag{5}$$

where $\lim_{n \to \infty} a_{1n}(t) = 1$ and n is the number of iterations.

(v): Multiply the envelope function $a_1(t)$ by $s_{1n}(t)$, and then yield a product function (PF),

$$PF_1(t) = a_1(t)s_{1n}(t). \tag{6}$$

Repeatedly, derive $PF_2(t)$ by subtracting $PF_1(t)$ from the original signal $x(t)$ and replicating all the above steps progressively, until the final signal becomes monotonic or unchanging which is a residue. As a whole, the original signal $x(t)$ can be decomposed with regard to

$$\sum_{p=1}^{k} PF_p(t) + u_k(t), \tag{7}$$

where $PF_p(t)$ is the product of the envelope function and frequency modulated signal, and $u_k(t)$ is the residue.

2.2   Temporal Convolutional Network (TCN)

The generic temporal convolutional network (TCN) architecture was introduced to solve sequence modeling tasks, where canonical recurrent networks occupy the main force before. As illustrated in [5], a TCN has two obvious differences: (1) the convolutions in the network should be causal, indicating it can only use the information from past time; (2) the input and output of the architecture should have the same length.

Causal Convolutions. For meeting the first principle above, causal convolutions are utilized, which means an output at time step t depends only on historical and current time step t, not on any future time $t + i$ ($i \in N^*$). To fulfill the second principle, TCNs employ a 1-D fully-convolutional network architecture, aiming to ensure higher layers have the same length as previous ones.

Dilated Convolutions. Apart from the aforementioned causal convolution, dilated convolutions are normally used within TCN to address the limitation of receptive field sizes. By increasing the receptive field at a faster rate, it helps to build networks for sequential tasks.

Residual Connections. Generally, a TCN model is made up of a 1-D fully-convolutional network and multiple residual blocks, which contains a branch leading out to a series of transformations F, whose outputs are added to the input $\mathbf{x}$ of the block. Besides, rectified linear unit (ReLU), batch normalization, and dropout are also applied in the block. Moreover, an additional 1×1 convolution is used to ensure unanimous input-output widths. Relying on such residual modules, training deep and larger TCNs becomes much easier.

3   Methodology

3.1   Problem Formulation

In essence, COVID-19 forecasting is a time series forecasting problem. The key to solve this problem is utilizing past observations to build a model that could capture the latent relationship and patterns well.

First, we denote a n driving series during time T as

$$\mathbf{X} = \left(\mathbf{x}^1, \mathbf{x}^2, \cdots, \mathbf{x}^n\right)^\top = (\mathbf{x}_1, \mathbf{x}_2, \cdots, \mathbf{x}_T) \in \mathbb{R}^{n \times T}, \tag{8}$$

where $\mathbf{x}^k = \left(x_1^k, x_2^k, \cdots, x_T^k\right)^\top \in \mathbb{R}^T$ represents a driving series of length T, and $\mathbf{x}_t = \left(x_t^1, x_t^2, \cdots, x_t^n\right)^\top \in \mathbb{R}^n$ denotes a vector of n exogenous input series at time t.

Generally, assuming the previous values of the target series as

$$\mathbf{y} = (y_1, \ldots, y_T) \in \mathbb{R}^T, \tag{9}$$

and the past values of n exogenous series as $(\mathbf{x}_1, \mathbf{x}_2, \cdots, \mathbf{x}_T) \in \mathbb{R}^{n \times T}$.

The goal is to predict the future values $y_{T+H} \in \mathbb{R}$ at a time point $T + H$ (H refers to the horizon of the prediction), which is fundamentally a one-step-ahead forecasting problem. Supposing $\hat{y}_{T+H}$ as the forecast of y_{T+H}, our model attempts to learn a nonlinear mapping function F from the past values to the future ones:

$$\hat{y}_{T+H} = F\left(y_1, \cdots, y_T, \mathbf{x}_1, \mathbf{x}_2, \cdots, \mathbf{x}_T\right) \tag{10}$$

3.2   Overview of Our Method

In this section, we demonstrate the general picture of our LMD-TCN model, which integrates LMD technique and TCN model in a framework. The flowchart of our model is as illustrated in Fig. 1. Firstly, apply LMD to decompose the original COVID-19 series into several sub-series, which have simpler frequency components and are relatively easy to model. Then, concatenate these PFs and one residue with the original COVID-19 series as the input sequences. Lastly, train the particular TCN network continuously, whereby the parameters of all neurons of the network are determined until achieving the desirable predictions.

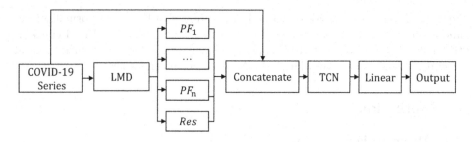

Fig. 1. The overview framework of our LMD-TCN model.

3.3   Time Series Decomposition

We apply LMD technique as the time series decomposition to extract the hidden features of the nonstationary and nonlinear COVID-19 signals. LMD could decompose the original COVID-19 series into two PFs and a residue, which represents a range of frequencies, revealing various periodic patterns of COVID-19. PFs offer an insight into the modulated characteristics, bringing about a more appropriate representation for the given modulated signal.

Figure 2 shows the LMD results of the original weekly new confirmed cases, which is decomposed into two PFs and one residue. PFs exhibit more high frequency components compared to original signals. Clearly, through the employment of time series decomposition, more beneficial characteristics hidden in the original data have been found, improving the training complexity greatly.

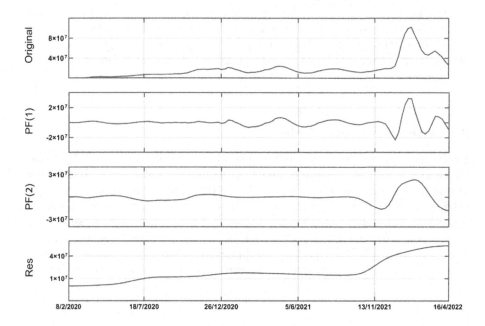

Fig. 2. LMD for weekly new confirmed cases.

3.4   Architecture Details

As shown in Fig. 3, we construct a simple LMD-TCN framework to solve the
COVID-19 forecasting problem. Our current model only includes one TCN block,
which is sufficient to learn ideal mappings from input to output. Actually, the
quantity of blocks could increase according to the complexity of given signals.
One block is made up of two 1×2 convolutional layers, each of which following
a weight norm layer and a ReLU activation layer separately. Parallelly, one 1×1
convolution is added while the input and output of TCN block have different
dimensions. The upcoming is two ReLU activation layers, between which is a skip
connection layer going from the original input. In the end, we use a linear layer to
decrease the high-dimensional features to one-dimensional vectors. In summary,
we could obtain accurate predictions in the future ranging through one-step-
ahead method by combining the given COVID-19 series with the corresponding
LMD decomposition results as input.

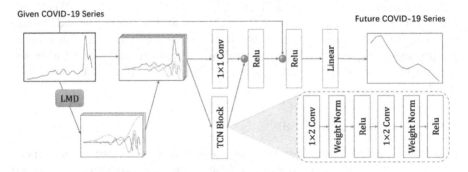

Fig. 3. The overall architecture of our LMD-TCN model.

4   Experiments

4.1   Dataset and Preprocessing

Worldwide daily new confirmed cases data was downloaded from the COVID-19
surveillance[2], including United States of America, India, Brazil, France, Germany, the United Kingdom, Russian Federation, Republic of Korean, etc. To
obtain better performance, we collected as many data points as possible, span-
ning from the birth of COVID-19 pandemic to nowadays. In addition, referring
to several similar COVID-19 forecasting methods [1,28], daily case counts are
aggregated to weekly dimension (see Fig. 4).

The data sources are weekly and ends on Saturday, beginning from Week
ending February 8, 2020 to Week ending April 16, 2022 (115 weeks). First, the
window size T is subtracted from the total data points as $(115 - T)$. Then, it is

---

[2] https://ourworldindata.org/coronavirus.

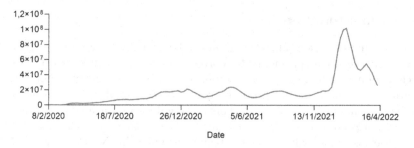

Fig. 4. Weekly new confirmed cases.

split into training set and testing set. The former set has 85% of the total sample points and the remaining 15% points belong to the latter set. For example, if we set $T = 21$ and forecasting horizon $H = 1$, the training duration spans from Week ending February 8, 2020 to Week ending January 8, 2022 (total 80 points), and the remaining time between Week ending January 15, 2022 and Week ending April 16, 2022 (total 14 points) is selected as the testing period. Before carrying out LMD decomposition, we firstly adopt min-max normalization as pre-processing method. Min-max normalization performs a linear transformation on the original data, which is needed in order to prevent inaccuracy of results.

4.2   Implementation Details

It should be noted that one-step-ahead prediction is performed in the experiments. We set training window size $T = 21$ and forecasting horizon $H = 1, 2$, and 3 weeks ahead at each time point. $H = 1, 2$, and 3 represents the short, medium and long term separately. According to Eq. 10, y_{T+H} is the target need to be predicted, and $(\mathbf{x}_1, \mathbf{x}_2, \cdots, \mathbf{x}_T) \in \mathbb{R}^T$ represents the LMD results. Additionally, as shown in Fig. 3, our model contains one TCN block and one linear layer with 512 hidden units correspondingly. Moreover, we set batch size as 16, epoch number as 300, and learning rate as 0.3. Besides, mean squared error (MSE) loss, Adam optimizer and stochastic initialization with 0 as mean and 1 as variance are utilized when training.

4.3   Evaluation Metrics

We employ four criteria: root mean squared log error (RMSLE) [30], mean absolute percentage error (MAPE) [18], Pearson correlation (PCORR) [7], and coefficient of determination (R^2) [6] to evaluate the forecasting performance. For convenience, $\hat{y}$ denotes the predicted values, $\bar{\hat{y}}$ denotes the average values of $\hat{y}$, y denotes the real values, and $\bar{y}$ denotes the average values of y.

RMSLE value only considers the relative error between the predicted and the actual value while neglecting the scale of data. This is mainly used when predictions have large deviations, which is the case with COVID-19 forecasting. MAPE measures a relative error by using absolute values to keep the positive and negative errors from canceling one another out. PCORR assigns a value between -1 and 1, where 0 is no correlation, 1 is total positive correlation, and -1 is total negative correlation. R^2 assesses how strong the linear relationship is between two variables. It usually takes any values between 0.0 to 1.0, where a value of 1.0 indicates a perfect fit, and a value of 0.0 indicates that the model fails to accurately model the data at all.

$$\text{RMSLE} = \sqrt{\frac{1}{n}\sum_{i=1}^{n}\left(\log\left(\hat{y}_i + 1\right) - \log\left(y_i + 1\right)\right)^2} \qquad (11)$$

$$\text{MAPE} = \frac{100}{n}\sum_{i=1}^{n}\frac{|y_i - \hat{y}_i|}{|y_i|} \qquad (12)$$

$$\text{PCORR} = \frac{\sum_{i=1}^{n}\left(\hat{y}_i - \overline{\hat{y}}\right)\left(y_i - \bar{y}\right)}{\sqrt{\sum_{i=1}^{n}\left(\hat{y}_i - \overline{\hat{y}}\right)^2}\sqrt{\sum_{i=1}^{n}\left(y_i - \bar{y}\right)^2}} \qquad (13)$$

$$R^2 = 1 - \frac{\sum_{i=1}^{n}\left(y_i - \hat{y}_i\right)^2}{\sum_{i=1}^{n}\left(y_i - \bar{y}\right)^2} \qquad (14)$$

4.4   Experimental Results

Our LMD-TCN model[3] can handle weekly new confirmed cases forecasting problem in the field of COVID-19. We only use the previous values of the target series $(y_1, \ldots, y_T) \in \mathbb{R}^T$ and their corresponding LMD components $(\mathbf{x}_1, \mathbf{x}_2, \cdots, \mathbf{x}_T) \in \mathbb{R}^T$ as inputs to train each model. To evaluate the forecasting performance of different methods, we make comparisons in terms of RMSLE, MAPE, PCORR, and R^2 with $H = 1$, 2, and 3.

From Table 1, one could conclude that our LMD-TCN model has a huge advantage over the other methods in all measures regardless of any horizon. Specifically, considering the value of RMSLE with $H = 1$, our method is ranked first, whereas, LogTrans is ranked second, followed by the TCN, LSTM, GRU, RNN, ARIMA, MLP, then XGBoost. RMSLE results reveal that our model has the smallest relative error between the predicted and ground truth. Focusing on the R^2 indicator, which refers to the correlation between prediction and the original COVID-19 series, our model is 0.9739 on horizon 1, while the second best result is 0.9687 obtained by LogTrans. It is noteworthy that the gap in R^2 between our model to the second best method becomes larger as horizon increases, and the gap is 0.0052, 0.0268, 0.2198 corresponding to $H = 1$, 2, and 3. We could draw the similar conclusion when comparing other criteria, which reflects the reliability and robustness of our LMD-TCN model.

---

[3] The source code of our method will be available after this paper is published.

Table 1. RMSLE, MAPE, PCORR and R^2 performance of different methods on weekly new confirmed cases data with horizon $H = 1$, 2, and 3. The best result for each row is **highlighted**. The second best result for each row is underlined.

Metric	Method								
	$H = 1$								
	ARIMA	XGBoost	MLP	RNN	LSTM	GRU	LogTrans	TCN	**Ours**
RMSLE	0.1001	0.2125	0.1251	0.0972	0.0898	0.0931	0.0641	0.0816	**0.0615**
MAPE	9.0300	20.3900	9.8745	8.1680	7.7225	7.6332	5.5838	6.9327	**5.5223**
PCORR	0.9828	0.8705	0.9683	0.9756	0.9792	0.9774	0.9872	0.9802	**0.9873**
R^2	0.9159	0.7024	0.9272	0.9472	0.9548	0.9514	0.9687	0.9593	**0.9739**
	$H = 2$								
	ARIMA	XGBoost	MLP	RNN	LSTM	GRU	LogTrans	TCN	Ours
RMSLE	0.2604	0.3220	0.3851	0.2227	0.3067	0.1767	0.1667	0.1897	**0.1309**
MAPE	26.0900	29.4300	24.8227	16.8576	19.7741	14.4121	13.1123	15.7061	**11.6827**
PCORR	0.9319	0.7186	0.8409	0.9113	0.8986	0.9336	0.9125	0.9045	**0.9451**
R^2	0.4274	0.3158	0.5695	0.7984	0.7008	0.8640	0.7642	0.8094	**0.8908**
	$H = 3$								
	ARIMA	XGBoost	MLP	RNN	LSTM	GRU	LogTrans	TCN	Ours
RMSLE	0.4657	0.3888	0.7195	0.3559	0.3737	0.4000	0.2433	0.3026	**0.2278**
MAPE	46.7600	33.3400	35.8315	23.6393	28.5128	29.5333	18.8598	21.3641	**17.6551**
PCORR	0.8329	0.5414	0.6843	0.7521	0.7769	0.7668	0.7580	0.7831	**0.8872**
R^2	−1.3772	−0.2868	−0.1219	0.4289	0.4208	0.3034	0.4943	0.5263	**0.7461**

Furthermore, we also depict the global curves of original and predicted weekly new confirmed cases with $H = 1$ in Fig. 5. Ground true means the original COVID-19 series. Prediction indicates the forecasting results by the corresponding method that only uses the previous y as input, neglecting other variables. LMD prediction is achieved by combing y with LMD decomposition results as inputs to train models. In fact, we have applied LMD technique to the other five deep learning methods, including MLP, RNN, LSTM, GRU, and LogTrans. Among which, the former four could train successfully but without improving accuracy significantly, the last one is unable to converge in this situation. Obviously, our model could produce the most visually pleasant fitting curves, which works in concert with the numerical results on Table 1.

In summary, our LMD-TCN can learn the precise mappings from given COVID-19 series to the future ones owing to the introduction of LMD technique into our network. Our model shows arrogant superiority to the other methods regardless of numerical results or visual performance. The results reveal that based on such time decomposition technique, a simple temporal convolutional architecture is more effective on COVID-19 forecasting tasks than recurrent and transformer architectures in some situations.

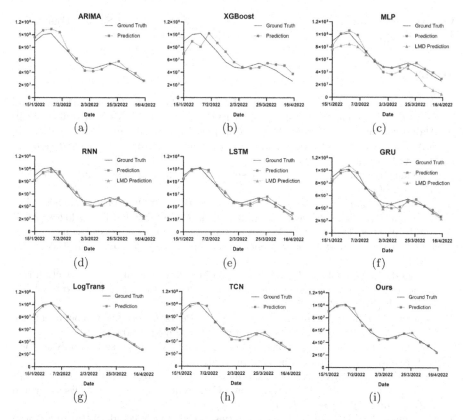

Fig. 5. Predicted results on weekly new confirmed cases with state-of-the-art methods ($H = 1$). Ground True means the original COVID-19 series. Prediction indicates the forecasting results by the corresponding method that only uses the previous y as input, neglecting other variables. LMD Prediction is achieved by combing y with LMD decomposition as input to train models. We only show methods suitable for LMD technique, ignoring those that fail to train if introducing LMD.

5   Conclusion

LMD decomposition can produce simpler frequency components and stronger correlations from original series which is an important cue for COVID-19 forecasting. To better explore these latent but effective components, we present an LMD-TCN model by combining LMD technique with the specific TCN architecture. The proposed method can explicitly model the precise mappings from given COVID-19 series to the future ones. It can thus provide accurate predicting results from short-term to long-term simultaneously. Experimental results show that our method outperforms the state-of-the-art methods on weekly new confirmed cases data. Numerical and visualization results also show the contribution of the proposed method. In the future, we plan to investigate how to handle more time series forecasting problems with our framework.

Acknowledgements. This work was supported by the Natural Science Foundation of Guangdong Province, China (2020A1515010761).

References

1. Al-Qaness, M.A., Ewees, A.A., Fan, H., Abd El Aziz, M.: Optimization method for forecasting confirmed cases of covid-19 in china. J. Clin. Med. **9**(3), 674 (2020)
2. Alabdulrazzaq, H., Alenezi, M.N., Rawajfih, Y., Alghannam, B.A., Al-Hassan, A.A., Al-Anzi, F.S.: On the accuracy of arima based prediction of covid-19 spread. Results Phys. **27**, 104509 (2021)
3. Almeida, R.: Analysis of a fractional seir model with treatment. Appl. Math. Lett. **84**, 56–62 (2018)
4. Anastassopoulou, C., Russo, L., Tsakris, A., Siettos, C.: Data-based analysis, modelling and forecasting of the covid-19 outbreak. PLoS ONE **15**(3), e0230405 (2020)
5. Bai, S., Kolter, J.Z., Koltun, V.: An empirical evaluation of generic convolutional and recurrent networks for sequence modeling. arXiv preprint arXiv:1803.01271 (2018)
6. Behnood, A., Golafshani, E.M., Hosseini, S.M.: Determinants of the infection rate of the covid-19 in the us using anfis and virus optimization algorithm (voa). Chaos, Solitons Fractals **139**, 110051 (2020)
7. Benesty, J., Chen, J., Huang, Y., Cohen, I.: Pearson correlation coefficient. In: Noise reduction in speech processing, pp. 1–4. Springer (2009)
8. Box, G.E., Jenkins, G.M., Reinsel, G.C., Ljung, G.M.: Time series analysis: forecasting and control. John Wiley & Sons (2015)
9. Chen, T., Guestrin, C.: Xgboost: a scalable tree boosting system. In: Proceedings of the 22nd ACM SIGKDD international Conference on Knowledge Discovery and Data Mining, pp. 785–794 (2016)
10. Chimmula, V.K.R., Zhang, L.: Time series forecasting of covid-19 transmission in Canada using lstm networks. Chaos, Solitons Fractals **135**, 109864 (2020)
11. Cho, K., Van Merriënboer, B., Bahdanau, D., Bengio, Y.: On the properties of neural machine translation: Encoder-decoder approaches. arXiv preprint arXiv:1409.1259 (2014)
12. Elman, J.L.: Finding structure in time. Cogn. Sci. **14**(2), 179–211 (1990)
13. Harko, T., Lobo, F.S., Mak, M.: Exact analytical solutions of the susceptible-infected-recovered (sir) epidemic model and of the sir model with equal death and birth rates. Appl. Math. Comput. **236**, 184–194 (2014)
14. Hochreiter, S., Schmidhuber, J.: Long short-term memory. Neural Comput. **9**(8), 1735–1780 (1997)
15. Huang, N.E., et al.: The empirical mode decomposition and the hilbert spectrum for nonlinear and non-stationary time series analysis. Proc. Roy. Soc. London. Series A: mathematical, physical and engineering sciences **454**(1971), 903–995 (1998)
16. Ioffe, S., Szegedy, C.: Batch normalization: accelerating deep network training by reducing internal covariate shift. In: International Conference on Machine Learning, pp. 448–456. PMLR (2015)
17. Li, S., et al.: Enhancing the locality and breaking the memory bottleneck of transformer on time series forecasting. In: Advances in Neural Information Processing Systems 32 (2019)
18. Makridakis, S., Hibon, M.: The m3-competition: results, conclusions and implications. Int. J. Forecast. **16**(4), 451–476 (2000)

19. Nair, V., Hinton, G.E.: Rectified linear units improve restricted boltzmann machines. In: ICML (2010)
20. Rahman, M.S., Chowdhury, A.H., Amrin, M.: Accuracy comparison of arima and xgboost forecasting models in predicting the incidence of covid-19 in bangladesh. PLOS Global Public Health **2**(5), e0000495 (2022)
21. Rosenblatt, F.: The perceptron, a perceiving and recognizing automaton Project Para. Cornell Aeronautical Laboratory (1957)
22. Shaban, W.M., Rabie, A.H., Saleh, A.I., Abo-Elsoud, M.: A new covid-19 patients detection strategy (cpds) based on hybrid feature selection and enhanced knn classifier. Knowl.-Based Syst. **205**, 106270 (2020)
23. Shoeibi, A., et al.: Automated detection and forecasting of covid-19 using deep learning techniques: a review. arXiv preprint arXiv:2007.10785 (2020)
24. Singh, V., Poonia, R.C., Kumar, S., Dass, P., Agarwal, P., Bhatnagar, V., Raja, L.: Prediction of covid-19 corona virus pandemic based on time series data using support vector machine. J. Discrete Math. Sci. Cryptography **23**(8), 1583–1597 (2020)
25. Smith, J.S.: The local mean decomposition and its application to eeg perception data. J. R. Soc. Interface **2**(5), 443–454 (2005)
26. Srivastava, N., Hinton, G., Krizhevsky, A., Sutskever, I., Salakhutdinov, R.: Dropout: a simple way to prevent neural networks from overfitting. J. Mach. Learn. Res. **15**(1), 1929–1958 (2014)
27. Vaswani, A., et al.: Attention is all you need. Advances in Neural Information Processing Systems 30 (2017)
28. Wang, L., Adiga, A., Venkatramanan, S., Chen, J., Lewis, B., Marathe, M.: Examining deep learning models with multiple data sources for covid-19 forecasting. In: 2020 IEEE International Conference on Big Data (Big Data), pp. 3846–3855. IEEE (2020)
29. Wibbens, P.D., Koo, W.W.Y., McGahan, A.M.: Which covid policies are most effective? a bayesian analysis of covid-19 by jurisdiction. PLoS ONE **15**(12), e0244177 (2020)
30. Zeroual, A., Harrou, F., Dairi, A., Sun, Y.: Deep learning methods for forecasting covid-19 time-series data: a comparative study. Chaos Solitons Fractals **140**, 110121 (2020)
31. Zhao, X., Barber, S., Taylor, C.C., Nie, X., Shen, W.: Spatio-temporal forecasting using wavelet transform-based decision trees with application to air quality and covid-19 forecasting. J. Appl. Stat., 1–19 (2022)
32. Chandra, R., Jain, A., Singh Chauhan, D.: Deep learning via lstm models for covid-19 infection forecasting in India. PLoS ONE **17**(1), e0262708 (2022)
33. Kumar, S., Sharma, R., Tsunoda, T., Kumarevel, T., Sharma, A.: Forecasting the spread of covid-19 using lstm network. BMC Bioinform. **22**(6), 1–9 (2021)

VMEKNet: Visual Memory and External Knowledge Based Network for Medical Report Generation

Weipeng Chen, Haiwei Pan$^{(\boxtimes)}$, Kejia Zhang, Xin Du, and Qianna Cui

College of Computer Science and Technology, Harbin Engineering University,
Harbin, People's Republic of China
{weipeng0703,panhaiwei,kejiazhang,dxxxx,cuiqianna}@hrbeu.edu.cn

Abstract. The main purpose of the medical report generation task is to generate a medical report corresponding to a given medical image, which contains detailed information of body parts and diagnostic results from radiologists. The task not only greatly reduces the workload of radiologists, but also helps patients get medical treatment in time. However, there are still many limitations in this task. First, the gap between image semantic features and text semantic features hinders the accuracy of the generated medical reports. Second, there are a large number of similar features in different medical images, which are not utilized efficiently and adequately. In order to solve the problems mentioned above, we propose a medical report generation model VMEKNet that integrates visual memory and external knowledge into the task. Specifically, we propose two novel modules and introduce them into medical report generation. Among them, the TF-IDF Embedding (TIE) module incorporates external knowledge into the feature extraction stage via the TF-IDF algorithm, and the Visual Memory (VIM) module makes full use of previous image features to help the model extract more accurate medical image features. After that, a standard Transformer processes the image features and text features then generates full medical reports. Experimental results on benchmark datasets, IU X-Ray, have demonstrated that our proposed model outperforms previous works on both natural language generation metrics and practical clinical diagnosis.

Keywords: Medical report generation · Transformer · TF-IDF algorithm · Visual memory

1 Introduction

Medical images, such as radiology and pathology images, are important for medical diagnosis and treatment [15]. For example, chest X-rays are often used to diagnose pneumonia, emphysema, heart disease, etc. A medical report, on the other hand, is a textual description of the information presented in a medical image, which includes detailed information about different body organs and the

© The Author(s), under exclusive license to Springer Nature Switzerland AG 2022
S. Khanna et al. (Eds.): PRICAI 2022, LNCS 13629, pp. 188–201, 2022.
https://doi.org/10.1007/978-3-031-20862-1_14

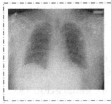

Findings: The lungs are clear bilaterally. Specifically, no evidence of focal consolidation, pneumothorax, or pleural effusion.. Cardio mediastinal silhouette is unremarkable. Visualized osseous structures of the thorax are without acute abnormality.

Impression: No acute cardiopulmonary abnormality.

Findings: The cardiac silhouette and mediastinal contours are within normal limits. There are low lung volumes with bronchovascular crowding. Otherwise the lungs are clear. There is no pneumothorax. No large pleural effusion.

Impression: No acute cardiopulmonary abnormality.

Fig. 1. Examples of medical report. Two different medical reports contain many similarities, which are indicated by the same color highlight. (Color figure online)

radiologist's diagnosis from medical images. Therefore, medical reports play an important role in the diagnosis of diseases and the treatment of patients. Figure 1 is an example of a chest X-ray report. A medical report often includes "Findings" and "Impression", "Findings" describes normal and abnormal features of organs in medical images, "Impression" indicates the clinical diagnosis inferred by the radiologist through "Finding". However, medical report writing is a time-consuming and error-prone task, especially for inexperienced radiologists, which may delay medical treatment for patients [20]. To reduce the burden on radiologists and improve the quality of medical report, automated medical report generation has become an urgent and attractive research direction in the field of artificial intelligence and clinical medicine. Given a medical image, the main purpose of the task is to generate a medical report, which contains detailed information and diagnostic results from the medical image.

The task most relevant to medical report generation is image captioning [1,6,7,10,11,16,18,24–26], which aims at generating a description of the input image automatically. However, medical report generation task is different from traditional image captioning in many ways. First, image captioning aims to describe visual scenes briefly in short sentences, while medical report generation task aims to generate long texts with professional medical terms. Second, feature extraction of medical images is difficult, hence the traditional image caption models cannot guarantee the accuracy and fluency of the generated medical reports. As a result, a number of novel methods are proposed for this task. In 2018, Jing et al. [14] proposed a co-attention approach that combines visual information with semantic information as input to decoder. The decoder adopts a hierarchical LSTM structure. In order to address the highly patterned nature of medical report, Chen et al. [5] proposed to introduce a Relational Memory (RM) and Memory-driven Conditional Layer Normalization (MCLN) into the standard Transformer [23].

Most recently, there has been a research trend to incorporate external knowledge in medical report generation tasks. Zhang et al. [28] incorporated knowledge at the architectural level using knowledge graph. CLARA [3] utilized a database to retrieve all sentences in the training set, followed by a decoder to generate reports. At the same time, models containing memory networks or memory-guide modules are another line of related research. For medical report generation task, there are also methods containing memory module. Banino et al. [2] proposed MEMO, an adaptive memory module for generating long texts. To make full use of similar patterns during the report generation process, Chen et al. [5] proposed a relational memory to enhance Transformer learning from previous patterns.

In this paper, our works focus on two main difficulties in medical report generation task: (1) due to the huge gap between image semantic features and text semantic features, the generated report is incomplete and inaccurate, (2) similar visual features present in different medical images are underutilized. In detail, in order to reduce the large gap between image semantic features and text semantic features, the TF-IDF Embedding (TIE) module is proposed to incorporate external knowledge into the feature extraction stage via the TF-IDF algorithm. The Visual Memory (VIM) module makes full use of previous image features, as a result, similar features in different medical images can be memorized during feature extraction, which assists in the encoding stage and guides the decoder to generate fluent and accurate medical reports. We implement quantitative and qualitative experiments to evaluate the performance of the model on the IU X-ray dataset. Overall, the main contributions in this paper can be summarized as:

(1) We propose a medical report generation model VMEKNet that integrates visual memory and external knowledge into the task.
(2) We propose a TF-IDF Embedding (TIE) module which incorporates external knowledge into the feature extraction process via the TF-IDF algorithm. And we propose a Visual Memory (VIM) module to record and make full use of previous image features.
(3) Quantitative and qualitative experiments results on benchmark dataset IU X-Ray show that our model outperforms previous works on both natural language generation metrics and practical clinical diagnosis.

2   Methodology

In this section, we present our proposed methodology. Like many previous image-to-text tasks, our model follows the standard Transformer [23] paradigm. Specifically, we obtain the patch features $P = \{p_1, p_2, \ldots, p_N\}, p_i \in \mathbb{R}^d$ and attention features $A = \{a_1, a_2, \ldots, a_N\}, a_i \in \mathbb{R}^d$, where both p_i and a_i are extracted from visual extractors and d is the size of the feature vector. After that, patch features processed by Visual Memory (VIM) module and attention features processed by TF-IDF Embedding (TIE) module are treated as inputs of the two encoders. The output of the decoder $Y = \{y_1, y_2, \ldots, y_T\}, y_t \in \mathbb{V}$ is the sequence of generated words, where y_t is t-th word in the generated sequence, T is the length of the whole words and V is the vocabulary of all possible words. The framework of our proposed model is shown in Fig. 2, where the details are illustrated in the following sections.

2.1   The Model Structure

Our model is similar to most medical report generation models with Transformer [23], which contains three major modules, i.e., the visual extractor, the encoder and the decoder, where the proposed VIM and TIE modules are mainly performed before the encoder. The descriptions for three modules are explained below.

Visual Extractor. Given a medical image **Img**, using a pre-trained Convolutional Neural Network (CNN) like VGG [22] or ResNet [12] could extract its visual features. CNN contains a series of feature extractors, and extractors of different network layers can capture unique visual features of different image levels, which represent different image information. This process is modeled as:

$$\{p_1, p_2, \ldots, p_N\} = f_{\text{layer}_1}(\text{Img}) \tag{1}$$

$$\{a_1, a_2, \ldots, a_N\} = f_{\text{layer}_2}(\text{Img}) \tag{2}$$

where $f_{\text{layer}_i}(\cdot)$ represents different layers of network mentioned above. After that, visual features will be used as input to subsequent modules.

Encoder. In our model, we apply two standard encoder modules from the origin Transformer [23], of which their inputs are patch features processed by VIM module and attention features processed by TIE module, respectively. After that, the hidden states encoded from two encoders are concatenated as the input for the subsequent decoder. The encoding process is modeled as:

$$\{h_1, h_2, \ldots, h_N\} = f_{e\_1}\left(\text{VIM}\left(p_1, p_2, \ldots, p_N\right)\right) \oplus f_{e\_2}\left(\text{TIE}\left(a_1, a_2, \ldots, a_N\right)\right) \tag{3}$$

where $f_{e\_i}(\cdot)$ represents i-th encoder.

Decoder. The backbone decoder in our model is from R2g [5], where they introduce Relational Memory (RM) module to improve the memory ability of the decoder and adjust the original Layer Normalization module with a Memory-driven Conditional Layer Normalization (MCLN) module. Therefore, the decoding process is as follows:

$$y_t = f_d\left((h_1, h_2, \ldots, h_N), \text{MCLN}\left(RM\left(y_1, y_2, \ldots, y_{t-1}\right)\right)\right) \tag{4}$$

where $f_d(\cdot)$ represents the decoder with RM and MCLN modules.

2.2   TF-IDF Embedding Module

The TF-IDF [21] algorithm (term frequency-inverse document frequency) is an effective method to evaluate how important certain words are to a document or corpus. The TF-IDF algorithm consists of TF and IDF, the former extracts high-frequency words from the input text as candidate keywords, while the latter applies weights to the former to extract the most important words.

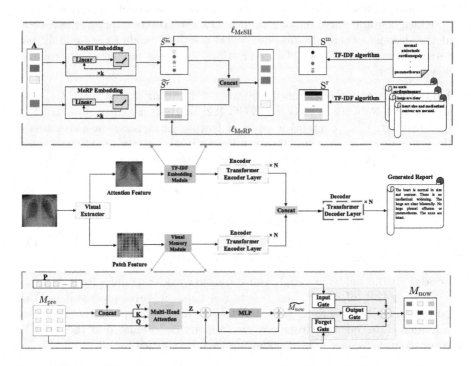

Fig. 2. The overall framework of our proposed model, with details of the visual extractor and decoder omitted. TF-IDF Embedding (TIE) module is indicated by the orange dash lines. Visual Memory (VIM) module is indicated by the yellow dash lines. In addition, the decoder in our model is from R2g [5] (Color figure online).

Inspired by TriNet [27], for medical report generation tasks, the corpus is the collection of all Medical Reports (MeRP), for each medical report there are some important keywords for summarizing the full report. In the meantime, Medical Subject Headings (MeSH) records the most important labels in medical images. Therefore, we set the semantic information from the Medical Reports (MeRP) and Medical Subject Headings (MeSH) as external knowledge for generating reports.

In doing so, we propose the TF-IDF Embedding (TIE) module to combine the TF-IDF algorithm with the feature extraction of model, an overview of TIE module is shown in Fig. 2. The module consists of two branches, the upper and lower branches utilize attention feature A from visual extractor to predict MeSH semantic feature and MeRP semantic feature, respectively. In order to leverage external knowledge, we minimize the loss between predicted MeSH & MeRP TF-IDF features and ground-truth TF-IDF features. The outputs of two branches are concatenated and then fed into the encoder as text semantic features.

For the upper branch, we utilize attention feature A to predict MeSH semantic feature $\widetilde{S^m}$. We first construct a MeSH vocabulary containing medical terms which summarize medical images. After that, for each MeSH we calculate TF-IDF values for all medical labels in MeSH corpus to build a ground-truth TF-IDF vector S^m. Among them the TF-IDF value $S^m_{i,j}$ of i-th tag g_i in j-th MeSH m_j is formulated as:

$$S^m_{i,j} = \frac{n_{i,j}}{\sum_k n_{k,j}} \times \log \frac{|M|}{|\{j:g_i \in m_j\}|} \tag{5}$$

where $n_{i,j}$ represents the frequency of tag g_i in MeSH m_j and $|M|$ denotes the total number of MeSH in the whole MeSH corpus. $|\{j : g_i \in m_j\}|$ is the number of MeSH containing tag g_i. After that, the process of predicting MeSH semantic features can be formalized as:

$$\widetilde{S^m} = W_m \cdot A \tag{6}$$

where A represents the attention feature and W_m is parameters for MeSH semantic feature embedding.

For the lower branch, we utilize attention feature A to predict MeRP semantic feature $\widetilde{S^r}$. We first define the corpus of medical reports (MeRP). After that, we construct a ground-truth TF-IDF vector S^r for each medical report. Among them the TF-IDF value $S^r_{i,j}$ of i-th word w_i in j-th medical report r_j is formulated as:

$$S^r_{i,j} = \frac{n_{i,j}}{\sum_k n_{k,j}} \times \log \frac{|R|}{|\{j:w_i \in r_j\}|} \tag{7}$$

where $n_{i,j}$ represents the frequency of word w_i in report r_j and $|R|$ denotes the number of reports in the whole medical report corpus. $|\{j : w_i \in r_j\}|$ is the number of reports containing word w_i. After that, the process of predicting MeRP semantic features can be formalized as:

$$\widetilde{S^r} = W_r \cdot A \tag{8}$$

where A represents the attention feature and W_r is parameters for MeRP semantic feature embedding.

After that, $\widetilde{S^m}$ and $\widetilde{S^r}$ are concatenated as text semantic features then fed into encoder.

2.3 Visual Memory Module

An obvious characteristic in the medical report generation task is high similarity. As shown in the Fig. 1, the two reports are similar since their features in the images are similar, too. For example, both two reports contain "the lungs are clear". Similar to practical medical diagnosis, doctors usually refer to similar medical images based on their experience to write a medical report more accurately and quickly. In order to utilize the similar features in different medical images, inspired by R2g [5], we propose the Visual Memory (VIM) module, which makes the model refer to previous features when extracting the features of current medical image, enhancing the feature-extraction capability of the model, an overview of VIM module is shown in Fig. 2.

For this purpose, we use a memory matrix M to record the previous image information in the process of feature extraction, which preserves important visual features. In the process of feature extraction for different images, information in M is gradually updated. For the patch features P extracted from visual extractor, the previous memory matrix M_{pre} will be combined with it as the query vector Q to form vector K and vector V, then all three vectors will be put into the Multi-Head Attention module together. For each head, vector query, key and value are formulated as: $Q = M_{\text{pre}} \cdot W_q$, $K = (M_{pre} \oplus P) \cdot W_k$, $V = (M_{pre} \oplus P) \cdot W_v$ where $M_{pre} \oplus P$ is concatenation of M_{pre} and P, W_q, W_k, W_v are parameters metrics. Multi-Head Attention module utilizes Q, K and V vectors to model the relationship between different visual features:

$$Z = \text{softmax}\left(\frac{Q \cdot K^T}{\sqrt{d_k}}\right) \cdot V \tag{9}$$

where d_{k} is the dimension of K and Z represents the output of Multi-Head Attention module. In order to prevent gradient vanishing or gradient exploding caused by deep network, we introduce residual connections to generate current memory matrix $\widetilde{M_{now}}$:

$$\widetilde{M_{now}} = f_{mlp}\left(Z + M_{pre}\right) + \left(Z + M_{pre}\right) \tag{10}$$

where $f_{mlp}(\cdot)$ is the multi-layer perceptron(MLP).

Then we use a gate mechanism to generate memory matrix M_{now} , which consists of input gate, forget gate and output gate. In order to balance P and M_{pre} , the input gate preserves important features of the current image and forget gate discards the information which is irrelevant to current image in the memory matrix. Input gate and forget gate are formalized as:

$$G_{\text{now}}^I = P \cdot W^I + \tanh\left(M_{\text{pre}}\right) \cdot U^I \tag{11}$$

$$G_{\text{now}}^F = P \cdot W^F + \tanh\left(M_{\text{pre}}\right) \cdot U^F \tag{12}$$

where W^I and W^F denote parameters for patch features in input gate and forget gate, respectively. U^I and U^F denote parameters for M_{pre} in input gate and forget gate, respectively. The output gate controls the generation of the memory matrix M_{now} for current image, which can be formalized as:

$$G_{\text{now}}^O = \widetilde{M_{now}} \cdot W^O \tag{13}$$

where W^O denotes parameters for output gate.

The final output of VIM module is formalized as:

$$M_{\text{now}} = \sigma\left(G_{\text{now}}^I\right) \odot P + \sigma\left(G_{\text{now}}^F\right) \odot M_{\text{pre}} + \sigma\left(G_{\text{now}}^O\right) \odot \widetilde{M_{now}} \quad (14)$$

where $\odot$ is Hadamard product and σ is the sigmoid function and M_{now} represents memory matrix containing features of the current image. After that, M_{now} is fed into encoder as the image semantic features.

2.4 Parameter Training

In our model, each training sample is a tuple (I, S, R) consists of the image I, the ground-truth TF-IDF semantic feature vector $S = [S^r; S^m]$ and the ground-truth report R. Each report in corpus contains M sentences, and each sentence consists of N words. Given a training sample, we obtain the patch features P and attention features A from visual extractors. After that, patch features processed by the VIM module and attention features processed by the TIE module are treated as inputs for two encoders, then the outputs of encoders are concatenated as hidden state h_t. For the decoder, given the hidden state h_t and a special START token, it will unroll for T times to generate word distribution $\widetilde{P_{word}}$ until the special token END appears. We train our model in an end-to-end manner, the loss function consists of three parts, namely the MeSH semantic feature loss ℓ_{MeSH}, the MeRP semantic feature loss ℓ_{MeRP} and the word generation loss ℓ_{word}. The loss function L for training is formalized as:

$$L = \lambda_{\text{MeSH}}\ell_{\text{MeSH}}\left(S^m, \widetilde{S^m}\right) + \lambda_{\text{MeRP}}\ell_{\text{MeRP}}\left(S^r, \widetilde{S^r}\right)$$

$$+\lambda_{\text{word}} \sum_{i=1}^{M}\sum_{j=1}^{N} \ell_{\text{word}}\left(P_{\text{word}}, \widetilde{P_{word}}\right) \quad (15)$$

where the word generation loss is the cross-entropy (CE) loss function, the MeSH semantic feature loss and the MeRP semantic feature loss are the mean square error (MSE) loss functions. $\lambda_{\text{MeSH}}, \lambda_{\text{MeRP}}, \lambda_{\text{word}}$ are loss weights.

3 Experiment Settings

3.1 Dataset

We conduct our experiments on the Indiana University Chest X-Ray (IU X-Ray) [8] which is a commonly used dataset for medical report generation tasks. It includes 7,470 images and 3,955 reports. The MeSH in this dataset is annotated by radiologists. For all medical reports, we follow the same procedure as Chen et al. [5] that we select reports containing two medical images and exclude reports without a "Findings" or "Impression" section. Then we divide the dataset into train/validation/test set by 7:1:2, set all letters to lower cases and remove all non-alpha tokens. After that, we obtain the top 30 medical labels as the MeSH vocabulary and the top 760 words occurring frequently as the MeRP vocabulary. For medical images in the dataset, we transform their size to 224 × 224 to fit the visual extractor as the input.

3.2   Baseline and Evaluation Metrics

In order to show the performance of our model, we leverage two approaches, (1) comparing our model with the baseline model and (2) evaluating the model with conventional natural language generation (NLG) metrics. First, we compare the performance of our model "VMEKNet" with the following medical report generation methods: R2g [5], CoAtt [14], CMN [4], CMAS-RL [13], SentSAT+KG [28]. Second, we evaluate the models mentioned above and VMEKNet with NLG metrics, which include BLEU [19], METEOR [9] and ROUGE-L [17]. The essence of BLEU is to examine the similarity between generated reports and ground-truth reports, METEOR considers the influence of synonyms on semantics, and ROUGE-L measures the fluency of generated reports.

3.3   Implementation Details

We train our model with PyTorch 1.10.0 on a single NVIDIA GeForce RTX 3090 GPU for experiments on the IU X-Ray dataset. During the training process, we train our model for 200 epochs with the batch size of 16. We adopt the Adam optimizer with gamma of 0.1 in an end-to-end method and set the learning rates to $5e-5$ and $1e-4$ for the visual extractor and other parameters, respectively. We adopt the ResNet101 [12] as visual extractor to extract features with the dimension set to 2048. For the TIE module, the dimensions of MeSH Embedding layer and MeRP Embedding layer are set to 30 and 760, respectively. For the VIM module, the number of heads in multi-head attention is set to 8, and the parameters in the input gate, forget gate and output gate are initialized randomly. For the decoder, we keep the parameters of the decoder and all details of RM and MCLN unchanged from R2g [5] for comparison. The loss weights λ_{MeSH}, λ_{MeRP}, λ_{word} are set to 1, 1 and 1, respectively. In order to prevent over-fitting, we adopt early-stopping and drop-out strategies. Note that the hyperparameters mentioned above are determined by validating the performance of the model on the validation set.

4   Experiment Results and Analyses

4.1   Comparison with Previous Studies

In this section, we compare the performance of our model (denoted as "Ours") with previous models mentioned in Sect. 3.2 on the same dataset IU X-Ray. The performance comparisons are shown in Table 1 on NLG metrics. According to Table 1, our model achieves the best performance in NLG metrics.

There are several findings concluded from different aspects. First, for medical report generation tasks, the Transformer-based model performs better than conventional Encoder-Decoder models, which can be illustrated by the comparison between "Ours" and "CoAtt". This may be attributed to the fact that the Transformer [23] is expert in handling long-text generation. Second, it is noticed that our model performs better than other models like "CMN" on NLG metrics, which demonstrates that VIM and TIE modules show excellent capability.

Table 1. Comparison results of our model (VMEKNet) with previous studies on the IU X-Ray dataset. The **best** results are highlighted.

Method	Year	BLEU-1	BLEU-2	BLEU-3	BLEU-4	METEOR	ROUGE-L
CoAtt [14]	2018	0.455	0.288	0.205	0.154	0.191	0.369
CMAS-RL [13]	2019	0.463	0.301	0.210	0.154	–	0.362
SentSAT+KG [28]	2020	0.441	0.291	0.203	0.147	–	0.367
R2g [5]	2020	0.467	0.303	0.210	0.155	**0.195**	0.371
CMN [4]	2021	0.501	0.316	0.217	0.158	0.194	0.380
VMEKNet (ours)	2022	**0.505**	**0.319**	**0.219**	**0.159**	**0.195**	**0.383**

4.2 Qualitative Results and Analyses

To further investigate the effectiveness of our model, we implement qualitative experiments on the IU X-Ray dataset. Figure 3 shows some examples of the generated reports and ground-truth reports associated with the input medical image. There are some findings concluded from different aspects.

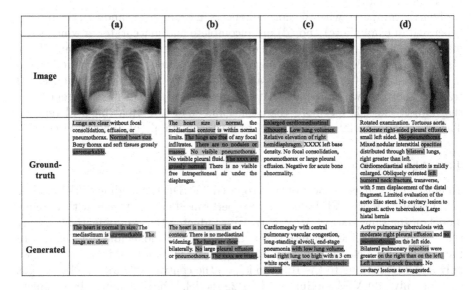

Fig. 3. Examples of generated reports given images in the IU X-Ray dataset. (a) and (b) are normal examples, while (c) and (d) are abnormal examples. In order to better show the quality of generated reports and compare with ground-truth reports, we mark different contents in the report with different colors highlight. (Color figure online)

First, it is observed that our model generates accurate medical reports for associated medical images. For example, as we can see from example (a), our model describes the image with "The heart is normal in size. The mediastinum is unremarkable. The lungs are clear", which is similar to the ground-truth "Lungs are clear without focal consolidation, effusion, or pneumothorax. Normal heart size. Bony thorax and soft tissues grossly unremarkable". This also provides a visual reference for the model performance obtained from Sect. 4.1 with NLG metrics.

Second, our model can generate similar medical reports for medical images containing similar features. For example, the medical images in example (a) and (b) both represent normal medical images, hence the two generated reports are extremely similar which consist of "Lungs are clear", "Normal heart size". It is believed that the addition of the memory network improves the performance of the model, further validating the effectiveness of the VIM module.

Third, note that for different medical images, our model generates accurate MeSH which summarizes the characteristics of disease in the image, thus generating a medical diagnosis. For example, in example (b) our model describes the image with "pleural effusion" and "pneumothorax", in example (c), our model predicts the disease "atelectasis". The reason behind this might be that we integrate external knowledge into the feature extraction process with the TIE module, which reduces the gap between image semantic features and text semantic features. Therefore, external knowledge provides an important reference for medical report generation.

Fourth, compared with the normal reports in example (a) and (b), the reports generated in example (c) and (d) are incomplete and inaccurate, in which some diseases are ignored. For example, in example(d), "active tuberculosis" and "large hiatal hernia" are decisive for the diagnosis of the patient, while they are ignored in generated reports. This may be attributed to the long-tailed distribution of training samples, which means that the number of normal medical reports in the dataset exceeds far more than the number of abnormal medical reports. Therefore, it is insufficient for model to learn enough about abnormalities.

4.3 Ablation Studies

To illustrate the effectiveness of the proposed TF-IDF Embedding (TIE) module and Visual Memory (VIM) module, we perform ablation studies with baseline model on the same dataset IU X-Ray. We conducted the experiments by setting the R2g [5] as baseline, because it is a highly scalable model and any changes to the model can be clearly reflected in the results. "Ours-no-VIM" means that we only add TIE module to the R2g model, on the contrary, "Ours-no-TIE" means that we only add VIM module to the R2g model. "Ours" denotes the complete model we propose, which includes both the TIE module and VIM module. The NLG metrics of ablation studies are shown in Table 2. At the same time, we implement qualitative experiments to verify the results.

There are several findings concluded from Fig. 4. First, both "Ours-no-TIE" and "Ours-no-VIM" models outperform R2g [5], which confirms that TIE module and VIM module are positive for improving the performance of the model. It is further shown that adding external knowledge to the model and making full use of the visual features of previous images helps the model learn sufficient visual features in the encoding stage, which guides the model to generate more accurate and comprehensive medical reports in the decoding stage. Second, compared

Table 2. Ablations studies results of our model on IU X-Ray dataset.

Method	BLEU-1	BLEU-2	BLEU-3	BLEU-4	METEOR	ROUGE-L
R2g [5]	0.467	0.303	0.210	0.155	**0.195**	0.371
Ours-no-VIM	0.489	0.313	0.217	0.158	0.190	0.375
Ours-no-TIE	0.478	0.310	0.211	0.156	0.188	0.372
VMEKNet (Ours)	**0.505**	**0.319**	**0.219**	**0.159**	**0.195**	**0.383**

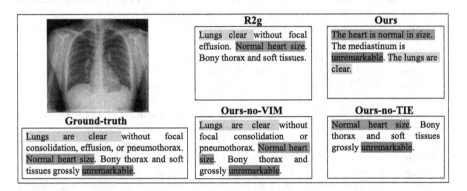

Fig. 4. Examples of generated reports from ablation studies.

with "Ours-no-TIE", "Ours-no-VIM" performs better, which demonstrates that TIE module shows more effectiveness than VIM module. The reason behind this might be that for the medical report generation task, the previous image features provided by VIM module need further mining, while external knowledge is easier for encoder to understand.

5   Conclusion and Future Work

In this paper, we propose a medical report generation model VMEKNet that integrates visual memory and external knowledge into the task. For this reason, we propose the TF-IDF Embedding (TIE) module to incorporate external knowledge via the TF-IDF algorithm and the Visual Memory (VIM) module to make full use of previous image features. Experimental results on the IU X-Ray dataset demonstrate that our model outperforms previous works, results of ablation studies show the effectiveness of TIE module and VIM module. As for the future work, first we would try to combine other external knowledge, such as knowledge graphs, with the model. Second, we aim to explore how the combination of external knowledge with image features affects the decoding stage. Third, we will evaluate the performance of our model on other datasets and practical clinical diagnosis.

Acknowledgments. This work is supported by the National Natural Science Foundation of China under (Grant No. 62072135), Innovative Research Foundation of

Ship General Performance (26622211), Ningxia Natural Science Foundation Project (2022AAC03346), Fundamental Research project (No. JCKY2020210B019), Fundamental Research Funds for the Central Universities (3072022TS0604).

References

1. Anderson, P., et al.: Bottom-up and top-down attention for image captioning and visual question answering. In: Proceedings of the IEEE Conference on Computer Vision and Pattern Recognition, pp. 6077–6086 (2018)
2. Banino, A., et al.: Memo: a deep network for flexible combination of episodic memories. arXiv preprint arXiv:2001.10913 (2020)
3. Biswal, S., Xiao, C., Glass, L.M., Westover, B., Sun, J.: Clara: clinical report auto-completion. In: Proceedings of The Web Conference 2020, pp. 541–550 (2020)
4. Chen, Z., Shen, Y., Song, Y., Wan, X.: Cross-modal memory networks for radiology report generation. arXiv preprint arXiv:2204.13258 (2022)
5. Chen, Z., Song, Y., Chang, T.H., Wan, X.: Generating radiology reports via memory-driven transformer. arXiv preprint arXiv:2010.16056 (2020)
6. Cornia, M., Stefanini, M., Baraldi, L., Cucchiara, R.: Meshed-memory transformer for image captioning. In: Proceedings of the IEEE/CVF Conference on Computer Vision and Pattern Recognition, pp. 10578–10587 (2020)
7. Dai, B., Fidler, S., Urtasun, R., Lin, D.: Towards diverse and natural image descriptions via a conditional GAN. In: Proceedings of the IEEE International Conference on Computer Vision, pp. 2970–2979 (2017)
8. Demner-Fushman, D., et al.: Preparing a collection of radiology examinations for distribution and retrieval. J. Am. Med. Inform. Assoc. **23**(2), 304–310 (2016)
9. Denkowski, M., Lavie, A.: Meteor 1.3: automatic metric for reliable optimization and evaluation of machine translation systems. In: Proceedings of the Sixth Workshop on Statistical Machine Translation, pp. 85–91 (2011)
10. Farhadi, A., et al.: Every picture tells a story: generating sentences from images. In: Daniilidis, K., Maragos, P., Paragios, N. (eds.) ECCV 2010. LNCS, vol. 6314, pp. 15–29. Springer, Heidelberg (2010). https://doi.org/10.1007/978-3-642-15561-1_2
11. Gao, L., Li, X., Song, J., Shen, H.T.: Hierarchical LSTMs with adaptive attention for visual captioning. IEEE Trans. Pattern Anal. Mach. Intell. **42**(5), 1112–1131 (2019)
12. He, K., Zhang, X., Ren, S., Sun, J.: Deep residual learning for image recognition. In: Proceedings of the IEEE Conference on Computer Vision and Pattern Recognition, pp. 770–778 (2016)
13. Jing, B., Wang, Z., Xing, E.: Show, describe and + conclude: on exploiting the structure information of chest x-ray reports. arXiv preprint arXiv:2004.12274 (2020)
14. Jing, B., Xie, P., Xing, E.: On the automatic generation of medical imaging reports. arXiv preprint arXiv:1711.08195 (2017)
15. Krupinski, E.A.: Current perspectives in medical image perception. Attention Percept. Psychophys. **72**(5), 1205–1217 (2010)
16. Li, Y., Liang, X., Hu, Z., Xing, E.P.: Hybrid retrieval-generation reinforced agent for medical image report generation. In: Advances in Neural Information Processing Systems, vol. 31 (2018)
17. Lin, C.Y.: Rouge: a package for automatic evaluation of summaries. In: Text summarization Branches Out, pp. 74–81 (2004)

18. Ordonez, V., Kulkarni, G., Berg, T.: IM2Text: describing images using 1 million captioned photographs. In: Advances in Neural Information Processing Systems, vol. 24 (2011)
19. Papineni, K., Roukos, S., Ward, T., Zhu, W.J.: Bleu: a method for automatic evaluation of machine translation. In: Proceedings of the 40th Annual Meeting of the Association for Computational Linguistics, pp. 311–318 (2002)
20. Pavlopoulos, J., Kougia, V., Androutsopoulos, I., Papamichail, D.: Diagnostic captioning: a survey. arXiv preprint arXiv:2101.07299 (2021)
21. Salton, G., Buckley, C.: Term-weighting approaches in automatic text retrieval. Inf. Process. Manag. **24**(5), 513–523 (1988)
22. Simonyan, K., Zisserman, A.: Very deep convolutional networks for large-scale image recognition. arXiv preprint arXiv:1409.1556 (2014)
23. Vaswani, A., et al.: Attention is all you need. In: Advances in Neural Information Processing Systems, vol. 30 (2017)
24. Vinyals, O., Toshev, A., Bengio, S., Erhan, D.: Show and tell: a neural image caption generator. In: Proceedings of the IEEE Conference on Computer Vision and Pattern Recognition, pp. 3156–3164 (2015)
25. Xu, K., et al.: Show, attend and tell: neural image caption generation with visual attention. In: International Conference on Machine Learning, pp. 2048–2057. PMLR (2015)
26. Xu, N., et al.: Multi-level policy and reward-based deep reinforcement learning framework for image captioning. IEEE Trans. Multimedia **22**(5), 1372–1383 (2019)
27. Yang, Y., Yu, J., Zhang, J., Han, W., Jiang, H., Huang, Q.: Joint embedding of deep visual and semantic features for medical image report generation. IEEE Trans. Multimedia (2021)
28. Zhang, Y., Wang, X., Xu, Z., Yu, Q., Yuille, A., Xu, D.: When radiology report generation meets knowledge graph. In: Proceedings of the AAAI Conference on Artificial Intelligence, vol. 34, pp. 12910–12917 (2020)

Detecting Video Anomalous Events with an Enhanced Abnormality Score

Liheng Shen$^{(\boxtimes)}$, Tetsu Matsukawa, and Einoshin Suzuki$^{(\boxtimes)}$

ISEE, Kyushu University, Fukuoka 819-0395, Japan
shen.liheng.020@s.kyushu-u.ac.jp, {matsukawa,suzuki}@inf.kyushu-u.ac.jp

Abstract. Detecting video anomalous events is vital for human monitoring. Anomalous events usually contain abnormal actions with exaggerated motion and little motion. We define the former and the latter
as dynamic anomalies and static anomalies, respectively. We define the
video data of events where a few persons perform diverse actions indoors
as Indoor Event Data (IED). Many frame prediction approaches have
succeeded in detecting dynamic anomalies. However, they are prone to
overlooking static anomalies in IED. To solve this problem, we propose
an Enhanced Abnormality Score (EAS), which is a combination of prediction, dynamic, appearance, and motion scores. To specifically target
static anomalies, we calculate a score to evaluate the dynamic degrees of
actions. We use an appearance score of a frame to detect static anomalies from appearance. This score is generated from a clustering-based
distance of a pre-trained CNN feature. We also use a motion score based
on flow reconstruction to balance the appearance score. We conduct
extensive experiments on two datasets involving indoor human activities.
Quantitative and qualitative experimental results show that our proposal
achieves the best performance among its variants and the state-of-the-art
methods.

Keywords: Video anomalous event detection · Frame prediction ·
Clustering · Flow reconstruction · Dynamic degree

1 Introduction

Human monitoring, especially human activities or events, has been drawing
attention in recent years [8,31]. As a fundamental task for human monitoring,
video anomalous event detection [39] is valuable due to its real-world applications
such as surveillance [34] and healthcare [5]. A model for video anomalous event
detection usually takes a single frame or sequence of frames as its input, then outputs frame-level labels [22,23,30], i.e., judging frames which describe whether an
event are normal or abnormal. Anomalous events are generally defined as events
which occur infrequently and largely deviate from expectations, e.g., "riding a
bike" is abnormal in an indoor environment [9,16]. Their detection is challenging
since gathering all kinds of rare yet diverse anomalous events is almost infeasible [2,22,29]. Therefore, the general idea is to train a one-class classifier which

© The Author(s), under exclusive license to Springer Nature Switzerland AG 2022
S. Khanna et al. (Eds.): PRICAI 2022, LNCS 13629, pp. 202–217, 2022.
https://doi.org/10.1007/978-3-031-20862-1_15

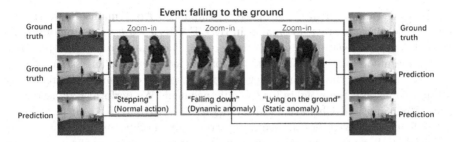

Fig. 1. A comparison between predicted frames and their ground truth. The two abnormal actions, i.e., "falling down" and "lying on the ground", and a normal action, i.e., "stepping", are components of the event. The frame of the static anomaly can be predicted as well as the frame of normal action, which is much better than that of the dynamic anomaly (see the face and arms).

can model frequently occurring behaviors using only normal, unlabeled training examples [2,36,39], and use it to detect anomalies in the test data.

Anomalous events usually include abnormal actions with exaggerated motion, e.g., "a person is falling", or little motion, e.g., "a person is lying on the ground". We call them "dynamic anomalies" and "static anomalies", respectively. To effectively detect an anomalous event, a model needs to be able to detect both dynamic and static anomalies from motion and appearance information. Many events in indoor scenarios, e.g., those in a student room and laboratory, usually involve fewer persons than in outdoor scenarios, e.g., those in an avenue and a subway station. We define the video data of indoor events involving a few persons as Indoor Event Data (IED). To detect anomalous events in IED, a model needs to handle features at fine-grained levels since appearance differences between frames are relatively small.

In video anomalous event detection, the frame prediction approach [22,25,30] has succeeded in detecting dynamic anomalies. This approach learns a CNN with an Auto-Encoder (AE) to model frames of normal events. Significant prediction errors between the prediction results and their corresponding ground truth indicate abnormalities. However, differences between consecutive frames are smaller in relatively static actions than in dynamic actions. Prediction errors between predicted frames and their ground truth in static anomalies are smaller than in dynamic anomalies. Thus, frames of static anomalies can be predicted almost as perfectly as normal cases, making the prediction model wrongly judge static anomalies as normal (Fig. 1). A recent method, Memory-guided Normality for Anomaly Detection (MNAD) [30], introduces a memory module to enhance discriminating anomalies from appearance, e.g., adding a score to the frame prediction model, which improves the model's ability to detect static anomalies. However, the scores are too small to detect static anomalies in IED. MNAD [30] makes most of the L2 distances between appearance features of testing data and trained memory items recording normal appearance prototypes extremely small, resulting in being insensitive to static anomalies.

To solve this problem, we propose an Enhanced Abnormality Score (EAS), which is sensitive to static anomalies in IED. EAS is a score consisting of prediction, dynamic, appearance, and motion scores. It enhances a score output by a prediction model on relatively static actions to avoid overlooking static anomalies. We calculate the dynamic degrees of frames to determine the relatively static actions and the weights for the enhancement. We perform Balanced Iterative Reducing and Clustering using Hierarchies (BIRCH) [41] on pre-trained CNN features to generate appearance scores for checking abnormalities [15]. Since BIRCH can generate micro clusters, the distances between the appearance features of testing data and trained cluster centroids, i.e., normal prototypes, are at fine-grained levels, which makes the score sensitive to static anomalies in IED. We also conduct flow reconstruction to obtain motion scores to alleviate outputting too high abnormality scores for the normal data not included in the training set.

In summary, the contributions of our paper are as follows.

- We selectively enhance the abnormality scores of the frame prediction model for the frames containing relatively static actions. We also design weights in the abnormality score calculation to better use the components.
- We introduce a clustering based appearance score and a flow reconstruction based motion score for the enhancement.
- We perform extensive experiments which show that our proposal achieves better performance than its variants and the state-of-the-art methods.

2   Related Work

We review the literature on methods of AE-based video anomalous event detection. There are two main groups, i.e., reconstruction and prediction. Similar to our proposal, several methods also perform clustering. Many methods cope with events equally in calculating abnormality scores.

Reconstruction and Prediction. With the powerful feature extraction capability of DNNs, AE-based methods have been blooming in recent years. Reconstruction-based AEs [3,14,26,27] use reconstruction errors to indicate anomalies from the assumption that anomalous data cannot be reconstructed as well as normal data. They use 3D ConvNet [14], CNN + RNN [3,26], or stacked RNN [27]. However, due to the high capacity of DNNs, AEs sometimes reconstruct abnormal frames well. Prediction-based AEs [22,25,38,42] compare predicted frames with their ground truth, where larger differences indicate anomalies. They are proposed to avoid a DNN reconstructing abnormal data as well as reconstructing normal data, enhancing anomaly detection performance [22]. Nevertheless, it is relatively straightforward for prediction-based AEs to predict the frame from consecutive frames with minor differences, resulting in overlooking static anomalies. MNAD [30] develops a memory module for an AE to enhance discriminating anomalies from appearance information. The memory module, which handles appearance information, improves the model's performance in detecting static anomalies. However, it is defective in processing IED.

Besides, some works perform AE-based prediction and reconstruction jointly [29,35,37]. However, they cannot avoid the aforementioned problems in dealing with IED.

Clustering. Several AE-based methods introduce clustering to exploit the advantages of both discriminative clustering methods and deep embedding models. They generally cluster intermidiate features of an AE [2,7,11,18]. Different from them, we cluster features extracted by a pre-trained CNN, which is independent of the AE's training.

Abnormality Score Calculation. Several methods apply parameter-based linear [1,9,12,30] and non-linear combinations [2,23,29,38] of different scores to calculate abnormality scores. However, these methods handle all the frames of events equally, rather than distinguishing them by their dynamic degree. Different from these methods, ours applies a different strategy to better target at relatively static and dynamic actions in video frames, improving the performance.

3   Proposal

We tackle video anomalous event detection, which takes frames as the input and outputs the label of each frame, i.e., normal or abnormal. We design our method based on the Frame Prediction (Frame-Pred) model [22]. We show an overview of our proposal in Fig. 2.

3.1   Frame Prediction Model

Let I and I^{ijc} both stand for an image, i.e., $I = \{I^{ijc}\} \in \mathbb{R}^{H \times W \times 3}$, where the indices i, j show spatial coordinate and H, W are image height and width respectively, and c indicates one of the 3 color channels (RGB)[1]. Given a video with consecutive t frames $I_1, I_2, ..., I_t$, the model predicts a future frame I_{t+1}. Suppose $\hat{I}_{t+1}$ denotes the predicted image at time $t+1$, while I_{t+1} is the ground truth. We use the frame prediction-based abnormality score $S_p(I_{t+1})$, which is defined as follows [22]:

$$S_p(I_{t+1}) = 1 - F_n\left(F_{psnr}(I_{t+1}, \hat{I}_{t+1})\right), \tag{1}$$

where $F_{psnr}(\cdot, \cdot)$ is Peak Signal to Noise Ratio (PSNR) defined as,

$$F_{psnr}(I, \hat{I}) = \frac{1}{3}\sum_{c=1}^{3}\left(10\log_{10}\frac{\left(\max_{i,j}\hat{I}^{ijc}\right)^2}{\frac{1}{HW}\sum_{i=1}^{H}\sum_{j=1}^{W}(I^{ijc} - \hat{I}^{ijc})^2}\right). \tag{2}$$

---

[1] We rescale the pixel values in the range $[-1, 1]$.

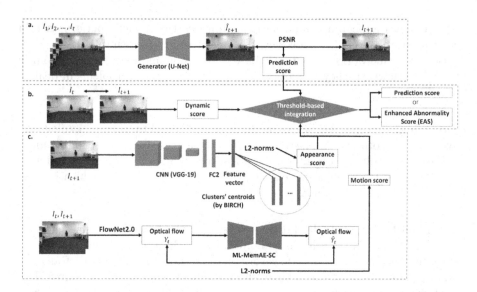

Fig. 2. Overview of our proposal. (a) A frame prediction model provides an abnormality score given previous frames. (b) Threshold-based abnormality score calculation. A dynamic score evaluates dynamic degree of the action in a frame. It also adjusts the degree of the enhancement on an abnormality score of a relatively static action. (c) A pre-trained CNN and clustering provide an abnormality score from an appearance view. A flow reconstruction model provides a motion score from a motion view.

A higher PSNR indicates high similarity between the predicted and ground-truth frames, indicating higher normality. $F_n(\cdot)$ is a normalization function that fits a score in the range $[0, 1]$ by the min-max normalization defined as follows:

$$F_n(x_t) = \frac{x_t - \min_t x_t}{\max_t x_t - \min_t x_t}, \tag{3}$$

where $\max_t x_t$ and $\min_t x_t$ are the maximum and minimum values of $x \in \mathbb{R}^1$ among all videos, respectively.

3.2 Appearance Score

To enhance detecting anomalies from the appearance aspect of a frame, we introduce an extra CNN. We regard a set of feature vectors extracted by the CNN on a training data set including only normal actions as normal appearance prototypes (Sect. 1). Inspired by Anomalous Image Region Detection (AIRD) [15], we train a clustering model independently from the AE's training via BIRCH [41]. BIRCH clusters image features efficiently and generates micro clusters. This model provides another object-level semantics which is independent of AE's training set, and serves as an appearance detector.

We define the appearance abnormality score $S_a(I_t)$ based on the $L2$-distance as follows:

$$S_a(I_t) = F_n\left(\|V_t - C_t\|_2^2\right). \tag{4}$$

On the training data, we input consecutive frames to the CNN frame by frame, and extract their feature vectors. BIRCH clusters those feature vectors and assigns the leaf nodes as the clusters' centroids $C_1, C_2, ..., C_t$.

On the test data, we input frames $I_1, I_2, ..., I_t$ and extract their features $V_1, V_2, ..., V_t$. We calculate L2 distances between the features and cluster centroids, and normalize those distances via Eq. (3) as the appearance abnormality score.

3.3 Motion Score

We use a flow reconstruction model to check the motion abnormality. A flow reconstruction model takes the input of optical flow (Y) and reconstructs it. Following [23], we use FlowNet2.0 [17] to extract optical flow. We use Multi-Level Memory-augmented Autoencoder with Skip Connections (ML-MemAE-SC) [23] due to its high performance in detecting motion anomalies from temporal information.

We define the motion abnormality score $S_m(I_t)$ as follows [23]:

$$S_m(I_t) = F_n\left(\|Y_t - \hat{Y}_t\|_2^2\right), \tag{5}$$

where $\hat{Y}_t$ is the reconstructed optical flow at time t, and Y_t is the ground truth.

3.4 Dynamic Score and Threshold-Based Integration

To measure the dynamic degree of video frames, we use the dynamic score $D(I_t)$ based on a difference of frames defined as follows:

$$D(I_t) = F_n\left(\left(\sum_{i=1}^{H}\sum_{j=1}^{W}\sum_{c=1}^{3} f(I_{t+1}^{ijc} - I_t^{ijc})^2\right)^{\frac{1}{2}}\right) \qquad f(x) = \begin{cases} 1, & x > \alpha, \\ x, & x \le \alpha. \end{cases} \tag{6}$$

The changed pixels indicate movement, e.g., an exaggerated motion usually causes many changed pixels. To eliminate the effect of a person's cloth color on the dynamic degree, we use the function $f(\cdot)$ to unify the changed pixel values. To counter the impact of the image noise and illumination variance, we introduce a threshold α. The larger the value of $D(\cdot)$ is, the more dynamic the action in the frame t is.

When the dynamic score is relatively high, i.e., the action is dynamic, we directly use the frame prediction score $S_p(I_t)$. Otherwise, i.e., when the action is relatively static, we take a weighted combination of $S_p(I_t)$ and a score of appearance and motion of the frame $S_{\text{am}}(I_t)$. This combination is the Enhanced Abnormality Score (EAS), represented by $S_{\text{pam}}(I_t)$.

Both abnormal actions and "unseen" normal actions contain "unfamiliar" appearances. $S_{\text{a}}(\cdot)$ shows a higher score for an abnormal action or a normal action that is largely different from the training set. The former case is desirable while the latter case brings destructive effects. For the same category of actions, the appearance may be very different, but the motion should be similar [13]. Thus, we take advantage of ML-MemAE-SC [23] to check motion abnormality to compensate for the destructive effects. We use the following score for the enhancement:

$$S_{\text{am}}(I_t) = \gamma S_{\text{a}}(I_t) + (1 - \gamma)S_{\text{m}}(I_t), \tag{7}$$

where $\gamma \in [0, 1]$ is a weight introduced for flexibility.

The (unnormalized) integrated abnormality score $S_{\text{inte}}^*(I_t)$ is defined as follows.

$$S_{\text{inte}}^*(I_t) = \begin{cases} S_{\text{p}}(I_t), & D(I_t) > \sigma, \\ S_{\text{pam}}(I_t) = D(I_t)S_{\text{p}}(I_t) + (1 - D(I_t))S_{\text{am}}(I_t), & D(I_t) \le \sigma, \end{cases} \tag{8}$$

where σ is a threshold to determine whether the actions in the input video frames are relatively static or dynamic.

As we explained in Sect. 1, the more static the action is, the more likely that the prediction model neglects static anomalies. We set $D(I_t)$ as a weight for the prediction score to handle this tendency. At last, we apply Eq. (3) as $S_{\text{inte}}(I_t) = F_{\text{n}}(S_{\text{inte}}^*(I_t))$.

4   Experiments

We extensively evaluate our proposed method by quantitative and qualitative analyses on two datasets, including a comparison with its variants and the state-of-the-art methods. We also check the parameter dependency.

4.1   Datasets and Evaluation Metric

Different from widely used public Video Anomaly Detection (VAD) datasets, e.g., UCSD Ped2 [28], CUHK Avenue [24], and ShanghaiTech [22], we use action recognition datasets (NTU RGB+D [32] and NTU RGB+D 120 [21]) which contain a larger number of categories of indoor human actions to constitute our benchmark. Those three VAD datasets lack indoor human activities, limiting their significance. On the other hand, detecting abnormal indoor human activities is vital for human monitoring [19,20].

NTU RGB+D [32] dataset includes 60 actions and NTU RGB+D 120 [21] is an extended dataset of the former dataset, which includes 120 actions. We reserve only the last 60 actions in NTU RGB+D 120 [21] to avoid repeating the NTU RGB+D [32] dataset. Each video clip in the original datasets includes the whole

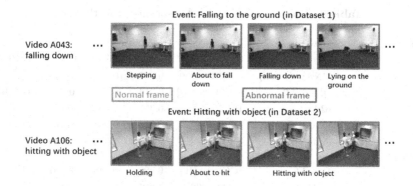

Fig. 3. Labeling the action recognition datasets [21,32] to constitute a frame-level VAD benchmark.

process of a main action, e.g., falling to the ground. To constitute a frame-level VAD benchmark, we label the corresponding frames of the abnormal actions in each video as "abnormal frames", and other frames as "normal frames". We regard the whole process of exaggerated, surprising, offensive, or severe actions as anomalous events (Fig. 3).

Dataset 1 is generated from NTU RGB-D [32]. We regard 9 actions[2] as abnormal and the remaining 51 actions as normal. Its training and test sets consist of 255 videos (24,917 normal frames) and 64 videos (5,509 normal and 771 abnormal frames), respectively.

Dataset 2 is generated from NTU RGB-D 120 [21]. We regard 11 actions[3] as abnormal and the remaining 49 actions as normal. Its training and test sets consist of 245 videos (17,193 normal frames) and 70 videos (3,982 normal and 701 abnormal frames), respectively.

We use the Area Under the ROC Curve (AUROC) and PR Curve (AUPRC) as evaluation metrics for frame-level video anomalous event detection since ROC and PR have their advantages and cannot be replaced by each other [4].

4.2 Implemtation Details

We implement the proposed method with Pytorch on a PC equipped with two RTX TITAN GPUs and an i9-10900KF CPU. We use the public codes of the

---

[2] The 9 actions are "throwing", "kicking something", "hopping", "jumping up", "falling down", "vomiting", "punching someone", "kicking someone", and "pushing someone".

[3] The 11 actions are "shooting at basket", "tennis bat swing", "running on the spot", "throwing up hat", "hitting with object", "grabbing stuff", "wielding knife", "knocking over", "shooting with gun", "stepping on foot", and "supporting somebody".

Table 1. Comparison with the state-of-the-art methods.

Type	Method	Ref	Dataset 1		Dataset 2	
			AUROC	AUPRC	AUROC	AUPRC
Appearance only	MNAD (recon)	CVPR'20 [30]	0.202	0.076	0.714	0.256
	QMem-L2	CVPR'20 [30]	0.574	0.265	**0.861**	**0.466**
	RIAD	PR'21 [40]	0.457	0.108	0.640	0.251
	VGG-19+BIRCH	Ours	0.706	0.228	0.705	0.336
Appearance and motion	Frame-Pred	CVPR'18 [22]	0.860	0.555	0.840	0.430
	MemAE	ICCV'19 [10]	0.422	0.140	0.857	0.366
	VEC	MM'20 [38]	**0.895**	0.592	0.816	0.434
	MNAD (pred)	CVPR'20 [30]	0.849	0.496	0.834	0.435
	HF^2-VAD	ICCV'21 [23]	0.891	**0.593**	0.853	0.465
	Proposed	Ours	**0.895**	**0.611**	**0.884**	**0.496**

prediction[4] and flow reconstruction models[5]. The structures and the training parameters remain the same as in the original paper [22,23].

We use the VGG-19 [33] pre-trained on the ImageNet dataset [6] due to its high capability in extracting object-level semantics. For each frame I, we extract vector (4096 dimension) of the second FC-Layer (FC2) as the feature vector $V \in \mathbb{R}^{4096}$.

We set threshold α in $D(\cdot)$ to 0.08 via pre-experiments and keep the parameters in BIRCH as its default. We manually set the threshold σ for $D(\cdot)$ to 0.2 and the weight γ for $S_a(\cdot)$ to 0.4.

4.3 Comparison with the State-of-the-Art

Table 1 compares our method with the state-of-the-art methods, for which we run the public codes[6] on our datasets with the default parameters. The bold figures indicate the best two scores.

Our proposal considers both spatial and temporal information and thus it easily surpasses the best baseline method at the top block. It also outperforms the relatively stronger methods, e.g., [23,38], at the bottom block as it better detects static anomalies. Thus, our proposal performs the best.

---

[4] Frame-Pred [22]: https://github.com/feiyuhuahuo/Anomaly_Prediction.

[5] HF^2-VAD (Flow Recon, ML-MemAE-SC) [23]: https://github.com/LiUzHiAn/hf2vad.

[6] MNAD [30]: https://github.com/cvlab-yonsei/MNAD
MemAE [10]: https://github.com/lyn1874/memAE
VEC [38]: https://github.com/yuguangnudt/VEC_VAD
RIAD [40]: https://github.com/plutoyuxie/Reconstruction-by-inpainting-for-visual-anomaly-detection.

Table 2. Ablation study of our proposal.

$S_p(\cdot)$	$S_a(\cdot)$	$S_m(\cdot)$	seg.	wt.	Dataset 1		Dataset 2	
					AUROC	AUPRC	AUROC	AUPRC
✓					0.860	0.555	0.840	0.430
	✓				0.706	0.228	0.705	0.336
		✓			0.875	0.546	0.847	0.442
✓	✓	✓			0.847	0.459	0.849	0.442
✓	✓	✓		✓	0.861	0.535	**0.882**	**0.496**
✓	✓	✓	✓		**0.890**	**0.608**	0.880	0.493
✓	✓	✓	✓	✓	**0.895**	**0.611**	**0.884**	**0.496**

At the top block, most methods show much lower scores in Dataset 1 than in Dataset 2. "QMem-L2" shows the best scores in Dataset 2. Meanwhile, its performance in Dataset 1 is low. We speculate the reason for the decrease of "QMem-L2" in Dataset 1 is that the training dataset largely affects the feature extraction ability of its encoder. Compared with the "QMem-L2", the performance of "VGG-19 + BIRCH" ($S_a(\cdot)$) is stable. Since CNN is pre-trained on the ImageNet dataset, it has a solid ability to identify object-level semantics

At the bottom block, most of the methods perform much better than those in the first block except for MemAE [10]. In MemAE [10], the normal examples which are not included in the training set are given too high abnormality scores due to the mechanism and are falsely detected as abnormal. Among those baseline methods except ours, HF^2-VAD [23] performs the best, as its integrated model based on flow reconstruction and frame prediction has a solid capability in extracting and inferring spatial and temporal information.

4.4 Ablation Study

To analyze the effect of each component in our proposal, we conduct an ablation study. We evaluate the combination of $S_p(\cdot)$, $S_a(\cdot)$, $S_m(\cdot)$, and the threshold-based calculation. We verify two parts independently for our threshold-based calculation: the threshold-based segmentation (seg.) and the dynamic score based weights (wt.). In the case when the former is not used, we only reserve $S_{pam}(\cdot)$. When the latter is not used, we take the average scores of $S_p(\cdot)$, $S_a(\cdot)$, and $S_m(\cdot)$ as $S_{pam}(\cdot)$.

Table 2 shows the results, where bold figures indicate the best two scores. We see that simply averaging the three components $S_p(\cdot)$, $S_a(\cdot)$, and $S_m(\cdot)$ performs no better than the baseline frame prediction model $S_p(\cdot)$. After adding dynamic score based weights (wt.) or threshold-based segmentation (seg.), the performance becomes better than $S_p(\cdot)$, which proves the significance of $D(\cdot)$. Our complete model achieves the best performance.

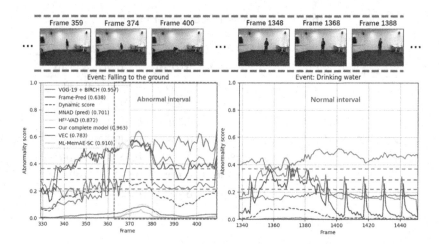

Fig. 4. Effect of $S_p(\cdot)$, $S_a(\cdot)$ and $S_m(\cdot)$. The green and red bounding boxes stand for normal and abnormal classes, respectively. The abnormality scores of each method are plotted in different colors. The numbers in brackets indicate methods' AUROCs in the event. Vertical red dotted lines denote the abnormal interval, while the rest is the normal interval. (Color figure online)

4.5   Qualitative Analysis

Superiority of our proposal. A model should give higher abnormality scores for abnormal data than normal data to avoid false detection. In Fig. 4 (left), Frame-Pred [22] and MNAD (pred) [30] detect dynamic anomalies effectively from frame #363–379, while detecting static anomalies poorly from frames #380–409. Their scores in frames #380–409 are lower than those in the normal interval, causing false detection. VEC [38] and HF²-VAD [23] show a similar trend but better performance. Although our model gives lower values for static anomalies than [22,30], its performance is the best. Note that these abnormality scores are normalized with Eq. (3). Since the abnormality scores for the abnormal interval are higher than those for the normal interval, the number of false detections is decreased.

Effect of $S_p(\cdot)$, $S_a(\cdot)$ and $S_m(\cdot)$. In Fig. 4 (left), the prediction model ($S_p(\cdot)$) shows the same curve as Frame-Pred [22]. "VGG-19 + BIRCH" ($S_a(\cdot)$) clearly detects the static anomalies, while "ML-MemAE-SC" ($S_m(\cdot)$) only detects the significant abnormal motion. With $S_a(\cdot)$, our model successfully discriminates anomalies among relatively static actions. It gives higher abnormality scores for the abnormal interval that corresponds to relatively static actions than those for the normal.

$S_a(\cdot)$ is sensitive to the diversity of the normal data, generating high abnormality scores for those normalities that do not appear during the training, as shown in the event "drinking water" (Fig. 4 (right)). $S_m(\cdot)$ in the event "drinking water" stably keeps low values. The motion information of this action is similar to the same category of actions in the training data. After combining $S_a(\cdot)$ and

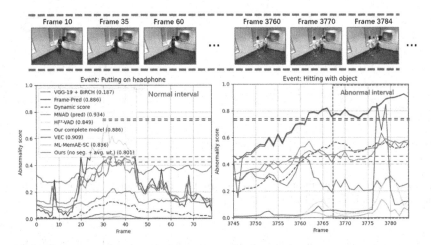

Fig. 5. Effect of threshold-based calculation. The figure's configuration is the same as Fig. 4. Note that methods' AUROCs shown on the left are for the event of "hitting with object".

$S_m(\cdot)$, our model's output shows lower abnormality scores in the normal interval than those in the abnormal interval, i.e., it exhibits a better performance.

Effect of Threshold-Based Calculation. In Fig. 5, "VGG-19 + BIRCH" ($S_a(\cdot)$) exhibits much lower performance on the two events. Our proposal without threshold-based calculation (represented as "Ours (no seg. + avg.wt.)") is thereby largely affected. Our proposal avoids such a problem via the threshold-based calculation. The threshold eliminates the impact of $S_a(\cdot)$ when the action is relatively dynamic, and the performance of our model is thereby retained. Compared to our complete model, "Ours (no seg. + avg.wt.)" achieves lower AUROC, and many of its abnormality scores in the abnormal interval are lower than the scores in the normal interval. Thus, our complete model is better than "Ours (no seg. + avg.wt.)", which proves the effect of the threshold-based calculation.

4.6 Parameter Dependencies

We investigate the dependency of the performance on the two parameters. In Fig. 6 (left), when the value of σ is set from 0 to 0.3, AUROC fluctuates. When σ is set to 0, our proposal's performance is the same as Frame-Pred [22]. To achieve the best overall performance in both Dataset 1 and Dataset 2, σ should be set from about 0.15 to 0.25, respectively. In this interval, our proposal outperforms HF^2-VAD [23], which achieves the best performance among all other baseline methods except ours (see Table 1). When the value of σ is larger than 0.3, AUROC keeps stable. We observe that our proposal still performs competitively among all other baseline methods.

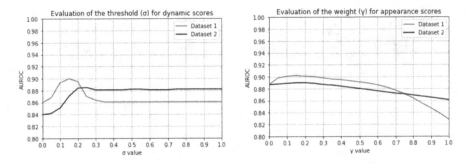

Fig. 6. Effect of the manually set parameters, i.e., the threshold (σ) for the dynamic score $(D(\cdot))$, and the weight (γ) of the appearance score $(S_a(\cdot))$.

In Fig. 6 (right), when the values of γ is set from 0 to 0.2, the AUROCs show a slight increase in both Dataset 1 and Dataset 2 since appearance scores improve the performance of detecting static anomalies. However, in our datasets, the normal data are much larger in volume than abnormal data. Some appearance scores $(S_a(\cdot))$ are too high for the normal data, which is not included in the training set. If γ is set lower than 0.7, our proposal reaches the best performance among all other baseline methods when considering both the results in Dataset 1 and Dataset 2 (see Table 1). It proves that without specifically assigning a value of γ, i.e., simply conducting an average fusion $(\gamma = 0.5)$ of the appearance and motion score, our proposal still performs better than the rest baseline methods. We find γ brings the potential to achieve higher performance of our proposal.

5   Conclusion

We have proposed a prediction-based model for video anomalous event detection. By introducing an extra appearance score calculated by CNN and BIRCH, our model enhances discriminating anomalies from appearance information to detect static anomalies better. Our model checks the abnormality of motion with flow reconstruction to compensate for overly discriminating the diversity of normal data caused by the appearance score. We also design a dynamic score to denote the dynamic degree of actions and a threshold-based calculation to specifically target relatively static and dynamic actions with different strategies. Extensive experiments on two datasets show the superiority of our proposed method compared with other baselines.

We will improve the calculation of the dynamic score since it may contradict our intuition under the influence of the sizes of human bodies and the number of people. Also, we will develop a module to replace the appearance and motion scores for better performance and less computation cost. We expect our model can be used by an autonomous mobile robot for significant practical value.

Acknowledgement. This work was partially supported by JST, the establishment of university fellowships towards the creation of science technology innovation, Grant Number JPMJFS2132.

References

1. Cai, R., Zhang, H., Liu, W., Gao, S., Hao, Z.: Appearance-motion memory consistency network for video anomaly detection. In: AAAI (2021)
2. Chang, Y., Tu, Z., Xie, W., Yuan, J.: Clustering driven deep autoencoder for video anomaly detection. In: Vedaldi, A., Bischof, H., Brox, T., Frahm, J.-M. (eds.) ECCV 2020. LNCS, vol. 12360, pp. 329–345. Springer, Cham (2020). https://doi.org/10.1007/978-3-030-58555-6_20
3. Chong, Y.S., Tay, Y.H.: Abnormal event detection in videos using spatiotemporal autoencoder. In: ISNN (2017)
4. Davis, J., Goadrich, M.: The relationship between precision-recall and ROC curves. In: ICML (2006)
5. Deguchi, Y., Takayama, D., Takano, S., Scuturici, V., Petit, J., Suzuki, E.: Skeleton clustering by multi-robot monitoring for fall risk discovery. J. Intell. Inf. Syst. **48**(1), 75–115 (2017)
6. Deng, J., Dong, W., Socher, R., Li, L., Li, K., Fei-Fei, L.: ImageNet: a large-scale hierarchical image database. In: CVPR (2009)
7. Dizaji, K.G., Herandi, A., Deng, C., Cai, W., Huang, H.: Deep clustering via joint convolutional autoencoder embedding and relative entropy minimization. In: ICCV (2017)
8. Dong, N., Suzuki, E.: GIAD: generative inpainting-based anomaly detection via self-supervised learning for human monitoring. In: PRICAI (2021)
9. Georgescu, M., Barbalau, A., Ionescu, R.T., Khan, F.S., Popescu, M., Shah, M.: Anomaly detection in video via self-supervised and multi-task learning. In: CVPR (2021)
10. Gong, D., et al.: Memorizing normality to detect anomaly: memory-augmented deep autoencoder for unsupervised anomaly detection. In: ICCV (2019)
11. Guo, X., Gao, L., Liu, X., Yin, J.: Improved deep embedded clustering with local structure preservation. In: IJCAI (2017)
12. Guo, X., et al.: Discriminative-generative dual memory video anomaly detection. CoRR abs/2104.14430 (2021). https://arxiv.org/abs/2104.14430
13. Han, T., Xie, W., Zisserman, A.: Self-supervised co-training for video representation learning. In: NeurIPS (2020)
14. Hasan, M., Choi, J., Neumann, J., Roy-Chowdhury, A.K., Davis, L.S.: Learning temporal regularity in video sequences. In: CVPR (2016)
15. Hatae, Y., Yang, Q., Fadjrimiratno, M.F., Li, Y., Matsukawa, T., Suzuki, E.: Detecting anomalous regions from an image based on deep captioning. In: VISIGRAPP (2020)
16. Hinami, R., Mei, T., Satoh, S.: Joint detection and recounting of abnormal events by learning deep generic knowledge. In: ICCV (2017)
17. Ilg, E., Mayer, N., Saikia, T., Keuper, M., Dosovitskiy, A., Brox, T.: FlowNet 2.0: evolution of optical flow estimation with deep networks. In: CVPR (2017)
18. Ionescu, R.T., Khan, F.S., Georgescu, M., Shao, L.: Object-centric auto-encoders and dummy anomalies for abnormal event detection in video. In: CVPR (2019)

19. Jalal, A., Kamal, S., Kim, D.: A depth video sensor-based life-logging human activity recognition system for elderly care in smart indoor environments. Sensors 14(7), 11735–11759 (2014)

20. Jalal, A., Kamal, S., Kim, D.: A depth video-based human detection and activity recognition using multi-features and embedded hidden Markov models for health care monitoring systems. Int. J. Interact. Multim. Artif. Intell. 4(4), 54–62 (2017)

21. Liu, J., Shahroudy, A., Perez, M., Wang, G., Duan, L., Kot, A.C.: NTU RGB+D 120: a large-scale benchmark for 3D human activity understanding. IEEE Trans. Pattern Anal. Mach. Intell. 42(10), 2684–2701 (2020)

22. Liu, W., Luo, W., Lian, D., Gao, S.: Future frame prediction for anomaly detection - a new baseline. In: CVPR (2018)

23. Liu, Z., Nie, Y., Long, C., Zhang, Q., Li, G.: A hybrid video anomaly detection framework via memory-augmented flow reconstruction and flow-guided frame prediction. In: ICCV (2021)

24. Lu, C., Shi, J., Jia, J.: Abnormal event detection at 150 FPS in MATLAB. In: ICCV (2013)

25. Lu, Y., Kumar, K.M., Nabavi, S.S., Wang, Y.: Future frame prediction using convolutional VRNN for anomaly detection. In: AVSS (2019)

26. Luo, W., Liu, W., Gao, S.: Remembering history with convolutional LSTM for anomaly detection. In: ICME (2017)

27. Luo, W., Liu, W., Gao, S.: A revisit of sparse coding based anomaly detection in stacked RNN framework. In: ICCV (2017)

28. Mahadevan, V., Li, W., Bhalodia, V., Vasconcelos, N.: Anomaly detection in crowded scenes. In: CVPR (2010)

29. Nguyen, T., Meunier, J.: Anomaly detection in video sequence with appearance-motion correspondence. In: ICCV (2019)

30. Park, H., Noh, J., Ham, B.: Learning memory-guided normality for anomaly detection. In: CVPR (2020)

31. Sargano, A.B., Angelov, P., Habib, Z.: A comprehensive review on handcrafted and learning-based action representation approaches for human activity recognition. Appl. Sci. 7(1) (2017)

32. Shahroudy, A., Liu, J., Ng, T.T., Wang, G.: NTU RGB+D: a large scale dataset for 3D human activity analysis. In: CVPR (2016)

33. Simonyan, K., Zisserman, A.: Very deep convolutional networks for large-scale image recognition. In: ICLR (2015)

34. Sultani, W., Chen, C., Shah, M.: Real-world anomaly detection in surveillance videos. In: CVPR (2018)

35. Tang, Y., Zhao, L., Zhang, S., Gong, C., Li, G., Yang, J.: Integrating prediction and reconstruction for anomaly detection. Pattern Recognit. Lett. 129, 123–130 (2020)

36. Vu, H., Nguyen, T.D., Le, T., Luo, W., Phung, D.Q.: Robust anomaly detection in videos using multilevel representations. In: AAAI (2019)

37. Ye, M., Peng, X., Gan, W., Wu, W., Qiao, Y.: ANOPCN: video anomaly detection via deep predictive coding network. In: MM (2019)

38. Yu, G., et al.: Cloze test helps: effective video anomaly detection via learning to complete video events. In: MM (2020)

39. Zaheer, M.Z., Mahmood, A., Astrid, M., Lee, S.-I.: CLAWS: clustering assisted weakly supervised learning with normalcy suppression for anomalous event detection. In: Vedaldi, A., Bischof, H., Brox, T., Frahm, J.-M. (eds.) ECCV 2020. LNCS, vol. 12367, pp. 358–376. Springer, Cham (2020). https://doi.org/10.1007/978-3-030-58542-6_22

40. Zavrtanik, V., Kristan, M., Skocaj, D.: Reconstruction by inpainting for visual anomaly detection. Pattern Recogn. **112**, 107706 (2021)
41. Zhang, T., Ramakrishnan, R., Livny, M.: BIRCH: a new data clustering algorithm and its applications. Data Min. Knowl. Discov. **1**(2), 141–182 (1997)
42. Zhou, J.T., Zhang, L., Fang, Z., Du, J., Peng, X., Xiao, Y.: Attention-driven loss for anomaly detection in video surveillance. IEEE Trans. Circuits Syst. Video Technol. **30**(12), 4639–4647 (2020)

Frequency Domain Based Learning with Transformer for Underwater Image Restoration

Danxu Wang[1] and Zhonglin Sun[2]($\boxtimes$)

[1] College of Intelligent Systems Science and Engineering,
Harbin Engineering University, Harbin, China
`wangdanxu2020@hrbeu.edu.cn`
[2] Queen Mary University of London, London, UK
`zhonglin.sun@qmul.ac.uk`

Abstract. Underwater images restoration is a corrective procedure aiming to eliminate the variations caused by the scattering and severe absorption of light when propagating in water. Holistic approaches dominate underwater image restoration by considering colour compensation on the blue channel through CNNs. In this paper, we discard the previous CNN-based network by employing Vision Transformer as the strong baseline for Underwater Image Restoration. To further boost the restoration, we investigate the impact of the frequency domain where higher frequencies represent more detailed information corresponding to the image, which hasn't been widely studied in this field. To this end, a novel loss function is adopted as the regularization defined in the spectral domain. By learning more detailed frequency information of the whole image, our proposed pipeline further enhances the accuracy of the baseline model achieving state-of-art performance on EUVP, UIEB and UFO-120 datasets.

Keywords: Under water Image Restoration · Frequency domain · Vision transformer

1 Introduction

Underwater images differ greatly from natural images in many ways. The images are extremely varied from what is seen in real scenes due to the scattering, diffraction and colour absorption when light propagates underwater. It is an influential topic in computer vision and ocean science with applications like robotics [12], rescue missions, artificial building inspection and ecological monitoring. With the advent of CNNs [15], the research undertaken for underwater has gained significant performance over the past prior-based methods. Several works [18,20,22] simply utilized the networks designed on top of other vision tasks, which ignore the properties of underwater images such as low contrast, blur and haze [28]. To better counter the characteristics of the underwater images, some efforts [17,32]

© The Author(s), under exclusive license to Springer Nature Switzerland AG 2022
S. Khanna et al. (Eds.): PRICAI 2022, LNCS 13629, pp. 218–232, 2022.
https://doi.org/10.1007/978-3-031-20862-1_16

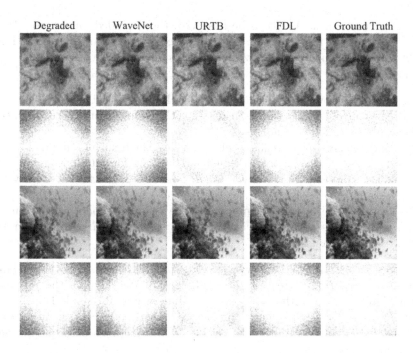

Degraded   WaveNet   URTB   FDL   Ground Truth

Fig. 1. Visualization of the learned images and their corresponding Spectrogram. The first column is the input degraded images, the second column is the result of WaveNet. The third column learned from without our FDL, the forth column is learned by adding FDL, the last column is the clean images.

proposed to process colour channels of the degraded images which proved to be effective. This work mostly keeps the eye on developing a new architecture and loss from the aspect of frequency domain for underwater image restoration.

Our focus first is to modify the CNN backbone with the recently introduced Vision Transformers [3,25] which have gained competitive results over CNNs [6] on other tasks. It is proven that the combination of CNN and Transformer would further boost the performance on other vision tasks [23,43], Thus, our first contribution is to investigate how Transformer would be of contribution for underwater restoration when simply employing the same loss function with CNN [32]. Despite the efforts on the color channels [17,32], we observed that there is little work focusing on learning more generalized images on the frequency domain [5]. An image with a very sharp overall variation in colour space will show a lot of high-frequency components in the frequency domain, and low-frequency components are often used to extract overall information [35]. Hence, our second motivation in this paper is to learn more realistic images via spectral regularization. Specifically, we designed the novel loss that minimizes the distance between the transformed output image and ground-truth image on the frequency domain. Fig 1 shows the degraded images obtained underwater, the output of our baseline model, the output after training on the frequency domain and the ground truth. As it can be observed, the degraded images are of less values on the high frequency domain compared to the clean images, and the model without frequency regularization will result in a circle of low value.

In summary, the contributions in this paper are as following:

1. We propose a novel Transformer-based block named URTB which, together with the convolutional layer, is utilized for the property of color degradation especially on different channels.
2. We aim to learn more realistic clear images via frequency domain where constraints are added on both detailed and overall information. Consequently, a new loss coined as Frequency Domain Loss (FDL) is added to the overall loss learning.
3. We conduct several experiments and prove that our model achieves much more competitive performance over previous state-of-the-art methods on several recent benchmarks.

Our paper is organized as follows. Section 2 provides brief reviews of related works in underwater image restoration. In Sect. 3, we describe the proposed network architecture with the proposed Underwater Residual Transformer Block(URTB), and the frequency domain loss function. In Sect. 4, we conduct experiments to demonstrate the effectiveness of our methods both qualitatively and quantitatively.

2   Related Work

This section gives a brief introduction about the methods of underwater image restoration which mainly focus on data-based methods, as well as the efforts on spectral-domain and the development of Vision Transformer.

2.1   Deep Learning for Underwater Image Restoration

Since the emergence of deep learning, data-driven approaches have been becoming the main trend to work on underwater images. There are several attempts proposed to adopt deep learning methods for underwater images [1,7,24,32,40]. In [40], the authors propose an end to end framework for underwater image enhancement, where a CNN-based network called UIE-Net is presented to conduct color-correction and haze removal. For fully exploiting the feature extracted, [7] develop a novel framework to aggregate the transmission and images domains via residual learning. In [24], the authors propose an underwater image enhancement solution through a deep residual framework consisting of CycleGAN, which generates synthetic underwater images for training purposes. In addition, Edge Difference Loss is proposed to learn more detailed edge information. Li [17] proposed a Transmission-Guided framework to enrich the feature representation which incorporates multi-colour characteristics. By learning diverse information about underwater images, the reverse medium transmission (RMT) map is adopted associated with the original image for being forwarded in the neural network. In [32], Sharma adopt the Convolutional Block Attention Module (CBAM) [42] to weigh the channel features extracted by the CNN with different receptive field sizes, and aggregate these features for obtaining the multi-contextual information with residual structure. However, these methods are designed based on shallow convolutional neural networks which sacrifice the superior performance offered by deep neural networks. Our contribution is to apply the vision transformer with booster performance to learn more generalization features.

2.2   Vision Transformer

As a pioneering work, Transformer which mainly consists of multi-head self-attention and linear layers was first introduced for natural language tasks in [38]. Later in [3], In vastly contrast to CNNs, Vision Transformer (ViT) offers superior performance by dividing the image into non-overlapping patches before processing the image. Compared to CNNs, ViT is proven to be sensitive to hyper-parameters and training strategy [36,37]. A lot of efforts have been proposed to train transformer more effective and efficient [25,43,45,46]. In SwinIR [23], The Swin transformer is employed for the task of image restoration due to its exceptional performance. And a residual Swin Transformer block(RSTB) is proposed with residual connection. In this paper, we follow [23] to adopt RSTB to see how Transformer works in underwater image restoration. To the best of our knowledge, this is the first work that applies the vision transformer to the task of underwater image restoration.

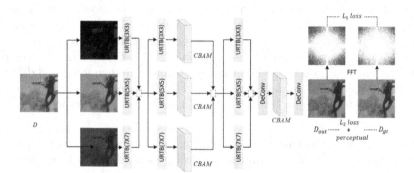

Fig. 2. The overview of our proposed network, where the input to the model is a degraded image and the output is a clean image. We use URTB, which will describe its basic structure in Sect. 3.2. Our model is trained on two domains: spatial and frequency

2.3   Frequency Domain

The above works for underwater image restoration focus mainly on the colour space of the degraded images in order to eliminate the blurriness and light absorption caused by propagation through the water. Those works more or less add regulations to learn more realistic clear images such as perceptual loss via a pre-trained VGG network [34] or an advanced network. This work [24] also proposed to learn more detailed edge through Edge Difference Loss. These approaches work in the spatial domain while ignoring the frequency domain, which includes overall and detailed information. Gupta [5] was the very preliminary approach to incorporating Fast Fourier Transformation (FFT) [27] with dark channels for underwater images. However, this approach simply adopts FFT on the Hazzard removed image but does not take advantage of the irresistible performance of deep learning. Besides, the authors of [31] added frequency domain to the network design and used attention mechanisms to obtain more generalized features. In this paper, we aim to add frequency regularization as the loss function to the learning process in an end-to-end manner.

3   Methodology

We first introduce our baseline in Sects. 3.1 and 3.2 and explain the difference between Underwater Residual Transformer Block(URTB) and RSTB [23]. Then in Sect. 3.3, we describe the proposed Frequency Domain Loss(FDL) defined in the spectral domain.

3.1   Network Architecture

Figure 2 shows our encoder-decoder model in which the encoder is a three-stage URTB block and the decoder is intended to enhance the reconstruction image. Let $D \in R^{H \times W \times C}$ $(C = 3)$ be the degraded image obtained underwater and $D_{gt} \in R^{H \times W \times C}$ $(C = 3)$ to be the corresponding clean ground truth image, where H and W represent the height and width. D_R, D_G and D_B are the red, green and blue channels of the input image D which are then fed into 3 different branches of the neural network where the only difference is the kernel size and the patch size for the convolution layer and transformer layer respectively.

Encoder. As for every channel in each stage, we adopt an Underwater Residual Transformer Block(URTB) to process the feature with different kernel size:

$$F'_{Mi} = H_{DF}(F_{Mi-1})_u \tag{1}$$

where $H_{DF}(\cdot)_u$ is the URTB whose details will be explained in Sect. 3.2, M represent RGB channels, u is the patch size, i is the index of stages. When it refers to first stage, D_R, D_G, D_B are equal to F_{R0}, F_{G0}, F_{B0}. Then we obtain the enhanced feature from the 3 branches of feature as:

$$F_{i+1} = F'_{Ri} \odot F'_{Gi} \odot F'_{Bi} \tag{2}$$

where $\odot$ is the concatenation operation. F_i is the multi-channel contextual feature after stage i. We replicate the URTB for three times to get further enhanced feature. One exception is stage 2 where CBAM [42] is adopted to generate the refined feature at the end of URTB for incorporating the channel information.

For the decoder part, we follow WaveNet [32] consisting of de-convolution layers and CBAM to reconstruct the high-quality clear output image.

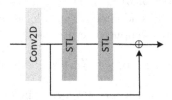

Fig. 3. The structure of the Underwater Residual Transformer Block (URTB). The feature is firstly processed through a convolution layer before it is sent to residual Swin Transformers

3.2 Underwater Residual Transformer Block (URTB)

As shown in Fig. 3, the Underwater Residual Transformer Block(URTB) is a block incorporating L a convolution layer and Swin Transformer layers (STL) [25] with the residual connection. Before sending features to transformer layers, we first use a $s \times s$ convolutional layer $H_{SF}(\cdot)_{s \times s}$ (s is receptive field size) to extract shallow feature as:

$$U_{Mi,0} = H_{SF}(F_{Mi-1})_{s*s} \qquad (3)$$

Using convolution before transformer to process the feature in vision task will result in more stable, generalized performance when training which has been proven in [43]. Given the output feature $U_{Mi,0}, M = R, G, B$ of the Convolution layer, the intermediate feature $U_{Mi,1}, U_{Mi,2}, ..., U_{Mi,L}$ of URTB is calculated as the following equation:

$$U_{Mi,j} = H_{STL1}(U_{Mi,j-1}), j = 1, 2, ..., L \qquad (4)$$

where H_{STL_j} is the j-th STL contained in URTB. Finally, the output of URTB is formulated by adding residual connections:

$$F'_{Mi} = U_{Mi,j} + U_{Mi,0} \qquad (5)$$

Skip connection provides integration of low-level and high-level features, which benefits training stability and performance. The URTB does not contain the convolution layer in comparison to the RSTB [23] due to a loss of performance which will be discussed in the ablation study 4.2.

Swin Transformer Layer. In this paper, we opt for the Swin Transformer Layer as the basic unit in UTRB which is famous for its effectiveness on other vision tasks e.g., classification [25], image restoration [23], self-supervised learning [44]. For the given image, we first split the image into non-overlapped windows where the window size is p, thus the feature dimension for each window is $p \times p \times C$ and the number of windows is $\frac{HW}{p \times p}$. Then multi-head self-attention which is the same as ViT [3] is adopted for each local window, the *query Q*, *key K* and *value V* matrices are computed respectively:

$$Q_{l,j} = X_{l,j}W_Q, \quad K_{l,j} = X_{l,j}W_K, \quad V_{l,j} = X_{l,j}W_V \tag{6}$$

where $X_l \in R^{p^2C}$ is the input feature of a local window at l-th layer, W_Q, W_K and W_V are the projection matrix. S is the number of heads, $j = 0, 1, 2, ..., S-1$ is the index of the head. Then self-attention is given by:

$$Att(Q_{l,j}, K_{l,j}, V_{l,j}) = SoftMax(Q_{l,j}K_{l,j}^T)/\sqrt{d} + B)V \tag{7}$$

d is a scale factor, B is the relative positional encoding to preserve spatial location. Finally, the output of multi-head attention is the concatenation of the S heads. Next, a multi-layer perceptron (MLP) which contains two linear layers with GELU activation is adopted for feature projection. The layer Norm and residual connections are adopted for modules which can be formulated as:

$$X = MSA(LN(X)) + X, X = MLP(LN(X)) + X \tag{8}$$

Swin Transformer also proposed to shift the window from layer to layer, allowing the spatial location of the feature in each layer to vary and interact with other features via MSA and MLP.

3.3 Frequency Domain Loss

The frequency domain is a vital domain in image process applications such as medical image reconstruction and de-noising. To our best knowledge, the application of frequency domain with deep learning has not been explored in the task of underwater image restoration. In the previous works, the reconstructed images are mainly optimized in the spatial domain where the loss is minimized on the distance between the output image D_{out} and the ground truth image D_{gt}. Normally the spatial loss function in our paper is L_2 loss defined as:

$$L_{sp} = \frac{1}{n} \sum_{n}^{1} \|D_{out} - D_{gt}\|_2^2 \tag{9}$$

n is the number of samples in a batch. To further enhance the learning quality of the generated image, we follow [32] to incorporate Perceptual loss L_{VGG} [11] which feeds the D_{out} and D_{gt} into a pre-trained VGG-16 [34] to get the embedding.

As Perceptual loss is just one aspect of training realistic images, we propose to convert the image into a spectrogram by using FFT and then constrain the converted image. When the image is converted into a spectrum, the low-frequency components correspond to the overall contour of the original image, while the high-frequency components represent the sharp and detailed texture information. Consequently, we require that the distance between the spectrogram of the generated image and the ground truth image in the frequency domain be closed such that the generated image is consistent with the ground truth in terms of overall contour and texture details. The function is written as:

$$L_{FDL} = \frac{1}{n} \sum_{n}^{1} |FFT(D_{out}) - FFT(D_{gt})| \tag{10}$$

The overall loss in our works is the combination of the above losses:

$$L = \alpha_1 * L_{sp} + \alpha_2 * L_{VGG} + \alpha_3 * L_{FDL} \tag{11}$$

where α_1, α_2 and α_3 are the scaling factors to adjust the respective loss components, contributing differently to the final loss.

4 Experiment

We begin by explaining the details of our experimental settings in this section, then present the results of our proposed method on several famous benchmarks, and then provide a series of ablation studies in order to illustrate the effectiveness of the proposed method. At last, the comparison with the state-of-art results is also conducted.

4.1 Implementation Details

Datasets. To fairly compare with other methods, we choose the publicly available benchmarks for training and evaluation, which are UIEB [19], EUVP [10] and UFO-120 [9] respectively. The UIEB dataset is comprised of 890 pairs of images with the resolution of which are obtained underwater while the reference images are generated by 12 image enhancement methods. EUVP dataset is a large scale dataset containing 11435 underwater degraded training pairs and 515 test pairs. For the UFO-120 dataset, the training samples are 1500 pairs and the test samples are 120 images. For the EUVP and UFO-120 datasets, PSNR, SSIM [41] and UIQM [29] are adopted as objective metrics for quantitative evaluation. As for EUVP, we report PSNR, SSIM, UIQM, NIQE [26], PCQI [39], UISM [29], VIF [33] and E [14].

Training Details. For training our network in association with our proposed loss, we choose AdamW [13] as our optimizer. The batch size is 5, the initial learning rate is 0.001 with Cosine learning rate decay, weight decay is 0.05. Number of heads in URTB is 2. We use 2 STL in the URTB. The number of total training epochs is 20. Our implementation is based on Pytorch [30] on a single Nvidia 3090 card. The kernel size in different branches are 3×3, 5×5 and 7×7, for patch size they are 6,8,10 respectively.

Table 1. The performance on EUVP datasets in terms of Network sizes and FLOPS

	Param	Flops	SSIM	PSNR	UIQM
WaveNet [32]	278.61k	18.13G	0.835	28.654	3.042
URTB	861.85k	55.46G	**0.840**	**29.017**	2.982
RSTB	945.08k	60.91G	0.803	27.626	3.013
WaveNet+CNN	895.83k	58.27G	0.806	27.614	**3.062**

Table 2. The results of FDL on EUVP datasets in terms of the numbers of STL block

	Param	Flops	SSIM	PSNR	UIQM
STL = 2	861.85k	55.46G	0.849	**29.377**	3.025
STL = 4	950.03k	60.37G	**0.854**	29.322	**3.067**
STL = 6	1.04M	65.27G	0.771	24.613	2.727

4.2 Ablation Study

We opt for a series of ablation experiments to illustrate the effectiveness of our choices for the proposed methods. The comparison are mainly conducted on EUVP datasets unless specified.

Impact of URTB over Baseline. Our first experiment is to validate the performance of the URTB over convolution neural networks(CNNs). In contrast to the Wavenet [32], our method adds a series of STLs after the convolutional layer as an image enhancement module. However, it introduces an extra number of parameters, which is unfair for comparing models with the same number of parameters. Due to this, we have added an extra convolutional layer in the WaveNet to construct the model of the same size as the URTB. As shown in Tab 1, we list the parameters of the WaveNet, URTB, RSTB and Wavenet+ CNN as well as their performance on the datasets. As it can be observed, with similar parameters and Flops, the URTB model outperforms the Wavenet+ CNN which demonstrates the effectiveness of the Transformer compared with CNNs.

Impact of Convolution in URTB. The difference between RSTB and URTB is that URTB removes the convolution layer at the end of RSTB. This is due to the fact that this layer of convolution is redundant, which results in a performance loss. For URTB the number of parameters are 861.85k and the flops are 55.46G, and it is 945.07k and 60.91G for RSTB, but more parameters does not result in a better performance, which also can be concluded in the Table 1.

Impact of Number of STL. We validate the choice of the number of STL in table 2 where the number is set to be 2,4,6 respectively. As shown, there is no significant difference between 2 and 4 layers of STL, however, when the number of layers reaches 6, performance deteriorates.

Table 3. The influence of hyper-parameters of losses on UFO-120 2X protocol

$\alpha_1 : \alpha_2 : \alpha_3$	SSIM	PSNR	UIQM
0.6: 0.35: 0.02	0.810 ± 0.06	27.40 ± 2.84	3.07 ± 0.49
0.6: 0.40: 0.02	0.819 ± 0.06	28.18 ± 3.08	3.06 ± 0.47
0.6: 0.45: 0.02	$\mathbf{0.822 \pm 0.06}$	$\mathbf{28.30 \pm 3.07}$	$\mathbf{3.10 \pm 0.48}$
0.6:0:0.02 (w/o FDL)	0.780 ± 0.07	26.49 ± 2.64	3.06 ± 0.45
0.6:0.45:0 (w/o Perceptual)	0.818 ± 0.06	28.18 ± 3.00	3.03 ± 0.48
0.1:0:0.02 (WaveNet [32] hyper-parameter)	0.774 ± 0.06	26.27 ± 3.00	3.00 ± 0.46

Impact of Frequency Domain. Herein, we experimented with the enhancement of the proposed FDL and with the impact of different choices of hyper-parameters on our task. As shown in Tab 3, for each of the three parameters α_1, α_2, α_3, we mainly change α_2 and devised 6 groups of combinations which are (1) 0.6:0.35:0.02, (2) 0.6:0.4:0.02, (3) 0.6:0.45:0.02, (4) the learning loss without FDL, (5) loss without Perceptual loss and (6) default loss in WaveNet [32]to explore the impact of FDL on the UFO-120-2X protocol. Comparison from the table shows that the (3) configuration yields the best results and learning on frequency domain really improves the accuracy.

4.3 Comparison with the SOTA

We chose two models with and without FDL to compare with the SOTA papers proposed recently on UIR.

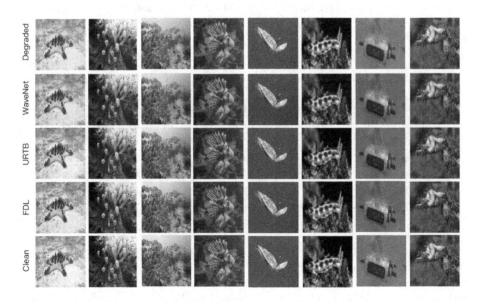

Fig. 4. Comparison of the proposed methods with WaveNet visually on EUVP dataset

Quantitative Results. We report the results trained and tested on various datasets including UIEB, EUVP and UFO-120 which are listed in Table 4, Table 5 and Table 6 respectively. On the EUVP dataset containing the most number of training samples of the task of image enhancement, compared with Deep WaveNet [32] which is the best published underwater image enhancement work, the baseline URTB has increased by 1.29% and 0.59% on PSNR and SSIM respectively. The URTB+FDL has improved by 2.54% and 1.55% on PSNR and SSIM respectively. Meanwhile, comparing our methods to other competitors, ours achieves the best results in terms of VIF and PCQI. On UIEB dataset which can be verified in Table 4, our proposed methods achieve the optimal results(0.8483) on SSIM, competitive results on PSNR evaluation (21.8088) which are better than CNN-based methods(WaveNet [32], Water-Net [19]). On the UFO-120 dataset, the results for underwater image super-resolution has been presented in Table 6. As observed, in 3 types of configuration 2x, 3x, 4x, not only our URTB+FDL module outperform other results than large margin, but also our baseline URTB has gained secondary performance. The only exception is the 2x configuration on UIQM, our models obtain 3.10(URTB+FDL) and 3.06(URTB) which is worse than Deep SESR [9].

Table 4. Evaluation results on UIEB dataset

Methods	SSIM	PSNR	UIQM
Water-Net [19]	0.68	20.14	2.55
UGAN [4]	0.67	23.67	2.70
Fusion-GAN [21]	0.68	**23.77**	2.58
Deep SESR [9]	0.57	16.65	2.98
Deep WaveNet [32]	0.80	21.57	-
URTB, ours	0.8253	21.7074	**3.0498**
URTB+FDL, ours	**0.8483**	21.8088	2.7641

Table 5. comparison with the SOTA results on EUVP datasets.

Methods	PSNR	SSIM	UIQM	NIQE	PCQI	UISM	VIF	E
UGAN-P [4]	26.54	.80	2.93	50.17	.704	6.83	.400	**7.54**
Funie-GAN-UP [10]	25.22	.78	2.93	**52.87**	.702	6.86	.394	7.50
Deep SESR [9]	27.08	.80	**3.09**	55.68	.679	7.06	.384	7.40
Deep WaveNet [32]	28.62	.83	3.04	44.89	.694	**7.06**	.438	7.38
URTB, ours	29.02	.84	2.98	43.75	**.849**	6.57	**.651**	7.14
URTB+FDL, ours	**29.38**	**.85**	3.03	50.40	.843	6.70	.633	7.15

Table 6. The comparison against the best results on UFO-120 dataset

Methods	PSNR			SSIM			UIQM		
	2X	3X	4X	2X	3X	4X	2X	3X	4X
SRCNN [2]	24.75 ± 3.7	22.22 ± 3.9	19.05 ± 2.3	$.72 \pm .7$	$.65 \pm .9$	$.56 \pm .12$	$2.39 \pm .35$	$2.24 \pm .17$	$2.02 \pm .47$
SRGAN [16]	26.11 ± 3.9	23.87 ± 4.2	21.08 ± 2.3	$.75 \pm .6$	$.70 \pm .5$	$.58 \pm .9$	$2.44 \pm .28$	$2.39 \pm .25$	$2.26 \pm .17$
SRDRM-GAN [8]	24.61 ± 2.8	-	23.26 ± 2.8	$.72 \pm .17$	-	$.67 \pm .19$	$2.59 \pm .64$	-	$2.57 \pm .63$
Deep SESR [9]	25.70 ± 3.2	26.86 ± 4.1	24.75 ± 2.8	$.75 \pm .8$	$.75 \pm .6$	$.66 \pm .5$	$3.15 \pm .48$	$2.87 \pm .39$	$2.55 \pm .35$
WaveNet [32]	25.71 ± 3.0	25.23 ± 2.7	25.08 ± 2.9	$.77 \pm .7$	$.76 \pm .7$	$.74 \pm .7$	$2.99 \pm .57$	$2.96 \pm .60$	$2.97 \pm .59$
URTB, Ours	26.49 ± 2.6	26.27 ± 2.7	25.23 ± 2.5	$.78 \pm .07$	$.77 \pm .07$	$.75 \pm .08$	$3.06 \pm .45$	$2.95 \pm .51$	$3.01 \pm .42$
FDL, Ours	28.30 ± 3.1	27.54 ± 3.0	27.35 ± 3.0	$.82 \pm .06$	$.80 \pm .07$	$.79 \pm .07$	$3.10 \pm .48$	$3.07 \pm .44$	$3.10 \pm .45$

Qualitative Results. We first visualise the results obtained from the training of our model on EUVP, showing in Fig. 4. We show the original images, the URTB baseline images, the URTB+FDL images, the ground truth images and the images obtained by Deep WaveNet [32]. Compared the URTB and Deep WaveNet [32], Our FDL training model tends to produce images with less colour distortion, especially in the background which can be observed from column 5 in Fig 4 where the output of WaveNet produces more dark results. Additionally, we can observe from Fig. 1 a certain high response to high frequencies in the spectrum generated by the URTB baseline and WaveNet [32] (highlighting near the edges of the image), which is not apparent in the original and ground truth images. By comparison, we find that our URTB+FDL model successfully removes the high response than the baseline. As for the UFO-120 dataset, we can observe from the comparison between URTB and WaveNet in Fig. 5 that WaveNet [32] trends to generate to more yellowish images while ours are more closer to the groundtruth images in terms of the overall color. We can conclude that training with the FDL, the colour shift has been relieved compared to without FDL.

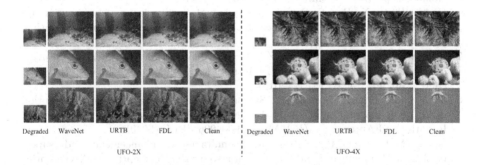

Degraded   WaveNet   URTB   FDL   Clean   Degraded   WaveNet   URTB   FDL   Clean

UFO-2X   UFO-4X

Fig. 5. Qualitative results on UFO-120 dataset

5   Conclusion

In this paper, we propose a novel framework that incorporates a model using the transformer as the baseline, and we propose a frequency domain-based loss function for reconstructing more realistic images. In particular, our baseline model uses the URTB module to further construct a deeper network, which consists of a series of Swin transformer layers and discards convolution compared to RSTB. And to our best knowledge, it is the first time of using Transformer in UIR. In addition, we employ the FFT to transform the output and reference images into the frequency domain, and then add an l1 loss to reduce the discrepancy between the reconstructed image and the real image. Extensive experiments have demonstrated numerically and visually the effectiveness of our proposed model and loss for underwater image enhancement and reconstruction tasks, achieving optimal results. Our future work will continue to explore the integration of the frequency domain with light-weight deep learning architectures.

References

1. Anwar, S., Li, C.: Diving deeper into underwater image enhancement: a survey. Sig. Process. Image Commun. **89**, 115978 (2020)
2. Dong, C., Loy, C.C., He, K., Tang, X.: Image super-resolution using deep convolutional networks. IEEE Trans. Pattern Anal. Mach. Intell. **38**(2), 295–307 (2015)
3. Dosovitskiy, A., et al.: An image is worth 16x16 words: transformers for image recognition at scale. arXiv preprint arXiv:2010.11929 (2020)
4. Fabbri, C., Islam, M.J., Sattar, J.: Enhancing underwater imagery using generative adversarial networks. In: 2018 IEEE International Conference on Robotics and Automation (ICRA), pp. 7159–7165. IEEE (2018)
5. Gupta, R., Farooqui, Z.: Underwater image clearance using dark channel and FFT enhancement. Int. J. Comput. Appl. **119**(23) (2015)
6. He, K., Zhang, X., Ren, S., Sun, J.: Deep residual learning for image recognition. In: Proceedings of the IEEE Conference on Computer Vision and Pattern Recognition, pp. 770–778 (2016)
7. Hou, M., Liu, R., Fan, X., Luo, Z.: Joint residual learning for underwater image enhancement. In: 2018 25th IEEE International Conference on Image Processing (ICIP), pp. 4043–4047. IEEE (2018)
8. Islam, M.J., Enan, S.S., Luo, P., Sattar, J.: Underwater image super-resolution using deep residual multipliers. In: 2020 IEEE International Conference on Robotics and Automation (ICRA), pp. 900–906. IEEE (2020)
9. Islam, M.J., Luo, P., Sattar, J.: Simultaneous enhancement and super-resolution of underwater imagery for improved visual perception. arXiv preprint arXiv:2002.01155 (2020)
10. Islam, M.J., Xia, Y., Sattar, J.: Fast underwater image enhancement for improved visual perception. IEEE Robot. Autom. Lett. **5**(2), 3227–3234 (2020)
11. Johnson, J., Alahi, A., Fei-Fei, L.: Perceptual losses for real-time style transfer and super-resolution. In: Leibe, B., Matas, J., Sebe, N., Welling, M. (eds.) ECCV 2016. LNCS, vol. 9906, pp. 694–711. Springer, Cham (2016). https://doi.org/10.1007/978-3-319-46475-6_43

12. Kim, K., Kim, J., Kang, S., Kim, J., Lee, J.: Object recognition for cell manufacturing system. In: 2012 9th International Conference on Ubiquitous Robots and Ambient Intelligence (URAI), pp. 512–514. IEEE (2012)

13. Kingma, D.P., Ba, J.: Adam: a method for stochastic optimization. arXiv preprint arXiv:1412.6980 (2014)

14. Kittaneh, O.A., Khan, M.A., Akbar, M., Bayoud, H.A.: Average entropy: a new uncertainty measure with application to image segmentation. Am. Stat. **70**(1), 18–24 (2016)

15. Krizhevsky, A., Sutskever, I., Hinton, G.E.: Imagenet classification with deep convolutional neural networks. Adv. Neural. Inf. Process. Syst. **25**, 1097–1105 (2012)

16. Ledig, C., et al.: Photo-realistic single image super-resolution using a generative adversarial network. In: Proceedings of the IEEE Conference on Computer Vision and Pattern Recognition, pp. 4681–4690 (2017)

17. Li, C., Anwar, S., Hou, J., Cong, R., Guo, C., Ren, W.: Underwater image enhancement via medium transmission-guided multi-color space embedding. IEEE Trans. Image Process. **30**, 4985–5000 (2021)

18. Li, C., Anwar, S., Porikli, F.: Underwater scene prior inspired deep underwater image and video enhancement. Pattern Recogn. **98**, 107038 (2020)

19. Li, C., et al.: An underwater image enhancement benchmark dataset and beyond. IEEE Trans. Image Process. **29**, 4376–4389 (2019)

20. Li, C., Guo, J., Guo, C.: Emerging from water: underwater image color correction based on weakly supervised color transfer. IEEE Sig. Process. Lett. **25**(3), 323–327 (2018)

21. Li, H., Li, J., Wang, W.: A fusion adversarial underwater image enhancement network with a public test dataset. arXiv preprint arXiv:1906.06819 (2019)

22. Li, J., Skinner, K.A., Eustice, R.M., Johnson-Roberson, M.: WaterGAN: unsupervised generative network to enable real-time color correction of monocular underwater images. IEEE Robot. Autom. Lett. **3**(1), 387–394 (2017)

23. Liang, J., Cao, J., Sun, G., Zhang, K., Van Gool, L., Timofte, R.: SwinIR: image restoration using swin transformer. In: Proceedings of the IEEE/CVF International Conference on Computer Vision, pp. 1833–1844 (2021)

24. Liu, P., Wang, G., Qi, H., Zhang, C., Zheng, H., Yu, Z.: Underwater image enhancement with a deep residual framework. IEEE Access **7**, 94614–94629 (2019)

25. Liu, Z., et al.: Swin transformer: hierarchical vision transformer using shifted windows. arXiv preprint arXiv:2103.14030 (2021)

26. Mittal, A., Soundararajan, R., Bovik, A.C.: Making a "completely blind" image quality analyzer. IEEE Sig. Process. Lett. **20**(3), 209–212 (2012)

27. Nussbaumer, H.J.: The fast Fourier transform. In: Nussbaumer, H.J. (ed.) Fast Fourier Transform and Convolution Algorithms, pp. 80–111. Springer, Heidelberg (1981). https://doi.org/10.1007/978-3-662-00551-4_4

28. Oakley, J.P., Satherley, B.L.: Improving image quality in poor visibility conditions using a physical model for contrast degradation. IEEE Trans. Image Process. **7**(2), 167–179 (1998)

29. Panetta, K., Gao, C., Agaian, S.: Human-visual-system-inspired underwater image quality measures. IEEE J. Ocean. Eng. **41**(3), 541–551 (2015)

30. Paszke, A., et al.: PyTorch: an imperative style, high-performance deep learning library. Adv. Neural. Inf. Process. Syst. **32**, 8026–8037 (2019)

31. Qin, Z., Zhang, P., Wu, F., Li, X.: FCANet: frequency channel attention networks. In: Proceedings of the IEEE/CVF International Conference on Computer Vision, pp. 783–792 (2021)

32. Sharma, P.K., Bisht, I., Sur, A.: Wavelength-based attributed deep neural network for underwater image restoration. arXiv preprint arXiv:2106.07910 (2021)
33. Sheikh, H.R., Bovik, A.C.: Image information and visual quality. IEEE Trans. Image Process. **15**(2), 430–444 (2006)
34. Simonyan, K., Zisserman, A.: Very deep convolutional networks for large-scale image recognition. arXiv preprint arXiv:1409.1556 (2014)
35. Song, S., Jaiswal, S., Shen, L., Valstar, M.: Spectral representation of behaviour primitives for depression analysis. IEEE Trans. Affect. Comput. (2020)
36. Steiner, A., et al.: How to train your VIT? Data, augmentation, and regularization in vision transformers. arXiv preprint arXiv:2106.10270 (2021)
37. Touvron, H., Cord, M., Douze, M., Massa, F., Sablayrolles, A., Jégou, H.: Training data-efficient image transformers & distillation through attention. In: International Conference on Machine Learning, pp. 10347–10357. PMLR (2021)
38. Vaswani, A., et al.: Attention is all you need. In: Advances in Neural Information Processing Systems, pp. 5998–6008 (2017)
39. Wang, S., Ma, K., Yeganeh, H., Wang, Z., Lin, W.: A patch-structure representation method for quality assessment of contrast changed images. IEEE Sig. Process. Lett. **22**(12), 2387–2390 (2015)
40. Wang, Y., Zhang, J., Cao, Y., Wang, Z.: A deep CNN method for underwater image enhancement. In: 2017 IEEE International Conference on Image Processing (ICIP), pp. 1382–1386. IEEE (2017)
41. Wang, Z., Bovik, A.C., Sheikh, H.R., Simoncelli, E.P.: Image quality assessment: from error visibility to structural similarity. IEEE Trans. Image Process. **13**(4), 600–612 (2004)
42. Woo, S., Park, J., Lee, J.-Y., Kweon, I.S.: CBAM: convolutional block attention module. In: Ferrari, V., Hebert, M., Sminchisescu, C., Weiss, Y. (eds.) ECCV 2018. LNCS, vol. 11211, pp. 3–19. Springer, Cham (2018). https://doi.org/10.1007/978-3-030-01234-2_1
43. Xiao, T., Dollar, P., Singh, M., Mintun, E., Darrell, T., Girshick, R.: Early convolutions help transformers see better. In: Advances in Neural Information Processing Systems, vol. 34 (2021)
44. Xie, Z., et al.: Self-supervised learning with swin transformers. arXiv preprint arXiv:2105.04553 (2021)
45. Yuan, K., Guo, S., Liu, Z., Zhou, A., Yu, F., Wu, W.: Incorporating convolution designs into visual transformers. arXiv preprint arXiv:2103.11816 (2021)
46. Yuan, L., et al.: Tokens-to-token VIT: training vision transformers from scratch on imagenet. arXiv preprint arXiv:2101.11986 (2021)

MMISeg: A Semi-supervised Segmentation Method Based on Mixup and Mutual Information for Cardiac MRI Segmentation

Yazhou Huang$^{(\boxtimes)}$, Hao Pan, and Zhiyu Zeng

Wuhan University of Technology, Wuhan, China
hyazoo@whut.edu.cn

Abstract. Since the task of annotating medical image labels is pixel-level and needs to be depicted by trained experts, there are few large-scale medical image datasets with annotations. Semi-Supervised Learning (SSL) has become the focus of research for medical image segmentation tasks. The key techniques for our Segmentation method are Mixup and Mutual Information (MMISeg), which involve consistency-based regularization and unsupervised representation learning. On the one hand, we utilize an interpolation-based method to mix unlabeled data, and minimize consistency regularization. On the other hand, by taking the feature of the encoder stage as global feature and the feature of the decoder stage as local feature, we maximize mutual information of global and local features which are from two different transformations of the same image, respectively. Experimental results show that MMISeg outperforms existing semi-supervised methods.

Keywords: Semi-supervised learning · Medical image segmentation · Mutual information · Mixup

1 Introduction

Deep learning gradually replaced the original method and became the mainstream image segmentation method. Especially in recent years, the proposal of Fully Convolutional Networks (FCN) [18] has greatly advanced the state-of-the-art in semantic image segmentation. Image segmentation is an important processing step for both natural images and medical images. Generally, such network contains a large number of trainable parameters and requires a large amount of labeled data for training. In the medical image segmentation domain, these data need to be large-scale pixel-wise annotated, but it is difficult to obtain a large labeled dataset due to pixel-wise annotation must made by trained experts, which is a time-consuming and tedious process. However, abundant unlabeled data is available. Semi-Supervised Learning (SSL) emerges as the times require. SSL-based methods utilize only few labeled data and compensating for the large

© The Author(s), under exclusive license to Springer Nature Switzerland AG 2022
S. Khanna et al. (Eds.): PRICAI 2022, LNCS 13629, pp. 233–246, 2022.
https://doi.org/10.1007/978-3-031-20862-1_17

portion of unlabeled data by generating pseudo labels. Surprisingly, the produced segmentation results are accurate and close to those fully supervised methods.

Mainstream SSL medical image segmentation frameworks are roughly divided into two categories. One of them employ consistency-based regularization [2,17, 22,23], and the other utilize unsupervised representation learning [7,21]. They have show a great potential at exploiting unlabeled data. The former approach based on consistency regularization,which leverages the principle transformation equivariant, i.e. $f(T(x)) = T(f(x))$ for a geometrical transformation T, which forces the unlabeled data x and its different transformed version $T(x)$ to produce similar prediction on the segmentation network f. The latter approach based on representation learning [4], which uses unlabeled data in a pre-training step to find an internal representation of images which is useful to the downstream analysis tasks [21].

Recently, a popular technique based on representation learning is contrastive learning [19,29]. Contrastive learning is a simple framework that learning positive/negative representations from data organized into positive/negative pairs. The positive pairs are usually consist of unlabeled data and its augmented version, and the negative pairs are usually consist of two different unlabeled data. This technique maximizes the similarity between the representation of positive pairs while minimizes the similarity among the representation of negative pairs [32]. However, the use of a continuous-variable representation that makes the estimation of the joint distribution of samples or their mutual information more difficult [21].

Deep clustering is a plausible solution, which based on a discrete representation [6,13]. In deep clustering, a network is trained with unlabeled data to map examples with similar semantic meaning to the same cluster label. Same as Generative Adversarial Networks (GANs), it also suffers from mode collapse which is possible that all samples are mapped to the same cluster. To alleviate this issue, [13] proposed an Information Invariant Clustering (IIC) algorithm based on Mutual Information (MI). The MI is used to measure the strength of the relationship between two variables X and Y, and is defined as:

$$MI(X;Y) = D_{KL}(p(X,Y)|p(X)p(Y)) \qquad (1)$$

Here KL is the KL divergence, $p(.)$ is the distribution of variable, $p(.,.)$ is the joint distribution of two variables. [20] applied the IIC algorithm to SSL segmentation. This IIC-based approach makes the framework more robust and increases the local smoothness of the segmentation and avoids mode collapse to a single class. Yet, only the output of the network is calculated IIC, and features from other layer are available.

MMISeg combines consistency-based regularization and unsupervised representation learning. On the one hand, we adapt interpolation-based consistency regularization [2], which mixes two unlabeled image and regularizes them. This idea was proposed by [2], which extended to an unsupervised setting by [5]. On the other hand, we utilize IIC-based representation learning to make the local features and global features between positive paris as close as possible. Our contribution can be summarized as follows:

1. We propose a novel and effective SSL strategy for medical images, such as cardiac Magnetic Resonance Imaging (MRI) images.
2. The proposed method in this paper combines consistency-based regularization and unsupervised representation learning, which can fully mine information from the abundant unlabeled data and improve the effectiveness and robustness of the model.
3. In this paper, we achieve Dice Similarity Coefficient (DSC) of 90.04% in ACDC dataset, 87.09% in MMWHS dataset, and the labeling rate is only 10% and 20% for each other.

2   Related Work

Semi-supervised Segmentation aims to utilize SSL to learn a model, which only employs a small amount of labeled data and a large amount of unlabeled data. In recent years, semi-supervised learning is applied to semantic segmentation widely. [1] is the first literature to introduce SSL framework into medical image segmentation, which adapted from the VGG-16 Net [25] and similar to the DeepLab architecture used in [10]. The framework generates pseudo labels after every iteration, which are refined using Conditional Random Field (CRF) [16]. Besides, there are methods based on data distillation [24]. It generates annotations on the unlabeled data using a model trained on a large amount of labeled data, and then all the annotations(existing or generated) are used to retrain the model. Adversarial learning [27] expands the training set by generating unlabeled or weakly labeled images through Generative Adversarial Networks (GANs). Thus it can obtain better image segmentation results with limited labeled data. Entropy minimization [31] reduces the difference between the original domain and the target domain by reducing the entropy value of the prediction result of the target domain image. Consistency regularization [23,28] enforces the model generates similar output for similar input, i.e. inject noise into the input data, and the output is as close as possible. Data augmentation [8,9] proposes an effective method for automatic data augmentation to synthesize labeled medical images by learning transformations to address the lack of labeled images.

Mixup [34] is a simple and data-agnostic way of data augmentation. By performing a simple linear transformation on the input data, the generalization ability of the model can be increased, and the robustness of the model to adversarial attacks can be improved. As a result, more approaches have been proposed. cutMix [33] considers the space of the image, and cuts a random rectangular area on one image to another to generate a new one. Manifold Mixup [30] extends input data mixing to output mixing of intermediate hidden layers. puzzleMix [15] adds saliency analysis to cutMix, calculates the saliency area of each sample, and only cuts the saliency region. patchUp [11] is based on the Manifold Mixup, and draws on the idea of cutMix cutting in the spatial dimension. It also cuts the output of the middle hidden layer, and exchanges or interpolates the middle hidden layer clipping blocks of two different samples. Co-Mixup [14] is based on puzzleMix, changing from mixing two samples to extracting saliency regions from multiple samples and mixing them.

Mutual Information (MI) is a concept in information theory used to measure the degree of interdependence between two random variables and is applied in deep learning widely. But MI has historically been difficult to calculate. Especially for high-dimensional spaces, the marginal distribution is inestimable. MINE [3] proposed a mutual information estimator, which achieves the estimation of mutual information between high-dimensional continuous random variables through gradient descent on neural networks. DIM [12] is based on MINE, which can simultaneously estimate and maximize the MI between global and local representations. Since the high estimation variance of MINE, several methods have been proposed to mitigate the drawback. [36] utilizes Jensen-Shannon (JS) divergence to maximize the mutual information between the input image and its latent representation. [26] clips the density ratios when estimating the partition function. To address the difficulty of directly estimating mutual information (MI) between high-dimensional variables and significant additional computational overhead, Information Invariant Clustering (IIC) [13] uses a clustering algorithm to cluster high-dimensional features into low-dimensional features and then maximize their mutual information.

3   Method

MMISeg consists of a fully supervised part and an unsupervised part. The main idea for fully supervised part is to enforce the output of the model as consistent as possible with the ground truth. Our unsupervised part combines consistency-based regularization and unsupervised representation learning. Which aims to mine information from the large amount of available unlabeled data. We then introduce our method through these two parts in greater detail.

3.1   Problem Definition

Image segmentation is a special classification task, the difference from traditional classification tasks is that it requires classification pixel by pixel. We split the dataset into a labeled part $D_l = (X_l, Y_l)$ of image-label samples $(x, y) \sim (X_l, Y_l)$, and a larger unlabeled part $D_u = (X_u, Y_u)$, where $X_l = \{x_i | i = 1, 2, ..., N\}, X_u = \{x_i | i = N + 1, N + 2, ...N + M\}, Y_l = \{y_i | i = 1, 2, ...N\}, x_i \in \mathbb{R}^{\Omega}, y_i \in \{1, ...C\}^{\Omega}$ and i denotes the image index. The ground truth Y_l are manually pixel-wise marked on the images X_l by experts, whereas the ground truth Y_u are unknown. Here, $\Omega = \{1, ...W\} \times \{1, ..., H\}$ is the image space and C is the number of segmentation classes. Our purpose is to train a model f parameterized by θ to predict the pixel-wise label map y from input image x.

3.2   Supervised Segmentation

For the fully supervised part, the most commonly used loss function for image segmentation task is the pixel-wise cross-entropy (CE) loss Eq. 2, which enforces

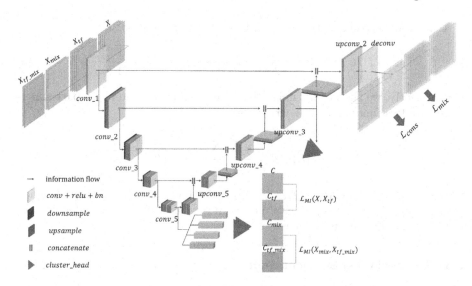

Fig. 1. The overall network architecture of our proposed method. Given a batch size unlabeled images X and their transformations X_{tf}, Mixing X as interpolated images X_{mix}, Mixing X_{tf} as interpolated images X_{tf_mix}. We maximize the MI between X and X_{tf}, X_{mix} and X_{tf_mix} to learn transformation-Invariant representation. The MI is obtained by multiple auxiliary clustering heads. At the same time, we utilize L_{cons} to enforce the consistency among different transformations. Naturally, L_{mix} ensures the consistency of the interpolated outputs, which help the model learn more robust features.

the output of model f to be consistent with y.

$$CE(p_i, y_i) = -\sum_{j=0}^{C-1} y_{ij} \log(p_{ij}) \qquad (2)$$

where y_i is the one-hot representation of the ground truth of sample i, when sample i belongs to class j, $y_{ij} = 1$, otherwise $y_{ij} = 0$, p_i is a predicted probability distribution for label y_i, p_{ij} denotes the predicted probability of the sample i belongs to class j, Specifically, the supervised part CE loss function can be written as:

$$L_{sup\_ce} = -\frac{1}{|D_l||\Omega|} \sum_{(x,y)\in D_l} \sum_{(i,j)\in \Omega} y_{ij} \log f_{ij}(x;\theta) \qquad (3)$$

However, since there is a lot of noise in medical images, the target region may only occupy a small part and the categories are extremely unbalanced, and we may not achieve good performance using only CE loss. The Dice Coefficient is an ensemble similarity measure function usually used to calculate the similarity of two samples which is equivalent to the F1 score. This measure ranges from 0 to 1, with higher value corresponding to better segmentation.

$$DICE(X,Y) = \frac{2TP}{2TP + FP + FN} = \frac{2|X \cup Y|}{|X| + |Y|} \qquad (4)$$

Consequently, we should maximize the Dice Coefficient. The other part supervised dice loss function can be written as:

$$L_{sup\_dice} = -\frac{1}{|D_l||\Omega|} \sum_{(x,y) \in D_l} \sum_{j=0}^{C-1} \frac{2\langle f_j(x; \theta), y_j \rangle}{\|f_j(x; \theta)\|_1 + \|y_j\|_1} \qquad (5)$$

where j denotes the class j, $f_j(x; \theta) \in \{0, 1\}^{\Omega}$ represents the predicted region of class j, $y_j \in \{0, 1\}^{\Omega}$ represents the ground truth of class j, $\langle ., . \rangle$ denotes dot product, and $\|.\|_1$ means L1 norm.

3.3   Unsupervised Segmentation

Consistency Regularization. Consistency Regularization is easily designed for classification tasks. For instance, the input image and its transformation and perturbation (rotation, flipping and cropping) should belong to the same class, i.e. classification task is transformation invariant. While in the segmentation task, once we transform or perturb the input image, the expected output for ground truth should have the same transformation or perturbation, i.e. segmentation task is transformation equivariant. Yet, convolutions are not transformation equivariant, meaning that if one rotates or flips the input, then the feature map does not necessarily rotate in a meaningful or easy to predict the manner [17]. Generally the transformations between input images T_1 and outputs T_2 are associated, so we introduce a transformation consistent scheme, which utilizes the same transformation $T_1 = T_2$ between input images and outputs, and enforces the ground truth and outputs as similar as possible. We use mean-squared (MSE) loss Eq. 6 to measure the distance between ground truth and output. The loss function can be expressed as:

$$MSE = \sum_{i}^{n} (y_i - \hat{y}_i)^2 \qquad (6)$$

Another form of expression for MSE loss is L2 norm. We deploy MSE loss on u and u_{tf}, u_{mix} and u_{tf_mix}. Therefore, the loss function of consistency regularization can be written as:

$$L_{cons} = \frac{1}{|X_u|} \sum_{u \in X_u} \sum_{x \in \Lambda} \|f(x_{tf}; \theta) - T(f(x; \theta))\|_2 \qquad (7)$$

where $\Lambda = \{u, u_{mix}\}$, u means the input image, x_{tf} means the transformation of input image, x_{mix} is obtained by interpolating and mixing input image, the same is true for x_{tf_mix}. $\|.\|_2$ denotes L2 norm. How to interpolate and mix images will be explained in Sect. 3.3.

Consistency-Based Regularization with Interpolation. In literature [5], the authors proposed that encouraging interpolated data-points to be more realistic, which improved the performance for feature learning and unsupervised clustering. It has also been demonstrated in [2] that the interpolation-based mixing technique improves unsupervised learning. Driven by this speculation and the aforementioned success, we adapt the interpolation-based mixing technique in our medical image segmentation method. Considering two unlabeled image $(u_1, u_2) \in X_u$, and then we can obtain another unlabeled image by interpolation $M_\alpha(u_1, u_2)$, where $M_\alpha(u_1, u_2) = \alpha u_1 + (1 - \alpha)u_2$, and the hyperparameter $\alpha \sim Beta(0.2, 0.2)$. This takes advantage of the fact that the network learns to predict a pixel-level segmentation mask for the input image, in addition to maintaining consistency between the output of the interpolated input and the interpolated output of the original input. Based on this idea, the Consistency-based Regularization with Interpolation technique can be summarized as:

$$M_\alpha(f(u_1; \theta), f(u_2; \theta)) \simeq f(M_\alpha(u_1, u_2); \theta) \tag{8}$$

Similarly, we use MSE loss Eq. 6 to measure the distance between them. Therefore, the loss function can be written as:

$$L_{mix} = \frac{1}{|X_u||\Lambda|} \sum_{(u_1,u_2) \in X_u} \sum_{(x_1,x_2) \in \Lambda} \|M_\alpha(f(x_1; \theta), f(x_2; \theta)) - f(M_\alpha(x_1, x_2); \theta)\|_2 \tag{9}$$

Here, $\Lambda = \{(u_1, u_2), (u_{tf1}, u_{tf2})\}$. We can enforce the consistency of the interpolated output and the output of interpolated input.

Global Mutual Information Loss. Considering unlabeled image $u \in X_u$, and its transformation version $u_{tf} = T(u)$, we assume that u and u_{tf} have similar contextual information. Transformation T is usually a simple geometrical transformation(rotation, flipping and cropping). For our baseline model UNet, we can divide it into two parts the encoder ϕ_{enc} and the decoder ϕ_{dec}. The high-level semantic features (global feature) $\phi_{enc}(u)$ and $\phi_{enc}(u_{tf})$ should be similar. We expect a high MI between them. Consequently, we maximize their mutual information:

$$\max_{\theta_{enc}} MI(\phi_{enc}(u); \phi_{enc}(u_{tf})) \tag{10}$$

where $MI(.;.)$ denotes the mutual information, and θ_{enc} is the learnable parameters of the encoder. While it is difficult to optimize directly Eq. 10 as the two variables are high-dimensional. Consequently, we utilize a clustering head and project the features into cluster probability distributions. According to the information bottleneck theory, we can obtain:

$$MI(g(\phi_{enc}(u)); g(\phi_{enc}(u_{tf}))) \leq MI(\phi_{enc}(u); \phi_{enc}(u_{tf})) \tag{11}$$

where $g(\phi_{enc}(.)) \in [0, 1]^K$ is the cluster probability distributions, g is the auxiliary clustering head, and K denotes the number of clusters. We use $P(z|u)$ to represent the cluster distributions of u, and $P(z_{tf}|u_{tf})$ to represent the cluster distributions of u_{tf}. The conditional joint distribution can be expressed as:

$$P(z, z_{tf}|u, u_{tf}) = g(\phi_{enc}(u)) \cdot g(\phi_{enc}(u_{tf}))^T \tag{12}$$

For all $u \in X_u$, the $K \times K$ joint probability distribution $P = P(z, z_{tf})$ can be approximately estimated as $P(z, z_{tf}|u, u_{tf})$. Meanwhile, according to Eq. 1, the global MI loss can be expressed as:

$$
\begin{aligned}
L_{MI}^{global} &= -\frac{1}{|X_u||\Lambda|} \sum_{u \in X_u} \sum_{x \in \Lambda} MI(P(z, z_{tf})) \\
&= -\frac{1}{|X_u||\Lambda|} \sum_{u \in X_u} \sum_{x \in \Lambda} P(z, z_{tf}) \log \frac{P(z, z_{tf})}{P(z) \cdot P(z_{tf})}
\end{aligned}
\tag{13}
$$

Here, $\Lambda = \{u, u_{mix}\}$, $z = g(\phi_{enc}(x))$, $z_{tf} = g(\phi_{enc}(x_{tf}))$. By optimizing the loss function, we can guarantee the contextual information similarity between input image and its transformation.

Local Mutual Information Loss. The features from the decoder are called the local features. Considering $\varphi^{(b)}(u) = \phi_{dec}^{(b)}(\phi_{enc}(u)) \in \mathbb{R}^{C_b \times H_b \times W_b}$ as the feature map of the b-th decoder block for an unlabeled image $u \in X_u$. For each position (i, j) of the local feature map, the feature vectors can be read off as $[\varphi^{(b)}(u)]_{i,j} \in \mathbb{R}^{C_b}$. The adjacent vectors can be defined as $[\varphi^{(b)}(u)]_{i+p,j+q}$, some small displacement $(p, q) \in \Delta^{(b)} \subset \mathbb{Z}^2$ The local features contain more spatial and structural information, i.e. it is regional. Therefore, we can assume that a patch in the input image shares information with its adjacent. By applying the same transformation T to $\varphi^{(b)}(u)$, the features can be paired and aligned at once. Based on this idea, our Mutual Information should be applied in $\varphi^{(b)}(u_{tf})$ and $T(\varphi^{(b)}(u))$. However, since the feature obtained directly from the decoder block is high-dimensional, we deploy linear projection head h for dimensionality reduction. It is worth noting that, in order not to destroy the spatial and structural information, h is 1×1 convolution and softmax. Therefore, we aim to maximize the MI between $h([\varphi^{(b)}(u_{tf})])$ and $h([T(\varphi^{(b)}(u))])$ The joint distribution for displacement $(p, q) \in \Delta^{(b)}$ can be estimated as:

$$P_{p,q}^{(b)} \approx \frac{1}{|X_u||\Lambda||\Omega|} \sum_{u \in X_u} \sum_{x \in \Lambda} \sum_{(i,j) \in \Omega} h([\varphi^{(b)}(x_{tf})]_{i,j}) \cdot h([T(\varphi^{(b)}(x))]_{i+p,j+q}) \tag{14}$$

where $\Lambda = \{u, u_{mix}\}$. Thus, for all decoder layers, the Local Mutual Information loss can be written as:

$$L_{MI}^{local} = -\frac{1}{|B|} \sum_{b=1}^{B} \frac{1}{|\Delta^{(b)}|} \sum_{(p,q) \in \Delta^{(b)}} MI(P_{p,q}^{(b)}) \tag{15}$$

Here, $MI(.)$ can be computed as Eq. 13.

3.4   Objective Function

For MMISeg, combining supervised part and unsupervised part, joint Eq. 3, Eq. 5, Eq. 7, Eq. 9, Eq. 13, and Eq. 15, the objective function can be expressed as:

$$
\begin{aligned}
L(\theta) &= L_{sup} + L_{unsup} \\
&= \lambda_1(L_{sup\_ce+sup\_dice}) + \lambda_2 L_{cons} + \lambda_3 L_{mix} + \lambda_4(L_{MI}^{global} + L_{MI}^{local})
\end{aligned}
\tag{16}
$$

where λ_1, λ_2 λ_3, and λ_4 are all hyperparameters that control the weights of each part of the loss respectively. We will discuss the effect of these hyperparameters on the experimental results later. By optimizing the loss, we can mine information from the abundance of unlabeled data, and then reach great performance. The overall network architecture of our proposed method is shown in Fig. 1.

4   Experiments and Results

4.1   Dataset and Evaluation Metrics

ACDC Dataset. Automated Cardiac Diagnosis Challenge (ACDC) provides short-axis cardiac MRI volumes of 100 patients, which can be divided into five subgroups: normal, previous myocardial infarction, dilated cardiomyopathy and abnormal right ventricle. For the entire cardiac cycle, there were only end-diastolic (ED) and end-systolic (ES) slices and corresponding manual references based on analysis by one clinical expert. The mutual reference annotations consist of three structures: left and right ventricle and myocardium. The dataset was split into train, validation, and test sets, and the 3D volumes were sliced into 2D slices. After eliminating invalid slices (i.e., slices that do not contain the target region), there are 1912 valid slices. Data augmentation includes cropping to 224 × 224 pixels, random horizontal flip, and random rotation.

MMWHS Dataset. Multi-Modality Whole Heart Segmentation Challenge provides 20 3D cardiac MRI volumes. The annotations consist of seven structures: left and right ventricle, left and right atrium, myocardium, ascending aorta and pulmonary artery. Same as the ACDC dataset, we can obtain 2898 slices. For data augmentation, we employ the same strategy as the ACDC dataset.

To evaluate the performance of MMISeg, we employ two broadly applicable metrics: Dice Similarity Coefficient (DSC) and Hausdorff Distance (HD). We will report the average of all the metric scores over all the classes for the ACDC dataset. Since the MMWHS dataset has seven structures, each slice may contain only a few of them, so we merely report these metrics for the whole heart.

4.2   Setup and Results

Driven by the excellent performance of U-Net in medical image segmentation, we employ U-Net as the baseline for MMISeg, which consists of five down-sampling layers and five up-sampling layers, implemented multi-scale feature fusion by skip connection. We use an ADAM optimizer with an initial learning rate of 0.001 to optimize the network learnable parameters. Following the existing works in literature [21], we apply global and local MI loss to three different layers: the last layer of the encoder ($conv\_5$) for global MI loss, and the last two layers from the decoder ($upconv\_3$ and $upconv\_2$) for local MI loss. While calculating MI loss, the weights of each layer are 0.5, 1.0, and 1.0 respectively, and remain unchanged throughout the experiment. We set the neighborhood size Δ to 3×3 for $upconv\_3$ and 7×7 for $upconv\_2$. Meanwhile, we fix the number of clusters of the decoder and encoder to $K = 10$, and deploy five clustering heads rather than a single head. To balance the different loss term in Eq. 16, we adapt the weights of $\lambda_1 = 1.0$, $\lambda_2 = 5.0$, $\lambda_3 = 1.0$, and $\lambda_4 = 0.1$. The labeling rates of the ACDC dataset and MMWHS dataset are 10% and 20% respectively.

The efficacy of MMISeg can be verified by comparison with other methods as shown in Table 1. By running with different random seeds, MMISeg obtains the highest mean DSC of 90.04% on the ACDC dataset and 87.09% on the MMWHS dataset. As shown in the Table 1, our method utilizes small labeled data and produces state-of-the-art performance in terms of DSC and HD. Although the improvement on the ACDC dataset is not obvious, the performance is boosted by 7.26% on the MMWHS dataset. Compared with our results, the labeling rate which is higher than our method [22] and lower than our method [21] achieve inferior performance. The impact of labeling rate and various hyperparameters on our experimental results will be introduced in Sect. 4.3.

Table 1. Comparison with other methods on the ACDC dataset and MMWHS dataset.

Method	ACDC			MMWHS		
	labeling rate (%)	DSC (%)	HD (mm)	labeling rate (%)	DSC (%)	HD (mm)
Entropy Min. [31]	5	72.32	–	13.3	49.44	–
Mean Teacher. [22]	5	84.10	–	13.3	55.57	–
Peng et al. [21]	5	85.76	-	13.3	55.75	-
Chaitanya et al. [7]	10	88.6	–	50	79.4	–
Adversarial Training. [35]	20	79.1	5.16	50	77.9	3.20
Basak et al. [2]	10	89.8	4.47	40	79.83	**3.05**
MMISeg.	10	**90.04**	**1.45**	20	**87.09**	3.24

4.3 Analysis of Our Method

Impact of Labeling Rate. Generally, higher labeling rate means greater performance, but the cost of obtaining annotated data is high. Therefore, it is critical to find a balance between labeling rate and performance. We conduct experiments on the ACDC dataset and MMWHS dataset respectively, and use DSC to measure the performance. As shown in Table 2, with only 5% labeling rate, we can get 86.72% DSC, far exceeding the performance of 1% labeling rate on the ACDC dataset. The improvement in labeling rate from 5% to 10% is also acceptable. However, the performance of 20% labeling rate did not improve significantly compared to 10% labeling rate. The difference is that as the labeling rate increases, the improvement in performance is considerable on the MMWHS dataset. We additionally explore the effect of larger labeling rate on the results, but as with the ACDC dataset, the improvement is inconsiderable at labeling rate 40%. We consider that it is worth sacrificing this little accuracy, but we only need less labeled data. Therefore, we choose 10% and 20% labeling rate on the ACDC dataset and MMWHS dataset, respectively.

Table 2. The validated DSC of different labeling rates on the ACDC dataset and MMWHS dataset. For ACDC dataset, RV, Myo and LV correspond to right ventricle, myocardium and right ventricle, respectively.

	ACDC				MMWHS
	RV	Myo	LV	Mean	
1%	16.21	40.36	54.45	43.25	57.61
5%	78.44	83.83	89.91	84.06	80.70
10%	**88.70**	88.00	93.44	90.04	84.17
20%	87.63	**89.99**	**94.04**	**90.55**	**87.09**

Impact of Hyperparameters. Experiences show that the choice of hyperparameters has a great influence on the experimental results. We carried out experiments on the ACDC dataset to explore the effect of hyperparameters $\lambda_1, \lambda_2, \lambda_3$, and λ_4 on performance. Following the existing works in literature [21], we find that the hyperparameter λ_4 which controls the local and global mutual information, should not be too large, and we fix it to 0.1. Since the hyperparameter λ_1 controls the weight of the supervised part, but our focus is on the unsupervised part, we keep $\lambda_1 = 1$ and only change the other hyperparameters. The results in Table 3 manifest there is little change in the performance when λ_2 is varied from 2.0 to 8.0. s λ_3 is more sensitive to segmentation performance, which reflects the importance of L_{mix} to our results from the side, as shown in Sect. 4.4. We can achieve the best performance when $\lambda_2 = 5.0$ and $\lambda_3 = 1.0$. These hyperparameters will be the basis of our subsequent ablation experiments.

Table 3. The validated mean DSC of different hyperparameters on the ACDC dataset. λ_2 controls the weight of L_{cons}, and λ_3 controls the weight of L_{mix}.

λ_2	λ_3		
	0.1	1.0	2.0
1.0	88.25	87.95	87.28
2.0	88.53	89.69	89.03
5.0	86.68	**90.04**	88.87
8.0	87.39	89.67	88.40

4.4   Ablation Experiment

For the unsupervised part, we have three items L_{cons}, L_{mix} and L_{MI}. According to Sect. 4.3, we fix $\lambda_1 = 1.0$, $\lambda_2 = 5.0$, $\lambda_3 = 1.0$, and $\lambda_4 = 0.1$. We ablate the use of L_{cons}, L_{mix} and L_{MI} by removing either. Results of the ablation experiments are summarized in Table 4. It can be seen that removing any part leads to a 1% to 2% drop in results, with the largest drop occurring when L_{mix} is removed. Therefore, L_{mix} is the most important part of our method, L_{cons} second and L_{MI} third.

Table 4. The validated DSC of ablation results on the ACDC dataset.

L_{cons}	L_{mix}	L_{MI}	ACDC			
			RV	Myo	LV	Mean
✓	✓		87.67	85.91	91.87	88.48
✓		✓	87.36	85.03	91.29	87.89
	✓	✓	86.35	86.25	92.02	88.21
✓	✓	✓	**88.70**	**88.00**	**93.44**	**90.04**

5   Conclusion

In this paper, we proposed a novel SSL medical image segmentation method, MMISeg, which combines consistency-based regularization and unsupervised representation learning, and validated the effectiveness of our proposed method on the ACDC dataset and MMWHS dataset. Therefore, it is believed that our proposed method can fully mine information from the abundant unlabeled data and improve the robustness of the model. Currently, we only apply our proposed method to cardiac MRI image segmentation, and our method is easily extended to other SSL problems in the medical image domain. Since MMISeg currently only supports 2D images, if you want to use it for 3D images for other medical domain, you need to slice the 3D images into 2D images first.

References

1. Bai, W., et al.: Semi-supervised learning for network-based cardiac MR image segmentation. In: Descoteaux, M., Maier-Hein, L., Franz, A., Jannin, P., Collins, D.L., Duchesne, S. (eds.) MICCAI 2017. LNCS, vol. 10434, pp. 253–260. Springer, Cham (2017). https://doi.org/10.1007/978-3-319-66185-8_29
2. Basak, H., Bhattacharya, R., Hussain, R., Chatterjee, A.: An embarrassingly simple consistency regularization method for semi-supervised medical image segmentation. arXiv preprint arXiv:2202.00677 (2022)
3. Belghazi, M.I., et al.: Mutual information neural estimation. In: International Conference on Machine Learning, pp. 531–540. PMLR (2018)

4. Bengio, Y., Courville, A., Vincent, P.: Representation learning: A review and new perspectives. IEEE Trans. Pattern Anal. Mach. Intell. **35**(8), 1798–1828 (2013)
5. Berthelot, D., Raffel, C., Roy, A., Goodfellow, I.: Understanding and improving interpolation in autoencoders via an adversarial regularizer. arXiv preprint arXiv:1807.07543 (2018)
6. Caron, M., Bojanowski, P., Joulin, A., Douze, M.: Deep clustering for unsupervised learning of visual features. In: Ferrari, V., Hebert, M., Sminchisescu, C., Weiss, Y. (eds.) Computer Vision – ECCV 2018. LNCS, vol. 11218, pp. 139–156. Springer, Cham (2018). https://doi.org/10.1007/978-3-030-01264-9_9
7. Chaitanya, K., Erdil, E., Karani, N., Konukoglu, E.: Contrastive learning of global and local features for medical image segmentation with limited annotations. Adv. Neural. Inf. Process. Syst. **33**, 12546–12558 (2020)
8. Chaitanya, K., Karani, N., Baumgartner, C.F., Becker, A., Donati, O., Konukoglu, E.: Semi-supervised and task-driven data augmentation. In: Chung, A.C.S., Gee, J.C., Yushkevich, P.A., Bao, S. (eds.) IPMI 2019. LNCS, vol. 11492, pp. 29–41. Springer, Cham (2019). https://doi.org/10.1007/978-3-030-20351-1_3
9. Chaitanya, K., Karani, N., Baumgartner, C.F., Erdil, E., Becker, A., Donati, O., Konukoglu, E.: Semi-supervised task-driven data augmentation for medical image segmentation. Med. Image Anal. **68**, 101934 (2021)
10. Chen, L.C., Papandreou, G., Kokkinos, I., Murphy, K., Yuille, A.L.: DeepLab: semantic image segmentation with deep convolutional nets, atrous convolution, and fully connected CRFs. IEEE Trans. Pattern Anal. Mach. Intell. **40**(4), 834–848 (2017)
11. Faramarzi, M., Amini, M., Badrinaaraayanan, A., Verma, V., Chandar, S.: Patchup: A regularization technique for convolutional neural networks. arXiv preprint arXiv:2006.07794 (2020)
12. Hjelm, R.D., et al.: Learning deep representations by mutual information estimation and maximization. arXiv preprint arXiv:1808.06670 (2018)
13. Ji, X., Henriques, J.F., Vedaldi, A.: Invariant information clustering for unsupervised image classification and segmentation. In: Proceedings of the IEEE/CVF International Conference on Computer Vision, pp. 9865–9874 (2019)
14. Kim, J.H., Choo, W., Jeong, H., Song, H.O.: Co-mixup: Saliency guided joint mixup with supermodular diversity. arXiv preprint arXiv:2102.03065 (2021)
15. Kim, J.H., Choo, W., Song, H.O.: Puzzle mix: exploiting saliency and local statistics for optimal mixup. In: International Conference on Machine Learning, pp. 5275–5285. PMLR (2020)
16. Krähenbühl, P., Koltun, V.: Efficient inference in fully connected CRFs with Gaussian edge potentials. In: 24th Proceedings of the International Conference on Advances in Neural Information Processing Systems (2011)
17. Li, X., Yu, L., Chen, H., Fu, C.W., Heng, P.A.: Semi-supervised skin lesion segmentation via transformation consistent self-ensembling model. arXiv preprint arXiv:1808.03887 (2018)
18. Long, J., Shelhamer, E., Darrell, T.: Fully convolutional networks for semantic segmentation. In: Proceedings of the IEEE Conference on Computer Vision and Pattern Recognition, pp. 3431–3440 (2015)
19. Van den Oord, A., et al.: Representation learning with contrastive predictive coding. arXiv preprint arXiv:1807.03748 2(3), 4 (2018)
20. Peng, J., Pedersoli, M., Desrosiers, C.: Mutual information deep regularization for semi-supervised segmentation. In: Proceedings of the Medical Imaging with Deep Learning, pp. 601–613. PMLR (2020)

21. Peng, J., Pedersoli, M., Desrosiers, C.: Boosting semi-supervised image segmentation with global and local mutual information regularization. arXiv preprint arXiv:2103.04813 (2021)
22. Perone, C.S., Ballester, P., Barros, R.C., Cohen-Adad, J.: Unsupervised domain adaptation for medical imaging segmentation with self-ensembling. Neuroimage **194**, 1–11 (2019)
23. Perone, C.S., Cohen-Adad, J.: Deep Semi-supervised segmentation with weight-averaged consistency targets. In: Stoyanov, D., et al. (eds.) DLMIA/ML-CDS - 2018. LNCS, vol. 11045, pp. 12–19. Springer, Cham (2018). https://doi.org/10.1007/978-3-030-00889-5_2
24. Radosavovic, I., Dollár, P., Girshick, R., Gkioxari, G., He, K.: Data distillation: towards omni-supervised learning. In: Proceedings of the IEEE Conference on Computer Vision and Pattern Recognition, pp. 4119–4128 (2018)
25. Simonyan, K., Zisserman, A.: Very deep convolutional networks for large-scale image recognition. arXiv preprint arXiv:1409.1556 (2014)
26. Song, J., Ermon, S.: Understanding the limitations of variational mutual information estimators. arXiv preprint arXiv:1910.06222 (2019)
27. Souly, N., Spampinato, C., Shah, M.: Semi supervised semantic segmentation using generative adversarial network. In: Proceedings of the IEEE International Conference on Computer Vision, pp. 5688–5696 (2017)
28. Tarvainen, A., Valpola, H.: Mean teachers are better role models: Weight-averaged consistency targets improve semi-supervised deep learning results. Advances in neural information processing systems 30 (2017)
29. Tian, Y., Krishnan, D., Isola, P.: Contrastive multiview coding. In: Vedaldi, A., Bischof, H., Brox, T., Frahm, J.-M. (eds.) ECCV 2020. LNCS, vol. 12356, pp. 776–794. Springer, Cham (2020). https://doi.org/10.1007/978-3-030-58621-8_45
30. Verma, V., et al.: Manifold mixup: better representations by interpolating hidden states. In: International Conference on Machine Learning, pp. 6438–6447. PMLR (2019)
31. Vu, T.H., Jain, H., Bucher, M., Cord, M., Pérez, P.: Advent: Adversarial entropy minimization for domain adaptation in semantic segmentation. In: Proceedings of the IEEE/CVF Conference on Computer Vision and Pattern Recognition, pp. 2517–2526 (2019)
32. Wang, X., Qi, G.J.: Contrastive learning with stronger augmentations. arXiv preprint arXiv:2104.07713 (2021)
33. Yun, S., Han, D., Oh, S.J., Chun, S., Choe, J., Yoo, Y.: CutMix: regularization strategy to train strong classifiers with localizable features. In: Proceedings of the IEEE/CVF International Conference On Computer Vision, pp. 6023–6032 (2019)
34. Zhang, H., Cisse, M., Dauphin, Y.N., Lopez-Paz, D.: mixup: Beyond empirical risk minimization. arXiv preprint arXiv:1710.09412 (2017)
35. Zhang, Y., Yang, L., Chen, J., Fredericksen, M., Hughes, D.P., Chen, D.Z.: Deep Adversarial networks for biomedical image segmentation utilizing unannotated images. In: Descoteaux, M., Maier-Hein, L., Franz, A., Jannin, P., Collins, D.L., Duchesne, S. (eds.) MICCAI 2017. LNCS, vol. 10435, pp. 408–416. Springer, Cham (2017). https://doi.org/10.1007/978-3-319-66179-7_47
36. Zhao, J., Lu, D., Ma, K., Zhang, Yu., Zheng, Y.: Deep Image clustering with category-style representation. In: Vedaldi, A., Bischof, H., Brox, T., Frahm, J.-M. (eds.) ECCV 2020. LNCS, vol. 12359, pp. 54–70. Springer, Cham (2020). https://doi.org/10.1007/978-3-030-58568-6_4

Dual-Stream Feature Fusion Network for Detection and ReID in Multi-object Tracking

Qingyou He[1,2(✉)] and Liangqun Li[1,2]

[1] ATR Key Laboratory, Shenzhen University, Shenzhen 518060, China
[2] Guangdong Key Laboratory of Intelligent Information Processing, Shenzhen University, Shenzhen 518060, China
heqingyou2020@email.szu.edu.cn

Abstract. Multi-object Tracking (MOT) focuses on associating detection boxes with previous results from the same detector using motion and appearance features. Recently, the Joint detection and embedding (JDE) paradigm is showing its efficiency to explore the potentially shared information between the tasks of detection and re-identification (ReID). However, formulating the tasks of detection and ReID into a shared feature fusion network may bring inevitable competition during training. To tackle this problem, we propose a novel dual-stream feature fusion network (DSFFN) to alleviate the competition between the two tasks and obtain better task-dependent feature expression. It forms the detection and ReID feature fusion tasks into a parallel network, and they only share the low-level feature information. Further, to solve the inconsistency across different scales of ReID embeddings and improve the awareness of important information, we propose a multi-scale cross-connected attention network (MSCCAN) for ReID feature fusion. At last, we modify the prediction head to be decoupled design to tackle the conflicts between multi-task. Our method obtains 78.8% MOTA and 74.3% IDF1 on MOT16 test sets, which outperforms the previous works and achieves state-of-the-art performance.

Keywords: Multi-object tracking · Dual-stream network · Feature fusion · Re-identification

1 Introduction

Multi-Object Tracking (MOT) plays a crucial role in computer vision society, with various practical applications ranging from video surveillance to autonomous driving. The goal of MOT is to connect the detection boxes between adjacent frames to form smooth trajectories. Since object detection [7,9,15,33] benefits a lot from the advances of deep learning and large-scale datasets [12,22], the most widely investigated MOT methods [3,16,28,30] usually follow the tracking-by-detection (TBD) paradigm, which divides MOT into two separate

© The Author(s), under exclusive license to Springer Nature Switzerland AG 2022
S. Khanna et al. (Eds.): PRICAI 2022, LNCS 13629, pp. 247–260, 2022.
https://doi.org/10.1007/978-3-031-20862-1_18

components: a detection model and an appearance embeddings model. However, the connection between detection and appearance feature extraction in TBD is not always elegant enough. Bochinski et al. [4] first obtained detection results from the object detector and then simply computed the IoU value between new detection boxes and the position of tracklets to achieve real-time association. Bewley et al. [3] introduced the Kalman filter to predict the current position using the previous states for smoother matching. There are also several works [6,30] following the tracking-by-detection paradigm that achieved good performance without appearance features. Though these methods using a weak matching strategy can achieve a high updating rate during tracking, their good performances seriously depend on perfect detection without uncertainties of the complex environment. Therefore, some researchers [16,28] began to focus on adding an extra network for appearance feature extraction to achieve a more robust association. Wojke et al. [26] adopted a simple CNN to extract ReID feature embedding after detection, and then used them for the data association. These methods proved that the appearance features are helpful in long-term tracking. But they have to crop the detection boxes after the detection step and perform forward inference in a separate model again to obtain ReID embeddings, which may lead to a massive computational redundancy. Thus, these two-step methods are difficult to realize real-time application in practical scenes.

Recently, with the development of multi-task learning, the one-shot methods [10,25,31] attract more attention due to their efficiency in localizing the objects and obtaining ReID features simultaneously in a unified network. The one-shot methods usually modify the prediction head to add extra output channels to indicate the ReID embeddings. However, the combination of the two different tasks of detection and ReID brings inevitable inherent competition and hurts the accuracy of detection. In the widely used one-shot methods, e.g. JDE [25], they usually distinguish the two tasks only in their prediction head. This means that detection and ReID share all features extracted by the same backbone and feature fusion network. However, detection expects the model has a high sensitivity for all valid objects whereas ReID tends to focus on the specific object. Thus, the different usages of these features by different tasks bring conflicts during learning. Zhang et al. [31] comprehensively analyzed the unfairness learning of the two tasks during training. They adopted an anchor-free detector to reduce ambiguous learning but the two tasks still shared the whole backbone and feature fusion network, which failed to tackle the competition between different tasks and still decreased the performance of its detector.

To solve the problem mentioned above, in this work, we first analyze the intrinsic reasons for the advantages and disadvantages of the one-shot method and conduct our research based on the widely used one-shot methods. We first propose a dual-stream feature fusion network (DSFFN) to separate the feature fusion operations of the tasks of detection and embedding. DSFFN allows both tasks to simultaneously obtain the desired task-dependent feature maps from their respective feature fusion networks. Meanwhile, we introduce a multi-scale cross-connected attention network (MSCCAN) to enhance the response value on the specific object. It consists of a cross-connected structure and several spatial attention and channel attention modules to improve the learning of important information. Further, we introduce the decoupled prediction head to alleviate the negative effects caused by the conflicts between multi-task. Moreover, our method still belongs to the one-shot method which can achieve end-to-end learning and output detection results and embeddings at the same time. In summary, the main contributions of our work are as follows:

1. A novel dual-stream feature fusion network (DSFFN) is proposed to finish the task-wise feature fusion for detection and ReID. Meanwhile, the prediction head is modified from coupled design to decoupled. These improvements reduce the competition between tasks and strengthen the representation capability of features.
2. A multi-scale cross-connected attention network (MSCCAN) is introduced in the ReID branch. It helps the network become more sensitive to the features of the specific target, which improves the reliability of the online association during long-term tracking.
3. Through extensive experiments, we verify the effectiveness of the proposed method and make considerable improvements to the one-shot method. Further, our method outperforms the state-of-the-art methods by a large margin on MOT16.

2   Method

Our goal is to leverage the efficiency of the joint detection and embedding paradigm and alleviate the competition between two tasks in a unified network. In this section, we present the details of our proposed framework, named dual-stream feature fusion network (DSFFN), including two parallel feature fusion networks for the tasks of detection and ReID respectively. Then, we introduce the multi-scale cross-connected attention network (MSCCAN) in the ReID branch to refine the ReID feature fusion and improve the awareness ability of the important information. Further, we modify the prediction head from coupled design to decoupled design.

2.1   Overview of JDE

JDE [25] employs YOLOv3 [20] as its object detector and then redesigns the prediction head to obtain detection results and the feature embeddings of each valid detection in a single network. After the input frames are processed by a backbone network, the feature maps are fed into a shared feature pyramid network (FPN) [11] to obtain multi-resolution features. This feature fusion process consists of a bottom-up pathway, a top-down pathway, and lateral connections. Then, the modified prediction head processes the extracted features and then outputs the detection results and ReID embeddings simultaneously.

2.2   Dual-stream Feature Fusion Network

Improvements of JDE are limited to adding an extra output branch in the prediction head to obtain detection results and ReID embeddings simultaneously. The main advantage is that it can use a unified network to finish the two tasks. However, these two different tasks share the same feature fusion network. Due to the large gap between the detection task and the ReID feature extraction task, during the back-propagation, the update of the weight parameters is always biased to one of the tasks. These limitations may directly lead to suboptimal learning during training and seriously hurt the performance of detection.

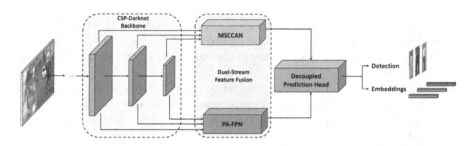

Fig. 1. Overview of the structure of our proposed method DSFFN. The input image is first fed into the backbone to extract multi-resolution features. Then the features are performed feature fusion operations in two separate networks to obtain task-dependent features. The obtained feature maps are processed by the decoupled prediction head to output detection results and ReID embeddings simultaneously.

To solve the problem and alleviate the competition between the two tasks, we propose a dual-stream feature fusion network (DSFFN), which can learn more representative features for detection and ReID, as can be seen in Fig. 1. It splits the original feature fusion network into two independent branches, which enables the detection task and the ReID task to obtain multi-scale fused features from the corresponding networks. We first replace the object detector in JDE from YOLOv3 [20] to YOLOX [9], which uses a stronger feature extraction backbone, CSP-Darknet, thus bringing better feature extraction performance. As shown in Figure 1, given an input video frame f_t, it undergoes a forward inference through the backbone network to yield feature maps of three different scales with 1/8, 1/16, and 1/32 down-sampling rates, which are denoted as $F_i|_{i=1,2,3}$. Then, we start from the backbone and extend two separate branches for extracting and detection and ReID features. These features are fed into DSFFN, including the fusion network Ψ and Φ for detection and ReID, respectively. Then, the features F_i from the same backbone are fused by separate feature fusion networks to obtain multi-scale detection features D_i and ReID features E_i, as shown in Eq. 1.

$$[D_i, E_i] = [\Psi(F_i), \Phi(F_i)], i = 1, 2, 3 \tag{1}$$

2.3   Multi-scale Cross-Connected Attention Network

FPN [11] in JDE [25] performs up-sampling operations to resize the feature maps in the top-down pathway and then fuses multi-level features simply using channel concatenation. However, due to the inconsistency across different feature scales, the fused features may retain redundant features but make important information invisible. Thus, we introduce a multi-scale cross-connected attention network (MSCCAN) to tackle the problem. For the detection branch, we adopt the same structure as YOLOX [9] with the PA-FPN feature fusion network for simplicity.

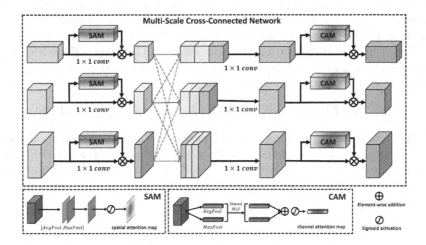

Fig. 2. Diagram of MSCCAN. We input multi-resolution features to it and then obtain the fused multi-scale feature map for ReID embeddings.

For the ReID branch, we use MSCCAN to aggregate multi-level features from different resolutions as shown in Fig. 2. The multi-scale structure is designed to provide exclusive ReID feature embeddings with different scale objects. In the network, the spatial attention module (SAM) and channel attention modules (CAM) are designed to learn more representative features. In other words, the combination of SAM and CAM in this network makes the trained model more sensitive to the features of specific objects.

In particular, as shown in Fig. 2, the MSCCAN branch obtains the input features $F_i|_{i=1,2,3}$ shared with the detection branch from the same backbone. Firstly, the SAM modules are adopted to aware of the position of the important information in the feature maps. The SAM operations are shown in Eq. 2.

$$S_i = \sigma(f^{7\times7}([AvgPool(\boldsymbol{F}_i); MaxPool(\boldsymbol{F}_i)])), i = 1, 2, 3 \qquad (2)$$

where σ represents the Sigmoid activation, $f^{7\times7}$ is the convolution layer with 7×7 kernel size. Specifically, we first perform avg-pooling and max-pooling on channel dimension to obtain a feature map with size $H \times W \times 2$, which are processed by a 7×7 convolution layer and a sigmoid activation to yield the spatial attention map S_i. Note that the original feature map are performed a 1×1 convolution to reduce the number of channels and followed an element-wise multiplication with the spatial attention map S_i, as shown in Eq. 3.

$$F'_i = f^{1 \times 1}(F_i) \otimes S_i, i = 1, 2, 3 \tag{3}$$

Then, we introduce the cross-connected concatenation to enhance information interaction between feature maps with different resolutions. We first resize the feature maps to the shape of the other level with up-sampling and down-sampling operations. For up-sampling, we apply the nearest interpolation to upscale the resolution and 1×1 convolution to reduce the number of channels. For down-sampling, we use 3×3 convolution with stride 2 to downscale and reduce the number of channels. After that, the operations of CAM are followed for each scale of feature maps to aggregate different information from different levels, the operations of the CAM are illustrated in Eq. 4.

$$C_i = \sigma(MLP(AvgPool(F_i)) + MLP(MaxPool(F_i))), i = 1, 2, 3 \tag{4}$$

The outputs of avg-pooling and max-pooling are first processed by a shared 1×1 convolution layer and then fused by element-wise addition and Sigmoid activation to obtain channel attention maps C_i. The channel attention maps are performed element-wise multiplications to finish the feature fusion task, as shown in Eq. 5.

$$F'_i = F_i \otimes C_i, i = 1, 2, 3 \tag{5}$$

2.4 Decoupled Prediction Head and Training Details

Further, the prediction head of JDE follows the coupled design of YOLOv3 [20], which leads to the existence of competition between classification and regression tasks. Therefore, we modify the coupled prediction head to a decoupled head, as shown in Fig. 3. In general, the design of the decoupled head is similar to YOLOX, but we add an extra branch for classification to predict the ID indexes of pedestrian objects corresponding to the extracted ReID feature. The learning of each decoupled prediction head is modeled as a multi-task learning problem. Note that the process of the classification is only performed during training.

To train the detection and ReID tasks in a unified network, we adopt a weighted sum of detection loss and ReID loss during training. Moreover, we set an additional learnable parameter $s = \{s_{det}, s_{id}\}$ for each part of the overall loss function, which can automatically adjust the weights and brings task-dependent uncertainty. The cost can be formulated as:

$$\mathcal{L} = \frac{1}{e^{s_{det}}}\mathcal{L}_{cls} + \frac{\lambda}{e^{s_{det}}}\mathcal{L}_{reg} + \frac{1}{e^{s_{id}}}\mathcal{L}_{id} \tag{6}$$

where λ is a balancing parameter. Specifically, we input a video frame f_i with its ground-truth labels L_k, where $L_k = (x_k, y_k, w_k, h_k, c_k)$. (x_k, y_k) represents

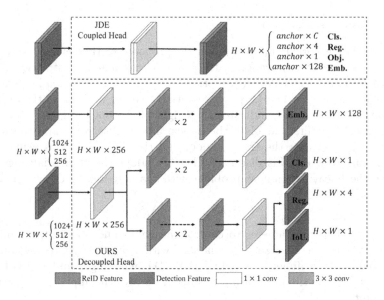

Fig. 3. The comparison of the coupled head of JDE and the decoupled head of our proposed method. The outputs are divided into two separate branches for detection and ReID to alleviate the conflict between multi-task. An additional IoU branch is added in regression branch for better localization capability.

the center position in the image and the (w_k, h_k) represents the size of the k-th bounding boxes. c_k indicates the ID index of the object in its bounding box. After processing the forward inference of the network, the decoupled prediction head outputs a 5-dimension vector $p = (x', y', w', h', s)$, where s indicates the confidence score of the existence of objects. Given a prediction box b_i, we calculate the intersection-over-union (IoU) value with the ground-truth box b_{gt}, and adopt IoU loss for bounding box regression, which can be defined as Eqs. (8–9). The α is set to 0.25 and γ is set to 0.

$$\mathcal{L}_{reg}(b_i) = \begin{cases} 1 - \text{IoU}(b_i, b_{gt}) & \text{if y=1} \\ 0 & \text{otherwise} \end{cases} \tag{7}$$

Though the class of objects is set to 1 (only pedestrians), we keep the classification branch in the prediction head for the extension of future work. Focal loss is adopted to calculate the classification errors:

$$\mathcal{L}_{cls} = -\alpha(1 - p_t)^\gamma log(p_t) \tag{8}$$

$$p_i = \begin{cases} p & \text{if y=1} \\ 1 - p & \text{otherwise} \end{cases} \tag{9}$$

2.5   Online Association

In this section, we briefly introduce how the proposed method is applied to MOT in this work. Specifically, we follow the same cascade matching strategy as JDE. We first initialize a tracklet with motion state $m_i = (x, y, \gamma, h, \dot{x}, \dot{y}, \dot{\gamma}, \dot{h})$ and a ReID embedding e_i, where (x, y) represents the center position of the object, γ is the aspect ratio, and h indicates the height of the bounding box. For a new coming frame, we first calculate the appearance similarity S_e and the motion similarity S_m between the tracklet pool and the new detections using cosine distance and Mahalanobis distance. Then we adopt the Hungarian algorithm to solve the linear assignment problem with the cost matrix C, which can be defined as:

$$C = \lambda S_m + (1 - \lambda) S_e \qquad (10)$$

where λ is a hyper parameter to control the importance of the two similarity metrics. When a certain tracklet is matched with new detection, its motion state is updated by the Kalman filter, while its ReID embedding is updated as Eq. 11, where α represents the momentum term, f_i^t indicates the appearance feature of the frame t.

$$e_i^t = \alpha e_i^{t-1} + (1 - \alpha) f_i^t \qquad (11)$$

3   Experiments

3.1   Implementation Details and Settings

Training. In this work, the training is performed in two steps. Specifically, we first mix multiple datasets and use them to train the detection branch, including CrowdHuman [23], MOT16 [17], and Cityperson [29]. The parameters of the backbone and feature fusion network are initialized with the COCO [12] pre-trained model. The batch size is set to 48 and the initial learning rate is set to 1×10^{-4}. After the first step of training, we freeze the parameters of the backbone and the feature fusion network of the detection branch. In other words, we only train MSCCAN and the decoupled prediction head in the second step. For data augmentation, we adopt mosaic, mix-up operations, and random-scale during training. We train our model with these augmentations for 70 epochs and add L1 loss for extra 10 epochs to obtain more accurate localization performance.

Evaluation and Metrics. We conduct the evaluation of our proposed method and the other methods on MOT16 and MOT17. To comprehensively evaluate the proposed method, we use multi-metrics to evaluate various aspects of trackers, including the CLEAR [2] metric and IDF1 [21] scores. CLEAR consists of basic metrics on MOT, including MOTA (Muti-Object Tracking Accuracy), MT (Most Tracked Objects Ratio), ML (Most Untracked Objects Ratio), FP (False Positive), FN (False Negative), IDsw (ID Switches), etc., while IDF1 score focuses on association performance.

Table 1. Component-wise ablation results on MOT16 train sets. (D+F) indicates combining DSFFN into the baseline and adopting FPN for the feature fusion in ReID branch. (D+F) indicates combining DSFFN into the baseline and adopting our proposed MSCCAN for the feature fusion in ReID branch. The results with the best performance are shown in **bold**.

Method	Backbone	MOTA ↑	IDF1↑	IDR↑	IDTP ↑	IDSw↓
JDE	YOLOv3	74.5	69.2	64.1	71963	1373
JDE	YOLOX	83.9	77.0	72.9	81850	494
Ours(D+F)	YOLOX	90.7	80.8	79.1	88866	492
Ours(D+M)	YOLOX	**91.4**	**83.1**	**82.1**	**92133**	**392**

3.2 Ablation Studies

To understand how these additional modules affect the tracking performance, we perform a series of experiments involving backbone, DSFFN, and MSCCAN on the MOT16 dataset. To avoid the influence of other factors, we adopt the same training settings and tracking strategy for all experiments in this section. We adopt JDE as our baseline method and then we compare its performance with our proposed method. The experimental results of ablation studies are listed in Table 1. IDR indicates identity recall rate, IDTP indicates the number of identity true positive, and IDsw is the number of identity switches during tracking.

For a fair comparison with JDE, we first replace the same object detector as ours. When equipped with a stronger detector, we can observe remarkable improvements in all aspects. Further, when the original feature fusion network is modified to the proposed DSFFN, we notice the improvements of +6.8% MOTA, +3.8% IDF1, and +6.2% IDR. At the same time, the number of ID switches is reduced sharply from 1373 to 494. These results verify the effectiveness of the dual-stream feature fusion network in alleviating the competition between the tasks of detection and ReID. Meanwhile, it can help to learn better task-dependent feature representations. Finally, when the proposed MSCCAN is combined with DSFFN, it yields +0.7% MOTA, +2.3% IDF1, and +3.0% IDR improvements, while further reducing the number of ID switches. It helps the network become more sensitive to the features of the specific target, which improves the reliability of the online association during long-term tracking.

3.3 Comparison with State-of-the-Art MOT Methods

In this section, we report our results on the testing sets of MOT16 and MOT17 using the "private detector" protocol since we use the same additional data as Fair [31] for training. We compare our proposed method with state-of-the-art MOT methods in recent years, and the results are shown in Table 2. Note that all results are evaluated by the official test server of the MOT challenge. Specifically, the compared MOT methods can be described in three classes: one-shot method, two-stage method, joint detection, and tracking method.

Table 2. Comparison with state-of-the-art multi-object tracking methods on the MOT16 benchmark. ⋆ indicates one-shot methods which integrate detection and embedding into a single network. ◇ indicates joint detection and tracking method without ReID embeddings. The other entries without special sign indicate two-stage methods. The results with the best performance are shown in **bold**.

Method	Year	MOTA↑	IDF1↑	MT↑	ML↓	FP↓	FN↓	IDsw↓
IOU [4]	2016	57.1	46.9	23.6	32.9	5702	70278	2167
SORT [3]	2016	59.8	53.8	25.4	22.7	8698	63245	1423
DeepSORT [26]	2017	61.4	62.2	32.8	18.2	12852	56668	781
TAP [32]	2017	64.8	73.5	38.5	21.6	12980	50635	571
RAN [8]	2018	63.0	63.8	39.9	22.1	13663	53248	**482**
◇Tracktor++ [1]	2019	56.2	54.9	20.7	35.8	**2394**	76884	617
◇Tube_TK [18]	2020	66.9	62.2	39.0	16.1	11544	47502	1236
◇CTracker [19]	2020	67.6	57.2	32.9	23.1	8934	48305	1897
⋆JDE [25]	2020	64.4	55.8	35.4	20.0	10642	52523	1544
⋆Fair [31]	2020	69.3	72.3	40.3	16.7	13501	41653	815
HTA [13]	2021	62.4	64.2	37.5	12.1	19071	47839	1619
TraDeS [27]	2021	70.1	64.7	37.3	20.0	8091	45210	1144
◇GSDT [24]	2021	66.7	69.2	38.6	19.0	14754	45057	959
◇MeMOT [5]	2022	72.6	69.7	44.9	16.6	14595	34595	845
OUTrack [14]	2022	74.2	71.1	44.8	13.8	13207	32584	1328
⋆CSTrack [10]	2022	75.6	73.3	42.8	16.5	9646	33777	1121
⋆**DSFFN**	OURS	**78.8**	**74.3**	**56.9**	**11.6**	14041	**23878**	763

Comparing with Joint Detection and Tracking Methods. Compared to these joint detection and tracking methods as shown in Table 2, our proposed method shows its superiority in long-term tracking. In summary, we obtain +11.2%–22.6% MOTA, +12.1–19.4% IDF1, and +17.9–36.2% MT improvements over these joint detection and tracking methods. Since they only focus on the association between adjacent frames and do not adopt any ReID module, which leads to fragmented trajectories. Thus, the two-stage methods usually perform better than the joint detection and tracking methods.

Table 3. Comparison with state-of-the-art one-shot methods on the MOT17 benchmark. The results with the best performance are shown in **bold**.

Method	Year	MOTA↑	IDF1↑	MT↑	ML↓	FP↓	FN↓	IDsw↓
JDE [25]	2020	63.0	59.5	35.7	17.3	39888	162927	6171
Fair [31]	2020	73.7	72.3	43.2	17.3	27507	117477	3303
CSTrack [10]	2022	74.9	72.6	41.5	17.5	**23847**	114303	3567
DSFFN	OURS	**79.4**	**73.9**	**55.2**	**12.2**	32616	**81385**	**2529**

Comparing with Two-Stage Methods. The two-stage methods have been widely investigated in recent years and we can find the obvious trend that they usually can achieve great performance. However, the difference in their tracking

Fig. 4. Visualization results of our proposed method on the test sets of MOT16. Each row indicates a set of the sample frames of a video sequence. Different colors of bounding boxes indicate different identities. Best viewed in color and zoomed in.

performance depends on the capabilities to extract ReID features. As shown in Table 2, on MOT16, we can observe that our proposed method remarkably outperforms all prior works based on the two-stage strategy. For example, when comparing with the latest state-of-the-art two-stage method, we outperform it by +4.6% MOTA and +3.2% IDF1. The improvement in the IDF1 score indicates that our proposed method has better learning capability on specific objects.

Comparing with One-Shot Methods. Since our research is performed based on the one-shot methods, we mainly focus on the improvements on them. As can be seen in Table 2, when evaluating on MOT16 test sets, our method achieves 78.8% MOTA, 74.3% IDF1, and 56.9% MT, which significantly outperforms +14.4% MOTA, +18.5% IDF1 over the baseline method JDE. Compared with Fair which adopts the same training data as our method, we also observe the improvements on +9.5% MOTA and +2.0% IDF1. Further, we extend our experiments to MOT17, as shown in Table 3. We observe a consistent trend with the results on MOT16. We obtain remarkable +5.7%–16.4% MOTA and +1.6%–14.4% IDF1 improvements over JDE and Fair. Thus, we conclude that the improvements are benefited from the design of our network, which indicates that the DSFFN and MSCCAN are helpful for the learning of task-dependent feature representation.

3.4 Qualitative Results

In this section, we visualize the qualitative result on MOT16 test sets as shown in Fig. 4. As can be seen in MOT16-01, MOT16-06, and MOT16-12, we observe the great capability of our method to tackle occlusion and assigning the correct identities with the help of reliable feature representation. At the same time, our method maintains great detection performance of tiny objects, as shown in MOT16-07 and MOT16-14. The results of MOT16-03 and MOT16-08 show the considerable performance under crowded scenes.

4   Conclusion

In this work, we propose a novel dual-stream feature fusion network (DSFFN) and adopt the decoupled design to the prediction head, which not only alleviates the competition between the tasks of detection and ReID but also improves the capabilities of better task-dependent feature expression. Further, we propose a multi-scale cross-connected attention network (MSCCAN) to reduce the inconsistency between different scales of feature maps and enhance the learning for specific identities. In summary, experiments on several datasets verify the superiority of our method, which outperforms the previous state-of-the-art methods. We believe that our research could further promote the development of the multi-object tracking society.

Acknowledgement. This work was supported by the National Natural Science Foundation of China (62171287, 61773267), Science & Technology Program of Shenzhen (Grant No. JCYJ20190808120417257).

References

1. Bergmann, P., Meinhardt, T., Leal-Taixe, L.: Tracking without bells and whistles. In: Proceedings of the IEEE/CVF International Conference on Computer Vision, pp. 941–951 (2019)
2. Bernardin, K., Stiefelhagen, R.: Evaluating multiple object tracking performance: the clear mot metrics. EURASIP J. Image Video Process. **2008**, 1–10 (2008)
3. Bewley, A., Ge, Z., Ott, L., Ramos, F., Upcroft, B.: Simple online and realtime tracking. In: 2016 IEEE International Conference on Image Processing (ICIP), pp. 3464–3468. IEEE (2016)
4. Bochinski, E., Senst, T., Sikora, T.: Extending IoU based multi-object tracking by visual information. In: 2018 15th IEEE International Conference on Advanced Video and Signal Based Surveillance (AVSS), pp. 1–6. IEEE (2018)
5. Cai, J., et al.: MeMOT: multi-object tracking with memory. In: Proceedings of the IEEE/CVF Conference on Computer Vision and Pattern Recognition, pp. 8090–8100 (2022)
6. Cao, J., Weng, X., Khirodkar, R., Pang, J., Kitani, K.: Observation-centric sort: Rethinking sort for robust multi-object tracking. arXiv preprint arXiv:2203.14360 (2022)
7. Carion, N., Massa, F., Synnaeve, G., Usunier, N., Kirillov, A., Zagoruyko, S.: End-to-end object detection with transformers. In: Vedaldi, A., Bischof, H., Brox, T., Frahm, J.-M. (eds.) ECCV 2020. LNCS, vol. 12346, pp. 213–229. Springer, Cham (2020). https://doi.org/10.1007/978-3-030-58452-8_13
8. Fang, K., Xiang, Y., Li, X., Savarese, S.: Recurrent autoregressive networks for online multi-object tracking. In: 2018 IEEE Winter Conference on Applications of Computer Vision (WACV), pp. 466–475. IEEE (2018)
9. Ge, Z., Liu, S., Wang, F., Li, Z., Sun, J.: YOLOX: exceeding yolo series in 2021. arXiv preprint arXiv:2107.08430 (2021)
10. Liang, C., Zhang, Z., Zhou, X., Li, B., Zhu, S., Hu, W.: Rethinking the competition between detection and ReID in multiobject tracking. IEEE Trans. Image Process. **31**, 3182–3196 (2022)
11. Lin, T.Y., Dollár, P., Girshick, R., He, K., Hariharan, B., Belongie, S.: Feature pyramid networks for object detection. In: Proceedings of the IEEE Conference on Computer Vision and Pattern Recognition, pp. 2117–2125 (2017)
12. Lin, T., et al.: Microsoft COCO: common objects in context. In: Fleet, D., Pajdla, T., Schiele, B., Tuytelaars, T. (eds.) ECCV 2014. LNCS, vol. 8693, pp. 740–755. Springer, Cham (2014). https://doi.org/10.1007/978-3-319-10602-1_48
13. Lin, X., Li, C.T., Sanchez, V., Maple, C.: On the detection-to-track association for online multi-object tracking. Pattern Recogn. Lett. **146**, 200–207 (2021)
14. Liu, Q., et al.: Online multi-object tracking with unsupervised re-identification learning and occlusion estimation. Neurocomputing **483**((2022)
15. Liu, Z., et al.: Swin transformer: Hierarchical vision transformer using shifted windows. In: Proceedings of the IEEE/CVF International Conference on Computer Vision. pp. 1001–110022 (2021)
16. Liu, Z., et al.: A strong baseline and batch normalization neck for deep person re-identification. IEEE Trans. Multim. **22**(10), 2597–2609 (2019)

17. Milan, A., Leal-Taixé, L., Reid, I., Roth, S., Schindler, K.: Mot16: a benchmark for multi-object tracking. arXiv preprint arXiv:1603.00831 (2016)
18. Pang, B., Li, Y., Zhang, Y., Li, M., Lu, C.: TubeTK: adopting tubes to track multi-object in a one-step training model. In: Proceedings of the IEEE/CVF Conference on Computer Vision and Pattern Recognition, pp. 6308–6318 (2020)
19. Peng, J., et al.: Chained-tracker: chaining paired attentive regression results for end-to-end joint multiple-object detection and tracking. In: Vedaldi, A., Bischof, H., Brox, T., Frahm, J.-M. (eds.) ECCV 2020. LNCS, vol. 12349, pp. 145–161. Springer, Cham (2020). https://doi.org/10.1007/978-3-030-58548-8_9
20. Redmon, J., Farhadi, A.: Yolov3: an incremental improvement. arXiv preprint arXiv:1804.02767 (2018)
21. Ristani, E., Solera, F., Zou, R., Cucchiara, R., Tomasi, C.: Performance measures and a data set for multi-target, multi-camera tracking. In: Hua, G., Jégou, H. (eds.) ECCV 2016. LNCS, vol. 9914, pp. 17–35. Springer, Cham (2016). https://doi.org/10.1007/978-3-319-48881-3_2
22. Shao, S., et al.: Objects365: a large-scale, high-quality dataset for object detection. In: Proceedings of the IEEE/CVF International Conference on Computer Vision, pp. 8430–8439 (2019)
23. Shao, S., et al.: Crowdhuman: a benchmark for detecting human in a crowd. arXiv preprint arXiv:1805.00123 (2018)
24. Wang, Y., Kitani, K., Weng, X.: Joint object detection and multi-object tracking with graph neural networks. In: 2021 IEEE International Conference on Robotics and Automation (ICRA), pp. 13708–13715. IEEE (2021)
25. Wang, Z., Zheng, L., Liu, Y., Li, Y., Wang, S.: Towards real-time multi-object tracking. In: Vedaldi, A., Bischof, H., Brox, T., Frahm, J.-M. (eds.) ECCV 2020. LNCS, vol. 12356, pp. 107–122. Springer, Cham (2020). https://doi.org/10.1007/978-3-030-58621-8_7
26. Wojke, N., Bewley, A., Paulus, D.: Simple online and realtime tracking with a deep association metric. In: 2017 IEEE International Conference on Image Processing (ICIP), pp. 3645–3649. IEEE (2017)
27. Wu, J., Cao, J., Song, L., Wang, Y., Yang, M., Yuan, J.: Track to detect and segment: an online multi-object tracker. In: Proceedings of the IEEE/CVF Conference on Computer Vision and Pattern Recognition, pp. 12352–12361 (2021)
28. Yu, F., Li, W., Li, Q., Liu, Yu., Shi, X., Yan, J.: POI: multiple object tracking with high performance detection and appearance feature. In: Hua, G., Jégou, H. (eds.) ECCV 2016. LNCS, vol. 9914, pp. 36–42. Springer, Cham (2016). https://doi.org/10.1007/978-3-319-48881-3_3
29. Zhang, S., Benenson, R., Schiele, B.: CityPersons: a diverse dataset for pedestrian detection. In: Proceedings of the IEEE Conference on Computer Vision and Pattern Recognition, pp. 3213–3221 (2017)
30. Zhang, Y., et al.: ByteTrack: multi-object tracking by associating every detection box. arXiv preprint arXiv:2110.06864 (2021)
31. Zhang, Y., Wang, C., Wang, X., Zeng, W., Liu, W.: FairMoT: on the fairness of detection and re-identification in multiple object tracking. Int. J. Comput. Vision 129(11), 3069–3087 (2021)
32. Zhou, Z., Xing, J., Zhang, M., Hu, W.: Online multi-target tracking with tensor-based high-order graph matching. In: 2018 24th International Conference on Pattern Recognition (ICPR), pp. 1809–1814. IEEE (2018)
33. Zhu, X., Su, W., Lu, L., Li, B., Wang, X., Dai, J.: Deformable DETR: deformable transformers for end-to-end object detection. arXiv preprint arXiv:2010.04159 (2020)

A Novel Approach for Pill-Prescription Matching with GNN Assistance and Contrastive Learning

Trung Thanh Nguyen[1,4], Hoang Dang Nguyen[1], Thanh Hung Nguyen[1], Huy Hieu Pham[2,3], Ichiro Ide[4], and Phi Le Nguyen[1(✉)]

[1] School of Information and Communication Technology, Hanoi University of Science and Technology, Hanoi, Vietnam
{thanh.nt176874,dang.nh194423}@sis.hust.edu.vn,
{hungnt,lenp}@soict.hust.edu.vn
[2] College of Engineering & Computer Science, Vin University, Hanoi, Vietnam
hieu.ph@vinuni.edu.vn
[3] VinUni-Illinois Smart Health Center, Vin University, Hanoi, Vietnam
[4] Graduate School of Informatics, Nagoya University, Nagoya, Japan
ide@i.nagoya-u.ac.jp

Abstract. Medication mistaking is one of the risks that can result in unpredictable consequences for patients. To mitigate this risk, we develop an automatic system that correctly identifies pill-prescription from mobile images. Specifically, we define a so-called pill-prescription matching task, which attempts to match the images of the pills taken with the pills' names in the prescription. We then propose PIMA, a novel approach using Graph Neural Network (GNN) and contrastive learning to address the targeted problem. In particular, GNN is used to learn the spatial correlation between the text boxes in the prescription and thereby highlight the text boxes carrying the pill names. In addition, contrastive learning is employed to facilitate the modeling of cross-modal similarity between textual representations of pill names and visual representations of pill images. We conducted extensive experiments and demonstrated that PIMA outperforms baseline models on a real-world dataset of pill and prescription images that we constructed. Specifically, PIMA improves the accuracy from 19.09% to 46.95% compared to other baselines. We believe our work can open up new opportunities to build new clinical applications and improve medication safety and patient care.

Keywords: Pill-prescription matching · Text-image matching · GNN · GCN · Contrastive learning

1 Introduction

A WHO report states that drug abuse, rather than illness, accounts for one-third of all deaths [1]. Additionally, roughly 6,000–8,000 persons per year pass

© The Author(s), under exclusive license to Springer Nature Switzerland AG 2022
S. Khanna et al. (Eds.): PRICAI 2022, LNCS 13629, pp. 261–274, 2022.
https://doi.org/10.1007/978-3-031-20862-1_19

away due to drug errors, according to Yaniv et al. [19]. Medical errors could seriously damage the treatment effectiveness, cause unfavorable side effects, or even lead to death. WHO has picked the theme Medication Without Harm for World Patient Safety Day 2022 to highlight the significance of taking medication properly. Drug abuse can be brought on by various factors, including using pills other than those prescribed. To this end, this study concentrates on the issue of matching the pill names in a prescription to the corresponding pills in an image, thereby detecting missing or mistaken pills. We call this the *pill-prescription matching* problem. The problem's context can be described as follows. The user has a prescription image and an image capturing pills that will be taken. We want to match each pill in the pill image with the corresponding name in the prescription.

The pill-prescription matching task is analogous to the well-known text-image matching task. In the text-image matching task, an input consists of an image containing numerous objects and a short paragraph of sentences. The text-image matching task aims to identify the keywords in the sentences and match them with the related objects in the image. The key issue in text-image matching is measuring the visual-semantic similarity between a text and an image. Frome et al. [5] proposed a feature embedding framework that uses Skip-Gram and Convolutional Neural Network (CNN) to extract cross-modal feature representations. Then, the ranking loss is applied so that the distance between mismatched text-image pairs is greater than that between matched pairs. Kiros et al. [12] utilized a similar approach that leverages the Long Short-Term Memory (LSTM) [10] to generate text representations. With the recent success of pre-training and self-supervised learning, text-image matching has profited from the rich visual and linguistic representation of pre-trained models on large-scale datasets for downstream tasks. Radford et al. [14] proposed a Contrastive Language-Image Pre-Training (CLIP) model to learn visual concepts under language supervision. It is trained using 400 million (text, image) pairs collected from the Web. Gao et al. [6] examined the text-image matching in cross-modal retrieval of the fashion industry. They used the pre-trained Bidirectional Encoder Representations from Transformers (BERT) [3] as the backbone network to learn high-level representations of texts and images.

However, the pill-prescription matching task differs from the general text-image matching task in the following aspects. First, unlike the common text-image matching task, pill names are typically lengthy phrases (instead of words like in the general text-image matching problem). Notably, the pill's name has almost no semantic meaning. Additionally, the same pill name might be expressed in a variety of ways (depending on the doctors). Moreover, many text boxes in the prescription (e.g., quantities, diagnostic, etc.) do not relate to the pill name. Therefore, the conventional text-image matching approaches are inadequate for the pill-prescription matching issue. To this end, we propose a novel approach for dealing with the pill-prescription matching problem. Our main idea is to leverage a Graph Neural Network (GNN) for capturing the spatial relationship of text boxes in the prescription, thereby highlighting text boxes that con-

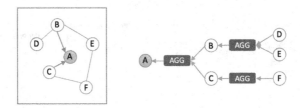

Fig. 1. The left side represents a graph, whereas the right side depicts the aggregation process of GraphSAGE (with two convolution layers) to generate the embedding vector for vertex A.

tain pill names. Moreover, we propose a cross-modal matching mechanism that employs a contrastive loss to encourage the distance between the mismatched pill image and pill name pairs while minimizing that of the matched pairs.

In summary, this work makes the following contributions:

1. We propose PIMA, a novel deep learning framework based on GNN and contrastive learning for the pill-prescription matching problem. To the best of our knowledge, we are the first to define and address this challenging task on a real-world dataset. The method is applicable for real-world scenarios in clinical practice to improve medication safety.
2. We conduct comprehensive experiments to demonstrate the effectiveness of the proposed approach on a real-world pill-prescription dataset. The proposed PIMA outperforms baseline methods with significant improvements in performance.

The remainder of the paper is organized as follows. We briefly introduce GraphSAGE, a GNN used in our proposed model in Sect. 2. The details of our proposed method are described in Sect. 3. We perform experiment to evaluate the proposal in Sect. 4 and conclude the paper in Sect. 5.

2 Preliminaries

This section introduces *Graph SAmple and aggreGatE* (GraphSAGE), which is one of the most well-known Graph Neural Network (GNN) developed by Hamilton et al. [7]. Similar to the convolution operation in Convolutional Neural Network (CNN), in the GraphSAGE, information relating to the local neighborhood of a node is collected and used to compute the node embeddings. For each node, the algorithm iteratively aggregates information from its neighbors. At each iteration, the neighborhood of the node is initially sampled, and the information from the sampled nodes is aggregated into a single vector. Specifically, at the k-th layer, the aggregated information $h_{N(v)}^k$ at a node v, based on the sampled neighborhood $N(v)$, can be expressed as:

$$h_{N(v)}^k = \mathrm{AGG}_k\left(\left\{h_u^{k-1}, \forall u \in N(v)\right\}\right),$$

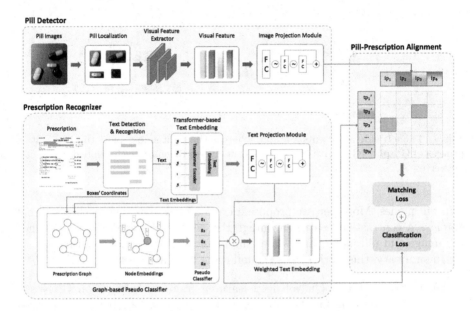

Fig. 2. Overview of PIMA, which consists of three modules: Pill Detector, Prescription Recognizer, and Pill-Prescription Alignment. The Pill Detector is responsible for extracting visual features from pill images. The Prescription Recognizer is responsible for embedding each text box on the prescription and highlighting those with pill names. Finally, the textual and visual data are fed into Pill-Prescription Alignment to produce a matching result.

where h_u^{k-1} is the embedding of node u in the previous layer. The aggregated embeddings of the sampled neighborhood $h_{N(v)}^k$ then is concatenated with the node's embedding at the previous layer h_v^{k-1} to form its embedding at the current layer as follows.

$$h_v^k = \sigma \left(W^k \cdot \text{CONCAT} \left(h_v^{k-1}, h_{N(v)}^k \right) \right),$$

where W^k is a trainable weight matrix and σ is a non-linear activation function. Figure 1 illustrates the aggregation process of GraphSAGE. GraphSAGE offers several aggregation methods, including mean, pooling, or neural networks (e.g. Long Short-Term Memory (LSTM) [10]).

3   Proposed Method

This section describes our proposed method named PIMA for the **PI**ll-prescription **MA**tching problem. We start by providing an overview of our solution in Sect. 3.1. We then describe the Pill Detector and Prescription Recognizer modules in Sects. 3.2 and 3.3, respectively. Finally, we explain the proposed loss function in Sect. 3.4.

3.1 Overview

Figure 2 illustrates the overview of our proposed model, which consists of three modules. The first module, named **Pill Detector**, uses Convolutional Neural Network (CNN) to create representations of pills. The second module, named **Prescription Recognizer**, is responsible for extracting the textual information. Specifically, this module utilizes a transformer model to create embedding of the text boxes. Moreover, we leverage a Graph Neural Network (GNN) to capture spatial information among the text boxes, thereby highlighting boxes representing the pill names. Finally, the textual and visual features are projected into a shared space before being fed into a Pill-Prescription Alignment module. In the **Pill-Prescription Alignment** module, we employ two loss functions. The first loss, a Binary Cross-entropy loss, is responsible for classifying the text boxes containing the pill name, while the second loss, a Contrastive loss, is responsible for matching the pill names with the associated pill images.

3.2 Pill Detector

The Pill Detector consists of two main components: Pill Localization and Feature Extraction. Firstly, an object detection model is applied to determine the location of every pill. Assuming that there are M pills cropped from an image, let's denote them as $\{p_1, ..., p_M\}$. We then leverage a CNN to extract visual features of the pills and obtain M feature vectors $\{\mathbf{ie}_1, ..., \mathbf{ie}_M\}$. These feature vectors are then projected onto the same hyper-plane with their counterpart in the prescription via an Image projection module. Consequently, we come up with the final representation of the pills as $\mathbf{IP} = [\mathbf{ip}_1, ..., \mathbf{ip}_M]$.

3.3 Prescription Recognizer

The Prescription Recognizer comprises three sub-modules: Text Recognition, Text Embedding, and Pseudo-Classification. Initially, the text recognition model is utilized to identify and localize each text box in the prescription. Suppose the prescription contains N text boxes, denoted as $\{s_1, ..., s_N\}$, then they are put through a Transformer-based text embedding module [18] to produce embedding vectors of the text boxes. On the one hand, these embedding vectors, along with the coordinates of the text boxes, are utilized to construct a graph representing the spatial relationship between the text boxes. This graph is used as the pseudo-classifier's input to highlight the boxes containing the pill names. On the other hand, these embedding vectors capture contextual information of the text boxes, which is used for matching with pill images.

Transformer-Based Text Embedding. Given a text box $s_i = [w_1^{(i)}, ..., w_{l_i}^{(i)}]$, where $w_t^{(i)}$ $(t = 1, ..., l_i)$ represents the token embedding of the t-th word of s_i, the text embedding of s_i, denoted by $\mathbf{te}_i$, is obtained by feeding $[w_1^{(i)}, ..., w_{l_i}^{(i)}]$ into a Transformer encoder. These text embeddings are then projected to the same hyper-plane as their counterparts in the pill images with the aid of a text projection module. Consequently, we get the final representations of the N text boxes as $\mathbf{TP} = [\mathbf{tp}_1, \cdots, \mathbf{tp}_N]$.

Graph-Based Pseudo Classifier. We noticed that a prescription contains numerous text boxes without pill names. Therefore, to improve the pill-prescription matching accuracy, a preprocessing step is required to highlight the boxes that are likely to contain pill names. For this, we create a binary classifier based on a GNN. Specifically, we first construct a graph G representing the spatial relationship between the text boxes, i.e., $G = \{V, E\}$, where $V = \{v_1, ..., v_N\}$, with v_i the i-th text box. The attribute of v_i is the text embedding $\mathbf{te}_i$. Two vertices, v_i and v_j, are connected if either v_i or v_j is the box with the shortest horizontal (or vertical) distance to the other. Any network can be used for this purpose, and investigating GNN is out of the scope of this paper. In this work, we utilize one of the most prominent GNN, namely GraphSAGE [7], to convert from graph space to vector space. Consequently, for every vertex v_i, we obtain a graph embedding vector h_i, which represents the relationship between v_i and its K-hop neighbors. Finally, these graph embedding vectors will then be input to a sigmoid layer to produce the classification results. In particular, the output of the pseudo-classifier is a vector $g = \langle g_1, ...g_N \rangle$, where g_i represents the likelihood that the i-th textbox has the pill name. This pseudo-classifier will be trained via classification loss (see Sect. 3.4).

Finally, the pseudo classification result is multiplied with the text embedding to obtain the weighted version, $\mathbf{TP}' = [g_1 \times \mathbf{tp}_1, ..., g_N \times \mathbf{tp}_N]$. It is worth noting that as g_i quantifies the likelihood that the i-th text box includes the pill name, the embedding vectors of the boxes having the pill name will be highlighted in the $\mathbf{TP}'$, while the remainder will be grayed out.

3.4   Pill-Prescription Alignment

This module receives visual representations of pill images from the Pill Detector and textual representations of text boxes from the Prescription Recognizer. It matches pill names and pill images to generate the final result. For this, we design an objective function consisting of two losses: classification loss and matching loss.

Classification Loss. We adopt Binary cross-entropy loss to identify whether or not a text box contains a pill name. We observe that the number of pill name boxes is significantly smaller than that of boxes without pill names. For this reason, we employ the following weighted cross-entropy loss to mitigate the bias.

$$\mathcal{L}_{\text{Classification}} = -\frac{1}{N} \sum_{i=1}^{N} w_i \left[y_i \log(g_i) + (1 - y_i) \log(1 - g_i) \right],$$

where y_i and g_i indicate the ground-truth label and the predicted result concerning a text box s_i, respectively; w_i represents the ratio of boxes with the label of $1 - y_i$. To be more specific, let n_1 be the number of text boxes containing a pill name, and N be the total number of the text boxes, then we have

$$w_i = \begin{cases} 1 - \frac{n_1}{N}, & \text{if the text box} s_i \text{contains a pill name,} \\ \frac{n_1}{N}, & \text{otherwise.} \end{cases}$$

Matching Loss. This loss aims to model the cross-modal similarity of pill name boxes and pill images' representations. The principle is to encourage the distance between the representations of mismatched pill names and pill image pairs while minimizing the gap between that of matched pairs. Specifically, let $\mathbf{ip}_i$ and $\mathbf{tp}_j$ be the representations of a pill image p_i and a text box s_j, respectively, then their similarity is defined by the cosine similarity as follows.

$$S(\mathbf{ip}_i, \mathbf{tp}_j) = \frac{\mathbf{ip}_i \cdot \mathbf{tp}_j}{\max(\|\mathbf{ip}_i\|_2 \cdot \|\mathbf{tp}_j\|_2, \epsilon)},$$

where ϵ is a small value which is responsible for avoiding division by zero. The matching loss is then defined as the sum of dis-similarities over all the matched pairs and similarities over all the mismatched pairs as follows.

$$\mathcal{L}_{\text{Matching}} = \frac{1}{M} \sum_{i=1}^{M} \left[\frac{1}{2} \sum_{j \notin \mathbb{P}_i} S(\mathbf{ip}_i, \mathbf{tp}_j)^2 + \frac{1}{2} \sum_{k \in \mathbb{P}_i} \max\left(0, m - S\left(\mathbf{ip}_i, \mathbf{tp}_k\right)\right)^2 \right],$$

where $\mathbb{P}_i$ is the set of all text boxes containing the pill name corresponding to the pill p_i, and m is a positive margin specifying the radius surrounding $S\left(\mathbf{ip}_i, \mathbf{tp}_k\right)$. In our method, we set m to 1 as the similarity values range from -1 to 1.

The total loss then is defined by the sum of the classification loss and the matching loss as follows.

$$\mathcal{L}_{\text{Total}} = \mathcal{L}_{\text{Matching}} + \lambda \mathcal{L}_{\text{Classification}}, \tag{1}$$

where λ is a hyper parameter that balances these two losses.

4   Experiments

In this section, we conduct comprehensive experiments to evaluate the proposed approach, PIMA. We carefully compare it to the state-of-the-art (SOTA) text-image matching methods under the same experimental settings. Moreover, we perform extensive ablation studies to provide a deeper understanding of some key properties of PIMA.

4.1   Dataset and Experimental Setup

To the best of our knowledge, there is currently no dataset publicly available for the pill-prescription matching task. This motivates us to build an open large-scale dataset containing pill images and the corresponding prescriptions[1]. In

---

[1] The dataset can be downloaded from our project Web-page at https://vaipe.org/# resource.

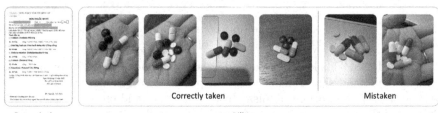

Prescription   Pill Images

Fig. 3. Representative examples from the pill image dataset. It was collected in real-world scenarios, where samples are taken in unconstrained environments.

Table 1. Details of the data partition.

Experimental scenario	Prescription images		Pill images	
	Train (%)	Test (%)	Train (%)	Test (%)
Scenario 1-1	69.55	30.45	70.58	29.42
Scenario 1-2	38.89	61.11	45.04	54.96
Scenario 1-3	3.86	96.14	6.12	93.88
Scenario 2-1, 2-2	69.55	30.45	72.40	27.60

particular, we collected $1,527$ prescriptions from anonymous patients in major hospitals between 2021 and 2022. After carefully checking data against the privacy concern, we performed the annotation process in which each pill image was assigned and annotated by a human annotator. We then separated the medication intakes for each prescription into morning, noon, and evening parts. For each pill intake, we took about 5 pictures of the pills. Consequently, we collected $6,366$ pictures of pills, and the unique number of pills was 107. Figure 3 shows several representative examples from our pill dataset. For algorithm development and evaluation, we divided the prescriptions and the corresponding pills into two subsets for training and testing. Details are described in Table 1.

Experimental Scenarios. We evaluate the performance of the proposed PIMA in two distinct circumstances. In the first scenario, we consider settings where medications are taken exactly as prescribed. We assess the precision with which our algorithm could assist users in matching the pills they have taken with their prescription names. The second scenario refers to circumstances in which the pills consumed do not correspond to the prescription. In such a scenario, we examine the accuracy with which our algorithm can identify pills that have been improperly used. Specifically, the percentage of pills incorrectly taken in the second scenario is set to 50%. To better investigate the performance of the proposed approach on different data distributions, we divide the two scenarios into sub-scenarios 1-1, 1-2, 1-3, 2-1, and 2-2, which are described in detail in the following.

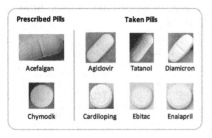
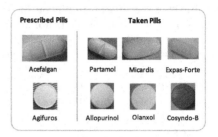

(a) Illustration for Scenario 2-1.   (b) Illustration for Scenario 2-2.

Fig. 4. Visualization of several changes in experimental Scenarios 2-1 and 2-2.

Scenario 1:

- Scenario 1-1. To split the prescription dataset where each prescription has multiple pill names, we use the stratified sampling method proposed by Sechidis et al. [17] into two datasets for training and testing.
- Scenario 1-2. The prescription data is split so that the training set only has prescriptions that do not overlap, and the test set has all the remaining data.
- Scenario 1-3. The prescription data is split so that a pill name only appears once in the training set, and the test set has all the remaining data.

Scenario 2: The training dataset is identical to the train set in Scenario 1-1; however, the test set in Scenario 2-1 contains 50% of random pill images that are very similar to the pills in the prescription (in terms of both color and shape); and the test set in Scenario 2-2 contains 50% of random pill images that have the same shape but a different color than the pills in the prescription. Figure 4 illustrates some examples.

Evaluation Metrics. To evaluate the effectiveness of PIMA, we report the final test accuracy using *F1-score* as the main metric, which is widely used in recognition tasks.

Training Details. In our implementation, the projection modules consist of two fully connected layers with the Gaussian Error Linear Units (GELU) activation [9]. The output dimension is set to 256. We use AdamW [13] as the optimizer and set the initial learning rate to 0.001. The factor λ (Eq. 1) is set as 1 for simplicity. We train the model with the batch size of 4 and the input image size of 224×224 pixels. The random rotation of $10°$ and horizontal flip are used as data augmentation techniques. All implementations are performed using the PyTorch framework, and the training process is conducted on a machine with an NVIDIA GeForce RTX 3080 GPU.

4.2   Experimental Results

We provide in this section our experimental results and the comparison between our approach and baseline methods. Because there is no other end-to-end method

Table 2. Experimental results on the test set of our pill image dataset with different CNN models. The best results are highlighted in **bold**.

CNN model	Number of parameters	Pretrained		Non-pretrained	
		Train (%)	Test (%)	Train (%)	Test (%)
Resnet-18 [8]	11.7M	99.87	86.06	67.39	67.27
Resnet-34 [8]	21.8M	96.28	82.27	68.01	66.68
Resnet-50 [8]	25.6M	86.08	77.04	68.39	67.27
ViT-Small/16 [4]	22.1M	99.44	66.47	61.07	56.59
MobileNet-V2 [16]	3.5M	99.39	89.48	75.96	70.63
MobileNet-V3-small [11]	2.5M	99.98	**90.18**	74.78	**71.65**
MobileNet-V3-large [11]	5.5M	99.93	90.01	70.31	70.30

Table 3. Experimental results on our pill dataset for the text-image matching task using CLIP model with different BERT pretrained models. Here, CNN model is `MobileNet-V3-small`. Best results are highlighted in **bold**.

BERT Model	Task	CNN Non-pretrained	
		Train (%)	Test (%)
BERT-base-uncased [3]	Fill-Mask	97.57	76.16
BERT-base-uncased-multilingual [3]		97.78	75.95
MiniLM-L12-v2 [15]	Sentence Similarity	98.14	76.52
MiniLM-L12-v2-multilingual [15]		97.76	**79.79**

like ours, the baselines are performed independently in a two-step process. A deep learning-based pill detector is firstly trained to recognize pills from images. The predicted pills are then compared with the correctly identified pill name in the prescription.

Baseline Performance. In this experiment, we train a set of SOTA Convolutional Neural Network (CNN) architectures (see Table 2) on our pill image dataset, in which the information from the prescription is not taken into account. Our experiments follow the Scenario 1-1 setting. During the training process, each learning model is initialized with pre-trained weights on the ImageNet dataset [2]. We also investigate the learning performance of CNN models on the pill image dataset when training from scratch. We obtain the highest performance with `Mobilenet-V3-small` model. It reports an F1-score of 90.18% when using ImageNet-trained deep features and an F1-score of 71.65% when trained from scratch, respectively.

CLIP Model. We use the SOTA model in text-image matching called Contrastive Language-Image Pre-training (CLIP) [14] as the second baseline model in this research. It has been proposed to learn visual concepts with language supervision. We train CLIP model on the pill image dataset with different pre-trained language models (e.g., BERT [3]), while the vision model is the `MobileNet-V3-small`, which has the best results on baseline classification. The

Table 4. Experiment results concerning Scenario 1 on our pill image dataset. PIMA significantly outperforms other SOTA methods. Best results are highlighted in **bold**.

Model	F1-score (%)		
	Scenario 1-1	Scenario 1-2	Scenario 1-3
Baseline	71.65	66.07	42.82
CLIP	79.79	72.63	48.17
PIMA w/o Graph	95.59	95.17	76.83
PIMA (our proposal)	**98.88**	**98.41**	**89.77**

Table 5. Matching accuracy concerning Scenario 2.

Model	Scenario 2-1			Scenario 2-2		
	F1(Cor) (%)	F1(Mis) (%)	F1(Avg) (%)	F1(Cor) (%)	F1(Mis) (%)	F1(Avg) (%)
CLIP	77.47	31.42	54.46	82.81	54.84	68.83
PIMA w/o Graph	96.11	30.06	63.09	97.24	55.45	76.35
PIMA (our proposal)	**96.85**	**62.10**	**79.48**	**97.99**	**94.35**	**96.17**

results for Scenario 1–1 are shown in Table 3. The results indicate that the pre-trained language models in different tasks (e.g., Fill-Mask, Sentence Similarity) are almost similar. The best test set result for the CNN model trained from scratch is 79.79%.

Based on the experimental results reported in Tables 2 and 3, we chose to use the trained from scratch CNN model `MobileNet-V3-small` and the pre-trained language model `MiniLM-L12-v2-multilingual` for our following experiments and comparisons.

Comparison with Baseline Approaches Scenario 1. Table 4 summarizes the results of the proposal PIMA and the baseline models concerning Scenarios 1-1, 1-2, and 1-3. For all scenarios, PIMA achieves the highest F1-score of 98.88%, 98.41%, and 89.77%, respectively. Even without using a GNN, PIMA w/o Graph still outperforms the others. Specifically, it outperforms the baseline classification by 23.94%, 29.10%, and 34.01%, respectively. In comparison with CLIP, PIMA improves the F1-scores by 19.09%, 25.78% and 41, 60% concerning Scenarios 1-1, 1-2, and 1-3, respectively. We observe that the proposed model achieves a high level of performance even when the number of pill images and prescription samples in Scenarios 1-2 and 1-3 are very limited.

Scenario 2. In this experiment, we set the threshold to consider an image and text pair matching correctly as α (with $\alpha = 0.8$ for all experimental scenarios). To ease the presentation, we denote F1(Cor) as the F1-score for matching pills that correctly taken with theirs corresponding names in the prescription. Besides, we use F1(Mis) to indicate the F1-score for detecting pills that are not in the prescription, and F1(Avg) to represent the mean of F1(Cor) and F1(Mis). The results of Scenarios 2-1 and 2-2 are shown in Table 5. As shown, PIMA achieves the highest average accuracy in both scenarios, 79.48% and 96.17%, respectively. Specifically, PIMA's F1(Cor) is higher than that of CLIP by 19.38% and 15.18%, respectively. In addition, PIMA improves the accuracy of detecting the use of wrong pills by 30.68% in Scenario 2-1 and 39.51% in Scenario 2-2 compared to PIMA. In comparison between F1(Cor) in the two scenarios, it can be seen that F1(Cor) in Scenario 2-1 is lower than that in Scenario 2-2 because the mistaken pills in Scenario 2-1 is much more similar to the prescribed pills. Finally, it can be observed that PIMA w/o Graph achieves a higher F1(Cor) than CLIP. However, the F1(Mis) of PIMA w/o Graph is similar to that of CLIP's.

4.3   Discussion

According to the experimental results, PIMA outperforms all other approaches in terms of both accuracy and convergence speed. As stated in the previous section, PIMA enhanced the F1 score in terms of accuracy from 19.05% to 46.95% compared to comparison benchmarks. These results are the consequence of contrastive learning's impacts. In fact, the baseline model separates pill and text box recognition into two distinct phases. The error in pill-prescription matching is then accumulated by the sum of the errors generated by the two phases. For the CLIP model, the matching loss only considers matched pairs. Specifically, it only intends to minimize the distance between pill images and pill names. This technique creates a paradox in the circumstance of pills with extremely similar appearances but significantly different names. Specifically, in such a case, the two similar visual representations are pulled back to nearly two completely different textual representations. In contrast to baseline and CLIP, PIMA employs contrastive loss, which takes into account both matched and mismatched pairs of pill names and images; additionally, we use weights while computing contrastive loss to balance the contribution of matched and mismatched pairs. This weighted contrastive loss increases the model's generalizability and avoids it from being skewed toward the mismatched cases. Thus, PIMA achieves higher precision.

Regarding convergence speed, Fig. 5a demonstrates that after only 50 epochs, PIMA has converged to an accuracy of about 97% for matching correctly taken pills. In contrast, CLIP only achieves an accuracy of approximately 80%. Although PIMA w/o Graph achieves significantly better performance than CLIP, its accuracy after 10 epochs is only about 88%, whereas that of PIMA is about 95%. Figure 5b depicts the convergence rate for the detection of mistaken pills. It is apparent that PIMA outperforms the other two significantly. In particular, after 50 epochs, PIMA achieves an accuracy of approximately 90%, whereas CLIP and PIMA w/o Graph only reach 50%. This can be explained by the GNN-based pseudo classifier's contribution. By having this classifier highlight text boxes containing medicine names, we have narrowed the search space for the matching issue, allowing PIMA to converge significantly more quickly than comparison benchmarks.

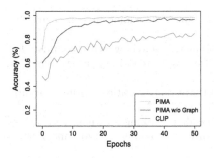

(a) Accuracy for matching correctly taken pills

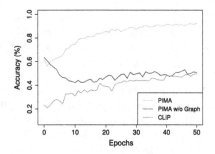

(b) Accuracy for detecting mistaken pills

Fig. 5. Convergence speed on Scenario 2-2.

5 Conclusion

We presented PIMA, a novel method to solve the pill-prescription matching task. The key idea behind the PIMA learning framework is the use of a Graph Neural Network (GNN) architecture and contrastive learning to jointly learn text and image representations in order to enhance pill-prescription matching performance. Our extensive experiments on a real-world pill dataset, including pill and prescription images, show that the proposed approach significantly outperforms baseline approaches, enhancing the matching F1-score from 19.05% to 46.95%. Additionally, we also demonstrated that the proposed PIMA is able to achieve a high level of performance while requiring less training costs compared to other benchmarks. We release our code at https://github.com/AIoT-Lab-BKAI/PIMA.

Acknowledgement. This work was funded by Vingroup Joint Stock Company (Vingroup JSC), Vingroup, and supported by Vingroup Innovation Foundation (VINIF) under project code VINIF.2021.DA00128.

References

1. Chang, W.J., Chen, L.B., Hsu, C.H., Lin, C.P., Yang, T.C.: A deep learning-based intelligent medicine recognition system for chronic patients. IEEE Access **7**, 44441–44458 (2019)
2. Deng, J., Dong, W., Socher, R., Li, L.J., Li, K., Fei-Fei, L.: ImageNet: a large-scale hierarchical image database. In: Proceedings of the 2009 IEEE Conference on Computer Vision and Pattern Recognition, pp. 248–255 (2009)
3. Devlin, J., Chang, M.W., Lee, K., Toutanova, K.: BERT: pre-training of deep bidirectional transformers for language understanding. Computation Research Repository arXiv Preprint, arXiv:1810.04805 (2018)
4. Dosovitskiy, A., et al.: An image is worth 16x16 words: transformers for image recognition at scale. Computation Research Repository arXiv Preprint, arXiv:2010.11929 (2020

5. Frome, A., et al.: DeViSE: a deep visual-semantic embedding model. Neural Inf. Process. Syst. **26**, 2121–2129 (2013)
6. Gao, D., et al.: FashionBERT: text and image matching with adaptive loss for cross-modal retrieval. Computation Research Repository arXiv Preprint, arXiv:2005.09801 (2020)
7. Hamilton, W., Ying, Z., Leskovec, J.: Inductive representation learning on large graphs. Neural Inf. Process. Syst. **30**, 1025–1035 (2017)
8. He, K., Zhang, X., Ren, S., Sun, J.: Deep residual learning for image recognition. In: Proceedings of the 2016 IEEE Conference on Computer Vision and Pattern Recognition, pp. 770–778 (2016)
9. Hendrycks, D., Gimpel, K.: Gaussian error linear units (GELUs). Computation Research Repository arXiv Preprint, arXiv:1606.08415 (2016)
10. Hochreiter, S., Schmidhuber, J.: Long short-term memory. Neural Comput. **9**, 1735–1780 (1997)
11. Howard, A., et al.: Searching for MobileNetV3. Computation Research Repository arXiv Preprint, arXiv:1905.02244 (2019)
12. Kiros, R., Salakhutdinov, R., Zemel, R.: Unifying visual-semantic embeddings with multimodal neural language models. Computation Research Repository arXiv Preprint, arXiv:1411.2539 (2014)
13. Loshchilov, I., Hutter, F.: Decoupled weight decay regularization. Computation Research Repository arXiv Preprint, arXiv:1411.2539 (2019)
14. Radford, A., et al.: Learning transferable visual models from natural language supervision **139**, 8748–8763 (2021)
15. Reimers, N., Gurevych, I.: Sentence-BERT: sentence embeddings using Siamese BERT-networks. In: Proceedings of the 2019 Conference on Empirical Methods in Natural Language Processing, pp. 3973–3983 (2019)
16. Sandler, M., Howard, A., Zhu, M., Zhmoginov, A., Chen, L.C.: MobileNetV2: inverted residuals and linear bottlenecks. In: Proceedings of the 2018 IEEE Conference on Computer Vision and Pattern Recognition, pp. 4510–4520 (2018)
17. Sechidis, K., Tsoumakas, G., Vlahavas, I.: On the stratification of multi-label data. In: Proceedings of the 2011 European Conference on Machine Learning and Knowledge Discovery in Databases, vol. 3, pp. 145–158 (2011)
18. Vaswani, A., et al.: Attention is all you need. In: 30th Proceedings of the Conference on Advances in Neural Information Processing Systems (2017)
19. Yaniv, Z., et al.: The national library of medicine pill image recognition challenge: an initial report. In: Proceedings of the 2016 IEEE Applied Imagery Pattern Recognition Workshop (2016)

A Robust Lightweight Deepfake Detection Network Using Transformers

Yaning Zhang[1], Tianyi Wang[2], Minglei Shu[1], and Yinglong Wang[1]($\boxtimes$)

[1] Shandong Artificial Intelligence Institute, Qilu University of Technology (Shandong Academy of Sciences), Jinan, China
shuml@sdas.org, wangylscsc@126.com

[2] Department of Computer Science, The University of Hong Kong, Hong Kong, China
tywang@cs.hku.hk

Abstract. Deepfake detection attracts widespread attention in the computer vision field. Existing efforts achieve outstanding progress, but there are still significant unresolved issues. Coarse-grained local and global features are insufficient to capture subtle forgery traces from various inputs. Moreover, the detection efficiency is not powerful enough in practical applications. In this paper, we propose a robust and efficient transformer-based deepfake detection (TransDFD) network, which learns more discriminative and general manipulation patterns in an end-to-end manner. Specifically, a robust transformer module is designed to study fine-grained local and global features based on intra-patch locally-enhanced relations as well as inter-patch locally-enhanced global relationships in face images. A novel plug-and-play spatial attention scaling (SAS) module is proposed to emphasize salient features while suppressing less important representations, which can be integrated into any transformer-based models without increasing computational complexity. Extensive experiments on several public benchmarks demonstrate that the proposed TransDFD model outperforms the state-of-the-art in terms of robustness and computational efficiency.

Keywords: Deepfake detection · Spatial attention scaling · Transformer

1 Introduction

The threat of face manipulated videos has raised widespread attention, especially after the advent of the deepfake technique that adopts deep learning tools. Deepfake can replace the face in the target video with the face in the source video using deep learning-based technologies such as autoencoder [14] and generative adversarial network (GAN) [8]. With these approaches, face generated videos are exceedingly simple to be generated on the condition that one can access a large amount of data spread widely on the Internet, which brings negative impacts on

---

Y. Zhang and T. Wang—Contributed equally to this work.

© The Author(s), under exclusive license to Springer Nature Switzerland AG 2022
S. Khanna et al. (Eds.): PRICAI 2022, LNCS 13629, pp. 275–288, 2022.
https://doi.org/10.1007/978-3-031-20862-1_20

individuals, organizations, and governments while greatly threatening the social stability [17]. Furthermore, with the sophistication and development of synthesis techniques, deepfake videos have become more realistic and it is challenging for human eyes to discern authenticity. The above challenges have driven the development of deepfake detection using deep neural networks (DNNs) [4,9,18,30]. Most of the existing efforts in common exploit the powerful data fitting capabilities of neural networks to mine discriminative features for deepfake detection. Deep learning-based detection approaches usually regard deepfake detection as a binary classification problem and employ convolutional neural networks (CNN) to analyze local features. However, the learned representations using CNN are not general enough since CNN seldomly focuses on global information. Furthermore, it is challenging to discern authenticity based on small local regions only. Recent work recognizes this problem and attempts to utilize a transformer-based model [28] to extract global emdeddings for capturing long-range manipulation traces. However, it usually analyze global characteristics in a coarse-grained manner, which may cause some image patches with weak artifacts to be rarely noticed due to face pose transitions. Therefore, coarse-grained global feature learning often serves as a suboptimal solution. In addition, the detection efficiency of the model is increasingly important in practical applications. Recent work has made significant advancements in deepfake detection performance, while state-of-the-art deepfake detectors also become gradually more expensive. For example, the advanced multi-attention (MAT) detector [29] requires 417.63M parameters and 224.38G floating-point operations per second (FLOPs) (20x more than Xception [21]) to realize state-of-the-art performance. Many face forgery detection models depend on on-device computation. Computational overhead is one of the main factors limiting the deployment of current networks in practical applications due to the inadequate computing power, large memory footprint, and severe battery consumption of the device. Based on these real-world resource restrictions, the model efficiency becomes increasingly important for face forgery detection. However, few approaches consider the computational complexity such as the number of parameters and FLOPs. Although some studies utilize the lightweight model Xception [3,16] to obtain remarkable results, their ability to study general representations is limited due to the coarse-grained local feature learning. As a result, these methods are insufficient to capture weak manipulated patterns owing to the diversity of forgery techniques.

Based on the discussion above, our method mainly solves the following two problems: (1) how to study more discriminative and general features for deepfake detection; (2) how to achieve state-of-the-art detection performance as efficiently as possible. In order to tackle these limitations, we propose a robust lightweight transformer-based deepfake detection (TransDFD) model. In detail, our model consists of two key components: the robust transformer module and the spatial attention scaling (SAS) technique. Robust transformer restricts locally-enhanced multi-head self-attention (LMSA) within each patch and boosts information flow across image patches by the spatial shuffle, thus learning fine-grained local and global representations. SAS flexibly refines spatial features to emphasize more significant manipulated artifacts, and vice versa. The main contributions of this work are summarized as follows:

- We propose a robust and lightweight TransDFD network for deepfake detection, which captures discriminative and comprehensive forgery traces with much fewer parameters and computational costs.
- The robust transformer is presented to learn fine-grained local and global features via focusing on intra-patch locally-enhanced relations and inter-patch locally-enhanced global relationships in face images.
- We design an innovative plug-and-play SAS technique to suppress less important representations while emphasizing more critical features, via a learnable diagonal matrix, which can be widely applied to boost the representation ability of transformers.
- Extensive experiments on several challenging datasets demonstrate the efficiency and robustness of our proposed model and feature visualizations show the generalizability and interpretability of our method.

2 Related Work

Most existing deepfake detection models utilize CNNs or attention mechanisms to capture local discriminative features. Rossler *et al.* [21] used the lightweight Xception, a standard CNN pre-trained on ImageNet, and transferred to the deepfake detection task, to extract local features. The TwoStream framework [18] applies two streams of Xception backbones which analyze the high-frequency feature and RGB content, respectively, for generalized face forgery detection. The representative forgery mining (RFM) [27], an attention-based data augmentation framework, exploits the Xception backbone to guide the detector to refine its attention for capturing local discriminative patterns. The multi-attentional (MAT) architecture [29] establishes a multi-attentional module to combine the low-level textural features and high-level semantic features. Kumar *et al.* [15] adopted multi-streamed CNNs to learn fine-grained local features, considering intra-patch local relations and inter-patch partial relationships within the face image. However, these models only extract local discriminative features and hardly consider the global relations among image patches. To address this problem, a convolutional vision transformer (CViT) framework [28] is proposed to integrate CNN and vision transformer (ViT) [6] for deepfake detection. Specifically, the CNN extracts local features while the ViT analyzes them to capture the inter-patch global dependencies at a coarse-grained level. We noted that, by contrast, our approach is capable of learning fine-grained local and global representations with fewer parameters and computational costs.

3 Approach

3.1 Network Architecture

The framework of our proposed TransDFD is illustrated in Fig. 1. TransDFD is composed of local feature extraction (LFE), robust transformer, and SAS.

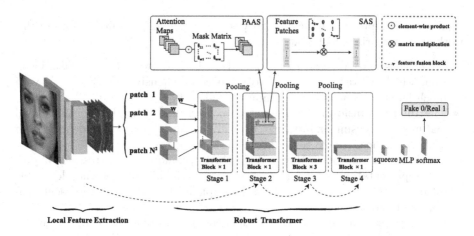

Fig. 1. The overall framework of TransDFD.

LFE adaptively filters the redundant information of a face image to obtain the refined feature map. Robust transformer (Sect. 3.3) utilizes transformer blocks to divide them into N^2 square patches with size $w \times w$ to encode feature vectors from a patch, thereby capturing fine-grained local and global representations. Meanwhile, the robust transformer employs the feature fusion block to analyze the refined feature map for obtaining local embeddings and supplementing them into fine-grained global representations. After that, SAS (Sect. 3.4) further refines elaborate embeddings using a learnable diagonal matrix. Finally, we squeeze the output of models and flatten them into feature vectors. The multiple layer perceptron (MLP) and softmax generate final detection results.

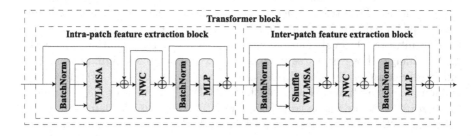

Fig. 2. The structure of the transformer block.

3.2   Local Feature Extraction

In order to filter redundant information irrelevant to the detection task in face images, LFE is designed to obtain fine feature maps in a simple and effective manner. In detail, the LFE module consists of the first two sequence blocks of VGG [24]. To save parameters and improve computation efficiency, the output channels of each convolutional layer in the first and second blocks in VGG are adjusted to 32 and 64, respectively. LFE extracts the delicate feature map $F_f \in \mathbb{R}^{C \times H \times W}$ as shown in Fig. 1 by inputting a facial image $F_i \in \mathbb{R}^{3 \times 224 \times 224}$, where H, W, C denotes the height, width, and channel of the feature map, respectively, and $H = W = 56$, $C = 64$. The F_f is then fed into the first transformer block and the first feature fusion block in the robust transformer module, simultaneously.

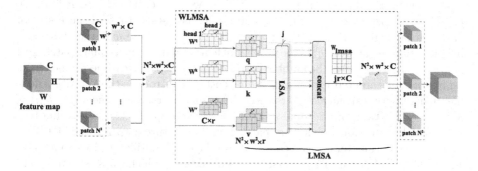

Fig. 3. The main workflow of the intra-patch feature extraction block.

3.3 Robust Transformer

Unlike the existing method [28] that utilizes the MSA mechanism to capture coarse-grained global features, inspired by the shuffle transformer [11] architecture with the novel window-based multi-head self-attention (WMSA) [10,16] mechanism and low costs, we propose a robust transformer module to focus on fine-grained local and global features learning. Figure 1 illustrates the architecture of the robust transformer module. Specifically, robust transformer contains four stages. Except for the first stage with L transformer blocks, each stage consists of a pooling layer, L transformer blocks, and a feature fusion block. Figure 2 shows the structure of the transformer block. Each transformer block includes two cascaded blocks: intra-patch feature extraction block and inter-patch feature extraction block. In particular, the former captures patch-level local enhancement relations by window-based locally-enhanced multi-head self-attention (WLMSA) module, obtaining fine-grained local representations, and the latter utilizes shuffle window-based locally-enhanced multi-head self-attention (Shuffle WLMSA) module to gain the fine-grained global embeddings via exploring patch-level locally-enhanced global relations. Through two cascaded blocks, transformer blocks analyze the local and global forgery patterns for each patch. To combine the advantages of CNNs in extracting local features and the benefits of transformer blocks in capturing long-range dependencies, the feature fusion block in each stage studies an input feature map through a convolutional layer with a kernel size of 2 and a stride of 2 to obtain downsampling and it is added element-wisely with the output of the last transformer block in this stage.

Transformer Block. Different from the traditional transformer block in ViT [6], we perform LMSA computation on each image patch in parallel, and the linear layers are replaced by the convolutional layers, which reduces the number of parameters and computational complexity. As Fig. 2 shows, the transformer block includes two cascaded blocks. The intra-patch feature extraction block aims to model patch-level locally-enhanced relations to obtain fine-grained local representations. The main workflow of the block is shown in Fig. 3. Without losing generality, given a feature map $F \in \mathbb{R}^{C \times H \times W}$, we first divide it into N^2 square patches with size $w \times w$, and each square patch is reshaped into a succession of flattened 2D feature patches to get $F_p \in \mathbb{R}^{N^2 \times w^2 \times C}$, where w is the width and height of square patches, w^2 is the number of feature patches in a square patch, and $N^2 = (H/w) \times (W/w)$ is the number of square patches. To study fine-grained local representations and reduce computational costs, we introduce the WLMSA module. In detail, we transform F_p into three different tensors, *i.e.*, a query $q = F_p W^q$, a key $k = F_p W^k$, and a value $v = F_p W^v$, where query, key, and value tensors are calculated for each square patch from the feature map F_p, and W^q, W^k, and W^v are parameters of the convolutional layer. We utilize LMSA to acquire $F_p' \in \mathbb{R}^{N^2 \times w^2 \times C}$ with fine-grained local embeddings, which implies that square patches are captured variously locally-enhanced relations between the respective internal characteristics in parallel. The LMSA is discussed in detail in the following section. Thereafter, we rearrange the square patches to their original spatial position to obtain F_s, *i.e.*, $F_p' \in \mathbb{R}^{N^2 \times w^2 \times C}$ is reshaped to $F_s \in \mathbb{R}^{C \times H \times W}$. Finally, we pass F_s into the neighbor-window connection (NWC) module and MLP module sequentially to obtain $V \in \mathbb{R}^{C \times H \times W}$. NWC consists of a convolutional layer with a kernel size equal to the image patch size to enhance connections among neighboring patches. The linear layer in the conventional MLP module [6] is adjusted to a convolutional layer with a kernel of 1×1 for economizing parameters. Intra-patch feature extraction block only analyzes patch-level local relationships without taking into account the global relations between image patches. To overcome the limitation, we present the inter-patch feature extraction block whose main workflow is similar to that shown in Fig. 3. In detail, we firstly split $V \in \mathbb{R}^{C \times H \times W}$ into w^2 square patches with size $N \times N$ to get $V_p \in \mathbb{R}^{w^2 \times N^2 \times C}$. To achieve spatial shuffle and inter-patch information communication, each new square patch with size $w \times w$ is composed of the feature patches at the same position in w^2 square patches with size of $N \times N$, carrying information for the overall patches with size of $N \times N$. That is to say, we rearrange $V_p \in \mathbb{R}^{w^2 \times N^2 \times C}$ to $V_f \in \mathbb{R}^{N^2 \times w^2 \times C}$. We introduce the Shuffle WLMSA module which has a similar pipeline to WLMSA and considers locally-enhanced global relations for each image patch in parallel to obtain $V_f' \in \mathbb{R}^{N^2 \times w^2 \times C}$ with fine-grained global features by inputting $V_f \in \mathbb{R}^{N^2 \times w^2 \times C}$. Afterward, we adjust the feature patches to the original positions for spatial alignment. *i.e.*, $V_f' \in \mathbb{R}^{N^2 \times w^2 \times C}$ is rearranged to $V_s \in \mathbb{R}^{w^2 \times N^2 \times C}$. Thereafter, we align image content spatially to obtain the feature map I. That is, $V_s \in \mathbb{R}^{w^2 \times N^2 \times C}$ is reshaped to $I \in \mathbb{R}^{C \times H \times W}$. Finally, we transfer I through the NWC and MLP modules to get $T \in \mathbb{R}^{C \times H \times W}$ which is then fed into the intra-patch feature extraction block in the subsequent transformer block.

LMSA. Inspired by [7], we find it beneficial to model locally-enhanced relations between adjacent signals within image patches when given the query, key, and value tensors. Since in the traditional MSA, each feature patch is equally accessible to any other ones and feature patches not in the neighborhood may also attend to each other with relatively large scores, as Fan *et al.* [7] proves mathematically, which potentially introduces noises to semantic modeling and overlooks the link among the surrounding signals. Therefore, a PAAS [20] technique is introduced to remove noise and study the relationships between adjacent feature patches within an image patch. Specifically, the MSA [11] produces the attention maps by formula $qk^T/\sqrt{r}+B$, and each value of attention maps denotes the correlation for any two feature patches in a square patch. We introduce a learnable position importance matrix $W_p \in \mathbb{R}^{w^2 \times w^2}$ to act as a soft attention mask. That is to say, we assign a learnable weight for each element of attention maps to learn the correlations between feature patches, adaptively, thereby eliminating the noises, which is defined as Eq. 1. A locally-enhanced self-attention (LSA), *i.e.*, a feature map with locally-enhanced information, is calculated by Eq. 1. Formally, the LMSA is computed as follows:

$$LSA = \text{softmax}((\frac{qk^T}{\sqrt{r}} + B) \odot W_p)v, \tag{1}$$

$$LMSA = [LSA_1; LSA_2; ...; LSA_j]W_{\text{lmsa}}, \tag{2}$$

where $q, k, v \in \mathbb{R}^{N^2 \times j \times w^2 \times r}$ are the query, key, and value tensors, respectively. w^2 is the number of feature patches in a square patch. j denotes the number of attention heads and $r = C/j$ denotes the dimension of the feature patch in head space. $B \in \mathbb{R}^{w^2 \times w^2}$ [23] is the relative position matrix. $\odot$ is the element-wise product. $W_{\text{lmsa}} \in \mathbb{R}^{jr \times C}$ is the learned parameter.

3.4 Spatial Attention Scaling

In order to learn detailed features, we devise the robust transformer module. However, the fine-grained embeddings obtained by Eq. 1 may contain noises as demonstrated by [7], we propose a SAS mechanism to further refine the representations. Specifically, our SAS method denotes that a diagonal matrix right-multiplies the output of LSA, which means that we assign a learnable weight to each spatial feature, and the spatial features of the same position in different channels share the weight. The LMSA in the robust transformer module is modified as follows:

$$F = diag(\lambda_1, \ldots, \lambda_{w^2})LSA, \tag{3}$$

$$LMSA = [F_1; F_2; ...; F_j]W_{\text{lmsa}}, \tag{4}$$

where the parameters λ_i are learnable weights for $i = 1, ..., w^2$. Diagonal matrix is initialized to follow a standard normal distribution. $F \in \mathbb{R}^{N^2 \times j \times w^2 \times r}$ is the feature map with refined characteristics. Formally, SAS does not alter the computational overhead of the network by adding these weights since they can be combined into the prior tensor of the LMSA as Eq. 3 demonstrates.

4 Experiments

4.1 Experiments Setting

Datasets. We carried out research on three benchmark databases, *i.e.*, FaceForensics++ (FF++) [21], Deepfake Detection Challenge (DFDC) [5], Deepfake Detection (DFD). FF++ includes 1,000 original videos from YouTube and 4,000 fake videos. The fake videos are generated by four algorithms: DeepFakes (DF) [1], Face2Face (F2F) [26], FaceSwap (FS) [2], and NeuralTextures (NT) [25]. FF++ has three qualities with distinct compression degrees, *i.e.*, raw, high quality (HQ), and low quality (LQ). We applied the HQ-type videos and the official splits, using 740 videos for training, 140 videos for validation, and 140 videos for testing. DFDC is a wide-scale deepfake dataset with a large number of clips and different quality levels. DFD is a deepfake detection dataset that utilizes publicly available deepfake generation methods to create over 3,000 manipulated videos from 28 actors in various scenes. The performance on the test set is reported.

Evaluation Metrics. We adopted the accuracy (ACC) and area under the receiver operating characteristic curve (AUC) as our evaluation criteria. Since most previous work rarely presents the metric of computation complexity, as a result, we computed the number of parameters and FLOPs of the models using the same setting.

Implementation Details. We used dlib [12] to crop the face regions as input facial images with size 224×224. The size w of square patches in the robust transformer module is set to 7. The depth L of the robust transformer is set to 6 with four phases with 1, 1, 3, and 1 transformer blocks and the attention heads j are set to 2, 4, 8, and 16, respectively. Furthermore, our model is trained with Adam optimizer [13] with learning rate 1e-4 and weight decay 1e-5. We utilized the scheduler to drop the learning rate by ten times every 15 epochs.

4.2 Comparison with the State of the Art

Within-Dataset Evaluation. We used FF++ for training and conducted the within-dataset evaluation. Results are displayed in Table 1. Our method consistently outperforms the recent mainstream models on four manipulation methods. In particular, our model outperforms the state-of-the-art, Xception, by 4.7% AUC, on the most difficult NT forgery technology that barely creates visible fabricated artifacts, illustrating the effectiveness of our proposed model. Furthermore, our method possesses the minimum number of parameters and FLOPs among all compared approaches as shown in Table 2. That is to say, our method is superior in terms of both computing efficiency and detection accuracy.

Table 1. Comparison with state-of-the-art methods on within-dataset. We trained on FF++ which consists of four manipulation techniques.

Method	DF		F2F		FS		NT		FF++	
	ACC	AUC	ACC	AUC	ACC	AUC	ACC	AUC	ACC	AUC
MAT [29]	90.70	97.43	90.64	97.75	90.82	97.02	77.65	85.56	87.50	94.85
CViT [28]	86.59	96.17	87.75	97.85	92.28	98.71	74.99	82.78	84.86	92.36
TwoStream [18]	91.08	97.39	91.54	97.96	90.82	96.39	79.12	86.65	88.17	94.93
Xception [21]	90.54	97.34	91.93	98.12	95.61	99.28	82.18	90.07	90.08	96.51
TransDFD(Ours)	**93.94**	**98.87**	**95.24**	**99.25**	**97.51**	**99.70**	**87.65**	**94.73**	**93.60**	**98.40**

Table 2. Comparison with state-of-the-art methods on cross-dataset evaluation.

Method	DFDC		DFD			
	ACC	AUC	ACC	AUC	Params(M)	GFLOPs
MAT [29]	63.16	69.56	77.63	85.18	417.63	224.38
CViT [28]	62.79	67.86	72.93	83.24	89.02	6.69
TwoStream [18]	59.93	64.80	75.77	83.79	53.24	13.79
Xception [21]	58.77	66.95	76.84	85.20	20.81	4.59
TransDFD(Ours)	**64.12**	**71.97**	**84.12**	**92.23**	**13.78**	**4.25**

Cross-Dataset Evaluation. To evaluate cross-dataset generalization, we trained the networks on FF++ and tested the models on DFDC and DFD. We can see that our proposed model constantly surpasses all of the compared opponents by a significant margin in Table 2. For instance, our method separately exceeds the state-of-the-art Xception which has few parameters and FLOPs by 5.0% and 7.0% AUC on DFDC and DFD, respectively. Different from Xception which merely employs the local information, our model considers the intra-patch relations and inter-patch global relations for fine-grained local and global representation, allowing various artifacts of the manipulated face can be noticed. Furthermore, compared to Xception, the computational costs and the number of parameters are also reduced by 0.3 G and 7.1 M, respectively. In comparison to CViT which also considers both local and global knowledge with transformer, our method confirms excellent performance both in computation overheads and AUC, validating the effectiveness of the fine-grained extraction of global features. Meanwhile, the gains are primarily due to our method's ability to learn richer forgery traces than compared opponents. Especially for the DFDC dataset, it is a more challenging benchmark since diverse generation technologies are applied to DFDC to achieve larger scale and higher diversity. The AUC of our method is 2.4%, 6.8%, 7.2%, and 5.0% higher than MAT, CViT, Two Stream, and Xception, respectively, on DFDC, which demonstrates the superior robustness of our model.

Table 3. Evaluation of each component in TransDFD on FF++. The models are trained from scratch on FF++. ST and RT denote shuffle transformer and robust transformer, respectively.

Datasets	Methods	Params(M)	GFLOPs	ACC	AUC
DF	ST	27.26	4.56	86.78	95.15
	RT	30.42	4.81	87.70	97.73
	LFE+RT	13.75	4.25	93.90	98.76
	LFE+RT+SAS	13.78	4.25	**93.94**	**98.87**
F2F	ST	27.26	4.56	83.46	92.98
	RT	30.42	4.81	88.96	97.44
	LFE+RT	13.75	4.25	94.38	99.17
	LFE+RT+SAS	13.78	4.25	**95.24**	**99.25**
FS	ST	27.26	4.56	84.80	92.73
	RT	30.42	4.81	93.19	98.10
	LFE+RT	13.75	4.25	96.79	99.48
	LFE+RT+SAS	13.78	4.25	**97.51**	**99.70**
NT	ST	27.26	4.56	72.57	78.10
	RT	30.42	4.81	77.61	86.00
	LFE+RT	13.75	4.25	84.92	92.90
	LFE+RT+SAS	13.78	4.25	**87.65**	**94.73**
FF++	ST	27.26	4.56	81.93	89.98
	RT	30.42	4.81	87.70	95.25
	LFE+RT	13.75	4.25	92.51	97.87
	LFE+RT+SAS	13.78	4.25	**93.60**	**98.40**

4.3 Ablation Study

To study the contribution of TransDFD components to learning ability, Table 3 shows the results of our ablation study, which investigates the effect of incrementally adding robust transformer, LFE, and SAS training components.

Effectiveness of Robust Transformer. We performed the experiments on FF++ to demonstrate that the robust transformer module is necessary. The results are listed in Table 3. It should be noted that the introduction of the robust transformer module consistently improves the ACC and AUC. We believe that the robust transformer module focuses on fine-grained local and global feature learning while paying attention to the local enhancement relationship between fine-grained features, guiding our model to explore more identifiable and comprehensive forgery areas.

Effectiveness of SAS. To confirm the effectiveness of our SAS method, our TransDFD model is trained with SAS and without SAS on FF++ and other

Table 4. Ablation results of transformer-based models. We trained on FF++ and tested on FF++, DFDC, and DFD.

Method	FF++		DFDC		DFD			
	ACC	AUC	ACC	AUC	ACC	AUC	Params(M)	GFLOPs
CViT w/o SAS	85.47	94.72	62.79	67.86	72.92	83.24	89.02	6.69
CViT w/ SAS	89.77	96.35	63.64	70.68	80.11	87.96	89.02	6.69
TransDFD w/o SAS	92.51	97.87	62.19	69.95	79.33	87.91	13.75	4.25
TransDFD w/ SAS	**93.60**	**98.40**	**64.12**	**71.97**	**84.12**	**92.23**	13.78	4.25

hyperparameters remain the same. In Table 3, we noticed that due to the introduction of SAS, the AUC of the model is increased by 2.7% on NT. From our perspective, SAS supervises the TransDFD model to concentrate on extensive facial forgery details as shown in Fig. 4. Besides, the parameters of TransDFD with SAS are only increased by 0.03M and the computational complexity is not changed, which lies in our SAS approach can be combined into the prior tensor of the LMSA as the Eq. 3 demonstrates. In order to prove that SAS can boost the performance of transformer-based models, we also conducted ablation experiments on within-dataset and cross-dataset. We show the quantitive results in Table 4, respectively. As we can see, SAS enhances the performance with few parameters and low computational overheads. Assuming that transformer-based models capture diverse global relationships without extra supervision, the SAS approach achieves this by assigning learnable parameters to global features, steering the model to highlight the most important representations and suppress less important ones. As a result, our SAS method boosts the attention of transformer-based models so as to improve their performance.

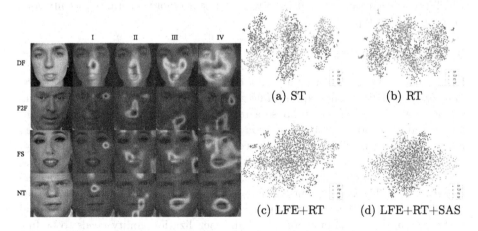

Fig. 4. The heatmap visualizations.

(a) ST (b) RT

(c) LFE+RT (d) LFE+RT+SAS

Fig. 5. The t-SNE visualizations.

4.4 Visualization

Visualization of Heatmap. We visualized the forgery traces captured by different settings using the Grad-CAM [22] on the FF ++ dataset, as Fig. 4 illustrates. Each row displays one manipulation approach. From top to bottom, the forgery types are DF, F2F, FS, and NT. The second to fifth columns display the results of four training schemes that have been listed in Table 3. Firstly, we compared the heatmap among different columns (training strategies): robust transformer (II) boosts the ability to capture long-range traces compared to the baseline (I). (III) compared with (II), the LFE module can push the model to locate more potential manipulation areas. In particular, (IV) relative to (III), our SAS technique enhances these candidate regions by exploring more regions of interest. Secondly, in comparison to various rows: It is commonly assumed that the most useful portions to discern are the mouth, nose, and eyes.

Cluster Visualization of Feature Map. We visualized the features generated by different models on the same FF++ test set by using the t-SNE [19]. As Fig. 5 shows, each color corresponds to a specific type of synthetic technique. We observe that the features learned by the shuffle transformer for each forgery method are concentrated in their respective regions and are not tightly grouped together. This phenomenon, on the one hand, indicates that different manipulations have various characteristic distributions, and on the other hand, shows that the shuffle transformer will separate fake data created by different forgery types even if we treated all fake samples as one class in the training stage. It clearly reveals that the features which shuffle transformer extracts contain the unique artifacts of each forgery algorithm, affecting its generalization ability. The feature distribution of different manipulations becomes rather compact due to the establishment of robust transformer and LFE. Moreover, owing to the introduction of our SAS mechanism, the fake sample are more mixed together, which proves that the TransDFD network can learn more general representations for each forgery type.

5 Conclusion

In this paper, we design a lightweight and robust network using transformers, namely, TransDFD, which applies fine-grained local and global feature learning for deepfake detection. We propose a robust transformer to extract the patch-level local and global embeddings via exploring intra-patch locally-enhanced relations and inter-patch locally-enhanced global relationships. We build a plug-and-play SAS method to identify salient forgery representations without increasing computational complexity, which enhances the performance of transformer-based models. The experiments on FF++, DFDC, and DFD demonstrate that we achieve state-of-the-art performance with few parameters and computational costs. The limitation of our model is that generalization ability needs to be further strengthened. In the future, we intend to explore self-supervised learning to extract critical information from complex datasets containing multiple manipulation techniques.

References

1. Deepfake. https://github.com/deepfakes/. Aaccessed 03 Sep 2020
2. Faceswap. https://github.com/MarekKowalski/FaceSwap. Accessed 03 Sep 2020
3. Chollet, F.: Xception: Deep learning with depthwise separable convolutions. In: 2017 IEEE Conference on Computer Vision and Pattern Recognition (CVPR), pp. 1800–1807 (2017). https://doi.org/10.1109/CVPR.2017.195
4. Dang, H., Liu, F., Stehouwer, J., Liu, X., Jain, A.K.: On the detection of digital face manipulation. In: 2020 IEEE/CVF Conference on Computer Vision and Pattern Recognition (CVPR), pp. 5780–5789, June 2020. https://doi.org/10.1109/CVPR42600.2020.00582
5. Dolhansky, B., et al.: The deepfake detection challenge dataset (2020)
6. Dosovitskiy, A., et al.: An image is worth 16 x 16 words: transformers for image recognition at scale. In: International Conference on Learning Representations, Austria (2021)
7. Fan, Z., et al.: Mask attention networks: rethinking and strengthen transformer. In: Proceedings of the 2021 Conference of the North American Chapter of the Association for Computational Linguistics: Human Language Technologies, pp. 1692–1701. Association for Computational Linguistics, June 2021
8. Goodfellow, I., et al.: Generative adversarial nets. In: Advances in Neural Information Processing Systems, pp. 2672–2680 (2014)
9. Güera, D., Delp, E.J.: Deepfake video detection using recurrent neural networks. In: 2018 15th IEEE International Conference on Advanced Video and Signal Based Surveillance (AVSS), pp. 1–6, November 2018. https://doi.org/10.1109/AVSS.2018.8639163
10. Huang, L., Yuan, Y., Guo, J., Zhang, C., Chen, X., Wang, J.: Interlaced sparse self-attention for semantic segmentation. arXiv preprint arXiv:1907.12273 (2019)
11. Huang, Z., Ben, Y., Luo, G., Cheng, P., Yu, G., Fu, B.: Shuffle transformer: rethinking spatial shuffle for vision transformer. arXiv preprint arXiv:2106.03650 (2021)
12. King, D.: dlib 19.22.1 (2021). https://pypi.org/project/dlib/. Accessed 29 Aug 2021
13. Kingma, D.P., Ba, J.: Adam: a method for stochastic optimization. In: 3rd International Conference on Learning Representations (ICLR). San Diego, CA, USA, Conference Track Proceedings, May 2015
14. Kingma, D.P., Welling, M.: Auto-encoding variational bayes. In: 2nd International Conference on Learning Representations (ICLR), pp. 14–16 (2014)
15. Kumar, P., Vatsa, M., Singh, R.: Detecting face2face facial reenactment in videos. In: 2020 IEEE Winter Conference on Applications of Computer Vision (WACV), pp. 2578–2586 (2020). https://doi.org/10.1109/WACV45572.2020.9093628
16. Li, L., et al.: Face x-ray for more general face forgery detection. In: 2020 IEEE/CVF Conference on Computer Vision and Pattern Recognition (CVPR), pp. 5000–5009 (2020). https://doi.org/10.1109/CVPR42600.2020.00505
17. London, U.C.: Deepfakes' ranked as most serious AI crime threat (2021). https://www.sciencedaily.com/releases/2020/08/200804085908.htm. Accessed 01 May 2021
18. Luo, Y., Zhang, Y., Yan, J., Liu, W.: Generalizing face forgery detection with high-frequency features. In: 2021 IEEE/CVF Conference on Computer Vision and Pattern Recognition (CVPR), pp. 16312–16321, June 2021. https://doi.org/10.1109/CVPR46437.2021.01605

19. Van der Maaten, L., Hinton, G.: Visualizing data using T-SNE. J. Mach. Learn. Res. **9**(11), 2579–2605 (2008)
20. Mao, X., et al.: Towards robust vision transformer. arXiv preprint arXiv:2105.07926 (2021)
21. Rössler, A., Cozzolino, D., Verdoliva, L., Riess, C., Thies, J., Niessner, M.: Face-forensics++: learning to detect manipulated facial images. In: 2019 IEEE/CVF International Conference on Computer Vision (ICCV), pp. 1–11 (2019). https://doi.org/10.1109/ICCV.2019.00009
22. Selvaraju, R.R., Cogswell, M., Das, A., Vedantam, R., Parikh, D., Batra, D.: Grad-cam: visual explanations from deep networks via gradient-based localization. In: 2017 IEEE International Conference on Computer Vision (ICCV), pp. 618–626, October 2017. https://doi.org/10.1109/ICCV.2017.74
23. Shaw, P., Uszkoreit, J., Vaswani, A.: Self-attention with relative position representations. In: Proceedings of the 2018 Conference of the North American Chapter of the Association for Computational Linguistics: Human Language Technologies, vol. 2, pp. 464–468, June 2021
24. Simonyan, K., Zisserman, A.: Very deep convolutional networks for large-scale image recognition. In: International Conference on Learning Representations, May 2015
25. Thies, J., Zollhöfer, M., Nießner, M.: Deferred neural rendering: image synthesis using neural textures. ACM Trans. Graph. (TOG) **38**(4), 1–12 (2019)
26. Thies, J., Zollhöfer, M., Stamminger, M., Theobalt, C., Nießner, M.: Face2face: real-time face capture and reenactment of RGB videos. In: 2016 IEEE Conference on Computer Vision and Pattern Recognition (CVPR), pp. 2387–2395, June 2016. https://doi.org/10.1109/CVPR.2016.262
27. Wang, C., Deng, W.: Representative forgery mining for fake face detection. In: 2021 IEEE/CVF Conference on Computer Vision and Pattern Recognition (CVPR), pp. 14918–14927. Nashville, TN, USA (2021). https://doi.org/10.1109/CVPR46437.2021.01468
28. Wodajo, D., Atnafu, S.: Deepfake video detection using convolutional vision transformer. arXiv preprint arXiv:2102.11126 (2021)
29. Zhao, H., Wei, T., Zhou, W., Zhang, W., Chen, D., Yu, N.: Multi-attentional deepfake detection. In: 2021 IEEE/CVF Conference on Computer Vision and Pattern Recognition (CVPR), pp. 2185–2194 (2021). https://doi.org/10.1109/CVPR46437.2021.00222
30. Zhou, P., Han, X., Morariu, V.I., Davis, L.S.: Two-stream neural networks for tampered face detection. In: 2017 IEEE Conference on Computer Vision and Pattern Recognition Workshops (CVPRW), pp. 1831–1839, July 2017. https://doi.org/10.1109/CVPRW.2017.229

A General Personality Analysis Model Based on Social Posts and Links

Xingkong Ma[1(✉)], Houjie Qiu[1], Shujia Yao[2], Xinyi Chen[1], Jingsong Zhang[1], Zhaoyun Ding[1], Shaoyong Li[1], and Bo Liu[1]

[1] College of Computer, National University of Defense Technology, Changsha, China
{maxingkong,qiuhoujie,xinyi_chen,
zhangjingsong17,zyding,shaoyongli}@nudt.edu.cn
[2] Shanxi University, Taiyuan, China

Abstract. Personality plays a vital role in psychological feature analysis, product recommendation, and mental health assessment. Analyzing personality based on social networks is becoming mainstream since it allows collecting user behaviors and continuously output personality prediction results in a non-intrusive manner. However, existing methods face either over-fitting problems due to the small-sized training datasets or inaccurate feature representation due to the limited information of the testee. This paper proposes a general personality analysis model based on posts and links in social networks, called GPAM. To solve the problem of insufficient training data, we use a user linkage technique to collect large-scale and high-quality labeled personality data in a short time. By introducing posts from high-influence friends, we propose a unified personality feature extraction model to represent the users without enough information. Under various parameter settings, the experimental results demonstrate that importing moderate posts from high-influence friends benefits state-of-the-art models. The average f1-scores of predicting both MBTI and Big Five in GPAM are higher than the latest model Trignet. Compared to without introducing extra posts, the average f1-scores of in GPAM improve at least 4% for wordless users and 51% for silent users.

Keywords: Personality analysis · Big five · MBTI · User linkage · Personality feature extraction

1 Introduction

Personality is the characteristic sets of behaviors, cognitions, and emotional patterns that evolve from biological and environmental factors [1]. Since personality is relatively stable, it plays a vital role in diverse fields, such as recruitment, counseling, personalized advertising, recommendation, mental health assessment, etc. For instance, Personality tests have become a recruitment trend in recent years. Data source from the Society for Industrial and Organizational Psychology [2] displays that 29% of employers use one or more forms of psychological measurement or assessment, and 13% of employers use personality tests. According

© The Author(s), under exclusive license to Springer Nature Switzerland AG 2022
S. Khanna et al. (Eds.): PRICAI 2022, LNCS 13629, pp. 289–303, 2022.
https://doi.org/10.1007/978-3-031-20862-1_21

to Psychology Today [3], around 80% of Fortune 500 companies use personality tests to assess their employees. Another example is the recommendation. Compared with content filtering or collaborative filtering, personality-aware recommendation systems solve the problems of the cold start and data sparsity [4] and have been applied to the recommendation of musics [5], books [6], etc.

Psychologists propose various models to describe the individual personality. Currently, two personality measurement models are considered to be reliable and operable. One is the Big Five model. It describes the personality trait using five dimensions: **O**penness, **C**onscientiousness, **E**xtraversion, **A**greeablenes, and **N**euroticism. The adjective definers of these dimensions can be found in [7]. The other is Myers Briggs Type Indicator (MBTI) [8]. It describes the personality from four dimensions of how a person interacts with the world (**E**xtraversion versus **I**ntroversion), gathers information (**S**ensing versus i**N**tuition), processes information (**T**hinking versus Feeling), and makes decisions (**J**udging versus **P**erception).

To evaluate individual personality, psychologists provide well-designed questionnaires to testees. This method has two disadvantages. Firstly, the answers to questionnaires are probably untruthful since testees tend to conceal their personality defects because of privacy protection. Secondly, it is difficult to expand to a large scale since the costs of time, human resources and money significantly increase with the growing number of testees.

Analyzing personality based on social networks has become a prevailing trend in recent years. However, most existing methods face the following two challenges. The first is the lack of labeled training data. Although several datasets [9–12] have been published on Internet, their sizes are small and the labels are doubtable, which leads to inadequate training and over-fitting problem. The second is that many users neither fill out their profiles nor frequently express themselves on social networks. It is hard to extract features from these users, which leads to inaccurate personality prediction.

To this end, we propose a general personality analysis model based on posts and links in social networks called GPAM. Generally speaking, we provide the following contributions: (1) We adopt a user linkage method to correlate the same person on different websites to collect labeled data. It allows to collect large-scale and high-quality trainging data quickly. (2) We propose a unified personality extraction model to extract features from users without enough posts. (3) We implement extensive experiments to verify the performance of GPAM under various parameter settings.

2   Related Works

Social networks encompass a large number of user information, such as age, gender, emotional state, address, education, posts, comments, friends, etc. Many researchers try to build a connection between social networks and personalities.

The first category is based on user expression. Pennebaker et al. [13] develop LIWC, a computerized text analysis program that outputs the percentage of words in a given text that falls into different psychological categories [14]. LIWC enlightens researchers to establish a linkage between linguistic patterns and personality or psychological state. Yang et al. [15] propose a recommending algorithm to players according to their identified personality traits. They compute the Pearson's Correlation Coefficients between the OCEAN personality traits and LIWC. Thus, the algorithm recommends games based on both user-user personality similarity and game-user personality similarity. SIMPA [16] detects self-referencing descriptions of personality in a target's text and utilizes these descriptions for personality assessment. Because of the ability to automatically extract features from texts, many researchers adopt deep learning methods to predict personality traits. HIE [17] first integrates heterogeneous information, including self-language usage, avatar, emoticon, and responsive patterns, then extracts semantic features through LIWC and Text-CNN. 2CLSTM [18] extracts user personality features by using LSTM concatenating with CNN. To avoid the post-order bias, Transformer-MD [19] proposes a post-order-agnostic encoder to put together the posts of a user to depict an overall personality profile. To exploit psycholinguistic knowledge, Trignet [20] constructs a heterogeneous tripartite graph by injecting structural psycholinguistic knowledge from LIWC, and proposes a flow graph attention network to obtain the embedding of posts. To alleviate the impact of polysemy in the personality detection tasks, SEPRNN [21] combines word embedding with contextual information to obtain precise semantics for words.

The second category is based on user profiles. Golbeck et al. [22] collect personal profiles of 279 Facebook users. The authors build a correlation between user attributes and the Big Five personality. Gu et al. [23] collect over six thousand profiles on Weibo in China. The results show that with the growth of age, the scores of conscientiousness and agreeableness increased, and openness and extroversion decreased. Besides, Wald et al. [24] analyzed the Big Five personality traits of Facebook users by using 31 profile attributes and 80 post attributes.

The third category is based on user behavior. Chittaranjan et al. [25] collects the usage data of 117 Nokia N95 smartphone users for 17 months. By extracting features from the logs of calls, short messages, Apps, Bluetooth, and profiles, they adopt multiple regression analysis techniques to analyze the correlation between the terminal data and personality. TECLA et al. [26] predicts temperaments and psychological types based on linguistic and behavioral analysis of Twitter data.

In conclusion, most existing methods do not consider two important issues that impact the perfomance of personality models. One is the small-sized training datasets. The other is the limited posts of testees. In GPAM, we propose a user linkage method and a unified personality extraction model to solve these issues.

3   Data Collection

The quantity and quality of labeled training data significantly affect the training and prediction of the personality model. As far as we know, there are mainly three data collection methods in existing works.

- The first is inviting social network users to answer questionnaires online and then crawling the social data of these users. Similar to the offline questionnaires, it is hard to extend to a large scale because of the privacy protection.
- The second is crawling the social data of the user who provides his/her Big Five score or MBTI type in the profile or posts [11]. Since the crawler has to search for users from the whole social network, the searching process leads to much time and resource costs.
- The third is crawling the user comments from personality forums like PersonalityCafe [27]. Users in these forums mainly talk about the behaviors or feelings of their personalities. Even if well-behaved personality prediction models are trained based on these discussions, they are not applicable to daily talking, including topics of economy, politics, society, living, etc.

To obtain a large-scale and high-quality labeled personality dataset, our basic idea is to link the same person from both personality websites and social networks. To increase the accuracy of user linkage, we choose famous persons as our targets. There are two reasons. The first is the personality types of famous persons easy to be collected from their funs or personality websites. The second is most famous persons ensure the authenticity of their social accounts through the real-name authentication system.

We firstly crawl the personality types of the Big Five and MBTI of famous persons from Personality-Database [28]. Note that ordinary people vote for these personality types. To avoid the wrong labeled personality type, we check the vote count over the threshold value. Secondly, since the famous person's nickname is the same as the real name, we can search for the real name and get the corresponding social network account from Facebook or Twitter with a high probability. Following the policy of Twitter API or Facebook API, it is easy to obtain each famous person's profile, posts, and links. Thus, we can collect both personality labels and social data from famous persons within a short time.

4   Personality Representation

As mentioned in Sect. 2, existing works extract personality features from user profile, expression, behavior, etc. However, a report from Twopcharts [29] shows that 44% of Twitter accounts have never sent a tweet, 30% of the accounts have sent 1–10 tweets, and only 13% of the accounts have written at least 100 tweets. Therefore, it is hard to collect enough data from most users, which leads to inaccurate feature representation.

Based on existing researches [30], personality type compatibility exists among individuals. Thus, we believe that introducing extra posts from high-influence friends to the users without enough posts is reasonable. There are two problems we need to solve. The first is how to measure the influence of each friend in the view of personalities. To this end, we propose an interaction-based influence sorting algorithm in Sect. 4.1. The second is how to fuse the personalities of high-influence friends into the testee's personality. To this end, we propose a unified feature extraction model in Sect. 4.2. Table 1 shows key notations used in this section.

Table 1. Key notations in GPAM

Parameters	Meanings
N_v	The number of feature vectors sampled from a user
N_{sp}	The number of sampled posts at a time
N_{xh}	The maximum number of high-influence friends
N_{nh}	The minimum post number of a high-influence friend publishes
N_{np}	The maximum post number a silent or wordless user publishes
N_{nr}	The maximum post number a silent or wordless user reserves
N_p	The post number of a user published

4.1 Interaction-based Influence Sorting

To select high-influence friends, we propose an interaction-based influence sorting algorithm (IISA) in this section. In specific, this algorithm follows three rules:

- Rule 1: Selecting following but not followers. For a testee, his/her following have much more influence than followers.
- Rule 2: Selecting the following who is mentioned in the posts of the testee. One may argue that why do not select the following whose post is given a like or commented by the testee. Theoretically, we are able to collect all posts from the following of the testee. However, it costs much time and resources in practice.
- Rule 3: Selecting the following with a large number of posts. Since the testee receives posts from the following, we suppose the influence of the following is in direct proportion to the number of posts.

Algorithm 1: *Interaction-based Influence Sorting*

```
Input   : FOWL: the following list.
Output: HIFL: the high-influence friend list.
; /*N_m : the mentioned times by the testee.                              */
1  for  each i in [0,FOWL.size()-1] do
2  |    if mentioned(testee, FOWL[i]) and (FOWL[i].N_p ≥ N_min) then
3  |    |    HIFL.append(FOWL[i])

4  if HIFL.size() ≥ N_xh then
5  |    sort HIFL by N_m of each item;
6  |    HIFL.remove(N_xh, HIFL.size()-1);
7  else
8  |    sort FOWL by N_m of each item;
9  |    for  each i in [0,FOWL.size()-1] do
10 |    |    if (HIFL.size() ≤ N_xh and FOWL[i].N_p ≥ N_min and
11 |    |    FOWL[i] ∉ HIFL) then
12 |    |    |    HIFL.append(FOWL[i])
```

The detailed process of IISA is shown in Algorithm 1. Firstly, if one following is mentioned by the testee, and his/her post number is bigger than the threshold

N_{min}, the following is appended to the high-influence friend list (Line 1–3). Note that we filter out the following with low activity, whose features are hard to be extracted, as mentioned at the beginning of this section. Secondly, if the size of the high-influence list is bigger than the threshold N_{xh}, we sort the list by the mentioned times and only keep the top N_{xh} items (Line 4–6). Thirdly, if the size of the high-influence list is less than N_{xh}, we sort the following by the number of posts and append the following with a bigger number of posts into the high-influence list (Line 7–12).

Take Fig. 1 as an example. Alice follows four friends, publishes three posts, and mentions Bob two times and Denise one time. Suppose $N_{min} = 100$ and $N_{xh} = 2$ in Algorithm 1, Bob and Denise are picked based on Rule 2. Suppose $N_{xh} = 3$, Bob, Denise and Eva are picked based on Rule 2 and 3.

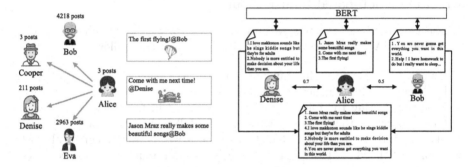

Fig. 1. Case of sorting friend influence   **Fig. 2.** Case of unified feature extraction

4.2   Unified Feature Extraction

In this section, we propose a unified feature extraction model. The basic idea is to fuse the personalities of high-influence friends into users without enough posts. We classify all users into three types. The first is the *silent user*, who does not publish any posts. The second is the *wordless user*, whose post number is between 1 to N_{np}, where N_{np} is a fixed threshold value. The third is the *active user*, whose post number is bigger than N_{np}.

The detailed process is shown in Algorithm 2. For each silent user, we pick posts from his/her high-influence friends based on their number of posts (Line 1–6). For a wordless user, we use the Bert model [31] to extract features (Line 8–10). Note that posts of each user are sampled into multiple groups, and a fixed-length vector represents each group. It brings two advantages. One is to avoid the vanishing gradient problem of long text, and the other is to increase the training samples. Next, the similarity weight between the wordless user and each high-influence friend is computed based on the maximum cosine distance among their feature vectors (Line 11–13). Each high-influence friend contributes a part of the posts to the testee based on the similarity until the total number of posts reaches the threshold N_{nr} (Line 14–17). Finally, the feature vectors of the testee are updated based on the new post list (Line 18). Note that active users do not append extra posts from friends in IISA.

Algorithm 2: *Unified Feature Extraction*

Input   : HIFL: the high-influence friend list of the testee.
Output: testee.vec: the list of feature vectors.

```
 1  if (testee.Np == 0) then
 2      for each i in [0,HIFL.size()-1] do
 3          TotalPosts += HIFL[i].Np;

 4      for each i in [0,HIFL.size()-1] do
 5          posts = pickPosts(HIFL[i].posts, HIFL[i].Np / TotalPosts * Nnr);
 6          testee.posts = testee.posts ∪ posts;

 7  if (testee.Np > 0 and testee.Np < Nnp) then
 8      testee.vec = sample(testee.posts, Nsp);
 9      for each i in [0,HIFL.size()-1] do
10          HIFL[i].vec = sample(HIFL[i].posts, Nsp);

11      for each i in [0,HIFL.size()-1] do
12          Sim[i] = cos(HIFL[i].vec, testee.vec);
13          TotalSim += Sim[i];

14      NeedPostNum = Nnr - testee.Np;
15      for each i in [0,HIFL.size()-1] do
16          posts = pickPosts(HIFL[i].posts, Sim[i] / TotalSim * NeedPostNum);
17          testee.posts = testee.posts ∪ posts;

18  testee.vec = sample(testee.posts, Nsp);
```

Take Fig. 2 as an example. Suppose Alice is a wordless user, and her high-influence friends are Denise and Bob. Firstly, each user's posts are transformed into a group of feature vectors through the Bert model. Secondly, we compute the similarities between Alice and her friends based on their feature vectors. Thirdly, based on their similarities, two posts from Denise and one post from Bob are appended to the post list of Alice. Finally, updated posts of Alice are transformed into new feature vectors through the Bert model.

5   Personality Model Training and Testing

The quantity of the labeled data greatly affects the training accuracy. According to the Algorithm 2, posts of each user are sampled and extracted as a group of fixed-length vectors, each of which is treated as a training or testing sample. By default, the sampling frequency of each user is in direct proportion to the number of posts.

We use multiple classifiers like SVM, XGBoost and Random Forest to train Big Five and MBTI models. Since the prediction results of different testing items may represent the same user, we use these prediction results to vote for the final label. As shown in Fig. 3, Denise has three testing vectors, each of which is classified into a personality type. Take MBTI for instance. These three vectors are classified into INFP, INTP, and INTJ types. After voting on each dimension, INTP is treated as the MBTI type of Denise.

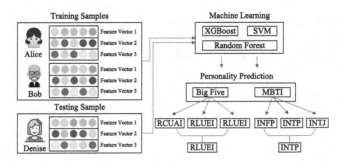

Fig. 3. Personality model training and testing

6 Experiment

6.1 Datasets

According to the user linkage method in Sect. 3, we collect 2007 users from Personality Database and Twitter. Although there are 16 personality labels in MBTI, we can build four binary classfiers rather than a multiple classifier with 16 labels, which brings higher classifying accuracy. Similarly, we build five binary classifiers for Big Five predication. Besides, the maximum gap of the label counts under the same dimension in MBTI and Big Five is not significant, which is propitious to build the classifiers.

Since we select high-influence friends through IISA in Sect. 4.1, it is critical to know the distributions of posts, following, and mentioned following in our dataset. According to the statistics, the post counts of 1.3% of users are zero, 8.3% of users are less than 50, and over 74% users are larger than 1000. The following counts of 3.7% of users are zero, 12.7% of users are less than 25, and over 73% users are larger than 100. The mentioned user counts of 15.8% of users are zero, 22.1% of users are less than 25, and over 60% users are larger than 100. In general, the distributions of numbers of post, following, and mentioned users are wide enough to verify the effectiveness of the feature extraction in Sect. 4.

6.2 Implemention

We deploy GPAM in a private server equipped with 24 processor cores, 64 GB memory, and a NVIDIA V100 GPU to reduce the training latency. For feature representation, we implement Doc2Vec and Bert. Both of them can transform texts into fixed-length vectors. For classification, we implement SVM, Random-Forest(RF), and XGBoost, which have been widely applied in the research and industry fields.

For the users with a large number of posts, we sample and transform these posts into multiple feature vectors as mentioned in Sect. 4.2. In the implementation, the sampling frequency is proportional to the number of posts for each user, and the detailed parameters are described in Sect. 6.3.

Remember that we propose an interaction-based influence sorting algorithm (IISA) in Sect. 4.1. In comparison, we implement another two strategies. One is the following with most posts first (MPF), and the other is the following with most followers first (MFF).

6.3 Parameters and Metrics

We measure GPAM under various parameter settings. To extract features from users, the number of sampled posts from a user at a time N_{sp} is set to 10, and the number of feature vectors sampled from a user N_v ranges from 1 to 20. One may argue that why do not increase N_v linearly with the number of posts. This is because it probably leads to unbalanced labels during training. For silent and wordless users mentioned in Sect. 4.2, the maximum number of posts they published N_{np} is set to 50. To append posts, the maximum number of high-influence friends of each user N_{xh} ranges from 5 to 20, the minimum post number of a high-influence friend publishes N_{nh} is set to 100. The maximum post number a silent or wordless user reserves N_{nr} is set to 100.

To evaluate the performance of GPAM, we compute average accuracy (AvgAcc), average precision (AvgPre), average recall (AvgRecall), and average f1-score (AvgF1) of all dimensions of MBTI and Big Five in each experiment.

6.4 Baseline Performance

This section tests the baseline performance of both MBTI and Big Five under various feature representation models and classification models. Our testees are users whose vote counts are larger than five and post counts are larger than 50. We train their posts and evaluate the performance of GPAM as the baseline. Besides, the state-of-the-art method Trignet [20] is also evaluated as a comparison. Specifically, we sample posts of users based on the parameters of N_v and N_{sp} in Sect. 6.3.

Table 2. Baseline performance of MBTI

Model	Avg. Acc	Avg. Pre	Avg. Recall	Avg. F1
Doc2Vec-SVM	61.88%	64.57%	64.57%	63.46%
Doc2Vec-RF	59.64%	62.20%	59.34%	56.91%
Doc2Vec-XGBoost	60.48%	63.07%	63.10%	62.22%
Bert-SVM	**63.31%**	**66.80%**	62.88%	60.94%
Bert-RF	62.50%	65.85%	63.91%	63.49%
Bert-XGBoost	62.39%	65.32%	**65.34%**	**64.53%**
Trignet	61.82%	59.91%	60.82%	59.95%

In the experiment of MBTI models, there are 10427 items for training, and 2075 items for testing. As shown in Table 2, the Bert-SVM model has the best AvgAcc (63.31%) and AvgPre (66.80%), and the Bert-XGBoost model has the best AVGRecall (66.55%) and AvgF1 (64.53%). For Doc2Vec and Bert, their average values of AvgF1 are 60.92% and 62.99%, respectively. For SVM, RF, and XGBoost, their average values of AvgF1 are 62.20%, 60.20%, and 63.38%, respectively.

In the experiment of the Big Five models, there are 6556 items for training and 992 items for testing. As shown in Table 3, the Bert-SVM model has the best AvgAcc (64.80%), AvgRecall (91.19%), and AvgF1 (75.23%), and the Bert-RF model has best AccPre (65.96%). For Doc2Vec and Bert, their average values of AvgF1 are 73.67% and 73.47%, which is 4% higher than Trignet on average. For SVM, RF, and XGBoost, their average values of AvgF1 are 74.39%, 73.51%, and 72.82%, respectively.

In general, GPAM show better performance than Trignet under different parameters. Bert shows slightly better performance than Doc2Vec on average since users the bidirectional transformer to solve the problem of polyseme. Besides, SVM and XGBoost offer marginally better performance than RF on average.

Table 3. Baseline performance of big five

Model	Avg. Acc	Avg. Pre	Avg. Recall	Avg. F1
Doc2Vec-SVM	64.26%	65.02%	85.47%	73.55%
Doc2Vec-RF	63.71%	64.04%	89.27%	74.25%
Doc2Vec-XGBoost	63.79%	64.91%	84.87%	73.22%
Bert-SVM	**64.80%**	65.06%	**91.19%**	**75.23%**
Bert-RF	64.06%	**65.96%**	81.95%	72.77%
Bert-XGBoost	63.68%	65.72%	81.30%	72.42%
Trignet	61.52%	65.60%	74.40%	69.52%

6.5 Impact of High-influence Friend Selection Strategies

In this section, we test the performance of both MBTI and Big Five models under three high-influence friend selection strategies, MFF, MPF, and IISA, mentioned in Sect. 6.2.

Table 4. Impact of high-influence friend selection strategies in MBTI

Strategy	Model	Avg. Acc	Avg. Pre	Avg. Recall	Avg. F1
MFF	Bert-SVM	63.89%	64.66%	58.66%	59.57%
	Bert-RF	62.70%	62.79%	60.17%	60.62%
	Bert-XGBoost	62.32%	61.96%	62.12%	61.73%
	Trignet	61.86%	60.02%	59.53%	59.50%
MPF	Bert-SVM	63.89%	64.42%	58.36%	59.48%
	Bert-RF	62.42%	62.75%	59.56%	60.34%
	Bert-XGBoost	62.13%	61.91%	61.90%	61.55%
	Trignet	60.43%	59.97%	58.04%	58.70%
IISA	Bert-SVM	**63.93%**	**65.55%**	60.11%	62.98%
	Bert-RF	63.20%	63.68%	60.50%	61.14%
	Bert-XGBoost	63.17%	63.22%	**67.18%**	**65.29%**
	Trignet	60.92%	59.34%	66.55%	62.42%

Table 5. Impact of high-influence friend selection strategies in big five

Strategy	Model	Avg. Acc	Avg. Pre	Avg. Recall	Avg. F1
MFF	Bert-SVM	64.93%	66.24%	90.81%	75.89%
	Bert-RF	64.45%	67.27%	82.18%	73.69%
	Bert-XGBoost	63.09%	67.03%	78.56%	72.11%
	Trignet	62.99%	66.95%	78.17%	72.02%
MPF	Bert-SVM	64.91%	66.02%	91.29%	76.01%
	Bert-RF	64.19%	67.18%	82.25%	73.62%
	Bert-XGBoost	62.93%	66.81%	78.83%	72.15%
	Trignet	62.00%	67.97%	74.83%	70.41%
IISA	Bert-SVM	65.02%	65.77%	**91.78%**	**76.18%**
	Bert-RF	**65.05%**	67.59%	83.08%	74.31%
	Bert-XGBoost	63.95%	67.23%	80.52%	73.15%
	Trignet	63.33%	**68.68%**	74.58%	71.40%

In the experiment of MBTI models, there are 1397 users in total, containing 396 wordless users. After introducing posts from high-influence friends, the training item sizes of MFF, MPF and IISA are 10090, 10105, and 8662, respectively, and the testing item sizes of MFF, MPF, and IISA are 3637, 3635, and 2325 respectively. As shown in Table 4, the Bert-SVM model using IISA has the best AvgAcc (63.93%) and AvgPre (65.55%), and the Bert-XGBoost using IISA has the best AvgRecall (62.18%) and AvgF1 (62.29%). Compared with the baseline in Table 2, the average AvgF1 of IISA in Table 4 increases slightly (62.98% vs. 63.13%, and 59.95% vs. 62.42%).

In the Big Five models experiment, there are 829 users in total and 177 users whose post numbers are less than 50. After post-transfer, the training item sizes of MFF, MPF, and IISA are 5942, 5932, and 6035, respectively, and the testing item sizes of MFF, MPF, and IISA are 2279, 2283, and 2281, respectively. As shown in Table 5, the Bert-RF model using IISA has the best AvgAcc (65.05%), Trignet using IISA has the best AvgPre (68.68%), and the Bert-SVM using IISA has the best AvgRecall (91.78%) and AvgF1 (76.18%). Compared with Table 3, the average AvgF1 of IISA and Trignet in Table 5 increases slightly (73.47% vs. 74.55%, and 69.52% vs. 71.40%)

In general, our strategy IISA has the best performance than MPF and MFF under different metrics. Besides, importing moderate posts from high-influence friends does not hurt and even benefits the state-of-the-art models.

6.6   Importing Posts for Users with Limited Posts

To evaluate the influence of introduced posts, we design three scenarios. In scenario 1, silent users import posts. In scenario 2, wordless users import posts. In scenario 3, both silent and wordless users import posts.

Table 6 shows the AvgF1 of MBTI models in different scenarios. In scenario 1, there are 1202 users in total, containing 95 silent users. The best AvgF1 for testing silent users reaches 54.64%, which is lower than the best AvgF1 of testing active users (61.31%). Nevertheless, this result is still remarkable since the personality of silent users can not be predicted in existing works. In scenario 2, there are 1413 users in total, containing 358 wordless users. The best AvgF1 for testing wordless users is 66.65%, which is better than the value of testing active users (62.29%). Because of IISA, wordless users are able to replenish posts from their mentioned following. In scenario 3, there are 1202 users in total, containing 391 wordless users and 61 silent users. Compared to the result of best AvgF1 values, it shows similar conclusions to the first and second scenarios.

Table 6. AvgF1 of MBTI models in different scenarios

Model	Scenario 1		Scenario 2		Scenario 3		
	Active users	Silent users	Active users	Wordless users	Active users	Silent users	Wordless users
Bert-SVM	55.61%	51.76%	56.98%	61.88%	57.33%	53.73%	57.23%
Bert-RF	59.37%	53.00%	61.14%	65.72%	60.68%	55.61%	60.45%
Bert-XGBoost	**61.31%**	**54.64%**	**62.29%**	**66.65%**	**61.86%**	**63.07%**	**65.91%**
Trignet	59.94%	53.82%	59.40%	59.14%	61.30%	61.24%	54.36%

Table 7 shows the Average F1 of Big Five models in different scenarios. In scenario 1, there are 717 users in total, containing 49 silent users. The best AvgF1 for testing silent users reaches 53.89%. In scenario 2, there are 837 users in total, containing 205 wordless users. Note that the best AvgF1 for testing wordless users is 79.62%, which is better than the value of testing active users (75.18%). In scenario 3, there are 862 users in total, containing 182 wordless users and 35

Table 7. Avg F1 of big five models in different scenarios

Model	Scenario 1		Scenario 2		Scenario 3		
	Active users	Silent users	Active users	Wordless users	Active users	Silent users	Wordless users
Bert-SVM	**75.73%**	**53.89%**	**75.18%**	**79.62%**	**74.52%**	**59.10%**	**78.77%**
Bert-RF	73.48%	53.51%	74.31%	76.34%	74.35%	53.09%	67.48%
Bert-XGBoost	72.64%	51.53%	73.15%	75.18%	73.03%	54.14%	66.62%
Trignet	67.90%	49.36%	70.72%	62.87%	71.78%	67.20%	49.86%

silent users. The best AvgF1 for testing silent users reaches 59.10%. Besides, the best AvgF1 for testing wordless users is over 4% than active users.

In general, GPAM shows better performance than Trignet in different scenarios. The imported posts from high-influence friends bring great gains for silent users.

7 Conclusion

This paper proposes GPAM, a general personality analysis model based on posts and links in social networks. GPAM proposes a user linkage technique to collect large-scale and high-quality labeled personality data shortly, and an unified feature extraction model to tackle the problem of inaccurate representation of users without enough posts. The experimental results demonstrate that importing moderate posts from high-influence friends greatly benefits silent and wordless users, and brings better performance than state-of-the-art model Trignet.

In the future, we plan to design various strategies for selecting posts from high-influence friends and extract personality features based on both LIWC and pretrain models. Besides, we plan to further extend our approach to predicting other personality models like Enneagram, Temperaments, Socionics, etc.

References

1. Corr, P.J., Matthews, G.: The Cambridge Handbook of Personality Psychology. Cambridge University Press, Cambridge (2020)
2. Employment testing (2022). https://www.siop.org/Business-Resources/Employment-Testing/Test-Use
3. Personality testing (2022). https://www.psychologytoday.com/intl/blog/credit-and-blame-work/200806/the-use-and-misuse-personality-tests-coaching-and-development
4. Dhelim, S., Aung, N., Bouras, M.A., Ning, H., Cambria, E.: A survey on personality-aware recommendation systems. arXiv preprint arXiv:2101.12153 (2021)
5. Schedl, M.: Deep learning in music recommendation systems. Front. Appl. Math. Stat. **5**, 44 (2019)
6. Annalyn, N., Bos, M.W., Sigal, L., Li, B.: Predicting personality from book preferences with user-generated content labels. IEEE Trans. Affect. Comput. **11**(3), 482–492 (2018)

7. McCrae, R.R., Costa, P.T.: Clinical assessment can benefit from recent advances in personality psychology. Am. Psychol. **41**(9), 1001 (1986)
8. Myers, I.B., McCaulley, M.H., Quenk, N.L., Hammer, A.L.: MBTI Manual: a Guide to the Development and Use of the Myers-Briggs Type Indicator. Consulting Psychologists Press, Mountain View (1998)
9. Kaggle mbti (2022). https://www.kaggle.com/datasnaek/mbti-type
10. Myperson dataset (2022). https://github.com/jcl132/personality-prediction-from-text
11. Plank, B., Hovy, D.: Personality traits on twitter-or-how to get 1,500 personality tests in a week. In: Proceedings of the 6th Workshop on Computational Approaches to Subjectivity, Sentiment and Social Media Analysis, pp. 92–98 (2015)
12. Twitter personality dataset (2022). https://github.com/monicamanda/twitter-personality-classification
13. Pennebaker, J.W., King, L.A.: Linguistic styles: language use as an individual difference. J. Pers. Soc. Psychol. **77**(6), 1296 (1999)
14. Tausczik, Y.R., Pennebaker, J.W.: The psychological meaning of words: LIWC and computerized text analysis methods. J. Lang. Soc. Psychol. **29**(1), 24–54 (2010)
15. Yang, H.C., Huang, Z.R.: Mining personality traits from social messages for game recommender systems. Knowl.-Based Syst. **165**, 157–168 (2019)
16. Gjurković, M., Vukojević, I., Šnajder, J.: SIMPA: statement-to-item matching personality assessment from text. Future Gener. Comput. Syst. **130**, 114–127 (2021)
17. Wei, H., et al.: Beyond the words: predicting user personality from heterogeneous information. In: Proceedings of the tenth ACM International Conference on Web Search and Data Mining, pp. 305–314 (2017)
18. Sun, X., Liu, B., Cao, J., Luo, J., Shen, X.: Who am i? personality detection based on deep learning for texts. In: 2018 IEEE International Conference on Communications (ICC), pp. 1–6. IEEE (2018)
19. Yang, F., Quan, X., Yang, Y., Yu, J.: Multi-document transformer for personality detection. In: Proceedings of the AAAI Conference on Artificial Intelligence, vol. 35, pp. 14221–14229 (2021)
20. Yang, T., Yang, F., Ouyang, H., Quan, X.: Psycholinguistic tripartite graph network for personality detection. In: Proceedings of the 59th Annual Meeting of the Association for Computational Linguistics and the 11th International Joint Conference on Natural Language Processing (Volume 1: Long Papers), pp. 4229–4239 (2021)
21. Xue, X., Feng, J., Sun, X.: Semantic-enhanced sequential modeling for personality trait recognition from texts. Appl. Intell. **51**(11), 7705–7717 (2021). https://doi.org/10.1007/s10489-021-02277-7
22. Golbeck, J., Robles, C., Turner, K.: Predicting personality with social media. In: CHI 2011 Extended Abstracts on Human Factors in Computing Systems, pp. 253–262 (2011)
23. Gu, H., Wang, J., Wang, Z., Zhuang, B., Su, F.: Modeling of user portrait through social media. In: 2018 IEEE International Conference on Multimedia and Expo (ICME), pp. 1–6. IEEE (2018)
24. Wald, R., Khoshgoftaar, T., Sumner, C.: Machine prediction of personality from Facebook profiles. In: 2012 IEEE 13th International Conference on Information Reuse & Integration (IRI), pp. 109–115. IEEE (2012)
25. Chittaranjan, G., Blom, J., Gatica-Perez, D.: Mining large-scale smartphone data for personality studies. Pers. Ubiquit. Comput. **17**(3), 433–450 (2013)
26. Lima, A.C.E., de Castro, L.N.: Tecla: a temperament and psychological type prediction framework from twitter data. PLoS ONE **14**(3), e0212844 (2019)

27. Personalitycafe. https://www.personalitycafe.com/
28. Personality database (2022). https://www.personality-database.com/
29. 44% of twitter accounts have never sent a tweet (2022). https://www.wsj.com/articles/BL-DGB-34255
30. Socionics relations. http://www.socionics.com/rel/rel.htm
31. Devlin, J., Chang, M.W., Lee, K., Toutanova, K.: Bert: pre-training of deep bidirectional transformers for language understanding. arXiv preprint arXiv:1810.04805 (2018)

Deception Detection Towards Multi-turn Question Answering with Context Selector Network

Yinan Bao[1,2], Qianwen Ma[1,2], Lingwei Wei[1,2], Ding Wang[1,2], Wei Zhou[1(✉)], and Songlin Hu[1,2]

[1] Institute of Information Engineering, Chinese Academy of Sciences, Beijing, China
{baoyinan,maqianwen,weilingwei,wangding,zhouwei, husonglin}@iie.ac.cn
[2] School of Cyber Security, University of Chinese Academy of Sciences, Beijing, China

Abstract. Deception occurring in multi-turn question answering (QA) circumstances such as interviews, court depositions, and online marketplaces, can cause serious consequences. Due to the lack of proper datasets and difficulty of finding deceptive signals, existing deception detection methods haven't utilized the QA contexts to detect deception. Previous methods that mainly focus on context-free deception detection cannot be applied to text-based QA contexts. Therefore, we design a novel Context Selector Network (CSN) to address the challenge of modeling the context-sensitive dependencies implied in multi-turn QA. We utilize BERT to obtain sentence embeddings first and then design a context selector to explore crucial deceptive signals implied in the QA contexts automatically. Towards real-life scenarios, we collect a high-quality dataset containing multi-turn QAs that consist of sequential dependent QA pairs. Compared with several state-of-the-art baselines, experimental results show the impressive effectiveness of the proposed model.

Keywords: Deception detection · Multi-turn QA · Context selector network · Text classification

1 Introduction

Deception often occurs in certain contexts of daily life, which can cause severe consequences and losses to individuals and society. Automatic deception detection methods towards multi-turn QA can benefit many applications, such as criminal interrogation, court depositions, interviews, and online marketplaces. However, text-based context deception detection has not been explored sufficiently [29] mainly due to the lack of proper datasets and difficulty of finding deceptive signals. To alleviate this problem, we focus on deception detection in a multi-turn QA which aims at classifying each QA pair as deception or not, through the analysis of the context.

Existing deception detection methods heavily rely on hand-crafted features including verbal [7,11,19,21,22,27,31,32] and non-verbal [6,18,25,28] cues explored from different modals, ignoring the use of semantic information implied in contexts and could not be applied to multi-turn QA data. Some tasks such as dialogue system [15] and

© The Author(s), under exclusive license to Springer Nature Switzerland AG 2022
S. Khanna et al. (Eds.): PRICAI 2022, LNCS 13629, pp. 304–315, 2022.
https://doi.org/10.1007/978-3-031-20862-1_22

Table 1. Part of a multi-turn QA example in the dataset. Q_i means the i_{th} question; A_i means the i_{th} answer. "T" means the QA pair is truthful and "F" means deceptive.

Turns		Theme: Sports
Turn-1	Q_1	What kind of ball sports do you like?
	A_1	Football. **(F)**
Turn-2	Q_2	Do you usually play ball? When and where do you play ball? How long does it take each time?
	A_2	I *don't play football* in my spare time. **(T)**
Turn-3	Q_3	Have you participated in any competition related to this sport?
	A_3	I have *never taken part in* a football match. **(T)**
Turn-4	Q_4	How well do you play? Have you received professional training?
	A_4	I *play football very well*. When I was in elementary school, I received two years of training in an amateur sports school. **(F)**
Turn-5	Q_5	Which star do you like in this sport? When did you like him/her?
	A_5	I like Ma Long. I liked him when I watched him play table tennis. **(T)**

multi-turn question answering [14, 30] seem to be similar to our task. However, they cannot be regarded as classification tasks, and cannot be directly applied to our task which is formed as a sentence-pair classification task. Thus, it is necessary to propose a novel approach for deceptive QA pairs recognition.

Intuitively, information implied in contexts is needed to understand the subjective beliefs of a speaker, which is an essential step to detect deceit [13]. For example, we cannot judge which QA pairs in Table 1 are deceptive or not without the given contexts. Furthermore, the features of deception are implicit and difficult to be detected. Due to the sparsity and complexity of latent deceptive signals, treating all of the context information equally will obstruct the model performance. As shown in Table 1, Turn-5 is relatively less relevant to Turn-2 while Turn-1, 3, and 4 are closely related to Turn-2. Taking all of the contexts into account probably hurt the model's ability to recognize deception.

We propose two hypotheses: (1) QA context is conducive to detect deceit. (2) Noises implied in QA context hinder the accurate identification of deception. To address these two assumptions, we use BERT [5] to get context-independent sentence embeddings and BiGRU [3] to get context-aware sentence embeddings. More importantly, a novel context selector is proposed to filter out noise in the contexts. Due to the lack of a proper dataset, we construct a multi-turn QA dataset containing sequential dependent QA pairs for the experiments. We design different questionnaires covering six daily life topics to collect deceptive and non-deceptive data. Our contributions are:

(1) We make the first attempt to tackle the multi-turn QA-style deception detection problem, and design a novel Context Selection Network (CSN) to explore deceptive signals implied in the contexts effectively.

(2) To fill the gap of deception detection in multi-turn QA, a newly collected dataset Deception QA is presented for the target task.

(3) Comparing with several deep learning-based baselines, our model achieves the best performance on the collected dataset, showing its effectiveness.

2 Related Work

2.1 Deception Detection

To address the problem of automatic deception detection, researchers have carried out a series of studies in different scenarios such as the social network scenario and daily life scenario.

Social network-based deception detection has been studied for a long period in the research community. Most of them utilize propagation pattern of deceptive information [2] and interactions between multiple users [17] to detect deception. However, these features don't exist in a multi-turn QA under the daily life situation. As a result, these methods cannot be applied to this new kind of task directly.

In addition, deception often occurs in the daily life scenario. Researchers have analyzed the features that can be used to detect deception. These features can be classified as linguistic features and interactions between individuals.

Linguistic Features: Some researches have shown the effectiveness of features derived from text analysis, which includes basic linguistic representations such as n-grams and Linguistic Inquiry and Word Count (LIWC) [19,22], and more complex linguistic features derived from syntactic CFG trees and part of speech tags [7,31]. Based on these research findings, many studies focused on text-based methods, recognizing deceptive languages in games [1,27], online reviews [20], news articles [26], and interviews [12].

Interactions Between Individuals: Apart from linguistic features implied in texts, interactions between individuals can also have a beneficial effect on detecting deceit. Tsunomori et al. [29] examined the effect of question types and individuals' behaviors on participants. Findings of the study show that specific questions led to more salient deceptive behavior patterns in participants which resulted in better deception detection performance.

These studies show that linguistic features and interaction between individuals in contexts contribute to deception detection. Therefore, deception detection in a text-based multi-turn QA is significant and reasonable. Although deceptive behavior often occurs in a multi-turn QA under daily life situation, due to the difficulty of finding deceptive signals and deception data collection and annotation, no work has been done on cues of deception drawing from text-based QA contexts. Unlike all the prior studies, this paper focuses on a novel task, that is, deception detection in a multi-turn QA. To the best of our knowledge, our work is the first attempt to perform deception detection in multi-turn QA.

2.2 Datasets Comparison

There have been a few of datasets based on different modalities developed for deception detection, such as text-based datasets [19,21,27,32], audio-based datasets [9,11] and multimodal-based datasets [24,25,28].

Some researchers proposed text-based datasets for deception detection. Ott et al. [21] developed the Ott Deceptive Opinion Spam corpus, which consists of 800 true reviews and 800 deceptive reviews. Mihalces et al. [19] collected data from three written deception tasks. Zhou and Sung [32] collected 1192 Mafia games from a popular Chinese website. de Ruiter and Kachergis [27] proposed the Mafiascum dataset, a collection of over 700 games of Mafia.

In addition to text-based datasets, some studies have developed audio-based datasets. Hirschberg et al. [9] were the first to propose audio-based corpus, which consists of 32 interviews averaging 30 min. Levitan et al. [11] collected a much larger corpus than it. However, these two datasets are not public available and free. Furthermore, it is hard to model the contextual semantics only based on the audio modality.

The multimodal datasets were all collected from public multimedia sources, such as public court trials [24], street interviews aired in television shows [25], and the Box of Lies game in a TV show [28]. The data cannot be annotated by the people who express deception or non-deception. The researchers labeled the data themselves after data collection, which may introduce human bias. Existing public multimedia sources also cannot provide adequate labeled samples for deep learning based deception detection methods. Moreover, compared with text data, processing multimodal data requires more computing resource.

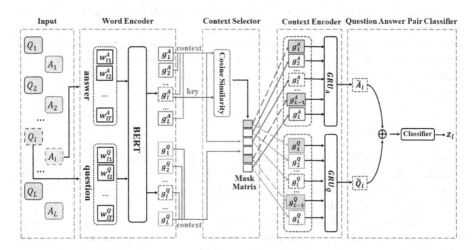

Fig. 1. Overview of the CSN. The red dashed box in the sequence indicates the target QA pair to be predicted. The black arrow in the context selector means obtaining a mask matrix after the cosine similarity module and blue arrows pointing to the mask matrix mean inputs to it. The dotted arrows pointing from mask matrix mean mask value is 0 and the corresponding contexts are masked, while solid arrows mean mask value is 1. (Color figure online)

3 Model

3.1 Problem Formalization

Suppose that we have a dataset $D = \{U_i, Y_i\}_{i=1}^N$, where $U_i = \{q_{il}, a_{il}\}_{l=1}^L$ represents a multi-turn QA with L QA pairs and every sentence in a multi-turn QA contains T words. N is the number of multi-turn QAs in the dataset. $Y_i = \{y_{il}\}_{l=1}^L$ where $y_{il} \in \{0, 1\}$ denotes the label of a QA pair. $y_{il} = 1$ means $\{q_{il}, a_{il}\}$ is deceptive, otherwise $y_{il} = 0$. Given the dataset, the goal of deception detection is to learn a classifier f : $U \to Y$, where U and Y are the sets of QA pairs and labels respectively, to predict the label of QA pairs based on the context information in a multi-turn QA.

3.2 Model Overview

We propose CSN that generates context-independent sentence embeddings first, and then selects contexts for the target question and answer respectively to filter out the noise, and then utilizes the context encoder to get context-aware sentence embeddings. As illustrated in Fig. 1, the proposed model consists of Word Encoder, Context Selector, Context Encoder, and Question Answer Pair Classifier.

3.3 Word Encoder

Since the form of data collection is to design questions first and then collect corresponding answers, we treat a multi-turn QA as a combination of one question sequence and one answer sequence. The l_{th} question and answer with T words in the i_{th} multi-turn QA are defined as $\{w_{l1}^Q, ..., w_{lT}^Q\}$ and $\{w_{l1}^A, ..., w_{lT}^A\}$ respectively. We feed both sentences into the pre-trained BERT and obtain context-independent sentence embeddings, which are defined as g_l^Q, g_l^A for the question and answer respectively. In the experiments, we also replace BERT with BiGRU which proves the effectiveness of BERT.

3.4 Context Selector

Given a multi-turn QA and its sentence representations, we treat the questions and answers as two contexts: $\mathcal{Q} = \{g_l^Q\}_{l=1}^L, \mathcal{A} = \{g_l^A\}_{l=1}^L$. We design a context selector to select contexts for target question and answer respectively in order to eliminate the influence of noise in the context.

We treat the answer of the QA pair to be predicted as key: g_l^A, to select the corresponding answer contexts. We use cosine similarity to measure text similarity between the answer key g_l^A and the answer context $\mathcal{A}$, which is formulated as:

$$s_{A_l} = \frac{\mathcal{A} g_l^{A\top}}{||\mathcal{A}||_2 ||g_l^A||_2}, \tag{1}$$

where s_{A_l} is the relevance score.

Then we use the score to form a mask matrix for each answer and assign the same mask matrix to the question contexts, aiming to retain the consistency of the masked answer sequence and question sequence, which is formulated as:

$$\tilde{s}_{A_l} = (\sigma(s_{A_l}) \geq \gamma), \tilde{s}_{Q_l} = \tilde{s}_{A_l}, \tag{2}$$

$$Q_l = \tilde{s}_{Q_l} \odot Q, A_l = \tilde{s}_{A_l} \odot A, \tag{3}$$

where $\odot$ is element-wise multiplication; σ is the sigmoid function; γ is the threshold and will be tuned according to the dataset. The sentences whose scores are below γ will be filtered out. Q_l and A_l are the final contexts for q_l and a_l.

The context selector can make the model focus on the more relevant contexts through filtering out the noise contexts and thus benefits the model of exploring context-sensitive dependencies implied in the multi-turn QA.

3.5 Context Encoder

Given the selected contexts of the target question and answer, we feed them to two BiGRUs respectively:

$$\tilde{Q}_l = \overleftrightarrow{GRU_Q}(Q_{(l(+,-)1)}, g_i^Q), \tag{4}$$

$$\tilde{A}_l = \overleftrightarrow{GRU_A}(A_{(l(+,-)1)}, g_i^A), \tag{5}$$

where $\tilde{Q}_l$ and $\tilde{A}_l$ represent the outputs of the q_l and a_l at the corresponding position in the two bidirectional GRUs. $\tilde{Q}_l$ and $\tilde{A}_l$ denote the context-aware embeddings of q_l and a_l respectively.

We use the two context encoders to model context dependencies between multiple answers and questions respectively. In this way, we can make full use of deceptive signals implied in the contexts to recognize deceptive QA pairs.

3.6 Question Answer Pair Classifier

Then, the context-aware embeddings of the target question and answer are concatenated to obtain the final QA pair representation:

$$h_l = [\tilde{Q}_l, \tilde{A}_l]. \tag{6}$$

Finally, the representation of the QA pair is fed into a softmax classifier:

$$z_l = softmax(Wh_l + b), \tag{7}$$

where W and b are trainable parameters.

The loss function is defined as the cross-entropy error over all labeled QA pairs:

$$\mathcal{L} = -\sum_{i=1}^{N}\sum_{l=1}^{L} y_{il} \ln z_{il}, \tag{8}$$

where N is the number of multi-turn QAs; L is the number of QA pairs in a multi-turn QA and y_{il} is the ground-truth label of the QA pair.

4   Deception QA Dataset Design

Our goal is to build a Chinese text-based collection of deception and non-deception data in the form of multi-turn QA, which allows us to analyze contextual dependencies between QA pairs concerning deception. We design questionnaires related to different topics about daily life and then recruit subjects to answer these questions.

4.1   Questionnaires Design

To collect deceptive and non-deceptive data, we design six different questionnaires covering six topics related to daily life. These six themes are sports, music, tourism, film and television, school, and occupation. For each questionnaire, we design different questions. The number of questions in each questionnaire varies from seven to ten. Specially, the first question in the questionnaire is directly related to the corresponding theme as shown in Table 1. The following questions are designed subtly so that they can be viewed as follow-up questions for the first question. There are also progressive dependencies between these questions.

4.2   Answers Collection

To obtain deceptive and non-deceptive data, we recruit 318 subjects from universities and companies to fill in the six questionnaires. The numbers of collected multi-turn QAs for each theme are 337, 97, 49, 53, 51, and 49 respectively.

Each subject is asked to answer the same questionnaire twice to make the distribution of deceptive and non-deceptive data as balanced as possible. For the first time, subjects need to tell the truth to the first question. For the second time, they need to tell lies to the same first question. Subjects are allowed to tell the truth or lies to the following questions casually, but the final goal is to convince others that the subjects' answers are all true. Questions in a questionnaire have sequential dependence, forcing the subjects to change their answers to the first question instead of other questions helps them better organize their expression to answer the following questions. In order to motivate subjects to produce high-quality deceptive and non-deceptive answers, we give them certain monetary rewards.

Similar to previous work [11], we ask the subjects to label their own answers. Subjects are asked to label their answers with "T" or "F". "T" means what they say is truth and "F" means deceptive.

4.3   Train/Dev/Test Split

We obtain 636 multi-turn QAs and 6113 QA pairs finally. After shuffling all of the multi-turn QAs, we divide the data into train set, development set, and test set randomly according to the ratio of 8:1:1. Table 2 shows dataset statistics.

Table 2. Statistics of train, dev and test sets of Deception QA.

	Train	Dev	Test	All
# QA Pairs (Multi-turn QAs)	4932 (512)	595 (62)	595 (62)	6113 (636)
Ave./Max. # QA Pairs/Multi-turn QA	9.61/10	9.60/10	9.60/10	9.61/10
Ave./Max. # Words/Question	9.44/18	9.45/18	9.45/18	9.45/18
Ave./Max. # Words/Answer	7.94/142	7.05/52	7.71/60	7.83/142
Truthful QA pairs	3172	353	419	3944
Deceptive QA pairs	1751	242	176	2169

5   Experiments

5.1   Experimental Settings

Deception QA dataset is a Chinese dataset. Jieba[1] is employed to segment text into Chinese words and Glove [23] is employed to get pre-trained word embeddings. Moreover, we use Chinese BERT and RoBERTa with whole word masking[2] [4]. For the context selector, γ is set to 0.63 according to the valid data. The performance is evaluated using standard Macro-Precision, Macro-Recall, and Macro-F1.

5.2   Baselines

The baselines are divided into two parts, according to whether take the context into consideration or not. Without considering the context, we compare our model with general text classification approaches: BiGRU [3], TextCNN [10], BERT [5] and RoBERTa [16]. Considering the context, we use BiGRU-CC, attBiGRU-CC, TextCNN-BiGRU, DialogueGCN [8], where CC means considering all the contexts and DialogueGCN is the state-of-the-art model of emotion recognition in conversation task. We propose CSN and CSN-BERT/-RoBERTa which have a subtlety-designed context selector to filter noise in the context.

5.3   Results and Analysis

Results in Table 3 can be divided into three parts. From top to the bottom, it shows the results that do not consider the contexts, consider all the contexts and perform contexts selection.

From the first part, we find that methods based on pre-trained language models (PLMs) are almost better than general text classification models. From the second part, we find that approaches considering the contexts perform much better than those who don't consider the contexts. This proves the effectiveness of the QA context to detect deception.

---

[1] https://github.com/fxsjy/jieba.

[2] https://github.com/ymcui/Chinese-BERT-wwm.

Table 3. Comparison of varying approaches.

Model	Macro-P	Macro-R	Macro-F1
BiGRU	56.47	50.96	45.11
TextCNN	60.64	51.98	47.11
BERT	57.06	58.41	56.11
RoBERTa	58.62	59.74	58.68
attBiGRU-CC	54.32	55.13	53.29
TextCNN-BiGRU	58.33	54.15	52.86
DialogueGCN	59.46	61.36	57.72
CSN-BERT	63.93	**66.64**	63.34
CSN-RoBERTa	**63.96**	65.03	**64.33**

Table 4. Ablation study on deception QA dataset.

Model	Macro-P	Macro-R	Macro-F1
CSN	**63.09**	**58.43**	**58.67**
BiGRU-CC	58.83	56.57	56.69
CSN-BERT	**63.93**	**66.64**	**63.34**
BERT-BiGRU-CC	59.18	59.99	59.38
CSN-RoBERTa	**63.96**	**65.03**	**64.33**
RoBERTa-BiGRU-CC	60.93	61.85	61.20

The model proposed by us achieves the best performance among all of the strong baselines. The Macro-F1 score of **CSN-RoBERTa** is 5.65% higher than that of **RoBERTa** and 6.61% higher than that of **DialogueGCN**. For other sequence-based approaches without the context selector, the Macro-F1 score of **CSN-RoBERTa** is 11.26% higher than them on average. It indicates that taking all of the contexts including noise can hurt the model performance. Besides context information, noise is another key factor that affects the ability of the model to recognize deception. The results indicate the effectiveness of our model.

From experimental results in Table 4, we can observe that removing the context selector results in performance degradation. The results of the ablation study on three models show that the Macro-F1 values of the models using the context selector is 3.02% higher than those of the models without context selector on average. This proves that the proposed context selector does help to improve the model's ability to recognize deceptive and non-deceptive QA pairs in a multi-turn QA.

5.4   Case Study

Table 5 shows an example that CSN-RoBERTa successfully predicted Turn-5 as deception by masking Turn-2, Turn-8, and Turn-9 while RoBERTa-BiGRU-CC which takes all of the contexts into consideration misclassified Turn-5.

Table 5. An example that CSN-RoBERTa successfully identified Turn-5 as deception but RoBERTa-BiGRU-CC failed. CSN-RoBERTa chose to mask the QA pairs written in blue in order to predict the label of Turn-5.

Turns		Theme: Sports
Turn-1	Q_1	What kind of ball sports do you like?
	A_1	Billiards. (**F**)
Turn-2	Q_2	When did you like this sport?
	A_2	I liked billiards when I was in college.(**T**)
Turn-3	Q_3	Why do you like this sport?
	A_3	Billiards is a very elegant sport. Girls who can play billiards are very cool. (**T**)
Turn-4	Q_4	Do you usually play ball? When and where do you play ball? How long does it take each time?
	A_4	When I was in college, I often went to the billiard hall near the school gate to play billiards for about an hour at a time. (**F**)
Turn-5	Q_5	Have you participated in any competition related to this sport?
	A_5	Yes, but I have never won any awards. (**F**)
Turn-6	Q_6	How well do you play? Have you received professional training?
	A_6	My level of billiards is average, not bad. (**F**)
Turn-7	Q_7	Which star do you like in this sport? When did you like him?
	A_7	Ding Junhui. He is a champion and plays billiards well. (**F**)
Turn-8	Q_8	Please introduce this star player.
	A_8	I don't know him very well, all I know is that he won the championship. (**T**)
Turn-9	Q_9	Please introduce some famous competitions and other famous star players related to this sport.
	A_9	Ding Junhui and snooker. Although I like playing billiards, I don't pay attention to the competitions. (**F**)

According to the example, we can find that the masked contexts can be regarded as noise which is less relevant to Turn-5. Turn-2 talked about the time when the subject liked billiards that is relatively irrelevant to the subject's experience in the game. Turn-7, Turn-8, and Turn-9 all talked about star players which could not provide effective information for judging whether Turn-5 is deceptive. Due to the inaccuracies of the model, only Turn-2, Turn-8, and Turn-9 are masked. This kind of noisy context can confuse the model and make it unable to classify Turn-5 correctly.

6 Conclusion

In this paper, we propose a novel task: deception detection in a multi-turn QA and a context selector network to model context-sensitive dependence. In addition, we build a high-quality dataset for the experiment. Empirical evaluation on the collected dataset indicates that our approach significantly outperforms several strong baseline approaches, showing that the QA contexts and the context selector do help the model effectively explore deceptive features. In the future, we would like to integrate user information to explore deeper deceptive signals in the multi-turn QA.

References

1. Azaria, A., Richardson, A., Kraus, S.: An agent for deception detection in discussion based environments. In: CSCW, pp. 218–227 (2015)
2. Bian, T., et al.: Rumor detection on social media with bi-directional graph convolutional networks. In: AAAI, pp. 549–556 (2020)
3. Cho, K., et al.: Learning phrase representations using RNN encoder-decoder for statistical machine translation. In: EMNLP, pp. 1724–1734 (2014)
4. Cui, Y., et al.: Pre-training with whole word masking for chinese BERT. arXiv: 1906.08101 (2019)
5. Devlin, J., Chang, M., Lee, K., Toutanova, K.: BERT: pre-training of deep bidirectional transformers for language understanding. In: NAACL-HLT, pp. 4171–4186 (2019)
6. Ding, M., Zhao, A., Lu, Z., Xiang, T., Wen, J.R.: Face-focused cross-stream network for deception detection in videos. In: Proceedings of the IEEE/CVF Conference on Computer Vision and Pattern Recognition, pp. 7802–7811 (2019)
7. Feng, S., Banerjee, R., Choi, Y.: Syntactic stylometry for deception detection. In: ACL, pp. 171–175 (2012)
8. Ghosal, D., Majumder, N., Poria, S., Chhaya, N., Gelbukh, A.F.: Dialoguegcn: A graph convolutional neural network for emotion recognition in conversation. In: EMNLP-IJCNLP, pp. 154–164 (2019)
9. Hirschberg, J., et al.: Distinguishing deceptive from non-deceptive speech. In: INTER-SPEECH, pp. 1833–1836 (2005)
10. Kim, Y.: Convolutional neural networks for sentence classification. In: EMNLP, pp. 1746–1751 (2014)
11. Levitan, S.I., et al.: Cross-cultural production and detection of deception from speech. In: WMDD@ICMI, pp. 1–8 (2015)
12. Levitan, S.I., Maredia, A., Hirschberg, J.: Linguistic cues to deception and perceived deception in interview dialogues. In: NAACL-HLT, pp. 1941–1950 (2018)
13. Li, D., Jr., E.S.: Discriminating deception from truth and misinformation: an intent-level approach. J. Exp. Theor. Artif. Intell. 32(3), 373–407 (2020)
14. Li, X., et al.: Entity-relation extraction as multi-turn question answering. In: ACL, pp. 1340–1350 (2019)
15. Liu, L., Zhang, Z., Zhao, H., Zhou, X., Zhou, X.: Filling the gap of utterance-aware and speaker-aware representation for multi-turn dialogue. In: AAAI, pp. 13406–13414 (2021)
16. Liu, Y., et al.: Roberta: A robustly optimized BERT pretraining approach. CoRR abs/arXiv: 1907.11692 (2019)
17. Lu, Y., Li, C.: GCAN: graph-aware co-attention networks for explainable fake news detection on social media. In: ACL, pp. 505–514 (2020)
18. Mathur, L., Mataric, M.J.: Unsupervised audio-visual subspace alignment for high-stakes deception detection. In: IEEE International Conference on Acoustics, Speech and Signal Processing, ICASSP 2021, Toronto, ON, Canada, 6–11 June 2021, pp. 2255–2259. IEEE (2021)

19. Mihalcea, R., Strapparava, C.: The lie detector: Explorations in the automatic recognition of deceptive language. In: ACL, pp. 309–312 (2009)
20. Ott, M., Cardie, C., Hancock, J.T.: Negative deceptive opinion spam. In: HLT-NAACL, pp. 497–501 (2013)
21. Ott, M., Choi, Y., Cardie, C., Hancock, J.T.: Finding deceptive opinion spam by any stretch of the imagination. In: ACL, pp. 309–319 (2011). https://www.aclweb.org/anthology/P11-1032/
22. Pennebaker, J.W., Francis, M.E., Booth, R.J.: Linguistic Inquiry and Word Count. Lawerence Erlbaum Associates, Mahwah, NJ (2001)
23. Pennington, J., Socher, R., Manning, C.D.: Glove: Global vectors for word representation. In: EMNLP, pp. 1532–1543 (2014)
24. Pérez-Rosas, V., Abouelenien, M., Mihalcea, R., Burzo, M.: Deception detection using real-life trial data. In: ICMI, pp. 59–66 (2015)
25. Pérez-Rosas, V., Abouelenien, M., Mihalcea, R., Xiao, Y., Linton, C.J., Burzo, M.: Verbal and nonverbal clues for real-life deception detection. In: EMNLP, pp. 2336–2346 (2015)
26. Pisarevskaya, D.: Deception detection in news reports in the russian language: Lexics and discourse. In: NLPmJ@EMNLP, pp. 74–79 (2017)
27. de Ruiter, B., Kachergis, G.: The mafiascum dataset: A large text corpus for deception detection. CoRR abs/ arXiv:1811.07851 (2018)
28. Soldner, F., Pérez-Rosas, V., Mihalcea, R.: Box of lies: Multimodal deception detection in dialogues. In: Burstein, J., Doran, C., Solorio, T. (eds.) NAACL-HLT, pp. 1768–1777 (2019)
29. Tsunomori, Y., Neubig, G., Sakti, S., Toda, T., Nakamura, S.: An analysis towards dialogue-based deception detection. In: Natural Language Dialog Systems and Intelligent Assistants, pp. 177–187 (2015)
30. Wang, X.D., Weber, L., Leser, U.: Biomedical event extraction as multi-turn question answering. In: LOUHI@EMNLP, pp. 88–96 (2020)
31. Xu, Q., Zhao, H.: Using deep linguistic features for finding deceptive opinion spam. In: COLING, pp. 1341–1350 (2012)
32. Zhou, L., Sung, Y.: Cues to deception in online chinese groups. In: HICSS-41, p. 146 (2008)

SIA-Unet: A Unet with Sequence Information for Gastrointestinal Tract Segmentation

Rongguang Ye, Ranmin Wang, Yantong Guo, and Lei Chen[(⊠)]

Guangdong University of Technology, Guangzhou, China
{3119007142,3121003517,3219007040,chenlei3}@gdut.edu.cn

Abstract. Magnetic resonance imaging (MRI) has been widely applied to the medical imaging diagnosis of various human body systems. Deep network-based medical image segmentation techniques for MRI can help patients receive more accurate and effective diagnoses. However, multiple consecutive two-dimensional MRIs have sequence information in reality. Different organs may appear specifically in a sequence of MRI data for the body part. Therefore, MRI sequence information is the key to improving the segmentation effect in deep network architecture design. In this paper, we propose the SIA-Unet, an improved Unet network that incorporates MRI sequence information. SIA-Unet also has an attention mechanism to filter the feature map's spatial data to extract valuable data. Extensive experiments on the UW-Madison dataset have been conducted to evaluate the performance of SIA-Unet. Experimental results have shown that with a coherent end-to-end training pipeline, SIA-Unet significantly outperforms other baselines. Our implementation is available at https://github.com/min121101/SIA-Unet.

Keywords: Magnetic resonance imaging · Medical image segmentation · Deep neural network

1 Introduction

In detecting gastrointestinal (GI) cancer using MRI, oncologists usually manually delineate the location of the intestinal and stomach, which is a labor-intensive and time-consuming process. With deep learning methods, it is possible to segment the intestinal and stomach to allow for faster treatment automatically [8,22], and therefore more patients can be treated effectively in a short period [5,13,14,23]. Automatic medical image segmentation can achieve results comparable to highly experienced radiologists [1,7]. Image segmentation has developed rapidly in recent years. Long et al. first used fully convolutional networks (FCNs) [9] for image segmentation. At the same time, Ronneberger et al. proposed a U-shaped network U-net [12] that uses channel dimension splicing

Supported by the National Natural Science Foundation of China (62006044).).

© The Author(s), under exclusive license to Springer Nature Switzerland AG 2022
S. Khanna et al. (Eds.): PRICAI 2022, LNCS 13629, pp. 316–326, 2022.
https://doi.org/10.1007/978-3-031-20862-1_23

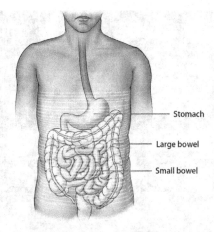

Fig. 1. The location of the small bowel, large bowel, and stomach in the human body.

in the feature fusion method. Unet has achieved accurate segmentation results in medical image segmentation problems [3,6]. Since the skip connection of the Unet model will bring too much redundant information, Zongwei et al. improved the skip connection of Unet and proposed Unet++ [24]. Subsequently, Attention Unet [11] and scSE-Unet [15] added different types of Attention to Unet to extract key information from the feature map. In particular, in the field of gastrointestinal tract segmentation, a number of deep learning-based detectors have been proposed in [4,19,20]. However, much of the gastrointestinal image data is in the format of MRIs, and these detectors do not exploit the seriality in MRIs.

Most MRI scans are sequence images [10]. Specific organs exist only in particular locations (Fig. 1), and there are also some scanned images without target organs, which affects neural network training. The main reason for this phenomenon is that the early images of MRI have not yet scanned the position of the organ. Most organs are located in the middle and late stages of the scan. For example, an MRI scan of a patient is shown in Fig. 2. The intestine appears in the middle stage, and the stomach only appears in the later scan stage. For the detection task of GI cancer, MRI's sequence information is crucial [2,21]. Although current image segmentation technology has been extensively studied, few studies in traditional 2D MRI scans can combine the sequence information of the scanned slices. To consider sequence information in 2D images, a feasible solution is to process the MRIs ourselves to obtain 3D data. However, rashly adding sequence information will inevitably generate redundant data. Thus, a specialized mechanism is needed to filter irrelevant information.

In this paper, we propose a simple yet effective model SIA-Unet by combining sequence information in MRI images. In SIA-Unet, multiple sequence images are first fused into the channel dimension, such that the original two-dimensional image has short-term sequence information. Furthermore, to efficiently extract

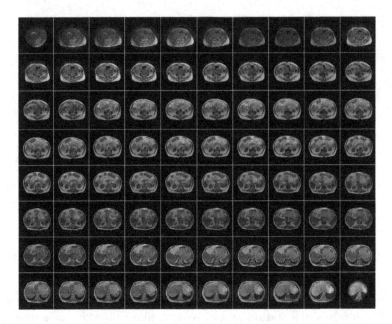

Fig. 2. Multiple slice images of an MRI scan. We found that the MRI scan results are from the abdomen to the chest of the human body. Red, grey, and blue represent the small bowel, large bowel, and stomach, respectively. The small and large bowel appear mid-scan, while the stomach appears late in the scan. (Color figure online)

information on the channel and spatial dimensions, scSE (The Spatial and Channel Squeeze & Excitation Block) attention mechanism [15] is used at the end of the skip connection and upsampling process, enabling the neural network to focus on segmentation regions while learning sequence information. Finally, we apply SIA-Unet to MRI images for GI segmentation to verify its performance.

The contributions of this work are summarized as follows:

1. We propose the SIA-Unet, a simple yet effective method to learn sequence MRI images. It enables images to have 3D information by combining multiple images of an MRI scan into the channel dimension.
2. Based on the sequence information extraction strategy, an attention mechanism is introduced; both of them synergistically extract, process, and filter channel and spatial information from GI scans.
3. Extensive experiments show that SIA-Unet outperforms four baselines by 1.5% on the UW-Madison dataset, achieving the highest performance.

2   Methodology

In this section, we propose a network called SIA-Unet for gastrointestinal tract segmentation. First, we describe how to exploit the sequence information from

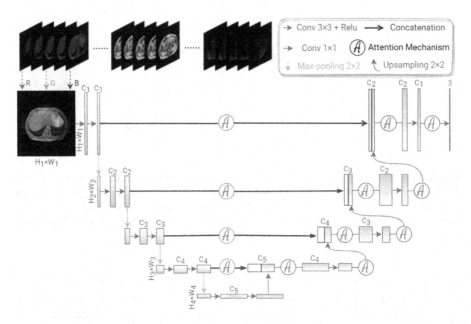

Fig. 3. The general framework of SIA-Unet. We first fuse multiple images of MRI scans into the channel dimension. In addition, grey and blue attention mechanisms are also added to the Unet. They function differently, but the main components are the same. Specific details are shown in Fig. 4. The grey attention mechanism in Unet's skip connections (scA) removes redundant information from previous data. The blue attention mechanism in up-sampling (usA) is used to complete the information calibration of the channel and spatial dimensions. (Color figure online)

MRI images. Second, we present an attention mechanism in Unet to further utilize channel and spatial data. An overview of SIA-Unet is shown in Fig. 3, where images are regenerated from MRI sequences before model training. After that, we add multiple attention mechanisms to Unet (their different colors indicate different effects).

2.1 Sequence Information Processing (SIP)

Since the results of an MRI scan are from the abdomen to the chest, different parts of the body will show different organs or even no organs. Therefore, the appearance of organs has a specific order and regularity, and it is crucial to use this prior information to improve the performance of GI tract segmentation. To allow the neural network to distinguish the position of the image on the human body, we plan to add sequence information to each image.

The data of a patient on MRI scan is $Slice = [Slice_1, Slice_2, \ldots, Slice_n]$, where $Slice_n$ represents a scanned slice, and its dimension is $[1, H, W]$. A scan slice does not contain any sequence information. As shown in Fig. 3, our approach preprocesses images before model training. Specifically, multiple serial slice

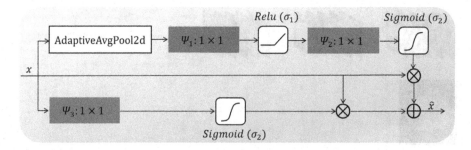

Fig. 4. Components of the attention mechanism. For x with input dimension $C \times H \times W$, it calculates the attention scores of the channels and spaces through the upper and lower branches, respectively. Then, multiply ($\otimes$) these two attention scores by x and add ($\oplus$) them to get the final $\hat{x}$. Ψ_1, Ψ_2, and Ψ_3 are all 1×1 convolution kernels. *Relu* and *Sigmoid* are two activation functions.

images are stacked on one channel, so that each image contains the MRI sequence data. Considering that consecutive slice data have almost the same information, we take an interval of j slices to extract a scan slice. After transformation, The ith MRI image is:

$$Slice_i = \begin{cases} [Slice_i, Slice_{i+j}, \ldots, Slice_{i+Nj}] & \text{if } i + Nj < n, \\ [Slice_i, Slice_{i+j}, \ldots, Slice_n] & \text{otherwise.} \end{cases} \quad (1)$$

where $Slice_i$ means that an image is extracted for every j MRI slice, and a total of N images is merged in the channel dimension. In this paper, we set N to 2, which means that each scan slice is processed into an RGB image (contains short-term sequence images), which is beneficial for the neural network to learn the sequence information of the MRI scan.

2.2 Attention Mechanism in U-Net

In order for the neural network to ignore unnecessary features and thus focus on segmenting organs, we introduce an attention mechanism [15] to exploit the channel and spatial information more deeply. As shown in Fig. 4, it is divided into two branches: (1) Spatial Squeeze and Channel Excitation ; (2) Channel Squeeze and Spatial Excitation.

Spatial Squeeze and Channel Excitation (cSE). It first passes the feature map x through the global average pooling layer, and the dimension of the feature map changes from $[C, H, W]$ to $[C, 1, 1]$. Then, a 1×1 convolutional layer is used to process the information with the *Relu* function[1] σ_1 to obtain a C-dimensional vector. Afterwards, a 1×1 convolutional layer and the *Sigmoid* function[2] σ_2 are

---

[1] $\sigma_1(x) = 1/(1 + e^{-x})$.
[2] $\sigma_2(x) = \max(0, x)$.

Table 1. Split train and Validation sets in the UW-Madison dataset. Empty means that there is no target organs in the slice image.

Set	Cases	Total image	#Empty	Divided by #image		
				small bowel	large bowel	stomach
Train	69	30128	17009	9014	11227	6743
Validation	16	8080	4706	2187	2858	1884

used to finalize the normalization of the information to obtain the attention score. Finally, multiply with the first x to complete the attention mechanism of the channel dimension. cSE can process channel dimension information to provide a feature map that is more conducive to neural network training.

Channel Squeeze and Spatial Excitation (sSE). The design of sSE is simple yet effective. The feature map first passes through the 1×1 convolutional layer, and the dimension of the feature map changes from $[C, H, W]$ to $[1, H, W]$. Then, a sigmoid function σ_2 is used to obtain the attention score of the spatial dimension. Finally, multiply the original x to complete the attention mechanism of the spatial dimension. sSE can filter the information of the spatial dimension, such that the neural network can focus more on cutting the target rather than the background.

In particular, in the initial Unet framework, the down-sampled feature maps are skip-connected with up-sampling, stacking in the channel dimension. Although the up-sampled feature map has a certain amount of information, it also carries too much redundant information. To filter the redundant information, as shown in Fig. 3, we incorporate two types of attention mechanisms into the Unet. Unlike scSE-Unet [15], we add a grey attention mechanism (usA) to the process of skip connection. usA suppresses the irrelevant features brought by the skip connection process. On the other hand, to enhance the neural network's perception of spatial and channel dimensions, we also added multiple blue attention mechanisms (scA). The pseudo-code of SIA-Unet is presented in Algorithm 1.

3 Experiment

3.1 Experimental Settings

Dataset. The dataset we used is a collection of MRI scans from multiple patients at the Carbone Cancer Center at the University of Wisconsin-Madison. We call it the UW-Madison dataset, which is divided as the training set and validation set. A scan of a patient is shown in Fig. 2. The summary information is shown in Table 1, in which 69 cases in the training set and 16 cases in the training set. The training set contains 30,128 scan slices (17,009 without GI organs), and the Validation set includes 8,080 scans (2,187 without GI organs).

Algorithm 1. SIA-Unet

1: **Input:** Dataset $\mathcal{D}$, model ϕ, mini-batch of image $\mathcal{M}$, channels $\mathcal{C}$, Stride $\mathcal{S}$, Sigmoid σ_1, Relu σ_1, Convolutional Layer $Conv$ and Encoder $\mathcal{E}$.

2: **for** each epoch $i = 0, 1, 2 \ldots n$ **do**

3:    **for** $\mathcal{M}$ in $\mathcal{D}$ **do**

4:       TRANSFORM($\mathcal{M}, \mathcal{C}, \mathcal{S}$) ▷ Combine multiple sequence images

5:       $\mathcal{M}' = \mathcal{E}(\mathcal{M}')$ ▷ The encoder extracts features

6:       $\mathcal{M}' = Unsample(\mathcal{M}', ATTENTION)$ ▷ Add attention to Unet

7:       $\mathcal{L} = 0.5 \times \mathcal{L}_{BCE} + 0.5 \times \mathcal{L}_{Tversky}$ ▷ Define the loss function

8:       Optimizing $\mathcal{L}$ using $Adam$ algorithm to update ϕ

9:    **end for**

10: **end for**

11: **function** TRANSFORM($\mathcal{M}, \mathcal{C}, \mathcal{S}$)

12:    **for** $c = 0, 1, 2 \ldots \mathcal{C}$ **do**

13:       $M[c, :, :] = M$.groupby(['case','day']).shift(-c*S).fillna(method="ffill")

14:    **end for**

15: **end function**

16: **function** ATTENTION($\mathcal{M}', \mathcal{H}, \mathcal{W}$)

17:    $Z = \frac{1}{H \times W} \sum_i^H \sum_j^W M'(i, j)$ ▷ After passing through the global pooling layer

18:    $U_{csE} = \mathcal{M}' \times \sigma_1(Conv(\sigma_2(Conv(Z))))$ ▷ Channel attention mechanism

19:    $U_{sSE} = \mathcal{M}' \times \sigma_2(Conv(\mathcal{M}'))$ ▷ Spatial attention mechanism

20:    $U_{scSE} = U_{csE} + U_{ssE}$

21:    **return** U_{scSE}

22: **end function**

Evaluation Metrics. We evaluate the performance of all methods with the Jaccard coefficient and Dice coefficient, two of the most commonly used metrics in medical image segmentation. Their equations can be expressed as:

$$\text{Jaccard} = \frac{A \cap B}{A \cup B} \tag{2}$$

$$\text{Dice} = \frac{2(A \cap B)}{A + B} \tag{3}$$

where A and B are binary matrices representing the ground-truth annotation and the predicted annotation, respectively.

Implementation Details. We use Unet as the architecture and use multiple backbones (i.e., VGG, EfficientNet) to verify the stability of SIA-Unet. We train the network for 20 epochs using the Adaptive Momentum Estimation (Adam) algorithm with a weight decay of 0.000001. The initial learning rate is 0.002, and the weights are changed with the cosine annealing learning rate; the initial temperature is 25, and the maximum temperature is 96.875. We use the Pytorch framework for training. And use data augmentation methods such as

HorizontalFlip, ShiftScaleRotate, and CoarseDropout. The loss function uniformly adopts the average of Binary Cross-Entropy ($\mathcal{L}_{BCE}$) and Tversky Loss ($\mathcal{L}_{Tversky}$) [16], $\mathcal{L}_{Tversky}$ is a classification Loss function used to solve the imbalance. The $\mathcal{L}_{BCE}$ is expressed as:

$$\mathcal{L}_{BCE} = -\sum_{j=1}^{C} \log\left(\widehat{p}_j\right), \quad \text{with } \widehat{p}_j = \begin{cases} p_j & \text{if } y_j = 1, \\ 1 - p_j & \text{otherwis.} \end{cases} \tag{4}$$

where C is the total number of categories, i.e., stomach, large bowel and small bowel, y_j is a binary distribution for each class j, p_j is the probability that the classifier estimates each class j.

We use one NVIDIA GeForce RTX 3090 GPU with 24G memory for training. Three sequence MRI images are fused into the channel dimension in our experiments.

Baseline. We use four baselines, including (I) Unet, (II) Unet++, (III) Attention Unet, and (IV) scSE-Unet.

(I) **Unet** [12]: One of the most widely used models in medical image segmentation. It adopts an encoder-decoder structure and skips connections to quickly train a high-accuracy network with only a small number of annotated images.

(II) **Unet++** [24]: An intensely supervised network that achieves a trade-off between the network training speed and accuracy in practical applications through pruning.

(III) **Attention Unet** [11]: An Attention Gate structure is added at the end of the skip connection, which suppresses irrelevant regions of the input image while highlighting the features of specific local areas.

(IV) **scSE-Unet** [15]: Adding attention to the channel and spatial dimensions can improve fine-grained semantic segmentation and smooth the segmentation boundary.

3.2 Main Result

To show the effectiveness of SIA-Unet, we conduct extensive experiments with two different backbones, i.e., VGG-16 [17] and EfficientNet-B0 [18]. As shown in Table 2, the Jaccard coefficient and Dice coefficient of SIA-Unet in Backbone as VGG are significantly higher than Unet by 2.2%. The Jaccard coefficient and Dice coefficient of LB, SB and ST are improved by around 1% to 3%, revealing that SIA-Unet promotes the detection of different organs. In addition to Unet, we also compare SIA-Unet with several other methods shown in Table 2, i.e., Unet++, Attention Unet, and scSE-Unet. The Jaccard coefficient and Dice coefficient of SIA-Unet are about 1.4% higher than the best model, Attention UnFet, and the LB lead is about 2.5% higher at most. SIA-Unet also achieves the best performance in EfficientNet-B0. As a result, SIA-Unet has good generalization ability on different backbones.

Table 2. Performance comparison of Unet [12], Unet++ [24], Attention Unet [11], scSE-Unet [15] and SIA-Unet in the UW-Madison dataset under different backbones (i.e. VGG-16 [17], EfficientNet-b0 [18]). LB, SB and ST denote the large bowel, small bowel and stomach, respectively.

Backbone	Method	Jaccard				Dice			
		Total	LB	SB	ST	Total	LB	SB	ST
VGG[17]	Unet	0.8604	0.8421	0.8211	0.9182	0.8894	0.8770	0.8536	0.9378
	Unet++	0.8642	0.8475	0.8309	0.9172	0.8931	0.8816	0.8635	0.9363
	Attention Unet	0.8691	0.8497	0.8366	0.9228	0.8974	0.8847	0.8690	0.9410
	scSE-Unet	0.8672	0.8500	0.8348	0.9179	0.8958	0.8841	0.8670	0.9373
	SIA-Unet	**0.8828**	0.8752	0.8465	0.9295	**0.9113**	0.9080	0.8800	0.9491
EfficientNet[18]	Unet	0.8536	0.8320	0.9170	0.8675	0.8886	0.8650	0.9369	0.8968
	Unet++	0.8505	0.8248	0.9166	0.8628	0.8849	0.8570	0.9363	0.8917
	Attention Unet	0.8500	0.8337	0.9211	0.8680	0.8839	0.8660	0.9404	0.8964
	scSE-Unet	0.8489	0.8199	0.9145	0.8604	0.8835	0.8533	0.9346	0.8900
	SIA-Unet	**0.8593**	0.8383	0.9210	0.8729	**0.8943**	0.8721	0.9416	0.9025

Table 3. The ablation study of each component of SIA-Unet, SIP indicates adding depth information to the original image (processing as a multi-channel image). scA and usA refer to the attention mechanisms at different positions in Fig. 3. The backbone used is VGG-16.

SIP	scA	usA	Jaccard				Dice			
			Total	LB	SB	ST	Total	LB	SB	ST
✗	✗	✗	0.8604	0.8421	0.8211	0.9182	0.8894	0.8770	0.8536	0.9378
✓	✗	✗	0.8748	0.8603	0.8382	0.9281	0.9035	0.8945	0.8699	0.9482
✓	✓	✗	0.8814	0.8714	0.8457	0.9300	0.9101	0.9051	0.8796	0.9497
✓	✓	✓	0.8828	0.8752	0.8465	0.9295	0.9113	0.9080	0.8800	0.9491

3.3 Ablation Study

We perform an ablation study to validate the effectiveness of each component in the method. SIA-Unet includes three components: SIP, scA, and usA. Table 3 shows the evaluation results of each component. It can be seen that when SIP is added, the Jaccard coefficient and the Dice coefficient increase by approximately 1.5% and 1.1%, respectively. Therefore, the sequence information of the MRI scan slices is crucial for the model. Especially for the organ with a large span such as LB (Jaccard coefficient increased by 2.2%). With scA and usA for information filtering, scA and usA can have approximately 0.6% and 0.1% improvement to the model. As a result, SIA-Unet combines three components to achieve a Jaccard coefficient of 0.8828 and a Dice coefficient of 0.9113.

4   Conclusion

This paper proposes SIA-Unet, a model dedicated to extracting and filtering channel and spatial dimension information. SIP integrates the MRIs of sequence scanned slices into the channel dimension, such that the original 2D images can have sequence features. Since SIP preprocessing will inevitably introduce redundant features, we add an attention mechanism (usA) to the end of Unet's skip connection to effectively filter the useless features of skip merge. At the same time, scA in the upsampling process can also filter redundant features due to convolution. The experimental results show that SIA-Unet has a more accurate segmentation effect.

References

1. Bai, W., et al.: Human-level cmr image analysis with deep fully convolutional networks (2017)
2. Gong, J., Kang, W., Zhu, J., Xu, J.: Ct and mr imaging of gastrointestinal stromal tumor of stomach: a pictorial review. Quant. Imaging Med. Surg. **2**(4), 274 (2012)
3. Guan, S., Khan, A.A., Sikdar, S., Chitnis, P.V.: Fully dense unet for 2-d sparse photoacoustic tomography artifact removal. IEEE J. Biomed. Health Inform. **24**(2), 568–576 (2019)
4. Horie, Y., et al.: Diagnostic outcomes of esophageal cancer by artificial intelligence using convolutional neural networks. Gastrointest. Endosc. **89**(1), 25–32 (2019)
5. Khened, M., Kollerathu, V.A., Krishnamurthi, G.: Fully convolutional multi-scale residual densenets for cardiac segmentation and automated cardiac diagnosis using ensemble of classifiers. Med. Image Anal. **51**, 21–45 (2019)
6. Li, X., Chen, H., Qi, X., Dou, Q., Fu, C.W., Heng, P.A.: H-denseunet: hybrid densely connected unet for liver and tumor segmentation from ct volumes. IEEE Trans. Med. Imaging **37**(12), 2663–2674 (2018)
7. Liao, F., Liang, M., Li, Z., Hu, X., Song, S.: Evaluate the malignancy of pulmonary nodules using the 3-d deep leaky noisy-or network. IEEE transactions on neural networks and learning systems **30**(11), 3484–3495 (2019)
8. Liu, K., Ye, R., Zhongzhu, L., Ye, R.: Entropy-based discrimination between translated Chinese and original Chinese using data mining techniques. PLoS ONE **17**(3), e0265633 (2022)
9. Long, J., Shelhamer, E., Darrell, T.: Fully convolutional networks for semantic segmentation. In: Proceedings of the IEEE Conference on Computer Vision and Pattern Recognition, pp. 3431–3440 (2015)
10. Motohara, T., Semelka, R.: Mri in staging of gastric cancer. Abdominal Radiol. **27**(4), 376 (2002)
11. Oktay, O., et al.: Attention u-net: Learning where to look for the pancreas. arXiv preprint arXiv:1804.03999 (2018)
12. Ronneberger, O., Fischer, P., Brox, T.: U-Net: Convolutional networks for biomedical image segmentation. In: Navab, N., Hornegger, J., Wells, W.M., Frangi, A.F. (eds.) MICCAI 2015. LNCS, vol. 9351, pp. 234–241. Springer, Cham (2015). https://doi.org/10.1007/978-3-319-24574-4_28
13. Roth, H.R., Lu, L., Lay, N., Harrison, A.P., Farag, A., Sohn, A., Summers, R.M.: Spatial aggregation of holistically-nested convolutional neural networks for automated pancreas localization and segmentation. Med. Image Anal. **45**, 94–107 (2018)

14. Roth, H.R., et al.: Hierarchical 3d fully convolutional networks for multi-organ segmentation. arXiv preprint arXiv:1704.06382 (2017)
15. Roy, A.G., Navab, N., Wachinger, C.: Concurrent spatial and channel 'Squeeze & Excitation' in fully convolutional networks. In: Frangi, A.F., Schnabel, J.A., Davatzikos, C., Alberola-López, C., Fichtinger, G. (eds.) MICCAI 2018. LNCS, vol. 11070, pp. 421–429. Springer, Cham (2018). https://doi.org/10.1007/978-3-030-00928-1_48
16. Salehi, S.S.M., Erdogmus, D., Gholipour, A.: Tversky loss function for image segmentation using 3d fully convolutional deep networks. In: Wang, Q., Shi, Y., Suk, H.-I., Suzuki, K. (eds.) MLMI 2017. LNCS, vol. 10541, pp. 379–387. Springer, Cham (2017). https://doi.org/10.1007/978-3-319-67389-9_44
17. Simonyan, K., Zisserman, A.: Very deep convolutional networks for large-scale image recognition. arXiv preprint arXiv:1409.1556 (2014)
18. Tan, M., Le, Q.: Efficientnet: Rethinking model scaling for convolutional neural networks. In: International Conference on Machine Learning, pp. 6105–6114. PMLR (2019)
19. Urban, G., et al.: Deep learning localizes and identifies polyps in real time with 96% accuracy in screening colonoscopy. Gastroenterology 155(4), 1069–1078 (2018)
20. Wang, D., et al.: Afp-net: Realtime anchor-free polyp detection in colonoscopy. In: 2019 IEEE 31st International Conference on Tools with Artificial Intelligence (ICTAI), pp. 636–643. IEEE (2019)
21. Wessling, J., Schreyer, A., Grenacher, L., Juchems, M., Ringe, K.: Incidental and" leave me alone" findings in the gi tract-part 1: Intestinal lumen and intestinal wall. Der Radiologe (2022)
22. Ye, R., Guo, Y., Shuai, X., Ye, R., Jiang, S., Jiang, H.: Licam: Long-tailed instance segmentation with real-time classification accuracy monitoring. J. Circ. Syst. Comput., 2350032 (2022)
23. Ye, R., Ye, R., Zheng, S.: Machine learning guides the solution of blocks relocation problem in container terminals. Trans. Res. Record p. 03611981221117157 (2022)
24. Zhou, Z., Rahman Siddiquee, M.M., Tajbakhsh, N., Liang, J.: UNet++: a nested U-Net architecture for medical image segmentation. In: Stoyanov, D., et al. (eds.) DLMIA/ML-CDS -2018. LNCS, vol. 11045, pp. 3–11. Springer, Cham (2018). https://doi.org/10.1007/978-3-030-00889-5_1

Co-contrastive Self-supervised Learning for Drug-Disease Association Prediction

Zihao Gao[1] , Huifang Ma[1,2(✉)] , Xiaohui Zhang[1] , Zheyu Wu[1] ,
and Zhixin Li[2]

[1] Northwest Normal University, Lanzhou, Gansu 730070, China
`mahuifang@yeah.net`
[2] Guangxi Normal University, Guilin, Guangxi 541004, China

Abstract. Prediction of drug-disease associations (DDAs), which aims
to identify new therapeutic opportunities for existing drugs, is becoming a promising proposition for drug discovery. Graph neural networks
(GNNs) as an emerging technique have shown superior capacity of dealing with drug-disease association prediction. However, existing GNNs-
based DDA prediction methods suffer from sparse supervised signals.
Inspired by the success of graph contrastive learning (GCL) in alleviating sparse supervised signals, we seek to leverage GCL to enhance
the prediction of DDAs. Unfortunately, most conventional GCL-based
models corrupt the raw data graph to augment data, which are unsuit-
able for DDA prediction. Meanwhile, these models may be ineffective
to capture the interactions between nodes, thus impairing the quality of
association prediction. To address the above issues, we propose a novel
Co-contrastive Self-supervised Learning (CSL) framework to tap potential candidate drugs for diseases. Technically, our framework first constructs three views. Then, two graph encoders are performed over the
three views, so as to capture both local and global structures simultaneously. Finally, we introduce a co-contrastive learning method and
co-train representations of the nodes to maximize agreement between
them, thus generating high-quality prediction results. What is more, we
integrate contrastive learning into the training, serving as an auxiliary
task to improve the prediction task. Evaluated by cross-validations, CSL
outperforms the baseline methods and the state-of-the-art methods on
three benchmark datasets.

Keywords: Drug-disease association prediction · Drug repositioning ·
Contrastive learning · Graph neural network

1 Introduction

Rapid advances in drug research and development over the past few decades,
as well as public health emergencies such as the outbreak of COVID-19, have
forced researchers to explore effective ways to counter these risks. Computer-
aided prediction of drug-disease associations (DDAs, *a.k.a.* drug repositioning)

© The Author(s), under exclusive license to Springer Nature Switzerland AG 2022
S. Khanna et al. (Eds.): PRICAI 2022, LNCS 13629, pp. 327–338, 2022.
https://doi.org/10.1007/978-3-031-20862-1_24

is becoming more appealing as it involves de-risked compounds, which could lead to lower total development expenses and shorter development schedules.

The earliest methods in this field formulate drug repositioning as a binary classification problem, where the drug-disease pairs are treated as instances, and the information about drugs and diseases is treated as features [1,2]. Then, classical classification models can be available to exploit drug repositioning methods. Afterward, the boom of deep learning provides alternatives, which employ multilayer perceptron (MLP) to learn the representations of data[3,4]. In recent years, graph convolutional networks (GCNs) [5] have attracted increasing attention and have been applied to DDA prediction tasks to learn the representation of drugs and diseases [6,7]. While promising, these approaches are still compromised by the same challe nge – sparsely labeled data, as wet experiment annotation is expensive and time-wasting. These data are insufficient to induce accurate representations of drugs and diseases in most cases, leading to suboptimal performance.

A contrastive learning paradigm from the computer vision domain is one approach to addressing these difficulties [8,9], which aims to construct similar and dissimilar view pairs via data augmentations, including cutout [10] and color distortion (including color dropping, brightness, contrast, saturation, hue) [11,12]. Some researchers have made a preliminary attempt at graph data [13,14]. However, contrastive learning on drug repositioning has its unique challenges: (1)In comparison to social or e-commerce networks with hundreds of millions of nodes, the graph of drug-disease associations has fewer nodes and more sparse edges (a number of diseases might only be treated by one drug). Therefore, techniques with node/edge dropout are completely unavailable for drug-disease association prediction. (2)When creating self-supervision signals, most existing methods generally assume that the neighbors are independent of each other, considering the global structure of the graph and ignoring the possible interactions between neighbor nodes. In some circumstances, the interactions between neighbor nodes could strengthen the properties of the target node in the graph. Modeling such interactions between neighbors reveals the potential correlation between them, which may be beneficial for the representation of the target node in a graph.

To overcome the mentioned limitations, we enrich the drug-disease association graph contrastive learning by incorporating the drug-drug similarity graph and disease-disease similarity graph, motivated by the fact that similar drugs tend to target similar diseases. On top of that, we propose a novel co-contrastive self-supervised learning (CSL) framework for drug-disease association prediction with three modules. The first module, *multi-source contrast view construction*, builds the known drug-disease association view, the drug-similarity, and disease-similarity views (applying the nearest neighbors) by using three sources of data. The second module, *context-aware neighborhood aggregation*, uses a bilinear graph neural network to encode complex local information in the drug-disease association view, and a global-aware attention mechanism to compensate for the receptive field issue in bilinear aggregation. The last module is *contrastive objec-*

tive, where we introduce a sampling mechanism to radically mine supervised signals for efficient co-contrastive learning. Furthermore, the prediction task and the contrastive learning task are unified under a *primary&auxiliary* learning paradigm.

Overall, the main contributions of this work are summarized as follows:

- We propose a novel co-contrastive self-supervised learning framework for drug-disease association prediction. By unifying the prediction task and the contrastive learning under this framework, the prediction performance can achieve significant gains.
- We consider the interaction between neighbor nodes (local) while creating self-supervision signals, and design a global-aware attention mechanism to capture high-order information in the other view. Moreover, the generated two distinct representations can improve contrastive performance even further.
- Extensive experiments show that our proposed model outperforms the SOTA methods and baseline methods and provides statistically significant gains on three benchmark datasets by conducting cross-validation.

2   The Proposed Method

We denote vectors by lowercase boldface, matrices by uppercase boldface, and sets by uppercase calligraphic font. Thus, let $\mathcal{R} = \{r_1, r_2, ..., r_N\}$ denotes the set of drugs, where N is the number of drugs; $\mathcal{D} = \{d_1, d_2, ..., d_M\}$ denotes the set of diseases, where M is the number of diseases. We embed each drug $r_i \in \mathcal{R}$ and disease $d_j \in \mathcal{D}$ into the same space. Our goal of DDA prediction is to learn a mapping function $f((r, d)|\omega) : \mathcal{E} \rightarrow [0, 1]$ from edges to scores, where ω is parameter, such that we can obtain the probability of a given drug treating a specific disease. Figure 1 displays the architecture of the proposed method.

2.1   Multi-source Contrast View Construction

DDA View. The drug-disease association view can be seen as an undirected graph $\mathcal{G} = \{\mathcal{V}, \mathcal{E}\}$, where $\mathcal{V}$ represents the set of nodes that correspond to drugs and diseases, $\mathcal{E} \subseteq \mathcal{V} \times \mathcal{V}$ denotes the set of edges indicating the existence of interaction between two kinds of nodes in $\mathcal{V}$. Furthermore, the graph $\mathcal{G}$ can be represented as an incidence matrix $\mathbf{A} \in \{0, 1\}^{N \times M}$, where $\mathbf{A}_{ij} = 1$ if drug r_i can treat disease d_j, otherwise $\mathbf{A}_{ij} = 0$.

Similarity View. Taking the construction of drug-similarity view as an example, with the similarity of drugs, for a certain drug node r_i, we can select drugs with the top-K highest similarity as the neighbor nodes which are the most similar to this drug. In this way, the drug-similarity view is denoted as $\mathcal{G}^R \in \{\mathcal{V}^R, \mathcal{E}^R\}$ with N drugs, and its adjacency matrix $\mathbf{A}^R \in \{0, 1\}^{N \times N}$, where $\mathbf{A}_{ij}^R = 1$ if drug r_j is the top-K nearest neighbor of drug r_i; otherwise $\mathbf{A}_{ij}^R = 0$. In the same way, the disease-similarity view is denoted as $\mathcal{G}^D \in \{\mathcal{V}^D, \mathcal{E}^D\}$ with M diseases, and its adjacency matrix $\mathbf{A}^D \in \{0, 1\}^{M \times M}$, where $\mathbf{A}_{ij}^D = 1$ if disease d_j is the top-K nearest neighbor of disease d_i; otherwise $\mathbf{A}_{ij}^D = 0$.

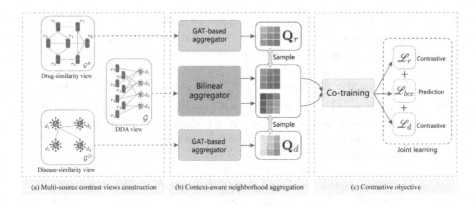

(a) Multi-source contrast views construction   (b) Context-aware neighborhood aggregation   (c) Contrastive objective

Fig. 1. An overview of the proposed CSL.

2.2 Context-Aware Neighborhood Aggregation

Node Feature Extraction. Each row of adjacency matrices of similarity views can act as the feature vector, but they may not sufficiently capture the graph structure, especially non-neighboring, higher-order connectivity. On this account, we run Random Walk with Restart[15] separately on drug similarity matrix $\mathbf{A}^R$ and disease similarity matrix $\mathbf{A}^D$ to introduce the topological context of each node into their initial vector representations. Specificlly, we follow [16] to extract node feature. After obtaining the steady-state, we set the feature vector $\mathbf{e}_v = \text{MLP}(\mathbf{x}_v^\infty)$ on $\mathbf{A}^V$ ($V \in \{R, D\}$) for drugs and diseases, where $\mathbf{e}_v \in \mathbb{R}^t$ denotes the updated node representation with t dimensions and MLP contains single hidden layer.

DDA View Encoder. GCN [5] is a neural network architecture which assumes that neighbouring nodes are independent of each other and utilizes the weighted sum to learn low-dimensional representations of nodes. Therefore, we first define a GA aggregetor for target node v (drug r or disease d) as:

$$\mathbf{h}_v^{(GA)} = \text{GA}(\{\mathbf{e}_i\}_{i\in\hat{\mathcal{N}}(v)}) = \sigma\left(\sum_{i\in\hat{\mathcal{N}}(v)} a_{vi}\mathbf{W}_g\mathbf{e}_i\right), \tag{1}$$

where GA$(\cdot)$ is the linear aggregator, $\hat{\mathcal{N}}(v) = \{v\} \cup \{i|\mathbf{A}_{vi} = 1\}$ denotes the extended neighbors of node v which contains the node v itself. σ is a non-linear activation function. a_{vi} is the weight of neighbor i and is defined as $\frac{1}{\sqrt{\hat{d}_v\hat{d}_i}}$, where $\hat{d}_v = |\hat{\mathcal{N}}(v)|$ and $\hat{d}_i = |\hat{\mathcal{N}}(i)|$. $\mathbf{W}_g$ is the weight matrix to do feature trasformation and σ is a non-linear activation function.

Nevertheless, GCN ignores the possible interactions between neighbor nodes and may fail to capture the signal when such interactions exist. At the same time, the multiplication of two vectors is an effective means to model the interaction [17], and it can emphasize the common properties and dilute the discrepant information. Thus, we define a BA aggregator for target node v as:

$$\mathbf{h}_v^{(BA)} = \mathrm{BA}(\{\mathbf{h}_i\}_{i\in\hat{\mathcal{N}}(v)}) = \sigma\left(\frac{1}{b_v}\sum_{i\in\hat{\mathcal{N}}(v)}\sum_{j\in\hat{\mathcal{N}}(v)\&i<j} \mathbf{e}_i\mathbf{W}_b \odot \mathbf{e}_j\mathbf{W}_b\right), \quad (2)$$

where $b_v = \frac{1}{2}\hat{d}_v(\hat{d}_v - 1)$ denote the number of interactions for the target node v, which normalizes the obtained representation to remove the bias of node degree. $\odot$ is element-wise product and $\mathbf{W}_b$ is the weight matrix to do feature trasformation.

Then, the encoder which is built on the DDA view for message passing between drugs and diseases extracts indirect interactions in the local structure. Specifically, for target node v, the DDA view encoder is defined as:

$$\mathbf{h}_v = \beta \times \mathbf{h}_v^{(GA)} + (1 - \beta) \times \mathbf{h}_v^{(BA)}, \quad (3)$$

where β is a hyper-parameter to trade off the strengths of the GA aggregator and BA aggregator.

Similarity View Encoder. Previous drug repositioning research assumed that similar drugs would treat the same disease, but dissimilar drugs might also treat the same disease. To fully exploit this potential correlation, we design a global-aware strategy based on an attention architecture, to obtain node representations considering various perspectives. The following two aspects are taken into account by the attention mechanism.

Firstly, we calculate the average representation of all nodes' embedding in the *drug similarity view* or *disease similarity view*, $\bar{\mathbf{e}}_v$ represents the average node information by average pooling. In order to explore the potential of drug treatment for non-indications, the node embedding and average information embedding are used to calculate the following attention score:

$$\epsilon_v = \mathrm{att}_1(\mathbf{W}_1\mathbf{e}_v \odot \bar{\mathbf{e}}_v), \quad (4)$$

where $\mathbf{W}_1$ is a transformation matrix and att_1 is a single-layer feedforward neural network with the LeakyReLU as activation function.

Apart from the above, we extend the message passing process by the attention mechanism.

$$\zeta_{vi} = \mathrm{att}_2(\mathbf{W}_2\mathbf{e}_v \| \mathbf{W}_2\mathbf{e}_i), \quad (5)$$

where $\mathbf{W}_2$ is a transformation matrix, $\|$ denotes the concatenation operation, $\mathbf{e}_i$ is the neighbor node representation of the node v and att_2 is a single-layer feedforward neural network applying the LeakyReLU nonlinearity.

Then, following the additive attention mechanism [18], we sum the node's global score and its local score to consider the factors of global and local simultaneously. To make coefficients easily comparable across different nodes, we employed the softmax function to normalize them across all choices of i. The attention coefficients δ_{vi} between node v and node i is computed as:

$$\delta_{vi} = softmax_v\left(\epsilon_v + \zeta_{vi}\right) = \frac{\exp\left(\epsilon_v + \zeta_{vi}\right)}{\sum_{j \in \mathcal{N}(v)} \exp\left(\epsilon_v + \zeta_{vj}\right)}, \tag{6}$$

where ϵ_v controls how much information the target node v can receive, and ζ_{vi} controls how much information the neighbor node i to v. In this way, we can get another representation of drugs and diseases. The calculation is define as:

$$\mathbf{q}_v = \sigma\left(\sum_{i \in \mathcal{N}(v)} \delta_{vi} \mathbf{W}_3 \mathbf{h}_i\right), \tag{7}$$

where $\mathbf{W}_3$ is the weight matrix.

2.3 Generating Prediction and Model Optimization

To reconstruct the associations between drugs and diseases, our decoder $f(\mathbf{e}_{r_i}, \mathbf{e}_{d_j})$ is formulated as follows:

$$\hat{y}_{r_i, d_j} = \mathrm{MLP}(\mathbf{e}_{r_i} \odot \mathbf{e}_{d_j}, \mathbf{h}_{r_i}, \mathbf{h}_{d_j}), \tag{8}$$

where $\hat{y}_{r_i, d_j}$ is the predicted probability score.

Owing to the known DDAs have been validated manually, they are highly reliable and important for improving prediction performance. However, the number of known drug-disease associations is far less than the number of unknown or unobserved drug-disease pairs. Hence, our proposed CSL learns parameters by minimizing the weighted binary cross-entropy loss as follows:

$$\mathcal{L}_{bce} = -\frac{1}{N \times M}\left(\eta \times \sum_{(i,j) \in \mathcal{S}_{rd}^+} \log \hat{y}_{r_i, d_j} + \sum_{(i,j) \in \mathcal{S}_{rd}^-} \left(1 - \log \hat{y}_{r_i, d_j}\right)\right), \tag{9}$$

where (i, j) indicates the pair of drug r_i and disease d_j, $\mathcal{S}_{rd}^+$ denotes the set of all known drug-disease association pairs and $\mathcal{S}_{rd}^-$ represents the set of all unknown or unobserved drug-disease association pairs. The balance factor $\eta = \frac{|\mathcal{S}_{rd}^-|}{|\mathcal{S}_{rd}^+|}$ imposes the importance of observed associations to reduce the impact of data imbalance, where $|\mathcal{S}_{rd}^-|$ and $|\mathcal{S}_{rd}^+|$ are the number of pairs in $\mathcal{S}_{rd}^-$ and $\mathcal{S}_{rd}^+$.

2.4   Contrastive Objective

Mining Self-Supervision Signals. In this section, we show how our framework mines informative self-supervision signals to enhance DDA prediction. Given a drug r_i and disease d_j in the DDA view, we choose their positive and negative drug samples within the same minibatch using its representation learned over the similarity view:

$$\mathbf{score}_r = softmax(\mathbf{Q}_d \mathbf{q}_r), \tag{10}$$

where $\mathbf{score}_r \in \mathbb{R}^M$ denotes the predicted probability of each disease being cured to the drug r in the similarity view.

With the computed probabilities, we can pick diseases with the top-K highest confidence as the positive samples. Formally, the positive sample selection is as follows:

$$\mathcal{S}_{r_i}^{d^+} = P_d^K \left(\mathbf{score}_{r_i}\right), \tag{11}$$

where P_d^K denotes picking the corresponding diseases d which are according to the top K probability scores with the highest confidence.

Then, we randomly select K negative samples from the diseases ranked in top 50% in $\mathbf{score}_{r_i}$ excluding the positives to contruct $\mathcal{S}_r^{d^-}$. These diseases can be viewed as hard negatives. In the same way, the information samples used for disease embeddings are selected to get $\mathcal{S}_{d_i}^{r^+}$ and $\mathcal{S}_{d_i}^{r^-}$.

Co-contrastive Learning. With the generated pseudo-labels, the self-supervised task used to refine encoders can be conducted through a contrastive object. We utilize NT-Xent [19] as our objective function to maximize the mutual information between the two views. The training objective for drug $\mathbf{h}_{r_i}$ is defined as:

$$\mathcal{L}_{r_i} = -\log \frac{\sum_{d_j \in \mathcal{S}_{r_i}^{d^+}} \left(e^{sim\left(\left(\mathbf{h}_{r_i},\mathbf{h}_{d_j}\right)\right)/\tau}\right)}{\sum_{d_j \in \mathcal{S}_{r_i}^{d^+}} \left(e^{sim\left(\mathbf{h}_{r_i},\mathbf{h}_{d_j}\right)/\tau}\right) + \sum_{d_k \in \mathcal{S}_{r_i}^{d^-}} \left(e^{sim\left(\mathbf{h}_{r_i},\mathbf{h}_{d_k}\right)/\tau}\right)}, \tag{12}$$

where τ denotes the temperature parameter and $sim(u,v)$ is the cosine similarity. In the same way, the training objective for disease $\mathbf{h}_{d_i}$ is defined as:

$$\mathcal{L}_{d_i} = -\log \frac{\sum_{r_j \in \mathcal{S}_{d_i}^{r^+}} \left(e^{sim\left(\left(\mathbf{h}_{d_i},\mathbf{h}_{r_j}\right)\right)/\tau}\right)}{\sum_{r_j \in \mathcal{S}_{d_i}^{r^+}} \left(e^{sim\left(\mathbf{h}_{d_i},\mathbf{h}_{r_j}\right)/\tau}\right) + \sum_{r_k \in \mathcal{S}_{d_i}^{r^-}} \left(e^{sim\left(\mathbf{h}_{d_i},\mathbf{h}_{r_k}\right)/\tau}\right)}, \tag{13}$$

Finally, we unify the prediction task with the auxiliary SSL task. The total loss $\mathcal{L}$ is defined as:

$$\mathcal{L} = \mathcal{L}_{bce} + \lambda(\mathcal{L}_r + \mathcal{L}_d), \tag{14}$$

where λ is hyperparameter to control the scale of the self-supervised graph co-training.

We optimize the model through the Adam optimizer [20] and initialize weights as described in [21]. To generalize effectively to the unobserved data, we trained the model in a denoising setup by randomly dropping out edges with a fixed probability. We also applied regular dropout [22] to the graph convolution layers.

3   Experiments

3.1   Experimental Settings

Datasets. We evaluate our model on three benchmark datasets: *Fdataset*[2], *Cdataset* [23] and *LRSSL* [24], which are often used in drug-disease association prediction. The basic statistics of the three datasets are shown in Table 1.

Table 1. Statistical details of the benchmark datasets.

Dataset	#Drugs	#Diseases	#Associations	Sparse ratio
Fdataset	593	313	1,933	0.0104
Cdataset	663	409	2,352	0.0087
LRSSL	763	681	3,051	0.0058

Baseline Methods. We compare our proposed CSL with various representative methods: (1) Matrix factorization and completion models including SCMFDD [25], BNNR [26], DRIMC [27]; (2) Deep learning-based models including NIM-CGCN [6], LAGCN [7], DRWBNCF [28].

Evaluation Metrics. We used the area under the receiver operating characteristic curve (AUROC) and the area under the exact recall curve (AUPR) as the main metrics because they allow measuring the performance of the method without any specific threshold.

Parameters Settings. Our proposed CSL model uses the Adam optimizer with an initial learning rate of 0.001 and batch size of 64. For pre-training, the restart probability α is set as 0.1. The temperature τ in *contrastive object* is set as 0.1. The hyperparameters of baseline methods are chosen as their optimal values provided by their publications.

3.2   Overall Performance

Following [6,26,27], we adopted 10-fold cross-validation (10-CV) to evaluate the performance of prediction methods. Table 2 reports the performance comparison results. We have the following observations:

- The methods based on matrix factorization and completion models has achieved better performance than expected on three datasets. Such performance might be attributed to a smaller number of nodes in DDA data compared to e-commerce and social recommendation data, which allows for the promising performance of matrix factorization and completion methods.
- Compared to NIMCGCN and LAGCN, the performance of DRWBNCF verifies that modeling neighbor interactions can improve representation learning. Surprisingly, in some cases, NIMCGCN and LAGCN achieve worse performance than BNNR and DRIMC. The reason might be that NIMCGCN ignores the interaction of nodes in heterogeneous networks, and LAGCN indiscriminately mixes the network topology information of different domains. Besides, both NIMCGCN and LAGCN are impacted by the long-tail distribution of data.
- The performance of our model on AUPR shows great improvement. CSL obtains the best average AUPR of 0.5215, which is 12.95% higher than DRWBNCF (the average AUPR is 0.4617). Benchmarking comparison results on three datasets show that CSL improves the prediction performance thanks to combining the information of the known drug-disease association with the neighborhood and neighborhood interaction information of drugs and diseases under the framework of contrastive learning.

Table 2. The average metrics of compared methods obtained in 10-CV.

Datast	Fdataset		Cdataset		LRSSL	
	AUROC	AUPR	AUROC	AUPR	AUROC	AUPR
SCMFDD	0.7748	0.0510	0.7921	0.0514	0.7783	0.0358
BNNR	0.9298	0.4372	0.9338	0.4702	0.9267	0.3152
DRIMC	0.9091	0.3096	0.9333	0.3894	0.9314	0.2661
NIMCGCN	0.8281	0.3385	0.8508	0.4326	0.8294	0.2670
LAGCN	0.8586	0.1188	0.9144	0.1849	0.9336	0.1109
DRWBNCF	0.9245	0.4845	0.9404	0.5589	**0.9345**	0.3416
CSL	**0.9352**	**0.5486**	**0.9468**	**0.6256**	0.9262	**0.3904**

3.3 Model Ablation

To evaluate the rationality of design sub-modules in our CSL framework, we consider three model variants as follows: (1) CSL without DDA view encoder (**w/o-DE**): We only use the similarity views to model drugs and diseases, removing the co-contrastive self-supervised learning. (2) CSL without similarity view encoder (**w/o-AE**): We only use the DDA view to model drugs and diseases, removing the drug-&disease-similarity view, interaction-aware similarity views and the co-contrastive self-supervised learning. (3) CSL without co-contrastive learning task (**w/o-CL**): We remove the co-contrastive self-supervised learning

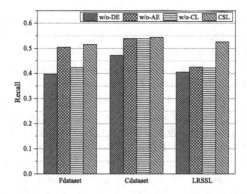

Fig. 2. The Recalls of all compared approaches obtained in 10-fold CV.

task and only use simple summing of drug/disease embeddings on two views to get the final embedding.

As can be observed in Fig. 2, each component contributes to the final performance. The DDA view encoder contributes the most. When only using the DDA view encoder, the model achieves a suboptimal performance which is much higher than the performance of the CSL without co-contrastive learning task on both the three datasets. This can demonstrate the effectiveness of modeling the interaction between neighbor nodes. By contrast, only using the similarity view encoder would lead to a huge performance degradation on three datasets. Surprisingly, removing the co-contrastive learning task and using the sum of drug/disease embeddings on two views to obtain the final embedding do not achieve suboptimal performance. This proves that contrastive learning can automatically mine labels, so as to maximize agreement between nodes in different view.

4   Conclusion

In this work, we recognize the limitations of the traditional DDA prediction and explored the potential of GCL to solve the limitations. In particular, we propose a novel *Co-contrastive Self-supervised Learning* (CSL) framework to tap candidate drugs for diseases. To be specific, we learn the representation of drugs and diseases on three relevant views and then introduce a co-contrastive learning method that can sample positive samples and dig hard negative samples to generate accurate node representations. Finally, we conducte extensive experiments on three benchmark datasets, justifying the advantages of our proposal regarding drug-disease association prediction.

Acknowledgment. This work is supported by Industrial Support Project of Gansu Colleges(No.2022CYZC-11), The National Natural Science Foundation of China (61762078, 61363058), Gansu Natural Science Foundation Project (21JR7RA114), and Northwest Normal University Young Teachers Research Capacity Promotion Plan (NWNU-LKQN2019-2).

References

1. Bleakley, K., Yamanishi, Y.: Supervised prediction of drug-target interactions using bipartite local models. Bioinformatics **25**(18), 2397–2403 (2009)
2. Gottlieb, A., Stein, G.Y., Ruppin, E., Sharan, R.: Predict: a method for inferring novel drug indications with application to personalized medicine. Mol. Syst. Biol. **7**(1), 496 (2011)
3. Öztürk, H., Özgür, A., Ozkirimli, E.: Deepdta: deep drug-target binding affinity prediction. Bioinformatics **34**(17), i821–i829 (2018)
4. Zeng, X., Zhu, S., Liu, X., Zhou, Y., Nussinov, R., Cheng, F.: Deepdr: a network-based deep learning approach to in silico drug repositioning. Bioinformatics **35**(24), 5191–5198 (2019)
5. Kipf, T.N., Welling, M.: Semi-supervised classification with graph convolutional networks. In: 5th International Conference on Learning Representations, ICLR. OpenReview.net, Toulon, France (2017)
6. Li, J., Zhang, S., Liu, T., Ning, C., Zhang, Z., Zhou, W.: Neural inductive matrix completion with graph convolutional networks for mirna-disease association prediction. Bioinformatics **36**(8), 2538–2546 (2020)
7. Yu, Z., Huang, F., Zhao, X., Xiao, W., Zhang, W.: Predicting drug-disease associations through layer attention graph convolutional network. Briefings in Bioinformatics **22**(4), bbaa243 (2021)
8. Wu, Z., Xiong, Y., Yu, S.X., Lin, D.: Unsupervised feature learning via non-parametric instance discrimination. In: 2018 IEEE Conference on Computer Vision and Pattern Recognition, CVPR. pp. 3733–3742. Computer Vision Foundation / IEEE Computer Society, Salt Lake City, UT, USA (2018)
9. Chen, T., Kornblith, S., Norouzi, M., Hinton, G.E.: A simple framework for contrastive learning of visual representations. In: Proceedings of the 37th International Conference on Machine Learning, ICML. Proceedings of Machine Learning Research, vol. 119, pp. 1597–1607. PMLR, Virtual Event (2020)
10. Devries, T., Taylor, G.W.: Improved regularization of convolutional neural networks with cutout. CoRR (2017). http://arxiv.org/abs/1708.04552
11. Howard, A.G.: Some improvements on deep convolutional neural network based image classification. In: Bengio, Y., LeCun, Y. (eds.) 2nd International Conference on Learning Representations, ICLR 2014 (2014)
12. Szegedy, C., et al.: Going deeper with convolutions. In: IEEE Conference on Computer Vision and Pattern Recognition, CVPR, pp. 1–9. IEEE Computer Society (2015)
13. Zhao, C., Liu, S., Huang, F., Liu, S., Zhang, W.: Csgnn: contrastive self-supervised graph neural network for molecular interaction prediction. In: Proceedings of the 30th International Joint Conference on Artificial Intelligence, IJCAI, pp. 3756–3763. IJCAI.org (2021)
14. Huang, C., et al.: Graph-enhanced multi-task learning of multi-level transition dynamics for session-based recommendation. In: 35th AAAI Conference on Artificial Intelligence, AAAI, pp. 4123–4130. AAAI Press, Virtual Event (2021)
15. Tong, H., Faloutsos, C., Pan, J.: Fast random walk with restart and its applications. In: Proceedings of the 6th IEEE International Conference on Data Mining ICDM, pp. 613–622. IEEE Computer Society, Hong Kong, China (2006)
16. Liu, L., Mamitsuka, H., Zhu, S.: Hpofiller: identifying missing protein-phenotype associations by graph convolutional network. Bioinformatics **37**(19), 3328–3336 (2021)

17. Zhu, H., et al.: Bilinear graph neural network with neighbor interactions. In: Proceedings of the 29th International Joint Conference on Artificial Intelligence, IJCAI, pp. 1452–1458. IJCAI.org (2020)
18. Bahdanau, D., Cho, K., Bengio, Y.: Neural machine translation by jointly learning to align and translate. In: 3rd International Conference on Learning Representations, ICLR, San Diego, CA, USA, (2015)
19. You, Y., Chen, T., Sui, Y., Chen, T., Wang, Z., Shen, Y.: Graph contrastive learning with augmentations. In: Advances in Neural Information Processing Systems 33: Annual Conference on Neural Information Processing Systems, NeurIPS, vol. 33, pp. 5812–5823 (2020)
20. Kingma, D.P., Ba, J.: Adam: a method for stochastic optimization. In: 3rd International Conference on Learning Representations, ICLR (2015)
21. Glorot, X., Bengio, Y.: Understanding the difficulty of training deep feedforward neural networks. In: Proceedings of the Thirteenth International Conference on Artificial Intelligence and Statistics, AISTATS, pp. 249–256. JMLR.org, Chia Laguna Resort, Sardinia, Italy (2010)
22. Srivastava, N., Hinton, G., Krizhevsky, A., Sutskever, I., Salakhutdinov, R.: Dropout: a simple way to prevent neural networks from overfitting. J. Mach. Learn. Res. **15**(1), 1929–1958 (2014)
23. Luo, H., et al.: Drug repositioning based on comprehensive similarity measures and bi-random walk algorithm. Bioinformatics **32**(17), 2664–2671 (2016)
24. Liang, X., et al.: Lrssl: predict and interpret drug-disease associations based on data integration using sparse subspace learning. Bioinformatics **33**(8), 1187–1196 (2017)
25. Zhang, W., et al.: Predicting drug-disease associations by using similarity constrained matrix factorization. BMC Bioinf. **19**(1), 1–12 (2018)
26. Yang, M., Luo, H., Li, Y., Wang, J.: Drug repositioning based on bounded nuclear norm regularization. Bioinformatics **35**(14), i455–i463 (2019)
27. Zhang, W., Xu, H., Li, X., Gao, Q., Wang, L.: Drimc: an improved drug repositioning approach using bayesian inductive matrix completion. Bioinformatics **36**(9), 2839–2847 (2020)
28. Meng, Y., Lu, C., Jin, M., Xu, J., Zeng, X., Yang, J.: A weighted bilinear neural collaborative filtering approach for drug repositioning. Briefings in Bioinformatics **23**(2), bbab581 (2022)

Obj-SA-GAN: Object-Driven Text-to-Image Synthesis with Self-Attention Based Full Semantic Information Mining

Ruijun Li[1(✉)], Weihua Li[1(✉)] [iD], Yi Yang[2] [iD], and Quan Bai[3] [iD]

[1] Auckland University of Technology, Auckland 1010, New Zealand
zjc0233@autuni.ac.nz, weihua.li@aut.ac.nz
[2] Hefei University of Technology, Hefei 230601, China
yyang@hfut.edu.cn
[3] University of Tasmania, Hobart 7005, Australia
quan.bai@utas.edu.au

Abstract. In recent years, text-to-image synthesis techniques have made considerable breakthroughs, but the progress is restricted to simple scenes. Such techniques turn out to be ineffective if the text appears complex and contains multiple objects. To address this challenging issue, we propose a novel text-to-image synthesis model called Object-driven Self-Attention Generative Adversarial Network (Obj-SA-GAN), where self-attention mechanisms are utilised to analyse the information with different granularities at different stages, achieving full exploitation of text semantic information from coarse to fine. Complex datasets are used to evaluate the performance of the proposed model. The experimental results explicitly show that our model outperforms the state-of-the-art methods. This is because the proposed Obj-SA-GAN model utilises textual information, which provides a better understanding of complex scenarios.

Keywords: Text-to-image synthesis · Attention · Self-Attention · Semantic mining · GAN

1 Introduction

With the explosive growth of information and the development of social media, people are inundated with information nowadays. Image can deliver the core information in a more effective way to the users than text-based information [1]. People also prefer to perceive image information rather than reading text. Hence, images play an increasingly indispensable role in the current information delivery process. However, most available high-quality images, such as cookbooks and movie posters, are created manually, turning out to be inefficient and expensive [17]. Motivated by this demand, it is significant to investigate how the machines

© The Author(s), under exclusive license to Springer Nature Switzerland AG 2022
S. Khanna et al. (Eds.): PRICAI 2022, LNCS 13629, pp. 339–350, 2022.
https://doi.org/10.1007/978-3-031-20862-1_25

can understand the semantic information in text and generate high-quality creative images.

Text-to-image synthesis aims to address this problem. It is a technique that automatically generates images based on textual information. Text-to-image synthesis encompasses two key research areas, i.e., Computer Vision (CV) and Natural Language Processing (NLP) [14]. The task of text-to-image synthesis typically includes two stages. First, the semantic sense is parsed from the text message, which directly determines whether the generated image satisfies the conditions given in the text message. Second, a generative model is utilised to synthesise a matched image from the parsed semantic sense [5]. There are a number of existing text-to-image synthesis models, and they have achieved remarkable success in many areas, such as medical image generation and computer-aided systems [18].

In the contemporary research field, there are a few dominant methods for the text-to-image task, including Variational Auto-Encoder (VAE), Deep Recurrent Attention Writer (DRAW), and approaches based on Generative Adversarial Networks (GAN) [27]. Specifically, VAE adopts statistical techniques to build the model and calculate the mean square error between the generated and genuine images [14]. DRAW is developed based on Convolutional Neural Networks (CNN) and attention mechanism. However, the resolutions of the images generated by these models are not clear enough to attain the desired results [5,28]. By contrast, GAN-based models can generally perform better [1,5,14,27]. The GAN model and its variants take simple text information as input and generate a high-quality image that matches it exceptionally well. However, such models are merely limited to simple datasets, which have only one object in each image, such as faces [28], birds [30] and flowers [15].

When textual information becomes more complex, having multiple objects in the text message, the GAN based models are likely to miss pivotal fine-grained information in the generation process, e.g., word-level semantic information. This leads to significant quality degradation of the generated images and the produced results fail to match the given semantic conditions [11]. For example, synthesising an image from the sentence "a woman is sitting on a chair at a table with a cup and cell phone" requires the generative model to achieve two objectives. First, it needs to identify all the objects, i.e., woman, chair, table, cup and cell phone. Second, it needs to rationalise the relationships between the objects, e.g., the woman sitting on the chair, the cup and the phone in her hands.

GAN models generally do not work well on complex images because they focus on learning the overall features of the images without paying attention to the corresponding objects. Taking a living room image as an example, GAN models fail to distinguish between the table and the bed in it but merely place some shapes and colours in a particular position of the synthesised images. In other words, after training, the model does not really understand the image but only remembers where place some appropriate shapes or colours. This also explains the reason for lacking clear details when synthesising complex images [30]. Therefore, it is challenging to deal with the relationships between objects when synthesising complex graphs. To alleviate this problem, some researchers developed the idea of analysing the relationships between objects specifically through an additional semantic layer before generating the images, where the image synthesis phase is based on the result of the semantic layer [7,11]. These models achieve improvements, but some important image features are missing. For example, when generating images from the sentence "a brown dog lying on bed with his banana toy", the banana toy was not synthesised.

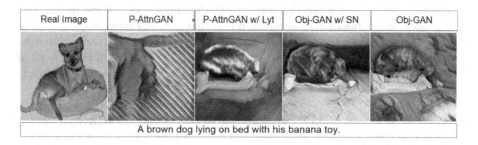

| Real Image | P-AttnGAN | P-AttnGAN w/ Lyt | Obj-GAN w/ SN | Obj-GAN |

A brown dog lying on bed with his banana toy.

Fig. 1. Synthesised images using object-driven image synthesis models [11].

In this paper, we recognise the importance of semantic layout for complex image synthesis and propose a generative model, namely, Object-Driven Self-Attention GAN (Obj-SA-GAN). It leverages Self-Attention (SA) mechanism to analyse text and then uses it to guide image synthesis. SA has two outstanding advantages over other architectures, i.e., Recurrent Neural Networks (RNN). SA extracts features from text sequences by treating the input x_i as key, value and query simultaneously, which can understand the elements in the sequence better [19]. Furthermore, the longest path for SA is $O(1)$, implying that it directly links any two words in a sentence through a single computational step. Thus, the distance between long-distance dependent features is greatly reduced, facilitating the effective use of these features.

The main contribution of this paper is that we propose an Obj-SA-GAN model for text-to-image synthesis. In particular, we use the SA to enhance the generated semantic layout, which makes our model more closely match the process of human drawing. In addition, we evaluate our model on the complex dataset MSCOCO, and the experimental results show that the proposed model outperforms the current popular generative models in terms of FID metrics and reaches a new milestone. This also addresses the performance issues of GAN models when being utilised in complex scenes.

The rest of the paper is organised as follows. In Sect. 2, related works are introduced, where the advantages and disadvantages of GAN and its common variants are summarised. In Sect. 3, we elaborate on the proposed Obj-SA-GAN model. In Sect. 4, we conduct extensive experiments to evaluate the performance of the proposed model and perform an ablation study to evaluate the contributions of each key component of our method. Finally, the research work is concluded in Sect. 5, and the directions for future research are explained.

2   Related Work

The generation of realistic images from textual descriptions brings great contributions to many real-world applications, such as healthcare, education, and computer-aided systems. Nowadays, a growing number of generative methods have been proposed for text-to-image synthesis. There are many existing generative models [2,4,6,9,10,13,18,21], where GAN-based models outperform the others in terms of the quality of the generated images and the semantic matching of the text [29,30]. However, the standard GAN model does not use mathematical models when building generators but rather a data-driven approach. The data is random, thus, the output of the GAN heavily relies on random vectors, leading to an uncontrolled process of image generation [27]. With the advent of the variants of GAN models, such as Conditional GAN (CGAN), the problem is getting alleviated [5,27].

Based on CGAN, the researchers have modified and optimised a set of GAN variants, such as Stack-GAN [8], StackGAN++ [25] and AttnGAN [1], which are based on the stacking or attentional architecture. Existing studies reveal that these models can produce high-quality images on simple datasets, such as CUB [15] and CelebA [23]. However, they do not perform well in complex datasets, such as COCO [30], containing multiple objects. Moreover, the GAN-based approach has low text utilisation and loses important fine-grained semantic information. A major challenge in synthesising complex images is to improve the accuracy of identifying relationships between objects. Hong et al. adopt semantic layers to analyse the connections between objects before generating images [7], having two phases, i.e., semantic layer and GAN-based image generation. However, the text message has been encoded into a single text vector, ignoring the fine-grained text information. The resulting images do not have enough details to support the generated results. Similarly, Li et al. design a two-phase model to synthesise images, where an object-driven GAN neural network is introduced by using part of the fine-grained information [11]. However, the improved model misses some important information when generating images, as demonstrated in Fig. 1. This reveals that their model still suffers from low text utilisation. We propose a new object-driven self-attention framework to improve the utilisation of fine-grained content.

The attention mechanism is much like the logic of seeing a picture, where people's attention is always focused on the important part of the image. This allows the attention mechanism to conserve resources and quickly obtain the most valuable information [20]. As the core theory of the most popular deep framework, i.e., Transformer, the self-attention mechanism turns out to be a very effective way to model context, which improves the attention mechanism, reduces the dependence on external information and is better at capturing the relevance within the data [23].

In summary, the classic GAN model maps textual information into a single text vector, ignoring word-level information. Both Hong and Li aim to improve the text utilisation of the model by introducing a semantic layer before image generation to achieve significant results in synthesising multi-object images.

Unfortunately, they used an LSTM model based on the RNN architecture for the semantic layer, so some fine-grained information is still missed when parsing the semantic information. However, attention mechanisms, in particular self-attention, can focus limited resources on the detailed information of an object to fully discover hidden connections. Inspired by these works, we intend to propose an object-driven SA GAN model that uses self-attention mechanisms to improve the text utilisation, theoretically enabling the synthesis of complex images better than baselines. This is the first research work to build a GAN generation model based on a self-attention and semantic layer.

3 Object-driven Self-Attention Generative Adversarial Network

The architecture of the proposed Obj-SA-GAN model is presented in Fig. 2. It takes a text description as input and extracts text information of different granularity at different stages, from coarse to fine. High-quality semantic layers are formed gradually and used to guide the downstream image synthesis task. The semantic generator includes two sub-generators: box and shape generator. The box generator parses the position and class information of the entity objects and determines the global layout of the generated images. The shape generator further refines the generated box sequence, outlining the general contour of each object. The image generator takes the text vector and the hidden feature map (hmap) generated by the semantic layer as inputs. In this stage, the semantic layer information is converted into pixels to form an image that conforms to the text semantics. This process is generally consistent with the original paper [11]. However, the difference is that we introduce the self-attention mechanism in the semantic generation part, making the generated semantic layer more accurate and detailed.

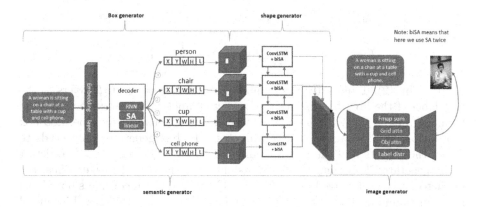

Fig. 2. The overall architecture of the proposed Obj-SA-GAN model.

3.1   Box Generator

The box generator defines a mapping from a text vector (s) to a sequence of boxes, namely,

$$B_{(1:t)} = B_1, B_2, \cdots, B_t \sim G_{box}(s) \tag{1}$$

It defines what kind of objects should be included in the picture and where to place these objects. The tth box annotation can be represented as $B_t = (b_t, l_t)$, where b_t refers to the coordinates of the top left corner of each object box (x, y) and the width and height of the box (w, h). l_t denotes the label information of the object. Figure 3 demonstrates the architecture of the box generator. Box generator is a seq2seq model based on the encoder-decoder architecture. A given sequence of text is first mapped to an embedding intermediate vector through an embedding layer, which generates an embedding vector for each text sequence. The embedding vector is then fed into a Self-Attention module. In the Self-Attention module, the model extracts key information for each object and generates a new set of vectors C_N, where N denotes the number of objects in the text. The Self-Attention module pays attention to each object and extracts the corresponding core information. It also allows to generate more accurate box sequences for each object.

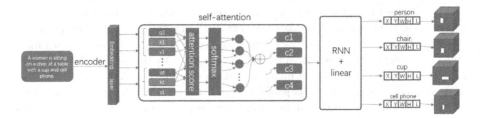

Fig. 3. The architecture of the box generator.

In order to train the box generator, we use Eq. (2) as the loss.

$$L_{(box)} = -\lambda_l \frac{1}{T} \sum_{t=1}^{T} l_t^* log p(l_t) - \lambda_b \frac{1}{T} \sum_{t=1}^{T} log p(b_t^*) \tag{2}$$

In Equation (2), T indicates the number of objects in the text, l_t^* refers to the true label of the box, l_t indicates the predicted label, and b_t^* describes the true bounding box (x, y, w, h). L_{box} measures the error between the generated box coordinates and the actual box coordinates. The box generator only needs to detect the objects and the corresponding positions. It does not need to detect if the generated bounding box is consistent with the actual image. Thus, the predicted b_t is not involved in the Eq. (2). The loss function considers both label loss and bounding box loss. The former describes a Negative Log Likelihood Loss (NLLLoss) to estimate the error related to the label, while the latter can be recognised as Squared Loss to estimate the error with the object box. In the current setting, we set $\lambda_l = \lambda_b = 1.0$.

3.2 Shape Generator

The shape generator is a further refinement of the box generator, which aims to predict the shape of an object in a given sequence of object box. Mathematically, $M_{(1:T)} = G_{shape}(B_{1:T}, Z_{1:T})$, where Z_T denotes a random noise vector. The shape generator is restricted by an instance constraint and a global constraint. The instance constraint ensures that the generated shape keeps consistent with the position of the previously generated box. The global constraint guarantees that generated shape fits the elements around it. The core component of the shape generator is a bidirectional convolutional LSTM (bi-convLSTM) model. The input is a feature map extracted from the box generator, followed by a bi-convLSTM block. We perform a self-attention operation before the forward and backward LSTMs. The hidden states in all steps are weighted to pay attention to the more important hidden state information in the entire text. This gives a better performance than using the bi-convLSTM alone.

A training strategy is employed to train the shape generator based on the GAN architecture. It consists of two components, instance-constrained discriminator (D_{inst}) and globally constrained discriminator (D_{global}), respectively. The loss function is formulated in Eq. (3)

$$l_{shape} = \lambda_i l_{inst} + \lambda_g l_{global} + \lambda_r l_{rec} \tag{3}$$

where l_{inst} and l_{global} denote the loss functions used by the two discriminators mentioned above. Both adopt the Binary Cross Entropy Loss (BCELoss) to measure the distance between the generated fake hamps and the real hmaps. l_{rec} refers to a perceptual loss, which measures the distance between the actual image and the generated image. In the current setting, we give λ_i=1.0 λ_g=1.0 and λ_r=10.0.

4 Experiments

In this section, extensive experiments are performed to evaluate the proposed Obj-SA-GAN model by using the MSCOCO dataset. Firstly, a brief description of the datasets is given. Secondly, we compare the performance of the Obj-SA-GAN model with state-of-the-art generative models. Thirdly, we perform ablation experiments to compare the contribution of each module of the model.

4.1 Setup

Datasets: The Microsoft Common Objects in Context 2014 (MS COCO-2014) dataset [12] and the ImageNet dataset [3] are utilised in this research.

- MS COCO was released in 2014. It is a collection of 164K images, which have been partitioned into the training set (82K), validation set (41K) and testing set (41K). The dataset is complex because most of the images possess at least two objects.
- ImageNet was released in 2009. It consists of 14 million images, covering most of the categories of images seen in life. ImageNet has more than 20K classifications, and each image is manually categorised.

Evaluation Metrics: we adopt Inception Score (IS) and Fréchet Inception Distance (FID) as evaluation metrics [7,11]. Both are acknowledged as standard metrics for evaluating the GAN-based generation model. Specifically, IS examined both the clarity and diversity of the resulting images. The higher the IS, the better the quality of the generated images. FID calculates the difference between the generated image and the original image. The smaller the difference, the better the generated image is.

Baselines: Two baselines are utilised as the counterparts of the proposed model.

- Inferring Semantic Layout for Hierarchical Text-to-Image Synthesis (Infer) [7] is a text-to-image synthesis model which integrates a semantic layer model with a generative model.
- Obj-GAN [11] is an improved model of Infer, which focuses on enhancing the image generator module of Infer. Object-driven attention is adopted in the GAN to synthesise images.

4.2   Experimental Results

In this subsection, we evaluate the proposed model by comparing it against a few state-of-the-art generative models quantitatively and qualitatively.

Performance Evaluation: Table 1 demonstrates the results of the quantitative comparison. It can be seen from the table that the proposed model outperforms all the baselines. In terms of FID, our Obj-SA-GAN model yields outstanding performance compared with the existing generative models. Regarding IS, the Obj-SA-GAN model also performs best, reaching approximately 32.26, almost twice the Infer baseline. According to the results, we can conclude that involving Self-Attention in the semantic layer can produce a significantly positive effect on the deep mining of relationships between objects because it fully utilises limited textual information.

Qualitative Analysis: In this subsection, qualitative analysis is conducted to visually and intuitively compare the results of each generated model. Figure 4 demonstrates the images generated by our model at different epochs. The input text is given as "a brown dog lying on bed with his banana toy". In Fig. 1, we have shown the actual image of the sample and the images generated by the four existing generative models. However, none of the generated images has any traces of a banana toy. In contrast, by applying our Obj-SA-GAN model, the shape of the banana becomes more apparent with the epoch increases. The result explicitly reveals that adding Self-Attention to the semantic layer can promote the model to generate an accurate and reasonable semantic layout, effectively guiding the image synthesis.

Table 1. Experimental results of varied models for Text-To-Image synthesis. Symbols ↑ and ↓ indicate the higher the best and the lower the best, respectively. n/a means that the indicator is not used in the article. we utilise **bold** indicates the experimental results of our proposed model. * indicates the best performance. The value that follows ± is the standard deviation.

Models	Inception ↑	FID ↓
Obj-SA-GAN	**32.26 ± 0.02 ***	**18.20 ***
Obj-GAN (baseline) [11]	29.89 ± 0.22	21.21
Infer (baseline) [7]	12.40 ± 0.08	n/a
P-AttnGAN 0 [11]	18.84 ± 0.29	59.02
P-AttnGAN 1 [11]	19.32 ± 0.29	54.96
P-AttnGAN 2 [11]	20.81 ± 0.16	48.47
Reed et al. [16]	7.88 ± 0.07	n/a
StackGAN [24]	8.45 ± 0.03	n/a
AttnGAN [22]	23.79 ± 0.32	28.76
vmGAN [26]	9.94 ± 0.12	n/a

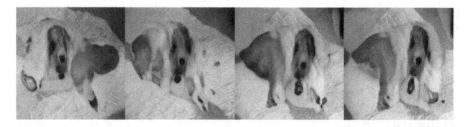

Text-input: A brown dog lying on bed with his banana toy

Two kids standing outside flying a kite during the day

Fig. 4. Generation results produced by our proposed model. The four subplots in each sample correspond to different epochs, ranging from 60 to 100.

Ablation Study: In this subsection, two ablation experiments are conducted to investigate the effectiveness of the Self-Attention module and shape generator, respectively. In Table 2, we statistically present the performance of the models by eliminating the Self-Attention module in box and shape generator, respectively.

It can be seen from the table that the FID of Obj-SA-GAN$_1$ appears close to Obj-SA-GAN$_2$. This reveals that the box and shape generator almost contribute equally to FID. As for IS, Obj-SA-GAN$_2$ reaches 32.54, nearly equal to the proposed model. This is because IS does not consider the semantic layout when evaluating the model.

Table 2. Ablation study of Obj-SA-GAN model

Models	Box attention	Shape attention	Inception	FID
Obj-SA-GAN	YES	YES	**32.26**	**18.25**
Obj-SA-GAN1	YES	NO	31.41	19.21
Obj-SA-GAN2	NO	YES	32.54	19.87

5   Conclusion and Future Work

In this paper, we proposed a novel text-to-image synthesis model, called the Obj-SA-GAN model, incorporating the attention and semantic layer. The proposed model adopts Self-Attention in the box and shape generator, which enhances text utilisation and deeply parses complex text descriptions, from coarse to fine, and gradually forms an accurate and fine-grained semantic layer to guide the global layout of the generated image. The proposed Obj-SA-GAN model can achieve excellent performance on the MSCOCO dataset, outperforming most existing generative models.

In the future, we plan to replace the multi-stage model with an end-to-end generative model. We also consider designing a novel quantitative assessment metric that can complement the Inception Score and other metrics.

References

1. Agnese, J., Herrera, J., Tao, H., Zhu, X.: A survey and taxonomy of adversarial neural networks for text-to-image synthesis. Wiley Interdisc. Rev.: Data Mining Knowl. Discovery **10**(4), e1345 (2020)
2. Bai, S., An, S.: A survey on automatic image caption generation. Neurocomputing **311**, 291–304 (2018)
3. Deng, J., Dong, W., Socher, R., Li, L.J., Li, K., Fei-Fei, L.: Imagenet: A large-scale hierarchical image database. In: 2009 IEEE Conference on Computer Vision and Pattern Recognition, pp. 248–255. IEEE (2009)
4. Esfahani, S.N., Latifi, S.: Image generation with gans-based techniques: A survey. Int. J. of Comput. Sci. Inf. Technol. **11**, 33–50 (10 2019). https://doi.org/10.5121/ijcsit.2019.11503
5. Frolov, S., Hinz, T., Raue, F., Hees, J., Dengel, A.: Adversarial text-to-image synthesis: A review. Neural Netw. **144**, 187–209 (2021)

6. Ghosh, B., Dutta, I.K., Totaro, M., Bayoumi, M.: A survey on the progression and performance of generative adversarial networks. In: 2020 11th International Conference on Computing, Communication and Networking Technologies (ICCCNT), pp. 1–8. IEEE (2020)
7. Hong, S., Yang, D., Choi, J., Lee, H.: Inferring semantic layout for hierarchical text-to-image synthesis. In: Proceedings of the IEEE Conference on Computer Vision and Pattern Recognition, pp. 7986–7994 (2018)
8. Huang, X., Li, Y., Poursaeed, O., Hopcroft, J., Belongie, S.: Stacked generative adversarial networks. In: Proceedings of the IEEE Conference on Computer Vision and Pattern recognition, pp. 5077–5086 (2017)
9. Karpathy, A., Fei-Fei, L.: Deep visual-semantic alignments for generating image descriptions. In: Proceedings of the IEEE Conference on Computer Vision and Pattern Recognition, pp. 3128–3137 (2015)
10. Lee, H., Ullah, U., Lee, J.S., Jeong, B., Choi, H.C.: A brief survey of text driven image generation and maniulation. In: 2021 IEEE International Conference on Consumer Electronics-Asia (ICCE-Asia), pp. 1–4. IEEE (2021)
11. Li, W., et al.: Object-driven text-to-image synthesis via adversarial training. In: Proceedings of the IEEE/CVF Conference on Computer Vision and Pattern Recognition, pp. 12174–12182 (2019)
12. Lin, T.-Y., et al.: Microsoft COCO: common objects in context. In: Fleet, D., Pajdla, T., Schiele, B., Tuytelaars, T. (eds.) ECCV 2014. LNCS, vol. 8693, pp. 740–755. Springer, Cham (2014). https://doi.org/10.1007/978-3-319-10602-1_48
13. Ning, X., Nan, F., Xu, S., Yu, L., Zhang, L.: Multi-view frontal face image generation: a survey. Concurrency and Computation: Practice and Experience, p. e6147 (2020)
14. Pavan Kumar, M., Jayagopal, P.: Generative adversarial networks: a survey on applications and challenges. Int. J. Multimedia Inform. Retrieval 10(1), 1–24 (2021)
15. Reed, S., Akata, Z., Yan, X., Logeswaran, L., Schiele, B., Lee, H.: Generative adversarial text to image synthesis. In: International conference on machine learning, pp. 1060–1069. PMLR (2016)
16. Reed, S., Akata, Z., Yan, X., Logeswaran, L., Schiele, B., Lee, H.: Generative adversarial text to image synthesis. In: International Conference on Machine Learning, pp. 1060–1069. PMLR (2016)
17. Shamsolmoali, P., et al.: Image synthesis with adversarial networks: a comprehensive survey and case studies. Inform. Fusion 72, 126–146 (2021)
18. Singh, N.K., Raza, K.: Medical image generation using generative adversarial networks: a review. Health Informatics: A Computational Perspective in Healthcare, pp. 77–96 (2021)
19. Vaswani, A., et al.: Attention is all you need. In: Advances in neural information processing systems, vol. 30 (2017)
20. Wang, F., Tax, D.M.: Survey on the attention based rnn model and its applications in computer vision. arXiv preprint arXiv:1601.06823 (2016)
21. Wu, X., Xu, K., Hall, P.: A survey of image synthesis and editing with generative adversarial networks. Tsinghua Sci. Technol. 22(6), 660–674 (2017)
22. Xu, T., et al.: Attngan: Fine-grained text to image generation with attentional generative adversarial networks. In: Proceedings of the IEEE conference on computer vision and pattern recognition, pp. 1316–1324 (2018)
23. Zhang, H., Goodfellow, I., Metaxas, D., Odena, A.: Self-attention generative adversarial networks. In: International Conference on Machine Learning, pp. 7354–7363. PMLR (2019)

24. Zhang, H., et al.: Stackgan: Text to photo-realistic image synthesis with stacked generative adversarial networks. In: Proceedings of the IEEE International Conference on Computer Vision, pp. 5907–5915 (2017)
25. Zhang, H., et al.: Stackgan++: realistic image synthesis with stacked generative adversarial networks. IEEE Trans. Pattern Anal. Mach. Intell. **41**(8), 1947–1962 (2018)
26. Zhang, S., et al.: Text-to-image synthesis via visual-memory creative adversarial network. In: Hong, R., Cheng, W.-H., Yamasaki, T., Wang, M., Ngo, C.-W. (eds.) PCM 2018. LNCS, vol. 11166, pp. 417–427. Springer, Cham (2018). https://doi.org/10.1007/978-3-030-00764-5_38
27. Zhou, R., Jiang, C., Xu, Q.: A survey on generative adversarial network-based text-to-image synthesis. Neurocomputing **451**, 316–336 (2021)
28. Zhou, Y., Shimada, N.: Generative adversarial network for text-to-face synthesis and manipulation with pretrained bert model. In: 2021 16th IEEE International Conference on Automatic Face and Gesture Recognition (FG 2021), pp. 01–08. IEEE (2021)
29. Zhu, B., Ngo, C.W.: Cookgan: Causality based text-to-image synthesis. In: Proceedings of the IEEE/CVF Conference on Computer Vision and Pattern Recognition, pp. 5519–5527 (2020)
30. Zhu, M., Pan, P., Chen, W., Yang, Y.: Dm-gan: Dynamic memory generative adversarial networks for text-to-image synthesis. In: Proceedings of the IEEE/CVF Conference on Computer Vision and Pattern Recognition, pp. 5802–5810 (2019)

Data Mining and Knowledge Discovery

APGKT: Exploiting Associative Path on Skills Graph for Knowledge Tracing

Haotian Zhang[1], Chenyang Bu[1](✉), Fei Liu[1,2](✉), Shuochen Liu[1],
Yuhong Zhang[1], and Xuegang Hu[1]

[1] Key Laboratory of Knowledge Engineering with Big Data (the Ministry of
Education of China), School of Information Science and Computer Engineering, Hefei
University of Technology, Hefei, China
chenyangbu@hfut.edu.cn, feiliu@mail.hfut.edu.cn
[2] Jianzai Tech, Hefei, China

Abstract. Knowledge tracing (KT) is a fundamental task in educational data mining that mainly focuses on students' dynamic cognitive states of skills. The question-answering process of students can be regarded as a thinking process that considers the following two problems. One problem is which skills are needed to answer the question, and the other is how to use these skills in order. If a student wants to answer a question correctly, the student should not only master the set of skills involved in the question, but also think and obtain the associative path on the skills graph. The nodes in the associative path refer to the skills needed and the path shows the order of using them. The associative path is referred to as the skill mode. Thus, obtaining the skill modes is the key to answering questions successfully. However, most existing KT models only focus on a set of skills, without considering the skill modes. We propose a KT model, called APGKT, that exploits skill modes. Specifically, we extract the subgraph topology of the skills involved in the question and combine the difficulty level of the skills to obtain the skill modes via encoding; then, through multi-layer recurrent neural networks, we obtain a student's higher-order cognitive states of skills, which is used to predict the student's future answering performance. Experiments on five benchmark datasets validate the effectiveness of the proposed model.

Keywords: Educational data mining · Knowledge tracing · Graph neural network

1 Introduction

Recent advances in intelligent tutoring systems have promoted the development of online education and generated a large amount of online learning data [1–3].

Chenyang Bu was supported in part by the National Natural Science Foundation of China under Grants 61806065 and 62120106008, and the Fundamental Research Funds for the Central Universities under Grant JZ2022HGTB0239. The source code is available at https://github.com/DMiC-Lab-HFUT/APGKT-PRICAI2022.

© The Author(s), under exclusive license to Springer Nature Switzerland AG 2022
S. Khanna et al. (Eds.): PRICAI 2022, LNCS 13629, pp. 353–365, 2022.
https://doi.org/10.1007/978-3-031-20862-1_26

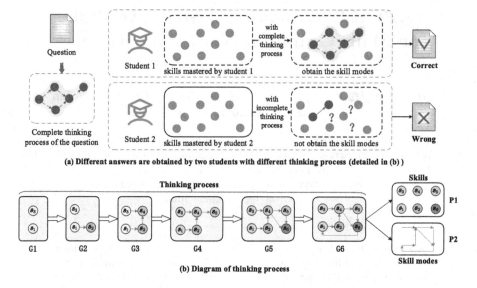

(a) Different answers are obtained by two students with different thinking process (detailed in (b))

(b) Diagram of thinking process

Fig. 1. (a) Instance of students answering questions. Given the same question, Student 1 and Student 2 provide different answers. Assuming that the skills mastery of the two students is similar, the student who cannot obtain the skill modes through thinking should have a higher probability of answering incorrectly. (b) Detailed thinking process of a student. G_i represents every thinking state and the arrow connecting two states represents a state transition, indicating a student's thinking and associative behavior.

Knowledge tracing (KT) is used to model students' dynamic mastery of skills based on their historical learning data and to infer their future answering performance, which is a fundamental and essential task in computer-aided educational systems and online learning platforms [4,5].

Bayesian knowledge tracing (BKT) [6] was the first KT model proposed by Corbett et al. It models students' cognitive states using the hidden markov model (HMM) with limited representation capabilities [7]. Subsequently, deep learning models, such as deep knowledge tracing (DKT) [8], were developed, which model a student's learning process as a recurrent neural network (RNN), significantly improving the prediction performance of the traditional Bayesian-based KT. With the development of graph neural networks (GNN) [9], GNN-based KT models [10,11], which use the natural graph structure existing in skills to model students' cognition, have attracted considerable attention. Although KT models have developed rapidly in recent years, limitations still exist.

Most of the existing KT models assume that students could obtain the correct answer only if they mastered all the skills; therefore, they use the cognitive state of the skills to predict a student's future answering performance. However, they ignore the thinking process of students. In addition to mastering skills, two points need to be considered to predict the future answering performance of a student: (1) finding the skills needed to answer a question among all the skills mastered, and (2) obtaining a reasonable order of use for these skills. If a student wants to answer a question correctly, the student should not only master the set of skills involved in the question but should also think and obtain the associative path on the skills graph, the nodes in which are the skills to be used, and the path showing the order of using them. Here, the associative path is referred to as the skill mode. If students only master the skills (e.g., $P1$ in Fig. 1(b)), the students cannot solve the problem because they may not establish an association between s_1 and s_2; they do not think of using s_2 to solve the problem. At this time, the students get stuck in processing the association from $G1$ to $G2$ shown in Fig. 1(b). Students may fail to establish an association between s_2, s_3, and s_4 as well. At this time, the student gets stuck in processing the association from $G2$ to $G3$ shown in Fig. 1(b). Students who do not master any of the processes in $P2$ may fail to solve the problem. Thus, obtaining skill modes is the key to answering questions successfully. As shown in Fig. 1(a), Student 1 and Student 2 provide different answers for the same question. Assuming that the skill mastery of the two students is similar, the student who cannot obtain the skill modes through thinking should have a higher probability of answering incorrectly (as shown in Fig. 1(a)). Students must use the skills they have mastered, the information in the question, and their experience to find the skills needed to answer a question and convert the thinking process into answers (as shown in Fig. 1(b)). This study assumed that students will have a higher probability of getting a question wrong if they only master the skills without mastering the skill modes.

APGKT is proposed considering skill modes (e.g., $P2$ in Fig. 1(b)) to improve performance of KT. The main contributions of this study are as follows:

- This study exploits the associative path on the skills graph for knowledge tracing (KT). The thinking process (i.e., obtaining the associative path) has been demonstrated to be indispensable for achieving a correct answer (detailed in Fig. 1). However, most of the existing KT models only consider whether the set of skills involved in the question have been mastered when predicting a student's future answering performance.
- The proposed APGKT model includes the concept of skill modes and higher-order cognitive states. Considering the dynamic process of students thinking and answering questions, the skills associated with a specific problem are considered as a whole to consider the organizational association. We combine the cognitive state of the skills and the skill modes into a higher-order cognitive state to accurately represent the cognitive processes of students.
- Extensive experiments on five public datasets proved that the prediction results of our model are better than those of baseline models, owing to the consideration of the thinking process during KT.

2   Related Work

In this section, related work regarding KT and the existing GNN-based KT models is introduced.

2.1 Knowledge Tracing

KT as a student modeling technique has attracted extensive research work. Existing KT models can be divided into three main categories: probabilistic models, logistic models, and deep learning-based models [1]. (1) **Probabilistic models**, which assume a Markov process to represent the learning process of students, are mainly of two types [1]: BKT [6] and DBKT [12]. They use unobservable nodes in the HMM to represent the knowledge state, and Bayesian networks and dynamic Bayesian networks for KT. (2) **Logistic models**, which assume that the probability of correctly answering questions can be expressed as a mathematical framework of students and skills parameters, are mainly of three types [1]: LFA [13], PFA [14], and KTM [15]. They use the output of the logistic regression function to represent the knowledge state, and logistic regression or factorization machines to model the knowledge state change. (3) **Deep learning-based models** adapt to complex learning processes, especially in the face of extensive interactive data [1], are being considered. Deep learning is a powerful tool to implement nonlinearity and feature extraction. DKT [8], the first deep learning-based model for KT, uses a RNN to model the cognitive state of students and has achieved excellent results. Subsequently, this model has been further developed into memory-aware [16], problem-aware [17–19], and attention [20–23] models [1], which use the interactive information in students' responses. Due to the natural graph structure of the KT task, GNN-based KT models have attracted researchers (detailed in Sect. 2.2).

2.2 GNN-based KT Models

GNNs, which process complex graph-structured data, have developed rapidly in recent years. In GNNs, a graph is a data structure that models a set of objects (nodes) and their relationships (edges). From the perspective of data structure, graph structures naturally exist within skills [10]. Therefore, combining the graph structure of the components (such as skills or questions) with relational inductive bias should improve the performance of KT models [1].

Recently, several KT-structure frameworks based on GNNs have been developed. For example, GKT [10] conceptualizes the underlying graph structure of skills into a graph to influence the updating process of the cognitive states of skills. HGKT [4] mines the hidden hierarchical relationships among exercises by constructing a hierarchical exercise graph. GIKT [11] aggregates the embedding of questions and skills through a graph convolutional network (GCN) to extract the higher-order information from them. By introducing the transfer of knowledge [24], SKT [25] further explores the knowledge structure and captures multiple relations in it to model the influence propagation among concepts. JKT [26] captures high-level semantic information and improves model interpretability by modeling the multi-dimensional relationships of "exercise-to-exercise" and "concept-to-concept" as graphs and fusing them with the "exercise-to-concept" relationship. Most existing GNN-based KT models only consider the graph structure within the set of skills involved in questions (e.g. $P1$ in Fig. 1(b)). Therefore,

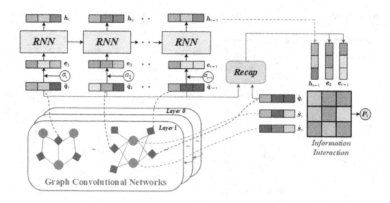

Fig. 2. Framework of the GIKT [11] model.

they lack the mining and utilization of information in the skill modes (e.g., $P2$ in Fig. 1(b)), which is what we focused on in this study.

2.3 GIKT

Our work is inspired by a graph-based interaction model for knowledge tracing (GIKT), and we refer readers to the reference [11] for more details about GIKT.

Embedding Propagation. GIKT models the relationship between questions and skills as a bigraph and uses multiple layers of GCN to aggregate their embeddings. After the GCN embedding propagation and aggregation processes, higher-order questions and skill-embedding representations $\tilde{q}$ and $\tilde{s}$ are obtained, respectively.

Student State Evolution. For each historical time t, GIKT obtains a representation of exercise e_t by concatting the embeddings of aggregated question $\tilde{q}_t$ and answer a_t. Then a long short-term memory network (LSTM) is used to learn the changes in the cognitive states h_t of students using e_t as input.

History Recap Module. GIKT uses a history recap module to select the history exercises related to the current answered questions to better represent the student's ability to answer the current specific question q_t. GIKT provides two methods for selecting history exercises I_e: hard and soft selections. The hard selection method only selects questions with skills identical to the current answered question each time and the soft selection method uses the similarity between the questions to select the top k-related problems with the highest correlations with the current question being answered.

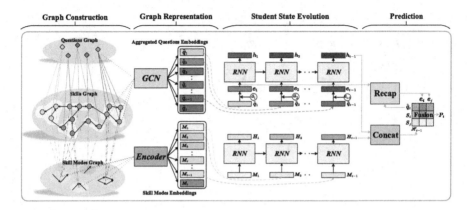

Fig. 3. Complete framework of the APGKT model. The first module on the left is the graph construction, the bottom of which is the skill modes graph we are concerned about. The next module is graph representation, where the efficient representation of the questions and the skill modes are obtained. In the student state evolution module, we obtain a student's cognitive state of skills and skill modes. Finally, the prediction module obtains the final prediction by fusing the higher-order cognitive state obtained by *Concat* and other state information.

Generalized Interaction Module. In this module, GIKT uses $\langle h_t, \tilde{q}_t \rangle$ to indicate the student's mastery of question q_t, $\langle h_t, \tilde{s}_j \rangle$ to indicate the student's mastery of related skill $s_j \in \mathcal{N}_{q_t}$, $\langle h_i, \tilde{q}_t \rangle$, and $\langle h_i, \tilde{s}_j \rangle$ to represent the interaction of the current student state with historical states. GITK considers the interaction information of all these states to obtain the predicted value.

3   APGKT: Proposed Model

In this section, we introduce the framework (detailed in Sect. 3.1) of our model, which includes graph construction and representation (detailed in Sect. 3.2), and student state evolution and prediction (detailed in Sect. 3.3).

3.1   Framework

The framework of the APGKT model is shown in Fig. 3. First, we construct a graph and obtain its representations (detailed in Sect. 3.2). We then obtain a student's higher-order cognitive states by splicing the cognitive state of skills and skill modes, which is then used to predict the performance of the student (detailed in Sect. 3.3). In the following sections, we describe in detail each module of our model.

3.2   Graph Construction and Representation

The structure of the graph is first described. Then, the construction of skill graph, the generation and representation of skill modes are detailed.

Structure of the Graph. To represent the relationship between questions, skills, and skill modes, we constructed a graph with three layers for three relationships (as shown in Fig. 3).

(1) **Three layers.** a) The top layer is a question graph that contains all the questions from the student's answer record. We represent these questions by $Q = \{q_1, q_2, ..., q_{n_q}\}$, where n_q denotes the total number of questions. b) The middle layer is a skills graph, which consists of the skills involved in all the questions. These skills are represented as $S = \{s_1, s_2, ..., s_{n_s}\}$, where n_s is the total number of skills. c) The bottom layer is a skill-mode graph, which contains all the obtained skill modes.

(2) **Three relations.** a) Each question q_i in the question graph is associated with a skill set in the skills graph, and we represent this skill set as $Sset_i = \{s_1^i, s_2^i, ..., s_{h_i}^i\}$, $h_i \geq 1$. $s_1^i, s_2^i, ..., s_{h_i}^i$ are skills related to question q_i and h_i indicates the number of skills related to question q_i. The skills in the skills graph are divided into several skill sets based on the questions. The relationship between questions Q and skills S is represented by a matrix QS. QS is a two-dimensional matrix of size $n_q \times n_s$, where $QS_{i,j} = 1$ indicates that q_i is related to s_j. b) The relationship between skills is constructed using several methods, which will be introduced in Sect. 3.2. This relationship is represented by a two-dimensional adjacency matrix SS of size $n_s \times n_s$, where n_s is the number of skills. $0 \leq SS_{i,j} \leq 1$ indicates the strength of the association between s_i and s_j. Note that $SS_{i,j}$ and $SS_{j,i}$ represent different relationships between the skills. c) The method for obtaining the relationship between skills and skill modes is introduced in Sect. 3.2. A skill may belong to different skill sets and different skill modes because it is simultaneously associated with different questions, and the number of skill modes equals the number of skill sets, as shown in Fig. 3.

Skills Graph Construction. APGKT needs to use the graph structure of skills when evaluating a student's proficiency in skills and skill modes. However, in most cases, the structure of the skills is not explicitly provided. Nakagawa et al. [10] introduced statistics-based and learning-based approaches for implementing the latent graph structure, of which the former are more efficient with less time consumption (detailed in Table 2 in [10]). From the aspect of statistics-based approaches, we assumed that the higher the frequency of two skills appearing together in the same question, the stronger the strength of the association between the two skills. This was not considered in the statistics-based approaches in [10]. Therefore, a frequency-based method is proposed in this subsection.

Frequency-based method generates a connected graph according to the number of times two skills appear together in the same question and the number of times two skills appear separately in different questions. This is calculated using Eq. (1).

$$SS_{i,j} = \frac{n_{i,j}}{\sum_{k=1}^{n_s} n_{i,k}}, \tag{1}$$

where $n_{i,j}$ represents the times two skills appear together in the same question.

Skill Modes Generation and Representation. Through the complete thinking process, the skill modes are obtained, which represent the associative paths on the skills graph (as shown in Fig. 1(b)). In this subsection, the generation and representation of the skill modes are designed.

Considering that students usually have a thinking process from easy to difficult when answering questions, we obtain an effective representation of the skill modes using the encoded association paths and difficulty levels of skills. Specifically, we first obtain the difficulty level of all the skills through statistical information using Eq. (2). Then, we obtain the ascending subscripts of the skills in $Sset_i$ according to the skill difficulty and referred to $Idx_i = \{i, j, ..., k\}$. We finally extract the local topological structure of $Sset_i$ in the SS using Eq. (3). That is, the values of the $i, j, ..., k$th row and $i, j, ..., k$th column in the SS are extracted and flattened to obtain the initial representation m_i of the skill mode.

$$Diff_{s_i} = \frac{n^i}{N^i}, \tag{2}$$

where n^i is the number of wrong answers to questions containing skill s_i and N^i is the number of questions containing skill s_i.

$$m_i = Flatten(\sum_{i' \in Idx_i} \sum_{j' \in Idx_i} SS_{i',j'}), \tag{3}$$

where Flatten indicates making multidimensional data one-dimensional.

We encode the initial representation of the skill modes through an encoder module to obtain the embedding of the skill modes M_i (Eq. (4)), and then calculate the mean squared error (mse) with the encoded m_i after decoding it to obtain the reconstruction loss $Reloss$ using Eq. (5). Finally, we minimize $Reloss$ to obtain an effective representation of the skill modes.

$$M_i = \sigma(W_M \times m_i + b_M) \tag{4}$$

$$Reloss = \frac{1}{n_q} \sum_{1}^{n_q} (M_i - m_i)^2 \tag{5}$$

In Eq. (4), σ indicates a nonlinear mapping, and W_M and b_M indicate the weights and biases, respectively, in the encoder that will be trained.

3.3 Student State Evolution and Prediction

For each time step t, the embedding of the aggregated question $\tilde{q}_t$ and skill modes M_t of q_t are provided as inputs into the LSTM to learn a student's mastery of skills and skill modes. Next, we connect the cognitive states of the student's skills and skill modes through the $Concat$ module to obtain the student's higher-order cognitive state $\mathcal{H}_t$ using Eq. (6). Finally, we incorporate the student's higher-order cognitive state $\mathcal{H}_t$ in (6) to improve the prediction of GIKT, and obtain the final prediction p_t as shown in Eq. (7) and Eq. (8) [11].

$$\mathcal{H}_t = [h_t, H_t], \tag{6}$$

where $[\cdot]$ represents vector concatenation.

$$\alpha_{i,j} = Softmax_{i,j}(W^T[f_i, f_j] + b), \tag{7}$$

$$p_t = \sum_{f_i \in I_e \cup \{\mathcal{H}_t\}} \sum_{f_j \in \mathcal{N}_{q_t} \cup \{\tilde{q}_t\}} \alpha_{i,j} g(f_i, f_j), \tag{8}$$

where p_t indicates the predicted result at time t, I_e indicates history exercises related to the q_t. $\mathcal{H}_t$ is the higher-order cognitive state of the student. $\tilde{\mathcal{N}}_{q_t}$ is the aggregated neighbor skill embedding of q_t. g represents the inner product.

APGKT is optimized by minimizing the cross-entropy loss between the predicted and the true values using gradient descent as shown in Eq. (9).

$$\mathcal{L} = -\sum_t (a_t \log p_t + (1 - a_t) \log(1 - p_t)), \tag{9}$$

where a_t represents the true value of the students' answer at time t.

4   Experiments

Experiments are conducted on five real-world datasets to demonstrate the effectiveness of the proposed model. First, the setup is introduced, including the datasets, baselines, and implementation details. Then, the comparing results and Nemenyi tests are presented. Finally, the parameters in the model are analyzed.

4.1   Setup

The setup of the experiments is introduced, including the five datasets, the compared baselines, and the implementation details.

Datasets. Five real-world datasets were used and their statistics are listed in Table 1. To verify the effectiveness of our model in the multi-skills scenario, we further processed the assist09 dataset, and only retained the questions involving multiple skills and students' answer records to form the dataset assist09-muti. The questions in CSEDM, FrcSub, Math1, and Math2 were all related to more than one skill, and there were no questions related to a single skill.

Comparison Baselines. To verify the effectiveness of our model, APGKT is compared with the following baselines: DKT [8], DKVMN [16], GKT [10], GIKT [11] (detailed in Sect. 2.3).

Table 1. Dataset statistics

Datasets	assist09	assist09-muti	CSEDM	FrcSub	Math1	Math2
Number of students	3002	1793	343	536	4209	3911
Number of questions	17705	3014	236	20	15	16
Number of skills	123	54	18	8	11	16

Table 2. Comparison in terms of AUC

Dataset	DKT [8]	DKVMN [16]	GKT [10]	GIKT [11]	APGKT (Our model)
assist09	0.6995	0.7112	0.7230	0.7742	**0.7767**
assist09-muti	0.6961	0.7106	0.7320	0.7763	**0.7817**
CSEDM	0.7543	0.7626	0.7647	0.7836	**0.7902**
FrcSub	0.8891	0.8729	0.8748	0.8982	**0.9059**
Math1	0.8349	0.8403	0.8456	0.8892	**0.8922**
Math2	0.8084	0.8159	0.8181	0.8681	**0.8695**

Implementation Details. The APGKT code was written using TensorFlow. The datasets were divided into training and testing sets in the ratio of 8:2. We set the length of skills, questions, and answer embeddings to 100, which were not pretrained but were randomly initialized and then optimized during training. The relationship between the skills was constructed using the Frequency-based method (detailed in Sect. 3.2). Finally, we used the Adam optimizer with a learning rate of 0.003 to optimize all the trainable parameters.

4.2   Results

Results including the mean AUC results, the Nemenyi tests, and the parametric analysis are illustrated in this subsection.

Comparison in Terms of AUC. We used AUC as the evaluation criterion, and Table 2 shows the AUC scores of the baseline models and our model. We observed that the AUC scores of APGKT were the highest (denoted in bold) for all the datasets, which demonstrates the effectiveness of the proposed method. On comparing the AUC scores of the models on the assist09 and assist09-muti datasets, we observed that our model performed better than the baseline models in multi-skill scenarios. This may be due to the abundant skill modes available in our model in multi-skill scenarios, which improves its predictive performance.

Nemenyi Test. In the experiments, Nemenyi tests [27] were conducted to statistically compare the five algorithms over five datasets (as shown in Fig. 4). The test results showed that our model performed better than other models.

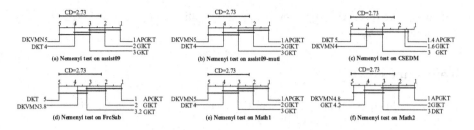

Fig. 4. Nemenyi test results of the proposed model and baselines. The results demonstrate the better performance of the proposed model.

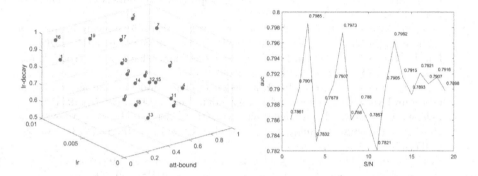

Fig. 5. Parameter analysis for APGKT. It is observed that our model outperforms the baselines although the parameters underwent constant changes.

Parametric Analysis. We also conducted parameter analyses on the CSEDM dataset to analyze the model's sensitivity to the parameters. Bayes opt (https://github.com/fmfn/BayesianOptimization) was used to tune the learning rate of Adam optimizer (lr), learning rate decay (lr-decay), and threshold for determining whether two questions are related (att-bound). They were initialized ranging from 0 to 1. It is observed that the performance of our model was superior to that of the baseline models although the parameters underwent constant changes.

5   Conclusion

Most of the existing KT models ignore the thinking process between specific skills, leading to suboptimal prediction performance. We introduced skill modes and higher-order cognitive states to solve this problem and proposed a novel model named APGKT. Specifically, we considered the dynamic process of students thinking and answering questions, and further explored the relationship between the specific skills involved in the questions. Extensive experiments on five public datasets verified that the proposed model outperformed the baseline models. Since the thinking process of students is actually a complex cognitive process, which is affected by many factors such as psychology, in the future, we will further explore the representation and application of the thinking process to improve the model.

References

1. Liu, Q., Shen, S., Huang, Z., Chen, E., Zheng, Y.: A survey of knowledge tracing, arXiv preprint arXiv:2105.15106 (2021)
2. Hu, X., Liu, F., Bu, C.: Research advances on knowledge tracing models in educational big data. J. Comput. Res. Develop. **57**(12), 2523–2546 (2020)
3. Bu, C., et al.: Cognitive diagnostic model made more practical by genetic algorithm, IEEE Transactions on Emerging Topics in Computational Intelligence (TETCI) (2022)
4. Tong, H., Wang, Z., Liu, Q., Zhou, Y., Han, W., HGKT: Introducing hierarchical exercise graph for knowledge tracing, arXiv preprint arXiv:2006.16915 (2020)
5. Liu, F., Hu, X., Bu, C., Yu, K.: Fuzzy Bayesian knowledge tracing. IEEE Trans. Fuzzy Syst. (TFS) **30**(7), 2412–2425 (2022)
6. Corbett, A.T., Anderson, J.R.: Knowledge tracing: Modeling the acquisition of procedural knowledge. User Model. User-Adap. Inter. **4**(4), 253–278 (1994)
7. Pelánek, R.: Bayesian knowledge tracing, logistic models, and beyond: An overview of learner modeling techniques. User Model. User-Adap. Inter. **27**(3), 313–350 (2017)
8. Piech, C., et al.: Deep knowledge tracing, in: Proceedings of International Conference on Neural Information Processing Systems (NeurIPS), pp. 505–513 (2015)
9. Bu, C., Lu, Y., Liu, F.: Automatic graph learning with evolutionary algorithms: an experimental study. In: Pham, D.N., Theeramunkong, T., Governatori, G., Liu, F. (eds.) PRICAI 2021. LNCS (LNAI), vol. 13031, pp. 513–526. Springer, Cham (2021). https://doi.org/10.1007/978-3-030-89188-6_38
10. Nakagawa, H., Iwasawa, Y., Matsuo, Y.: Graph-based knowledge tracing: Modeling student proficiency using graph neural network, In: Proceedings of IEEE/WIC/ACM International Conference on Web Intelligence (WI), IEEE, pp. 156–163 (2019)
11. Yang, Y., et al.: GIKT: A graph-based interaction model for knowledge tracing. In: Hutter, F., Kersting, K., Lijffijt, J., Valera, I. (eds.) ECML PKDD 2020. LNCS (LNAI), vol. 12457, pp. 299–315. Springer, Cham (2021). https://doi.org/10.1007/978-3-030-67658-2_18
12. Käser, T., Klingler, S., Schwing, A.G., Gross, M.: Dynamic bayesian networks for student modeling. IEEE Trans. Learn. Technol. **10**(4), 450–462 (2017)
13. Cen, H., Koedinger, K., Junker, B.: Learning factors analysis – a general method for cognitive model evaluation and improvement. In: Ikeda, M., Ashley, K.D., Chan, T.-W. (eds.) ITS 2006. LNCS, vol. 4053, pp. 164–175. Springer, Heidelberg (2006). https://doi.org/10.1007/11774303_17
14. Pavlik, P.I., Cen, H., Koedinger, K.R.: Performance factors analysis-a new alternative to knowledge tracing, In: Proceedings of Conference on Artificial Intelligence in Education: Building Learning Systems That Care: From Knowledge Representation to Affective Modelling, IOS Press, NLD, pp. 531–538 (2009)
15. Vie, J.J., Kashima, H.: Knowledge tracing machines: Factorization machines for knowledge tracing, In: Proceedings of the AAAI Conference on Artificial Intelligence (AAAI), vol. 33, pp. 750–757 (2019)

16. Zhang, J., Shi, X., King, I., Yeung, D.Y.: Dynamic key-value memory networks for knowledge tracing, In: Proceedings of International Conference on World Wide Web (WWW), ACM, pp. 765–774 (2017)

17. Liu, Q., et al.: Finding fimilar exercises in online education systems, In: Proceedings of ACM SIGKDD International Conference on Knowledge Discovery & Data Mining, KDD '18, Association for Computing Machinery, New York, NY, USA, pp. 1821–1830 (2018)

18. Liu, Q., et al.: Finding fimilar exercises in online education systems, In: Proceedings of ACM SIGKDD International Conference on Knowledge Discovery & Data Mining, KDD '18, Association for Computing Machinery, New York, NY, USA, pp. 1821–1830 (2018)

19. Liu, Q., et al.: EKT: exercise-aware knowledge tracing for student performance prediction. IEEE Trans. Knowl. Data Eng. (TKDE) 33(1), 100–115 (2019)

20. Pandey, S., Karypis, G.: A self-attentive model for knowledge tracing, CoRR abs/1907.06837 (2019). http://arxiv.org/abs/1907.06837

21. Wang, X., Mei, X., Huang, Q., Han, Z., Huang, C.: Fine-grained learning performance prediction via adaptive sparse self-attention networks. Inf. Sci. 545, 223–240 (2021)

22. Zhu, J., Yu, W., Zheng, Z., Huang, C., Tang, Y., Fung, G.P.C.: Learning from interpretable analysis: attention-based knowledge tracing. In: Bittencourt, I.I., Cukurova, M., Muldner, K., Luckin, R., Millán, E. (eds.) AIED 2020. LNCS (LNAI), vol. 12164, pp. 364–368. Springer, Cham (2020). https://doi.org/10.1007/978-3-030-52240-7_66

23. Shin, D., Shim, Y., Yu, H., Lee, S., Kim, B., Choi, Y.: SAINT+: Integrating temporal features for ednet correctness prediction, In: Proceedings of LAK21: International Learning Analytics and Knowledge Conference, LAK21, Association for Computing Machinery, New York, NY, USA, pp. 490–496 (2021)

24. Royer, J.M.: Theories of the transfer of learning. Educ. Psychol. 14(1), 53–69 (1979)

25. Tong, S., et al.: Structure-based knowledge tracing: An influence propagation view, In: Proceedings of IEEE International Conference on Data Mining (ICDM), IEEE, pp. 541–550 (2020)

26. Song, X., Li, J., Tang, Y., Zhao, T., Chen, Y., Guan, Z.: JKT: a joint graph convolutional network based deep knowledge tracing. Inf. Sci. 580, 510–523 (2021)

27. Demšar, J.: Statistical comparisons of classifiers over multiple data sets. J. Mach. Learn. Res. 7, 1–30 (2006)

Features Fusion Framework
for Multimodal Irregular Time-series
Events

Peiwang Tang[1,2] and Xianchao Zhang[3,4(✉)]

[1] Institute of Advanced Technology, University of Science and Technology of China,
Hefei 230026, China
tpw@mail.ustc.edu.cn
[2] G60 STI Valley Industry & Innovation Institute, Jiaxing University, Jiaxing
314001, China
[3] Key Laboratory of Medical Electronics and Digital Health of Zhejiang Province,
Jiaxing University, Jiaxing 314001, China
zhangxianchao@zjxu.edu.cn
[4] Engineering Research Center of Intelligent Human Health Situation Awareness
of Zhejiang Province, Jiaxing University, Jiaxing 314001, China

Abstract. Some data from multiple sources can be modeled as multi-modal time-series events which have different sampling frequencies, data compositions, temporal relations and characteristics. Different types of events have complex nonlinear relationships, and the time of each event is irregular. Neither the classical Recurrent Neural Network (RNN) model nor the current state-of-the-art Transformer model can deal with these features well. In this paper, a features fusion framework for multimodal irregular time-series events is proposed based on the Long Short-Term Memory networks (LSTM). Firstly, the complex features are extracted according to the irregular patterns of different events. Secondly, the nonlinear correlation and complex temporal dependencies relationship between complex features are captured and fused into a tensor. Finally, a feature gate are used to control the access frequency of different tensors. Extensive experiments on MIMIC-III dataset demonstrate that the proposed framework significantly outperforms to the existing methods in terms of AUC (the area under Receiver Operating Characteristic curve) and AP (Average Precision).

Keywords: Features fusion · LSTM · Multimodal · Time-series

1 Introduction

In general terms, a modality refers to the way in which something happens or is experienced [2]. To our best knowledge, many existing works have demonstrated that Neural Network can achieve an excellent result in single modality processing such as image classification [23], speech synthesis [13], natural language processing [26]. In the field of data, multimodal is used to represent different forms of

© The Author(s), under exclusive license to Springer Nature Switzerland AG 2022
S. Khanna et al. (Eds.): PRICAI 2022, LNCS 13629, pp. 366–379, 2022.
https://doi.org/10.1007/978-3-031-20862-1_27

data, or different formats of the same form, which generally represents text, picture, audio and video [11,22]. Hence, multimodal data processing have attracted a wide attention from the academia, especially for multimodal fusion which is one of the original topics in multimodal machine learning [2]. Neural Networks is expected to tackle the multimodal fusion problem [18] and has been used extensively to fuse information for text, image and audio [14,15], gesture recognition [17], and video or image description generation [21,27], since the earliest investigation of AVSR [20]. However, almost of all these studies focus on text, images or speech modes rather than multimodal time-series which is a critical ingredient across many domains, so how to effectively process multimodal data still need further study. Many methods have been launched to process simple single mode time-series data [1,29], which have achieved the best result in their respective field. But they have no way to directly use multimodal time-series data, for example multisensor data, medical time-series data.

The problem of features fusion is challenging in multimodal irregular time-series data processing [4]. For example, for clinical data, patient's electronic health records can be abstracted into thousands of interrelated medical events with temporal information, including complex allergy history, family genetic history, drug list, hospitalization records and other historical records. Different event has almost absolutely different frequency of recording. E.g. patient's hospitalization records may be only once a few years, but medication records could be many times a year. Not only different events have different recording frequencies, but also the same type events have significant differences in their different nature. For example, attributes of drug taking events such as drug type, dose and test events include specific indicators and comparison results with normal range values. In order to integrate the features of these events, we must describe these dependencies.

In order to solve the above problems in multimodal irregular time-series events, in this paper, the following contributions is presented in this paper: (1) We propose a new features fusion method to deal with multimodal data, where the features of complex data are fused into a common feature subspace. This method can be applied to different multimodal data. (2) We explore different encoding methods for temporary features, and found a method to embed the temporary features into the non-temporary features, which allows us to better deal with time-series data (3) We propose a model called FG-LSTM which developed from the Recurrent Neural Network such as Phased LSTM [16] to deal with the problem of irregular time-series data. Our proposed model filters the input features by feature gate while recording the complex temporal relationship between different features. (4) We compare with other models, and the experiment results based on the real data demonstrate that the prediction performance of our model is significantly improved.

2   Related Work

2.1   Multimodal Fusion Problem

Multimodal fusion mainly refers to the comprehensive processing of multimodal data by computer, which is responsible for fusing the information of each mode to perform target prediction [22]. Tensor Fusion Network (TFN) [28]is a multimodal network for features fusion through matrix operation to directly fuse the three features vectors of the data with three modes (such as text, image and audio). However, since TFN calculates the correlation between the elements of different modes through the tensor outer product between modes, it will greatly increase the dimension of features tensor and result in a too large model that is difficult to train. Low-rank Multimodal Fusion [14] uses a low rank matrix to decompose the weight, and hence the TFN process is changed into a single linear transformation of each mode. Then the received multi-dimensional point by Low-rank Multimodal Fusion can be regarded as the sum of multiple low rank vectors, and thus the number of parameters in the model is reduced. Although Low-rank Multimodal Fusion is an upgrade of TFN, once the features are too long, it is still easy to explode parameters. Multimodal Adversarial Representation Network [10] adds a dual discriminator countermeasure network based on multimodal fusion (ordinary attention fusion), which captures dynamic commonness and invariance respectively. Multimodal Bottleneck Transformer [15] uses a shared token between two Transformer, so that this token becomes a communication bottleneck of different modes to save computational attention. In this way, multimodal interaction can be limited to several shared tokens. Compared with the above researches, we pay more attention to multimodal time-series events, and the above researches can also be regarded as special cases of multimodal time-series events.

2.2   Time-series Forecasting

Recurrent neural network (RNN) is a neural network used to process sequence data. Theoretically, RNN can store long-term memory and update the previous state according to the current input at any time, but in fact, it is very difficult. In another word, RNN is difficult to solve the problem of long-term dependence [5]. LSTM [6] is a special RNN, which is mainly to solve the problems of gradient disappearance and gradient explosion in the process of long sequence training. Compared with ordinary RNN, LSTM has better performance in long sequences, but LSTM can only maintain a long-term dependence within about 50 time steps. Phased LSTM [16] can solve the problem that LSTM can not process irregular input sequences. By integrating different sampling frequencies or irregularly sampled data on phase gate, Phase LSTM can remember signals with different periods, and the state can propagate for a long time. When the processing sequence reaches thousands of steps, LSTM is almost unavailable, while Phased LSTM performs well. But Phased LSTM is not suitable for modeling the complex event sequence with thousands of event types. HE-LSTM [12] is proposed to deal with heterogeneous temporal events in long-term dependence, but it can only extract event types while the features relationship of events can not be obtained. Transformer [26] is a powerful architecture that can achieve excellent performance on a variety of sequential learning tasks, which does not perform recursion on the sequence, but processes the feedforward model of the whole sequence simultaneously. Recent research shows that transformer has the potential to improve the prediction ability [24]. However, transformer has some serious problems that make it unable to be directly applied to multimodal irregular time-series data, such as quadratic time complexity, high memory utilization and the inherent limitations of encoder-decoder architecture [29]. In addition to the above problems, the biggest problem of Transformer is that the model contains no recurrence and no convolution, which results in the input tensor can not contain the time relationship of the input sequence effectively [3].

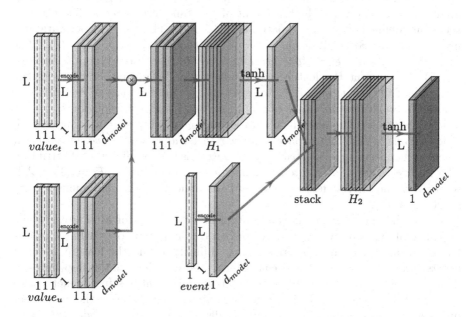

Fig. 1. The non-temporal features fusion method.

3   Methodology

For time-series $\mathbf{S}$ in a given scene, the features of the sequence are consist of dynamic events $\{\mathbf{E}_t\}_{1 \le t \le L}$ with length L, and each event occurs at the same or different time. We arrange it according to the chronological order of events. Among the events that occur at the same time, the events recorded earlier are arranged in front. Each time-series **S** corresponds to a discrete label, which indicates the state of the object at a certain time in the future. For example, in Clinical Endpoint Prediction Task, 0 or 1 indicates the patient's status (death or not) at a certain point in time in the future. So prediction of the results of time-series **S** with this corresponding discrete label is defined as the classification of time-series **S**.

3.1 Features Fusion

Each time-series **S** contains many types of events, and each event has its own time of occurrence. We use $\mathcal{S}$ to represent the feature space where **S** is located, $\mathcal{E}$ to represent non-temporal information, that is, the feature space where the events is located, and $\mathcal{T}$ to represent the feature space where temporal information is located. Formally, a sequence $S = [E_1, E_2, \ldots, E_L]$, defines each element as $E_i = (e_i, t_i)$, with $e_i \in \mathcal{E}$ being the non-temporal features at time i and $t_i \in \mathcal{T}$ as an temporal features, and t_i is the interval between the occurrence time of this event and the time when the first event of this time-series occurs. The features vector are defined over a joint space : $\mathcal{S} := (\mathcal{E} \times \mathcal{T})$. The resulting permutation-invariant set is: $\mathbf{S}_E = \{E_1, E_2, \ldots, E_L\} = \{(e_1, t_1), (e_2, t_2), \ldots, (e_L, t_L)\}$. For each event we define $e_i = (type, attribute)$, where $type$ is the type of event, we use $\mathcal{F}_t$ to represent the feature space where type is located; $attribute$ is the attribute of the event, we use $\mathcal{F}_a$ to represent the feature space where attribute is located. So the feature space of event : $\mathcal{E} := (\mathcal{F}_t \times \mathcal{F}_a)$, $\mathcal{E}$ is obviously a joint space, where $\mathcal{F}_t$ is the discrete feature space and $\mathcal{F}_a$ is the continuous feature space. Similarly, attribute consists of two parts: $attribute = (value_t, value_u)$, where $value_t$ is the type of attribute, and $value_u$ is the specific value of attribute. The feature vector of attribute are defined over a joint space : $\mathcal{F}_a := (\mathcal{V}_t \times \mathcal{V}_u)$, where $\mathcal{V}_t$ is the discrete feature space of $value_t$ and $\mathcal{V}_u$ is the continuous feature space of $value_u$.

For each type of event, it can contain multiple types of attributes. While for different types of events, it may contain the same type of attributes or different types of attributes. Therefore, it is difficult to find the feature space of events directly, and we need to characterize the complex relationship between different events. We demonstrate the non-temporal features fusion method as shown in Fig. 1, where d_{model} is the encoded dimension: (1) Select the first three-dimensional feature of attribute, fill up the deficiencies with 0, encode $value_t$ and $value_u$ as V_t, V_u respectively, and then use $V_t \times V_u$ to get a new three-dimensional feature; (2) Use 1×1 convolution kernel to increase the dimension of the features obtained in the previous step, and then use 1×1 convolution kernel to reduce the dimension to one-dimensional features after being processed by the $tanh$ activation function; (3) Stack the features obtained in the previous step with the features encoded by event, then use 1×1 convolution kernel to increase the dimension, after processing by the $tanh$ activation function, use 1×1 convolution kernel to reduce the dimension to obtain the one-dimensional non-temporal features. For $\mathcal{V}_u$ of continuous feature space, we do not simply encode $value_u$ with convolution or fully connected layers, instead encode $value_u$ with the help

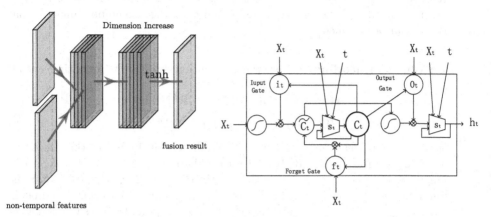

Fig. 2. Temporal and non-temporal features fusion methods

Fig. 3. FG-LSTM Model

of $\mathcal{V}_t$ of discrete feature space, as shown in the formula:

$$V_u = W_{v_t} \times value_u + B_{v_t} \tag{1}$$

where $W_{v_t} \in \mathbb{R}^{L_W \times d_{model}}$ and $B_{v_t} \in \mathbb{R}^{L_B \times d_{model}}$ is the tensor after embedding $value_t$, and $V_u \in \mathbb{R}^{L_V \times d_{model}}$ is the result after encoding $value_u$.

For the fusion of temporal and non-temporal features, many studies directly adopt the additive method, such as the most famous Transformer architecture [26]. The fusion of temporal and non-temporal features is not a simple additive relationship, so the method shown in the Fig. 2 is proposed. Firstly, stack the temporal and non-temporal features, then increase the dimension of the two features used 1×1 convolution structure. After processing by the *tanh* activation function, we eventually fuse features into one-dimensional tensor on another 1×1 convolution structure.

Because the time interval between events is not equal, and the time of each event is a very important feature that can not be ignored. We add "time encoding" to the input embeddings and use two methods to encode time:

Function Encoding. We use sine and cosine functions of different frequencies just as "positional encoding" [26]:

$$FE_{(time,2i)} = sin\left(time/10000^{2i/d_{model}}\right) \tag{2}$$

$$FE_{(time,2i+1)} = cos\left(time/10000^{2i/d_{model}}\right) \tag{3}$$

where i is the dimension, $i \in \{1, \ldots, d_{model}/2\}$. That is, each dimension of the time encoding corresponds to a sinusoid. We chose this function because for any fixed time offset k, FE_{time+k} can be represented as a linear function of FE_{time}. The time encoding have the same dimension d_{model} as the embeddings, so that the two can be summed.

Convolution Encoding. We use the convolution structure to learn time encoding:

$$\mathbf{H} = tanh(Conv1d(T^L)) \in \mathbb{R}^{L \times d_{model}/2} \tag{4}$$

$$\mathbf{T} = tanh(Conv1d(\mathbf{H})) \in \mathbb{R}^{L \times d_{model}} \tag{5}$$

For the temporal features with length L and dimension 1, that is, the size $L \times 1$, use the convolution kernel of 1×1 to learn the matrix with size $1 \times d_{model}/2$, change the temporal features into the matrix with size $L \times d_{model}/2$. After the $tanh$ activation function, use the convolution kernel of 1×1 to learn the matrix with size $d_{model}/2 \times d_{model}$ again, and change the temporal features into a matrix with the size of $L \times d_{model}$. Finally get the temporal features with the size of $L \times d_{model}$ after $tanh$ activation function.

3.2 Model Architecture

Long short-term memory (LSTM) [6] is an important ingredient for modern deep RNN architectures. The FG-LSTM extends the LSTM model by adding a new feature gate s_t, and the Fig. 3 shows the FG-LSTM model. The x_t is the input features at time t, and others are basically consistent with ordinary LSTM. The feature gate has two factors: a feature filter and a time gate.

The combination of features and time gates only allows the features of certain kinds of features to be input into the neuron, and makes the neuron open only in a specific cycle. This ensures that each neuron will only capture the features of specific types of events and sample them, which solves the problem of poor training effect caused by the complexity and diversity of time and long event sequence.

The opening and closing of this feature gate is controlled by the features and time. Updates to the cell state c_t and h_t are permitted only when the gate is open. We proposed a particularly successful formulation of the feature gate as following:

$$s_t = ReLU(W_{hs} \tanh(W_{xh}x_t + b_h) + b_s) \odot k_t \tag{6}$$

where $W_{xh} \in \mathbb{R}^{d_{model} \times h}, W_{hs} \in \mathbb{R}^{h \times s}$, $b_h \in \mathbb{R}^{1 \times h}$ and $b_s \in \mathbb{R}^{1 \times s}$ are the parameters to be learned, h is hidden size, s is output size. $ReLU$ and $tanh$ is the activation function, x_t is the tensor input at time t, and k_t is the time gate [16].

Compared with traditional RNN and other excellent variants of RNN [9], FG-LSTM can choose to update the learned parameters at the time point t of irregular sampling. This allows the FG-LSTM to work with asynchronously sampled irregular time-series data. We can then rewrite the regular LSTM cell update equations for c_t and h_t, using proposed cell updates $\tilde{c}_t$ and $\tilde{h}_t$ mediated by the feature gate s_t :

$$i_t = \sigma_i(x_t W_{xi} + h_{t-1} W_{hi} + w_{ci} \odot c_{t-1} + b_i) \tag{7}$$

$$f_t = \sigma_f(x_t W_{xf} + h_{t-1} W_{hf} + w_{cf} \odot c_{t-1} + b_f) \tag{8}$$

$$\tilde{c}_t = f_t \odot c_{t-1} + i_t \odot \tanh_c(x_t W_{xc} + h_{t-1} W_{hc} + b_c) \tag{9}$$

$$c_t = s_t \odot \tilde{c}_t + (1 - s_t) \odot c_{t-1} \tag{10}$$

$$o_t = \sigma_o(x_t W_{xo} + h_{t-1} W_{ho} + w_{co} \odot c_t + b_o) \tag{11}$$

$$\tilde{h}_t = o_t \odot \tanh_h(\tilde{c}_t) \tag{12}$$

$$h_t = s_t \odot \tilde{h}_t + (1 - s_t) \odot h_{t-1} \tag{13}$$

To sum up, for a neuron, only when it meets the type conditions of the corresponding feature gate, and the features information in its sampling period, neron will be updated. Therefore, it can be considered that this neuron represents the state of a certain type of features in a certain sampling period. This is because the feature gate s_t, can be seen as a binary classifier to chose the cluster of features types responsible for each neuron. In addition, neurons do not update any information in the closing stage and maintain a perfect memory of past information, i.e. $c_j = c_{j-\Delta}$ if $k_t = 0$ for $t_{j-\Delta} \leq t \leq t_j$. Therefore, other neurons that track other features can directly use the information of this set of features, even if they are far away from each other in sequence indexing. Because of this special mechanism, FG-LSTM can have much diverse and longer memory for modeling the dependency of multiple features.

We use a Softmax layer to predict the true label $\hat{y}_t$ of the learned features tensor of sequence in the given decision times. This consists of two linear transformations with a *ReLU* activation in the middle.

$$y_t = softmax(max(0, h_t W_1 + b_1)W_2 + b_2) \tag{14}$$

We use cross-entropy to calculate the classification loss of the prediction y_t and true label $\hat{y}_t$ of each sample as follows:

$$Loss(\hat{y}_t, y_t) = \frac{1}{L} \sum_{1 \leq t \leq L} (\hat{y}_t \times \ln y_t + (1 - \hat{y}_t) \times \ln(1 - y_t)) \tag{15}$$

We can sum up the losses of all the samples in one minibatch to get the total loss for back propagation.

4   Experiments

The dataset used in this experiment is generated by Intensive Care Unit patient medical record data (MIMIC-III) of Beth Israel Deaconess Medical Center in the United States [7]. More than 20000 patient samples in MIMIC-III were

Table 1. The Dataset Distribution

Dataset	Target 0	Target 1	Total
training set	475291	59328	534619
validation set	61698	6540	68238
evaluation set	143373	19622	162995

extracted from the dataset, covering more than 4000 kinds and a total of more than 20 million multimodal irregular time-series data. In the experiment, the dataset is divided into training set, validation set and evaluation set, with a ratio of 7 : 1 : 2. Table 1 shows the data distribution of the dataset, which is divided into two classes. All experiments were implemented by Pytorch [19], optimized by Adam optimization algorithm [8], with the learning rate of 0.0001 and the other parameters are selected as default parameters. We set the random number seed to 1 to ensure the repeatability of the experimental results. Unless otherwise specified, d_{model} (the dimension after features coding) is 256, the batchsize is 128. The detailed parameter settings of different experiments are described below. All the experiments are conducted on a single Nvidia RTX 3090 GPU (24GB memory), which is sufficient for all the baselines.

Table 2. Results of different non-temporal features fusion methods on different models, among them, different non-temporal feature fusion methods perform the best results, we use bold numbers in black, and underlined numbers are the best results in different models of the same fusion method.

Model		LSTM	Bi-LSTM	Phased LSTM	HE-LSTM	Transformer	Informer	FG-LSTM	Count
Our Method	AUC	**75.63**	**75.59**	**72.52**	74.21	**75.69**	**76.05**	<u>**78.85**</u>	12
	AP	**34.96**	**34.92**	**30.45**	32.44	**34.31**	**34.93**	<u>**38.90**</u>	
Other Method	AUC	68.59	70.36	68.95	**76.35**	64.23	75.91	<u>76.37</u>	2
	AP	25.94	26.85	26.63	**34.80**	21.71	32.85	<u>36.42</u>	
Count		0	0	0	0	0	0	4	–

4.1   Evaluating Metrics

AUC (the area under Receiver Operating Characteristic curve) and AP (Average Precision) [25] are uesd in this paper. AUC is the area of ROC curve and the x-axis, and AP is the area of PRC (precision recall curve) and the x-axis, both of which are robust to the imbalanced data of positive and negative samples.

4.2   Comparing Methods

Because the proposed FG-LSTM is a variant based on the classical LSTM [6], we choose the classical LSTM and three other excellent variants including BI-LSTM, Phase LSTM [16] and HE-LSTM [12]. Recently, Transformer architecture has achieved the best performance in many problems, so we discuss the ability of Transformer related architecture to deal with multimodal irregular time-series. We chose the vanilla Transformer [26] and further select one of excellent variants in it called Informer [29]. Because our experiment does not involve the generation process, therefore, only the encoder part of the Transformer architecture is used, and get the final output directly through a fully connected feed-forward network. For LSTM related architectures, only use one layer. For Informer, the number of layers in the original author's open source code is selected, that is, $n = 2$. For Transformer, in order to better compare with Informer, we selecte the same encoder layers as Informer. In addition, d_{model} is changed to 256, which is consistent with LSTM architecture, and there is no change in the parameter settings of Transformer related architecture.

4.3 Experimental Result

Non-temporal Features Fusion Methods. In many previous studies, the processing methods of features from different feature spaces are only simple addition. According to this idea, a method is proposed as a comparative experiment, as shown below:

$$x = V_e + sum\left(V_t \times V_u\right) \tag{16}$$

where $V_e \in \mathbb{R}^{L_e \times d_{model}}$, $V_t \in \mathbb{R}^{L_t \times d_{model}}$ and $V_u \in \mathbb{R}^{L_u \times d_{model}}$ are the tensor encoded by $event$, $value_t$ and $value_u$ respectively. In this experiment, the coding method without considering the temporary features. We uniformly choose the (2) (3) proposed above. For the fusion method of temporal features and non-temporal features, the addition method is directly selected, and the rest are discussed in detail below.

Table 2 shows the experimental results of AUC and AP on Table 1 dataset with different model architectures and different non-temporal features fusion methods. It is obvious that, compared with the common methods, the proposed method of non-temporary features fusion has better performance. Except for the best performance in HE-LSTM framework, our proposed method has advantages in all other frameworks. The most obvious improvement is the Transformer framework, which has increased by 17.84% in AUC and 58.03% in AP. However, for the excellent Informer framework proposed for single-modal time-series, the improvement is not very obvious. The AUC and AP have only increased by 0.18% and 6.33% respectively, which shows that the Informer framework is not very sensitive to feature fusion methods. If we do not pay much attention to features fusion methods, Informer framework is indeed a good choice. For our proposed model FG-LSTM, the best performance of all models is obtained in different non-temporal feature fusion methods, and the AUC and AP are also improved by 3.24% and 6.80% respectively. Although the improvement is not very obvious, it also proves the superiority of our proposed model itself. In general, different feature fusion methods have great impact on the performance of different models, but excellent models are not particularly sensitive to feature fusion methods.

Table 3. Results of different temporal features fusion methods on different models.

Model	FE						CE					
	add		conv-add		*conv − add*		add		conv-add		*conv − add*	
	AUC	AP	AUC	AP	AUC	AP	AUC	AP	AUC	AP	AUC	AP
LSTM	75.63	34.96	*76.88*	*36.38*	76.87	36.35	**79.47**	**39.50**	79.09	38.56	79.18	38.53
Bi-LSTM	75.59	34.92	*78.28*	*37.67*	76.98	37.46	79.04	38.56	77.95	36.06	**79.64**	**39.43**
Phased LSTM	72.52	30.45	*74.82*	*33.57*	72.83	30.69	76.34	34.03	74.54	32.90	**78.01**	**36.89**
HE-LSTM	74.21	32.44	*76.78*	*34.73*	75.46	33.24	**77.06**	**35.86**	76.79	34.72	75.47	34.37
Transformer	75.69	34.31	*76.14*	*34.88*	75.85	34.87	**76.41**	**35.19**	75.65	34.22	76.26	35.13
Informer	76.05	34.93	*76.19*	*35.66*	75.96	34.86	**78.11**	**35.29**	75.99	34.90	76.05	34.12
FG-LSTM	78.85	38.90	*80.67*	*41.94*	78.47	38.01	79.33	39.09	**81.20**	**42.69**	80.89	41.59
Count	0		0		0		8		2		4	

Temporal and Non-temporal Features Fusion Methods. The advanced of the proposed non-temporal features fusion method has been proved. Therefore, in this experiment, we verify the progressiveness of our proposed temporal and non-temporal features fusion method. In order to explore whether it is necessary to upgrade the dimension, we set up a group of control experiments to fuse the two features after stack directly with the help of 1×1 convolution kernel.

Table 3 shows our experimental results. Where **FE** is function encoding, **CE** is convolution encoding, **add** is a direct addition method, **conv-add** is our method, and *conv − add* is a comparative method without dimension upgrading. For the **FE** method without learning parameters, it can be seen that the **conv-add** method has achieved the most advanced experimental results in different models, while the *conv − add* method without dimension upgrading is not as good as the **conv-add** method. But it is still better than the direct addition method in many models. For the **CE** method of learning parameters, it can be seen no matter what kind of temporal and non-temporal feature fusion method, **CE** is better than **FE**, but none of the three feature fusion methods always has best performance in all models. Because our upgraded **conv-add** method also has parameters to learn, we believe that as long as the dataset is larger, the upgraded **conv-add** method can still be better than other methods in different models. Finally, for different models, different time coding methods and different feature fusion methods are used. Our FG-LSTM model is better than other models, which is enough to prove the robustness of our FG-LSTM. It also shows that the variants of LSTM are not necessarily inferior to the models of Transformer series.

Experimental Comparison of Different Length Time-Series. In order to verify the proposed model in this paper has stronger ability to capture the temporal dependence between features than other models, in this experiment, different models are input with different lengths of time-series data, ranging from 100 to 800. For the temporal feature coding method, choose **CE**. For the non-temporal feature fusion method, use our own method. For the tem-

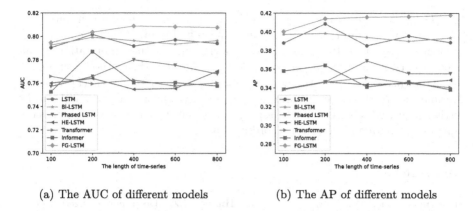

(a) The AUC of different models   (b) The AP of different models

Fig. 4. The performance of different models on different time-series length.

poral and non-temporal feature fusion method, choose the *conv* − *add* method
without dimension upgrading. Figure 4(a) and Fig. 4(b) show the results of this
experiment, for Transformer, when the length of time-series is 600 and 800, the
Transformer failure for the out-of-memory, so we set the *batchsize* is 64 to make
24GB memory enough. From the experimental results, we can draw the following
conclusions:

Firstly, the time-series information is effective for the prediction results.
When the input length is less than 400, most models will be improved with
the increase of the length of the input sequence. Secondly, compared with other
models, FG-LSTM is better at capturing the timing dependency in time-series.
When the sequence length exceeds 400 and becomes longer and longer, the performance of the model is not improved much in AUC, but the AP is still improved
steadily. However, other models can not capture the timing dependence under
ultra long sequences, so they have not been greatly improved, and even the effect
has become worse. Finally, we can see that the classical LSTM model is superior
to Transformer and its variant model Informer, which shows that the time-series
information extraction of Transformer series models is still slightly insufficient.

5 Conclusion

This paper proposes a features fusion framework and FG-LSTM model updated
on the basis of LSTM. The model can well deal with multimodal irregular time-
series data. At the same time, we also explore how to better encode time features
and how to better integrate temporal features and non-temporal features, which
is particularly important for irregular time-series data. Firstly, through the temporal features coding method and features fusion framework, the representation
tensor obtained by the model can fuse the features and temporal dependency
between different non-temporal information, effectively capture the temporal
dependency under ultra long sequences and the feature information of a minority events. Then, input the representation tensor of the obtained time-series into

the FG-LSTM, due to the existence of feature gates, the model can automatically adapt to the multi-scale sampling frequency of multi-source complex data, asynchronously track the temporal information and feature information of different events. Finally, the experiments demonstrate that the method proposed in this paper has better performance than other typical methods on real datasets. The method in this paper is promising to expand and popularize, and can be further migrated to diverse fields, especially for multi-source asynchronous sampling sensor data and behavior recording data.

References

1. Armandpour, M., Kidd, B., Du, Y., Huang, J.Z.: Deep personalized glucose level forecasting using attention-based recurrent neural networks. arXiv preprint arXiv:2106.00884 (2021)
2. Baltrušaitis, T., Ahuja, C., Morency, L.P.: Multimodal machine learning: A survey and taxonomy. IEEE Trans. Pattern Anal. Mach. Intell. **41**(2), 423–443 (2018)
3. Dai, Z., Yang, Z., Yang, Y., Carbonell, J.G., Le, Q.V., Salakhutdinov, R.: Transformer-xl: Attentive language models beyond a fixed-length context. In: ACL (1) (2019)
4. Fu, Y., Cao, L., Guo, G., Huang, T.S.: Multiple feature fusion by subspace learning. In: Proceedings of the 2008 International Conference on Content-based Image and Video Retrieval, pp. 127–134 (2008)
5. Hochreiter, S., Bengio, Y., Frasconi, P., Schmidhuber, J., et al.: Gradient flow in recurrent nets: the difficulty of learning long-term dependencies (2001)
6. Hochreiter, S., Schmidhuber, J.: Long short-term memory. Neural Comput. **9**(8), 1735–1780 (1997)
7. Johnson, A.E., et al.: Mimic-iii, a freely accessible critical care database. Sci. data **3**(1), 1–9 (2016)
8. Kingma, D.P., Ba, J.: Adam: A method for stochastic optimization. Computer Science (2014)
9. Koutnik, J., Greff, K., Gomez, F., Schmidhuber, J.: A clockwork rnn. In: International Conference on Machine Learning, pp. 1863–1871. PMLR (2014)
10. Li, X., et al.: Adversarial multimodal representation learning for click-through rate prediction. In: Proceedings of The Web Conference 2020, pp. 827–836 (2020)
11. Liu, J., Li, T., Xie, P., Du, S., Teng, F., Yang, X.: Urban big data fusion based on deep learning: an overview. Inform. Fusion **53**, 123–133 (2020)
12. Liu, L., Shen, J., Zhang, M., Wang, Z., Liu, Z.: Deep learning based patient representation learning framework of heterogeneous temporal events data. Big Data Res. **5**(1), 2019003 (2019)
13. Liu, P., et al.: Vara-tts: Non-autoregressive text-to-speech synthesis based on very deep vae with residual attention. arXiv preprint arXiv:2102.06431 (2021)
14. Liu, Z., Shen, Y., Lakshminarasimhan, V.B., Liang, P.P., Zadeh, A.B., Morency, L.P.: Efficient low-rank multimodal fusion with modality-specific factors. In: Proceedings of the 56th Annual Meeting of the Association for Computational Linguistics (Volume 1: Long Papers) (2018)
15. Nagrani, A., Yang, S., Arnab, A., Jansen, A., Schmid, C., Sun, C.: Attention bottlenecks for multimodal fusion. In: Advances in Neural Information Processing Systems, vol. 34 (2021)

16. Neil, D., Pfeiffer, M., Liu, S.C.: Phased lstm: Accelerating recurrent network training for long or event-based sequences. In: NIPS (2016)
17. Neverova, N., Wolf, C., Taylor, G., Nebout, F.: Moddrop: adaptive multi-modal gesture recognition. IEEE Trans. Pattern Anal. Mach. Intell. **38**(8), 1692–1706 (2015)
18. Ngiam, J., Khosla, A., Kim, M., Nam, J., Lee, H., Ng, A.Y.: Multimodal deep learning. In: ICML (2011)
19. Paszke, A., et al.: Pytorch: an imperative style, high-performance deep learning library. Adv. Neural. Inf. Process. Syst. **32**, 8026–8037 (2019)
20. Potamianos, G., Neti, C., Gravier, G., Garg, A., Senior, A.W.: Recent advances in the automatic recognition of audiovisual speech. Proc. IEEE **91**(9), 1306–1326 (2003)
21. Ramesh, A., et al.: Zero-shot text-to-image generation. arXiv preprint arXiv:2102.12092 (2021)
22. Ren, Z., Wang, Z., Ke, Z., Li, Z.: Wushour·Silamu: Survey of multimodal data fusion. Comput. Eng. Appl. **57**(18), 16 (2021)
23. Tan, M., Le, Q.: Efficientnet: Rethinking model scaling for convolutional neural networks. In: International Conference on Machine Learning, pp. 6105–6114. PMLR (2019)
24. Tsai, Y.H.H., Bai, S., Yamada, M., Morency, L.P., Salakhutdinov, R.: Transformer dissection: An unified understanding for transformer's attention via the lens of kernel. In: Proceedings of the 2019 Conference on Empirical Methods in Natural Language Processing and the 9th International Joint Conference on Natural Language Processing (EMNLP-IJCNLP), pp. 4344–4353 (2019)
25. Turpin, A., Scholer, F.: User performance versus precision measures for simple search tasks. In: Proceedings of the 29th annual international ACM SIGIR conference on Research and development in information retrieval, pp. 11–18 (2006)
26. Vaswani, A., et al.: Attention is all you need. In: Advances in Neural Information Processing systems, pp. 5998–6008 (2017)
27. Wu, C., et al.: Visual synthesis pre-training for neural visual world creation. arXiv preprint arXiv:2111.12417 (2021)
28. Zadeh, A., Chen, M., Poria, S., Cambria, E., Morency, L.P.: Tensor fusion network for multimodal sentiment analysis. arXiv preprint arXiv:1707.07250 (2017)
29. Zhou, H., Zhang, S., Peng, J., Zhang, S., Li, J., Xiong, H., Zhang, W.: Informer: Beyond efficient transformer for long sequence time-series forecasting. In: Proceedings of AAAI (2021)

A Multi-output Integration Residual Network for Predicting Time Series Data with Diverse Scales

Hao Li[1,2], Mingjian Tang[3], Kewen Liao[4], and Jie Shao[1,2(✉)]

[1] University of Electronic Science and Technology of China, Chengdu 611731, China
hao_li@std.uestc.edu.cn, shaojie@uestc.edu.cn
[2] Sichuan Artificial Intelligence Research Institute, Yibin 644000, China
[3] Westpac Banking Corporation, Sydney, NSW 2000, Australia
ming.tang@westpac.com.au
[4] Australian Catholic University, North Sydney, NSW 2060, Australia
kewen.liao@acu.edu.au

Abstract. Deep learning methods can fit the observation history over different time series with multiple levels of representations from huge dataset. However, it is challenging to directly train deep neural networks on a raw dataset with a large number of time series, as the different time-series have diverse scales. We initiate the study of an effective deep residual framework named MIR-TS for time series prediction with multi-output integration on time series data with diverse scales. Specifically, we leverage the residual module that constrains the original input average close to 0 to transform the original input, so that the distribution of features changes from sparse to dense. Compared with the traditional residual network, this approach improves the generalization of model via residual reuse, capturing more detailed features of time series to improve prediction. The results on the M3 and TOURISM benchmarks show that MIR-TS achieves a consistent better or highly comparable performance across different time series frequencies.

Keywords: Neural networks · Nonlinear time series · Diverse scales · Deep learning · Residual network

1 Introduction

As an important part of time series analysis [13,20,26], time series prediction plays a crucial role in statistics, finance, economics, engineering, and computer science. According to the number of time-related variables, time series prediction problems are divided into univariate prediction and multivariate prediction. In this study, we focus on univariate time series. Most traditional univariate time series prediction methods, such as autoregressive integrated moving average (ARIMA) model [6] and exponential smoothing [12,29], are local prediction method [5] that means the prediction cannot share information across different time series.

© The Author(s), under exclusive license to Springer Nature Switzerland AG 2022
S. Khanna et al. (Eds.): PRICAI 2022, LNCS 13629, pp. 380–393, 2022.
https://doi.org/10.1007/978-3-031-20862-1_28

With the rapid development of deep learning, various novel deep learning methods [10, 22, 23, 28] have shown much potential for chaotic and long-history time series prediction. Most deep learning methods are trained as global models [5] since in general they require a lot of data to train with. However, as pointed out in [24], deep learning methods often produce inferior prediction results for short-history time series. Time series with short observation history widely exist in practice (e.g., less frequently recorded/sampled, highly summarized, or truncated due to data out of date), and prediction of such time series is in urgent need (e.g., prediction of the trend of new infectious diseases such as COVID-19).

Among these prediction methods, N-BEATS [22] stands out in achieving state-of-the-art results on large datasets such as M4 [18] (a dataset with large number of short-history time series) by deep residual networks. Unlike previous deep learning methods, N-BEATS uses sliding windows and residual networks to convert time series prediction into an ordinary regression problem, avoiding the lack of available historical data on training. However, when training with data of limited size (in the magnitude of hundreds or thousands of time series) such as M3 [17], N-BEATS does not show consistently satisfactory results despite its complicated learning and functional structure. A possible reason is that N-BEATS is a deep prediction structure, which is hard to train on time series data with diverse scales if lacking of enough number of time series. One technique to tackle time series data with diverse scales on small dataset is data augmentation [24]. However, according to the result of [4], there is no method better than others on each dataset. Redesigning a flexible and generic data augmentation method is also an open challenge for time series prediction, which means it must be careful to select a method to generate new time series. Applying normalization method is another way to handle time series data with diverse scales, but it is useless for N-BEATS [22]. Therefore, it demands a simple and more effective deep learning architecture in the context of time series data with diverse scales.

In this work, we propose a multi-output integration residual framework named MIR-TS to handle time series data with diverse scales. First, MIR-TS applies the Naive method [19] as a base prediction to reduce the difference of deep models' outputs. Then, for each residual module, we use three fully connected (FC) layers to remove the original input average of the module. Thus, the residual average will be close to 0 by using original input minus the output of FC layers. Next, we leverage the independent predictors to deal with different residuals and obtsain different outputs. Finally, the model output is computed by adding all outputs and base prediction together, which can increase the generalization of model with residual reuse. Our main contributions are summarized as follows:

- We use the residual module to make features gather around 0, which improves the prediction ability to tackle time series data with diverse scales.
- We propose a simple multi-output residual architecture to improve the generalization of model by residual reuse.
- Extensive experiments demonstrate a consistent prediction performance of MIR-TS across different time-series datasets and frequencies.

2   Related Work

2.1   Time Series Prediction Methods

Traditionally, time series prediction methods are derived from statistics and signal processing theories. The simplest prediction method is Naive, and more variants include SNaive and Naive2 [19]. Furthermore, common classic statistical models are ARIMA [6] and exponential smoothing [12,29]. For instance, the Theta method [1] which was the winner of M3 competition, decomposes a time series into two theta-lines and combines them for prediction. The dynamic optimized theta model (DOTM) [9] and EXP [25] are variants of the original Theta model which achieve great performance on M3. Recently, researchers tend to combine and ensemble statistical and machine learning methods for prediction [19,27]. Such methods require manual selection of statistical model parameters and machine learning architectures on different time series. Recently, deep time series prediction models have been investigated based on long short-term memory (LSTM) or transformer. Compared with traditional statistical methods, they can train the same model with different time series to share information. The most noteworthy of the LSTM-based models is DeepAR [10]. The transformer-based work proposed by [15] uses convolution to extract the features of multiple time steps for self-attention, achieving great results for long-history time series data such as electric power load prediction. Most of the above methods require long-history data to fit the model. Unfortunately, deep learning methods do not have obvious performance advantages over statistical methods in short time series. Recently, a seq2seq model called N-BEATS [22] was proposed for short-history data. N-BEATS uses a multi-output deep residual framework to achieve state-of-the-art on the M4 benchmark [18] with lots of short time series. However, as confirmed in our experiments N-BEATS does not generalize well on time series data with diverse scales. Different from N-BEATS, we redesign the residual structure, reducing the over-fitting on time series data with diverse scales and achieving better prediction performance. Meanwhile, MIR-TS provides more accurate prediction by effectively training with ordinary regression and multi-output ensemble compared with traditional methods.

2.2   Deep Residual Neural Network

The classic residual network structure, ResNet [11], can build a deep convolutional neural network from dozens of layers to hundreds by using the residual of the previous module as the input of the next module. DenseNet [14] further develops the ResNet model, which applied all previous residuals as the input of the next module to improve the residual reuse of the module. The emergence of ResNet and DenseNet has improved the features representation ability of convolutional neural networks, which enables convolutional networks to achieve an accuracy that exceeds human levels in image recognition tasks. In the research of time series, WaveNet [21] uses residual connects and dilated casual convolutional layer to represent time series. Compared with ResNet that only uses the last residual as the predictor input, MIR-TS leverages all residuals for prediction, which improves the residual reuse with multi-output structure.

3 Problem Statement

Time series prediction aims at using historical data to predict the time series values for a range of time in future. This study focuses on the univariate discrete time series prediction problem. Unlike the LSTM-based statistical prediction method [10] that uses long-history data for autoregression, we regard the time series prediction method as an ordinary regression problem.

To be more specific, we want to learn an approximation function $y_{pred} = f(x)$ to minimize the error between evaluations and true values of future, where x is a time-irrelevant feature. Because x is not directly from the time series, we also need to learn a feature extraction function $x = g(y_{ob})$, where y_{ob} is the historical observations of time series. A simple idea is using a sliding window of fixed size to obtain a subsequence from time series, and then splitting it into two parts by a cut-point. Next, we can extract time-irrelevant feature from part before cut-point and use the feature to estimate the values of the part after cut-point. The above statement can be formulated as: given a length-N_i observation history $[y_{i,1}, ..., y_{i,N_i}]$ from the time series set and a length-T prediction range, the goal is to predict the T unknown values $y_{target} = [y_{i,N_i+1}, ..., y_{i,N_i+T}]$. The input of the neural network model is a fixed length-H window before the first prediction value, denoted as $y_{in} = [y_{i,N_i-H+1}, ..., y_{i,N_i}]$. Let L denote loss function, the overall goal is to minimize $\sum_{(y_{target},y_{in})\sim D} L(y_{target}, f(g(y_{in})))$. This approach is inconsistent with the statistical method that uses all observed points as the input.

MAPE (mean absolute percentage error) and sMAPE (symmetric MAPE) are commonly used metrics to evaluate prediction performance, where $\hat{y}$ represents corresponding predicted values.

$$MAPE = \frac{100}{T} \sum_{t=1}^{T} \frac{|y_{i,N_i+t} - \hat{y}_{i,N_i+t}|}{|y_{i,N_i+t}|}, \tag{1}$$

$$sMAPE = \frac{200}{T} \sum_{t=1}^{T} \frac{|y_{i,N_i+t} - \hat{y}_{i,N_i+t}|}{|y_{i,N_i+t}| + |\hat{y}_{i,N_i+t}|}. \tag{2}$$

According to official recommendations, for different datasets either MAPE or sMAPE can be used to better measure the performance.

4 Our Proposed Method

As shown in Fig. 1, MIR-TS can be regarded as a multi-output residual network, in which each residual connects to an independent predictor. MIR-TS uses residual to shift the original input average to close to 0, which makes the predictor have more ability to process time series data with diverse scales. Unlike N-BEATS [22], the feature embedding (we call it residual module in this study) and predictor are different modules in MIR-TS. This makes the feature embedding module have the ability of generating more detailed features and the predictor be able to predict better with residual.

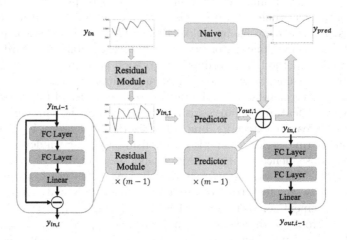

Fig. 1. The structure of MIR-TS, where input is a fixed-size subsequence cut from a time series. First, the module will output the corresponding residuals with multi-output residual modules. The residual average will be close to 0 compared with original input average. Next, these residuals will be input to multiple independent predictors, respectively. Finally, the prediction results are added to obtain the final prediction. The FC layers of residual model have same structure with predictors but the matrix weights are different.

4.1   Data Processing

We focus on training deep learning model to predict time series data with diverse scales, so each time series's value range is different. In order to make MIR-TS focus on predicting non-linear trend instead of mean values of time series, we must restrict the output range of MIR-TS. Thus, we first consider transforming the target to be predicted y_{target} and then use the neural network to predict it. Considering a linear transform $T(x) = a + bx$, let $y'_{target} = T(y_{target})$ and using MAPE (Eq. 1) as metric, the new optimization goal is:

$$MAPE' = \frac{100}{T} \sum_{t=1}^{T} \frac{|a + by_{i,N_i+t} - \hat{y}_{i,N_i+t}|}{|a + by_{i,N_i+t}|} \tag{3}$$

It is obvious that MAPE and MAPE' are not equal. Thus, training model with MAPE' will lead to bias when we measure the model's performance on the test set with MAPE. If we use SMAPE as the metric, there will be a similar conclusion as MAPE. On the contrary, there will be no bias if T is used to transform y_{out}, because the final prediction is $T(y_{out})$ so that the metric has the same form for both training and test. In time series forecasting, a most used transformation is MaxMin: $T(x) = x(MaxV - MinV) + MinV$, where, $MaxV$ and $MinV$ are the maximum and minimum values of the observed time series. However, the value of $b = MaxV - MinV$ could be very large, which means $|y_{out}|/|y_{in}| << 1$. This will cause the absolute value of the weight of the neural network too small such that the error will increase. Thus, the coefficient b is set up to 1 to avoid the error's increase. Then, we only need to select the coefficient a to provide a suitable base statistical prediction for the network. A suggestion is the Naive prediction [19] that only uses the last value as the prediction and is easy to add to the deep learning framework. The ablation study in Sect. 5.5 demonstrates that the Naive prediction provides a better initialization than others such as mean of input window. Thus, in this study, the final prediction is denoted by:

$$y_{out} = y_{na} + f(g(y_{in})), \qquad (4)$$

where y_{na} is the Naive prediction.

4.2 Residual Module

In this section, we describe the component of residual module, and analyze its effect.

Let input $y_{in} = y_a + y_{re}$, where y_a is the original input average, and y_{re} is the residual. Thus, by applying residual operation, we could represent:

$$\hat{y}_{re} = y_{in} - R(y_{in}), \qquad (5)$$

where $\hat{y}_{re}$ and $R(y_{in})$ are the estimated values of y_{re} and y_a respectively. The architecture of the residual module is depicted in the bottom left of Fig. 1. The residual modules consist of three FC layers, and the activation of the first two layers is ReLU, where $ReLU(x) = max(0, x)$. The last FC layer does not use the activation function, so we call it the linear layer. The following equations describe the operation of the residual module:

$$
\begin{aligned}
z_1 &= FC_1(y_{in}) = ReLU(L_1(y_{in})), \\
z_2 &= FC_2(z_1) = ReLU(L_2(z_1)), \\
R(y_{in}) &= L_3(z_2), \\
L_i(x) &= W_i x + b_i (i = 1, 2, 3),
\end{aligned} \qquad (6)
$$

where W_i is the matrix of linear transform and b_i is bias. The linear layer transforms the input to the weighted average of input in time, and it removes some part of fluctuating features. The role of ReLU is similar to a half-wave filter, and it could be applied to remove half-wave features further. Thus, if we use two ReLU functions, all fluctuating features will be removed. Thus, the residual $\hat{y}_{re}$ has a similar shape with the original input but its average is close to 0, which can effectively process time series on time series data with diverse scales. Section 5.4 demonstrates this phenomenon further.

4.3   Model with Single Residual and Single Predictor

Through the residual operation, we get dense feature compared with original input. Then, we use independent predictor to process this feature. The predictor also has three FC layers, and its structure is shown in the bottom right of Fig. 1. Let the input of predictor be $y'_{in} = \hat{y}_{re}$, the final prediction is:

$$
\begin{aligned}
y_{out} &= y_{na} + f(g(y'_{in})) \\
&= y_{na} + f(g(y_{in} - R(y_{in}))).
\end{aligned} \tag{7}
$$

For simplicity, we assume the first two layers of predictor is the feature extraction g and the last linear layer is f, and then we can approximately analyze y_{out} by the Taylor formula with Peano's remainder:

$$
\begin{aligned}
y_{out} &= y_{na} + f(g(y_{in} - R(y_{in}))) \\
&= y_{na} + f(g(y_{in})) - f(g(R(y_{in}))) \\
&\quad + J_{f \circ g}(R(y_{in}))(y'_{in}) + o(|y'_{in}|^2) \\
&= y_{na} + f(g(y_{in})) - f(g(R(y_{in}))) \\
&\quad + W_f J_g(R(y_{in}))(y'_{in}) + o(|y'_{in}|^2).
\end{aligned} \tag{8}
$$

Here, W_f denotes the weight matrix of f, $J_{f \circ g}$ represents Jacobian matrix of composite function $f \circ g$, J_g represents Jacobian matrix of function g, and $o()$ is the small O in Landau notation. Noted that $W_f J_g(R(y_{in}))(y'_{in}) = f(J_g(R(y_{in}))(y'_{in})$, the final predictor can be divided into three parts. The first is the prediction from base statistical prediction y_{na}, the second is original signal prediction $f(g(y_{in}))$ minus the prediction with input average $f(g(R(y_{in})))$, and the last is reshape of (y'_{in}). The coefficients of reshape are generated by $f(J_g(R(y_{in})))$, which is helpful for re-adjusting the prediction values of the second part about input average.

4.4   Integration of Different Prediction Residual Networks

The original ResNet only uses the last residual as the input of the predictor. In order to improve residual reuse ability, we design a multi-output integration structure. We first introduce the following notations: R_i denotes the i-th residual module, P_i denotes the i-th predictor, $\hat{y}_{in,i}$ denotes the i-th estimated values, $y_{out,i}$ denotes the i-th prediction, g_i denotes the i-th feature extraction function, f_i is the i-th regression function, and y_{pred} denotes the final prediction. Then, we can write the model output as:

$$
\hat{y}_{in,i} = \hat{y}_{in,i-1} - R_i(\hat{y}_{in,i-1})(\hat{y}_{in,0} = y_{in}), \tag{9}
$$

$$
y_{out,i} = P_i(\hat{y}_{in,i}). \tag{10}
$$

Then, the prediction vector is as follows:

$$
y_{pred} = y_{na} + \sum_{i=1}^{m} y_{out,i}. \tag{11}
$$

Table 1. M3 information: the number of time series based on frequency, and statistics based on frequency.

	Yearly	Quarterly	Monthly	Others
Number	645	756	1428	174
Min-Length	20	24	66	71
Max-Length	47	72	144	104
Mean-Length	28.4	48.9	117.3	76.6
STD Mean	1571.6	1350.3	1776.5	4850.6

Table 2. TOURISM information: the number of time series based on frequency, and statistics based on frequency.

	Yearly	Quarterly	Monthly
Number	518	427	366
Min-Length	11	30	91
Max-Length	47	130	333
Mean-Length	24.4	99.6	298
STD Mean	2041387.8	371021.1	28674.8

By using the Taylor's formula in the same way, y_{pred} can be represented as:

$$y_{pred} = y_{na} + \sum_{i=1}^{m} [f_i(g_i(\hat{y}_{in,i-1})) - f_i(g_i(R_i(\hat{y}_{in,i-1})))$$
$$+ W_{f_i} J_{g_i}(R_i(\hat{y}_{in,i-1}))(\hat{y}_{in,i}) + o(|\hat{y}_{in,i}|^2)]. \tag{12}$$

Let $f(y_{in})$ represents $\sum_{i=1}^{m} f_i(g_i(\hat{y}_{in,i-1}))$, $R(y_{in})$ denotes $\sum_{i=1}^{m} f_i(g_i(R_i$ $(\hat{y}_{in,i-1})))$, and $reshape = \sum_{i=1}^{m} W_{f_i} J_{g_i}(R_i(\hat{y}_{in,i-1}))(\hat{y}_{in,i})$, then y_{pred} also can split into three parts y_{na}, $f(y_{in}) - R(y_{in})$ and $reshape$. It further confirms that MIR-TS can be regarded as an extension of a single output model with better generalization by reusing residual.

5 Empirical Results

5.1 Dataset

We use two benchmark datasets M3 and TOURISM, both of which have time series data with diverse scales. **M3** [17] is a diverse dataset: the time series come from business, financial and economic domains. It includes 645 annual series (the average length is 28.4), 756 quarter series (the average length is 48.9), 1428 month series (the average length is 117.3), and other frequency series (the average length is 76.6). **TOURISM** [2] was released in a Kaggle competition and the all of 1311 time series were supplied by governmental tourism organizations. It includes 518 annual series (the average length is 24.4), 427 quarter series (the average length is 99.6), and 366 monthly series (the average length is 298). Table 1 and Table 2 also give information of time series scales on the M3 and TOURISM datesets. STD mean (the standard deviation of the mean of each series) on two datasets shows that it has large differences in scale of time series on the same frequency.

Table 3. The results represent the average sMAPE performance on the M3 test set (lower values are better). Bold denotes the best result, and * denotes the second best. The ± values show 95% confidence intervals.

	Yearly(645)	Quarterly(756)	Monthly(1428)	Others(174)	Average(3003)
Naive2	17.88	9.95	16.91	6.30	15.47
ARIMA	17.73	10.26	14.81	5.06	14.01
Theta	17.14	9.77	13,86	4.60	13.19
DOTM	15.94	9.28	13.74	4.58	12.90
EXP	16.39	8.98	13.43	5.46	12.71
LGT	15.23*	n/a	n/a	4.26	n/a
N-BEATS	16.2	8.92	13.45*	4.19	12.64
ResNet	15.56	**8.89**	13.51	**4.09**	12.61*
MIR-TS (ours)	**15.236 ± 0.090**	8.926 ± 0.059*	**13.270 ± 0.041**	4.104 ± 0.061*	**12.421 ± 0.030**

5.2   Experiment Setup and Comparison Baselines

We follow official settings both of M3 and TOURISM competitions for splitting training and test sets. The ensemble methods are commonly used for improving the accuracy and stability on time series prediction. To achieve the best result, we select lengths from 2/3 times of prediction range as input window size on M3, and the input size from 2/3/4/5 times of prediction range on TOURISM. We follow the N-BEATS setup for every fixed input window, using SMAPE/MAPE/MASE as loss function on M3 training stage to get the different model, and we use MAPE as loss function on TOURISM training stage. For every fixed input window and loss function, we use the bagging method [7] to obtain final results (conducting ten experiments with different random seeds and applying median as result). For the M3 experiment, the FC layer sizes of first two layers are set at 512, and the number of residual modules is set at 30. For the TOURISM experiment, the first two FC layer sizes are 256 and the residual module number is 20. For both M3 and TOURISM, we train individual model for each frequency. We set the batch size as 1024 and the learning rate as 0.001 for both experiments. We use the last horizon-length data in the training set as the validation set to select hyperparameters.

The average results of each frequency domain can be found in Table 3 and Table 4. On M3, we compare against Naive2 [19] (similar with the Naive method but data are seasonally adjusted if needed, by applying a classical multiplicative decomposition, and a 90% autocorrelation test is performed to decide whether the data are seasonal), Theta [1], EXP [25], and LGT [24] (a hybrid data augmentation approach). On TOURISM, we compare against three statistical methods: SNaive [19], Theta [1], SaliMali [8] (the winner of the Quarterly/Monthly TOURISM competition), Stratometrics (the second place method of the TOURISM competition), and LeeCBaker [3] (a combination method). MIR-TS is implemented and trained in PyTorch, and we use one TITAN X GPU for model training. The source code and data are available at https:// github.com/HaoLi980405/MIR-TS.

Table 4. The results represent the average MAPE performance on the TOURISM test set (lower values are better). Bold denotes the best result, and * denotes the second best. The ± values show 95% confidence intervals.

	Yearly(518)	Quarterly(427)	Monthly(366)	Average(1311)
SNaive	23.61	16.46	22.56	21.25
Theta	23.45	16.15	22.11	20.88
ARIMA	28.03	16.23	21.13	20.96
LeeCBaker	22.73	15.14	20.19	19.35
Stratometrics	23.15	15.14	20.37	19.52
SaliMali	n/a	14.83*	19.64	n/a
N-BEATS	**21.43**	14.90	19.45*	18.65*
ResNet	22.48	14.93	19.51	18.85
MIR-TS (ours)	21.50 ± 0.395*	**14.76 ± 0.129**	**19.05 ± 0.115**	**18.38 ± 0.159**

5.3   Prediction Results

Due to the randomness in sampling input data and initializing the model parameters of experiments, we conduct five experiments on each model and report 95% confidence intervals by t-distribution. We apply the result of five experiments to conduct one-sided test for significance, which shows that MIR-TS achieve the best average results on both M3 ($\alpha = 0.005$) and TOURISM ($\alpha = 0.025$), where α is the significance level. According to Table 3, MIR-TS achieves state-of-the-art or same level performance across all frequencies except Monthly. In particular, the result of MIR-TS is significantly increased by 6% compared with the best learning-based N-BEATS method and by 11.2% over the winner Theta model of M3 on M3 Yearly data. MIR-TS achieves the same level result with the hybrid method LGT, which achieves the best result on M3 annual data. However, LGT misses the Quarterly and Monthly results to be generalizable. In other words, MIR-TS also achieves the state-of-the-art results on Yearly frequency while being more generalizable. In particular, MIR-TS achieves the state-of-the-art results on Monthly (improved 4.4% over Thata model and 1.3% over N-BEATS) and Others (increased 1.9% over N-BEATS and 12.8% over Theta). On Quarterly frequency, MIR-TS also achieves top-3 result. In addition, the variance of both models is relatively small.

From Table 4 on the less diverse TOURISM dataset, MIR-TS is better than N-BEATS on Monthly frequency data (increased 1.5% over N-BEATS and 1.7% over the third best result). It also achieves the best average performance on the whole dataset (increased 1.4% over N-BEATS and 2.5% over the third best result). Another finding is that MIR-TS achieves top-3 results across all frequencies. In summary, the MIR-TS model has demonstrated consistent superior prediction performance across different frequencies on M3 and TOURISM. MIR-TS has achieved a performance improvement of 1%-3% compared with N-BEATS in several frequencies with a small number of time series (Yearly and Others on M3, and Monthly on TOURISM). These results demonstrate that MIR-TS can perform well for general datasets and achieve the best results for time series data with diverse scales.

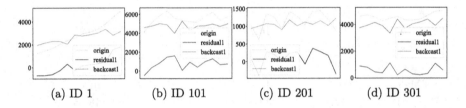

| (a) ID 1 | (b) ID 101 | (c) ID 201 | (d) ID 301 |

Fig. 2. Examples of comparison of residual module1 output, residual1, and original time series. All four time series come from the M3 dataset, with IDs 1, 101, 201, 301. The horizontal axis represents time, and the vertical axis represents the corresponding value at each moment.

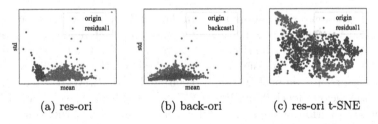

| (a) res-ori | (b) back-ori | (c) res-ori t-SNE |

Fig. 3. (a) and (b) are the distribution mean and standard deviation. In (a), the red points represent original input of the model, and the blue points represent the residual after the first residual module. In (b), the red points represent original input of the model, and the green points represent the output of the first residual module. (c) is t-SNE output, where red points denote the t-SNE output of original input and blue points denote the t-SNE of residuals. (Color figure online)

5.4   Effect of Residual Structure

In order to verify the effect of the residual module, we select four time series data from the annual data of M3 to investigate their first residual module outputs and corresponding residuals. Figure 2 shows the linear layer output of first residual module (backcast1), the first residual (residual1), and the original input of model. We find the ratio between backcast1 and the original input average is close to 1, which causes the residual1 average to around 0. It verifies our analysis of residual effect in methodology. Then, Fig. 3(c) shows the t-SNE output [16] of the original inputs and residuals. The results show data distribution of residuals is more even than that of original inputs, which reduces the impact of the long and short tails problem. These reveal that the residual module has the ability to transform time series data with diverse scales to dense (Fig. 3(a) and Fig. 3(b) also show the evidence about this). Because all of the residual averages are close to 0, the predictor can learn more common features across different time series.

Table 5. Results of different base statistical predictions on the TOURISM-Monthly dataset.

Based	MAPE
None	19.61
Naive	19.21
Mean	19.48
Max	29.61
Min	21.61

5.5   Effect of Different Base Statistical Predictions and Multi-output Structure

This section describes the effect of different base statistical predictions on the results and the effect of multi-output structure. None means that the result does not contain the base statistical prediction. Naive means that the base statistical prediction is the Naive prediction. Mean, Max and Min are the average, maximum and minimum of input window respectively. We conduct five experiments and use bagging for results. According to Table 5, Naive is significantly better than other methods, and thus we set it as the base statistical prediction in all experiments. ResNet can be regarded as a residual model with single output. Comparing all results of MIR-TS with ResNet from Table 3 and Table 4, MIR-TS can achieve 1.5% increase on M3 average result, and 2.5% on TOURISM Yearly. On each frequency data on both M3 and TOURISM, it also achieves 1–3% increase over ResNet. These results demonstrate that MIR-TS can achieve better results than the single-output model.

6   Conclusion

This paper proposed a multi-output residual-based deep learning framework MIR-TS to effectively learn time series features and predict on time series data with diverse scales. Theoretical analysis and the changing pattern of the residual confirm that our residual structure can capture and aggregate the time-series characteristics to handle time series data with diverse scales and predict more accurately. We leverage multi-output residual-based deep learning framework to reuse residual in order to improve the generalization of model. The results demonstrate MIR-TS can achieve state-of-the-art performance on time series data with diverse scales. We plan to extend MIR-TS with more complicated architecture and thoroughly test the framework for more time series forecasting problems.

Acknowledgements. This work is supported by the National Natural Science Foundation of China (No. 61832001) and Australian Research Council (No. DP220101420).

References

1. Assimakopoulos, V., Nikolopoulos, K.: The theta model: a decomposition approach to forecasting. Int. J. Forecast. **16**(4), 521–530 (2000)
2. Athanasopoulos, G., Hyndman, R.J., Song, H., Wu, D.C.: The tourism forecasting competition. Int. J. Forecast. **27**(3), 822–844 (2011)
3. Baker, L.C., Howard, J.: Winning methods for forecasting tourism time series. Int. J. Forecast. **27**(3), 850–852 (2011)
4. Bandara, K., Hewamalage, H., Liu, Y., Kang, Y., Bergmeir, C.: Improving the accuracy of global forecasting models using time series data augmentation. Pattern Recogn. **120**, 108148 (2021)
5. Benidis, K., et al.: Neural forecasting: introduction and literature overview. CoRR abs/2004.10240 (2020)
6. Box, G.E.P., Jenkins, G.M., MacGregor, J.F.: Some recent advances in forecasting and control. J. Roy. Stat. Soc. Ser. C (Appl. Stat.) **23**(2), 158–179 (1974)
7. Breiman, L.: Bagging predictors. Mach. Learn. **24**(2), 123–140 (1996)
8. Brierley, P.: Winning methods for forecasting seasonal tourism time series. Int. J. Forecast. **27**(3), 853–854 (2011)
9. Fiorucci, J.A., Pellegrini, T.R., Louzada, F., Petropoulos, F., Koehler, A.B.: Models for optimising the theta method and their relationship to state space models. Int. J. Forecast. **32**(4), 1151–1161 (2016)
10. Flunkert, D.S.V., Gasthaus, J., Januschowski, T.: DeepAR: probabilistic forecasting with autoregressive recurrent networks. Int. J. Forecast. **36**(3), 1181–1191 (2020)
11. He, K., Zhang, X., Ren, S., Sun, J.: Deep residual learning for image recognition. In: 2016 IEEE Conference on Computer Vision and Pattern Recognition, CVPR 2016, pp. 770–778 (2016)
12. Holt, C.C.: Forecasting seasonals and trends by exponentially weighted moving averages. Int. J. Forecast. **20**(1), 5–10 (2004)
13. Hu, H., Tang, M., Bai, C.: DATSING: data augmented time series forecasting with adversarial domain adaptation. In: CIKM 2020: The 29th ACM International Conference on Information and Knowledge Management, pp. 2061–2064 (2020)

14. Huang, G., Liu, Z., van der Maaten, L., Weinberger, K.Q.: Densely connected convolutional networks. In: 2017 IEEE Conference on Computer Vision and Pattern Recognition, CVPR 2017, pp. 2261–2269 (2017)
15. Li, S., et al.: Enhancing the locality and breaking the memory bottleneck of transformer on time series forecasting. In: Advances in Neural Information Processing Systems 32: Annual Conference on Neural Information Processing Systems 2019, NeurIPS 2019, pp. 5244–5254 (2019)
16. van der Maaten, L., Hinton, G.: Visualizing data using t-SNE. J. Mach. Learn. Res. **9**(86), 2579–2605 (2008)
17. Makridakis, S., Hibon, M.: The M3-competition: results, conclusions and implications. Int. J. Forecast. **16**(4), 451–476 (2000)
18. Makridakis, S., Spiliotis, E., Assimakopoulos, V.: The M4 competition: results, findings, conclusion and way forward. Int. J. Forecast. **34**(4), 802–8081 (2018)
19. Makridakis, S., Spiliotis, E., Assimakopoulos, V.: The M4 competition: 100,000 time series and 61 forecasting methods. Int. J. Forecast. **36**(1), 54–74 (2020)
20. Montori, F., Liao, K., Jayaraman, P.P., Bononi, L., Sellis, T., Georgakopoulos, D.: Classification and annotation of open internet of things datastreams. In: Hacid, H., Cellary, W., Wang, H., Paik, H.-Y., Zhou, R. (eds.) WISE 2018, Part II. LNCS, vol. 11234, pp. 209–224. Springer, Cham (2018). https://doi.org/10.1007/978-3-030-02925-8_15
21. van den Oord, A., et al.: WaveNet: a generative model for raw audio. In: The 9th ISCA Speech Synthesis Workshop, p. 125 (2016)
22. Oreshkin, B.N., Carpov, D., Chapados, N., Bengio, Y.: N-BEATS: neural basis expansion analysis for interpretable time series forecasting. In: 8th International Conference on Learning Representations, ICLR 2020 (2020)
23. Smyl, S.: A hybrid method of exponential smoothing and recurrent neural networks for time series forecasting. Int. J. Forecast. **36**(1), 75–85 (2020)
24. Smyl, S., Kuber, K.: Data preprocessing and augmentation for multiple short time series forecasting with recurrent neural networks. In: 36th International Symposium on Forecasting (2016)
25. Spiliotis, E., Assimakopoulos, V., Nikolopoulos, K.: Forecasting with a hybrid method utilizing data smoothing, a variation of the theta method and shrinkage of seasonal factors. Int. J. Prod. Econ. **209**, 92–102 (2019)
26. Sun, H., et al.: Fast anomaly detection in multiple multi-dimensional data streams. In: 2019 IEEE International Conference on Big Data (IEEE BigData), pp. 1218–1223 (2019)
27. Wang, L., Wang, Z., Qu, H., Liu, S.: Optimal forecast combination based on neural networks for time series forecasting. Appl. Soft Comput. **66**, 1–17 (2018)
28. Wang, Y., Smola, A., Maddix, D.C., Gasthaus, J., Foster, D., Januschowski, T.: Deep factors for forecasting. In: Proceedings of the 36th International Conference on Machine Learning, ICML 2019, pp. 6607–6617 (2019)
29. Winters, P.R.: Forecasting sales by exponentially weighted moving averages. Manag. Sci. **6**(3), 324–342 (1960)

PLAE: Time-Series Prediction Improvement by Adaptive Decomposition

Jufang Duan$^{(\boxtimes)}$ ⓘ, Yi Wang ⓘ, and Wei Zheng ⓘ

Lenovo Research, Beijing, China
{duanjf2,wangyi50,zhengwei25}@lenovo.com

Abstract. Univariate time-series forecasting is a kind of commonly encountered yet tough problem. Most of the forecast algorithms' performance is constrained by the limited information due to the single input dimension. No matter how capable a forecast algorithm is, an accurate output cannot be rendered on an unpredictable time-series. This paper presents PLAE (Predictability Leveraging Auto-Encoder), a Seq2Seq model for univariate time-series data aiming to enhance the accuracy of the given algorithm without dimensional adaptation. The main idea is decomposing the original input data into a group of more predictable microscopic time-series on which the forecast algorithm can deliver a more accurate output. And the final prediction is rendered by aggregating those components back to the original one-dimension. Experiments on three public data sets and one real-world data set show that PLAE can improve the forecast accuracy for 23.38% in terms of MAPE and 19.76% in terms of RMSE. Besides, experimental evidence shows that PLAE's adaptive non-linear decomposition mechanism outperforms the pre-defined additive decomposition *w.r.t.* both forecasting performance and components' interpretability.

Keywords: Time-series prediction · Time-series decomposition · Predictability measure · Accuracy enhancement

1 Introduction

Time-series prediction is a widespread task in many industries, like weather forecast, stock price prediction and sales prediction, *etc.* Here, we focus our research on univariate time-series prediction whose definition is shown in [11]. This type of problem looks uncomplicated in a glance but is hard to solve because of the limitation of the input data dimension and the resultant low predictability.

Most of the readily available time-series forecast algorithms [7,16,25,34] are trained on historical observation and the corresponding features, trying to find out implicit patterns that can contribute to the forecast result. However, no feature is available when problems are limited in the univariate realm which significantly reduces the predictability. Apart from the algorithms mentioned above, ARIMA and its revisions [4,6] are a group of algorithms originally designed

© The Author(s), under exclusive license to Springer Nature Switzerland AG 2022
S. Khanna et al. (Eds.): PRICAI 2022, LNCS 13629, pp. 394–407, 2022.
https://doi.org/10.1007/978-3-031-20862-1_29

for univariate time-series forecasting. They forecast on an autoregressive basis, which means the accuracy of the output relies heavily on the historical observation. In another word, if the data is not sufficiently predictable, the forecast result will be far from accuracy.

One of the most applied methods to enhance the predictability of the input data is time-series decomposition. By decomposing the original time-series into more predictable components like seasonality or long-term trend, the forecast accuracy can be improved. Huang *et al.* [15] introduce the Empirical Mode Decomposition (EMD) and prove its usability in non-stationary data. However, the decomposed components usually show little interpretability, requiring expert knowledge to be enrolled. Methods like STL [9] decompose the input data into a group of more interpretable pre-defined components on an additive basis. And forecast algorithms like Prophet [28] also implement decomposition on the similar idea. However, the pre-defined decomposition performs bad under certain circumstances. For example, if a time-series shows little seasonal characteristic, the seasonality component given by STL will be insignificant, leaving only the other two components to contribute.

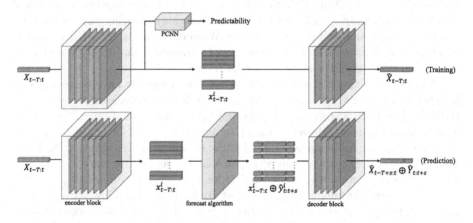

Fig. 1. The workflow of PLAE.

This work presents PLAE (Predictability Leveraging Auto-Encoder), a Seq2Seq model based on an architecture consisting of decomposition, prediction, and aggregation, aiming to enhance the forecast accuracy of the existing algorithms without requiring dimensional adaptation. The decomposition implements non-linear mapping on the input data, generating a bunch of *microscopic time-series* that are highly predictable. The prediction is made independently on each microscopic time-series before being aggregated back to the one-dimensional form. When training, the model learns the self-mapping from $X_{t-T:t}$ to $\hat{X}_{t-T:t}$ with the aim of maximising the average predictability of the microscopic time-series $[x^1_{t-T:t}, x^2_{t-T:t}, ..., x^k_{t-T:t}]$. Here X is the input univariate time-series, $\hat{X}$ is the prediction, T is the length of the look-back window, s is the forecast step, and $x^i_{t-T:t} \in R^T, i = 1, 2, ..., k$ is the generated microscopic time-series with a total number of k. The predictability is obtained by a pre-trained network, PCNN (Predictability Calculation Neural Network), whose details are shown in Sect. 3.1. During the prediction stage, $x^i_{t-T:t}$ is formed by the trained encoder and a s-step-forward forecast is made on it. The final prediction, $\hat{Y}_{t:t+s}$, is gained by mapping the concatenation of $x^i_{t-T+s:t}$ and the prediction $\hat{y}^i_{t:t+s}$ back to the one-dimensional form through the trained decoder. The workflow of PLAE is illustrated in Fig. 1

The main contributions of this paper are twofold: (1) We propose a quantitative predictability measure for univariate time-series data ameliorating the bias in the previous research. (2) We come up with PLAE, a Seq2Seq model for univariate time-series that can improve the forecast accuracy of existing forecast algorithms.

2   Related Works

At any time, parametric time-series forecasting algorithms are baseline choices in the industry, *e.g.* ARMA [21] and ARIMA [4]. They utilise moving average and differentiation for auto-regressive modeling. There are also other popular models, *e.g.* exponential smoothing [13] and Holt-Winters methods [5]. All the models mentioned above are lack of sufficient model parameters and their performance usually cannot match the state-of-the-art models.

Besides statistical methods, decision tree-based models have become popular choices in recent years, especially gradient boosting decision trees method (GBDT) like XGBoost [7] and LightGBM [16]. They are competitive in real-world time-series tasks. However, the performance of GBDT-like models is highly influenced by exogenous variables and feature engineering. Therefore, GBDT-like models have bottleneck when no covariate is available, and they are hard to deal with time-series data with complicated hidden patterns automatically.

Neural networks might be the hottest topic in the machine learning field, especially for the time-series forecasting. The trend of neural network structures have been updated constantly, *e.g.* Vanilla NN [27], CNN [3] and LSTM [2], *etc.* RNN and LSTM, which are often considered as the corner stone for deep learning time-series forecasting, empower the network to learn historical patterns auto-regressively. However, some experiments show that RNN and LSTM performs inadequately for long sequence time-series forecasting problem [34]. After that, Du *et al.* [10] figure that the Seq2Seq structure can obtain even higher performance. Beyond that, Li *et al.* [19] firstly introduce Transformer blocks to the time-series field and achieve impressive performance on many of the public data sets. Nevertheless, transformer-like models still cannot impress the industry because they need intricate structure tuning, and the model is hard to converge when time-series data becomes sophisticated. Due to the inadequate performance mentioned above, we are encouraged to find an adaptable method that can leverage the power of the existing forecast algorithms.

In addition, many recent researches were proposed in different aspects. Zhu *et al.* [35] suggest that the prediction of the macroscopic time-series can be leveraged by the clustering of the microscopic time-series. However, the relationship between macroscopic and microscopic time-series is fixed and pre-defined with required extra knowledge. Chen *et al.* proposed DeepTCN [8] which basically uses dilated causal convolution and Seq2Seq structure, and provides probabilistic forecasting. However, the implicit yet strong assumption of i.i.d. condition on all the subjects is needed, which is not usually satisfied in real-world cases. Salinas *et al.* [25] proposed DeepAR, which uses an auto-regressive encoder-decoder structure to offer probabilistic forecasting. DeepAR's performance is highly relied on assumptive data distribution, and the specific scale factor will affect performance directly. In practice, these settings need strong assumption and intricate hyper-parameters tuning.

Another issue correlated with our work is quantitative predictability measuring. Most of the existing measures are based on information theory and deliver a notional upper-bound of predictability. Molgedey *et al.* [22] use n-gram conditional entropy to measure the uncertainty of predicting the next k steps based on the observation. They show that predictability can be enhanced by basing the prediction on longer blocks of observation. Garland *et al.* [14] divide the observation into two parts: redundancy and entropy generation. They show that the more redundancy in time-series data, the more predictable it should be. Their work, together with the work by Pennekamp *et al.* [24], introduces permutation entropy [1] to measure the uncertainty, which (1) can discretise the real-valued time-series into categorical data suitable for entropy calculation; (2) is robust to observational noise and requires no prior knowledge. Song *et al.* [26] use an estimator of actual entropy based on Lempel-Ziv data compression [17] to measure the uncertainty and they show that the temporal information revealed by the actual entropy contributes a lot to predictability calculation. Further, Fano's inequality [23] is used to define the upper-bound of predictability. However, Xu *et al.* [32] point out that the inconsistency of the logarithm base and ambiguous description in calculating the Lempel-Ziv estimator may lead to misunderstandings and the overestimation of predictability.

3   Proposed Method

3.1   Predictability Measures

Methodology. For a certain time-series, the predictability is the probability that an appropriate algorithm can deliver a correct answer based on the observation. The most intuitive method of predictability measuring is by looking at the forecast accuracy certain algorithms can achieve. Unfortunately, this method is unreasonable in two ways. First, it is hard to tell that the chosen algorithm is arguably "the appropriate algorithm". Second, forecast accuracy on different test windows may vary a lot and it is irrational to choose one specific test window over others.

Song *et al.* [26] show a quantitative method of predictability measuring. This information theory-based predictability measure is given by Eq. (1), where S is the actual entropy, N is the number of different values and Π is the predictability. By solving Eq. (1), the predictability Π can be obtained.

$$S = -\Pi \log_2 \Pi - (1 - \Pi) \log_2 (1 - \Pi) + (1 - \Pi) \log_2 (N - 1) \qquad (1)$$

However, certain bias exists when this measure is utilised on time-series data and the main reason is that it fails to capture the time dependencies. Consider the time-series shown in Eq. (2), where $\epsilon_t \sim N(0, 1)$ denotes the white Gaussian noise. Using Eq. (1), the result would be 44.80% showing that the time-series is quite unpredictable. The reason is that the strong trend pattern is ignored during the actual entropy calculation, making the entropy to be overestimated at 4.65 which further leads to a low level of predictability.

$$y(t) = x(t) + 4 \sin x(t) + \epsilon_t \qquad (2)$$

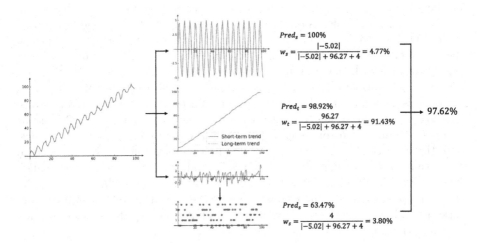

Fig. 2. Process of predictability measuring

In order to fix this bias, we introduce a new method whose process is as follows. First, the temporal information is extracted by Fourier seasonal decomposition [18] and exponential smoothing, retaining seasonality and trend, respectively. Under the assumption of long-term trend is totally predictable, the predictability is defined as 100% minus the average absolute bias between long-term trend (trend component smoothed with a window length equals to 5, which is a heuristic method that works well in our experiment) and the trend component. Because of the periodicity, the seasonal component's predictability is 100%. Then, density-based clustering [12] is implemented on the residue and transforms the continuous time-series into discrete value set based on its distribution. The quantitative measure given by Eq. (1) is then utilised on the clustering result to get the predictability of the residue. The final predictability of the time-series is calculated by the absolute volume weighted average of the predictability of those three components. Using this method, the predictability of Eq. (2) is measured at 97.62% which is a lot more reasonable. The process of this calculation is illustrated in Fig. 2.

PCNN. In this part, we discuss PCNN, a neural network fitting the predictability measure mentioned above in a differentiable form.

Apart from the temporal information required by most time-series analysis approaches, our predictability measure also requires local information when calculating the actual entropy. Intuitively, a neural network extracting both temporal and spatial information is suitable here. PCNN adopts the similar network architecture with CRNN [20], an image-based sequence recognition model introduced by Liao et al.. Here, the two-dimensional convolutional layers and pooling layers are replaced by their one-dimensional form. By training the parameters of the convolutional layers, PCNN can find the local information around each time step before temporal information is extracted by the bi-directional LSTM. The network configuration is shown in Table 1, where k, s, and p stand for kernel size, stride, and padding size, respectively.

Table 1. PCNN configuration summary

Type	Configuration
Dense	#hidden units: 64
Dense	#hidden units: 64
Dense	#hidden units: 512
Bidirectional-LSTM	#hidden units: 256
Bidirectional-LSTM	#hidden units: 256
Max Pooling	window: 1×2, s: 1
Convolution	#maps: 256, k: 1×11, s: 1, p: 5
Batch Normalization	–
Convolution	#maps: 256, k: 1×7, s: 1, p: 3
Max Pooling	window: 1×2, s: 1
Convolution	#maps: 128, k: 1×11, s: 1, p: 5
Max Pooling	window: 1×2, s: 1
Convolution	#maps: 128, k: 1×11, s: 1, p: 5
Input	–

When training, we artificially generate the training data by randomly creating seasonality, trend and residue as well as their corresponding weights before the final aggregation. Labels are calculated by our newly proposed predictability measure. In our work, PCNN is trained on 400,000 artificially generated time-series data for 2,000 epochs. The training on 4 T V100 GPUs takes approximately 2 days.

3.2 PLAE

To begin with, PLAE follows an architecture which consists of three parts: decomposition, prediction, and aggregation. The basic idea is to decompose the input data into a bunch of highly predictable microscopic time-series on which the predictions are delivered, and then aggregate them together to form the final answer. Note that the prediction is made separately on each microscopic time-series whose dimension is the same as the input's, meaning the original forecast algorithm can be used without dimensional adaptation. This three-step-workflow is illustrated in Fig. 3.

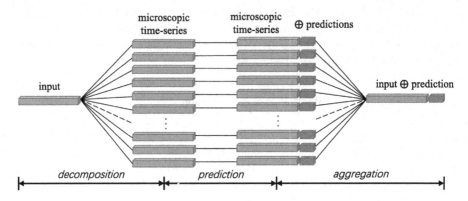

Fig. 3. The general forecast framework consisting of decomposition, prediction and aggregation.

PLAE implements the decomposition through the encoder block and PCNN. The encoder block maps the original input $\boldsymbol{X}_{t-T:t} \in R^T$ to the k microscopic time-series $\boldsymbol{x}_{t-T:t} \in R^{k,T}$ with two targets: (1) maximising the average predictability of each microscopic time-series measured by PCNN and (2) penalising the similarities across all microscopic time-series. The first target aims to enhance the predictability as much as possible and the second target encourages the network to search for different types of decomposition results. With these two targets being optimised, the model is trained to generate k highly predictable univariate microscopic time-series and each of them captures one certain kind of predictable motif. The aggregation in PLAE is implemented through the decoder which fits the non-linear mapping from the microscopic time-series back to the input data. The detail of PLAE is illustrated in Fig. 4.

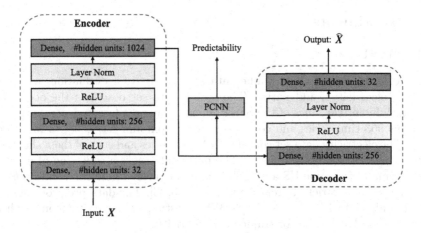

Fig. 4. The detailed structure of PLAE.

Overall, the training of PLAE simultaneously (1) minimising the loss of self-mapping, (2) maximising the average predictability of the microscopic time-series and (3) minimising the similarities among microscopic time-series. The loss function can be formulated as Eq. (3), where $Pred(\bullet)$ represents the predictability given by the pre-trained PCNN and $CM(\boldsymbol{x})$ represents the correlation matrix of the encoder output $\boldsymbol{x}$. Even though the $CM(\boldsymbol{x})$ can only depict the linear correlation among each pair of microscopic time-series, our experimental analysis shows it can enforce the PLAE to find microscopic time-series of different kind. The 0.01 multiple of the predictability loss term prevents the training from overly focusing on predictability, whose unexpected result is to deliver a bunch of highly predictable but meaningless microscopic time-series, *e.g.* perfectly smoothed trend or different types of periodical sequences. The training epoch is set to be 200 in our tests.

$$loss = MSE(\boldsymbol{X}, \hat{\boldsymbol{X}}) + 0.01 \times [1 - \frac{1}{k}\sum_{i=1}^{k} Pred(\boldsymbol{x})] + \|CM(\boldsymbol{x})\|_1 \qquad (3)$$

In the prediction stage, since the predictability is the theoretical upper-bound of the forecast accuracy, more accurate output should be delivered on the newly generated forecast subjects, *i.e.*, microscopic time-series, even though the forecast algorithm remains unchanged. For the ith microscopic time-series, after the prediction is made, the concatenation of $\boldsymbol{x}_{t-T+s:t}^i$ and $\hat{\boldsymbol{y}}_{t:t+s}^i$ may serve as the ith component of the decoder input. Since the decoder output is the concatenation of $\hat{\boldsymbol{X}}_{t-T+s:t}$ and $\hat{\boldsymbol{Y}}_{t:t+s}$, the final prediction can be rendered explicitly.

4 Experiments

4.1 Test Data

Public Data Sets. Three public data sets are used for evaluation, which are traffic[1], electricity[2], and parts[3]. The traffic data set describes the occupancy rate of different car lanes of the San Francisco bay area freeways across time. It contains 963 time-series and covers the range from Jan 1st, 2008, to Mar 30th, 2009. The electricity data set contains 370 time-series and each of them shows the power consumption every quarter. The parts data set is a collection of monthly parts demand from one US automobile manufacturer. These three data sets are widely used in a variety of relative works [8,25,33]. The data pre-processing we adopt is aligned with Chen *et al.* [8]. When testing, we forecast 3 months ahead for parts and 24 h ahead for traffic and electricity.

Real-World Data Set. A real-world time-series data set is also selected to show the effectiveness of our method in practice. We adopt internal configurable-to-order sales data (referred as sales) as the forecast subject. It contains 533 weekly sales from Apr 4th, 2018, to Oct 17th, 2021. When testing, we leave the last 13 weeks of data as the forecast targets.

4.2 PLAE Against Direct Forecasting

To begin with, we list all the forecast algorithms whose accuracy under both direct forecasting and PLAE forecasting would be shown and analysed. The forecast algorithms we choose are (1) Auto ARIMA, which is a representative linear model; (2) TSB [29], which is an industrial well-accepted demand forecast algorithm. (3) GBDT Regressor, which is a widely used ensemble learning algorithm; (4) Wen *et al.* [31], which combines time-series clustering and deep neural networks; (5) Informer [34], which is a state-of-the-art time-series forecasting algorithm derived from the famous Transformer model [30].

The evaluation metrics are mean absolute percent error (MAPE) and root mean square error (RMSE). The test results are shown in Table 2.

It is obvious that, compared with forecasting directly, using PLAE can significantly leverage the forecast accuracy of the outputs. Despite the various accuracy of direct forecasting, we can see a general phenomenon that when forecasted by PLAE the results can be a lot better. Considering the percentage of improvement measured by MAPE, GBDT regressor on PLAE leads its direct forecasting result for an average of 27.52%, followed by Wen *et al.* (27.51%), Auto ARIMA (26.18%), TSB (21.32%) and Informer (14.38%). When measured by RMSE, the order of percentage improvement remains unchanged. Again, the algorithm with the most significant accuracy enhancement is GBDT regressor (with 31.27%

[1] https://archive.ics.uci.edu/ml/datasets/PEMS-SF.
[2] https://archive.ics.uci.edu/ml/datasets/ElectricityLoadDiagrams20112014.
[3] https://robjhyndman.com/expsmooth/.

Table 2. PLAE against direct forecasting

		Sales		Traffic		Electricity		Parts	
		MAPE	RMSE	MAPE	RMSE	MAPE	RMSE	MAPE	RMSE
Auto ARIMA	Direct	31.41%	2986.84	30.04%	0.13	35.09%	1130.45	61.34%	1.10
	PLAE	18.54%	2116.57	17.72%	0.12	34.10%	892.36	49.12%	1.03
TSB	Direct	26.15%	2672.56	55.32%	0.26	65.27%	2316.15	34.67%	1.07
	PLAE	23.13%	2097.36	56.76%	0.29	21.42%	1397.51	31.50%	1.05
GBDT Regressor	Direct	26.27%	2780.05	31.61%	0.13	28.21%	707.78	54.67%	0.89
	PLAE	14.49%	1728.18	27.38%	0.11	23.20%	318.49	36.02%	0.74
Wen *et al.*	Direct	25.37%	2736.36	56.28%	0.25	57.97%	978.93	45.77%	0.68
	PLAE	11.86%	1448.76	48.61%	0.18	31.08%	686.22	47.24%	0.68
Informer	Direct	24.99%	2628.85	28.54%	0.14	26.25%	722.90	44.32%	0.66
	PLAE	23.70%	2497.35	25.62%	0.11	24.89%	647.62	27.95%	0.57

improvement), followed by Wen *et al.* (25.98%), Auto ARIMA (16.06%), TSB (12.88%) and Informer (12.62%). Vertically, it shows the average amount that PLAE can enhance on each forecast subject. Consider the percentage of improvement measured by MAPE first. We can see the percentage improvements are ranging from 15.13% (on the traffic) to 31.16% (on sales), with 27.87% on the electricity and 19.38% on the parts locating in between. When measured by the average percentage RMSE improvement, the results are 28.11%, 12.19%, 31.21% and 7.54% for sales, the electricity, the traffic, and the parts, respectively. Overall, PLAE can improve 23.38% in terms of MAPE and 19.76% in terms of RMSE. The comparison between direct forecasting and PLAE forecasting shows that the accuracy improvement does have achieved and PLAE can leverage the existing algorithms' performance.

The difference of predictability on the forecast subjects explains the reason for accuracy enhancement. Table 3 lists the average one-step-forward predictability of what these two methods forecast on.

Table 3. Predictability on forecast subjects

Method	Sales	Traffic	Electricity	Parts
Direct	76.34%	78.51%	73.26%	65.20%
PLAE	**90.58%**	**89.29%**	**92.21%**	**88.19%**

Obviously, PLAE enhances the original low predictability to a higher degree. The improvement on sales, traffic, electricity, and parts are 14.24%, 10.78%, 18.95%, and 22.99%, respectively. Since the predictability is the theoretical upper-bound of the forecast accuracy, the same algorithm can deliver a more accurate prediction on a more predictable forecast subject.

4.3   PLAE Against Fixed Decomposition Based Forecasting

Unlike most of the industrial well-accepted methods that decompose the input data into a set of pre-defined components, PLAE gives the adaptive decomposition on a trainable basis, learning to find the most predictable components that capture different motifs. In this part, we compare PLAE against two other methods which deliver prediction based on a fixed decomposition. Specifically, we choose STL and Prophet. STL is a decomposition method widely used on sequential data. It decomposes the input data into seasonality, trend, and residue before the predictions being made on each of them. Prophet also decomposes the input data in an additive way but with four components, *i.e.*, trend, periodic changes, holidays and idiosyncratic changes. The comparable analysis between PLAE and the other two methods can deliver a experimental conclusion on whether the trainable decomposition based forecasting outperforms the fixed decomposition based forecasting.

Since STL is a decomposition method *per se*, certain forecast algorithm has to be addressed for each component. Here, the forecast algorithm is selected through backtest, whose step is equal to the forecast step, on the trend component and residue, respectively. For both STL based forecasting and Prophet, we tuned the hyper-parameters by grid searching. Results are shown in Table 4.

Table 4. PLAE against fixed decomposition based forecasting

	Sales		Traffic		Electricity		Parts	
	MAPE	RMSE	MAPE	RMSE	MAPE	RMSE	MAPE	RMSE
STL based forecasting	35.40%	3018.08	46.56%	0.23	27.31%	805.42	41.21%	0.79
Prophet	29.97%	2661.73	47.11%	0.23	33.79%	880.71	49.74%	0.84

On average, PLAE outperforms the STL based forecasting for 17.06%, 11.34%, 0.37%, and 2.84% in terms of MAPE, and 1040.44, 0.07, 16.98, and -0.02 in terms of RMSE on sales, traffic, electricity, and parts, respectively. And PLAE outperforms the Prophet for 11.63%, 11.89%, 6.85%, and 11.37% in terms of MAPE, and 684.09, 0.07, 92.27, and 0.03 in terms of RMSE on sales, traffic, electricity, and parts, respectively. Across the four data sets, PLAE has a percentage of improvement for 20.20% (*w.r.t.* MAPE) and 15.75% (*w.r.t.* RMSE) over the STL based forecasting, and 26.80% (*w.r.t.* MAPE) and 17.19% (*w.r.t.* RMSE) over the prophet. Because of the constantly accurate predictions Informer delivers, we consider PLAE forecasting using Informer (namely PLAE-Informer) as a high-performance forecast algorithm *per se*. The PLAE-Informer outperforms the STL based forecasting for 11.70%, 20.94%, 2.42%, and 13.26% in terms of MAPE, and 520.73, 0.12, 157.80, and 0.22 in terms of RMSE on sales, traffic, electricity, and parts, respectively. And it outperforms the Prophet for 6.27%, 21.49%, 8.90%, and 21.79% in terms of MAPE, and 164.38, 0.12, 233.09, and 0.2 in terms of RMSE on sales, traffic, electricity, and parts, respectively.

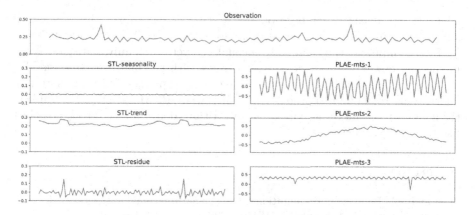

Fig. 5. The decomposition given by STL and PLAE

We also implement a visualised analysis on the microscopic time-series. The decomposed results on a random picked time-series from the traffic data set are shown in Fig. 5. For PLAE, only three pieces of the microscopic time-series with the largest weight are demonstrated.

For this certain input data, the seasonality given by STL is small in value, leaving this total predictable component insignificant compared with trend and residue. The residue, however, is quite large. Since the residue component often appear to be chaotic, this may drag the combined forecast accuracy quite a lot. PLAE, on the other hand, delivers a quite predictable yet interpretable decomposition. The PLAE-mts-1 component shows a strong seasonal pattern. The PLAE-mts-2 component shows the long-term trend. The PLAE-mts-3 component shows a constant gain with a seasonal fluctuation. It is obviously that the microscopic time-series decomposed by PLAE is much more predictable than the three components decomposed by STL, which further leads to the outperforming *w.r.t.* the forecast accuracy on the decomposed series. This visualised analysis shows the adaptive non-linear decomposition outperforms the predefined additive decomposition in both performance and interpretability.

5   Conclusion and Future Work

In this paper, we introduce PLAE, a predictability enhancement-based Seq2Seq model for univariate time-series forecasting. PLAE aims to improve the performance of the readily available algorithms without dimensional adaptation. The concept of PLAE is to build an auto-encoder-like architecture whose encoder decomposes the input data into a group of microscopic time-series with improved predictability, and the decoder renders aggregated final output from the microscopic time-series predictions. Experiments on three public data sets and one real-world data set show that PLAE can improve 23.38% of MAPE and 19.76% RMSE compared with forecasting directly. We also experimentally prove the adaptive non-linear decomposition makes PLAE outperform the pre-defined additive decomposition in forecasting performance as well as interpretability.

PLAE empowers the commonly encountered yet tough univariate time-series prediction, however, it currently cannot work with the multivariate data. Our future work is to push the univariate quantitative predictability measure into multivariate realm and to propose the multivariate PLAE. We think it will help the multivariate time-series forecasting algorithms deliver better predictions just like what PLAE does now.

References

1. Bandt, C., Pompe, B.: Permutation entropy: a natural complexity measure for time series. Phys. Rev. Lett. **88**(17), 174102 (2002)
2. Bao, W., Yue, J., Rao, Y.: A deep learning framework for financial time series using stacked autoencoders and long-short term memory. PloS One **12**(7), e0180944 (2017)
3. Borovykh, A., Bohte, S., Oosterlee, C.W.: Conditional time series forecasting with convolutional neural networks. arXiv preprint arXiv:1703.04691 (2017)
4. Box, G.E., Jenkins, G.M., Reinsel, G.C., Ljung, G.M.: Time Series Analysis: Forecasting and Control. Wiley, Hoboken (2015)
5. Chatfield, C.: The holt-winters forecasting procedure. J. Roy. Stat. Soc. Ser. C (Appl. Stat.) **27**(3), 264–279 (1978)
6. Chen, K.Y., Wang, C.H.: A hybrid SARIMA and support vector machines in forecasting the production values of the machinery industry in Taiwan. Expert Syst. Appl. **32**(1), 254–264 (2007)
7. Chen, T., Guestrin, C.: XGBoost: a scalable tree boosting system. In: Proceedings of the 22nd ACM SIGKDD International Conference on Knowledge Discovery and Data Mining, pp. 785–794 (2016)
8. Chen, Y., Kang, Y., Chen, Y., Wang, Z.: Probabilistic forecasting with temporal convolutional neural network. Neurocomputing **399**, 491–501 (2020)
9. Cleveland, R.B., Cleveland, W.S., McRae, J.E., Terpenning, I.: STL: a seasonal-trend decomposition. J. Off. Stat **6**(1), 3–73 (1990)
10. Du, S., Li, T., Horng, S.J.: Time series forecasting using sequence-to-sequence deep learning framework. In: 2018 9th International Symposium on Parallel Architectures, Algorithms and Programming (PAAP), pp. 171–176. IEEE (2018)
11. Esling, P., Agon, C.: Time-series data mining. ACM Comput. Surv. (CSUR) **45**(1), 1–34 (2012)
12. Ester, M., Kriegel, H.P., Sander, J., Xu, X., et al.: A density-based algorithm for discovering clusters in large spatial databases with noise. In: KDD, vol. 96, pp. 226–231 (1996)
13. Gardner, E.S., Jr.: Exponential smoothing: the state of the art. J. Forecast. **4**(1), 1–28 (1985)
14. Garland, J., James, R., Bradley, E.: Model-free quantification of time-series predictability. Phys. Rev. E **90**(5), 052910 (2014)
15. Huang, N.E., et al.: The empirical mode decomposition and the Hilbert spectrum for nonlinear and non-stationary time series analysis. Proc. Roy. Soc. Lond. Ser. A Math. Phys. Eng. Sci. **454**(1971), 903–995 (1998)
16. Ke, G., et al.: LightGBM: a highly efficient gradient boosting decision tree. In: Advances in Neural Information Processing Systems 30, pp. 3146–3154 (2017)

17. Kontoyiannis, I., Algoet, P.H., Suhov, Y.M., Wyner, A.J.: Nonparametric entropy estimation for stationary processes and random fields, with applications to English text. IEEE Trans. Inf. Theory **44**(3), 1319–1327 (1998)
18. Kumar, U., De Ridder, K.: GARCH modelling in association with FFT-ARIMA to forecast ozone episodes. Atmos. Environ. **44**(34), 4252–4265 (2010)
19. Li, S., et al.: Enhancing the locality and breaking the memory bottleneck of transformer on time series forecasting. In: Advances in Neural Information Processing Systems 32, pp. 5243–5253 (2019)
20. Liao, M., Lyu, P., He, M., Yao, C., Bai, X.: Mask TextSpotter: an end-to-end trainable neural network for spotting text with arbitrary shapes. IEEE Trans. Pattern Anal. Mach. Intell. **43**(2), 532–548 (2019)
21. McLeod, A.I., Li, W.K.: Diagnostic checking ARMA time series models using squared-residual autocorrelations. J. Time Ser. Anal. **4**(4), 269–273 (1983)
22. Molgedey, L., Ebeling, W.: Local order, entropy and predictability of financial time series. Eur. Phys. J. B Condens. Matter Complex Syst. **15**(4), 733–737 (2000)
23. Navet, N., Chen, S.H.: On predictability and profitability: would GP induced trading rules be sensitive to the observed entropy of time series? In: Brabazon, A., O'Neill, M. (eds.) Natural Computing in Computational Finance. SCI, vol. 100, pp. 197–210. Springer, Heidelberg (2008). https://doi.org/10.1007/978-3-540-77477-8_11
24. Pennekamp, F., et al.: The intrinsic predictability of ecological time series and its potential to guide forecasting. Ecol. Monogr. **89**(2), e01359 (2019)
25. Salinas, D., Flunkert, V., Gasthaus, J., Januschowski, T.: DeepAR: probabilistic forecasting with autoregressive recurrent networks. Int. J. Forecast. **36**(3), 1181–1191 (2020)
26. Song, C., Qu, Z., Blumm, N., Barabási, A.L.: Limits of predictability in human mobility. Science **327**(5968), 1018–1021 (2010)
27. Tang, Z., De Almeida, C., Fishwick, P.A.: Time series forecasting using neural networks vs. Box-Jenkins methodology. Simulation **57**(5), 303–310 (1991)
28. Taylor, S.J., Letham, B.: Forecasting at scale. Am. Stat. **72**(1), 37–45 (2018)
29. Teunter, R.H., Syntetos, A.A., Babai, M.Z.: Intermittent demand: linking forecasting to inventory obsolescence. Eur. J. Oper. Res. **214**(3), 606–615 (2011)
30. Vaswani, A., et al.: Attention is all you need. In: Advances in Neural Information Processing Systems 30 (2017)
31. Wen, M., Li, P., Zhang, L., Chen, Y.: Stock market trend prediction using high-order information of time series. IEEE Access **7**, 28299–28308 (2019)
32. Xu, P., Yin, L., Yue, Z., Zhou, T.: On predictability of time series. Phys. A Stat. Mech. Appl. **523**, 345–351 (2019)
33. Yu, H.F., Rao, N., Dhillon, I.S.: Temporal regularized matrix factorization for high-dimensional time series prediction. In: Advances in Neural Information Processing Systems 29 (2016)
34. Zhou, H., et al.: Informer: beyond efficient transformer for long sequence time-series forecasting. In: Proceedings of the AAAI Conference on Artificial Intelligence, vol. 35, pp. 11106–11115 (2021)
35. Zhu, Z., et al.: MixSeq: connecting macroscopic time series forecasting with microscopic time series data. In: Advances in Neural Information Processing Systems 34 (2021)

GMEKT: A Novel Graph Attention-Based Memory-Enhanced Knowledge Tracing

Mianfan Chen[1], Wenjun Ma[1], Shun Mao[1], and Yuncheng Jiang[1,2(✉)]

[1] School of Computer Science, South China Normal University, Guangzhou, China
{2020023007,shunm,jiangyuncheng}@m.scnu.edu.cn, mawenjun@scnu.edu.cn
[2] School of Artificial Intelligence, South China Normal University, Foshan, China

Abstract. Knowledge Tracking (KT) attempts to predict students' learning performance by tracking their changing knowledge state based on their past performance on exercises. Existing KT models primarily use knowledge concepts while ignoring the latent information of exercises, particularly for possible changes in students' learning processes. This paper proposes a novel Graph attention-based Memory-Enhanced Knowledge Tracing (GMEKT) model to address these issues, employing the Graph Attention Network (GAT) and a novel fusion method to extract additional rich information from the exercises. In detail, we first create a dynamic adjacency matrix as the input of the graph attention network to alleviate the sparsity. Then a memory module based on self-attention and gating network is developed to trace the evolution of the knowledge state and memory unit when students do the exercises. Finally, we conduct extensive experiments on public datasets to validate the proposed model's effectiveness. Compared to the state-of-the-art KT models, GMEKT outperforms them by more than 2.67% in AUC.

Keywords: Knowledge state · Knowledge tracing · Graph attention network · Educational data mining

1 Introduction

Nowadays, knowledge tracking can provide more brilliant educational services to students by tracking their knowledge states, such as recommending individualized learning paths [10]. Current studies use numerous ways to assess students' knowledge levels and learning preferences based on historical learning interactions. In these methods, knowledge tracing uses machine learning for sequence modeling and monitors student knowledge states' changes using educationally associated data, which is widely used in various online tutoring systems and received increasing attention [9].

Existing KT approaches [17,22] typically model knowledge concepts rather than exercises, resulting in the loss of latent information contained in the exercises. As illustrated in Fig. 1, a knowledge concept may correspond to multiple

© The Author(s), under exclusive license to Springer Nature Switzerland AG 2022
S. Khanna et al. (Eds.): PRICAI 2022, LNCS 13629, pp. 408–421, 2022.
https://doi.org/10.1007/978-3-031-20862-1_30

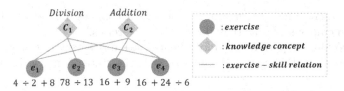

Fig. 1. A simple graph of exercises and knowledge concepts.

exercises, and an exercise may contain numerous knowledge concepts. If they only consider the skills used in the exercises and ignore their characteristics, their performance may suffer a loss. Unfortunately, data sparsity is a serious issue because students can only answer a portion of massive exercises. A challenge in KT is determining how to mine the potential representative information of the exercises.

The recent models focus on exploiting latent information of exercises via graphs. For example, Graph-based Knowledge Tracing (GKT) [14] constructs a skill relation graph to learn their relationship. Graph-based Interaction Knowledge Tracing (GIKT) [21] employs bipartite graphs with Graph Convolutional Network (GCN) to acquire higher-order information for exercises and knowledge concepts. However, combining the two methods to improve the model's predictive performance is unusual. In contrast, Some studies concentrate on the students' learning process while ignoring the exercise's potential information. Individual Estimation Knowledge Tracing (IEKT) [11] proposes modeling students by combining student characteristics such as cognitive level and knowledge acquisition sensitivity to exercises. Collaborative Knowledge Tracing (CoKT) [12] obtains the inter-student information by retrieving the records and sub-sequences of students with similar question-answering experiences.

To model the student learning process based on the hidden information, we propose a novel Graph attention-based Memory-Enhanced Knowledge Tracing (GMEKT), predicting students' performance via a graph attention network [18] based embedding and memory module. Specifically, (1) we utilize graph attention networks to obtain efficient exercise representations from exercise-knowledge concepts to get the relationship between exercises and knowledge concepts and build a dynamic adjacency matrix of each batch to alleviate the sparsity problem of exercises; (2) we improve the feature embedding of the exercise to mine the latent information of the exercise; (3) we add a memory module based on CNN, self-attention, and gating network to track the changes in student's knowledge state and memory units by simulating their learning process. The memory module can update the student's state by interacting with the current exercise and the knowledge state at the current time step.

Our main contributions are summarized as follows:

(1) We propose a novel fusion approach with graph attention networks and build a dynamic adjacency matrix with each batch.

(2) We present a memory module to model the changes in students' knowledge and memory states as they perform the exercises.
(3) We conduct experiments on four benchmark datasets, and the experimental results show that our model outperforms the state-of-the-art baselines.

2   Related Work

Existing knowledge tracking models can be divided into traditional machine learning models and deep learning models.

Traditional machine learning models in KT are classified into two types: Bayesian knowledge tracing [4] and cognitive diagnostic models. Bayesian knowledge tracing used hidden Markov models to simulate students' learning of various knowledge concepts. Its knowledge state is binary, mastery or not, but this state cannot fully reflect the complexity of learning. In contrast, cognitive diagnostic models are concerned with learning parameters from historical data to make predictions. Item Response Theory [2] predicted the probability of correct answers based on student ability and question difficulty. Performance Factors Analysis [16] predicted student's performance by counting correct and incorrect attempts at skills, and Knowledge Tracing Machines [19] used Factorization Machines to integrate learning-related side information.

Deep learning is widely used in knowledge tracing tasks. The classic Deep Knowledge Tracing (DKT) [17] first used long short-term memory (LSTM) [6] to model students' exercise sequences and outperform other traditional knowledge tracking models such as BKT and PFA. Later, additional DKT variants were proposed, such as DKT+ [13], which introduced forgetting features into DKT to improve the model's performance. The Dynamic Key-Value Memory Network (DKVMN) [22] used a Memory-Augmented Neural Network to record the learner's proficiency with each underlying concept. In light of the DKT model's inability to track mastery of each knowledge concept and the DKVMN's failure to capture the dependencies of long sequences of student practice records, the Sequential Key-Value Memory Networks (SKVMNs) [1] were proposed. The Self Attentive Knowledge Tracing (SAKT) [15] was the first to propose using transformers for knowledge tracking. To capture the presentation of the exercise, the Context-Aware Attentive Knowledge Tracing (AKT) [5] model employed a monotonic attention network and Rasch model-based embedding. To better grasp the students' mastery of the exercises, Individual Estimation Knowledge Tracing (IEKT) [11] introduced the cognition level estimation module and knowledge acquisition sensitivity estimation module to knowledge tracing. Collaborative Knowledge Tracing (CoKT) [12] made predictions based on the integration of the intra-student and inter-student information.

Although the KT models discussed above all highlight their respective advantages and achieve good results, they either lack modeling of the learning process or representations to enrich the exercises further. Compared to the preceding models, our model employs a graph attention network and vector fusion to improve the presentations of exercises. Still, it also uses a memory module to simulate students' learning process, thereby improving prediction performance.

3   Method

This section will go over our model GMEKT in detail, with an overview architecture shown in Fig. 2. To begin, we define the problem of knowledge tracking and then describe the embedding input module, student knowledge state update, and prediction module.

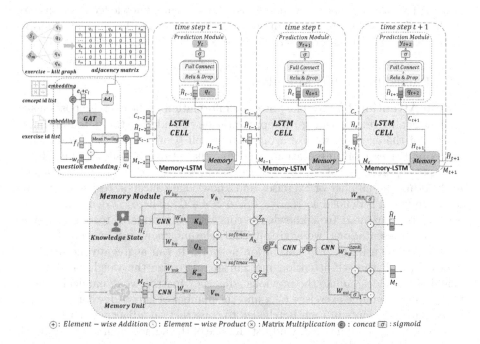

Fig. 2. The architecture of the GMEKT. Exercise embedding's output x_i is the model's exercise input, and the memory module's details can be seen at the bottom of the figure. Q_h, K_h, and V_h are the query, key, and value based on the knowledge state feature's convolution. Furthermore, the aggregated feature Z_h is obtained by performing self-attention on H_t and another feature Z_m, with Z_m is calculated by querying on K_m and V_m. In this case, both K_m and V_m are mappings of the memory M_{t-1}. The aggregated feature Z is obtained by convolution combining Z_h and Z_m.

Problem Definition. Knowledge tracking aims to determine whether the student can complete the next exercise correctly based on previous answers or the student's knowledge state. Since students have completed a series of exercises in the knowledge tracking task, we can construct the students' learning sequence as $x = (e_1, a_1), (e_2, a_2), ..., (e_t, a_t)$ and the new exercise as e_{t+1}, where e_i represents the exercise ID and $a_i \in \{0, 1\}$ represents whether the student answered the question correctly, and the final goal is to predict the probability $p(a_{t+1} = 1|x, e_{t+1})$.

3.1 Overview Architecture

GMEKT is made up of three modules, as shown in Fig. 2: the exercise input module, the student's knowledge state update module, and the predicting module.

The exercise's input module first obtains the embedding through GAT and then fuses with the feature embedding to further mine the exercise's rich information. LSTM and a memory module assist the student's knowledge state update module. Finally, the predicting module seeks to forecast the student's performance on the next exercise based on the student's current knowledge state.

3.2 Embedding Input Module

Graph Attention Layer. The potential information of the exercise poses a significant challenge in learning its representation. To address the potential information of the exercise, we use a bipartite graph $\mathcal{G}$ of exercises and knowledge concepts. For ease of presentation, we define the set of exercises and knowledge concepts separately as $\mathcal{E} = (e_1, e_2, ..., e_n)$ and $\mathcal{C} = (c_1, c_2, ..., c_m)$, with n and m denoting the number of exercises and knowledge concepts, respectively. The bipartite graph is defined as $\{(e, r_{ec}, c)|e \in \mathcal{E}, c \in \mathcal{C}\}$, where r_{ec} denotes whether an exercise is related to a knowledge concept. Furthermore, to obtain better exercise representations, we aggregate the relevant knowledge-concept features of the exercise using a graph attention network. It can aggregate the neighbor nodes through the self-attention mechanism to realize the weight of different neighbors. Besides, unlike the previous adjacency matrix, we dynamically count the number of unique exercises E_{uni} and the number of knowledge concepts C_{uni} based on all students in each batch size to construct an adjacency matrix $\boldsymbol{Adj}$. As a result, we can dynamically adjust the size of the adjacency matrix per batch to address the sparsity issue.

The exercise set is then represented by an embedding matrix $\boldsymbol{E} \in \mathbb{R}^{n \times 2d}$, where d is the dimension, and the knowledge concept set is represented by an embedding matrix $\boldsymbol{C} \in \mathbb{R}^{m \times 2d}$. We concatenate the exercise embedding and knowledge concept embedding corresponding to each batch's adjacency matrix. Finally, the input embedding and adjacency matrix are received using the original GAT network. Furthermore, we reconstitute the obtained output embedding into the batch's exercise sequence embedding via the id mapping relationship, and the final GAT output embedding is as follows:

$$g = \text{batchnorm}(\text{GAT}([\boldsymbol{E}_{\text{batch}}, \boldsymbol{C}_{\text{batch}}], \boldsymbol{Adj})). \tag{1}$$

The [,] is the operation that concatenates two vectors and $\boldsymbol{E}_{\text{batch}}$ and $\boldsymbol{C}_{\text{batch}}$ indicate the embeddings of unique exercises and knowledge concepts done by all students in the batch respectively.

Embedding Fusion. Inspired by IRT [2], GMEKT's input embedding takes the exercise sequence embedding output by GAT and the exercise's feature embedding with mean pooling can extract the latent meaning of both better than simple summation. Furthermore, we use a multi-layer perception to integrate the exercise feature embedding further. As a result, at time step t, we build the exercise embedding as follows:

$$e_t = \text{MeanPooling}(g_{et} + \omega_t \cdot (W_1^T f_t + b_1)). \tag{2}$$

The $g_{et} \in \mathcal{R}^d$ is the GAT exercise sequence embedding at time step t. $\omega_t \in \mathcal{R}^d$ is the feature embedding of exercise, $f_t \in \mathcal{R}^{2d}$ is the embedding that summarizes exercise information. The weight matrix is $W_1 \in \mathcal{R}^{2d \times d}$, and the bias term is $b_1 \in \mathcal{R}^d$. Then, for the answer a_t, which is either 0 or 1, we expand it to an all-zero or all-one vector $a_t \in \mathcal{R}^a$, where a is also a dimension. Finally, we concatenate them as x_t input vectors for our model, as shown in the exercise embedding of Fig. 2.

3.3   Student Knowledge State Update

Knowledge tracking is sequential for each step, and different exercises may have correlations. We use LSTM [6] to learn the students' knowledge state from the exercise input vectors to capture the change in students' knowledge state doing exercises. The following are the implementation specifics:

$$H_t = \text{LSTM}(x_t, \hat{H}_{t-1}), \tag{3}$$

where H_t and $\hat{H}_{t-1}$ represent students' knowledge state, the knowledge state output of the memory module at the previous time step respectively. We can get a vague estimation of students' knowledge state using LSTM. Furthermore, inspired by SA-convLSTM [8], we introduce a memory unit M and memory module in LSTM to simulate the changes of memory and knowledge state during students' learning process, allowing it to learn the accurate knowledge state of students and thus improve prediction accuracy.

Memory Module. To more accurately track the students' knowledge state and the changes in their memory units, we design a memory module to achieve this purpose. The input of the module is the previous time step's memory unit M_{t-1} and the current time step's knowledge state H_t. The CNN and self-attention are used to aggregate the features. Then, using a gating mechanism, Z and the original input H_t are used to update the memory. CNN is primarily used to extract the essential features of the current knowledge state and memory unit related to the knowledge involved in the exercise and can improve the model's expressive ability. Self-attention is used to extract the features of high importance in the current knowledge state. By multiplying the matrix between query Q_h and key K_m, the similarity score e_m between knowledge state embedding and memory unit embedding is calculated. All weights used for feature aggregation are obtained by the SoftMax function along each row:

$$e_m = Q_h^T K_m,$$

$$\alpha_{mij} = \frac{\exp(e_{mij})}{\sum_{K=1}^{N} \exp(e_{mij})}, i, j = 1, 2, ..., N. \tag{4}$$

Then, the i-th feature $\boldsymbol{Z}_m$ is calculated by a weighted sum across all N locations, which is defined as follow:

$$\boldsymbol{Z}_{mi} = \sum_{j=1}^{N} \alpha_{mij} \boldsymbol{W}_{mv} \boldsymbol{M}_{(t-1)j}, \tag{5}$$

where $\boldsymbol{M}_{(t-1)j}$ is the memory's j-th column and $\boldsymbol{Z}_h$ can be generated in the same way. Finally, with $\boldsymbol{Z} = \boldsymbol{W}_z[\boldsymbol{Z}_h, \boldsymbol{Z}_m]$, the aggregated feature $\boldsymbol{Z}$ can be obtained. Furthermore, we use a gating mechanism to update the memory unit so that it can capture long-term dependencies between exercise content and exercise order. The aggregated feature $\boldsymbol{Z}$ and the original input $\boldsymbol{H}_t$ are applied to the input gate i_t' and the fused feature g_t'. In addition, the forget gate is replaced with $1 - i_t'$ to reduce parameters. The following is the specifics of the updating process:

$$\begin{aligned} i_t' &= \sigma(\boldsymbol{W}_{zi}\boldsymbol{Z} + \boldsymbol{W}_{hi}\boldsymbol{H}_t + \boldsymbol{b}_i), \\ g_t' &= \tanh(\boldsymbol{W}_{zg}\boldsymbol{Z} + \boldsymbol{W}_{hg}\boldsymbol{H}_t + \boldsymbol{b}_g), \\ \boldsymbol{M}_t &= (1 - i_t') \circ \boldsymbol{M}_{t-1} + i_t' \circ g_t', \end{aligned} \tag{6}$$

where $\circ$ is the dot product. Finally, the memory module's output knowledge state $\hat{\boldsymbol{H}}_t$ is a dot product of the output gate o_t' and updated memory $\boldsymbol{M}_t$, which can be expressed as follows:

$$\begin{aligned} o_t' &= \sigma(\boldsymbol{W}_{zo}\boldsymbol{Z} + \boldsymbol{W}_{ho}\boldsymbol{H}_t + \boldsymbol{b}_o), \\ \hat{\boldsymbol{H}}_t &= o_t' \circ \boldsymbol{M}_t. \end{aligned} \tag{7}$$

3.4 Prediction

We predict the student's performance in the next exercise e_{t+1} using the student's knowledge state $\hat{\boldsymbol{H}}_t$ obtained from the memory module. We concatenate them first, then pass them through two layers of a fully connected network, ReLU, and dropout. Finally, we proceed through the sigmoid activation layer:

$$y_{t+1} = \sigma([\hat{\boldsymbol{H}}_t, e_{t+1}]). \tag{8}$$

To optimize our model, we choose the cross-entropy log loss to minimize the loss between the predicted correct answer probability $\hat{y}_t$ and the student's actual answer label y_t:

$$\mathcal{L} = -\sum_{t=1}^{T}(y_t \log \hat{y}_t + (1 - y_t)\log(1 - \hat{y}_t)). \tag{9}$$

4 Experiments

In this section, we conduct extensive experiments to evaluate our model's performance on four public datasets. To demonstrate the effectiveness of our added modules, we perform ablation experiments on the modules of our model. Finally, we further assess the performance of our model.

Table 1. Dataset statistics.

Dataset	ASSIST2009	ASSIST2012	ASSIST2017	EdNet-KT1
Students	3, 884	29, 018	1, 709	5, 000
Exercises	17, 737	53, 019	3, 162	12, 104
Concepts	123	265	102	189
Interactions	337, 559	2, 711, 813	942, 816	622, 421
Avg. length	81.19	93.45	551.68	111.69

4.1 Datasets

We assess our model's effectiveness using four real-world datasets (see Table 1) that are commonly used in KT tasks, all of which collect students' practice-answer history. The following are their specifics.

- **Assistments 2009(ASSIST2009)**[1] was came from ASSISTments online education platform during the school year 2009–2010.
- **Assistments 2012(ASSIST2012)**[2] was gathered from ASSISTments during the 2012–2013 school year, where each exercise is only related to one skill, but one skill corresponds to several exercises.
- **Assistments Challenge(ASSIST2017)**[3] was used in the ASSISTments data mining competition in 2017.
- **EdNet-KT1**[4] was collected by Choi *et al.* [3]. The entire dataset is massive, with 131,441,538 records and 784,309 students involved. So we take 5000 students from it and assign each exercise to more than one skill.

4.2 Baseline Model

GMEKT is compared to several state-of-the-art methods. The following are their specifics:

- **DKT** [17] leveraged recurrent neural network to assess student knowledge state. Moreover, we use LSTM to implement it.
- **DKVMN** [22] had a key matrix to store latent knowledge concepts and a dynamic value matrix to update the corresponding knowledge state.
- **DKT+** [13] was a variant of DKT [17], considering the impact of forgetting behavior to DKT.
- **SAKT** [15] introduced the self-attention model to capture the correlation of relevant exercises from previous interactions to make predictions.

---

[1] https://sites.google.com/site/assistmentsdata/home/assistment-2009-2010-data.
[2] https://sites.google.com/site/assistmentsdata/home/2012-13-school-data-with-afect.
[3] https://sites.google.com/view/assistmentsdatamining/dataset.
[4] http://ednet-leaderboard.s3-website-ap-northeast-1.amazonaws.com/.

- **GIKT** [21] used a graph convolutional network to capture exercise representations from the relation graph of exercise and knowledge concepts and a recap module to capture long-term dependencies.
- **AKT** [5] leveraged a monotonic attention mechanism to summarize learner performance and uses Rasch model to capture differences among exercises.
- **IEKT** [11] incorporated the learner characteristics into the model by considering learners' cognition levels and knowledge acquisition sensitivity.
- **COKT** [12] retrieved the sequences of peer students who have similar question-answering experiences to obtain the inter-student information and predict their correctness in answering questions.

Table 2. AUC and ACC values of all comparison methods on all datasets.

Method	ASSIST2009		ASSIST2012		ASSIST2017		EdNet-KT1	
	AUC	ACC	AUC	ACC	AUC	ACC	AUC	ACC
DKT [17]	0.7325	0.7148	0.7279	0.7354	0.7205	0.6901	0.6822	0.6875
DKVMN [22]	0.7318	0.7152	0.7236	0.7331	0.7102	0.6839	0.6745	0.6846
DKT+ [13]	0.7428	0.7183	0.7352	0.7313	0.7213	0.6917	0.7029	0.6933
SAKT [15]	0.6898	0.6861	0.7248	0.7383	0.6613	0.6705	0.6915	0.6935
GIKT [21]	0.7647	0.7283	0.7686	0.7503	0.7448	0.6989	0.7324	0.7013
AKT [5]	0.7665	0.7302	0.7694	0.7517	0.7582	0.7089	0.7366	0.7089
IEKT [11]	0.7573	0.7232	0.7371	0.7325	0.7489	0.7013	0.7356	0.7078
COKT [12]	0.7685	0.7329	0.7435	0.7385	0.7911	0.7339	0.7399	0.7102
GMEKT	**0.7791**	**0.7453**	**0.7795**	**0.7616**	**0.8178**	**0.7520**	**0.7467**	**0.7124**

4.3   Implementation Details

First, we set all input sequences to a fixed length of 100 for four public datasets, where longer-than-fixed-length sequences are divided into several short sequences, and the short sequences are filled with zero vectors for the fixed length. Besides, we removed the student's question whose sequence length is less than three from all datasets. Second, we chose the area under the receiver operating characteristic (ROC) curve (AUC) and Accuracy (ACC) as evaluation metrics, which are widely used in existing KT research. Finally, we set some necessary parameters. The hidden state dimension d of LSTM is 128 and answer's dimension a is 50, the batch size is 64, and all trainable parameters are optimized by Adam algorithm with a learning rate of 0.002, the self-attention dimension is 64, and GAT's hyper-parameters alpha is 0.003, dropout is 0.1 and n_heads is 2. We added a dropout layer with a dropout rate of 0.1 in the prediction module to prevent over-fitting. In addition, our exercise input embedding includes a dropout layer with 0.05 in feature embedding.

In our experiments, we used standard 5-fold cross-validation across four datasets in all methods. For each fold, 60%, 20%, and 20% of students are divided into the training set, validation set, and test set, respectively. The average result of all folds is regarded as the final result. All experiments are performed on a 14-core Intel Core i7-12700H CPU and an NVIDIA GeForce RTX 3080 Ti GPU (16G VRAM). In addition, this model is implemented with Pytorch and python 3.7.

4.4 Experimental Results

Our five-fold AUC and ACC average results are shown in Table 2. More specifically, our model outperforms other models by at least 0.68% in AUC, demonstrating its effectiveness.

On the ASSIST2017 dataset, our model outperforms other models significantly, including a 2.67% improvement in AUC and a 1.81% improvement in ACC over the state-of-the-art model. Since each student's exercise sequence in ASSIT2017 is relatively long, our model excels at capturing students' long historical learning interactions. In addition, our model's performance on the other three datasets is also better than existing approaches, verifying the effectiveness of the proposed model.

4.5 Ablation Study

We conduct ablation experiments on six variants of the model to validate the effects of the graph attention network, the new fusion method of GAT's exercise vector and feature vector, and the memory module in GMEKT. The details of these variants are shown in Table 3:

Table 3. Ablation study on four datasets.

Method	ASSIST2009		ASSIST2012		ASSIST2017		EdNet-KT1	
	AUC	ACC	AUC	ACC	AUC	ACC	AUC	ACC
GMEKT-RGM	0.7334	0.7151	0.7247	0.7308	0.7210	0.6912	0.7034	0.6910
GMEKT-RM	0.7469	0.7203	0.7365	0.7337	0.7382	0.6952	0.7145	0.6962
GMEKT-RGF	0.7605	0.7285	0.7402	0.7356	0.7866	0.7268	0.7318	0.7009
GMEKT-RG	0.7632	0.7301	0.7532	0.7441	0.7904	0.7310	0.7357	0.7048
GMEKT-RF	0.7668	0.7312	0.7683	0.7510	0.8033	0.7395	0.7397	0.7097
GMEKT-RMP	0.7727	0.7378	0.7746	0.7563	0.8155	0.7478	0.7450	0.7102
GMEKT	**0.7791**	**0.7453**	**0.7795**	**0.7616**	**0.8178**	**0.7520**	**0.7467**	**0.7124**

GMEKT-RGM(Remove Graph Attention Network and Memory Module) only uses the embedding vector mapped by the exercise id and uses LSTM to model the student's knowledge state.

GMEKT-RM (Remove Memory Module) removes the memory module and uses the fusion input of GAT's exercise vector and feature vector.

GMEKT-RGF (Remove Graph Attention Network and Feature embedding) removes the exercise feature vector and the GAT's exercise vector, only use the embedding vector mapped by the exercise ID.

GMEKT-RG (Remove Graph Attention Network) only uses the exercise feature vector as the input vector, which differs from the input of GMEKT-RGF.

GMEKT-RF (Remove Feature embedding) uses the GAT's exercise vector and the memory module, which removes the exercise feature vector.

GMEKT-RMP (Remove MeanPooling) uses GAT's exercise vector plus exercise feature vector as the input vector and uses the memory module.

Table 3 shows that our model GMEKT outperforms all variant models, proving that our added modules are practical. Furthermore, when the graph attention module is removed, GMEKT-RG and GMEKT-RGF drop by about 2%, demonstrating that our model can learn the exercise representation well. Second, after removing the memory module, we see a significant decrease, indicating that our proposed model can use the memory module to update students' knowledge state during the learning process effectively.

4.6   Length Analysis and Visualization

To investigate the effect of different fixed lengths on our model, we evaluate our method's performance with AKT and COKT on all datasets with four different lengths: 20, 50, 80, and 100 (see Fig. 3). Shorter learning sequences of students often determine that the model cannot learn better performance. When the length is 20, GMEKT can slightly outperform AKT and COKT. As the length increases, GMEKT can also maintain good performance. Clearly, GMEKT can better simulate students' knowledge states even in short learning sequences for better predictions with a certain application value.

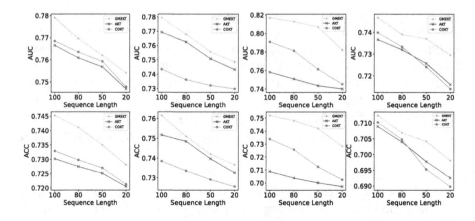

Fig. 3. Comparison results of the influence of sequence lengths on four datasets.

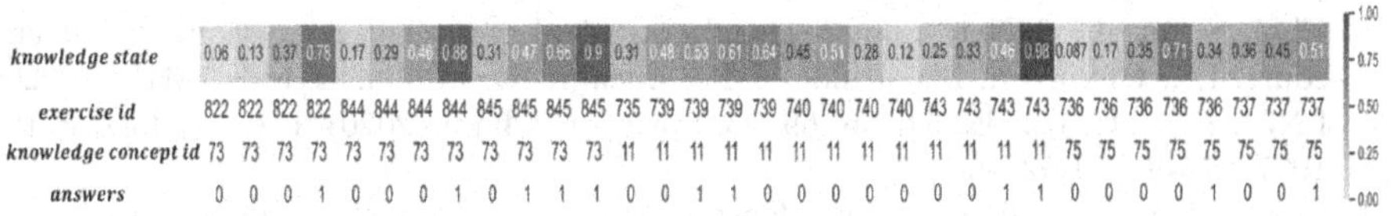

knowledge state	0.06 0.13 0.37 0.75 0.17 0.29 0.46 0.88 0.31 0.47 0.66 0.9 0.31 0.48 0.63 0.61 0.64 0.45 0.51 0.28 0.12 0.25 0.33 0.46 0.98 0.087 0.17 0.35 0.71 0.34 0.36 0.45 0.51
exercise id	822 822 822 822 844 844 844 844 845 845 845 845 735 739 739 739 739 740 740 740 740 743 743 743 743 736 736 736 736 736 737 737 737
knowledge concept id	73 73 73 73 73 73 73 73 73 73 73 73 11 11 11 11 11 11 11 11 11 11 11 11 11 75 75 75 75 75 75 75 75
answers	0 0 0 1 0 0 0 1 0 1 1 1 0 0 1 1 0 0 0 0 0 0 1 1 0 0 0 0 1 0 0 1

Fig. 4. Visualization cases of student's individualized knowledge tracing result.

We visualize the process of knowledge tracking for a student in Assistments2017 (see Fig. 4). Among them, 11 means multiplication, 73 means fractions, 75 means inequality-solving, and the probability in the knowledge state represents the student's mastery of the current exercise and knowledge concept. Students' grasp of knowledge concepts 73 may be under-performed due to the difficulty of the different exercises. In addition, we notice that the student's progress in mastering the deeper concepts of inequality-solving is slow, which shows that the student cannot understand the concepts proficiently.

5 Conclusion

This paper proposes Graph attention-based Memory-Enhanced Knowledge Tracing (GMEKT), a novel knowledge tracing model for modeling students' knowledge state and predicting student performance. We first use graph attention networks to obtain the exercise's embedding through dynamic adjacency matrix. A novel fusion approach is then used to improve the representation further. Besides, we present a memory module to model how students' knowledge states and memory states during the learning process. Experimental results show that GMEKT outperforms the state-of-the-art KT models.

In future work, we will continue to investigate better ways of representing the exercise's information. For example, we will also explore how the contrastive learning [7] can be further refined in the KT, which is an interesting question.

Acknowledgement. The works described in this paper are supported by The National Natural Science Foundation of China under Grant Nos. 61772210 and U1911201; Guangdong Province Universities Pearl River Scholar Funded Scheme (2018); The Project of Science and Technology in Guangzhou in China under Grant No. 202007040006.

References

1. Abdelrahman, G., Wang, Q.: Knowledge tracing with sequential key-value memory networks. In: Proceedings of the 42nd International ACM SIGIR Conference on Research and Development in Information Retrieval, pp. 175–184 (2019)
2. Ebbinghaus, H.: Memory: a contribution to experimental psychology. Ann. Neurosci. **20**(4), 155 (2013)

3. Choi, Y., et al.: EdNet: a large-scale hierarchical dataset in education. In: Bittencourt, I.I., Cukurova, M., Muldner, K., Luckin, R., Millán, E. (eds.) AIED 2020. LNCS (LNAI), vol. 12164, pp. 69–73. Springer, Cham (2020). https://doi.org/10.1007/978-3-030-52240-7_13

4. Corbett, A.T., Anderson, J.R.: Knowledge tracing: modeling the acquisition of procedural knowledge. User Model. User Adapt. Interact. **4**(4), 253–278 (1994)

5. Ghosh, A., Heffernan, N., Lan, A.S.: Context-aware attentive knowledge tracing. In: Proceedings of the 26th ACM SIGKDD International Conference on Knowledge Discovery and Data Mining, pp. 2330–2339 (2020)

6. Hochreiter, S., Schmidhuber, J.: Long short-term memory. Neural Comput. **9**(8), 1735–1780 (1997)

7. Lee, W., Chun, J., Lee, Y., Park, K., Park, S.: Contrastive learning for knowledge tracing. In: The World Wide Web Conference, pp. 2330–2338 (2022)

8. Li, B., Tang, B., Deng, L., Zhao, M.: Self-attention ConvLSTM and its application in RUL prediction of rolling bearings. IEEE Trans. Instrum. Meas. **70**, 1–11 (2021)

9. Liu, Q., Shen, S., Huang, Z., Chen, E., Zheng, Y.: A survey of knowledge tracing. arXiv preprint arXiv:2105.15106 (2021)

10. Liu, Q., et al.: Exploiting cognitive structure for adaptive learning. In: Proceedings of the 25th ACM SIGKDD International Conference on Knowledge Discovery and Data Mining, pp. 627–635 (2019)

11. Long, T., Liu, Y., Shen, J., Zhang, W., Yu, Y.: Tracing knowledge state with individual cognition and acquisition estimation. In: Proceedings of the 44th International ACM SIGIR Conference on Research and Development in Information Retrieval, pp. 173–182 (2021)

12. Long, T., et al.: Improving knowledge tracing with collaborative information. In: Proceedings of the Fifteenth ACM International Conference on Web Search and Data Mining, pp. 599–607 (2022)

13. Nagatani, K., Zhang, Q., Sato, M., Chen, Y.Y., Chen, F., Ohkuma, T.: Augmenting knowledge tracing by considering forgetting behavior. In: The World Wide Web Conference, pp. 3101–3107 (2019)

14. Nakagawa, H., Iwasawa, Y., Matsuo, Y.: Graph-based knowledge tracing: modeling student proficiency using graph neural network. In: 2019 IEEE/WIC/ACM International Conference on Web Intelligence (WI), pp. 156–163. ACM (2019)

15. Pandey, S., Karypis, G.: A self-attentive model for knowledge tracing. In: Proceedings of the 12th International Conference on Educational Data Mining, pp. 384–389 (2019)

16. Pavlik Jr, P.I., Cen, H., Koedinger, K.R.: Performance factors analysis-a new alternative to knowledge tracing. In: International Conference on Artificial Intelligence in Education, pp. 531–538 (2009)

17. Piech, C., et al.: Deep knowledge tracing. In: Advances in Neural Information Processing Systems, pp. 505–513 (2015)

18. Velickovic, P., Cucurull, G., Casanova, A., Romero, A., Lio, P., Bengio, Y.: Graph attention networks. In: 6th International Conference on Learning Representations, ICLR. OpenReview.net (2018)

19. Vie, J.J., Kashima, H.: Knowledge tracing machines: factorization machines for knowledge tracing. In: Proceedings of the AAAI Conference on Artificial Intelligence, vol. 33, pp. 750–757 (2019)

20. Wu, Z., Pan, S., Chen, F., Long, G., Zhang, C., Philip, S.Y.: A comprehensive survey on graph neural networks. IEEE Trans. Neural Netw. Learn. Syst. **32**(1), 4–24 (2020)

21. Yang, Y., et al.: GIKT: a graph-based interaction model for knowledge tracing. In: Hutter, F., Kersting, K., Lijffijt, J., Valera, I. (eds.) ECML PKDD 2020. LNCS (LNAI), vol. 12457, pp. 299–315. Springer, Cham (2021). https://doi.org/10.1007/978-3-030-67658-2_18

22. Zhang, J., Shi, X., King, I., Yeung, D.Y.: Dynamic key-value memory networks for knowledge tracing. In: The World Wide Web Conference, pp. 765–774 (2017)

Dual-VIE: Dual-Level Graph Attention Network for Visual Information Extraction

Junwei Zhang, Hao Wang$^{(\boxtimes)}$, and Xiangfeng Luo

School of Computer Engineering and Science, Shanghai University, Shanghai, China
wang-hao@shu.edu.cn

Abstract. Visual Information Extraction (VIE) is a task to extract key information from document images such as waybills and receipts. Existing methods typically combine multi-modal information including textual, visual, layout features and achieve promising results on datasets in various domains. However, previous methods treat the VIE task as a token-level sequence labelling problem and have not explicitly modelled the relationship between bounding boxes. VIE heavily depends on the context, especially the relationship between key-value pairs. To address this problem, in this paper, we propose a dual-level graph attention model that combines coarse-grained and fine-grained information. At the fine-grained token level, we force the graph attention network to focus on its local token neighbours within a bounding box. At the coarse-grained bounding box level, we encourage further information interaction between bounding boxes and pay more attention to the potential key-value pairs. To the best of our knowledge, our method may be the first attempt to jointly model the correlation between bounding boxes and tokens under a unified fine-tuning framework. Experimental results show that the proposed method significantly surpasses previous methods. Compared to the strong baseline LayoutLM, our method improves the F1-score by about 3% on both datasets. Our method is an important complement to existing VIE methods.

Keywords: Visually rich documents · Layout modeling · Graph attention network

1 Introduction

Visual Information Extraction (VIE) aims to extract key information from document images (waybills, invoices) rather than plain text. However, the diversity of document formats and layouts makes it difficult for machines to understand the document contexts. In VIE, textual information [1], visual information [2] and layout information [3] are critical to the understanding of a document.

Currents VIE systems simply treat the VIE task as a sequential tagging or classification problem and implement it through the named entity (NER) [4]

© The Author(s), under exclusive license to Springer Nature Switzerland AG 2022
S. Khanna et al. (Eds.): PRICAI 2022, LNCS 13629, pp. 422–434, 2022.
https://doi.org/10.1007/978-3-031-20862-1_31

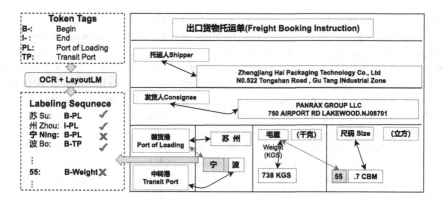

Fig. 1. An example shows the extraction error of the vanilla LayoutLM model used for visual information extraction on the Freight-BI dataset. Freight-BIs are often written in Chinese and English and the positions of text blocks are flexible and not fixed. Keys of entities are labeled with green boxes, values of entities are labeled with blue boxes, and key-value pairs are labeled with bidirectional arrows. LayoutLM models predict token labels in a sequential processing manner. Therefore, they are susceptible to overfitting, as the model may rely more on token-level spatial and semantic associations. (Color figure online)

framework. However, treating the document content as a simple linear sequence loses most of the valuable non-sequential information of the document (e.g., location, visual, layout). The main challenge for VIE is to effectively extract the textual, layout, and visual features of a document and obtain key and value representations with richer non-textual information. [1,5–7] modeled the layout structure of documents by using graph convolutional networks. These methods have achieved superior results by considering visual features. However, most previous methods are limited to model token-level semantic and spatial associations. For example, LayoutLM models [8] predict token labels in a sequential processing manner, more relying on spatial and semantic associations between tokens. They have not noticed that the layout information between bounding boxes might be an important clue for the inference of the relationship between key-value pairs. As shown in Fig. 1, the recognition of the value of "Port of Loading" and "Transit Port" is difficult, since the document may contain similar text fragments both in format and in semantic (e.g., "Port of origin" and "Port of discharge", the values of weight and volume/size), it raises the ambiguity which is difficult to distinguish. Therefore, token-level layout and visual features might be not sufficient to distinguish between the value of "Port of Loading" and "Transit Port".

In our preliminary experiments, we find that studying the correlation between keys and values, i.e., bounding-box-level layout features, may be enhance the VIE task concerning the following observations and considerations: (1) Text in document images usually appears as key-value pairs. If the corresponding value for a particular key can be found, the class can be determined naturally. (2) The value corresponding to a key usually appears on the lower or right side of the key. (3) Although there may be multiple similar texts in a document image (e.g., shipper's address, recipient's address, weight and volume), the spatial relationship between keys and values are strong hint which can help the model make prediction. (4) Considering the bounding-level positional relationship between keys and values can significantly simplify the learning process of the model.

In this paper, we propose a dual-level graph attention network framework, which captures both the coarse- and fine-grained multi-modal information, including textual, visual and spatial features at the same time. In addition, our model pays more attention to key-value pair candidates by using a k-nearest-neighbour (KNN) graph network. The main contributions of our research are summarized as follows:

- We propose a dual-level graph attention network that can effectively model the token- and bounding-box-level multi-modal information. The model can also capture the correlation between keys and values using k-nearest-neighbour (KNN) graph network.
- For each granularity, our approach can effectively fuse multi-modal features (including text, visual, layout and entity relevance), bringing significant accuracy improvements and surpassing existing methods.
- We manually annotated a freight booking instruction dataset containing more than 4,500 images and more than 20 categories with the help of OCR tools. The code of the proposed method and the dataset will be made public later.

2   Related Work

Traditional approaches extract key information based on feature engineering. However, this approach [3,9] uses only text and location information and requires the construction of complex feature engineering. Rule-based approaches rely heavily on predefined templates or rules, require much effort, and are not scalable for most document understanding problems because of the complex and diverse forms of real-life document layouts. Most modern approaches treat VIE as a sequential labelling problem. It is much more difficult for a machine to distinguish classes of entities from complex documents without ambiguity than for a typical NER task. One of the main reasons is that frameworks, such as BIL-STM+CRF, only operate on plain text and do not combine visual information with document layout information to obtain a richer feature representation.

Recently, several studies in the VIE task have attempted to take full advantage of features not yet exploited in complex documents. A study proposed Convolutional Universal Text Information Extractor (CUTIE) [10]. CUTIE treats the document understanding task as an image semantic segmentation task. A grid is created, and the text is placed in cells corresponding to the position of the text in the image. The goal is to extract useful information using the position and content of the text. However, this work uses only text features and does not involve image features. Although [2,11] uses images for feature extraction, it only focuses on image features and does not consider text features.

Inspired by BERT [8,12] proposed the LayoutLM approach. It applies the architecture of BERT to pre-trained models for text and layout on many documents and incorporates visual features. Similar to LayoutLM, [13] proposes the LAMBERT model. Although the above two pre-trained language models for document processing perform well in several downstream tasks, they only considers the relationship between all tokens in a document. They does not consider the potential relationship between two text segments, which is crucial for extracting key information in VIE.

Due to the great success of graphical neural networks [14,15] in unstructured data tasks, more and more research is focused on using GNN to solve the problem of document structure modelling and improve document understanding. In [1,5–7,16] GNN are used to model the layout information of a document. With the messages passed between nodes, the model can understand the general layout of each document, which helps in subsequent entity extraction. [17] proposed a lexicon-based graphical neural network that treats Chinese NER (named entity recognition) as a node classification task. Moreover, the models proposed by [1], and [5] model the document layout structure by GNN and finally input to a BiLSTM CRF model for decoding, which, although proved to be effective, however, both of them only used textual features and did not use visual features. In [1], each node in the graph is connected to the remaining nodes, so the graph convolution aggregates useless and redundant information between the nodes and introduces noise. Unlike fully connected graphs, [6] predicts the connections between nodes by graph learning and dynamically updates the parameters of the adjacency matrix, which also improves the results. Although the above graph-based methods have all achieved good results, these methods using GNN to encode textual and visual information are hardly guaranteed to learn the relationships between key-value pairs well. However, our method explicitly learns the relationship between key-value pairs between bounding boxes, which in turn improves the effectiveness of VIE.

3 Proposed Model

In this section, we will describe our proposed method in detail. Our method considers the bounding-box-level and the token-level textual and visual features at the same time when encoding the node representation of the graph. Then, the nodes are aggregated by constructing a position-based matrix and a feature similarity-based matrix to assign different weights to the features of neighbouring nodes so that the graph convolution can better learn the embedding representation of bounding box nodes. Finally, we employ a decoder part with BILSTM and CRF to predict labels.

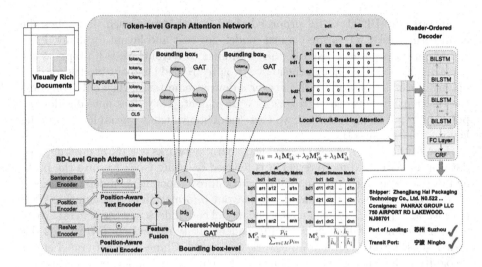

Fig. 2. Our Dual-Level graph attention network using both coarse- and fine-grained layout information.

3.1 Token-Level Graph Attention Network

To obtain token-level features, we employ LayoutLM to generate token-level representations which contains semantic, layout, and visual information (Fig. 2).

Universal Multi-modal Encoder. The LayoutLM model is used as the backbone network to extract the fused multi-modal features. Given a document $D = \{bd_1, bd_2, \ldots, bd_M\}$, where bd_i denotes the i-th bounding box. $L = \{l_1, l_2, \ldots, l_M\}$, l_i stands for the number of tokens in the i-th bounding box after performing tokenization using a Bert Tokenizer. The i-th bounding box that contains l_i tokens can be represented as:

$$bd_i = W_{1:N}[start : start + l_i - 1] = \{w_{start}, \ldots, w_j, \ldots, w_{start+l_i}\}, 1 \le i \le n \tag{1}$$

$$start = \sum_{i'=1}^{i'=i-1} l_{i'}, 1 \le i \le n \tag{2}$$

Namely, w_j stands for the j-th token in bd_i; $start$ is the index of the start token in bd_i. Then, the initial token embeddings are obtained by using the LayoutLM encoder. We encode document D regardless of bounding box boundaries as follows:

$$H_{0:n} = LayoutLM(W_{0:N}) = LayoutLM([CLS]||bd_1|| \ldots ||bd_M) \tag{3}$$

where $||$ indicates the concatenation operation on all text blocks, and H_0 indicates an special document embeddings at the $[CLS]$ position. Then, we collect all token embeddings generated by LayoutLM with respect to the indices of tokens in the document.

Local Circuit-Breaking Attention. Given a graph $G = (V, E)$, G represents an bounding box, in which $v_j \in V$ and $j \in \{1, 2, ..., n\}$. v_j denotes a node (token) in the bounding box. To force the graph attention network focus on its local neighbourhood, we facilitates token correlations within the bounding box using the Circuit-Breaking mechanism. For each bounding box, we encourage the interaction between the tokens inside the bounding box while prevent information passing from the outside bounding boxes. This results in a fully-connected subgraph for each bounding box. $e_{j\tilde{j}}$ denotes an edge between tokens v_j and $v_{\tilde{j}}$, which is computed as

$$
e_{j\tilde{j}} = \begin{cases} 1, & \text{if } v_j \in bd_i \quad \text{and} \quad v_{\tilde{j}} \in bd_i \\ 0, & \text{if } v_j \notin bd_i \quad \text{or} \quad v_{\tilde{j}} \notin bd_i \end{cases} \tag{4}
$$

which means that token nodes in the current bounding box are connected, but none of them are connected with any token out of the current bounding box.

Graph Convolution. For all tokens, we perform graph convolution with the Circuit-Breaking attention:

$$
h_j^{(t+1)} = \delta(\sum_{\tilde{j}=1}^{N} \alpha_{j\tilde{j}} W h_{\tilde{j}}^{(t)} \otimes e_{j\tilde{j}}) \tag{5}
$$

where $h_j^{(t+1)}$ is the aggregation and update of $h_j^{(t)}$. $h_{\tilde{j}}$ is the hidden state of node v_j's neighbour $v_{\tilde{j}}$. $\otimes$ is denotes the operation of element-wise multiplication. δ is an activation function and $\alpha_{j\tilde{j}}$ is the attention coefficient which indicates the importance of node j to node $\tilde{j}$. The coefficients is computed by:

$$
\alpha_{j\tilde{j}} = \frac{exp(\delta(V^T[W h_j \oplus W h_k]))}{\sum_{n \in N} exp(\delta(V^T[W h_j \oplus W h_n]))} \tag{6}
$$

3.2 BD-Level Graph Attention Network

Position-Aware Text Encoder. Since the document presents the text content in a 2D structure, it is necessary to encode the text given its layout information. Following LayoutLM, we normalize and discretize all coordinates to integers in the range $[0, 1000]$. Then, we use two positional embedding layers to encode x-axis features and y-axis features, respectively. Given the normalized position features of the i-th bounding box $bd_i - < x_0, x_1, y_0, y_1, w, h >$, where w is the horizontal length and h is the vertical length of bd_i, respectively. Then, we pass six position features through the two layout embedding layers. Finally, the encoded embeddings are aggregated to construct the 2D layout embedding p_i

$$
p_i = [Emb_x(x_0, x_1, w) \,||\, Emb_y(y_0, y_1, h)], 1 \le i \le t \tag{7}
$$

where $\|$ indicates a concatenation operation. Emb_x and Emb_y are two position embedding layers regarding to x-axis and y-axis. To generate BD-text representations, we use a pre-trained SentenceBert model [18] to encode the plain texts into parallel vectors. Compared to Bert, SentenceBert can generate semantically-rich sentence embeddings. The final sentence embedding is computed by combining the SentenceBert embeddings with projected position embeddings via an affine transformation $Proj$ as follows:

$$S_i = SentenceBert(bd_i) + Proj(p_i), 1 \le i \le t \tag{8}$$

Position-Aware Visual Encoder. Given a document image I, scaled to 224×224, we extract visual features from the entire image using a visual encoder with ResNet [19] inside as the backbone network. Then, we extract the region of interest (ROI) using the $ROIAlign$ operation based on the coordinates of the bounding box. The process of visual feature extraction for the i-th bounding box can be represented as:

$$V_i = ROIAlign[ResNet(I), bd_i] + Proj(p_i), 1 \le i \le t \tag{9}$$

Feature Fusion. The bounding box features of the nodes in the final BD-level graph are added as follows:

$$\tilde{h}_i = \sigma(S_i \oplus V_i), 1 \le i \le t \tag{10}$$

where σ is an activation function and $\oplus$ denotes the concatenation operator.

Spatial Distance Matrix. To enhance the information interaction between keys within the potential key-value pairs candidates, and reduce the interference between different key-value pairs, we construct the adjacency matrix $\mathbf{M}^p \in \mathbb{R}^{T \times T}$ based on the Euclidean distance between the bounding boxes. For all nodes adjacent to node i, M is the number of bounding boxes in a document. $p_{i\tilde{i}}$ denotes the Euclidean distance between nodes i and $\tilde{i}$. $\mathbf{M}^p_{i\tilde{i}}$ denotes the Euclidean distance between node i and node $\tilde{i}$ after normalization:

$$\mathbf{M}^p_{i\tilde{i}} = \frac{p_{i\tilde{i}}}{\sum_{m \in M} p_{im}} \quad \text{w.r.t.} \quad p_{i\tilde{i}} = \frac{exp(-p_{i\tilde{i}})}{\sum_{m \in M} exp(-p_{im})} \tag{11}$$

Semantic Similarity Matrix. Analogously, M^q denotes the Spatial Distance Matrix, the semantic matrix $\mathbf{M}^q \in \mathbb{R}^{T \times T}$ based on feature similarity. The elements in $\mathbf{M}^p$ contiguously update during the learning of graph neural network. M^q_{ij} denotes the feature similarity of node i and node $\tilde{i}$:

$$\mathbf{M}^q_{i\tilde{i}} = \frac{\tilde{h}_i \cdot \tilde{h}_{\tilde{i}}}{\left\| \tilde{h}_i \right\| \cdot \left\| \tilde{h}_{\tilde{i}} \right\|} \tag{12}$$

K-Nearest-Neighbour Graph Attention Network. Differing from previous work [1] that they build a fully connected graph neural network, we porpose a K-Nearest-Neighbour (KNN) graph attention layer by cascading a self-attention layer to focus only on its neighbour nodes, especially for key nodes. We use four nearest nodes. Graph convolution is formulated using the four-headed scaled-dot attention. Given a node v_i and encoder representation $\tilde{h}_i$ after feature fusion, the output of each layer can be represented as:

$$\tilde{h}_i^{(t+1)} = \delta(\sum_{k \in Nt(M,i,K)} \gamma_{ik} W \tilde{h}_k^{(t)}) \tag{13}$$

where v_k stands for one of the neighbour nodes of v_i. $Nt(M, i, K)$ is the set of the indices of the K-nearest neighbour nodes for v_i. $\gamma_{ik} = \lambda_1 \mathbf{M}_{ik}^r + \lambda_2 \mathbf{M}_{ik}^p + \lambda_3 \mathbf{M}_{ik}^q$, $\lambda_1, \lambda_2, \lambda_3$ satisfying: $\lambda_1 + \lambda_2 + \lambda_3 = 1$, $\mathbf{M}_{ik}^p \in \mathbf{M}^p, \mathbf{M}_{ik}^q \in \mathbf{M}^q$, are the two matrices constructed as mentioned above. $\tilde{h}_k^{(t)}$ is the hidden layer representation of the neighboring nodes of node v_k at the time step t. $\tilde{h}_i^{(t+1)}$ sums up the neighboring node features as well as its own features. W is a linear layer and δ is an activation function. Following [20], we also use multi-headed attention to improve the model's performance. The coefficient of $\mathbf{M}_{i\tilde{i}}$ for arbitrary $\tilde{i}$ to i can be expressed as:

$$\mathbf{M}_{ik}^r = \frac{exp(\delta(V^T[W\tilde{h}_i \oplus W\tilde{h}_k]))}{\sum_{m \in M} exp(\delta(V^T[W\tilde{h}_i \oplus W\tilde{h}_m]))} \tag{14}$$

δ is a LeakyReLU function. W and V variables are trainable parameters. The representations at different graph convolution layers are concatenated to form the final representation. For each token, we stitch coarse-grained BD-level graph embeddings, fine-grained token-level graph embeddings, and LayoutLM embeddings.

$$\vec{H}_{0:n} = \vec{w}_{0:n} \oplus \vec{h}_{0:n} \oplus \vec{\tilde{h}}_{0:n} \tag{15}$$

3.3   Reader-Ordered Decoder

In our preliminary experiments, we found that the reading order, which controls the sequence in which the content is presented to the user, has a great influence on the VIE performance. Thus, it is necessary to model the order of bounding boxes. To utilize the order information of OCR sequences, we feed the outputs $\vec{H}_{0:n}$ into the standard BiLSTM-CRF layer.

$$z_{1:n} = BiLSTM(\vec{H}_{1:n}; 0, \theta_{lstm}) \tag{16}$$

where $\vec{z}_j \in \mathbb{R}^{n \times d}$ is obtained by splicing the features of the three components mentioned above.

A conditional random field (CRF) is used to generate a family of conditional probability for the sequence. Given the tokenwise sequence of final states

$z_{1:n}^{final} = \left[z_1^{final}, z_2^{final}, \ldots, z_n^{final} \right]$, and the probability disritibution of a label $\hat{y} = \left[\hat{l}_1, \hat{l}_2 \ldots, \hat{l}_n \right]$ sequence can be defined as the follows:

$$p(\hat{y} \mid z) = \frac{exp(\sum_{i=1}^n W_{(l_{i-1},l_i)} z_i^{final} + b_{(l_{i-1},l_i)})}{\sum_{y' \in Y(s)} exp(\sum_{i=1}^n W_{(l'_{i-1},l'_i)} z_i^{final} + b_{(l'_{i-1},l'_i)})} \tag{17}$$

where W and b are the weight and bias parameters and $\hat{Y}$ are the set of all arbitrary label sequences. Decoding of CRF layer is to search the output sequence y^* having the highest conditional probability for testing. Our model parameters of whole networks are jointly trained by minimizing the following loss function:

$$y^* = \underset{y \in \hat{Y}}{argmax} - \sum_{i=1}^n log(p(y_i \mid z_i)) \tag{18}$$

4   Experiments

4.1   Datasets

We conducted experiments on two real-world datasets, FUNSD and Freight-BI. The FUNSD dataset is a widely-used public dataset to evaluate VIE models. Their statistics are presented in Table 1. Note that the layout divergence of these two datasets is very large.

Table 1. Statistics of training and testing datasets used in this paper. We also give the averaged number and the standard derivation with respect to the counts of keys, values, bounding boxes and tokens.

Dataset	Training	Testing	Entities	Key	Value	BD	Token
FUNSD	149	50	4	17.8 ± 14.4	21.7 ± 12.1	47.9 ± 26.3	234.4 ± 104.7
Freight-BI	3,375	1,125	20	18.7 ± 28.2	26.5 ± 8.9	71.6 ± 28.2	441.0 ± 213.7

FUNSD [21] is a dataset for understanding forms in noisy scanned documents. It consists of 199 accurate, complete, scanned form images with annotations. The dataset is divided into 149 training samples and 50 test samples, which has 4 entities to extract (i.e., Question, Answer, Header and Other).

Freight Booking Instruction (Freight-BI) dataset consists of 4500 images of shipping bills and contains 20 types of entities. Examples include consignor, consignee, date, address, phone number, etc. The layout is complex and varied, with no fixed template. There is much noise in the documents, including the fact that the bottom of the waybill usually contains complexly formatted sub-tables and many fields with similar content but different semantics in it.

4.2   Implementation Details

Networks Setting. The model is trained from using the Adam optimizer with a learning rate of 0.0005. The feature extractor for catching image features is implemented by ResNet-101, we set the number of graph convolution layers to 2 and 8 heads for the multi-head attention. We use the text-lines which have already been annotated in the datasets as the text segments.

Label Generation. For the Freight Booking Instruction, with the help of the OCR annotation tool, the coordinates of each bounding box are annotated, and each bounding box is annotated with predefined entity types. We have predefined 20 entity types, including shipper and consignee address, consignee phone, port of origin, etc. For the FUNSD data, the corresponding annotation files have been provided. For the above two datasets, we use BIO annotation for the token in the text of each bounding box.

4.3   Baseline Method

In order to verify the performance of our proposed method, we compared the performance of the model with the baseline models: Bert [12], BERT-CRF [22] Bert+BILSTM+CRF, BERT+ResNet, BERT+ResNet+BILSTM+CRF, LAMBERT [13], LAMBERT+ResNet, LAMBERT+ResNet+BILSTM+CRF, LayoutLM [8]. ResNet is used to extract visual features. Where + indicates model combination (Figs. 3 and 4).

Table 2. Precession(Prec), Recall(Rec), F1-score performance comparisons from FUNSD and Freight-BI datasets.

Method	FUNSD			Freight-BI		
	Prec	Rec	F1	Prec	Rec	F1
BERT	45.61	59.14	51.50	63.46	69.30	66.26
BERT+CRF	46.74	59.14	65.26	65.85	71.91	68.75
BERT+BILSTM+CRF	50.06	57.71	55.61	67.61	70.57	69.06
BERT+ResNet	47.32	61.98	53.67	67.75	72.54	72.07
BERT+ResNet+BILSTM+CRF	55.40	57.90	56.62	69.43	77.74	77.29
LAMBERT	41.47	52.57	46.37	75.56	83.34	79.42
LAMBERT+ResNet	44.09	57.67	49.97	78.41	86.09	82.07
LAMBERT+ResNet+BILSTM+CRF	51.31	60.15	55.38	82.44	87.67	84.77
LayoutLM	77.51	83.56	80.42	83.92	87.22	85.54
Dual-VIE	**83.17**	**83.75**	**83.46**	**86.59**	**90.57**	**88.54**

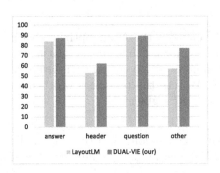

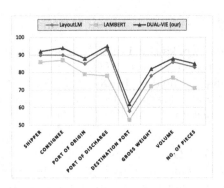

Fig. 3. Comparison of state-of-the-art models in terms of F1-score for FUNSD categories.

Fig. 4. Comparison of state-of-the-art models in terms of F1-score on the Freight-BI categories.

Table 3. Ablation studies of individual component.

Model	FUNSD	Freight-BI
full model	**83.46**	**88.54**
w/o token-level CB-GAT	82.68	87.80
w/o BD-level KNN-GAT	82.80	87.72
w/o Reader-ordered	82.64	87.63

Results on Two Dataset. As shown in Table 2, higher performance is achieved with the introduction of graphical features compared to the traditional information extraction method using only text. It is worth noting that in the LAMBERT paper, image features are not considered, and in our experiments, the model effect is greatly improved after adding image features. LAMBERT does not work too well in FUNSD dataset, probably because of the size of the dataset. Meanwhile, LayoutLM achieves a better performance when using text, layout and image information simultaneously. Our method achieves best results and outperforms LayoutLM by significant margins (3.02% on FUNSD dataset, 3% on Freight-BI dataset) due to consideration of different granularity features.

Ablation Studies. As shown in Table 3, we analyzed the impact of each component of the model on the model results, including the token granularity graph neural network, bounding box granularity graph neural network and Reader-ordered. We set the change in the F1 value of the model when these three modules are not considered. Without the token granularity graph neural network, the model is not good enough to carry out the information interaction between tokens within a bounding box, the result drops to the F1 score of 0.78 on FUNSD dataset and 0.74 on Freight-BI dataset. Since the bounding box granularity graph neural network can model the relationship between key-value pairs. Without it, the result drops to the F1 score of 0.66 on FUNSD dataset and 0.82 on Freight-BI dataset. Without Reader-ordered constraint on label prediction, the result drops to the F1 score of 0.82 on FUNSD dataset and 0.91 on Freight-BI dataset.

5 Conclusion

This paper propose a novel dual-level graph neural network model for visual information extraction. The model leverages both token-level and bounding-box-level layout information to extract keys and values. We investigate the proper way to aggregate textual, visual and positional features at each granularity. Furthermore, our model can focus on the potential key-value pair candidates. Experiment results on two VIE datasets show that coarse-grained spaitial information is important for VIE tasks, especially for the documents with complex layouts as in the Freight-BI dataset. This study provides a novel perspective for extracting structural information from documents. In future research, we will consider features such as font size and color in visually rich documents to enhance model performance.

Acknowledgement. The research reported in this paper was supported in part by the Shanghai Science and Technology Young Talents Sailing Program Grant 21YF1413900; Shanghai Municipal Science and Technology Committee of Shanghai Outstanding Academic Leaders Plan 20XD1401700; National Key Research and Development Program of China 2021YFC3300602.

References

1. Liu, X., Gao, F., Zhang, Q., Zhao, H.: Graph convolution for multimodal information extraction from visually rich documents. In: Proceedings of the 2019 Conference of the North American Chapter of the Association for Computational Linguistics: Human Language Technologies, Volume 2 (Industry Papers), pp. 32–39 (2019)
2. Katti, A.R., et al.: Chargrid: Towards understanding 2D documents. In: Proceedings of the 2018 Conference on Empirical Methods in Natural Language Processing, pp. 4459–4469 (2018)
3. Simon, A., Pret, J.C., Johnson, A.P.: A fast algorithm for bottom-up document layout analysis, vol. 19, pp. 273–277. IEEE (1997)
4. Lample, G., Ballesteros, M., Subramanian, S., Kawakami, K., Dyer, C.: Neural architectures for named entity recognition. In: Proceedings of NAACL-HLT, pp. 260–270 (2016)
5. Qian, Y., Santus, E., Jin, Z., Guo, J., Barzilay, R.: Graphie: a graph-based framework for information extraction. In: Proceedings of NAACL-HLT, pp. 751–761 (2019)
6. Yu, W., Lu, N., Qi, X., Gong, P., Xiao, R.: Pick: processing key information extraction from documents using improved graph learning-convolutional networks. In: 2020 25th International Conference on Pattern Recognition (ICPR). pp. 4363–4370. IEEE (2021)

7. Gal, R., Ardazi, S., Shilkrot, R.: Cardinal graph convolution framework for document information extraction. In: Proceedings of the ACM Symposium on Document Engineering 2020, pp. 1–11 (2020)

8. Xu, Y., Li, M., Cui, L., Huang, S., Wei, F., Zhou, M.: Layoutlm: pre-training of text and layout for document image understanding. In: Proceedings of the 26th ACM SIGKDD International Conference on Knowledge Discovery & Data Mining, pp. 1192–1200 (2020)

9. Schuster, D., et al.: Intellix-end-user trained information extraction for document archiving. In: 2013 12th International Conference on Document Analysis and Recognition, pp. 101–105. IEEE (2013)

10. Zhao, X., Niu, E., Wu, Z., Wang, X.: Cutie: learning to understand documents with convolutional universal text information extractor. arXiv e-prints pp. arXiv-1903 (2019)

11. Guo, H., Qin, X., Liu, J., Han, J., Liu, J., Ding, E.: Eaten: Entity-aware attention for single shot visual text extraction. In: 2019 International Conference on Document Analysis and Recognition (ICDAR), pp. 254–259. IEEE (2019)

12. Kenton, J.D.M.W.C., Toutanova, L.K.: Bert: pre-training of deep bidirectional transformers for language understanding. In: Proceedings of NAACL-HLT, pp. 4171–4186 (2019)

13. Garncarek, Ł., et al.: LAMBERT: layout-aware language modeling for information extraction. In: Lladós, J., Lopresti, D., Uchida, S. (eds.) ICDAR 2021. LNCS, vol. 12821, pp. 532–547. Springer, Cham (2021). https://doi.org/10.1007/978-3-030-86549-8_34

14. Kipf, T.N., Welling, M.: Semi-supervised classification with graph convolutional networks. arXiv preprint arXiv:1609.02907 (2016)

15. Velickovic, P., Cucurull, G., Casanova, A., Romero, A., Lio, P., Bengio, Y.: Graph attention networks. Stat **1050**, 20 (2017)

16. Cheng, M., Qiu, M., Shi, X., Huang, J., Lin, W.: One-shot text field labeling using attention and belief propagation for structure information extraction. In: Proceedings of the 28th ACM International Conference on Multimedia, pp. 340–348 (2020)

17. Gui, T., et al.: A lexicon-based graph neural network for Chinese NER. In: Proceedings of the 2019 Conference on Empirical Methods in Natural Language Processing and the 9th International Joint Conference on Natural Language Processing (EMNLP-IJCNLP), pp. 1040–1050 (2019)

18. Reimers, N., Gurevych, I.: Sentence-Bert: sentence embeddings using Siamese Bert-networks. In: Proceedings of the 2019 Conference on Empirical Methods in Natural Language Processing and the 9th International Joint Conference on Natural Language Processing (EMNLP-IJCNLP), pp. 3982–3992 (2019)

19. He, K., Zhang, X., Ren, S., Sun, J.: Deep residual learning for image recognition. In: Proceedings of the IEEE Conference on Computer Vision and Pattern Recognition, pp. 770–778 (2016)

20. Vaswani, A., et al.: Attention is all you need. In: Advances in Neural Information Processing Systems, vol. 30 (2017)

21. Jaume, G., Ekenel, H.K., Thiran, J.P.: FUNSD: a dataset for form understanding in noisy scanned documents. In: 2019 International Conference on Document Analysis and Recognition Workshops (ICDAR), vol. 2, pp. 1–6. IEEE (2019)

22. Souza, F., Nogueira, R., Lotufo, R.: Portuguese named entity recognition using Bert-CRF. arXiv preprint arXiv:1909.10649 (2019)

Temporal Edge-Aware Hypergraph Convolutional Network for Dynamic Graph Embedding

Da Huang[1,2] and Fangyuan Lei[1,2(✉)]

[1] School of Electronic and Information, Guangdong Polytechnic Normal University,
Guangzhou 510665, China
leify@gpnu.edu.cn
[2] Guangdong Provincial Key Laboratory of Intellectual Property & Big Data,
Guangzhou 510665, China

Abstract. Graph embedding is a critical aspect of network analysis that helps to advance various real-world applications such as social recommendation and protein structure prediction. Most of the existing graph embedding methods are designed for static graphs while many real-world graphs intrinsically behave as dynamic graphs. Recent works try to combine graph neural networks(GNN) with recurrent neural networks to address this issue. However, these methods can not independently utilize GNN models to cope with dynamic graphs and they ignore the inner edge-level correlations in dynamic graphs. To tackle these problems, we propose a novel dynamic graph embedding framework in this paper, called DynHyper. Specifically, we introduce a temporal hypergraph construction to capture the local structure information and temporal dynamics simultaneously. Then, we employ a hyperedge projection to obtain edge-level correlations. Further, we propose a temporal edge-aware hypergraph convolution to transmit and aggregate the messages in the temporal hypergraph. We conduct our experiments on seven real-world datasets to evaluate the effectiveness of DynHyper in both link prediction and node classification tasks. Experimental results show that DynHyper significantly outperforms all baselines, especially on the more complex datasets.

Keywords: Graph convolutional networks · Dynamic graph embedding · Hypergraph learning

1 Introduction

Graphs have a great capacity to model the relationship among entities, successfully applied in many fields, such as social network [10], finance analysis [15], and biological network [24]. Many academics are attempting to extend neural network models to graphs as a result of deep learning's extraordinary performance. These neural network models, also known as graph network embedding,

© The Author(s), under exclusive license to Springer Nature Switzerland AG 2022
S. Khanna et al. (Eds.): PRICAI 2022, LNCS 13629, pp. 435–449, 2022.
https://doi.org/10.1007/978-3-031-20862-1_32

have emerged as a prominent method for graphs. The key idea of graph network embedding is to map node representation into a low-dimensional latent space, which preserves the similarity of nodes based on their local structure. These graph network embedding algorithms have been used by numerous academics for a variety of applications, including node classification, link prediction, and network visualization [1,3,5,7,22,23,27].

Although existing graph network embedding methods provide excellent performance, they are primarily developed for static graphs where nodes and edges remain unchanged over time. In most cases, however, networks behave as dynamic graphs in the actual world. For example, as new friendship contacts grow, new communication events such as emails and text messages are streamed on social networks. In e-commerce networks, new goods and ratings arise daily. In financial networks, transactions are streamed in computational finance, and supply chain relationships are always changing. In these dynamic graphs, nodes and edges are constantly evolving. The evolution trend of dynamic graphs can be recorded by a temporal sequence made up of a series of graph snapshots. Compared with static graphs, dynamic graphs have an additional dimension(i.e., the time dimension) that adds temporal dynamics to them. As a result, dynamic graph embedding is presented as a solution to the major issue of dynamic graphs, which is capturing temporal dynamics adequately.

Recently, several efforts, like DynmaicTraid [28], DynGEM [6], and TIMER [26], use some smoothness regularization to capture temporal dynamics. The premise behind these strategies is that dynamic graphs change slowly and thus they are unable to address dynamic graphs with abrupt changes. More recently, with the remarkable success of graph convolutional networks(GCN), some researchers focus on extending the GNNs to dynamic graphs by combining GCN with RNN components(e.g., LSTM or GRU), such as WD-GCN [14], EvolveGCN [17], and GANE [20]. However, these current GCN methods are designed for simple graphs that only represent pair-wise relationships among nodes. Thus, these GCN methods can not handle dynamic graphs composed of a series of simple graph snapshots independently, forcing them to resort to RNN components. Therefore, these approaches based on mixed architectures may break the internal link between topological information and temporal dynamics. Additionally, these methods only focus on capturing information from nodes and ignore edge information of graphs which is also an essential component of graph information.

To tackle the above issues, we propose a novel dynamic graph embedding framework, called DynHyper. First, we design a temporal hypergraph to model a dynamic graph that contains the characteristic of both local structure and temporal dynamics. Compared with simple graphs, hypergraphs can describe multiple relationships among nodes, and thereby we construct temporal hypergraphs to represent the correlation of nodes including local structure and temporal dynamics. To be specific, the main difference between simple graphs and hypergraphs lies in that hypergraphs contain hyperedges, which can connect an arbitrary number of nodes. Hence, we employ a hyperedge to connect nodes in the same time step, which is enclosed with the local structure information. Interactions between distinct hyperedges can indicate temporal interactions between nodes, allowing us to capture temporal dynamics in our model. In addition, edge information is an indispensable part of the graph. Therefore, we introduce a hyperedge projection for temporal hypergraphs to capture edge-level correlations of hypergraphs. The hyperedge projection aims to convert hyperedges to nodes, which preserves edge-level relationships of temporal hypergraphs and can integrate message-passing schemes for nodes. Finally, we propose the temporal edge-aware hypergraph convolution to operate message aggregation and transmission to update node embeddings on the temporal hypergraph. DynHyper's effectiveness is demonstrated by experimental results on seven real-world datasets in link prediction and node classification tasks.

In a nutshell, our key contributions can be summarized as follows:

- We introduce a temporal hypergraph construction to capture the local structure information and temporal dynamics simultaneously for dynamic graphs and a hyperedge projection to obtain edge-level relationships for temporal hypergraphs.
- We propose a temporal edge-aware hypergraph convolutional network that can execute message passing in dynamic graphs autonomously and effectively without the need for RNN components.
- We conduct our experiments on seven real-world datasets in link prediction and node classification tasks to evaluate the effectiveness of DynHyper. Our findings show superior predictive performance, compared to the state-of-the-art methods in dynamic graph embedding.

2   Related Work

Dynamic graph embedding plays a crucial role in network analysis, which aids in the advancement of many real-world applications such as social recommendation and protein structure prediction. Roughly, we classify them into three streams: random walk methods, autoencoder-based methods, and GNNs-based methods.

Random walk methods aim to apply random walks to generate node sequences and incrementally update the node embedding affected by temporal evolution [9,13,25]. For instance, dynnode2vec [13] employs the evolve random walks that only generate the walks for the changed nodes and proposes a dynamic skip-gram model, where the previous embedding is initialized as the weight for the next graph snapshot. For autoencoder-based methods, one seeks to minimize the reconstruct loss of a given graph snapshot. For example, DynGEM [6] proposes an incremental fully-connected network that can share the parameters between two consecutive networks to capture temporal evolution. The other aims to minimize the reconstruct loss between the previous graph snapshots and the future graph snapshot. For instance, dyngraph2vecAE [4] introduces the autoencoder network with the reconstruct loss between the adjacency mapped by the previous graph embeddings and the adjacency in the next time step.

Recently, the popular way to cope with dynamic graph embedding is to combine the GNNs model with temporal components(e.g., LSTM). GCRN-M1 [19] first employs graph convolution to obtain node embedding and then feed them into an RNN to capture temporal dynamics. The distinction between WD-GCN [14] and GCRM-M1 [19] lies in that WD-GCN utilizes the separate LSTM components per node. EvolveGCN [17] aims to use an RNN to evolve the parameter of the GNNs model, significantly reducing the mode size(i,e, the model parameters). DySAT [18] employs a self-attention mechanism with the GNNs model to joint learn representation along the dimensions of both local structure and temporal dynamics. GANE [20] utilizes tensor factorization to obtain temporal pattern similarity of nodes and incorporates it into the graph attention network for capturing temporal dynamics.

3   Preliminaries

Notations. A dynamic graph network is defined as a series of static graph network snapshots collected at each time step t, i.e., $\mathbb{G} = \{G^1, G^2, \ldots, G^T\}$, where T denotes the total number of time steps. Each graph snapshot $G^t = (V^t, E^t)$ is a weight undirected graph network made of a node-set V^t, an edge set E^t, and a weighted adjacency matrix A^t at each time step t.

Problem Formulation. In this subsection, we formally define the problem of dynamic graph embedding. Given a dynamic graph G, dynamic graph embedding aims to learn mappings $f^t : \{G^1, G^2, \ldots, G^t\} \longrightarrow R^{|V^t| \times d}$ so that they obtain the latent representation $Z^t = f^t(G^1, G^2, \ldots, G^t)$, where $Z^t \in R^{|V^t| \times d}$ and d denotes the embedding dimensionality. Here, each row vector $Z_v^t \in R^d$ is the low dimensional embedding of node v, which preserves local topological proximities and temporal evolutionary pattern information up to time step t.

4   Methodology

In this section, we present our proposed framework for dynamic graph embedding, as illustrated in Fig. 1. The proposed framework includes three major parts. First, we introduce the temporal hypergraph to capture both local structure information and temporal dynamics for dynamic graphs. Then, we use a hyperedge projection to obtain edge-level relationships. After that, we utilize the temporal edge-aware hypergraph convolution to aggregate information and pass on them among nodes to update nodes embedding, illustrated in the following sections.

4.1   Temporal Hypergraph Construction

In this subsection, we discuss temporal hypergraph construction. Note that, a dynamic graph contains a series of graph snapshots. The major challenge for

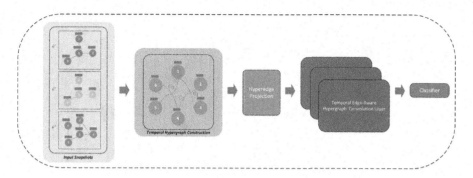

Fig. 1. An overview of our proposed framework. Given snapshot graphs $\{G^1, G^2, G^3\}$ as input, we first generate the temporal hypergraph based on time steps. To be specific, the temporal hypergraph contains all original nodes from input snapshots and hyperedges. A hyperedge is composed of the nodes from the same time step, i.e., e_1, e_2, e_3. Then, those hyperedges in the temporal hypergraph are operated by a hyperedge projection. After that, we utilize the temporal edge-aware hypergraph convolution to aggregate information and pass on them among nodes to update nodes embedding.

dynamic graph embedding is to capture temporal evolution among these graph snapshots. The prior works mainly focus on restoring to RNN or Transformer to capture temporal dynamics indirectly, which splits the internal connection between topological information and temporal dynamics. To address this issue, we aim to directly capture both temporal dynamics and topological information through the properties of the hypergraph.

For a given dynamic graph $\mathbb{G} = \{\mathbb{V}, \mathbb{E}\}$, where $\mathbb{V} = \{V^1, V^2, \ldots, V^t\}$ denotes a series of node sets and $\mathbb{E} = \{E^1, E^2, \ldots, E^t\}$ denotes a series of edge sets. We assume that historical observations start from time step 1 to time step τ. First, note that $V^1 \subseteq V^2 \subseteq \ldots \subseteq V^\tau$, V^τ contains all nodes in graph snapshots up to time step τ, so we define V^τ as a hypernode set of the temporal hypergraph. Second, we aim to construct hyperedges of the temporal hypergraph. More specifically, a hyperedge $e \in E^\tau$ is formed by linking a centroid node and its first-order neighbors at the same time step, where $E^\tau = \{e_{v_i}^m | m \in \{1, .., \tau\}, v_i \in V^\tau\}$ is the hyperedge set of the temporal hypergraph and m denotes a certain time step. For example, if a hyperedge connects v_1, v_2 and v_3, it can be denoted as $e_{v_1}^m = \{v_1, v_2, v_3 | v_2, v_3 \in N(v_1), v_1, v_2, v_3 \in G^m\}$, where v_1 is assigned as a centroid hypernode, and $N(v_1)$ is the first-order neighbors' set of hypernode v_1. Based on the discussion above, we define the temporal hypergraph as $H^\tau = (V^\tau, E^\tau, W)$, where W denotes weight matrix for hyperedge, $|V^\tau|$ is the number of hypernodes, and $|E^\tau|$ is the number of hyperedges. For simplicity, we use $|V|$ and $|E|$ to represent $|V^\tau|$ and $|E^\tau|$ respectively. Formally, the temporal hypergraph can be represented by an incidence matrix $H \in R^{|V| \times |E|}$:

$$H(v_i, e_{v_j}^m) = \begin{cases} 1, & \text{if } v_i \in e_{v_j}^m \\ 0, & \text{otherwise} \end{cases} \tag{1}$$

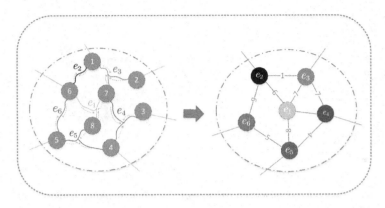

Fig. 2. An example of a hyperedge projection.

4.2 Hyperedge Projection

In this subsection, we further explore the edge-level correlations in hypergraphs. The temporal hypergraph is designed to obtain temporal dynamics of dynamic graphs, but it cannot well reflect the edge-level correlations in dynamic graphs. Thus, we introduce a hyperedge projection to extract edge-level correlations for dynamic graphs. The key idea of hyperedge projection is to capture edge-edge correlations of the temporal hypergraph. Figure 2 shows an example of a hyperedge projection. Specifically, the hypernodes connected to the same hyperedge are uniformly mapped into an edge that is defined as a node in the new graph. The hypernode projection can be formally written as follows:

$$P = D_e^{-1} H^T X \qquad (2)$$

where $P \in R^{|V| \times M}$ is the hyperedge projection embedding of the original hypernode representation X, H^T is the transpose matrix of the incidence matrix H, and $D_e \in R^{|E| \times |E|}$ denotes the hyperedge degree matrix. Then, these new nodes are connected if they contain the same hypernode. For example, in Fig. 2, e_5 connects e_6 by the green line with the number 5, denoting that they contain the same hypernode v_5. In other words, these nodes connected are neighbors if they share the same hypernodes. Compared to hyperedges, edges only connect two nodes in this new graph. In a way, we convert the temporal hypergraph to a simple graph by the hyperedge projection and can easily integrate message-passing schemes for nodes, which preserves the original edge-level correlations of the temporal hypergraph.

4.3   Temporal Edge-Aware Hypergraph Convolution

In this section, we introduce the details of the message passing process via temporal edge-aware hypergraph convolution. In our work, if nodes have not initial feature, each node v is initialized by a one-hot vector $x_v \in R^M$, where M is the number of nodes in G^τ. Then, an update operation for each node v is conducted in the temporal hypergraph, which contains intra-hyperedge aggregation and inter-hyperedge aggregation. The intra-hyperedge aggregation can be formulated as:

$$z_e = \sum_{v \in e} \frac{x_v}{\delta(e)} \tag{3}$$

where z_e is the hyperedge representation through the intra-hyperedge aggregation, x_v is the initial representation of the node v, and $\delta(e)$ denotes the degree of the hyperedge $|e|$. Afterward, the inter-hyperedge aggregation can be expressed as:

$$z_v = \sum_{e \in S} \frac{z_e}{d(v)} \tag{4}$$

where z_v is the embedding of the node v through the inter-hyperedge aggregation, S is the set of hyperedges containing the node v, and $d(v)$ denotes the number of hyperedges containing the node v. These two steps can merge and be rewritten as:

$$Z = D_e^{-1} H^T D_v^{-1} H X \tag{5}$$

where $Z \in R^{|E| \times M}$ is the embedding of hypernodes, $H \in R^{|V| \times |E|}$ denotes the incident matrix, the original hypernode representation $X \in R^{|V| \times M}$, and $D_v \in R^{|V| \times |E|}$ denotes hypernode degree matrix. We observe that this update operation is equal to the simplified hypergraph convolution [2]. Then, we further extend this operation to capture the edge-level correlations in the temporal hypergraph. According to the hypernode projection mentioned in Sect. 4.2, we utilize the hypernode projection to replace the original hypernode representation X with P in the convolution rule as follows:

$$Z_{\text{edge}} = D_e^{-1} H^T D_v^{-1} H P \tag{6}$$

where $Z_{edge} \in R^{|E| \times M}$ is the edge-level embedding of hypernodes. After capturing the edge-level correlations of the temporal hypergraph, we remap the edge-level embedding into the node-level embedding which is assigned to each node in the dynamic graph:

$$Z_{node} = H Z_{edge} \tag{7}$$

where $Z_{node} \in R^{|V| \times M}$ is the node-level embedding of hypernodes. Then, we utilize the renormalization trick introduced by [11] and employ a learnbale matrix. The complete temporal hypergraph propagation rule can be written as follows:

$$\begin{aligned} \tilde{Z} &= \sigma \left(D_v^{-1/2} Z_{node} D_v^{-1/2} \Theta \right) \\ &= \sigma \left(D_v^{-1/2} H D_e^{-1} H^T D_v^{-1} H P D_v^{-1/2} \Theta \right) \end{aligned} \tag{8}$$

where $\tilde{Z} \in R^{|E| \times d}$ is the final embedding of hypernodes, $\Theta \in R^{|E| \times d}$ denotes the model parameters matrix, d denotes the embedding dimensionality, and $\sigma(\cdot)$ denotes the activation function (e.g. *ELU*).

Table 1. The statistics of datasets

Dataset	#nodes	#edges	#features	#labels	#time steps
UCI	1,809	16,822	–	–	13
Enron	143	2,347	–	–	12
Yelp	6,569	95,361	–		12
ML-10M	20,537	43,760	–		13
Alibaba	5,640	53,049	19	–	11
Epinions	9,368	231,537	44	–	9
Primary School	242	20,009	–	11	40

4.4 Loss Function

In this subsection, we introduce the objective function that enables node representations to capture dynamic topological evolution during training our model. Inspired by DySAT [18], our model encourages nodes sampled in the fixed-length random walk to obtain similar representations. Formally, we use a binary cross-entropy loss to optimize the model parameters as follows:

$$L = \sum_{v \in V} (\sum_{u \in N_{walk}(v)} - \log \left(\sigma \left(< \tilde{z}_w, \tilde{z}_v > \right) \right)$$
$$- \beta \cdot \sum_{u' \in P_n(v)} \log \left(1 - \sigma \left(< \tilde{z}_{u'}, \tilde{z}_v > \right) \right)) \tag{9}$$

where $\tilde{z}_v$ is the final embedding of a node v, $\sigma(\cdot)$ denotes the sigmoid function, $< \cdot >$ denotes the inner product. $N_{walk}(v)$ is the positive nodes' set of a node v sampled by the random walk, and $P_n(v)$ is the negative nodes' set of a node v sampled by a negative sampling function based on the degree of nodes. β is the negative sample value to balance positive and negative samples.

5 Experiments and Analysis

5.1 Experimental Setup

Datasets. To evaluate the performance of our model, we use seven public real-world datasets in our experiments. The datasets are summarized in Table 1. UCI [16]is an online social network. Links of this network denote the massage sent between peer users, i.e., nodes. Enron [12] contains a set of email messages concerning the Enron corporation, which is represented as an email communication network. Nodes of network denote the addresses and links denote there's an interaction between these email addresses. Yelp[1]: is a rating network of users and businesses where links connect users and businesses if users score the businesses. ML-10M [8] consists of users and tags that users applied to certain movies. The links of this network denote there's an interaction between users and movies. Alibaba[2] is an e-commerce network, consisting of users and items. The edge between user and item denotes the click interaction. Epinions[3] denotes a trusted network between users. The edge of the network indicates the trust correlation between users. Primary School [21] represents the contact network. The link of this network is constructed from the interactions between teachers and students.

Baselines. We compare our proposed model with the following state-of-the-art dynamic graph embedding methods: (1) DynAE [4] utilizes an autoencoder framework based on dense layers; (2) DynAERNN [4] is based on DynAE, which uses recurrent neural networks to capture temporal dynamics of dynamic graphs; (3) DynGEM [6] adopts an incremental autoencoder framework for a dynamic graph based on the last graph snapshot; (4) DySAT [18]: DySAT aims to simultaneously capture the local structure information and temporal dynamics based on the self-attention mechanism; (5) EvolveGCN [17] uses the GCN to learn local structure information for each graph snapshot and employs the GRU or LSTM to update parameters of GCN to capture temporal evolution based on different graph snapshots; (6) GAEN [20] incorporates node temporal pattern similarities based on the tensor factorization technique and neighborhood attention to learn the node embedding for dynamic graphs.

Settings. In our experiments, we evaluate the performance of our model in both link prediction and node classification tasks. For link prediction, we train a logistic regression classifier to predict the existence of links at the time step $t + 1$ based on the embeddings learned from previous networks up to time step t. We randomly sample 60% of nodes for training. We utilize 20% of nodes to tune hyperparameters of our model and the remaining 20% of nodes for testing. We utilize the Mean Accuracy(ACC) and the Mean Area Under the ROC Curve (AUC) as our evaluation metrics of link prediction. For node classification, we randomly sample 20% of nodes as a validation set. Then, we use 30%, 50%, and 70% of nodes as train sets respectively, the corresponding remaining nodes are used as test sets. We also train a logistic regression classifier to map nodes into different categories based on the embeddings learned from previous networks up to time step t. We employ the Mean Accuracy(ACC) as our evaluation metrics of node classification. We use mini-batch gradient descent with Adam. For hyperparameters, we set batch size as 512, the embedding dimensionality d as 128, the

---

[1] https://www.yelp.com/dataset/.
[2] https://tianchi.aliyun.com/competition/entrance/231719/information/.
[3] https://cse.msu.edu/~tangjili/trust.html.

learning rate as 10^{-3}, the weight decay as 5×10^{-4}, the max epoch as 20, and negative sample ratio β as 0.01. We conduct our experiments on a machine with the Intel Core i9-9960X (3.10GHz) CPU, 128 Gb of RAM, and four NVIDIA 2080Ti GPU cards, which are implemented in Python 3.6 with Tensorflow.

Table 2. The predictive performance of link prediction task in terms of AUC and ACC on UCI, Enron, Yelp, ML-10M, Alibaba, and Epinions. The results are the mean and standard deviation of 5 different runs. OOM denotes running out of memory on our machine.

Method	Metric	UCI	Enron	Yelp	ML-10M	Alibaba	Epinion
DynAE	ACC	69.05 ± 0.08	68.22 ± 1.09	60.00 ± 0.07	64.75 ± 0.31	75.84 ± 0.03	74.53 ± 0.21
	AUC	85.94 ± 0.26	72.64 ± 0.16	64.17 ± 0.16	91.14 ± 0.21	87.51 ± 0.20	94.17 ± 0.03
DynAERNN	ACC	68.92 ± 1.34	67.36 ± 0.40	54.77 ± 0.67	74.55 ± 0.32	76.21 ± 0.39	74.71 ± 0.94
	AUC	82.73 ± 0.58	75.56 ± 0.14	56.74 ± 0.87	76.57 ± 0.86	82.74 ± 0.28	82.03 ± 1.52
DynGEM	ACC	71.01 ± 1.19	66.99 ± 0.34	60.98 ± 0.06	OOM	75.42 ± 0.60	83.82 ± 0.61
	AUC	84.29 ± 1.88	72.90 ± 1.36	67.33 ± 0.04	OOM	87.31 ± 0.43	91.88 ± 1.04
EvolveGCN	ACC	72.26 ± 0.45	66.14 ± 1.09	61.03 ± 0.29	79.35 ± 0.32	72.63 ± 0.08	81.01 ± 0.57
	AUC	79.58 ± 0.28	72.12 ± 1.08	64.94 ± 0.23	87.28 ± 0.79	79.56 ± 0.11	89.07 ± 0.38
DynSAT	ACC	68.47 ± 0.05	74.17 ± 1.03	65.76 ± 0.23	82.40 ± 0.66	67.52 ± 0.15	89.13 ± 0.14
	AUC	82.77 ± 0.08	82.97 ± 1.03	71.84 ± 0.65	92.86 ± 0.15	75.34 ± 0.15	96.14 ± 0.52
GANE	ACC	72.86 ± 0.94	$\mathbf{78.99 \pm 0.66}$	62.38 ± 0.11	OOM	77.00 ± 0.02	74.85 ± 0.55
	AUC	80.59 ± 0.74	86.08 ± 0.50	65.76 ± 0.18	OOM	85.45 ± 0.23	82.20 ± 2.09
DynHyper(ours)	ACC	$\mathbf{75.04 \pm 0.16}$	76.21 ± 0.38	$\mathbf{69.90 \pm 0.71}$	$\mathbf{82.86 \pm 0.61}$	$\mathbf{83.08 \pm 0.04}$	$\mathbf{91.58 \pm 0.29}$
	AUC	$\mathbf{87.81 \pm 0.13}$	$\mathbf{87.26 \pm 0.39}$	$\mathbf{76.61 \pm 0.04}$	$\mathbf{94.14 \pm 0.15}$	$\mathbf{90.58 \pm 0.03}$	$\mathbf{99.10 \pm 0.01}$

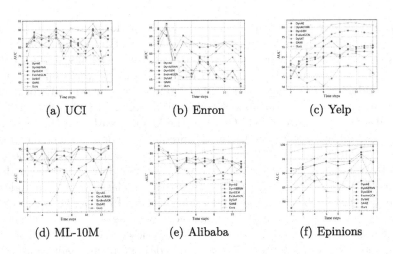

(a) UCI   (b) Enron   (c) Yelp

(d) ML-10M   (e) Alibaba   (f) Epinions

Fig. 3. The results of six datasets in link prediction task in terms of AUC at various time steps.

Table 3. The predictive performance of the node prediction task in terms of ACC on Primary School at different train ratios. The results are the mean and standard deviation of 5 different runs.

Dataset	Primary School		
Train ratios	30%	50%	70%
DynAE	47.19 ± 0.02	47.25 ± 0.05	46.05 ± 0.04
DynAERNN	46.85 ± 0.14	46.99 ± 0.18	46.99 ± 0.04
DynGEM	50.01 ± 0.08	51.05 ± 0.11	50.84 ± 0.26
EvolveGCN	42.75 ± 0.30	45.16 ± 0.23	46.20 ± 0.24
DySAT	60.72 ± 0.38	63.72 ± 0.24	64.85 ± 0.39
GANE	55.17 ± 0.19	57.82 ± 0.09	59.26 ± 0.10
DynHyper(ours)	$\mathbf{63.39 \pm 0.09}$	$\mathbf{65.86 \pm 0.17}$	$\mathbf{67.01 \pm 0.13}$

5.2   Experimental Results

Link Prediction. In this subsection, we discuss the performance of our model in the link prediction task compared with state-of-the-art methods. Experimental results are illustrated in Table 2. Table 2 shows that DynHyper consistently outperforms baselines in all datasets except that GANE outperforms DynHyper on the Enron dataset under ACC. These results indicate the effectiveness of DynHyper in link prediction. For example, as compared to the best approach of baselines(i.e., DySAT) on the Yelp dataset, we get roughly a 5% improvement in both AUC and ACC. Note that GANE gains better performance than DynHyper on the Enron dataset. GANE obtains node temporal patterns via tensor factorization to improve performance, which may be more successful on tiny datasets like Enron having only 143 nodes. However, DynHyper tries to capture the edge-level correlations on datasets, which may perform better in large datasets rather than small ones. As the result shows, DynHyper obtains about 94% AUC and 99% AUC on ML-10M and Epinions datasets respectively, which are much larger datasets than the Enron dataset. Based on the abovementioned, this might be the reason why our approach on Enron is inferior to GANE. Besides, DynGEM employs the smoothness regularization to capture temporal dynamics that can not address the network with abrupt change. Users' communications on UCI typically span longer periods, showing that the network is smooth. However, rating behaviors on Yelp, tend to be erratic and connected with events like restaurant openings and discounted promotions, indicating a network with abrupt change. Thus, we observe that DynGEM obtain a relatively better performance on UCI than the performance on Yelp. The predictive results of DynHyper are consistently superior to DynGEM on all the datasets, especially Yelp, demonstrating that DynHyper performs well in both smooth and abrupt networks.

Furthermore, we seek to analyze the detailed performance of these methods at each time step. The results are reported in Fig. 3. First, we note that DynHyper is inferior to some baselines at the initial time step on some datasets, such as

Enron and Alibaba. The potential reason is that these datasets do not form a lot of edge-level relationships at the initial time step. Additionally, we find that as the time step is increased, DynHyper's performance improves. Moreover, DyperHyper is consistently superior to all baselines at each time step on some datasets, such as Yelp and Epinions. This finding might be caused by these datasets containing more edge-level correlations. It is worth noticing that Yelp and Epinions have more links than other datasets.

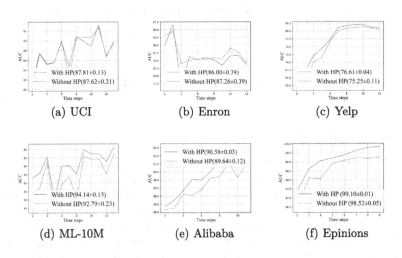

(a) UCI   (b) Enron   (c) Yelp

(d) ML-10M   (e) Alibaba   (f) Epinions

Fig. 4. Experimental results for ablations

Node Classification. In this subsection, we compare DynHyper's performance to that of state-of-the-art approaches in the node classification task. Due to the lack of dynamic graphs datasets with node labels, we use the Primary School dataset with different train ratios to fully use this dataset for evaluation. Table 3 shows the results of the experiments. DynHyper achieves a consistent 2%~3% ACC improvement on Primary School at different train ratios, demonstrating DynHyper's effectiveness in node classification. In addition, approaches with the RNN component, such as DynAERNN and EvolveGCN, perform poorly in node classification. DynAERNN is even superior to DynAE, suggesting that Combination with the RNN component is ineffective at capturing temporal dynamics in the node classification task.

Ablation Study. In this subsection, we conduct ablation studies to evaluate the contribution of the hyperedge projection(HP) of our model. HP aims to capture edge-level relationships of datasets to improve performance. To better demonstrate this, we compare the performance between our model with HP and our model without HP at various time steps. The compared results are shown in

Fig. 4. According to Fig. 4, DynHyper with HP outperforms DynHyper without HP on most datasets. As discussed above, the Enron dataset is a small dataset having 143 nodes while HP is much more effective with big datasets. As a result, we note that DynHyper without HP is superior to DynHyper without HP on the Enron dataset.

6   Conclusion

In this paper, we propose a dynamic embedding framework to address dynamic graphs, named DynHyper. We introduce temporal hypergraph construction to capture effectively temporal dynamics for dynamic graphs. Additionally, we propose a hyperedge projection to obtain edge-level relationships of temporal hypergraphs. Furthermore, We propose a temporal edge-aware hypergraph convolutional network to independently and effectively conduct the message passing in dynamic graphs without any RNN components. Experimental results confirm that DynHyper has great performance in both link prediction and node classification tasks, especially on the more complex datasets. Our future work aims to extend our work to address more complex dynamic graphs, such as those with changeable attributed nodes.

Acknowledgments. This work was partly supported by the Guangdong Provincial Key Laboratory of Intellectual Property and Big Data (2018B030322016), the National Natural Science Foundation of China (U1701266), Special Projects for Key Fields in Higher Education of Guangdong, China(2021ZDZX1042), the Natural Science Foundation of Guangdong Province, China(2022A1515011146), Key Field R&D Plan Project of Guanzhou(202206070003).

References

1. Cai, H., Zheng, V.W., Chang, K.C.C.J.I.T.O.K., Engineering, D.: A comprehensive survey of graph embedding: problems, techniques, and applications. IEEE Trans. Knowl. Data Eng. **30**(9), 1616–1637 (2018)
2. Feng, Y., You, H., Zhang, Z., Ji, R., Gao, Y.: Hypergraph neural networks. In: Proceedings of the AAAI Conference on Artificial Intelligence. vol. 33, pp. 3558–3565 (2019)
3. Fu, S., Liu, W., Zhang, K., Zhou, Y.: Example-feature graph convolutional networks for semi-supervised classification. Neurocomputing **461**, 63–76 (2021)
4. Goyal, P., Chhetri, S.R., Canedo, A.J.K.B.S.: dyngraph2vec: capturing network dynamics using dynamic graph representation learning. Knowl.-Based Syst. **187**, 104816 (2020)
5. Goyal, P., Ferrara, E.J.K.B.S.: Graph embedding techniques, applications, and performance: a survey. Knowl.-Based Syst. **151**, 78–94 (2018)
6. Goyal, P., Kamra, N., He, X., Liu, Y.: Dyngem: Deep embedding method for dynamic graphs. arXiv preprint arXiv:1805.11273 (2018)
7. Hamilton, W.L., Ying, R., Leskovec, J.: Representation learning on graphs: methods and applications. IEEE Data Eng. Bull. **40**(3), 52–74 (2017)

8. Harper, F.M., Konstan, J.A.: The movielens datasets: History and context. ACM Trans. Interact. Intell. syst. (TIIS) **5**(4), 1–19 (2015)
9. Heidari, F., Papagelis, M.: EvoNRL: evolving network representation learning based on random walks. In: Aiello, L.M., Cherifi, C., Cherifi, H., Lambiotte, R., Lió, P., Rocha, L.M. (eds.) COMPLEX NETWORKS 2018. SCI, vol. 812, pp. 457–469. Springer, Cham (2019). https://doi.org/10.1007/978-3-030-05411-3_37
10. Jiang, Y., Ma, H., Liu, Y., Li, Z., Chang, L.: Enhancing social recommendation via two-level graph attentional networks. Neurocomputing **449**, 71–84 (2021)
11. Kipf, T.N., Welling, M.: Semi-supervised classification with graph convolutional networks. In: 5th International Conference on Learning Representations, ICLR 2017, Toulon, France, April 24–26, 2017, Conference Track Proceedings. OpenReview.net (2017)
12. Klimt, B., Yang, Y.: The Enron corpus: a new dataset for email classification research. In: Boulicaut, J.-F., Esposito, F., Giannotti, F., Pedreschi, D. (eds.) ECML 2004. LNCS (LNAI), vol. 3201, pp. 217–226. Springer, Heidelberg (2004). https://doi.org/10.1007/978-3-540-30115-8_22
13. Mahdavi, S., Khoshraftar, S., An, A.: dynnode2vec: scalable dynamic network embedding. In: 2018 IEEE International Conference on Big Data (Big Data), pp. 3762–3765. IEEE (2018)
14. Manessi, F., Rozza, A., Manzo, M.J.P.R.: Dynamic graph convolutional networks. Pattern Recogn. **97**, 107000 (2020)
15. Mizerka, J., Stróżyńska-Szajek, A., Mizerka, P.J.F.R.L.: The role of bitcoin on developed and emerging markets-on the basis of a bitcoin users graph analysis. Finan. Res. Lett. 35, 101489 (2020)
16. Panzarasa, P., Opsahl, T., Carley, K.M.: Patterns and dynamics of users' behavior and interaction: network analysis of an online community. J. Am. Soc. Inform. Sci. Technol. **60**(5), 911–932 (2009)
17. Pareja, A., et al.: Evolvegcn: evolving graph convolutional networks for dynamic graphs. In: Proceedings of the AAAI Conference on Artificial Intelligence, vol. 34, pp. 5363–5370 (2020)
18. Sankar, A., Wu, Y., Gou, L., Zhang, W., Yang, H.: DYSAT: deep neural representation learning on dynamic graphs via self-attention networks. In: Proceedings of the 13th International Conference on Web Search and Data Mining, pp. 519–527 (2020)
19. Seo, Y., Defferrard, M., Vandergheynst, P., Bresson, X.: Structured sequence modeling with graph convolutional recurrent networks. In: Cheng, L., Leung, A.C.S., Ozawa, S. (eds.) ICONIP 2018. LNCS, vol. 11301, pp. 362–373. Springer, Cham (2018). https://doi.org/10.1007/978-3-030-04167-0_33
20. Shi, M., Huang, Y., Zhu, X., Tang, Y., Zhuang, Y., Liu, J.: GAEN: graph attention evolving networks. In: Proceedings of the Thirtieth International Joint Conference on Artificial Intelligence (IJCAI) (2021)
21. Stehlé, J., et al.: High-resolution measurements of face-to-face contact patterns in a primary school. PLoS ONE **6**(8), e23176 (2011)
22. Tian, X., Ding, C.H., Chen, S., Luo, B., Wang, X.: Regularization graph convolutional networks with data augmentation. Neurocomputing **436**, 92–102 (2021)
23. Wang, S., Fu, K., Sun, X., Zhang, Z., Li, S., Jin, L.: Hierarchical-aware relation rotational knowledge graph embedding for link prediction. Neurocomputing **458**, 259–270 (2021)
24. Wang, Y., You, Z.H., Yang, S., Li, X., Jiang, T.H., Zhou, X.J.C.: A high efficient biological language model for predicting protein-protein interactions. Cells **8**(2), 122 (2019)

25. Yu, W., Cheng, W., Aggarwal, C.C., Zhang, K., Chen, H., Wang, W.: Netwalk: a flexible deep embedding approach for anomaly detection in dynamic networks. In: Proceedings of the 24th ACM SIGKDD International Conference on Knowledge Discovery & Data Mining, pp. 2672–2681 (2018)
26. Zhang, Z., Cui, P., Pei, J., Wang, X., Zhu, W.: Timers: error-bounded SVD restart on dynamic networks. In: Thirty-Second AAAI conference on artificial intelligence (2018)
27. Zheng, W., Qian, F., Zhao, S., Zhang, Y.: M-GWNN: multi-granularity graph wavelet neural networks for semi-supervised node classification. Neurocomputing **453**, 524–537 (2021)
28. Zhou, L., Yang, Y., Ren, X., Wu, F., Zhuang, Y.: Dynamic network embedding by modeling triadic closure process. In: Proceedings of the AAAI Conference on Artificial Intelligence, vol. 32 (2018)

Performance Improvement Validation of Decision Tree Algorithms with Non-normalized Information Distance in Experiments

Takeru Araki$^{(\boxtimes)}$ [ID], Yuan Luo [ID], and Minyi Guo [ID]

Department of Computer Science and Engineering, Shanghai Jiao Tong University,
Shanghai, China
{t23akeru,yuanluo}@sjtu.edu.cn, guo-my@cs.sjtu.edu.cn

Abstract. The performance of ID3 algorithm in decision tree depends
on the information gain but it has a drawback because of tending to select
attributes with many values as the branching attributes. The gain ratio
(especially in C4.5) is proposed to improve the information gain, but it
does not always improve the performance, nor is it always defined. Some
scientists use normalized information distance to improve the gain ratio,
however, it is ineffective. In this paper, we investigate two non-normalized
information distance selection criteria to replace the information gain and
the gain ratio and conduct detailed experiments on 13 datasets classified
into four types with theoretical analysis. Surprisingly, on the datasets
where the number of values of each attribute differ greatly i.e. in Type1
and Type2, non-normalized information distance-based algorithms can
increase the accuracy of about 15–25% of ID3 algorithm. The first reason is that more values for an attribute does not reduce the distances,
which is suggested by Mántaras. The second reason is that the conditional entropy which is the opposite one used in the information gain
can bring balance to the multi-valued biased values. Furthermore, our
methods can maintain results comparable to those of existing algorithms
on other cases. **Compared to the gain ratio, the algorithms with
non-normalized information distances conquer the drawback
much better on Type1 datasets, which is strongly confirmed
by experiments and corresponding analysis.** It can be presumed
that "normalization" improvement methods such as normalized information distance and the gain ratio are not always effective.

Keywords: Decision tree · ID3 algorithm · Information distance ·
Information gain · Gain ratio

1 Introduction

In recent years, with the great boom in artificial intelligence, "machine learning," the heart of artificial intelligence technology, is a field that has attracted

© The Author(s), under exclusive license to Springer Nature Switzerland AG 2022
S. Khanna et al. (Eds.): PRICAI 2022, LNCS 13629, pp. 450–464, 2022.
https://doi.org/10.1007/978-3-031-20862-1_33

a great deal of attention. Decision tree is one of the classic learning methods in machine learning, and there has been a surge and renewed interest in learning decision trees due to their attractive property of being interpretable [2,6,8,15]. ID3 algorithm, the earliest proposal for decision tree by Quinlan, is a type of supervised learning algorithm designed for general purposes [13]. ID3 algorithm uses the concept of information entropy in information theory to select branching attributes by the information gain [16]. However, the method that uses this information gain tends to select attributes with many values [19]. This is because the information gain of this type of attribute is larger than the others. However, the attributes with more values are not always optimal [17,20,22].

Some scientists have already tried to fix the problem of "tending to use attributes with more values." Quinlan defined the gain ratio to improve the performance of the information gain, but it has some weak points such as the fact that it cannot be defined in some cases [14,22], which is discussed later in this paper. Several studies have attempted to introduce the concept of attribute importance by incorporating it into the calculation of information entropy. Some improvements rarely increased the accuracy but could simplify the trees [9,12,17,19,21]. Other scientists have proposed methods that incorporate Hellinger distance and K-L divergence into the calculation of the splitting criteria and have evaluated their performances compared to various splitting criteria. They, however, have yet to achieve a significant improvement in accuracy [1,5,18]. Some studies have attempted to incorporate information distance into the calculation of segmentation criteria; Ben-Gal et al. proposed new splitting criteria based on information distance and attempted to improve the performances of the information gain and the gain ratio. The results sometimes showed advantages against the other criteria in terms of average depth and classification accuracy, but in other cases, they fell short of the expectations [3]. Mántaras et al. formally proved that the use of normalized information distance and non-normalized information distance as criteria does not bias to select multi-valued attributes. Comparing the gain ratio and normalized information distance, they showed that not only they almost could get equal accuracy, but also that normalized information distance can simplify the tree construction by experiments [4].

Prior research has attempted various remedies to the problem of "tending to use attributes with more values." and some have tested new criteria based on information distance [3,4]. However, they have not experimented with simple (non-normalized) information distance before normalization and other calculations. They have shown that it is not effective so much to utilize normalized information distance to improve the gain ratio. In this paper, we experimentally show the performances of non-normalized information distance (D_1) that is not used in the experiments by either Mántaras et al. or Ben-Gal et al. and another similar distance (D_2) that is seldom investigated in other research. These two non-normalized information distances can in many cases surprisingly produce much higher accuracy than the gain ratio or the normalized information distance on imbalanced datasets. We analyze the causes theoretically. Specifically, 13 different UCI datasets are classified into four types, five datasets are provided which are randomly shuffled for each dataset so that the training data part and testing data part are separated differently. The performances of our decision tree algorithms are tested by the fine-grained experiments for each type compared to ID3 algorithm and the gain ratio-based algorithm.

The remainder of this paper is organized as follows. In Sect. 2, we present definition of the four types of datasets used in the experiments of this paper (Definition 1). In Sect. 3, we investigate the weak point of ID3 algorithm that we improve in this paper and analyze its cause (Proposition 3). In Sect. 4, we confirm the criterion gain ratio (Definition 4), a proposed improvement to ID3 algorithm presented by Quinlan [14]. Section 5 presents the definition of two non-normalized information distances D_1 and D_2 used in this paper (Definition 6) and their advantages (Theorem 7, Proposition 8). Section 6 shows the results of our detailed experiments with some specific decision tree diagrams and analysis between non-normalized information distances and the gain ratio. Section 7 concludes this paper.

2   Types of Datasets

In this paper, **all the random variables are discrete.** In this section, we define the four types of the datasets to finely analyze each decision tree algorithm.

Definition 1. Assume that dataset S has n attributes and symbol A is the set of the attributes that dataset S has. Let N_{A_k} be the number of the values that the kth attribute A_k ($1 \leq k \leq n$) has and let N_{Class} be the number of the values that the class of dataset S has. To classify each dataset under four types, we define the variance V at first:

$$V(A) = \frac{1}{n} \sum_{k=1}^{n} \left(N_{A_k} - \overline{N_A} \right)^2 \quad \text{where} \quad \overline{N_A} = \frac{1}{n} \sum_{k=1}^{n} N_{A_k} \quad \text{for all } A_k \in A. \quad (1)$$

Type1 - 4 are the types of the datasets used in our experiments, the definitions of which are below, where $max(A)$ means the number of values for the attribute with the most values (Table 1).

Type1: $V(A) > 1$ and $max(A) > N_{Class}$. The range taken by each N_{A_k} for A_k is large (in other words, each N_{A_k} for A_k is very different from each other) and the largest N_{A_k} is larger than N_{Class}.

Type2: $V(A) > 1$ and $max(A) < N_{Class}$. The range taken by each N_{A_k} for A_k is large (in other words, each N_{A_k} for A_k is very different from each other) and the largest N_{A_k} is smaller than N_{Class}.

Type3: $V(A) = 0$ and $max(A) = min(A) = N_{Class}$. All the N_{A_k} and N_{Class} are the same.

Type4: The others.

Table 1. The information of the specific datasets of Type4 we use

Dataset	$V(A)$	$max(A)$	N_{Class}
Nursery Dataset	0.839	5	5
Balance Scale Dataset	0	5	3
Car Evaluation Dataset	0.3	4	2
Hayes-Roth Dataset	0.25	4	3
Tic-Tac-Toe Endgame Dataset	0	3	2
Chess (King-Rook vs. King-Pawn) Dataset	0.028	3	2
Primary Tumor Dataset	0.154	3	18

3   Disadvantage of ID3 Algorithm

In this section, we investigate ID3 algorithm and consider why it favors attributes with many values. At first, we take a look at the formula of the information gain which is used in ID3 algorithm as the selection criterion.

Definition 2. Symbol A is used to express the set of attributes that dataset S has. Let A_k be the kth attribute dataset S has and let $Class$ be the class of dataset S. N_{A_k} denotes the number of the values that the kth attribute A_k $(1 \leq k \leq n)$ has and N_{Class} denotes the number of the values that the class of dataset S has. A_{k_i} $(1 \leq i \leq N_{A_k})$ expresses the ith value of attribute A_k and $Class_j$ $(1 \leq j \leq N_{Class})$ expresses the jth value of class $Class$, then for each attribute A_k, the information gain $Gain$ is:

$$Gain(A_k) = H(Class) - H(Class|A_k) \qquad \text{for all } A_k \in A, \qquad (2)$$

where the entropy and the conditional entropy H are:

$$H(Class) = - \sum_{j=1}^{N_{Class}} P(Class_j) \log_2 P(Class_j), \text{ where } P(Class_j) = \frac{|X \cap Class_j|}{|X|}, (3)$$

$$H(Class|A_k) = \sum_{i=1}^{N_{A_k}} H(Class|A_k = A_{k_i})P(A_{k_i}), \qquad (4)$$

where $P(A_{k_i}) = \dfrac{|X \cap A_{k_i}|}{|X|}$ and

$$H(Class|A_k = A_{k_i}) = - \sum_{j=1}^{N_{Class}} P(Class_j|A_k = A_{k_i}) \log_2 P(Class_j|A_k = A_{k_i}).$$

ID3 algorithm uses the largest information gain as the selection criterion, however, selecting the largest information gain essentially equals selecting the smallest conditional entropy, since $H(Class)$ is always the same for each information gain $Gain(A_k)$ [10].

In Proposition 3, we show the conditional entropy of the attribute with less values can be larger than that with more values.

Proposition 3. Let A'_k be an attribute constructed from attribute A_k by splitting each value into two. (For example, the ith value A_{k_i} in A_k is split into two types of values $A'_{k_{i_1}}$ and $A'_{k_{i_2}}$ in A'_k.) Then we have that

$$H(Class|A_k) \geq H(Class|A'_k). \tag{5}$$

Proof. Since $N_{A'_k} = 2N_{A_k}$, A'_k is the attribute that has more values than A_k. Thus, the number of the terms of $H(Class|A'_k = A'_{k_i})$ is more than that of $H(Class|A_k = A_{k_i})$. It also can be presumed that $H(Class|A'_k = A'_{k_i})$ for split attribute A'_k relatively tends to lead to zero or small compared to $H(Class|A_k = A_{k_i})$ of non-split attribute A_k. The more terms of $H(Class|A'_k = A'_{k_i})$ which are zero or small number, the smaller $H(Class|A'_k)$ can be calculated. Therefore, $H(Class|A_k) \geq H(Class|A'_k)$. The proof is completed.   □

Since $H(Class|A'_k)$ can be smaller than $H(Class|A_k)$, the attributes with more values tend to be preferred to be selected as the splitting attribute over attributes with fewer values. This phenomenon can happen when $V(A)$ is large, in other words when each N_{A_k} for A_k is very different from each other. Thus, especially on Type1 and Type2 datasets, the accuracy of ID3 algorithm relatively tends to be low because of this disadvantage.

4   Gain Ratio

Quinlan defined the gain ratio (especially in C4.5) to overcome the disadvantage of ID3 algorithm [14].

Definition 4. Let *Gain* be the information gain (Definition 2). A_k denotes the kth attribute dataset S has, and N_{A_k} denotes the number of the values of the kth attribute A_k ($1 \leq k \leq n$). The gain ratio *GainRatio* is:

$$GainRatio(A_k) = \frac{Gain(A_k)}{H(A_k)}, \tag{6}$$

where the entropy H is:

$$H(A_k) = - \sum_{i=1}^{N_{A_k}} P(A_{k_i}) \log_2 P(A_{k_i}), \quad \text{where} \quad P(A_{k_i}) = \frac{|X \cap A_{k_i}|}{|X|}. \tag{7}$$

Here $H(A_k)$ is often called split information. This gain ratio remedies the problem of ID3 algorithm which is that "tending to use attributes with more values." However, the gain ratio may not always be defined because the denominator i.e. $H(A_k)$ can be zero in some cases. The comparison of the accuracy and the analysis between the non-normalized information distance-based selection criteria and the gain ratio are shown in Sect. 6.

5 Information Distance-Based Splitting Criteria

In this section, we investigate the distance concept and analyze why non-normalized information distances can overcome the weak point of ID3 algorithm that we have shown before. Firstly, to be the distance, it must satisfy the following distance axioms [11].

Definition 5. A set E provided with a metric is called a metric space. If a function $d : E \times E \to \mathbb{R}$ such that for all $x, y, z \in E$ satisfies all the conditions below, it can be called a distance.

- d is non-negative: $d(x,y) \geq 0$ with equality if and only if $x = y$,
- d is symmetric: $d(x,y) = d(y,x)$,
- d verifies the triangular inequality: $d(x,y) \leq d(x,z) + d(z,y)$.

5.1 Non-normalized Information Distances (Proposed Methods)

We use two types of non-normalized information distances D_1 and D_2 based on the information theory introduced by Houllier [7].

Definition 6. Assume that S and Y are random variables. Let $H(X,Y)$ be the joint entropy of random variables S and Y and let $I(X;Y)$ be the mutual information of random variables S and Y. The two types of the non-normalized information distances D_1 and D_2 are

$$D_1(X,Y) = H(X,Y) - I(X;Y) = H(X|Y) + H(Y|X), \tag{8}$$
$$D_2(X,Y) = max(H(X), H(Y)) - I(X;Y) = max(H(X|Y), H(Y|X)). \tag{9}$$

It is proved that both D_1 and D_2 satisfy distance axioms in [7]. We use these D_1 and D_2 as the new selection criteria. The attribute whose D_1 or D_2 is the smallest is used as the splitting attribute of the branching of the decision tree.

5.2 Advantages of Distances

This part shows the two reasons why the non-normalized information distance-based selection criteria can overcome the disadvantage of ID3 algorithm.

Firstly, we show the reason why D_1 and D_2 are hardly affected by the attributes with many values by quoting the theorem in [4]. We rewrite the formulas of D_1 and D_2 for dataset S. Since the variable A_k has distribution which can be normalized as the probability distribution, A_k can be dealt as a discrete random variable, so does the *Class*:

$$D_1(A_k, Class) = H(Class|A_k) + H(A_k|Class), \tag{10}$$
$$D_2(A_k, Class) = max(H(Class|A_k), H(A_k|Class)). \tag{11}$$

Theorem 7. More values on attributes do not lead to smaller distances. Let A'_k be an attribute split from attribute A_k into two and the data with attribute A_k are also divided into two parts accordingly. Then we have that

$$D_1(A_k, Class) \leq D_1(A'_k, Class), \tag{12}$$

$$D_2(A_k, Class) \leq D_2(A'_k, Class). \tag{13}$$

Proof. Let $A'_{k_{i_1}}$ and $A'_{k_{i_2}}$ be the values divided into two from the ith value A_{k_i} of the kth attribute. Firstly, we take a look at the case of D_1. $D_1(A_k, Class) = H(Class|A_k) + H(A_k|Class) = -\sum_{j=1}^{N_{Class}} \sum_{i=1}^{N_{A_k}} P(Class_j, A_{k_i}) \log_2 \frac{P(Class_j, A_{k_i})}{P(A_{k_i})} - \sum_{i=1}^{N_{A_k}} \sum_{j=1}^{N_{Class}} P(Class_j, A_{k_i}) \log_2 \frac{P(Class_j, A_{k_i})}{P(Class_j)}$, however, the two terms

$$P(Class_j, A_{k_i}) \log_2 \frac{P(Class_j, A_{k_i})}{P(A_{k_i})} \tag{14}$$

and

$$P(Class_j, A_{k_i}) \log_2 \frac{P(Class_j, A_{k_i})}{P(Class_j)} \tag{15}$$

in $D_1(A_k, Class)$ are replaced with

$$P(Class_j, A'_{k_{i_1}}) \log_2 \frac{P(Class_j, A'_{k_{i_1}})}{P(A'_{k_{i_1}})} + P(Class_j, A'_{k_{i_2}}) \log_2 \frac{P(Class_j, A'_{k_{i_2}})}{P(A'_{k_{i_2}})} \tag{16}$$

and

$$P(Class_j, A'_{k_{i_1}}) \log_2 \frac{P(Class_j, A'_{k_{i_1}})}{P(Class_j)} + P(Class_j, A'_{k_{i_2}}) \log_2 \frac{P(Class_j, A'_{k_{i_2}})}{P(Class_j)} \tag{17}$$

in $D_1(A'_k, Class)$. Because the examples of A_{k_i} is split randomly into $A'_{k_{i_1}}$ and $A'_{k_{i_2}}$, we have $\frac{P(Class_j, A'_{k_{i_1}})}{P(A'_{k_{i_1}})} = \frac{P(Class_j, A'_{k_{i_2}})}{P(A'_{k_{i_2}})} = \frac{P(Class_j, A_{k_i})}{P(A_{k_i})}$, so the terms (14) and (16) are equal. But (15) is greater than (17), because when $p = p_1 + p_2$ and $p, p_1, p_2 \in [0, 1]$ we have that $\log_2 p \geq \log_2 p_1$ and $\log_2 p \geq \log_2 p_2$. Therefore $D_1(A_k, Class) \leq D_1(A'_k, Class)$. For D_2, $D_2(A_k, Class) = max(H(Class|A_k), H(A_k|Class)) = max(-\sum_{j=1}^{N_{Class}} \sum_{i=1}^{N_{A_k}} P(Class_j, A_{k_i}) \log_2 \frac{P(Class_j, A_{k_i})}{P(A_{k_i})}, -\sum_{i=1}^{N_{A_k}} \sum_{j=1}^{N_{Class}} P(Class_j, A_{k_i}) \log_2 \frac{P(Class_j, A_{k_i})}{P(Class_j)})$. Thus, if (14) and (16) are greater than (15) and (17), then $D_2(A_k, Class) = D_2(A'_k, Class)$, otherwise, $D_2(A_k, Class) \leq D_2(A'_k, Class)$. Therefore, both $D_1(A_k, Class) \leq D_1(A'_k, Class)$ and $D_2(A_k, Class) \leq D_2(A'_k, Class)$ are proved.   □

Consequently, this analysis can be the reason why D_1 and D_2 are scarcely affected by the attributes with many values when the range taken by each N_{A_k} is large such as Type1 and Type2 datasets.

Secondly, we explain why D_1 and D_2 perform better than the information gain, especially in the case of Type1. Here we show the formula of $H(A_k|Class)$ as well.

Definition 8. Let $Class$ be the class of dataset S and let A_k be the kth attribute dataset S has. N_{Class} denotes the number of the values that the class of dataset S has and N_{A_k} denotes the number of the values that the kth attribute A_k $(1 \leq k \leq n)$ has. $Class_j$ $(1 \leq j \leq N_{Class})$ expresses the jth value of class $Class$ and A_{k_i} $(1 \leq i \leq N_{A_k})$ expresses the ith value of attribute A_k, then the conditional entropy is:

$$H(A_k|Class) = \sum_{j=1}^{N_{Class}} H(A_k|Class = Class_j)P(Class_j), \tag{18}$$

where $\quad P(Class_j) = \dfrac{|X \cap Class_j|}{|X|} \quad$ and

$$H(A_k|Class = Class_j) = -\sum_{i=1}^{N_{A_k}} P(A_{k_i}|Class = Class_j)\log_2 P(A_{k_i}|Class = Class_j).$$

Proposition 9. The conditional entropy $H(A_k|Class)$ which is the opposite conditional entropy used in the information gain can bring balance to the non-normalized information distance-based selection criteria on Type1 datasets.

Proof. The difference between the information gain and non-normalized information distances D_1 and D_2 is that D_1 and D_2 calculate not only $H(Class|A_k)$ but also $H(A_k|Class)$ [3]. Under the case of Type1, for attribute A_k such as $N_{A_k} > N_{Class}$, because the number of the terms to calculate $H(A_k|Class = Class_j)$ is more than the number of the terms to calculate $H(Class|A_k = A_{k_i})$, $H(A_k|Class)$ tends to be larger than $H(Class|A_k)$. Though $H(Class|A_k)$ has as many terms as $H(A_k|Class = Class_j)$ to calculate, each term to calculate $H(Class|A_k)$ is multiplied by $P(A_{k_i})$, the total number of each $P(A_{k_i})$ is one. Therefore the number of the terms to calculate $H(Class|A_k)$ can scarcely affect the scale of $H(Class|A_k)$. The term $H(Class|A_k = A_{k_i})$ can easily be small when $N_{A_k} > N_{Class}$ even if it is not reasonable to be a splitting attribute. However, as we have explained, $H(A_k|Class)$ can be large instead when $N_{A_k} > N_{Class}$. D_1 can be balanced by adding the large $H(A_k|Class)$ to the small $H(Class|A_k)$. Therefore D_1 can avoid favoring attributes with many values without rational reason under the case of Type1. For D_2, since D_2 prefers the larger one between $H(Class|A_k)$ and $H(A_k|Class)$, it is easy to assume that D_2 also can avoid being affected by $H(Class|A_k)$ that is calculated as small without rational reason. Hence, it can be expected that D_2 performs as well as D_1 under the case of Type1. This advantage should not be applied to Type2 datasets because Type2 is that $N_{A_k} < N_{Class}$. The proof is completed.   □

6 Experiments

We have shown the non-normalized information distances D_1 and D_2, and the possibility that they can improve the performances of the existing algorithms in some cases. In this section, we show the experiments using 13 practical UCI datasets with different backgrounds and the decision tree algorithms with D_1 and

D_2 can increase the accuracy by about 15–25%, especially on Type1 and Type2 datasets. We also can notice that they even perform as well as ID3 algorithm and the algorithm using the gain ratio on the datasets of Type3 and Type4.

The way of our experiments is below.

- If the dataset has missing value, we remove the examples including the missing values from the dataset to convert the original dataset into the dataset which has no missing values.
- We shuffle the examples to avoid being the biased datasets because some are initially sorted by some columns, which leads to bias in the datasets. We use the five shuffled datasets and verify the accuracy.
- For each dataset of the experiments, we take different proportions 75% for training and the remaining 25% for testing.
- We classify each dataset under four types as shown in Sect. 2.

6.1   Result Examples for Each Dataset Type

We show a part of the details of some experiments. One thing we have to notice is that, in the experiments, the numbers N_{A_k} in the training dataset might be different from the numbers N_{A_k} in the original datasets. It is because when dividing the datasets into the training part and the testing part, some values can only exist in either of them.

Type1

Table 2. The results for five experiments of Breast Cancer Dataset (removed the examples including missing values, $V(A) = 9.278$ and $max(A) = 11$, $N_{Class} = 2$)

Dataset	Information gain	Gain ratio	D_1	D_2
breast-cancer pattern 1	38.57%	50.00%	60.00%	62.86%
breast-cancer pattern 2	44.29%	40.00%	57.14%	60.00%
breast-cancer pattern 3	47.14%	42.86%	70.00%	67.14%
breast-cancer pattern 4	35.71%	50.00%	61.43%	61.43%
breast-cancer pattern 5	52.86%	51.43%	65.71%	70.00%

Table 3. The results for five experiments of Lymphography Dataset ($V(A) = 3.624$ and $max(A) = 8$, $N_{Class} = 4$)

Dataset	Information gain	Gain ratio	D_1	D_2
lymphography pattern 1	59.46%	64.86%	83.78%	81.08%
lymphography pattern 2	67.57%	72.97%	75.68%	67.57%
lymphography pattern 3	51.35%	67.57%	62.16%	62.16%
lymphography pattern 4	67.57%	62.16%	81.08%	64.86%
lymphography pattern 5	43.24%	45.95%	81.08%	64.86%

Type2

Table 4. The results for five experiments of Soybean (Large) Dataset (removed the examples including missing values, $V(A) = 1.064$ and $max(A) = 7$, $N_{Class} = 15$)

Dataset	Information gain	Gain ratio	D_1	D_2
soybean-large pattern 1	74.63%	89.55%	89.55%	83.58%
soybean-large pattern 2	71.64%	73.13%	80.60%	73.13%
soybean-large pattern 3	70.15%	86.57%	89.55%	85.07%
soybean-large pattern 4	76.12%	86.57%	82.09%	86.57%
soybean-large pattern 5	71.64%	89.55%	86.57%	83.58%

Type3

Table 5. The results for five experiments of Congressional Voting Records Dataset (removed the examples including missing values, $V(A) = 0$ and $max(A) = min(A) = N_{Class} = 2$)

Dataset	Information gain	Gain ratio	D_1	D_2
congressional-voting pattern 1	94.83%	94.83%	93.10%	96.55%
congressional-voting pattern 2	94.83%	94.83%	94.83%	98.28%
congressional-voting pattern 3	94.83%	94.83%	94.83%	96.55
congressional-voting pattern 4	91.38%	91.38%	91.38%	91.38%
congressional-voting pattern 5	93.10%	93.10%	91.38%	91.38%

Type4

Table 6. The results for five experiments of Car Evaluation Dataset ($V(A) = 0.3$ and $max(A) = 4$, $N_{Class} = 2$)

Dataset	Information gain	Gain ratio	D_1	D_2
car-evaluation pattern 1	95.37%	95.37%	94.44%	94.44%
car-evaluation pattern 2	98.15%	98.15%	97.45%	97.45%
car-evaluation pattern 3	96.76%	97.22%	95.37%	96.06%
car-evaluation pattern 4	96.30%	96.99%	96.30%	96.30%
car-evaluation pattern 5	97.22%	97.22%	96.99%	96.99%

According to Table 2, 3, 4, 5 and 6, algorithms with non-normalized information distances D_1 and D_2 improve the performance of the information gain better than the gain ratio in most cases on Type1 and Type2 datasets. Especially on Type1 datasets, they increase the accuracy a lot (about 15–25%). Compared between Type1 and Type2, it is seen that the improvement in Type1 is bigger than that in Type2. This is considered because of Proposition 9, which is mentioned in Sect. 5.2. On the other hand, on Type3 and Type4 datasets, D_1 and D_2 seldom show many advantages against the information gain. However, they also do not decrease the accuracy so much. For some cases, they show even better accuracy than the information gain and the gain ratio.

6.2   Advantage of Distances Compared to Gain Ratio

Here we take a look how non-normalized information distances are the better splitting criteria than the gain ratio.

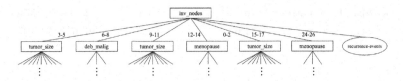

Fig. 1. A part of the tree generated by the information gain (ID3 algorithm) for breast-cancer pattern 1

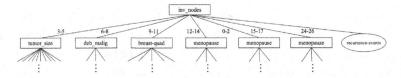

Fig. 2. A part of the tree generated by the gain ratio for breast-cancer pattern 1

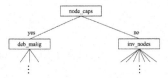

Fig. 3. A part of the tree generated by using D_1 for breast-cancer pattern 1

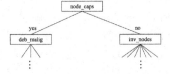

Fig. 4. A part of the tree generated by using D_2 for breast-cancer pattern 1

Table 7. Each information gain (IG), gain ratio (GR), D_1, and D_2 in breast-cancer pattern 1 which is sorted respectively (in descending order for information gain and gain ratio, in ascending-order for D_1 and D_2)

Attributes(N_{A_k}) : IG	Attributes(N_{A_k}) : GR	Attributes(N_{A_k}) : D_1	Attributes(N_{A_k}): D_2
inv_nodes(7) : 0.0974	inv_nodes(7) : 0.0759	node_caps(2) : 1.4717	node_caps(2) : 0.8160
deb_malig(3) : 0.0766	node_caps(2) : 0.0741	irradiate(2) : 1.5525	irradiate(2) : 0.8373
node_caps(2) : 0.0525	deb_malig(3) : 0.0501	breast(2) : 1.8614	breast(2) : 0.9934
tumor_size(11) : 0.0515	irradiate(2) : 0.0418	menopause(3) : 1.9532	menopause(3) : 1.0961
irradiate(2) : 0.0312	tumor_size(11) : 0.0174	inv_nodes(7) : 1.9565	inv_nodes(7) : 1.1853
age(6) : 0.0202	menopause(3) : 0.0103	deb_malig(3) : 2.2440	deb_malig(3) : 1.4520
menopause(3) : 0.0114	age(6) : 0.0099	breast-quad(5) : 2.8140	breast-quad(5) : 1.9483
breast-quad(5) : 0.0028	breast-quad(5) : 0.0014	age(6) : 2.8772	age(6) : 2.0289
breast(2) : 0.0005	breast(2) : 0.0005	tumor_size(11) : 3.7279	tumor_size(11) : 2.9109

Since $GainRatio(A_k) = \frac{Gain(A_k)}{H(A_k)}$, the disadvantages of the gain ratio are:

- if $H(A_k)$ is zero, the gain ratio cannot be defined, and
- it may choose attributes with very low $H(A_k)$ rather than those with high $Gain$ [4].

As shown in Table 7 and the trees (Fig. 1, 2, 3 and 4), the gain ratio can overcome the problem "tending to favor the attribute with many values" to some extent thanks to being divided by the entropy $H(A_k)$. However, the selection criteria of non-normalized information distances D_1 and D_2 are seldom affected by many values in the attributes. Their accuracies are higher than that of the gain ratio. It is deemed that the effectiveness to add $H(A_k|Class)$ to $H(Class|A_k)$ (to replace $H(Class|A_k)$ for $H(A_k|Class)$ for non-normalized information distance D_2) is higher than that of what the information gain divided by $H(A_k)$. In addition, D_1 and D_2 do not have the cases not to be defined. Therefore, it can be said that non-normalized information distances D_1 and D_2 should have more advantages to be used as the selection criteria than the gain ratio.

6.3 Comprehensive Experimental Results

We show more results in the other experiments. The examples including missing values are removed from the datasets. The dataset names are below.

Type1: Breast Cancer, Lymphography, Mushroom.
Type2: Soybean (Large).
Type3: Congressional Voting Records, SPECT Heart.
Type4: Nursery, Balance Scale, Car Evaluation, Hayes-Roth, Tic-Tac-Toe Endgame, Chess (King-Rook vs. King-Pawn), Primary Tumor.

For each dataset, we prepare five different datasets which are sorted differently by shuffling them. The summary of the results is below. Let $PF(C)$ be the performance (accuracy) of the algorithm with criterion C. Here IG and GR mean the information gain and the gain ratio respectively.

Table 8. The numbers of the cases that the existing algorithms are better than the non-normalized information distance-based algorithms

Accuracy	Type1	Type2	Type3	Type4	Total
$PF(IG) > PF(D_1)$	0/15	0/5	5/10	17/35	22/65
$PF(IG) > PF(D_2)$	1/15	0/5	3/10	16/35	20/65
$PF(GR) > PF(D_1)$	1/15	2/5	6/10	16/35	25/65
$PF(GR) > PF(D_2)$	2/15	3/5	5/10	19/35	29/65

Table 9. The numbers of the cases that the existing algorithms as good as the non-normalized information distance-based algorithms

Accuracy	Type1	Type2	Type3	Type4	Total
$PF(IG) = PF(D_1)$	5/15	0/5	3/10	9/35	17/65
$PF(IG) = PF(D_2)$	6/15	0/5	1/10	12/35	19/65
$PF(GR) = PF(D_1)$	5/15	1/5	3/10	10/35	19/65
$PF(GR) = PF(D_2)$	5/15	2/5	2/10	8/35	17/65

Table 10. The numbers of the cases that the existing algorithms are better than the non-normalized information distance-based algorithms multiplied by 1.1

Accuracy	Type1	Type2	Type3	Type4	Total
$PF(IG) > PF(D_1) \times 1.1$	0/15	0/5	1/10	0/35	1/65
$PF(IG) > PF(D_2) \times 1.1$	0/15	0/5	0/10	0/35	0/65
$PF(GR) > PF(D_1) \times 1.1$	0/15	0/5	1/10	0/35	1/65
$PF(GR) > PF(D_2) \times 1.1$	0/15	0/5	0/10	1/35	1/65

According to Table 8 and 9, the non-normalized distance-based algorithms (D_1 and D_2) perform better than the algorithms with the information gain or the gain ratio in most cases, especially on Type1 and Type2 datasets. Table 10 is the comparison between the pure accuracies of the existing criteria and the those of D_1 and D_2 multiplied by 1.1. It is shown to avoid to care about that the algorithms with D_1 and D_2 slightly lose against those of the information gain and the gain ratio. Consequently, it can be said that the non-normalized distance-based algorithms perform well on not only Type1 and Type2 datasets for sure, but also on Type3 and Type4 datasets.

7   Conclusion

In conclusion, surprisingly, non-normalized information distances D_1 and D_2 are the better criteria than other proposed splitting criteria such as the gain ratio or normalized information distances. They can overcome the problem that "existing decision tree algorithms tend to select the attribute with many values when splitting" in many cases. In this paper, we divide 13 datasets into four types and shuffle each dataset to create five patterns for precise decision tree experiments. The results show that decision trees using non-normalized information distances D_1 and D_2 significantly increase the accuracy (15–25%) than those using the information gain and the gain ratio on imbalanced datasets (Type1 and Type2) with larger differences in the number of values each attribute has. Besides, they can perform almost as equally as the existing criteria even on the datasets which are not imbalanced (Type3 and Type4). The decision tree algorithms using non-normalized information distances as the splitting criteria in this study may lead to improvements in a variety of recent complex machine learning algorithms. The results also suggest that methods such as "normalization" does not necessarily make algorithms better, and it is expected that this idea can be applied to algorithms other than decision trees. In the future, we plan to analyze the differences between the two non-normalized information distances (D_1 and D_2) used in this paper in detail and to study the application of decision trees that use these non-normalized information distances as the splitting criteria.

Acknowledgements. This work was supported in part by Shanghai Municipal Science and Technology Key Project 20511100300.

References

1. Akash, P.S., Kadir, M.E., Ali, A.A., Shoyaib, M.: Inter-node hellinger distance based decision tree. In: IJCAI, pp. 1967–1973 (2019)
2. Bastani, O., Kim, C., Bastani, H.: Interpreting blackbox models via model extraction. arXiv preprint arXiv:1705.08504 (2017)
3. Ben-Gal, I., Dana, A., Shkolnik, N., Singer, G.: Efficient construction of decision trees by the dual information distance method. Qual. Technol. Quant. Manag. **11**(1), 133–147 (2014)
4. López DeMántaras, R.: A distance-based attribute selection measure for decision tree induction. Mach. Learn. **6**(1), 81–92 (1991)
5. Dong, M., Liu, M., Jing, C.: One-against-all-based hellinger distance decision tree for multiclass imbalanced learning. Frontiers of Information Technology & Electronic Engineering **23**(2), 278–290 (2022)
6. Frosst, N., Hinton, G.: Distilling a neural network into a soft decision tree. arXiv preprint arXiv:1711.09784 (2017)
7. Houllier, M., Luo, Y.: Information distances over clusters. In: Zhang, L., Lu, B.-L., Kwok, J. (eds.) ISNN 2010. LNCS, vol. 6063, pp. 355–364. Springer, Heidelberg (2010). https://doi.org/10.1007/978-3-642-13278-0_46
8. Hu, X., Rudin, C., Seltzer, M.: Optimal sparse decision trees. In: Advances in Neural Information Processing Systems, vol. 32 (2019)

9. Jin, C., De-Lin, L., Fen-Xiang, M.: An improved id3 decision tree algorithm. In: 2009 4th International Conference on Computer Science & Education, pp. 127–130. IEEE (2009)
10. Korn, G.A., Korn, T.M.: Mathematical handbook for scientists and engineers: definitions, theorems, and formulas for reference and review. Courier Corporation (2000)
11. Li, M., Chen, X., Li, X., Ma, B., Vitányi, P.M.B.: The similarity metric. IEEE Trans. Inf. Theory **50**(12), 3250–3264 (2004)
12. Liang, X., Qu, F., Yang, Y., Cai, H.: An improved id3 decision tree algorithm based on attribute weighted. In: International Conference on Civil, Materials and Environmental Sciences, pp. 613–615 (2015)
13. Quinlan, J.R.: Discovering rules by induction from large collections of examples. Expert Systems in the Micro Electronics Age (1979)
14. Quinlan, J.R.: Induction of decision trees. Mach. Learn. **1**(1), 81–106 (1986)
15. Sarpatwar, K., et al.: Privacy enhanced decision tree inference. In: Proceedings of the IEEE/CVF Conference on Computer Vision and Pattern Recognition Workshops, pp. 34–35 (2020)
16. Shannon, C.E.: A mathematical theory of communication. Bell Syst. Tech. J. **27**(3), 379–423 (1948)
17. Soni, V.K., Pawar, S.: Emotion based social media text classification using optimized improved id3 classifier. In: 2017 International Conference on Energy, Communication, Data Analytics and Soft Computing (ICECDS), pp. 1500–1505. IEEE (2017)
18. Chong, S., Cao, J.: Improving lazy decision tree for imbalanced classification by using skew-insensitive criteria. Appl. Intell. **49**(3), 1127–1145 (2019)
19. Wang, Y., Li, Y., Song, Y., Rong, X., Zhang, S.: Improvement of id3 algorithm based on simplified information entropy and coordination degree. Algorithms **10**(4), 124 (2017)
20. Wang, Z., Liu, Y., Liu, L.: A new way to choose splitting attribute in id3 algorithm. In: 2017 IEEE 2nd Information Technology, Networking, Electronic and Automation Control Conference (ITNEC), pp. 659–663. IEEE (2017)
21. Yuxun, L., Niuniu, X.: Improved id3 algorithm. In: 2010 3rd International Conference on Computer Science and Information Technology, vol. 8, pp. 465–468. IEEE (2010)
22. Zhu, L., Yang, Y.: Improvement of decision tree ID3 algorithm. In: Wang, S., Zhou, A. (eds.) CollaborateCom 2016. LNICST, vol. 201, pp. 595–600. Springer, Cham (2017). https://doi.org/10.1007/978-3-319-59288-6_59

The Time-Sequence Prediction via Temporal and Contextual Contrastive Representation Learning

Yang-yang Liu and Jian-wei Liu[✉] ⓘ

Department of Automation, China University of Petroleum, Beijing, Beijing, China
yangyang-liu@student.cup.edu.cn, liujw@cup.edu.cn

Abstract. The time series classification tasks have commonly faced the problem, i.e., lower labelled time series data and higher labelling costs. Regarding this issue, some researchers try introducing representation learning into the time series classification task. Moreover, recently the researcher proposed a model called TS-TCC. TS-TCC combines transformer and representation learning and has achieved promising performance. Therefore, we will predict the Time-sequence via Temporal and Contextual Contrastive Representation Learning (PTS-TCC). PTS-TCC tends to perform better than TS-TCC in robustness. PTS-TCC consists of four modules: cluster module, data hidden representation learning module, temporal hidden representation learning module, and contextual hidden representation learning module. Extensive quantitative evaluations of the HAR (Human Activity Recognition), Epilepsy (Epilepsy Seizure Prediction) and Sleep-EDF (Sleep Stage Classification) datasets verify the effectiveness of our proposed PTS-TCC. In contrast to SOTA, the average accuracy rate of PTS-TCC improves by 5% in HAR, Epilepsy and Sleep-EDF.

Keywords: Representation learning · Time series classification · Cluster

1 Introduction

The time series classification task is different from the conventional classification task. Time series classification aims to classify ordered sequences, which are ordered in chronological order. For example, ECG/EEG signal classification, action sensor data classification, etc. Recent research have suggested that the time series classification task gradually became the most important research task in the time series field. Many time series classification models [12, 18, 19] are proposed and get better results. All of these types of models use methods that are deep learning to learn data features.

Indeed, it is not easy to gather so many labelled time series data. Likewise, manual labelling is hard and unrealistic. Therefore, we do not have enough labelled time-series data to train the deep learning model.

As discussed above, the problem of insufficient labelling data in time series classification tasks is important. One way to overcome this problem is to use the self-supervised

© The Author(s), under exclusive license to Springer Nature Switzerland AG 2022
S. Khanna et al. (Eds.): PRICAI 2022, LNCS 13629, pp. 465–476, 2022.
https://doi.org/10.1007/978-3-031-20862-1_34

hidden representation learning method. Elle et al. [2] propose an unsupervised Time-Series representation learning framework via Temporal and Contextual Contrasting (TS-TCC). TS-TCC implements the classification tasks on the unlabeled time series data. Furthermore, TS-TCC gets better test accuracy than the previous supervised time series classification model.

In order to improve the robustness of the model based on the TS-TCC [2], we propose predicting the Time-sequence via Temporal and Contextual Contrastive Representation Learning (PTS-TCC). PTS-TCC consists of several modules: cluster module, data hidden representation learning module, temporal hidden representation learning module, and contextual hidden representation learning module. Different from TS-TCC, PTS-TCC uses cluster and informer to enhance model robustness. As we know, the informer [3] can learn better temporal hidden representation than the transformer. Moreover, our Clustering module treats data in the same cluster as the positive example of the input data and the rest in other clusters as the negative example to enhance the model's discriminative capacity. The experimental result has shown that PTS-TCC has improved the average test accuracy by at least 4% while maintaining good robustness on the HAR, Epilepsy and Sleep-EDF dataset. The contributions of this work are shown as follows:

(1) The idea of clustering is introduced into the PTS-TCC model to enhance the model's discriminative capacity. The purpose of improving the robustness of the model can be achieved;
(2) We use the informer, which performs better in time series forecast tasks, to enhance the model's capacity to learn hidden temporal representation. With this, we can accomplish the goal that improves the model's robustness;
(3) For PTS-TCC, our experimental results demonstrate the state-of-the-art performance on the robustness and test accuracy indexes.

2   Related Work

One of the most popular tasks in time series research is the task of time series classification (TSC) for decades. Lines J et al. [4] used the nearest neighbour classifier and distance measurement method to solve the TSC task in 2015. DTW is the most distance measurement method in the TSC task when using an artificial neural network as a classifier. Furthermore, [4] also proves that neural networks using different distance metrics combine to superior to sets of individual components. Literature [4] has contributed to the development of the ensembles method. Since then, the gathering method can be classified into ensembles of decision-making trees [6, 7] and ensembles of the discriminative classifier. These ensemble methods have a common feature that transfers the time sequence into a new feature space [8]. In 2015, A method that an ensemble of 35 classifiers called COTE [9] improved performance in the time series classification task. Literature [10] proposes HIVE-COTE based on COTE. However, HIVE-CODE loses its practical application value in the case of a large data set.

Recently, researchers have been trying to apply deep learning to TSC task solving with the successful application of deep learning models in various classification tasks [11]. Literature [12] uses convolutional neural networks to solve the TSC task for the first time in 2017. After that, the deep learning model used in the TSC task can be categorized into the Generative deep learning classification model and Discriminant Deep Learning Classification Model [13]. Generative deep learning classification models [14, 15] need unsupervised training before using classifier learning weight. Discriminant Deep Learning Classification Model [16, 17] is a classifier that can directly learn the mapping between the original inputs of a time series (or its hand-designed features) and the probability distribution of class variables in the dataset. With the development of deep learning, Discriminant Deep Learning Classification Model use back-propagation to train the deep learning model to get the feature, rather than manual design.

As we all know, the deep learning model needs large label data. However, labelled time series data in actual industrial acquisitions are small and expensive to label. TS-TCC [20] has been proposed, using representation learning to model the TSC task with unlabeled time series data. TS-TCC gets a better result in unlabeled time series data classification tasks than the previous model, which uses supervised learning. Inspired by [20]'s work, we propose the PTS-TCC with data augmentation methods and the self-attention mechanism. PTS-TCC differs from TS-TCC in that PTS-TCC uses a cluster model and informer, which has good performance in the field of time series, to reinforce the model's learning of features.

3   The Proposed PTS-TCC Model

In this section, we will introduce PTS-TCC in detail, and the structure is shown in Fig. 1. Our model aims to solve unlabeled time series data classification tasks. Firstly, we use a clustering algorithm to group the time series data. Secondly, we use a deep learning model and data augmentation methods to learn the deep feature and the underlying dependency relationships of data. This step is mainly composed of three parts: (1) We use the data augmentation method and neural network to learn the time series data hidden representation; (2) We use an informer to learn the hidden temporal representation of time series data; (3) We use non-linear projection head to learn hidden contextual representation. Finally, we need to minimize the loss function of PTS-TCC to get the appropriate weights of the model.

The main components of the PTS-TCC model and the effect of each module, and the transfer of inter-module parameters are as follows:

(1) Cluster module. The cluster module's primary role is to generate clustering for the input time series sequence, which can enhance the discriminative capacity of learning data features and improve the robustness of the model. The cluster model's input is time-sequence $X = \{x_1, x_2, ..., x_n\}$. After the clustering module, we get the output vector $X' = \{x_1^1, x_2^1, ..., x_1^i, x_2^i, ..., x_1^k, ..., x_{N_k}^k\}, i \in k$.

(2) Data hidden representation learning modules. The data hidden representation learning module's primary role is to reinforce the modelling capacity of learning data features. In this module, the input vector is $X' = \{x_1^1, x_2^1, ..., x_1^i, x_2^i, ..., x_1^k, ..., x_{N_k}^k\}, i \in k$. After applying the different data augmentation strategies of PTS-TCC, we will get two output data hidden representation vectors, Z^s and Z^w.

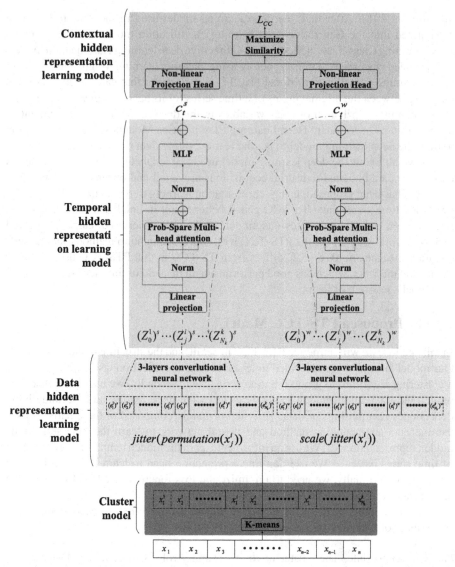

Fig. 1. The structure of PTS-TCC. PTS-TCC consists of four parts: cluster module, data hidden representation learning module, temporal hidden representation learning module, and contextual hidden representation learning module.

(3) Temporal hidden representation learning module. The temporal hidden representation learning module's primary role is to enhance the modelling of the dependency relationship of time series data and improve the robustness of PTS-TCC. In this module, the input vector is Z^s and Z^w. After being processed by the temporal hidden representation learning module, we will get two output temporal hidden representation vectors, c^s and c^w.

Table 1. Nomenclature

Terms	Meaning	Terms	Meaning
x_j^i	The j-th data of the i-th cluster	N_o	the number of data in the other cluster as c_t^i
N_k	the amount of all data in the k-th cluster	$c_j^{m^-}$	the m-th data in the other cluster as c_t^i
$sim(\cdot)$	similarity measure function	$c_t^{j^+}$	represents the j-th data in the same cluster as c_t^i
N_i	the number of data in the same cluster as c_t^i	τ	augmentation family
c_t^i	the input data at time t	/	/

(4) Contextual hidden representation learning module. The contextual hidden representation learning module's primary role is to learn more discriminative representations and improve the robustness of PTS-TCC. In this module, the input vector is c^s and c^w. After being handled by the contextual hidden representation learning module, we will get the similarity between c^s and c^w (Eq. (13)).

(5) Minimizing loss function (e.g. Equation (1)). Among the Eq. (1), λ_1 and λ_2 are the hyper-parameters of PTS-TCC, i.e., the trade-off parameters of every loss function. L^s and L^w are the loss function of different data augmentation strategies. L_{CC} is the loss function of the contextual hidden representation learning model (Table 1).

$$L = \lambda_1 \cdot (L^s + L^w) + \lambda_2 \cdot L_{CC} \tag{1}$$

3.1 Cluster Module

We introduce the idea of clustering to learn better dependencies between data and improve the robustness of the model. Considering the size of the dataset and the convergence speed and interpretability of the clustering algorithm, we chose k-means as the clustering method.

The cluster module's input is time-sequence $X = \{x_1, x_2, ..., x_n\}$. After the clustering module, we get the output vector $áX' = \{x_1^1, x_2^1, ..., x_1^i, x_2^i, ..., x_1^k, ..., x_{N_k}^k\}, i \in k$.

We can get positive sample similarity (e.g., Eq. (2)) and full sample similarity (e.g., Eq. (3)) based on the above step.

$$sim_{positive} = \sum_{j=1}^{N_i} \exp(sim(c_t^i, c_t^{j^+})/\tau) \tag{2}$$

$$sim_{all} = \sum_{j=1}^{N_i} \exp(sim(c_t^i, c_j^{j^+})/\tau) + \sum_{m=1}^{N_o} \exp(sim(c_t^i, c_j^{m^-})/\tau) \tag{3}$$

3.2 Data Hidden Representation Learning Module

The data hidden representation learning module consists of two data augmentation strategies and a convolutional neural network [20]. Firstly, the input vector needs to go through two kinds of data augmentation strategies (Eq. (4) and Eq. (5)). And then, the vector was input into the convolutional neural network (Eq. (6) and Eq. (7)). The $jitter(\cdot)$ function represents adding a normal distribution (with a mean of 0 and a standard deviation of 0.8) into the input vector. The $permutation(\cdot)$ function represents a random displacement from the input vector slicing. The $scale(\cdot)$ function represents multiplying the input variable by a random variable [21]. The $Conv(\cdot)$ function represents a convolution neural network.

$$E^s(X') = jitter(permutation(X')) \tag{4}$$

$$E^w(X') = scale(jitter(X')) \tag{5}$$

$$Z^s = Conv(E^s(X')) \tag{6}$$

$$Z^w = Conv(E^w(X')) \tag{7}$$

Based on the feedback structure in the red dotted line in Fig. 1, we derive the data hidden representation learning's loss function (Eq. (8) and Eq. (9)). In the Eq. (8) and Eq. (9), L^w represents the loss function corresponding to the weak enhancement policy in the t-to-$t + H$ period; L^s represents the loss function corresponding to the weak enhancement policy in the t-to-$t + H$ period; z_t^i represents the i-th data hidden representation vector at t time; c represents the temporal hidden representation vector from the temporal hidden representation learning module; $W(\cdot)$ is a linear layer that can map c_t^i to the same dimension as $(z_t^i)^s$.

$$L^s = -\frac{1}{H} \sum_{h=1}^{H} \log \frac{\exp((W_h((c_t^i)^s)))^T (z_{t+h}^i)^w)}{\sum_{n \in N_{t,h}} \exp((W_h((c_t^i)^s))^T (z_n^i)^w)} \tag{8}$$

$$L^w = -\frac{1}{H} \sum_{h=1}^{H} \log \frac{\exp((W_h((c_t^i)^w)))^T (z_{t+h}^i)^s)}{\sum_{n \in N_{t,r}} \exp((W_h((c_t^i)^w))^T (z_n^i)^s)} \tag{9}$$

3.3 Temporal Hidden Representation Learning Module

We use the temporal hidden representation learning module to learn the temporal hidden representation vector. The temporal hidden representation learning module's every layer may be divided into Prob-Sparse Multi-Head Attention (PMHA) [3] and Multilayer Perceptron (MLP). PMHA's main role is to learn the temporal features of the time series sample (Eq. (10)). MLP's (Eq. (11)) main role is learning data features and dependencies between data. Moreover, MLP consists of two RELU active functions and a fully connected layer with dropout. Lastly, re-operating all L layer's results to get the final result c_t (Eq. (12)). The effect of the $Norm(\cdot)$ is normalizing the input data

$$\tilde{\Phi} = PMHA(Norm(W(Z))) \tag{10}$$

$$\Phi = MLP(Norm(\tilde{\Phi})) + \tilde{\Phi} \tag{11}$$

$$c_t = \Phi_L^0 \tag{12}$$

3.4 Contextual Hidden Representation Learning Module

The contextual hidden representation learning module consists of two non-linear projection heads. The non-linear projection head maps the contexts into the space where the contrasting contextual operation is applied. We can get the loss function of the contextual hidden representation learning module (Eq. (13)).

$$L_{CC} = -\sum_{i=1}^{N} \log \frac{\sum_{j=1}^{N_i} \exp(sim(c_t^i, c_j^{j^+})/\tau)}{\sum_{j=1}^{N_i} \exp(sim(c_t^i, c_j^{j^+})/\tau) + \sum_{m=1}^{N_o} \exp(sim(c_t^i, c_j^{m^-})/\tau)} \tag{13}$$

4 Experiment

4.1 Parameters and Preprocessing

We normalized the time series data to eliminate the undesirable effects of singular data in the time series. We use the Max-Min normalization method to normalize the data in this experiment. The Max-Min normalization method mainly performs a linear transformation on the original data. We assume that $\min x$ and $\max x$ are the minima and maximum values of x. The original value x is mapped to the valued x^{norm} in the interval [0,1] through the min-max normalization method, and the formula is shown in Eq. (14).

$$x' = \frac{x - \min x}{\max x - \min x} \tag{14}$$

4.2 Baseline and Data-Set

We compare our proposed PTS-TCC method with the following baselines: (1) SSL-ECG [25]; (2) CPC [26]; (3) SimCLR [27]; (4) TS-TCC [20]. Furthermore, we use Human Activity Recognition [22], Epilepsy Seizure Prediction [23], and Sleep Stage Classification [24] as the dataset. Table 3 introduces the parameters of three datasets.

Human Activity Recognition [22]. The UCI HAR dataset is activity recognition based on smartphone sensor data. It was created with the experimental team from the University of Genoa, Italy, in 2012. The data was collected from 30 volunteers aged 19 to 48. These people wore smartphones strapped to their waists and performed six everyday activities (Walking, Walking Upstairs, Walking Downstairs, Sitting, Standing, and Lying). The records exercise data of 6 normal activities through mobile phone software developed. The motion data recorded is x, y, and z accelerometer data (linear acceleration) and gyroscope data (angular velocity) from the smartphone, sampled at 50 Hz (50 data points per second). Each volunteer performed two activity sequences, the first with the device on the left side of the waist and the second with the smartphone placed by the user according to their preferences. At the same time, the video of each volunteer performing the activity was recorded, and the sports category was manually marked according to these videos and sensor data later (Table 2).

Table 2. The specific parameter values on the HAR, Epilepsy and Sleep-EDF dataset.

Hyperparameter symbols	Dataset values		
	Har	Sleepedf	Epilepsy
input_channels	9	1	1
kernel_size	8	25	8
stride	1	3	1
final_out_channels	128	128	128
num_classes	6	5	2
dropout	0.35	0.35	0.35
features_len	18	127	24
num_epoch	40	40	40
beta1	0.9	0.9	0.9
beta2	0.99	0.99	0.99
lr	3e−4	3e−4	3e−4
batch_size	128	128	128
jitter_scale_ratio	1.1	1.5	0.001
jitter_ratio	0.8	2	0.001
max_seg	8	5	5
temperature	0.2	0.2	0.2
hidden_dim	100	64	100
timesteps	6	120	10

Epilepsy Seizure Prediction [23]. The Epilepsy dataset contains EEG recordings from 500 subjects; each subject's brain activity was recorded for 23.6 s. The original dataset

Table 3. Parameters of the dataset (Human Activity Recognition, Epilepsy Seizure Prediction, and Sleep Stage Classification) used in the experiment.

Dataset	Train set	Test set	Validation set	Class	Length	Channel
HAR	5881	2947	1471	6	128	9
Epilepsy	7360	2300	1840	2	178	1
SleepEDF	27425	6805	8078	5	3000	1

is labelled into five classes. Since four categories do not include seizures, we combine them into one category.

Sleep Stage Classification [24]. The Sleep Stage Classification dataset classifies input EEG signals into five categories: Wake (W), Non-rapid eye movement (N1, N2, N3), and Rapid eye movement (REM). Sleep-EDF includes an overnight PSG sleep recording during which a single EEG channel (i.e. Fpz-Cz) was sampled at 100 Hz.

4.3 Results and Discussion

Table 4. The experiment results of 10-fold cross-validation in HAR, Epilepsy, and Sleep-EDF datasets.

Data	HAR	Epilepsy	Sleep-EDF
1-fold	0.9424	0.9926	0.9001
2-fold	0.9447	0.9922	0.9028
3-fold	0.9476	0.9931	0.9006
4-fold	0.9460	0.9931	0.9036
5-fold	0.9512	0.9926	0.9020
6-fold	0.9427	0.9922	0.9036
7-fold	0.9492	0.9909	0.8962
8-fold	0.9489	0.9926	0.9045
9-fold	0.9401	0.9926	0.8935
10-fold	0.9476	0.9922	0.9026
Mean	0.9460	0.9924	0.9009

In this section, we will use discrete coefficients to measure the model's degree of volatility in three datasets. Furthermore, we use test accuracy to evaluate the model's performance in every dataset. In addition, we use 10-fold cross-validation to measure the reliability and stability of the model. The results of the 10-fold cross-validation are shown in Table 4. Table 5 shows the test accuracy (the accuracy here is the average of multiple experiments), mean, standard deviation, and discrete coefficient of the baseline model (SSL-ECG, CPC, SimCLR, TS-TCC) and our model.

Derive from Table 5's experiment data, and we will find: (1) PTS-TCC's test accuracy is higher than baseline in HAR, Epilepsy, and Sleep-EDF; (2) PTS-TCC's mean test accuracy is five per cent higher than baseline in HAR, Epilepsy, and Sleep-EDF; (3) PTS-TCC's discrete coefficient is lower than baseline in HAR, Epilepsy, and Sleep-EDF.

The above phenomenon suggests a conclusion that our model improves the model's test accuracy while ensuring robustness in the unlabeled time series dataset. This conclusion is because our model uses the idea of cluster and informer. Compared with TS-TCC, our model can learn more comprehensive hidden representation information from data. Moreover, it can further deepen the model's learning of data features and dependencies between data. Hence, the model's robustness and generalization ability are improved, and test accuracy is increased.

Table 5. The experiment results on HAR, Epilepsy, and Sleep-EDF datasets. We show the test accuracies, means, standard deviations, and discrete coefficients of the baseline model (e.g. SSL-ECG, CPC, SimCLR, TS-TCC) and our model.

Method\Data	Test accuracy			Mean	Standard deviation	Discrete coefficient
	HAR	Epilepsy	Sleep-EDF			
SSL-ECG	0.6534	0.8915	0.7458	0.7636	0.1200	0.1572
CPC	0.8385	0.9444	0.8282	0.8704	0.0643	0.0739
SimCLR	0.8097	0.9353	0.7891	0.8447	0.0791	0.0937
TS-TCC	0.9037	0.9554	0.83	0.8964	0.0630	0.0703
PTS-TCC [ours]	**0.9460**	**0.9924**	**0.9009**	**0.9464**	**0.0458**	**0.0483**

5   Conclusions and Future Work

In this paper, we propose to Predict the Time-sequence via Temporal and Contextual Contrastive Representation Learning (PTS-TCC), which is adaptable for time series representation learning and classification tasks. PTS-TCC consists of a cluster module, data augmentation strategy for representation learning, and prob-sparse self-attention operation of the informer. This structure of PTS-TCC allows our model can learn better data features and dependencies between data. Hence, our model can improve the test accuracy based on better robustness. The experimental results illustrate that our model is generally superior to the baseline models. In future work, we will explore the representation learning on the asynchronous event sequences.

References

1. Ching, T., Himmelstein, D.S., Beaulieu-Jones, B.K., et al.: Opportunities and obstacles for deep learning in biology and medicine. J. R. Soc. Interface **15**(141), 20170387 (2018)

2. Eldele, E., Ragab, M., Chen, Z., et al.: Time-series representation learning via temporal and contextual contrasting. arXiv preprint arXiv:2106.14112

3. Zhou, H., Zhang, S., Peng, J., et al.: Informer: Beyond efficient transformer for long sequence time-series forecasting. In: AAAI (2021)

4. Lines, J., Bagnall, A.: Time series classification with ensembles of elastic distance measures. Data Min. Knowl. Disc. **29**(3), 565–592 (2014). https://doi.org/10.1007/s10618-014-0361-2

5. Bagnall, A., Lines, J., Bostrom, A., Large, J., Keogh, E.: The great time series classification bake off: a review and experimental evaluation of recent algorithmic advances. Data Min. Knowl. Disc. **31**(3), 606–660 (2016). https://doi.org/10.1007/s10618-016-0483-9

6. Baydogan, M.G., Runger, G., Tuv, E.: A bag-of-features framework to classify time series. IEEE Trans. Pattern Anal. Mach. Intell. **35**(11), 2796–2802 (2013)

7. Deng, H., Runger, G., Tuv, E., et al.: A time series forest for classification and feature extraction. Inf. Sci. **239**, 142–153 (2013)

8. Kate, R.J.: Using dynamic time warping distances as features for improved time series classification. Data Min. Knowl. Disc. **30**(2), 283–312 (2015). https://doi.org/10.1007/s10618-015-0418-x

9. Bagnall, A., Lines, J., Hills, J., et al.: Time-series classification with COTE: the collective of transformation-based ensembles. IEEE Trans. Knowl. Data Eng. **27**(9), 2522–2535 (2015)

10. Lines, J., Taylor, S., Bagnall, A.: Hive-cote: the hierarchical vote collective of transformation-based ensembles for time series classification. In: ICDM. IEEE, pp: 1041–1046 (2016)

11. LeCun, Y., Bengio, Y., Hinton, G.: Deep learning. Nature **521**(7553), 436–444 (2015)

12. Gamboa, J.C.B.: Deep learning for time-series analysis. arXiv preprint arXiv:1701.0188 (2017)

13. Ismail Fawaz, H., Forestier, G., Weber, J., Idoumghar, L., Muller, P.-A.: Deep learning for time series classification: a review. Data Min. Knowl. Disc. **33**(4), 917–963 (2019). https://doi.org/10.1007/s10618-019-00619-1

14. Bengio, Y., Yao, L., Alain, G., et al.: Generalized denoising auto-encoders as generative models. In: Advances in Neural Information Processing Systems (2013)

15. Hu, Q., Zhang, R., Zhou, Y.: Transfer learning for short-term wind speed prediction with deep neural networks. Renewable Energy **85**, 83–95 (2016)

16. Uemura, M., Tomikawa, M., Miao, T., et al.: Feasibility of an AI-based measure of the hand motions of expert and novice surgeons. Computational and mathematical methods in medicine (2018)

17. Geng, Y., Luo, X.: Cost-sensitive convolution based neural networks for imbalanced time-series classification. arXiv preprint arXiv:1801.04396 (2018)

18. Lin, S., Runger, G.C.: GCRNN: Group-constrained convolutional recurrent neural network. IEEE Trans. Neural Networks Learn. Syst. **29**(10), 4709–4718 (2017)

19. Serrà, J., Pascual, S., Karatzoglou, A.: Towards a universal neural network encoder for time series. In: CCIA, pp: 120–129 (2018)

20. Eldele, E., Ragab, M., Chen, Z., et al.: Time-series representation learning via temporal and contextual contrasting. In: IJCAI (2021)

21. Um, T.T., Pfister, F.M.J., Pichler, D., et al.: Data augmentation of wearable sensor data for parkinson's disease monitoring using convolutional neural networks. In: Proceedings of the 19th ACM International Conference on Multimodal Interaction, pp: 216–220 (2017)

22. Anguita, D., Ghio, A., Oneto, L., Parra, X., Reyes-Ortiz, J.L.: A public domain dataset for human activity recognition using smartphones. In: ESANN (2013)

23. Andrzejak, R.G., Lehnertz, K., Mormann, F., et al.: Indications of nonlinear deterministic and finite-dimensional structures in time series of brain electrical activity: dependence on recording region and brain state. Phys. Rev. E Stat. Nonlin. Soft Matter Phys. **64**(6), 061907 (2001)

24. Eldele, E., et al.: An attention-based deep learning approach for sleep stage classification with single-channel EEG. IEEE Trans. Neural Syst. Rehabil. Eng. (2021)
25. Etemad, A., Sarkar, P.: Self-supervised ECG representation learning for emotion recognition. IEEE Trans. Affective Comput. (2020)
26. van den Oord, A., Li, Y., Vinyals, O.: Representation learning with contrastive predictive coding. arXiv preprint arXiv:1807.03748 (2018)
27. Chen, T., Kornblith, S., Norouzi, M., Hinton, G.: A simple framework for contrastive learning of visual representations. In: ICML (2020)

Managing Dataset Shift by Adversarial Validation for Credit Scoring

Hongyi Qian[1]($\boxtimes$) (ID), Baohui Wang[2], Ping Ma[2], Lei Peng[3], Songfeng Gao[3], and You Song[1,2]($\boxtimes$) (ID)

[1] School of Computer Science and Engineering, Beihang University, Beijing 100191, People's Republic of China
{qianhongyi,songyou}@buaa.edu.cn
[2] School of Software, Beihang University, Beijing 100191, People's Republic of China
{wangbh,maping}@buaa.edu.cn
[3] HuaRong RongTong (Beijing) Technology Co., Ltd, Beijing 100033, People's Republic of China
{penglei,gaosongfeng}@chamc.com.cn

Abstract. The inconsistency between the distribution of training data and the data that need to be predicted is very common in credit scoring scenarios, which is called dataset shift. The macroeconomic environment and risk control strategies are likely to evolve over time, and the behavior patterns of borrowers may also change. The model trained with past data may not be applicable to the recent stage. Although dataset shift can cause poor model performance, the vast majority of studies do not take this into account. In this study, we propose a method based on adversarial validation, in which partial training set samples with the closest distribution to the predicted data are selected for cross-validation to ensure generalization performance. In addition, the remaining training samples with inconsistent distribution are also involved in the training process, but not in the validation, which makes full use of all the data and further improves the model performance. To verify the effectiveness of the proposed method, comparative experiments with several other data split methods are conducted with the Lending Club dataset. The experimental results demonstrate the importance of dataset shift problem in the field of credit scoring and the superiority of the proposed method.

Keywords: Dataset shift · Data distribution · Credit scoring · Adversarial validation · Cross-validation

1 Introduction

With the rapid development of internet finance in recent years, users can simply use online platforms to complete peer-to-peer transactions. How to effectively evaluate the borrowers' solvency and reduce default risk has become an important research area in the academic and business community [8]. At this stage, with the continuous development of intelligent machine learning methods, credit

© The Author(s), under exclusive license to Springer Nature Switzerland AG 2022
S. Khanna et al. (Eds.): PRICAI 2022, LNCS 13629, pp. 477–488, 2022.
https://doi.org/10.1007/978-3-031-20862-1_35

scoring models have made a series of progress in balanced sampling method [14], feature selection [11], and ensemble model [13]. These advancements have allowed credit scoring to reach new heights of accuracy, but the vast majority of them still use the traditional cross-validation schemes for data segmentation [18,19]. The whole dataset is randomly split without considering the dataset shift problem.

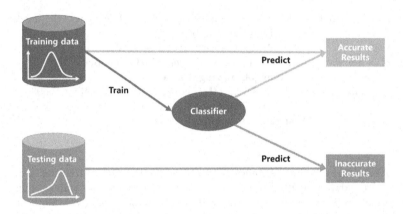

Fig. 1. Classifier performance loss caused by different data distribution.

Dataset shift [17] is an important topic in machine learning. As shown in Fig. 1 it refers to the scenario where the joint distribution of inputs and outputs is inconsistent during the training and testing phases. This inconsistency is usually caused by sample selection bias, which can lead to a loss in the generalization performance of the model on new data. Applications such as demand prediction [7], customer profiling for marketing [7], and recommender systems [7] are susceptible to dataset shift. This phenomenon is particularly evident in the non-stationary environments such as credit scoring [1], where changes in the macroeconomic environment and risk control strategies can invalidate models trained with past data.

However, there are few studies on dataset shift in the field of credit scoring. For example, Maldonado et al. [12] proposed an algorithmic-level machine learning solution, using novel fuzzy support vector machine (FSVM) strategy, in which the traditional hinge loss function is redefined to account for dataset shift. To our best knowledge, no data-level machine learning solution has been proposed to solve the dataset shift problem in the field of credit scoring.

The main reason why the dataset shift problem has not been highlighted in the credit scoring field is that the major credit scoring public datasets in the past do not provide the timestamp information of the samples. Such as German [4], Australian [4], Taiwan [4,20], Japan [4] in the UCI repository[1]

---

[1] https://archive.ics.uci.edu/ml/index.php.

and PAKDD[2], Give Me Some Credit[3], Home Credit Default Risk[4] provided in the data mining competitions. As a result, researchers are unable to construct the training and testing sets in chronological order. However, that can be changed with the release of the Lending Club[5] dataset. Lending Club is a US peer-to-peer lending company, headquartered in San Francisco, California, and it provided a large number of real credit data for practitioners and scholars to study. The provided data have specific timestamp information that allows researchers to easily study the effect of dataset shift.

The goal of this study is to propose a data-level machine learning solution to deal with the problem of dataset shift in credit scoring scenarios. To sum up, the main contributions of this study are as follows:

i. This study is the first solution based on a data-level machine learning approach to address the dataset shift problem in the credit scoring field. This study recommends paying more attention to the impact of data distribution on the model effectiveness, rather than just minimizing the classification error.

ii. The method used to solve the dataset shift problem in this study is based on adversarial validation. Researchers at Uber [15] have previously proposed a method that uses adversarial validation to filter features to deal with dataset shift. They use the feature importance obtained from adversarial validation to filter the most inconsistently distributed features sequentially. However, there is a trade-off for this method between the improvement of generalization performance and losing information. On the contrary, the method proposed in this study based on adversarial validation can make full use of all data to improve the model generalization performance.

iii. Experiments on Lending Club data showed that the proposed method in this study achieves the best results compared to the existing methods that commonly use cross-validation or timeline filtering to partition data.

The rest of this paper is organized as follows. Section 2 presents some theoretical background of dataset shift. Section 3 details the adversarial validation based method to help balance the training and testing sets. Section 4 shows the design details and results of the experiments and discusses them. Section 5 gives the conclusion and illustrates the direction for future research.

2 Dataset Shift

2.1 Definition of Dataset Shift

The term *dataset shift* was first introduced by J. Quionero-Candela et al. [17]. In this study, *dataset shift* is represented for the situation where the data used to train the classifier and the environment where the classifier is deployed do not follow the same distribution, which means $P_{train}(y, x) \neq P_{test}(y, x)$.

---

[2] https://pakdd.org/archive/pakdd2009/front/show/competition.html.
[3] https://www.kaggle.com/c/GiveMeSomeCredit.
[4] https://www.kaggle.com/c/home-credit-default-risk/data.
[5] https://www.lendingclub.com/.

2.2 Types of Dataset Shift

A classification problem consists of three parts, namely a set of features or covariates x, a target variable y, and joint distribution $P(y, x)$. There are three different types of shift, depending on which probabilities change or not:

- **Covariate shift** represents the situation where training and testing data distribution may differ arbitrarily, but there is only one unknown target conditional class distribution. In other words, it appears only in $X \to Y$ problems, and is mathematically defined as the case where $P_{train}(y \mid x) = P_{test}(y \mid x)$ and $P_{train}(x) \neq P_{test}(x)$.
- **Prior probability shift** is the reverse case of covariate shift. It appears only in $Y \to X$ problems, and is defined as the case where $P_{train}(x \mid y) = P_{test}(x \mid y)$ and $P_{train}(y) \neq P_{test}(y)$.
- **Concept shift** happens when the relationship between the input and class variables changes, which is defined as

$$P_{train}(y \mid x) \neq P_{test}(y \mid x) \text{ and } P_{train}(x) = P_{test}(x) \text{ in } X \to Y \text{ problems.}$$
$$P_{train}(x \mid y) \neq P_{test}(x \mid y) \text{ and } P_{train}(y) = P_{test}(y) \text{ in } Y \to X \text{ problems.}$$

2.3 Causes of Dataset Shift

There are many possible reasons for dataset shift, the two most important of which are as follows:

Reason 1. Sample selection bias is a systematic defect in the data collection or labeling process, where the training set is obtained by a biased method and this non-uniform selection will cause the training set to fail to represent the real sample space. Joaquin et al. [16] give a mathematical definition of sample selection bias:

- $P_{train} = P(s = 1 \mid y, x)P(x)$ and $P_{test} = P(y \mid x)P(x)$ in $X \to Y$ problems.
- $P_{train} = P(s = 1 \mid x, y)P(y)$ and $P_{test} = P(x \mid y)P(y)$ in $Y \to X$ problems.

where s is a binary selection variable that decides whether an instance is included in the training samples ($s = 1$) or rejected from it ($s = 0$).

In the credit scoring literature it goes by the name of reject inference, because potential credit applicants who are rejected under the previous model are not available to train future models [2].

Reason 2. Non-stationary environments is often caused by temporal or spatial changes, and is very common in real-world applications. Depending on the classification problem's type, non-stationary environments can lead to different kinds of shift:

- In $X \to Y$ problems, a non-stationary environment could create changes in either $P(x)$ or $P(y \mid x)$, generating covariate shift or concept shift, respectively.
- In $Y \to X$ problems, it could generate prior probability shift with a change in $P(y)$ or concept shift with a change in $P(x \mid y)$.

Non-stationary environments often appears in adversarial classification problems such as network intrusion detection [10], spam detection [3] and fraud detection [5]. The presence of an adversary trying to bypass the existing classifier introduces any possible dataset shift, and the bias can change dynamically.

3 Methodology

3.1 Adversarial Validation

Adversarial validation is a method to detect dataset shift, which requires training a binary classifier and judging whether the sample is from the training set or the testing set. Specifically, the process of adversarial validation can be divided into three steps:

i. For the original dataset $\{train\_X, train\_y, val\_X, val\_y\}$, remove the old label column $\{train\_y, val\_y\}$, and add a new label column that marks the source of the data $\{train\_y_s, val\_y_s\}$, labeling the samples in the training set as 0 (*i.e. train*$\_y_s = 0$) and the samples in the testing set as 1 (*i.e. train*$\_y_s = 1$).
ii. Train the classifier on the dataset $\{train\_X, train\_y_s, val\_X, val\_y_s\}$ with the newly labeled column. The output of the classifier is the probability that the sample belongs to the testing set. In this study, 5-fold cross-validation is used.
iii. Observe the results of the classifier. The performance of the classifier indicates the consistency of data distribution. The higher the accuracy of classifier, the more inconsistent the distribution of training set and testing set.

3.2 Using Adversarial Validation Results to Deal with Dataset Shift

The method proposed based on adversarial validation in this study can not only judge whether the dataset distribution is consistent, but also further balance the training and testing sets. A total of two schemes are proposed in this study.

Method 1. Use only the data with the top-ranked adversarial validation results for 5-fold cross-validation.

The samples inconsistent with the distribution of the testing set can be removed from the training process. In particular, the training data can be divided into two parts by the adversarial validation results according to a certain threshold value. The samples that are more consistent with the testing set distribution are called $data\_X_a = \{train\_X_a, val\_X_a\}$, and the remaining samples are called $data\_X_b$. $P_{data\_X_a} \approx P_{test\_X} \neq P_{data\_X_b}$, and only $data\_X_a$ is reserved for 5-fold cross-validation. As a result, model evaluation metrics on the validation data should have similar results on the testing data, which means that if the model works well on the validation data, it should also work well on the testing data.

Method 2. All data are used for training, and only the data with the top-ranked adversarial validation results are used for validation.

Although **Method 1** alleviates the problem of inconsistent data distribution between training and testing sets, it has defects in data utilization. Only $data\_X_a$ data was used in the whole training process, and $data\_X_b$ data was wasted. To solve this problem, $data\_X_b$ is added to the training data of each fold in the process of 5-fold cross-validation to assist training, but it does not participate in the validation. This not only maintains the consistency of validation and testing results, but also makes full use of all data.

4   Experimental Study

4.1   Data Collection

The dataset used in this study comes from Lending Club, and the time range is from 2018M1[6] to 2020M9 over a period of 33 months. The original dataset contains 276,685 samples with a positive sample ratio of 21.93%[7]. The timestamp information helps divide training and testing sets in strict chronological order. Specifically, the data of 18 months from 2018M1 to 2019M6 are taken as the training set, which contains 247,276 samples in total. The data from 2019M7 to 2020M9 were taken as the testing set, including 29,409 samples.

Many original features in the Lending Club data have a high proportion of missing values, and some of the remaining variables are unavailable to an investor before deciding to fund the loan. As a result, including the target variable "loan_status", 25 variables are actually used for modeling. These variables include basic personal information, credit history and loan information.

4.2   Model and Hyperparameters Set-up

As a modern gradient boosting decision tree (GBDT) [6] library, LightGBM [9] is chosen as the modeling tool, and the same hyperparameters are used for both the adversarial validation and credit scoring modeling phases. Unless otherwise noted, the default model setting is used. Specifically, for category variables, we employ the LightGBM built-in support. For other hyperparameters, "num_boost_round" is set to 50000, which is a relatively large value. Meanwhile, by setting the parameter "early_stopping_rounds" to 200, the model will stop training if the AUC for validation data doesn't improve in the last 200 rounds. It not only ensures sufficient training, but also prevents over-fitting. Besides, "max_depth", "colsample_bytree", "subsample" are set as 4, 0.8 and 0.8 respectively.

---

[6] The representation of time in this study consists of two parts, for example, 2018M1 represents January 2018.

[7] The samples with "Charged off" and "Fully Paid" status are taken as positive and negative samples respectively, all loans with other status have been filtered out as their final status are unknown.

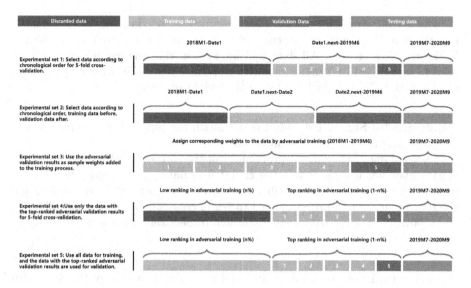

Fig. 2. Experimental setup, including 5 experimental sets, comparing a variety of models' performance on the testing set, which is trained on data divided by time or by adversarial validation results.

4.3 Experiment Set-up

As shown in Fig 2, a total of 5 sets of experiments are set up. The testing set data of each experiment are all from 2019M7 to 2020M9, while the training and validation sets are divided in different ways.

Experimental Set 1. Select data according to chronological order for 5-fold cross-validation.

A fixed time point is set and only data after that time point are used for the 5-fold cross-validation. Specifically, the starting month of the cross-validation data was selected from 2018M1 to 2019M6 for a total of 18 experiments. In these experiments, the starting point selection 2018M1, which uses all data for training can be used as a benchmark.

Experimental Set 2. Select data according to chronological order, training data before, validation data after.

Experiment set 2 only used data closer to the testing set for validation. Specifically, there are three choices of data time ranges, which are to use all data, 2018M6 and subsequent data, 2018M12 and subsequent data. These three groups of data will be divided into training and validation data according to the sequence of timeline, for a total of $17 + 11 + 5 = 33$ experiments.

Experimental Set 3. Use the adversarial validation results as sample weights added to the training process.

The output probability of the adversarial validation classifier to the samples, i.e., the similarity with the testing set samples, is directly used as the weight in the training process. All data will be used in this one experiment, and no need to be divided by time or quantile. Specifically, set the "weight" parameter in LightGBM Dataset API to change the weight of each instance.

Experimental Set 4. Use only the data with the top-ranked adversarial validation results for 5-fold cross-validation.

The ranking of the output probability of the sample by the adversarial validation classifier is regarded as the criterion of data partitioning. Data that is more inconsistent with the distribution of the testing set will be discarded, and the remaining data will be subjected to 5-fold cross-validation. Specifically, 0%, 5% ... 90%, 95% of the data were discarded, respectively, for a total of 20 experiments.

Experimental Set 5. All data are used for training, and only the data with the top-ranked adversarial validation results are used for validation.

Experimental Set 4 brings about the problem of wasting data. This can also harm the model performance, especially when the amount of discarded data is large. Experimental Set 5 adds these discarded data that are inconsistent with the testing set distribution into the cross-validation training data, but does not participate in the validation. This not only addresses the problem of dataset shift, but also makes full use of all data. Similarly, the data are also divided according to the output probability ranking of the samples by the adversarial validation classifier, and the number of experiments is the same as in Experimental Set 4, with a total of 20 experiments.

4.4   Results and Discussion

Results and Analysis of Experimental Set 1. Figure 3 (a) shows the results of Experimental Set 1. With the increase of the starting month of the selected data, the AUC of the validation set shows a trend of gradual decline, and the decline speed increases with the decrease of the selected data. However, for the testing set, the AUC fluctuated steadily when the selected data started before 2019M2, and only after that did it start to show a significant decreasing trend. This confirms that the problem of dataset shift does exist, adding data far from the testing set to the training process can only improve offline validation performance rather than the predicted score on the testing set.

The 5-fold cross-validation with all the data could be used as a benchmark, which the AUC of the testing set was 0.7237. Among all the experiments of Experimental Set 1, the selection of 2018M2 and later data for cross-validation is the best, with the testing set AUC reaching 0.7256.

Results and Analysis of Experimental Set 2. As shown from Fig. 3 (b) to (d), regardless of the selection range of training validation data starts from 2018M1, 2018M7, or 2019M1, with the gradual increase of data divided into the training set, the AUC of validation set and testing set both show an increasing trend, and the gap between them gradually decreases. This indicates that postponing the time point of splitting the training and validation sets can improve both the performance of the model and the consistency of the validation and testing set results.

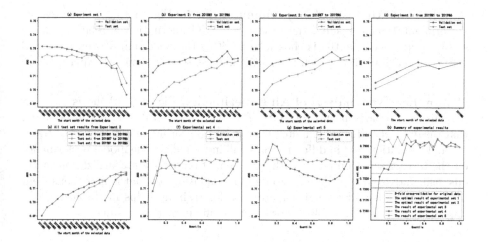

Fig. 3. Summary of experimental set results.

Figure 3 (e) integrates the testing set AUC results of the three sub-experiments, and the optimal results that can be achieved by all three are relatively close. The best result occurs when using the data from 2018M7 to 2019M5 as the training set and the 2019M6 data as the validation set, the testing set AUC reaches 0.7220. This result is lower than using all the original data directly for 5-fold cross-validation, since the 2019M6 data, which is closest to the testing set distribution, is only involved in the validation and not in training.

Results and Analysis of Experimental Set 3. The AUC result of adversarial validation is 0.9681, much higher than 0.5, which indicates that the classifier can easily distinguish the training data from the test data, and the two are indeed inconsistent in distribution. The final AUC obtained for the validation and testing set are 0.7149 and 0.7202, respectively, which is rather inferior to the benchmark of using the full data directly for the 5-fold cross-validation. This indicates that changing only the sample weights without changing the sample selection does not effectively solve the dataset bias problem.

Results and Analysis of Experimental Set 4. As shown from Fig. 3 (f), with the increase of the probability quantile of adversarial validation, the testing set AUC showed a gradual rise at first, and then a relatively stable fluctuation. When the quantile selection is 75%, the maximum testing set AUC can reach is 0.7315, which is an improvement compared with the previous three experiments. When the quantile is small, the performance of the model is greatly reduced due to the lack of available training data, exposing the drawback that this method fails to make full use of all data.

Results and Analysis of Experimental Set 5. Figure 3 (g) illustrates the Experimental Set 5 results, the testing set AUC fluctuation is relatively more stable. When the quantile is chosen to be 40%, the maximum testing set AUC value can reach 0.7327, which is also the highest score among all experiments.

Comprehensive Analysis of All Experiments. Figure 3 (h) shows the comprehensive comparison of the results of all 5 experimental sets. It can be noted that the dataset shift problem does exist in credit scoring, and dividing the training and validation sets in different ways will indeed affect the model performance on the testing set. Compared with other partitioning or data utilization methods, using adversarial validation to build a validation set that is more consistent with the test set and involving more data for training helps in stabilizing and improving the results. Table 1 shows the specific numerical results.

Table 1. Comparison of optimal testing set results of each experimental set. CV refers to cross-validation and ADV refers to adversarial validation.

Training methods	AUC
Baseline: CV for original data	0.7237
Experimental set 1: CV for recent data	0.7256
Experimental set 2: only use recent data for validation	0.7220
Experimental set 3: use the ADV results as sample weights	0.7203
Experimental set 4: CV for data with top-ranked ADV results	0.7315
Experimental set 5: CV for original data and only use data with top-ranked ADV results for validation	**0.7327**

5   Conclusion and Future Work

This study proposes a method based on adversarial validation to deal with the dataset shift problem in the credit scoring field. Only the training samples whose distribution is consistent with the testing set are used for cross-validation to ensure the model generalization performance. Furthermore, to make full use of all data information to further improve model performance, the remaining training samples whose distribution is inconsistent with the testing set are also added into the training process of each fold of cross-validation, but not involved in the validation.

Experiments on the Lending Club dataset showed that the proposed method is more helpful in improving performance in scenarios where the data distribution of the training set and the testing set are inconsistent, rather than dividing data in chronological order. This work demonstrates the importance of the dataset shift problem in credit scoring. For the sake of performance on new data, it recommends paying more attention to the impact of data distribution on the model effectiveness, rather than just minimizing the classification error.

In the future work plan, more ways to exploit adversarial validation partitioned data can be explored. Transfer learning, which aims to improve the performance of models in different but related target domains, would be a good choice. In addition to credit scoring, the application of adversarial validation can be explored in other data distribution inconsistency scenarios.

References

1. Castermans, G., Martens, D., Gestel, T.V., Hamers, B., Baesens, B.: An overview and framework for PD backtesting and benchmarking. J. Oper. Res. Soc. **61**(3), 359–373 (2010)
2. Crook, J.N., Banasik, J.: Does reject inference really improve the performance of application scoring models. J. Bank. Finance **28**, 857–874 (2004)
3. Dalvi, N., Domingos, P., Mausam, Sanghai, S., Verma, D.: Adversarial classification. In: Proceedings of the Tenth ACM SIGKDD International Conference on Knowledge Discovery and Data Mining, pp. 99–108. KDD 2004. Association for Computing Machinery, New York (2004)
4. Dua, D., Graff, C.: UCI machine learning repository (2017)
5. Fawcett, T., Provost, F.J.: Adaptive fraud detection. Data Min. Knowl. Disc. **1**, 291–316 (2004)
6. Friedman, J.H.: Greedy function approximation: a gradient boosting machine. Ann. Stat. **29**(5), 1189–1232 (2001)
7. Gama, J., Žliobaitundefined, I., Bifet, A., Pechenizkiy, M., Bouchachia, A.: A survey on concept drift adaptation. ACM Comput. Surv. **46**(4), 1–37 (2014)
8. Karlan, D., Zinman, J.: Microcredit in theory and practice: using randomized credit scoring for impact evaluation. Science **332**(6035), 1278–1284 (2011)
9. Ke, G., et al.: LightGBM: a highly efficient gradient boosting decision tree. Adv. Neural Inf. Process. Syst. **30**, 3147–3155 (2017)
10. Kolcz, A., Teo, C.H.: Feature weighting for improved classifier robustness. In: CEAS 2009 (2009)
11. Kozodoi, N., Lessmann, S., Papakonstantinou, K., Gatsoulis, Y., Baesens, B.: A multi-objective approach for profit-driven feature selection in credit scoring. Decis. Support Syst. **120**, 106–117 (2019)
12. Maldonado, S., López, J., Vairetti, C.: Time-weighted fuzzy support vector machines for classification in changing environments. Inf. Sci. **559**, 97–110 (2021)
13. Marqués, A.I., García, V., Sánchez, J.S.: Exploring the behaviour of base classifiers in credit scoring ensembles. Expert Syst. Appl. **39**(11), 10244–10250 (2012)
14. Niu, K., Zhang, Z., Liu, Y., Li, R.: Resampling ensemble model based on data distribution for imbalanced credit risk evaluation in P2P lending. Inf. Sci. **536**, 120–134 (2020)

15. Pan, J., Pham, V., Dorairaj, M., Chen, H., Lee, J.Y.: Adversarial validation approach to concept drift problem in user targeting automation systems at uber. arXiv preprint arXiv:2004.03045 (2020)
16. Quiñonero-Candela, J., Sugiyama, M., Schwaighofer, A., Lawrence, N.D.: When training and test sets are different: characterizing learning transfer (2009)
17. Quionero-Candela, J., Sugiyama, M., Schwaighofer, A., Lawrence, N.D.: Dataset Shift in Machine Learning. The MIT Press (2009)
18. Song, Y., Wang, Y., Ye, X., Wang, D., Yin, Y., Wang, Y.: Multi-view ensemble learning based on distance-to-model and adaptive clustering for imbalanced credit risk assessment in P2P lending. Inf. Sci. **525**, 182–204 (2020)
19. Xia, Y., Liu, C., Da, B., Xie, F.: A novel heterogeneous ensemble credit scoring model based on bstacking approach. Expert Syst. Appl. **93**, 182–199 (2018)
20. Yeh, I.C., Lien, C.H.: The comparisons of data mining techniques for the predictive accuracy of probability of default of credit card clients. Expert Syst. Appl. **36**(2), 2473–2480 (2009)

Linking Check-in Data to Users on Location-aware Social Networks

Yujie Li[1], Yu Sang[2], Wei Chen[1]([✉]), and Lei Zhao[1]

[1] School of Computer Science and Technology, Soochow University, Suzhou, China
{robertchen,zhaol}@suda.edu.cn
[2] School of Artificial Intelligence and Computer Science, Jiangnan University,
Wuxi, China
7213107001@stu.jiangnan.edu.cn

Abstract. Linking check-in data to their owners can benefit many downstream tasks, such as POI (Point of Interest) recommendation, destination prediction, and route planning, since we can obtain redundant information for each user after linking. Consequently, we formulate and investigate the novel problem CUL (Check-in-User Linking) in this work. Notably, the main difference between CUL and the existing problem TUL (Trajectory-User Linking) is that the trajectories used in TUL are continuous, while the check-in records in CUL are discrete. To tackle the problem CUL effectively, we develop a model entitled CULVAE (Check-in-User Linking via Variational Autoencoder). Firstly, a well-designed grid index is applied to organize the input check-in records. Then, an encoding module is developed to embed a user with corresponding grids. Next, a decoding module is proposed to generate a low-dimensional representation of each user. Finally, a multi-class classifier is proposed to link check-in records to users based on the output of the decoding module. We conduct extensive experiments on four real-world datasets, and the results demonstrate that our proposed model CULVAE performs better than all state-of-art approaches.

Keywords: Check-in Data · Social networks · Variational autoencoder

1 Introduction

The ubiquitous GPS-enabled devices (e.g., mobile phones and bracelets) and the flourish of location-aware social networks (e.g., Facebook and Twitter) bring the convenience for acquiring large-scale user-related check-in data. Due to the abundant information and user characteristics involved in these data, there has been increasing attention paid to check-in based studies, such as POI recommendation [6,23], route planning [16], and cross-platform user account linkage [3,4].

As the fundamental and an indispensable component of the above-mentioned studies, the management and analysis of check-in data is increasingly being a significant study nowadays. In view of this, we formulate and investigate a novel problem namely CUL (**C**heck-in-**U**ser **L**inking), i.e., linking check-in data to

© The Author(s), under exclusive license to Springer Nature Switzerland AG 2022
S. Khanna et al. (Eds.): PRICAI 2022, LNCS 13629, pp. 489–503, 2022.
https://doi.org/10.1007/978-3-031-20862-1_36

users who generate them. We argue that the study is different from the existing work TUL (**Trajectory-User Linking**) [11,26] and the main reasons are as follows. The points in trajectories generated by cars, trucks, buses, and GPS-equipped animals are usually automatically sampled by GPS devices with fixed and short time intervals. However, the check-in data collected from social networks are usually very sparse and have no fixed time interval, since the generation of these data is determined by users' willingness instead of the GPS devices. Consider the example in Fig. 1, the trajectories τ_1 and τ_2 generated by vehicles are continuous, while the check-in records from r_1 to r_8 generated by users on social networks are discrete. Due to the rich sequential information contained by trajectories, existing studies for TUL have developed many methods, which have senior performance in modeling sequence information, based on RNN (Recurrent Neural Network) [25], LSTM (Long Short-Term Memory) [14], and GRU (Gated Recurrent Unit) [9].

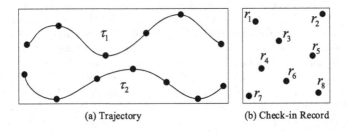

(a) Trajectory   (b) Check-in Record

Fig. 1. An example of trajectory and check-in record

Despite the great contributions made by the above-mentioned studies, we claim that their proposed sequential model-based approaches are ineffective for CUL, and the reason is twofold. From the spatial perspective, we can model the route behaviors of users based on the continuous sample points of trajectories, yet such behaviors are hard to obtain with irregular discrete check-in records. From the temporal perspective, as the time interval between adjacent sample points in a trajectory is fixed and short, we can model users' temporal behaviors effectively with sequential methods, while the irregular time interval between different check-in records brings the great challenge for modeling such behaviors. Having observed the difference between trajectory and check-in record from Fig. 1 and the drawbacks of existing work, we formula the novel problem CUL and develop a model called CULVAE. Although this study can serve a wide range of applications, following inevitable problems bring great challenges for it.

Irregularity. To illustrate the problem more clearly, we conduct an analysis on four real-world check-in datasets, i.e., Brightkite and Gowalla provided by [8], Foursquare and Twitter provided by [4]. The distributions of distance and time interval, i.e., $dist(l)$ and $dist(t)$, between three consecutive check-in records r_i,

r_{i+1}, and r_{i+2} of a user are presented in Fig. 2 (a) and (b) respectively, where $dis(l)$ and $dis(t)$ are calculated as follows:

$$dis(l) = |Euclidean(l_{i+2}, l_{i+1}) - Euclidean(l_{i+1}, l_i)|$$
$$dis(t) = ||t_{i+2} - t_{i+1}| - |t_{i+1} - t_i||$$

where l_i and t_i denote the location and time-stamp of the record r_i respectively. Observed from Fig. 2(a), the distance between three consecutive check-in records is irregular, as the probability of $dis(l) \geq 10km$ is large. Meanwhile, we observe the same irregular distribution of time interval from Fig. 2(b), where the probability of $dis(t) \geq 10000s$ is much larger than that of others.

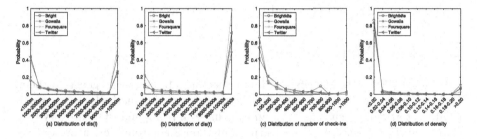

Fig. 2. An analysis for the problems of irregularity and data sparsity

Data Sparsity. We also conduct experiments on the above-mentioned datasets to illustrate the data sparsity problem from two different perspectives, i.e., the distribution of the total number of check-ins of each user and the corresponding density, where the density is defined as the number of check-in record in per km^2. Observed from Fig. 2(c) and (d), most users have less than 100 check-in records and the density of most users is less than 0.02. Moreover, although there are some users having more than 1000 check-ins and with a density greater than 0.02, the probability is small.

Obviously, the irregularity and data sparsity problem will deeply weaken the performance of sequential models, such as RNN, LSTM, and GRU. In view of this, we develop the model CULVAE based on VAE (Variational Autoencoder) [18]. The reason for adopting VAE here is that an individual's mobility pattern usually centers at some personal geographical regions (e.g., home region and work region) on location-aware social networks [3, 24], and the Gaussian distribution used in VAE can model this pattern effectively. Specifically, the developed model CULVAE contains the following four steps. Firstly, we divide the space into grid cells, and each user is represented by a set of grids that he/she has visited. Secondly, we develop an encoding module to embed users based on above-mentioned grids. Thirdly, a decoding module is proposed to rebuild the input of encoder and output the low-dimensional representation of a user. Finally, we design a linking module by incorporating MLP (Multilayer Perceptron) and softmax to link check-in records to their owners based on the output of the decoding module. To sum up, we make the following contributions in this work.

- To the best of our knowledge, we are the first to formulate and investigate the problem CUL.
- To address the problem CUL effectively, we propose a novel model entitled CULVAE based on Variational Autoencoder.
- We conduct extensive experiments on four real-world datasets, and the results demonstrate the superiority of our proposed model CULVAE over the state-of-art methods.

In the rest of the paper, we review related work in Sect. 2 and formulate the problem in Sect. 3. Section 4 introduces the details of CULVAE, followed by the experimental study in Sect. 5, and the paper is concluded in Sect. 6.

2   Related Work

The task of TUL is to identify and link trajectories to users who generate them. Different from the traditional mobility pattern recognition methods that use artificially set attributes such as check-in time interval [7,15] and POI category [13], Gao et al. [11] realize the deep learning method for automatic feature extraction of trajectories and understanding of human mobility models. Specifically, they develop models TULER-LSTM, TULER-GRU, and Bi-TULER based on LSTM, GRU, and Bidirectional LSTM respectively. In the following work, the semi-supervised model TULVAE [26] learns the latent semantics of sequential trajectories through a variational autoencoder, and utilizes the newly generated trajectory encoding to achieve linking. Sun et al. [22] propose an end-to-end attention recurrent neural learning framework TULAR, which introduces the learning approach Trajectory Semantic Vector (TSV) via unsupervised location representation learning and recurrent neural networks to reckon the weight of parts of source trajectory. At the same time, the model DeepTUL [20], which is composed of a feature representation layer and a neural network with an attention mechanism, is proposed by combining multiple features that govern user mobility and learning from labeled historical trajectory to capture the multi-periodic nature of user mobility. In recent advances, to tackle the problem of defending against location attacks, such as de-anonymization and location recovery, the model STULIG [27], which characterizes multiple latent aspects of human trajectories and their labels into separate latent variables, is developed based on deep probabilistic generative models. Specifically, the model can generate synthetic plausible trajectories, thus protecting users' actual locations while preserving the meaningful mobility information for various machine learning tasks. Despite the significant contributions made by the above studies, there has been no work linking discrete check-in records to users, thus we formulate and investigate the problem.

3   Preliminaries

3.1   Variational Autoencoders

The generation model VAE consists of an encoder and a decoder, given an input x, the encoder is represented as $p(z|x)$, where $p(z)$ is the probability of obtaining the latent vector z by randomly sampling from the Gaussian distribution, and the decoder is represented as $q(x|z)$. The output rebuilt from the set of latent vectors is expected to be similar to the original input, i.e., the probability of output equal to the input is expected as high as possible, and the problem is transformed into the maximization of $\sum_x \log p(x)$, i.e.,

$$max \sum_x \log p(x), \quad p(x) = \int_z p(z)p(x|z)dz \tag{1}$$

As the maximum likelihood estimation $p(x)$ cannot be calculated directly, VAE [19] uses variational distribution $q(z|x)$ to approximate the posterior distribution $p(z|x)$, i.e. minimizing the Kullback-Leibler (KL) divergence of $q(z|x)$ and $p(z|x)$:

$$\begin{aligned} \log p(x) &= \mathbf{E}_{z \sim q(z|x)}[\log p(x,z) - \log q(z|x)] + \mathbf{KL}[q(z|x) \parallel p(z|x)] \\ &\geq \varepsilon^d(t) = \mathbf{E}_{z \sim q(z|x)}[\log p(x,z) - \log q(z|x)] \\ &= \mathbf{E}_{z \sim q(z|x)}[\log p(x|z)] - \mathbf{KL}[q(z|x) \parallel p(z)] \end{aligned} \tag{2}$$

Next, the optimization of VAE is transformed into maximize the evidence lower bound (ELOB) $\varepsilon^d(t)$.

3.2   Problem Formulation

Definition 1. *Check-in Record.* *Let $r = (u, l, t)$ be a check-in record generated by a user u, where $l = (lat, lng)$ represents the location information of r, lat and lng denote the longitude and latitude respectively, and t is the time-stamp.*

Notably, we investigate the CUL problem based on the location information of check-in records, while the time information is not taken into account. This is because the experimental results in [2] have demonstrated that the time information is a negative factor for effective user behavior modeling in the face of the data sparsity problem introduced in Sect. 1.

Given a set of check-in records $\mathcal{R} = \{r_1, r_2..., r_m\}$ generated by a set of users $U = \{u_1, u_2..., u_n\}$ on location-aware social networks, this study aims to learn a mapping function that links check-in records to their owners: $\mathcal{R} \mapsto U$.

4   Proposed Model CULVAE

The overview of our proposed model CULVAE is presented in Fig. 3(a), which contains the following four steps. Firstly, a grid index is designed to organize the

input data. Then, an encoder is proposed to embed each user with corresponding grid cells and calculate the latent distributions of users. Next, a decoder is
developed to rebuild the input of the encoder and optimize the representation
of the latent distributions. Finally, a linking module is proposed to link check-in
records to users based on the latent distributions of VAE.

4.1 Grid Index

We first construct a grid index to organize the input data instead of encoding
each discrete check-in record directly and the reasons are as follows. In real
life, although the sequential behaviors are hard to model due to the irregularity
problem discussed in Sect. 1, we can model the distribution of check-in records
with a Gaussian function from the spatial perspective effectively, since a user's
mobility pattern usually centers in some specific areas, such as home region and
work region [3, 24]. Additionally, we can reduce the size of the input data by only
considering grid cells visited by a user, and this will accelerate the convergence
of our proposed model.

Observed from Fig. 3(b), we divide the space into 5×5 grid cells. Given
$\mathcal{R} = \{\mathcal{R}_{u_1}, \mathcal{R}_{u_2}\}$, where $\mathcal{R}_{u_1}$ and $\mathcal{R}_{u_2}$ denote the set of check-in records of u_1 and
u_2 respectively. Next, u_1 and u_2 can be represented as $G(u_1) = \{g_{10}, g_{11}, g_{13}, g_{24}\}$
and $G(u_2) = \{g_1, g_4, g_{13}, g_{15}, g_{21}\}$ respectively, by assigning each cell a unique
numerical id from bottom to top and from left to right. Obviously, the size of
grid representation (i.e., $|G(u_1)| + |G(u_2)| = 9$) is smaller than that of $|\mathcal{R}|$ (i.e.,
$|\mathcal{R}(u_1)| + |\mathcal{R}(u_2)| = 18$).

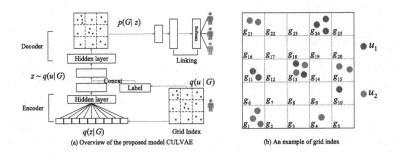

(a) Overview of the proposed model CULVAE   (b) An example of grid index

Fig. 3. Model architecture and grid index

4.2 Encoder

Although we can reduce the size of input data with grid representation $G(u)$
based on the index in Fig. 3(b), treating each grid in $G(u)$ equally is not appropriate. By way of illustration, u_2 has three check-in records in g_1, but only one
check-in record of u_2 falls into g_4, thus g_1 and g_4 are not equally important
for u_2. Additionally, the popular areas (e.g., shopping mall and cafeteria) are
more attractive and usually contain more check-in records than personal private

places, such as home and office. This phenomenon leads to the low peculiarity of grids related to popular areas. To fully explore this feature and model the characteristics of each user more effectively, we assign different weights to grids in $G(u)$ based on the idea of *TF-IDF*.

Specifically, *TF-IDF* has been widely used in data mining and NLP, where *TF* refers to the word frequency and *IDF* denotes the inverse document frequency. Given a user u, the *TF* value of the j-th grid of $G(u)$ is defined as:

$$tf_{ij} = \frac{n_{ij}}{\sum_k n_{ik}} \tag{3}$$

where n_{ik} is the number of check-in records of u in grid g_i and k is the number of different grids in $G(u)$. The *TF-IDF* value of the j-th grid of $G(u)$ is given as:

$$idf_{ij} = \log \frac{|U|}{|\{i : g_j \in G(u)\}|} \tag{4}$$

where $|U|$ represents the number of users, $|\{i : g_j \in G(u)\}|$ denotes the number of users having check-in record in grid g_j. Finally, the corresponding *TF-IDF* value is defined as:

$$tf\text{-}idf_{ij} = tf_{ij} \times idf_{ij} \tag{5}$$

Following the calculation of the *TF-IDF* value and given a user u with $G(u) = \{g_i, \cdots, g_l\}$, we can obtain the input, which is defined as $Input(u)$, of the encoder related to u by concatenating all $tf\text{-}idf_{g_i}$,

$$Input(u) = Concat(tf\text{-}idf_{g_i}, \cdots, tf\text{-}idf_{g_l}) \tag{6}$$

Then, we apply a two-layer MLP to embed $Input(u)$ into a low-dimensional space, and the output x is defined as:

$$x = MLP(Input(u)) \tag{7}$$

Next, we can obtain the mean vector M_X and variance vector S_X by calculating the mean and variance for each x_i in $X = \{x_1, x_2, \cdots, x_n\}$. Then, we apply the Gaussian distribution function to construct the latent distribution of VAE, i.e.,

$$z = \mathcal{N}(M_X, S_X^2) \tag{8}$$

In the semi-supervised learning task, the latent distribution z is concatenated with the user's label $id(u)$ to get the latent distribution z_u related to u, i.e.,

$$z_u = Concat(z, id(u)) \tag{9}$$

Next, z_u will be fed into the following decoder and more details are discussed as follows.

4.3   Decoder

After encoding the check-in data and obtaining labeled and unlabeled latent distributions z_u and z, we optimize the decoder of CULVAE. Specifically, we use two latent distributions z_1, z_2 to rebuild the latent distribution z. The value of z is generated by the prior distribution $p(z)$ that satisfies the Gaussian distribution, and the joint distribution $p(G, z_1, z_2)$ related to u can be decomposed into $p(G|z_1, z_2)p(z_1|z_2)p(z_2)$ [17]. The Kullback-Leibler (KL) divergence between $q(z|G, u)$ and $p(z|G, u)$ is required to be close to 0, as our goal is to approximate the true posterior $p(z|G, u)$ with $q(z|G, u)$, and this KL divergence is defined as:

$$KL[q(z|G, u)||p(z|G, u)] = \mathbb{E}_{z \sim q}[\log q(z|G, u)$$
$$- \log p(G|z, u) - \log p(u) - \log p(z) + \log p(G, u)] \quad (10)$$

The problem of minimizing the KL divergence is transformed into maximizing the following **ELOB**$\varepsilon_1^g(G, u)$:

$$\log p(G, u) \geq \mathbb{E}_{z \sim q}[\log p(z) + \log p(G|u, z) - \log q(z|G, u)]$$
$$= \mathbb{E}_{z \sim q}[\log p(G|u, z)] - KL[q(z|G, u)||p(z)] = \varepsilon_1^g(G, u) \quad (11)$$

where $KL[q(z|G, u)||p(z)]$ denotes the KL divergence between the latent posterior $q(z|G, u)$ and the prior distribution $p(z)$ [26] and $\mathbb{E}_{z \sim q}[\log p(u)]$ is ignored here, as it is a constant. Next, the maximization of **ELOB**$\varepsilon_1^g(G, u)$ is transformed into minimizing $KL[q(z|G, u)||p(z)]$, which is disassembled with following method:

$$KL[q(z|G, u)||p(z)] = KL[q(z, G, u)||q(z)p(G, u)]$$
$$+ \beta KL[q(z)|| \prod_j q(z_j)] + \sum_j KL[q(z_j||p(z_j))] \quad (12)$$

where the first item $KL[q(z, G, u)||q(z)p(G, u)]$ is the mutual information term in InfoGAN [5]. The second term $\beta KL[q(z)|| \prod_j q(z_j)]$ is called Total Correlation, it is considered in β-TCVAE [1], where a heavier penalty can lead to better disentanglement, the larger the value, the greater the correlation. The third item $\sum_j KL[q(z_j||p(z_j))]$ is called dimension-wise KL, it mainly prevents each latent distribution from being too far away from the corresponding prior.

When faced with unlabeled check-in records, we use a classifier $q(u|z)$, which is constructed in the next linking module, to generate a predicted label, and get the following **ELOB**$\varepsilon_2^g(G)$:

$$\log p(G) \geq \mathbb{E}_{z \sim q}[\log p(G|u, z) + \log p(z) - \log q(u, z|G)]$$
$$= \sum_u q(u|x)(\varepsilon_1^g(G, u)) + H(q(u|G)) = \varepsilon_2^g(G) \quad (13)$$

where $H(q(u|G))$ is the entropy of information. Finally, the function of the overall extended **ELOB** is defined as:

$$\varepsilon = - \sum_{G, u \sim \widetilde{p_G}} \varepsilon_1^g(G, u) + a[\log q(u|\mathbf{G})] - \sum_{G \sim \widetilde{p_u}} \varepsilon_2^g(G) \quad (14)$$

where the hyperparameter a controls the weight of labeled data learning. From this, we obtain the final objective function of semi-VAE. $\widetilde{p_G}$ and $\widetilde{p_u}$ represent the empirical distribution of labeled and unlabeled subsets of check-in data respectively.

4.4 Linking

The above VAE-based semi-supervised learning model is trained to learn the characteristics of each set of check-in records, thus the latent distribution z used to restore corresponding records contains key information of users. Next, we use the latent distribution z to replace the original check-in records during linking.

Specifically, the proposed linking module is composed of a two-layer Multi-Layer Perception(MLP) and softmax. In general, check-in-user linking can be viewed as a multi-class classification problem. The input of the MLP is the latent distribution z after the check-in records are fed into the VAE. Let the output of the MLP is $Y = \{y_1, y_2, ..., y_n\}$. Then the probability that the check-in data generated by user u_i is $p(y_i)$ in softmax, and it is defined as $p(y_i) = \frac{exp(y_i)}{\sum_{j=1}^{n} exp(y_j)}$.

4.5 Training

The VAE optimization process may encounter serious gradient disappearance and we use the activation function Leaky-ReLU (i.e., $f(x) = max(ax, x)$) to alleviate it. At the same time, the data will be batch standardized [28] before being transmitted to the latent distributions. In the linking module, we apply cross-entropy as the loss function and use Back Propagation and Adam to optimize our proposed model.

5 Experiments

5.1 Datasets

BHT and **GOW**. Brightkite[1] and Gowalla[2] were once location-based social networking websites, where users shared their locations by checking-in. We randomly select 739 and 1026 users with 402748 and 356266 check-in records from the datasets provided by [8] to study the performance of our proposed approaches. **FQ** and **TW**. Foursquare and Twitter are currently popular social networks, where users can share statues associated with location information. These two datasets contain 862 and 1717 users with 187795 and 785300 check-in records respectively. For each dataset, we divide check-in records of a user into training set and test set according to the ratio of 7:3.

---

[1] https://snap.stanford.edu/data/loc-brightkite.html.
[2] https://snap.stanford.edu/data/loc-Gowalla.html.

5.2   Compared Methods

We compare the performance of our model CULVAE with those of the following approaches. (1) Trajectory-User Linking methods: TULER [11], TULVAE [26], STULIG [27], and TULAR [22]. These approaches need to embed unique grids into low-dimensional space through word vectors firstly, and then encode check-in records according to timestamps. (2) Graph embedding methods: DeepWalk [21], Node2vec [12], and BiNE [10]. These approaches are also suitable for learning the relationship between users and check-in data, as we can construct a bipartite graph between them with the grid index introduced in Sect. 4.1.

5.3   Parameter Settings

For all TUL methods, each grid cell is embedded into a 250-dimensional vector. The learning rate and the dropout rate are set to 0.0005 and 0.5 respectively. TULER, TULAR, TULVAE, and STULIG adopt two-layer stacked RNNs. *ReLU* is the activation function and *Adam* is the optimizer for all models. The batch size of all methods on datasets BHT, GOW, and FQ is 64, and the size is set to 32 on dataset TW. Notably, we report the best performance of all compared methods in this section.

5.4   Experimental Results

Table 1 presents the performance of all methods on four datasets, where the best results are highlighted in bold. From the table, we have the following observations. (1) TULAR performs better than other TUL methods, as it implements training with arbitrary length trajectories, while TULER-LSTM, TULER-GRU, BiTULER, TULVAE, and STULIG set a fixed length for all trajectories, which may lead to the loss of information. (2) Graph embedding approaches (i.e., DeepWalk, Node2vec, and BiNE) have better results than all TUL methods. This is because the latter are designed for continuous trajectories, and these sequential models cannot handle discrete check-in records effectively, while the former can extract more effective user features with the bipartite graph constructed based on our proposed grid index. (3) Without surprise, the model CULVAE performs better than all compared methods, as we use the latent distribution z instead of the check-in records as the input of the link module, and the application of the objective function of semi-supervised VAE and KL divergence disentanglement enables the latent distribution to obtain better user representation.

Table 1. Comparison of CULVAE with others methods on four datasets

Method	BHT			GOW		
	ACC@1	ACC@5	Macro-F1	ACC@1	ACC@5	Macro-F1
TULER-LSTM	54.95%	62.47%	53.10%	61.26%	70.32%	59.03%
TULER-GRU	55.01%	62.61%	53.83%	61.18%	69.52%	59.93%
BiTULER	55.28%	63.07%	55.29%	62.54%	70.81%	61.20%
TULVAE	59.43%	68.14%	59.13%	66.70%	74.56%	64.86%
STULIG	62.81%	71.40%	60.98%	67.52%	76.16%	65.40%
TULAR	64.24%	73.86%	62.10%	71.89%	78.67%	68.75%
DeepWalk	80.92%	91.20%	77.44%	88.50%	96.20%	86.25%
Node2vec	84.98%	94.08%	80.76%	90.80%	97.50%	85.86%
BiNE	83.36%	93.23%	80.94%	88.00%	96.60%	85.45%
CULVAE	**87.60%**	**94.45%**	**85.18%**	**92.70%**	**97.81%**	**91.78%**
Method	FQ			TW		
	ACC@1	ACC@5	Macro-F1	ACC@1	ACC@5	Macro-F1
TULER-LSTM	34.71%	45.12%	32.49%	41.91%	57.76%	38.23%
TULER-GRU	34.40%	45.46%	32.53%	42.12%	58.28%	38.68%
BiTULER	35.87%	45.67%	33.43%	42.63%	58.66%	39.42%
TULVAE	38.01%	49.49%	34.69%	46.14%	63.40%	43.15%
STULIG	39.25%	51.08%	36.81%	47.04%	65.45%	44.28%
TULAR	40.74%	53.46%	38.93%	49.63%	68.57%	46.30%
DeepWalk	60.90%	74.59%	57.11%	61.09%	83.40%	53.68%
Node2vec	63.23%	75.99%	57.76%	75.31%	90.60%	66.48%
BiNE	63.69%	75.41%	59.98%	71.87%	89.87%	66.60%
CULVAE	**67.30%**	**76.68%**	**65.58%**	**77.16%**	**91.10%**	**73.43%**

5.5   Ablation Study

To investigate the benefits brought by different components of CULVAE, we conduct the ablation study and compare the performance of the following methods. (1) CULVAE-SD: the method eliminates semi-supervised learning and the application of disentanglement, and adopts unsupervised learning to complete the generation task. (2) CULVAE-S: the approach only leverages the disentanglement. (3) CULVAE-D: the approach only leverages semi-supervised learning without the application of disentanglement. (4) CULVAE: our proposed model employs both semi-supervised learning and disentanglement.

From Fig. 4, all other methods perform better than CULVAE-SD, as both semi-supervised learning and disentanglement are not considered in it. Additionally, we can observe that the results of CULVAE-D are higher than those of CULVAE-S, which proves that semi-supervised learning brings more improvement than disentanglement for our model. This is because the latent distribution

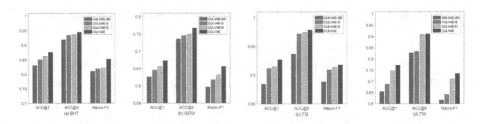

Fig. 4. Results of ablation study

of VAE based on semi-supervised learning can learn the location features of each user with an irregular distribution more effectively. Specifically, in the generation task, the latent distribution generated by the encoder is concatenated with the user's label, which makes the generation process more directional. During the optimization of VAE, the objective function guides these latent distributions to describe users' check-in records, which leads to the effective characterization of users' features. Furthermore, the highest ACC@1, ACC@5, and Macro-F1 of CULVAE demonstrates the necessity of considering both semi-supervised learning and disentanglement.

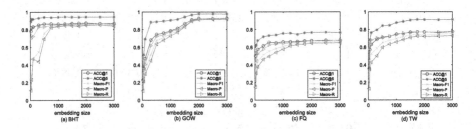

Fig. 5. Performance of CULVAE w.r.t. varied embedding size

5.6   Parametric Experiment

The embedding size of the latent distribution is a key parameter for our proposed model. Figure 5 presents the results of CULVAE with different embedding sizes on four datasets. Observed from which, the larger this parameter, the better representation of user features. The reason is that we can collect more abundant and useful information from the check-in records with a larger embedding size of the latent distribution. Meanwhile, when the size of the latent distribution exceeds a certain value, the metrics tend to be stable, and it leads to the slower convergence of the model. Consequently, we set the embedding size to 1000, 2000, 2000, and 2000 for BHT, GOW, FQ, and TW respectively.

   The size of the check-in dataset refers to the number of records to be considered. By way of illustration, the range 0–10 in Fig. 6 means that we only consider users that have less than 10 check-in records, and > 500 denotes all users having

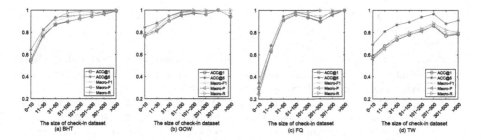

Fig. 6. Performance of CULVAE with different sizes of check-in dataset

more than 500 records. Without surprise, we observe the increasing tendency of the experimental results with the increase of this number. This is because more information is extracted with a larger number of check-in records. Additionally, the occasional drop in Fig. 6 may be caused by the noise information contained by the given dataset.

6 Conclusion and Future Work

Linking check-in records to theirs owners on location-aware social networks can serve a wide range of applications, such as POI recommendation, location prediction, and route planning, thus we formulate and investigate the problem CUL in this work. To alleviate the problems of irregularity and data sparsity, we develop a novel semi-supervised model namely CULVAE, which contains four different modules, i.e., grid division, encoder, decoder, and linking. The experiments conducted on four real-world datasets demonstrate the higher performance of CULVAE than that of the state-of-art approaches. In the future, we can investigate the problem CUL across multiple platforms, since many users share statues on different social networks.

Acknowledgements. This work is supported by the National Natural Science Foundation of China under Grant No. 61902270, and the Major Program of the Natural Science Foundation of Jiangsu Higher Education Institutions of China under Grant No. 19KJA610002.

References

1. Chen, R.T., Li, X., Grosse, R., Duvenaud, D.: Isolating sources of disentanglement in vaes. In: NeurIPS, pp. 2615–2625 (2019)
2. Chen, W., Wang, W., Yin, H., Zhao, L., Zhou, X.: HFUL: a hybrid framework for user account linkage across location-aware social networks. VLDB J. (2022). https://doi.org/10.1007/s00778-022-00730-8
3. Chen, W., Yin, H., Wang, W., Zhao, L., Hua, W., Zhou, X.: Exploiting spatio-temporal user behaviors for user linkage. In: CIKM, pp. 517–526 (2017)

4. Chen, W., Yin, H., Wang, W., Zhao, L., Zhou, X.: Effective and efficient user account linkage across location based social networks. In: ICDE, pp. 1085–1096 (2018)
5. Chen, X., Duan, Y., Houthooft, R., Schulman, J., Sutskever, I., Abbeel, P.: Info-GAN: interpretable representation learning by information maximizing generative adversarial nets. In: NeurIPS, pp. 2180–2188 (2016)
6. Chen, Y., Wang, X., Fan, M., Huang, J., Yang, S., Zhu, W.: Curriculum meta-learning for next poi recommendation. In: SIGKDD, pp. 2692–2702 (2021)
7. Cheng, R., Pang, J., Zhang, Y.: Inferring friendship from check-in data of location-based social networks. In: ASONAM, pp. 1284–1291 (2015)
8. Cho, E., Myers, S.A., Leskovec, J.: Friendship and mobility: user movement in location-based social networks. In: KDD, pp. 1082–1090 (2011)
9. Chung, J., Gulcehre, C., Cho, K., Bengio, Y.: Empirical evaluation of gated recurrent neural networks on sequence modeling. arXiv preprint arXiv:1412.3555 (2014)
10. Gao, M., Chen, L., He, X., Zhou, A.: BiNE: bipartite network embedding. In: SIGIR, pp. 715–724 (2018)
11. Gao, Q., Zhou, F., Zhang, K., Trajcevski, G., Luo, X., Zhang, F.: Identifying human mobility via trajectory embeddings. In: IJCAI, vol. 17, pp. 1689–1695 (2017)
12. Grover, A., Leskovec, J.: node2vec: scalable feature learning for networks. In: SIGKDD, pp. 855–864 (2016)
13. Hang, M., Pytlarz, I., Neville, J.: Exploring student check-in behavior for improved point-of-interest prediction. In: SIGKDD, pp. 321–330 (2018)
14. Hochreiter, S., Schmidhuber, J.: Long short-term memory. Neural Comput. $9(8)$, 1735–1780 (1997)
15. Hsieh, H.P., Li, C.T., Lin, S.D.: Exploiting large-scale check-in data to recommend time-sensitive routes. In: UrbComp, pp. 55–62 (2012)
16. Hu, G., Shao, J., Ni, Z., Zhang, D.: A graph based method for constructing popular routes with check-ins. World Wide Web $21(6)$, 1689–1703 (2018)
17. Kingma, D.P., Mohamed, S., Rezende, D.J., Welling, M.: Semi-supervised learning with deep generative models. In: Advances in Neural Information Processing Systems, pp. 3581–3589 (2014)
18. Kingma, D.P., Welling, M.: Auto-encoding variational bayes. In: ICLR, pp. 1–14 (2014)
19. Kingma, D.P., Welling, M.: Auto-encoding variational bayes. In: ICLR, pp. 1–14 (2014)
20. Miao, C., Wang, J., Yu, H., Zhang, W., Qi, Y.: Trajectory-user linking with attentive recurrent network. In: AAMAS, pp. 878–886 (2020)
21. Perozzi, B., Al-Rfou, R., Skiena, S.: DeepWalk: online learning of social representations. In: SIGKDD, pp. 701–710 (2014)
22. Sun, T., Xu, Y., Wang, F., Wu, L., Qian, T., Shao, Z.: Trajectory-user link with attention recurrent networks. In: ICPR, pp. 4589–4596 (2020)
23. Yin, H., Zhou, X., Cui, B., Wang, H., Zheng, K., Nguyen, Q.V.H.: Adapting to user interest drift for poi recommendation. IEEE Trans. Knowl. Data Eng. $28(10)$, 2566–2581 (2016)
24. Yuan, Q., Cong, G., Ma, Z., Sun, A., Nadia, M.T.: Who, where, when and what: discover spatio-temporal topics for Twitter users. In: KDD, pp. 605–613 (2013)
25. Zaremba, W., Sutskever, I., Vinyals, O.: Recurrent neural network regularization. CoRR abs/1409.2329 (2014)
26. Zhou, F., Gao, Q., Trajcevski, G., Zhang, K., Zhong, T., Zhang, F.: Trajectory-user linking via variational autoencoder. In: IJCAI, pp. 3212–3218 (2018)

27. Zhou, F., Liu, X., Zhang, K., Trajcevski, G.: Toward discriminating and synthesizing motion traces using deep probabilistic generative models. IEEE Trans. Neural Networks Learn. Syst. **32**(6), 2401–2414 (2021)
28. Zhu, Q., Bi, W., Liu, X., Ma, X., Li, X., Wu, D.: A batch normalized inference network keeps the KL vanishing away. In: ACL, pp. 2636–2649 (2020)

Robust Subspace Clustering Based on Latent Low-rank Representation with Weighted Schatten-p Norm Minimization

Qin Qu[1], Zhi Wang[1(✉)], and Wu Chen[2]

[1] College of Computer and Information Science, Southwest University, Chongqing, China
chiw@swu.edu.cn
[2] School of Software, Southwest University, Chongqing, China

Abstract. Subspace clustering, which aims to cluster the high-dimensional data samples drawn from a union of multiple subspaces, has drawn much attention in machine learning and computer vision. As a typical subspace clustering method, latent low-rank representation (LLRR) can handle high-dimensional data efficiently. However, the nuclear norm in its formulation is not the optimal approximation of the rank function, which may lead to a suboptimal solution for the original rank minimization problem. In this paper, a weighted Schatten-p norm (WSN), which can better induce low rank, is used to replace the nuclear norm in LLRR, resulting in a novel latent low-rank representation model (WSN-LLRR) for subspace clustering. Furthermore, considering both the accuracy and convergence rate, we present an efficient optimization algorithm by using the alternating direction method of multipliers (ADMM) to solve the proposed model. Finally, experimental results on several real-world subspace clustering datasets show that the performance of our proposed method is better than several state-of-the-art methods, which demonstrates that WSN-LLRR can get a better accurate low-rank solution.

Keywords: Subspace clustering · Latent low-rank representation · Weighted schatten-[spsdollar1dollarsps] norm

1 Introduction

Subspace clustering aims to cluster the high-dimensional data samples drawn from a union of multiple subspaces, into their corresponding low-dimensional subspaces. It has various real-world applications in computer vision [12], machine learning [8], image processing [17], etc. Recently, the low-rank representation (LRR) [9,10] based subspace clustering technique has been widely studied owing to its ability to capture the global structures of the high-dimensional data. LRR aims at seeking the lowest-rank representation of all data jointly by solving a rank minimization problem [9,10].

© The Author(s), under exclusive license to Springer Nature Switzerland AG 2022
S. Khanna et al. (Eds.): PRICAI 2022, LNCS 13629, pp. 504–515, 2022.
https://doi.org/10.1007/978-3-031-20862-1_37

However, LRR may suffer from the issue of insufficient sampling [11]. To overcome this drawback, Liu et al. [11] suggested using the latent low-rank representation (LLRR) model, which considers both the observed and the unobserved data came from the same collection of low-rank subspaces. This problem can be formulated as:

$$\min_{Z} rank(Z) \quad s.t. \quad X_O = [X_O, X_H]Z, \tag{1}$$

where X_O and X_H are the observed and the unobserved data matrix, respectively. The concatenation (along column) of the X_O and X_H is used as the dictionary. Unfortunately, the problem (1) is NP-hard. To make the above NP-hard problem solvable, researchers suggested relaxing the rank function with some convex functions. For example, LRR [9,10], LLRR [11], and LRRSC [3] replace the rank function with the nuclear norm, which is defined as the sum of all singular values of a matrix.

However, the obtained results may be the suboptimal solution since the nuclear norm process all the singular values equally. Therefore, recently researchers have developed several more efficient non-convex surrogate functions to approximate the rank function [16,21–23]. In [16], Nie et al. proposed the Schatten-p norm to enforce the low-rank regularization. Based on the Schatten-p norm, Zhang et al. [27] and Cao et al. [2] presented the Schatten-p norm regularized LRR (SPM) and LLRR (Sp-LLRR) for the subspace clustering problem, respectively. However, the Schatten-p norm ignores the importance of different rank components, which ultimately affects the improvement of the clustering performance. To alleviate such a problem, Xie et al. [23] proposed the weighted Schatten-p norm, which assigns suitable weights to different singular values. In [26], Zhang et al. proposed the weighted Schatten-p norm and l_q-norm regularized LRR (WSPQ) for subspace clustering. Although WSPQ can achieve better low-rank properties and robustness to various noises, it is only an enhanced version of LRR and can not handle the issue of insufficient sampling.

In this paper, a novel LLRR model for the subspace clustering problem, namely, weighted Schatten-p norm regularized LLRR (WSN-LLRR), is proposed. It can obtain a low-rank representation of all the high-dimensional data samples more accurately than LLRR and overcomes the issue of insufficient sampling in WSPQ. Benefiting from these merits, the proposed model can effectively improve the subspace clustering performance. However, the introduced weighted Schatten-p norm is a non-convex low-rank regularizer, leading to a non-convex, non-smooth optimization problem and is not trivial to solve. To solve the above problem, we design an efficient optimization algorithm by using the alternating direction method of multipliers (ADMM) [1,13] framework. The proposed optimization algorithm has promising accuracy and convergence speed. Meanwhile, experimental results on Extended Yale B, ORL, and COIL-20 datasets, show that our proposed subspace clustering method can obtain better clustering performance than the state-of-the-art algorithms.

2   Related Work

2.1   Low Rank Representation (LRR)

Given an observed data matrix $X = [x_1, x_2, ..., x_n] \in \mathbb{R}^{d \times n}$ drawn from a union of multiple different subspaces, each data vector $x_i \in \mathbb{R}^{n \times 1}$ denotes a data sample and can be represented by the linear combination of the other data vectors. LRR aims at finding the lowest-rank representation of all data jointly by solving a rank minimization problem [9,10]. LRR replaces the rank function with the nuclear norm, and optimizes the following constraint problem:

$$\min_{Z} \|Z\|_* + \lambda \|E\|_{2,1} \quad s.t. \quad X = XZ + E, \tag{2}$$

where $\|E\|_{2,1} = \sum_{j=1}^{d} \sqrt{\sum_{i=1}^{n} E_{ij}^2}$ denotes the $l_{2,1}$-norm to model the error $E \in \mathbb{R}^{d \times n}$, $\lambda > 0$ is a balance parameter. The optimal solution Z^* to the problem (2) is block-diagonal that can uncover the structure of subspaces [9].

Considering that the nuclear norm in problem (2) may lead to the obtained solution deviating from the optimal solution for the original rank minimization problem, and the $l_{2,1}$-norm can not model different noises, Zhang et al. [26] proposed the weighted Schatten-p norm and l_q-norm regularized LRR (WSPQ) for subspace clustering:

$$\min_{Z} \|Z\|_{w,S_p}^p + \lambda \|E\|_q \quad s.t. \quad X = XZ + E. \tag{3}$$

where $\|Z\|_{w,Sp}^p = \sum_{i=1}^{n} w_i \sigma_i^p$ $(0 < p \le 1)$ is the weighted Schatten-p norm of the coefficient matrix Z, $w = [w_1, w_2, ..., w_n]$ is a non-negative weights vector, and $\|E\|_q = \sum_{i=1}^{d} \sum_{j=1}^{n} |E_{ij}|^q$. Although WSPQ can achieve better low-rank properties and robustness to different noise, it is only an enhanced version of LRR and can not handle the issue of insufficient sampling.

2.2   Latent Low Rank Representation (LLRR)

To address the issue mentioned above, Liu et al. [11] suggested using the latent low-rank representation (LLRR) model, in which both the observed and the unobserved data sampled from the same collection of low-rank subspaces, are considered to construct the dictionary. Such a model can be formulated as:

$$\min_{Z} \|Z\|_* + \|L\|_* + \lambda \|E\|_1 \quad s.t. \quad X = XZ + LX + E, \tag{4}$$

where $Z \in \mathbb{R}^{n \times n}$ and $L \in \mathbb{R}^{d \times d}$ denotes the coefficient matrix, $\lambda > 0$ is a trade-off parameter, l_1-norm is used to model the error term E, here $\|E\|_1 = \sum_{i=1}^{d} \sum_{j=1}^{n} |E_{ij}|$. The optimal solution Z^* to the problem (4) is also block-diagonal that can be used for subspace clustering.

3 Robust Subspace Clustering Based on Weighted Schatten-p Norm Minimization

3.1 The Proposed Model

We formally introduce the proposed non-convex weighted Schatten-p norm regularized LLRR model (WSN-LLRR), i.e.,

$$\min_{Z,L,E} \|Z\|_{w,S_p}^p + \|L\|_{w,S_p}^p + \lambda\|E\|_1 \quad s.t. \quad X = XZ + LX + E. \tag{5}$$

The weighted Schatten-p norm introduced in our model can better induce low rank, therefore, our model can obtain a low-rank representation of all the high-dimensional data samples more accurately than the LLRR model.

3.2 Optimization

The problem (5) is non-convex, non-smooth, and difficult to solve. To address this issue, we design an efficient optimization algorithm by using the ADMM framework. By introducing two auxiliary variables J and S, problem (5) can be reformulated as the following equivalent problem:

$$\min_{Z,L,J,S,E} \|J\|_{w,S_p}^p + \|S\|_{w,S_p}^p + \lambda\|E\|_1$$

$$s.t. \quad X = XZ + LX + E, Z = J, L = S. \tag{6}$$

The above model can be transformed into the following augmented Lagrangian function form:

$$\Gamma(J,S,Z,L,E,Y_1,Y_2,Y_3,\mu)$$
$$= \|J\|_{w,S_p}^p + \|S\|_{w,S_p}^p + \lambda\|E\|_1 + \langle Y_1, X - XZ - LX - E\rangle + \langle Y_2, Z - J\rangle$$
$$+ \langle Y_3, L - S\rangle + \frac{\mu}{2}(\|X - XZ - LX - E\|_F^2 + \|Z - J\|_F^2 + \|L - S\|_F^2), \tag{7}$$

where $Y_1 \in \mathbb{R}^{d\times n}, Y_2 \in \mathbb{R}^{n\times n}$, and $Y_3 \in \mathbb{R}^{d\times n}$ are the augmented Lagrangian multipliers, $\mu > 0$ is the penalty parameter, $\langle\cdot,\cdot\rangle$ and $\|\cdot\|_F$ are the matrix inner product and Frobenius norm of a matrix, respectively. We can alternatively update the variables J, S, Z, L, E while fixing the others as follows:

$$
\begin{cases}
J_{k+1} = & \arg\min_J \frac{1}{\mu_k}\|J\|_{w,S_p}^p + \frac{1}{2}\|J - (Z_k + \frac{Y_{2,k}}{\mu_k})\|_F^2 & (8)\\[2mm]
S_{k+1} = & \arg\min_S \frac{1}{\mu_k}\|S\|_{w,S_p}^p + \frac{1}{2}\|S - (L_k + \frac{Y_{3,k}}{\mu_k})\|_F^2 & (9)\\[2mm]
Z_{k+1} = & \arg\min_Z \|J_{k+1} - (Z + \frac{1}{\mu_k}Y_{2,k})\|_F^2 & \\[2mm]
 & +\|E_k - (X - XZ - L_kX + \frac{1}{\mu_k}Y_{1,k})\|_F^2 & (10)\\[2mm]
L_{k+1} = & \arg\min_L \|S_{k+1} - (L + \frac{1}{\mu_k}Y_{3,k})\|_F^2 & \\[2mm]
 & +\|E_k - (X - XZ_{k+1} - LX + \frac{1}{\mu_k}Y_{1,k})\|_F^2 & (11)\\[2mm]
E_{k+1} = & \arg\min_E \frac{\lambda}{\mu_k}\|E\|_1 + \frac{1}{2}\|E - (X - XZ_{k+1} - L_{k+1}X + \frac{Y_{1,k}}{\mu_k})\|_F^2 & (12)
\end{cases}
$$

(1) Update J: problem (8) is a weighted Schatten-p norm minimization problem and can be translated into multiple independent subproblems, which are described in Lemma 1.

Lemma 1. *(see [23]) Let $Y = U\Sigma V^T$ be the SVD of $Y \in \mathbb{R}^{d \times n}$, where $\Sigma = diag$ $(\sigma_1, \sigma_2, ..., \sigma_r)$, $r = min(d, n)$, and all the singular values are in non-ascending order. Then, the optimal solution to the following problem:*

$$\min_{X \in \mathbb{R}^{d \times n}} \lambda \|X\|_{w,S_p}^p + \frac{1}{2}\|X - Y\|_F^2 \tag{13}$$

will be $X^* = U\Sigma^* V$ with $\Sigma^* = diag(\delta_1, \delta_2, ..., \delta_r)$, where δ_i is given by solving the following problem:

$$\min_{\delta_1, ..., \delta_r} \sum_{i=1}^{r}[\frac{1}{2}(\delta_i - \sigma_i)^2 + \lambda w_i \delta_i^p] \quad s.t. \quad \delta_i \geq 0, \text{ and } \delta_i \geq \delta_j, \text{ for } i \leq j. \tag{14}$$

If the weights w_i $(i = 1, ..., r)$ are in non-descending order, problem (14) can be decoupled into r independent l_p-norm minimization problems:

$$\min_{\delta_i \geq 0} f_i(\delta) = \frac{1}{2}(\delta_i - \sigma_i)^2 + \lambda w_i \delta_i^p, \quad i = 1, 2, ..., r, \tag{15}$$

then, each subproblem can be solved by the generalized soft-thresholding (GST) algorithm [28], which is shown in Lemma 2.

Lemma 2. *(see [28]) Given $y \in \mathbf{R}$, p, and $\lambda > 0$, an optimal solution to*

$$\min_x \frac{1}{2}(x - y)^2 + \lambda |x|^p, \tag{16}$$

is described as:

$$x^* = \begin{cases} 0 & |y| \leq \tau_p^{GST}(\lambda) \\ sgn(y)S_p^{GST}(|y|; \lambda) & |y| > \tau_p^{GST}(\lambda) \end{cases}, \tag{17}$$

where $\tau_p^{GST}(\lambda) = [2\lambda(1-p)]^{\frac{1}{2-p}} + \lambda p[2\lambda(1-p)]^{\frac{p-1}{2-p}}$, and $S_p^{GST}(|y|; \lambda)$ can be derived by solving the following problem:

$$S_p^{GST}(|y|; \lambda) - |y| + \lambda p[S_p^{GST}(|y|; \lambda)]^{p-1} = 0 \tag{18}$$

Based on the prior knowledge that the larger singular values of a matrix are more important than the smaller ones since they provide the major information of a matrix, therefore, the larger singulars should be shrunk less and the smaller ones should be shrunk more. Following the suggestions in [6,23], we set the weights as: $w_i = C\sqrt{dn}/(\sigma_i(J) + \varepsilon)$, where $C > 0$ is a constant, $\varepsilon = 10^{-16}$ is to avoid dividing by zero.

(2) Update S: problem (9) is also a weighted Schatten-p norm minimization problem, which can be solved in the same way as problem (8).

Algorithm 1. Solving problem (7) by ADMM

Input: Data matrix X, parameters λ, p

Initialization: $Z = J = 0, L = S = 0, E = 0, Y_1 = 0, Y_2 = 0, Y_3 = 0, \mu = 10^{-6}, max_\mu = 10^{10}, \rho = 1.5, \varepsilon = 10^{-6}, k = 0$
1: **while** not converged **do**
2:    Sequentially update J, S, Z, L, E by solving problem (8), (9), (10), (11), (12), respectively;
3:    Update the multipliers as:
      $Y_1 = Y_1 + \mu(X - XZ - LX - E)$, $Y_2 = Y_2 + \mu(Z - J)$, $Y_3 = Y_3 + \mu(L - S)$;
4:    Update the parameter μ as: $\mu = min(\rho\mu, max_\mu)$;
5:    Check the convergence condition:
      $\|X - XZ - LX - E\|_\infty < \varepsilon$, $\|Z - J\|_\infty < \varepsilon$, $\|L - S\|_\infty < \varepsilon$,
6: **end while**
Output Coefficient matrix Z^*

---

(3) Update Z: problem (10) is a standard quadratic optimization problem with closed-form solution:

$$Z_{k+1} = (I + X^TX)^{-1}(X^T(X - L_kX - E_k) + J_{k+1} + \frac{(X^TY_{1,k} - Y_{2,k})}{\mu_k}) \quad (19)$$

(4) Update L: similar to problem (10), problem (11) is also a standard quadratic optimization problem with closed-form solution:

$$L_{k+1} = ((X - XZ_{k+1} - E_k)X^T + S_{k+1} + \frac{(Y_{1,k}X^T - Y_{3,k})}{\mu_k})(I + XX^T)^{-1} \quad (20)$$

(5) Update E: problem (12) is a l_1-norm minimization problem with closed-form solution. We first define $Q = X - XZ_{k+1} - L_{k+1}X + \frac{Y_{1,k}}{\mu_k}$, then E_{k+1} can be calculated element-wisely, and each $(E_{k+1})_{ij}$ can be obtained as follows:

$$(E_{k+1})_{ij} = \begin{cases} Q_{ij} - \frac{\lambda}{\mu_k}sgn(Q_{ij}) & if \ |Q_{ij}| < \frac{\lambda}{\mu_k} \\ 0 & otherwise \end{cases}. \quad (21)$$

Finally, we summarize the overall optimization procedure of problem (7) in Algorithm 1.

3.3 The Complete Clustering Algorithm

As in [9,11], the coefficient matrix Z^* solved in Algorithm 1 is used to conduct subspace clustering. We first calculate the skinny SVD of Z^*, denoted as $Z^* = U^*\Sigma^*(V^*)^T$, then, the affinity matrix W is defined via $[W]_{ij} = ([HH^T]_{ij})^{2a}$, where $H = U^*(\Sigma^*)^{\frac{1}{2}}$, a is a parameter usually chosen from $\{2, 3, 4\}$. Finally, spectral clustering techniques such as Normalized Cuts (NCut) [20] could be applied on W to produce the final clustering results.

3.4   Complexity Analysis

For a data matrix X of size $d \times n$, the time costs of the complete clustering algorithm is mainly at updating J, S, Z, L and E in Algorithm 1. Updating both J and S needs to calculate the SVD, which costs $\mathcal{O}(n^3)$ and $\mathcal{O}(d^3)$, respectively. The GST algorithm in updating J and S costs $\mathcal{O}(Kn)$ and $\mathcal{O}(Kd)$, respectively, where K is the number of iterations in the GST algorithm. Updating Z and L costs $\mathcal{O}(dn^2)$ and $\mathcal{O}(d^2n)$, respectively. Updating E costs $\mathcal{O}(n^3)$. Therefore, the overall computational complexity of the proposed clustering algorithm is $\mathcal{O}(k(d^3 + 2n^3 + d^2n + dn^2 + Kd + Kn))$, where k denotes the number of iterations in Algorithm 1.

4   Experiments

4.1   Settings

In this section, we conduct experiments to evaluate the performance of our proposed model on three representative benchmark datasets: the Extended Yale B dataset [5], the ORL dataset [18], and the COIL-20 dataset [15]. We compared our proposed WSN-LLRR algorithm against several state-of-the-art subspace clustering methods including SSC [4], LRR [9], LLRR [11], ARM [7], WSPQ [26], LRRSC [3], and FLLRR [24]. The clustering results of all methods are generated from the source codes provided by the authors, and the parameters are set according to the original papers. In our method, we select λ from $\{10^{-5}, 10^{-4}, 10^{-3}, 10^{-2}, 10^{-1}, 10^0, 10^1\}$, and choose p from 0.1 to 1 with interval 0.1.

Three standard clustering metrics, clustering accuracy (ACC) [14], normalized mutual information (NMI) [14], and adjusted rand index (AR) [25] are used to evaluate the clustering performance. The ACC is defined as:

$$ACC = \frac{N(accurately\ clustered\ samples)}{N(total\ of\ clustered\ samples)}. \tag{22}$$

The NMI of A and B is defined as follows:

$$NMI(A, B) = \frac{I(A, B)}{\sqrt{H(A)H(B)}}, \tag{23}$$

where $I(, \cdot,)$ and $H(\cdot)$ denote the mutual information and information entropy, respectively. The definition of AR [19] is as:

$$AR = \frac{\binom{n}{2}(a+d) - [(a+b)(a+c) + (c+d)(b+d)]}{\binom{n}{2}^2 - [(a+b)(a+c) + (c+d)(b+d)]}, \tag{24}$$

where n is the number of objects. We define M and N as the true partition and clustering results, respectively, then, a is the number of objects in a pair placed in the same group in M and the same group in N, b is the number of objects in a pair placed in the same group in M and different groups in N, c is the number of objects in a pair placed in the same group in N and different groups in M, and d is the number of objects in a pair placed in different groups in M and different groups in N.

All the experimental results are produced in MATLAB R2014a on a desktop PC with Windows Server 2008, an Intel (R) Xeon(R) CPU E5-2680 2.40GHz, and 256 GB RAM. We conduct each experiment 10 times and record the average result.

4.2   Experiments on Extended Yale B Dataset

This dataset contains 38 different individuals, each consisting of 64 frontal face images with 192×148 pixels shooted under different lights condition, For ease the computational cost and memory, these images are downsampled to 48×42 pixels. The first 10 individuals of this dataset, namely EYaleB 10, are used in this experiment, therefore, there are 640 images in this subset and the raw pixels of each image are organized into a vector with dimensions 2016-D (48×42). The experimental results by competing methods are shown in Table 1, where the best results are highlighted in bold. It can be seen that our proposed method outperforms other competitive approaches in terms of the three metrics. Specifically, the improvement of our proposed method is significant against LLRR and FLLRR. This is because the weighted Schatten-p norm in WSN-LLRR can approximate the actual rank of data better. The reason why WSPQ and ARM get better results than LRR is their better rank approximation. LRRSC introduces the symmetric constraint in LRR and obtains the second-best results.

Table 1. Clustering results of competing methods (%) for EYaleB 10 dataset

Metrics	Methods							
	LRR	SSC	LLRR	ARM	WSPQ	LRRSC	FLLRR	Ours
ACC	79.06	76.88	86.56	94.53	94.38	96.09	86.72	**96.41**
NMI	82.84	76.31	82.43	91.11	90.97	92.14	91.07	**92.97**
AR	69.10	60.90	67.11	86.92	86.56	91.38	84.55	**91.84**

Table 2. Clustering results of competing methods (%) for ORL dataset

Metrics	Methods							
	LRR	SSC	LLRR	ARM	WSPQ	LRRSC	FLLRR	Ours
ACC	72.50	77.00	77.25	78.25	79.50	79.25	75.50	**82.50**
NMI	85.47	89.32	87.52	89.49	89.85	90.82	89.01	**91.85**
AR	58.96	68.79	66.25	68.88	70.67	72.15	68.02	**75.38**

4.3   Experiments on ORL Dataset

There are 40 different individuals in the ORL dataset, each subject contains 10 facial images shooted under different illumination and facial expression. Each image is downsampled to 40 × 30 pixels. The raw pixels of each image are organized into a vector with dimensions 1200-D. Because the differences between each image of an individual are much more complex, this dataset is more challenging. In this experiment, we use the whole dataset. Table 2 shows the clustering results. One can see that our proposed method achieves the best results in terms of the three metrics. Specifically, WSN-LLRR improves the ACC, NMI, and AR of the other methods by at least 3.25%, 1.03%, and 3.23%, respectively. This validates the efficiency of our proposed method over the other competing methods.

Table 3. Clustering results of competing methods (%) for COIL-20 8 dataset

Metrics	Methods							
	LRR	SSC	LLRR	ARM	WSPQ	LRRSC	FLLRR	Ours
ACC	78.47	80.04	80.56	**81.25**	78.65	81.08	80.73	**81.25**
NMI	85.71	91.46	90.32	88.49	84.55	**91.70**	88.44	89.84
AR	76.39	80.51	80.38	76.84	75.75	**81.85**	79.40	76.99

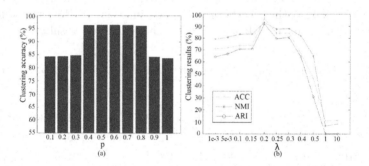

Fig. 1. Clustering results on the EYaleB 10 dataset (%) with varying p and λ.

4.4   Experiments on COIL-20 Dataset

The COIL-20 dataset contains 1440 object images with a black background, which come from 20 subjects. Images of each subject were shooted at pose intervals of 5 °C, finally, resulting in a total of 72 different images. We resize the images and put the pixels of each image into a vector with dimension 1024-D (32×32). The first 8 classes of this dataset, namely COIL-20 8, are used to conduct experiments. Therefore, there are 576 images in the subset and we construct the data matrix with size 1024×576. Table 3 shows the experimental results.

It can be seen that our proposed WSN-LLRR and ARM achieve the best result in terms of ACC, namely 81.25%, which achieves a higher value of 0.17% than the second-best result of LRRSC. In terms of NMI, WSN-LLRR also achieves comparable results. LRRSC achieves the best results concerning AR.

4.5 Parameter Selection

The proposed model WSN-LLRR has two important parameters p and λ, where p is to guarantee the low-rank property of the coefficient matrix, and λ is used to balance the effects between the data term and the low-rank terms. The EYaleB 10 dataset is utilized to test the effectiveness of p and λ. Experimental results are given below of the clustering accuracy variation under the varying p values in steps of 0.1. The vertical axis denotes the clustering accuracy subject to p. From Fig. 1 (a), one can see that, when $p = 0.6$, the proposed method achieves relatively better clustering accuracy. In theory, the closer p is to 0, the closer the weighted Schatten-p norm is to the rank function, therefore, an intuitive way to set p is that p should be set to a small value. However, we usually do not choose such a strategy in practice since noises and outliers in data will destroy the low-rank property of the data matrix, therefore, the strong low-rank constraint is not suitable. In addition, the parameter λ greatly affects the clustering performance of our proposed method. Figure 1 (b) shows the experimental results on the EYaleB 10 dataset in terms of ACC, NMI, and ARI. When λ ranging from 0.1 to 1, ACC varies between 96.41% to 10.78%. This reminds we need to select λ carefully.

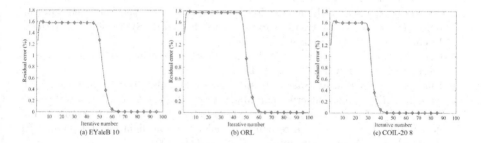

Fig. 2. Convergence curves of WSN-LLRR on three datasets.

4.6 Convergence Analysis

It is not easy to analyze the convergence property of the proposed WSN-LLRR theoretically since the non-convex nature of the weighted Schatten-p norm. In this subsection, we provide quantitative results to prove the model's convergence. For each iteration in the optimization process, we record the relative residual error: $\frac{\|X-XZ-LX-E\|_F}{\|X\|_F}$. Figures 2 (a), (b), and (c) shows the relationship between relative residual error and iterative number on the EYaleB 10, ORL, and COIL-20 8 datasets, respectively. One can see that the relative errors can close to 10^{-6} within 100 iterations on three datasets, which verifies the good convergence property of the proposed WSN-LLRR model.

5   Conclusion

In this paper, a new robust subspace clustering model based on latent low-rank representation and the weighted Schatten-p norm is proposed. Specifically, the proposed model is better to induce low rank than the nuclear norm in the standard LLRR model. Moreover, an efficient optimization algorithm based on the ADMM framework is presented to solve the proposed model. Finally, experimental results on Extended Yale B, ORL, and COIL20 datasets show that the proposed model can get higher clustering accuracy than other state-of-the-art methods. In addition, we discuss the selection of parameters and verify the proposed model can reach convergence within relatively few iterations. Our future work is to do more theoretical research on the selection of parameters and apply the proposed model to multi-view data.

References

1. Boyd, S., Parikh, N., Chu, E., Peleato, B., Eckstein, J., et al.: Distributed optimization and statistical learning via the alternating direction method of multipliers. Found. Trends® Mach. learn. **3**(1), 1–122 (2011)
2. Cao, J., Fu, Y., Shi, X., Ling, B.W.K.: Subspace clustering based on latent low rank representation with schatten-p Norm. In: 2020 2nd World Symposium on Artificial Intelligence (WSAI), pp. 58–62. IEEE (2020)
3. Chen, J., Mao, H., Sang, Y., Yi, Z.: Subspace clustering using a symmetric low-rank representation. Knowl.-Based Syst. **127**, 46–57 (2017)
4. Elhamifar, E., Vidal, R.: Sparse subspace clustering: algorithm, theory, and applications. IEEE Trans. Pattern Anal. Mach. Intell. **35**(11), 2765–2781 (2013)
5. Georghiades, A.S., Belhumeur, P.N., Kriegman, D.J.: From few to many: illumination cone models for face recognition under variable lighting and pose. IEEE Trans. Pattern Anal. Mach. Intell. **23**(6), 643–660 (2001)
6. Gu, S., Xie, Q., Meng, D., Zuo, W., Feng, X., Zhang, L.: Weighted nuclear norm minimization and its applications to low level vision. Int. J. Comput. Vis. **121**(2), 183–208 (2017)
7. Kang, Z., Peng, C., Cheng, Q.: Robust subspace clustering via tighter rank approximation. In: Proceedings of the 24th ACM International on Conference on Information and Knowledge Management, pp. 393–401 (2015)
8. Khachatryan, A., Müller, E., Stier, C., Böhm, K.: Improving accuracy and robustness of self-tuning histograms by subspace clustering. IEEE Trans. Knowl. Data Eng. **27**(9), 2377–2389 (2015)
9. Liu, G., Lin, Z., Yan, S., Sun, J., Yu, Y., Ma, Y.: Robust recovery of subspace structures by low-rank representation. IEEE Trans. Pattern Anal. Mach. Intell. **35**(1), 171–184 (2012)

10. Liu, G., Lin, Z., Yu, Y., et al.: Robust subspace segmentation by low-rank representation. In: ICML. Citeseer. vol. 1, p. 8 (2010)
11. Liu, G., Yan, S.: Latent low-rank representation for subspace segmentation and feature extraction. In: 2011 International Conference on Computer Vision, pp. 1615–1622. IEEE (2011)
12. Lu, L., Vidal, R.: Combined central and subspace clustering for computer vision applications. In: Proceedings of the 23rd International Conference on Machine Learning, pp. 593–600 (2006)
13. Luo, X., Wu, H., Wang, Z., Wang, J., Meng, D.: A novel approach to large-scale dynamically weighted directed network representation. IEEE Trans. Pattern Anal. Mach. Intell. 1 (2021)
14. Manning, C., Raghavan, P., Schütze, H.: Introduction to information retrieval. Nat. Lang. Eng. 16(1), 100–103 (2010)
15. Nene, S.A., Nayar, S.K., Murase, H., et al.: Columbia object image library (coil-20) (1996)
16. Nie, F., Huang, H., Ding, C.: Low-rank matrix recovery via efficient schatten p-Norm minimization. In: Twenty-sixth AAAI Conference on Artificial Intelligence (2012)
17. Ren, Z., Wu, B., Zhang, X., Sun, Q.: Image set classification using candidate sets selection and improved reverse training. Neurocomputing 341, 60–69 (2019)
18. Samaria, F.S., Harter, A.C.: Parameterisation of a stochastic model for human face identification. In: Proceedings of 1994 IEEE Workshop on Applications of Computer Vision, pp. 138–142. IEEE (1994)
19. Santos, J.M., Embrechts, M.: On the use of the adjusted rand index as a metric for evaluating supervised classification. In: Alippi, C., Polycarpou, M., Panayiotou, C., Ellinas, G. (eds.) ICANN 2009. LNCS, vol. 5769, pp. 175–184. Springer, Heidelberg (2009). https://doi.org/10.1007/978-3-642-04277-5_18
20. Shi, J., Malik, J.: Normalized cuts and image segmentation. IEEE Trans. Pattern Anal. Mach. Intell. 22(8), 888–905 (2000)
21. Wang, Z., et al.: Large-scale affine matrix rank minimization with a novel nonconvex regularizer. IEEE Trans. Neural Netw. Learn. Syst. 33(9), 4661–4675 (2022)
22. Wang, Z., Wang, W., Wang, J., Chen, S.: Fast and efficient algorithm for matrix completion via closed-form 2/3-thresholding operator. Neurocomputing 330, 212–222 (2019)
23. Xie, Y., Gu, S., Liu, Y., Zuo, W., Zhang, W., Zhang, L.: Weighted schatten p-norm minimization for image denoising and background subtraction. IEEE Trans. Image Process. 25(10), 4842–4857 (2016)
24. Yu, S., Yiquan, W.: Subspace clustering based on latent low rank representation with frobenius norm minimization. Neurocomputing 275, 2479–2489 (2018)
25. Zhang, S., Wong, H.S., Shen, Y.: Generalized adjusted rand indices for cluster ensembles. Pattern Recognit. 45(6), 2214–2226 (2012)
26. Zhang, T., Tang, Z., Liu, Q.: Robust subspace clustering via joint weighted schatten-p Norm and LQ norm minimization. J. Electron. Imaging 26(3), 033021 (2017)
27. Zhang, X., Xu, C., Sun, X., Baciu, G.: Schatten-q regularizer constrained low rank subspace clustering model. Neurocomputing 182, 36–47 (2016)
28. Zuo, W., Meng, D., Zhang, L., Feng, X., Zhang, D.: A generalized iterated shrinkage algorithm for non-convex sparse coding. In: Proceedings of the IEEE International Conference on Computer Vision, pp. 217–224 (2013)

Evolutionary
Computation/Optimisation

Speeding up Genetic Programming Based Symbolic Regression Using GPUs

Rui Zhang[1], Andrew Lensen[2], and Yanan Sun[1(✉)]

[1] Sichuan University, Chengdu 610000, China
zhang_ray@stu.scu.edu.cn, ysun@scu.edu.cn
[2] Victoria University of Wellington, Wellington 6140, New Zealand
andrew.lensen@ecs.vuw.ac.nz

Abstract. Symbolic regression has multiple applications in data mining and scientific computing. Genetic Programming (GP) is the mainstream method of solving symbolic regression problems, but its execution speed under large datasets has always been a bottleneck. This paper describes a CUDA-based parallel symbolic regression algorithm that leverages the parallelism of the GPU to speed up the fitness evaluation process in symbolic regression. We make the fitness evaluation step fully performed on the GPU and make use of various GPU hardware resources. We compare training time and regression accuracy between the proposed approach and existing symbolic regression frameworks including gplearn, TensorGP, and KarooGP. The proposed approach is the fastest among all the tested frameworks in both synthetic benchmarks and large-scale benchmarks.

Keywords: Symbolic regression · Genetic programming · Parallel algorithm · Graphics processing unit (GPU) · Compute unified device architecture (CUDA)

1 Introduction

Exploring and learning relationships from data is the central challenge of the sciences. Among various methods [33,34] for achieving this goal, symbolic regression [3] which can represents such relationships as a concise and interpretable function is the most popular [32]. It has a wider range of applications in curve fitting [14], data modeling [17], and material science [35].

Symbolic regression is achieved as an optimization problem. Given a dataset (X, y), symbolic regression is achieved by optimizing an interpretable function $f(X) : \mathbb{R}^n \to \mathbb{R}$ to minimize the loss $D(f(X), y)$. Achieving symbolic regression has two common approaches: Genetic Programming (GP) method [23] and neural network (NN) method [6,24,28]. As one of the Evolutionary Algorithms (EA), GP optimizes solutions by imitating the evolution procedure in nature and aims to find global optima. GP is a generalized heuristic search technique used to optimize a population of computer programs according to a fitness function that determines the program's ability to perform a task. Due to its flexible

© The Author(s), under exclusive license to Springer Nature Switzerland AG 2022
S. Khanna et al. (Eds.): PRICAI 2022, LNCS 13629, pp. 519–533, 2022.
https://doi.org/10.1007/978-3-031-20862-1_38

representation and good global search ability, GP is the mainstream method for solving symbolic regression problems. The advantage of GP-based symbolic regression compared to the recent neural network (NN) methods [6, 24, 28] is that: the black-box-like solutions provided by NNs are hard to explain and interpret by users. In GP-based symbolic regression, each candidate solution in the population is represented as an expression tree, and the evolutionary process of all participating programs is visible to the user. The user can intuitively discover the characteristics of the data by the features of the different participating programs. Therefore, GP can evolve programs with the potential for interpretability. On the other hand, GP can automatically evolve structures and parameters of programs, which can eliminate the need for the manual design of NN structures.

However, GP is known for its poor scalability. The main reason is that the fitness of each GP program is evaluated on the whole dataset in each generation, causing the GP algorithm to be computationally expensive and time-consuming. Thus, fitness evaluation is the bottleneck of GP in large-scale problems [8]. There are various previous works to optimize the fitness evaluation step of GP, such as caching fitness results of subtree [19], eliminating the need for fitness [7], and computational parallelization. In symbolic regression problems, using computational parallelization is the most effective way to speed up the fitness evaluation step, especially performing parallelizing through GPUs, which can execute thousands of threads in parallel and excel at processing multiple threads using Single Instruction Multiple Thread (SIMT) [11] intrinsic. The existing GPU approaches can be broadly grouped into these two categories:

1) Performing data vectorization and leveraging existing data vectorization interfaces. TensorGP [5] and KarooGP [30] are two common GPU-enabled GP frameworks that support symbolic regression. Both of them are based on the Tensorflow [1] interface. KarooGP adopts the Graph Execution Model [15] of Tensorflow and consequently has a slow execution speed. TensorGP requires a dataset in tensor type, and it does not support regression in real-world datasets well due to this limitation.

2) Directly leveraging GPU parallelization by involving more threads in the computation of the fitness evaluation phase. A SIMD interpreter [22] is developed to evaluate the whole population of GP in parallel. The interpreter computes the intermediate value of the current node each time the kernel is launched, which avoids the use of *switch-case* statements on the GPU to identify the type of the node. However, the frequent launching of kernel functions will cause the delay. Chitty [9] improves the stack structure and stores the prefix on the shared memory. Although better performance is obtained compared to that without memory access restrictions, they do not make greater use of the GPU hardware resources.

To better leverage the multi-threaded parallel computing capability of the GPU in GP-based symbolic regression, this paper proposes a GPU parallel approach to accelerate the fitness evaluation of GP-based symbolic regression. We use the constant memory for program storage, global memory for the stack that records the temporary fitness results, and shared memory for the parallel metric reduction. The whole dataset and the evaluated program are stored in the device-side memory so that the fitness evaluation step of the proposed method can be performed entirely on the GPU. In the fitness evaluation process of a single GP program, the loss of the program in each fitness case will be executed simultaneously using the GPU parallelism. The experiment results demonstrate that the proposed approach outperforms other GP-based symbolic regression frameworks in execution speed without degradation in regression accuracy. The idea and the novel data structures of the proposed parallel algorithm can be used not only in symbolic regression but also can be generalized to similar stack-based GP methods. The contributions of this work are:

1) We create the GPU acceleration in the fitness evaluation step by using the CUDA C/C++ layer and the code is released at the following address: https://github.com/RayZhhh/SymbolicRegressionGPU.
2) We accelerate the fitness evaluation step by optimizing data structures for symbolic regression on the device side and performing a parallel metric reduction on the GPU, which fully leverages the GPU computational capability.
3) We evaluate the proposed approach against common CPU and GPU frameworks through synthetic datasets and real-world datasets. The proposed approach turns out to be the fastest among all regression tasks.

2   Background and Related Work

This section introduces the GP algorithm and its application in symbolic regression. We also introduce existing GP frameworks that support symbolic regression algorithms.

2.1   Genetic Programming

GP has four major steps: population initialization, selection, mutation, and evaluation. GP algorithm uses random mutation, crossover, a fitness function, and multiple generations of evolution to resolve a user-defined task. GP programs are often represented as syntax tree [29]. The structure of the syntax tree is defined by [29] as follows:

- The 'leaves' of the syntax tree are called terminals. They are variables, constants, and no-parameter functions in the program.
- The inner nodes of the tree are called functions.
- The depth of a node is the number of edges that need to be traversed to reach the node starting from the tree's root node (which is assumed to be at depth 0).
- The depth of a tree is the depth of its deepest leaf (terminal).

2.2   Existing GP Frameworks

The gplearn [31] is implemented based on the *scikit-learn* [27] machine learning framework. According to [4], gplearn can also perform parallelization, but the parallelization can be used only on the mutation step. Our tests did not find that gplearn's multithreading parameters could effectively improve the computing speed. We disabled this parameter in our later benchmarks. DEAP [13] is another GP framework implemented by Python that provides CPU-based parallelization.

TensorGP and KarooGP are two GPU supported frameworks. Both frameworks are based on the interface of TensorFlow [1] for data vectorization. In the fitness evaluation step, TensorGP represents terminal and variable as the tensor with the same dimension as the input dataset. The metric is calculated by tensor operations (such as tensor multiplication, tensor addition, etc.) provided by Tensorflow. The required dataset of TensorGP is limited to a tensor for a set of points uniformly sampled in the problem domain. So it will be inapplicable when facing real-world problems since the required tensor can not be constructed. Different from TensorGP which leverages the tensor calculation interface, our work makes more intuitive use of GPU parallelism by having threads perform calculations on each data point. TensorGP adopts the Eager Execution Model [2] of TensorFlow, while KarooGP adopts the Graph Execution Model [15] of Tensor-Flow, which means that in KarooGP, each internal program has to be compiled into a DAG (Directed Acyclic Graph) before having fitness calculation. According to our experimental results and the conclusion in [4], TensorGP turns out to be much faster than KarooGP.

Several papers [4,5] adopt Pagie polynomial [26] as the speed benchmark for GP-based symbolic regression frameworks. Pagie polynomial is considered to be challenging to approximate and it is recommended by several GP benchmark articles [16,25]. According to the results in [4], TensorGP (GPU) is faster than other CPU and GPU frameworks including gplearn, KarooGP, and DEAP.

3   The Proposed Symbolic Regression Algorithm

In this section, we first explain the challenge in implementation. Then, we demonstrate the process of our algorithms in chronological order of execution.

3.1   Challenge Faced

Directly porting the CPU code logic to the GPU produces only limited performance improvement. This is because the warp divergence and unconstrained memory access will greatly influence the performance of the GPU. Warp divergence occurs when threads in a warp execute different code blocks. If they execute different *if-else* branches, all threads are blocked at the same time except the one that is executing, which affects performance. The proposed algorithm avoids warp divergence and also achieves coalesced data access by optimizing data structures. Modern GPU architectures provide various components (e.g., constant memory, global memory, and shared memory) with different features. Our work takes the advantage of different components according to specific computing tasks to make full use of the computing resources provided by the GPU.

[9] improves the stack structure and stores the prefix on the shared memory. The improvement made in our work is that all blocks in the grid evaluate the same program. Since there will not be a situation where each block evaluates a different program, we store the programs in constant memory and leverage the on-chip cache for memory access acceleration. This avoids the transfer from global memory to shared memory. Our modification may result in GPU computational resources not being fully used on small-size datasets, while larger datasets will ensure that the evaluation of a program will take up all GPU computational resources.

The flow chart of the proposed algorithm is shown in Fig. 1. In the proposed algorithm, the initialization, selection, and mutation steps are executed on the CPU; the fitness evaluation step, which is the most expensive component in most GP algorithms, is executed on the GPU.

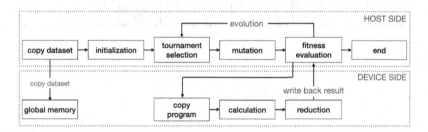

Fig. 1. Process of the proposed algorithm. Memory allocation and free parts on the GPU are ignored.

3.2   Memory Allocation and Dataset Transfer

This step is the initialization of the framework. Since the dataset will not be modified on the device memory, we transfer it to the device side at the beginning. This avoids the delay caused by memory transfer between the host side and device side during fitness evaluation. We also allocate stack memory space in the global memory and two arrays for a program in the constant memory, which can be reused for the fitness evaluation of each generation. On the device side, threads access memory in warp units. If threads of a warp read data with contiguous addresses, CUDA will coalesce their accesses, performing only one memory access request. Therefore, we design data structures for the stack and the dataset on the device side that support coalesced memory access.

We first allocate device-side memory space through *cudaMallocPitch()*, then the dataset is converted into the column-major type (shown in Fig. 2) and transferred to device-side memory through *cudaMemcpy2D()*. For column-major storage, each time when threads access variables, the entire row of the dataset is accessed. As the memory addresses of elements in a row are contiguous, coalesced memory access is available. To achieve coalesced memory access, we also

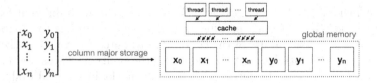

Fig. 2. The column-major storage of the dataset on the device side memory can achieve the coalesced access.

do not allow threads to allocate independent stack memory. Instead, we consolidate the stack memory space they need. In our implementation, the stack structure is essentially a *1D* array. Our stack structure is shown in Fig. 3, with 512 threads per block used in this work.

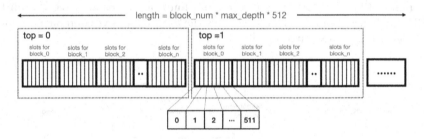

Fig. 3. Device-side stack allocation.

As shown in Fig. 3, if *stack_top* is zero currently, all the threads will access memory space in the box on the left side. And so on, if *stack_top* is one, threads will access memory in the box on the right side. Memory access like this can lead to a coalesced memory access that will greatly improve memory access efficiency. The program will not be modified on the GPU, and it will be accessed by all the threads. In our implementation, a program is stored in constant memory on the GPU, where a single memory-read request to constant memory can be broadcast to nearby threads, which saves memory-read-request times and speeds up the memory access efficiency. In addition, caches can save data of constant memory, so consecutive reads to the same address will not generate additional memory access.

3.3   Population Initialization and Selection

Both initialization and selection are carried out on the CPU. Although the GPU is based on the SIMT (Single Instruction Multiple Threads) architectures, the performance of the GPU cannot be effectively utilized because threads will perform different tasks and execute different instructions when initializing programs, which affects the performance. The proposed approach supports a user-defined function set, as well as the three initialization methods including full initialization, growth initialization, and ramped half-and-half [20]. In the selection step, the proposed approach only provides tournament selection [10,21]. The proposed approach also provides a *parsimony_ coefficient* parameter inspired by [31] to prevent the bloating of programs.

In our implementation, we adopt an elitist preservation approach where the candidate program with the best fitness of each generation goes directly into the next generation. Elitist preservation can ensure that the fitness of the next generation population is not inferior to the current population.

3.4 Mutation

Mutations take place on the CPU because each program is different that using a GPU is not applicable. The proposed approach supports five mutation types:

- Crossover mutation: A random subtree of the parent tree is replaced by a random subtree of the donor tree.
- Subtree mutation: A random subtree of the parent tree is replaced by a random subtree of a randomly generated tree.
- Hoist mutation: Suppose A is a subtree of the parent tree, B is the subtree of A, hoist mutation replaces A with B.
- Point mutation: A node of the parent tree is replaced by a random node.
- Point replace mutation: Any given node will be mutated of the parent tree.

Note that hoist mutation can lead to a decrease in program depth, which can prevent the program from bloating. Since the stack structure we mentioned earlier limits the maximum depth of the program. To avoid overflow during fitness evaluation, if we find that the depth of a program exceeds the specified maximum depth after mutation, the hoist mutation will be repeatedly performed on the program until the depth of the program is less than the specified depth.

3.5 Fitness Evaluation

The fitness evaluation process is the most complicated part of our algorithm. In this step, the CPU and GPU need to work together. The CPU is responsible for data copy, and the GPU is responsible for data calculation. A program is first converted into a prefix expression. Then, it will be transferred to the constant memory allocated before. The process is illustrated in Fig. 4. The prefix is represented by two arrays that record the values and the types for nodes in the prefix. The element 'u' denotes that the node is a unary function; 'b' denotes a binary function; 'v' denotes a variable; 'c' denotes a constant. Nodes in different types will correspond to different stack operations in the kernel function.

The metric calculation and reduction steps are performed on the GPU. Each thread is responsible for calculating the predicted value for a data point with the help of our device-side stack. The reverse iteration begins from the last node to the first node of the program. For each node in the iteration, we make the corresponding operation according to the type of the node. If the node is a terminal, the thread simply pushes its value into the stack. If the node is a function, the thread calculates the value according to the function type and pushes the result into the stack.

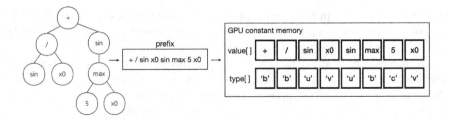

Fig. 4. Program transfers to the device-side memory. Each expression tree is represented by a prefix and each node of the prefix is identified by two tokens.

In the metric calculation step, each thread is responsible for the difference value calculating between the predicted value and its corresponding real value. The proposed approach supports three metric types, they are:

- MAE (Mean Absolute Error)
- MSE (Mean Squared Error)
- RMSE (Root Mean Squared Error)

The metric result computed by each thread will be stored in the shared memory, which is an on-chip memory that offers fast access speed.

In the reduction step, each block is responsible for the sum of losses calculated by its internel threads. The results of blocks are stored in a device-side array allocated in the global memory, which is then copied to the host side. Figure 5 shows the reduction process on the device-side and host-side.

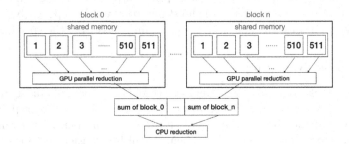

Fig. 5. Reduction on the GPU and the CPU.

After we get the sum of losses calculated by each thread, we will calculate the final loss result according to the specified loss function. The above procedures complete the evaluation of a single program, so these steps will be repeated until all programs in the population obtain fitness. Note that the bank conflict needs to be avoided in parallel reduction design, which occurs when multiple threads simultaneously access different addresses of the same bank. Our implementation ensures that threads in a warp are scattered across different banks during the shared memory access to avoid bank conflict. The kernel function of the proposed algorithm is shown in Algorithm 1.

4   Experiments and Results

This section presents our experimental results on synthetic datasets and large-scale real-world datasets.

Algorithm 1: Kernel function

Input: prefix, stack, dataset, realValue, result
Output: none
for *node in prefix* **do**
  | doStackOperation(node, stack, dataset);
end
metric = square(stack.top() - realValue);
sharedMem[threadID] = metric;
synchronize();
for *i in [256, 128, 64, 32, 16 , 8, 4, 2, 1]* **do**
  | // the loop is expanded in our inplementation
  | **if** *threadID < i* **then**
  | | sharedMem[threadID] += sharedMem[threadID + i];
  | **end**
  | synchronize();
end
result[blockID] = sharedMem[0];

Table 1. Hardware and software specifications in synthetic benchmarks and large-scale benchmarks.

Component	Specification	Component	Specification
CPU	AMD Ryzen 5 5600H	CUDA Tool Kit Version	11.5
GPU	NVIDIA RTX 3050 Laptop	OS	Windows 11
GPU RAM	4.0 GB	Host RAM	16.0 GB

4.1   Benchmarks on Synthetic Datasets

We compare the average execution times between gplearn (CPU), TensorGP (GPU), KarooGP (GPU), and the proposed approach. We also test the best fitness after 50 iterations under different dataset sizes [4]. All tests employed in synthetic benchmark concern the approximation of the Pagie Polynomial [26] function defined by Eq. 1, following the conventions of GP community [4,16,25].

$$f(x,y) = \frac{1}{1 + x^{-4}} + \frac{1}{1 + y^{-4}} \qquad (1)$$

We generate 7 datasets of different size from $64 \times 64 = 4,096$ data points to $4096 \times 4096 = 16,777,216$ by uniformly subsampling data points from the domain $(x, y) \in [-5, -5] \times [-5, -5]$. Framework parameters are listed in Table 2.

Table 2. Parameters for benchmarks.

Parameter	Value	Parameter	Value
Population size	50	Generations	50
Tournament size	3	Fitness metric	RMSE
Maximum initial depth	10	Maximum allowed depth	10
Crossover probability	0.9	Function set	$+, -, \times, \div$, sin, cos, tan
Mutation probability	0.08	Initialization method	Ramped Half and Half

Table 3. Average execution time of 30 runs on NVIDIA GeForce RTX 3050 Laptop GPU for various frameworks (lower is better). The symbol of "DNF" denotes that the test does not finish within three hours. The symbol of "MAF" denotes that the memory allocation failed on the GPU. The bold marks the minimum execution time for each test.

Framework	4,096	16,384	65,536	262,144	1,048, 576	4,194,304	16,777,216
Our approach	**0.152**	**0.215**	**0.193**	**0.331**	**0.886**	**3.034**	**11.851**
TensorGP (GPU)	5.655	6.873	6.236	6.473	6.535	17.334	MAF
KarooGP (GPU)	27.42	47.92	60.08	123.97	367.21	DNF	DNF
Gplearn (CPU)	1.731	2.936	8.897	53.006	174.228	DNF	DNF

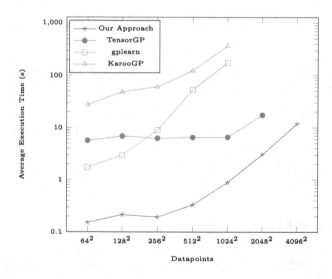

Fig. 6. Log-Log Plot of Execution Time for various frameworks on NVIDIA RTX 3050 Laptop GPU (Lower is better).

In our synthetic dataset experiment, we first compare the execution time of different frameworks in different dataset sizes. We ran each experiment 30 times and calculated the average execution time. The experimental results are shown in Table 3 and Fig. 6.

It can be seen from Table 3 that the proposed approach performs a faster training speed than other GPU and CPU frameworks for different sizes of datasets. Compared to gplearn which only supports CPU execution, the proposed approach achieves a maximum speedup of 170× acceleration on the fourth dataset (1,048,576 data points). The proposed approach is also faster than the two GPU-supported frameworks across each dataset. To discuss the influence of GPU models on the proposed algorithm, we also compare the execution speed on different GPUs. The hardware and software specifications are shown in Table 4. As shown in Table 5, the proposed approach is faster than TensorGP (GPU) in all GPU models.

Table 4. Hardware and software specifications in various GPUs tests.

Component	Specification	Component	Specification
CPU	Intel Xeon Gold 6310 @ 2.1 GHz	RAM	32.0 GB
CUDA Tool Kit Version	11.0	OS	Ubuntu 18.04.5

From these tests, we notice that under different GPU models, TensorGP did not show an increasing trend in the dataset of 64^2 to 1024^2 data points. This may be because the GPU-based tensor calculating interface provided by Tensorflow works well for large-scale tensors, but there is little optimization for smaller tensors. For the proposed algorithm, the regression time in 64^2 to 512^2 data points are similar, and the regression time of 512^2 to 4096^2 dataset is close to linear growth, this is because datasets less than 512^2 data points in our test do not use up all the computing resources provided by the GPU, and the computing resources of the GPU have been exhausted for datasets in larger sizes that more computing tasks have to line up and show a linear growth of the regression time. We also notice that TensorGP has a much more memory consumption than the proposed method. The memory allocation for the 4096^2 dataset failed on the RTX 3050 Laptop GPU with four GB of device memory. This is because that tensor is a complex data structure, so the encapsulation of the dataset requires extra memory space.

Table 5. Execution times on various GPUs in seconds (lower is better). The bold marks the minimum execution time for each test.

Framework	GPU	64^2	128^2	256^2	512^2	1024^2	2048^2	4096^2
TensorGP	RTX 2080 Ti	5.751	5.834	5.428	5.03	5.503	8.168	28.31
Our approach		**0.086**	**0.085**	**0.114**	0.149	0.353	1.138	3.561
TensorGP	RTX 3090	9.014	8.769	8.551	9.338	9.618	8.7	14.482
Our approach		0.099	0.094	0.155	**0.148**	**0.32**	**0.806**	**2.605**
TensorGP	NVIDIA A100	7.984	6.834	7.568	7.234	6.934	7.301	19.413
Our approach		0.139	0.140	0.184	0.173	0.354	0.847	2.686
TensorGP	RTX A6000	8.602	8.454	9.290	7.593	8.528	8.133	22.072
Our approach		0.154	0.138	0.167	0.234	0.470	1.225	3.486

We also analyze the regression accuracy of the proposed approach under different dataset sizes (shown in Table 6). Compare with the corresponding fitness results according to Table 6, the regression accuracy of the proposed approach on synthetic datasets is close to TensorGP. Therefore, on the premise of similar regression accuracy, the proposed approach is faster than TensorGP in execution speed.

4.2   Large-Scale Benchmarks

We run large-scale benchmarks on two datasets usually used to compare gradient boosting frameworks. In particular, we consider the Airline [18] and YearPredictionMSD [12] datasets with 115M and 515K rows respectively.

Since both of these two datasets are not able to transform to a *Tensor* form that TensorGP needs, experiments are carried out only on the proposed approach, KarooGP, and gplearn. Each framework will run three times for each dataset, and we record the execution time and best fitness after 50 generations of these experiments.

Table 6. Table showing the best RMS Error after 50 iterations.

Size	Our approach	TensorGP	Size	Our approach	TensorGP
4,096	0.233 ± 0.045	0.274 ± 0.048	1,048,576	0.242 ± 0.052	0.253 ± 0.066
16,384	0.258 ± 0.041	0.211 ± 0.065	4,194,304	0.246 ± 0.045	0.237 ± 0.078
65,536	0.246 ± 0.047	0.265 ± 0.058	16,777,216	0.247 ± 0.060	–
262,144	0.240 ± 0.052	0.239 ± 0.050			

A total 18 runs were performed on gplearn, KarooGP, and the proposed approach. Karoo GP did not finish on the Airline dataset in less than an hour. So we only compared with gplearn on the Airline dataset. Table 7 lists the regression accuracy and average execution time in seconds after 50 iterations.

Table 7. Table containing mean execution time and best fitness across three runs for gplearn, KarooGP, and the proposed approach on Airline and Year datasets. The symbol of "DNF" denotes that the test do not finish within an hour.

	Airline time	Airline fitness	Year time	Year fitness
Our approach	4.099	37.806	0.629	21.779
Gplearn	251.178	37.757	150.119	22.045
KarooGP	DNF	DNF	772.822	22.063

We notice that the regression accuracy of different frameworks was similar across these two datasets, the proposed approach achieves a speedup of 200× acceleration compared to gplearn and a 1200× acceleration compared to KarooGP on the YearPredictionMSD dataset. Through these tests, we conclude that our algorithm can effectively improve the execution speed through GPU parallelization under the premise of achieving similar regression accuracy.

5   Summary

This paper introduces a GPU parallelization algorithm to accelerate the GP-based symbolic regression. We optimize memory access by using column-major storage for the dataset, and a stack space that supports coalesced access for threads. We also implement a GPU-side reduction that avoids bank conflict. After training, the proposed approach preserves the best program in the last generation and its corresponding metric. This program can be considered the optimal solution to the symbolic regression. Our experimental results show that the proposed approach performs faster execution speed than gplearn, TensorGP, and KarooGP. This indicates that the proposed algorithm can effectively improve the execution speed of symbolic regression through parallel computation in the fitness evaluation step. In particular, the fast execution speed on large datasets indicates that the proposed method has the potential to allow GP-based symbolic regression to be applied to large problems that it currently is not able to be.

References

1. Abadi, M., Agarwal, A., Barham, P., et al.: TensorFlow: large-scale machine learning on heterogeneous distributed systems (2016)
2. Agrawal, A., Modi, A.N., Passos, A., et al.: TensorFlow eager: a multi-stage, python-embedded DSL for machine learning. CoRR abs/1903.01855 (2019)
3. Awange, J.L., Paláncz, B.: Symbolic Regression, pp. 203–216. Springer International Publishing, Cham (2016)
4. Baeta, F., Correia, J.A., Martins, T., et al.: Speed benchmarking of genetic programming frameworks. In: Proceedings of the Genetic and Evolutionary Computation Conference, pp. 768–775. GECCO 2021. Association for Computing Machinery, New York, NY, USA (2021)
5. Baeta, F., Correia, J., Martins, T., Machado, P.: TensorGP – genetic programming engine in TensorFlow. In: Castillo, P.A., Jiménez Laredo, J.L. (eds.) EvoApplications 2021. LNCS, vol. 12694, pp. 763–778. Springer, Cham (2021). https://doi.org/10.1007/978-3-030-72699-7_48
6. Biggio, L., Bendinelli, T., Neitz, A., Lucchi, A., Parascandolo, G.: Neural symbolic regression that scales. CoRR abs/2106.06427 (2021). arxiv:2106.06427
7. Biles, J.A.: Autonomous GenJam: eliminating the fitness bottleneck by eliminating fitness. In: Proceedings of the Genetic and Evolutionary Computation Conference Workshop Program, vol. 7 (2001)
8. Cano, A., Zafra, A., Ventura, S.: Speeding up the evaluation phase of GP classification algorithms on GPUs. Soft Comput. 16, 187–202 (2012)
9. Chitty, D.M.: Improving the performance of GPU-based genetic programming through exploitation of on-chip memory. Soft Comput. 20, 661–680 (2016)
10. Chitty, D.M.: Exploiting tournament selection for efficient parallel genetic programming. In: Lotfi, A., Bouchachia, H., Gegov, A., Langensiepen, C., McGinnity, M. (eds.) UKCI 2018. AISC, vol. 840, pp. 41–53. Springer, Cham (2019). https://doi.org/10.1007/978-3-319-97982-3_4
11. Cook, S.: CUDA Programming: A Developer's Guide to Parallel Computing with GPUs, 1st edn. Morgan Kaufmann Publishers Inc., San Francisco, CA, USA (2012)

12. Dua, D., Graff, C.: UCI machine learning repository (2017). https://archive.ics. uci.edu/ml
13. Fortin, F.A., De Rainville, F.M., Gardner, M., Parizeau, M., Gagné, C.: DEAP: evolutionary algorithms made easy. J. Mach. Learn. Res. Mach. Learn. Open Source Softw. **13**, 2171–2175 (2012)
14. Lee, K.H., Yeun, Y.S.: Genetic programming approach to curve fitting of noisy data and its application in ship design. Trans. Soc. CAD/CAM Eng. **9** (2004)
15. Handley, S.: On the use of a directed acyclic graph to represent a population of computer programs. In: Proceedings of the First IEEE Conference on Evolutionary Computation. IEEE World Congress on Computational Intelligence, pp. 154–159, vol. 1 (1994)
16. Harper, R.: Spatial co-evolution: quicker, fitter and less bloated. In: Proceedings of the 14th Annual Conference on Genetic and Evolutionary Computation, pp. 759–766. GECCO 2012. ACM (2012)
17. Icke, I., Rosenberg, A.: Multi-objective genetic programming projection pursuit for exploratory data modeling (2010). https://doi.org/10.48550/ARXIV.1010.1888
18. Ikonomovska, E.: Airline dataset: for evaluation of machine learning algorithms on non-stationary streaming real-world problems (2009). https://kt.ijs.si/elena_ ikonomovska/data.html
19. Keijzer, M.: Alternatives in subtree caching for genetic programming. In: Keijzer, M., O'Reilly, U.-M., Lucas, S., Costa, E., Soule, T. (eds.) EuroGP 2004. LNCS, vol. 3003, pp. 328–337. Springer, Heidelberg (2004). https://doi.org/10.1007/978-3-540-24650-3_31
20. Koza, J.: Genetic programming: on the programming of computers by means of natural selection. Complex Adap. Syst. **1** (1992)
21. Koza, J.: Genetic programming as a means for programming computers by natural selection. Stat. Comput. **4**(2), 87 (1994)
22. Langdon, W.B., Banzhaf, W.: A SIMD interpreter for genetic programming on GPU graphics cards. In: O'Neill, M., et al. (eds.) EuroGP 2008. LNCS, vol. 4971, pp. 73–85. Springer, Heidelberg (2008). https://doi.org/10.1007/978-3-540-78671-9_7
23. Langdon, W.B., Poli, R., McPhee, N.F., et al.: Genetic programming: an introduction and tutorial, with a survey of techniques and applications. In: Computational Intelligence: A Compendium, pp. 927–1028. Studies in Computational Intelligence, Springer, Heidelberg (2008). https://doi.org/10.1007/978-3-540-78293-3_22
24. Martius, G., Lampert, C.H.: Extrapolation and learning equations. CoRR abs/1610.02995 (2016). arxiv:1610.02995
25. McDermott, J., White, D.R., Luke, S., et al.: Genetic programming needs better benchmarks. In: Proceedings of the 14th Annual Conference on Genetic and Evolutionary Computation, pp. 791–798. GECCO 2012. Association for Computing Machinery, New York, NY, USA (2012)
26. Pagie, L., Hogeweg, P.: Evolutionary consequences of coevolving targets. Evolut. Comput. **5**(4), 401–418 (1997)
27. Pedregosa, F., Varoquaux, G., Gramfort, A., et al.: Scikit-learn: machine learning in python. J. Mach. Learn. Res. **12**, 2825–2830 (2012)
28. Petersen, B.K., et al.: Deep symbolic regression, version 1.0, December 2019. https://doi.org/10.11578/dc.20200220.1, https://www.osti.gov//servlets/ purl/1600741
29. Poli, R., Langdon, W.B., McPhee, N.F.: A field guide to genetic programming. Published via http://lulu.com and freely available at http://www.gp-field-guide.org.uk (2008)

30. Staats, K., Pantridge, E., Cavaglia, M., et al.: TensorFlow enabled genetic programming. In: Proceedings of the Genetic and Evolutionary Computation Conference Companion, pp. 1872–1879. GECCO 2017. Association for Computing Machinery, New York, NY, USA (2017)
31. Stephens, T.: Genetic programming in python with a scikit-learn inspired api: Gplearn (2016). https://github.com/trevorstephens/gplearn
32. Tohme, T., Liu, D., Youcef-Toumi, K.: GSR: a generalized symbolic regression approach (2022). https://doi.org/10.48550/ARXIV.2205.15569, arxiv:2205.15569
33. Tohme, T., Vanslette, K., Youcef-Toumi, K.: A generalized Bayesian approach to model calibration. Reliabil. Eng. Syst. Saf. **204**, 107–141 (2020). https://doi.org/10.1016/j.ress.2020.107141
34. Tohme, T., Vanslette, K., Youcef-Toumi, K.: Improving regression uncertainty estimation under statistical change. CoRR abs/2109.08213 (2021). arxiv:2109.08213
35. Wang, Y., Wagner, N., Rondinelli, J.M.: Symbolic regression in materials science. MRS Communications (2019). https://doi.org/10.48550/ARXIV.1901.04136

High-Dimensional Discrete Bayesian Optimization with Intrinsic Dimension

Shu-Jun Li[1], Mingjia Li[1], and Hong Qian[1,2(✉)]

[1] School of Computer Science and Technology, East China Normal University,
Shanghai 200062, China
hqian@cs.ecnu.edu.cn
[2] National Key Laboratory for Novel Software Technology, Nanjing University,
Nanjing 210023, China

Abstract. Bayesian optimization (BO) has achieved remarkable success in optimizing low-dimensional continuous problems. Recently, BO in high-dimensional discrete solution space is in demand. However, satisfying BO algorithms tailored to this issue still lack. Fortunately, it is observed that high-dimensional discrete optimization problems may exist low-dimensional intrinsic subspace. Inspired by this observation, this paper proposes a Locality Sensitive Hashing based Bayesian Optimization (LSH-BO) method for high-dimensional discrete functions with intrinsic dimension. Via randomly embedding solutions from intrinsic subspace to original space and discretization, LSH-BO turns high-dimensional discrete optimization problems into low-dimensional continuous ones. Theoretically we prove that, with probability 1, there exists a corresponding optimal solution in the intrinsic subspace. The empirically results on both synthetic functions and binary quadratic programming task verify that LSH-BO surpasses the compared methods and possesses the versatility across low-dimensional and high-dimensional kernels.

Keywords: Black-box optimization · Intrinsic subspace · Locality sensitive hashing

1 Introduction

Bayesian Optimization (BO) [5,8] is a principled method to optimize the black-box problems formulated as $x^* = \arg\min_{x \in X} f(x)$. In black-box optimization (also called derivative-free or zeroth-order optimization), the gradient of objective functions f is hard to access, and one can only optimize via sampling solutions and modeling the underlying objective functions with the sampled solutions

This work is supported by National Natural Science Foundation of China (No. 62106076), Natural Science Foundation of Shanghai (No. 21ZR1420300), "Chenguang Program" sponsored by Shanghai Education Development Foundation and Shanghai Municipal Education Commission (No. 21CGA32), and National Key Laboratory for Novel Software Technology at Nanjing University (No. KFKT2021B14). Hong Qian is the corresponding author of this paper.

© The Author(s), under exclusive license to Springer Nature Switzerland AG 2022
S. Khanna et al. (Eds.): PRICAI 2022, LNCS 13629, pp. 534–547, 2022.
https://doi.org/10.1007/978-3-031-20862-1_39

x and their evaluated function values $f(x)$. Bayesian optimization is pervasive in machine learning and scientific computing [20,27]. In those scenarios, the objective function are often expensive to evaluate, while BO is able to find out a satisfied solution with limited evaluation budget since it invokes Gaussian process (GP) [23] to model the underlying objective functions.

Despite the success of Bayesian optimization, notably, BO is mainly applied to the low-dimensional and continuous solution space due to its limitation of scalability and continuity of Gaussian process. Two aspects account for this limitation. For the issue of scalability, BO suffers from the high cost of each iteration and the large number of iteration [25]. With the increasing dimensionality of solution space, the solution space expands exponentially and more solutions need to be sampled in order to well fit the underlying GP model. The computational complexity of posterior distribution in GP drastically increases with the increasing number of sampled solutions. Furthermore, the acquisition functions that determine which solution should be sampled are also high dimensional. Maximizing the high-dimensional acquisition functions is challenging and the optimizing result of acquisition functions affects the quality of final solution to be returned by BO. For the issue of continuous solution space, BO uses Gaussian process that relies on the smoothness defined on a kernel function as the surrogate model and is mainly applied to continuous variables [1]. In discrete solution space, BO often rounds the real number to the nearest integer. GP treats the change between two consecutive integers as continuous but ignores that the objective function is indeed piece-wise for discrete variables. For categorical variables, the ordinal relationship between variable values does not exist, and the standard kernels in GP usually ignore the ordinal relationship. Besides, discrete solution space brings extra difficulty in optimizing the acquisition functions [28].

Bayesian optimization in high-dimensional and discrete solution space is in demand. For example, the drug discovery problem that is abstracted into a molecular selection and ranking problem [20], protein sequence design so that it can bind to a specific substance [28], and bike sharing company deciding whether or not to place a bike station at a government given space [1], etc. In those scenarios, the optimization tasks are black-box, discrete and sometimes high dimensional. Therefore, it is necessary and urgent to extend the success of Bayesian optimization from low-dimensional continuous solution space to high-dimensional discrete solution space.

On one hand, many high-dimensional Bayesian optimization algorithms focus on continuous solution space. One mainstream of these existing work is based on random embedding [30]. The embedding-based methods [16,19,22,30] assume that the objective function value is affected by a minority of decision variables, whereas the other decision variables only have a limited or even no effect on the function value. Namely, the objective function has an (approximate) low-dimensional intrinsic subspace. When functions possessing a low-dimensional intrinsic subspace, random embedding enables BO to optimize in the low-dimensional continuous space while evaluate in the original high-dimensional continuous solution space. On the other hand, the existing discrete

BO approaches focus on the modification of covariance kernels [9,21] or the substitution of surrogate models [1,2,12,28], e.g., tree models. However, these discrete BO algorithms suffer from the issue of high-dimensional scalability. Thus, high-dimensional discrete Bayesian optimization algorithms still lack.

Fortunately, it is observed that high-dimensional discrete (or even categorical) optimization problems may also exist low-dimensional intrinsic dimension. For the categorical hyper-parameters in solvers of mixed integer programming that is NP-hard, only a part of categorical hyper-parameters have a significant impact on the overall performance of solvers [13,30]. Inspired by this observation, this paper aims to address high-dimensional discrete Bayesian optimization problem, and the realistic low intrinsic dimension assumption is added to make it tractable.

In this paper, we propose a Locality Sensitive Hashing based Bayesian Optimization (LSH-BO) method to handle the challenges from both high dimensionality and discreteness. The LSH-BO method focuses on the objective functions with low intrinsic dimension. Via randomly embedding solutions from intrinsic subspace to original space, LSH-BO turns high-dimensional discrete optimization problems into low-dimensional continuous ones. There are two ingredients in LSH-BO, embedding matrix (from high dim to low dim) and discretization (from discrete to continuous). Blending them together separates optimization and evaluation and enables us to perform optimization in low-dimensional continuous space while evaluation in original high-dimensional discrete space. The contribution of this paper is three folds.

- Propose a simple yet effective LSH-BO to handle high-dimensional optimization over categorical or discrete solution space with intrinsic dimension. LSH-BO makes the problem tractable via turning high-dimensional discrete optimization into low-dimensional continuous one.
- Theoretically prove that, with probability 1, there exists a corresponding optimal solution in the intrinsic subspace.
- Empirically verify that LSH-BO surpasses the compared methods and possesses the versatility across low-dimensional and high-dimensional kernels.

The rest of the paper reviews the related work, recaps Bayesian optimization, introduces the proposed LSH-BO and its theoretical result, presents experiment result, and finally gives a conclusion.

2   Related Work

To address the challenge of discrete search space, there are mainly two lines of research. The first way is to modify the covariance kernels to make GP adapt to the categorical space. In [9], a modified kernel is proposed to handle discrete space by transforming the points to their closest integer values in the kernel. In [21], a GP based method COMBO generates a combinatorial graph to quantify the "smoothness" of functions and utilizes the diffusion kernel to model the high-order interactions between variables. The second way to handle discrete problems is to substitute surrogate model to avoid dealing with GP in categorical space. Both SMAC [12] and Tree-structured Parzen Estimator (TPE) [2] adopt tree-shaped model as their surrogate model. SMAC is based on random forests [4] to model categorical problems. By using random walks to optimize the discontinuous and non-differentiable acquisition function, it can deal with up to 76 discrete variables [12,25]. TPE [2] models each input dimension independently by a kernel density estimator and mainly suffers from lack of accuracy. Also, its performance on high dimensional problems is unsatisfactory. Instead of using tree-shaped model, the AMORTIZED BO [28] uses neural networks to build the surrogate model. With the increase of dimensionality, designing and training neural networks become more difficult. BOCS [1] uses sparse Bayesian linear regression as the surrogate model for BO in binary discrete domain and is able to learn the interactions among categorical variables automatically. However, the computational complexity of interactions highly relies on the input dimension, thus as the dimensionality of problem grows, its performance becomes undesirable.

To handle the challenge of high dimensionality, one mainstream of the existing work is based on random embedding and assumes that the objective function has a low-dimensional intrinsic subspace. In [30], a well-known random embedding method REMBO is proposed to embed the original problem into a low dimensional search space and then search for the optimum in the intrinsic subspace. In [22], a sequential random embeddings approach is proposed to deal with the high dimensional functions with approximately intrinsic subspace. In [19], a novel embedding strategy, the hashing-enhanced subspace BO algorithm, is proposed with a theoretical justification of a bounded error in kernel before and after applying embedding. In [16], it summaries the current mainstream linear embedding technology. It is worth noting that most embedding-based methods only focus on the continuous domain.

This paper follows the line of embedding-based methods. The proposed LSH-BO differs from REMBO in the following aspects. First, LSH-BO deals with the binary categorical domain while REMBO mainly focuses on the continuous domain. The experiment of REMBO on discrete problems only scales to 47 dimensions. Second, the choice of kernels are different. REMBO only uses high dimensional kernels in discrete problems while both of the high dimensional and low dimensional kernels can be used in LSH-BO. Third, this paper applies a different strategy to handle the challenge of discrete search space. We use LSH which has the property of preserving similarity, while REMBO simply rounds real number to integer which may not have such a property. Other ways to deal with high dimensional optimization problems include utilizing the concept of trust-region, e.g., CASMOPOLITAN [29], and decomposition-based methods, e.g., Add-GP-UCB [14] and G-Add-GP-UCB [24].

3   Preliminaries: Bayesian Optimization

Bayesian optimization is a principled method to optimize black-box functions which mainly consists of two parts: surrogate model that learns the underlying objective function by Bayesian rule, and acquisition function that guides us to select the next point to evaluate by trading off exploration and exploitation.

BO invokes Gaussian process (GP) [23] as the surrogate model. GP defines a distribution over function space which the underlying objective function may be contained. GP is fully characterized by its mean and covariance function. Given sampled solutions, prior on mean and covariance function, and a new solution, GP has a closed form to update mean and covariance function so as to obtain the posterior distribution over the function space analytically [8].

The popular acquisition functions include probability of improvement (PI) [15], expected improvement (EI) [18] and upper confidence bounds (UCB) [7]. PI has the form $PI(x) = P(f(x) \geq f(x^*) + \xi) = \phi(m(x) - f(x^*) - \xi/\sigma(x))$, where $\phi(\cdot)$ is the normal cumulative distribution function and ξ is a trade-off parameter to avoid PI getting stuck in a local optimum. Instead of taking the probability of improvement into account as in PI, EI makes use of the amount of improvement. It can be evaluated in the form $EI(x) = (\mu(x) - f(x^*))\Phi(Z) + \sigma(x)\phi(z)$ if $\sigma(x) \geq 0$, otherwise $EI(x) = 0$, where $Z = m(x) - f(x^*) - \xi/\sigma(x)$, and $\phi(\cdot)$ and $\Phi(\cdot)$ represents the PDF (probability density function) and CDF (cumulative distribution function) of the standard normal distribution respectively. Another widely-used acquisition function is UCB. $UCB(x) = \mu(x) + \kappa\sigma(x)$, where $\mu(\cdot)$ and $\sigma(\cdot)$ are mean and standard deviation, and κ is a positive parameter to balance exploration and exploitation.

4   Bayesian Optimization with Locality Sensitive Hashing

Problem Setup. Let $f\colon X \to \mathbb{R}$ be a costly-to-evaluate black-box function f over binary structured domain $X = \{0,1\}^D$. Consider the optimization problem $x^* = \arg\min_{x\in\{0,1\}^D} f(x)$. It is worth noting that D could scale up to thousands or even millions. Such properties (discrete and high dimension) bring a great challenge to optimization. To this end, this paper proposes a Locality Sensitive Hashing based Bayesian Optimization (LSH-BO) method which turns the high dimensional discrete optimization problem into a low dimensional continuous one, and then effectively deals with it.

Specifically, we first define a new search space with a low dimension and then construct a function that maps vectors in the low dimensional space to the original space via Locality Sensitive Hashing (LSH) [6]. LSH is a function if for any x and y we have $\Pr(f(x) = f(y)) = \text{sim}(x, y)$, where $\text{sim}(x, y) \in [0, 1]$ is some defined similarity between x and y. In another words, LSH is a class of functions with the property of similarity preservation for some pairwise similarity. In LSH-BO, we use the cosine similarity. Then, the standard BO is applied to search for the optimal point in this new search space and solution evaluation is conducted in the original high dimensional space.

Intrinsic Dimension in Discrete Solution Space. Before presenting the details of LSH-BO, we redefine the concept of intrinsic low dimension mentioned in related work. The motivation is that, in categorical search space, linear addition and subtraction is not closed, e.g., categorical variables "apple" plus "pear" is meaningless. Therefore, the classic definition in REMBO [30] with linear intrinsic subspace is not suitable for objective functions. We define the intrinsic entry, constant entry and intrinsic dimensionality as follows

Definition 1. *Given a function $f \colon \{0,1\}^D \to \mathbb{R}$, an entry t is said to be an intrinsic entry, with t is an integer that $1 \leq t \leq D$, if there exists a $(x_1, \ldots, x_{t-1}, x_{t+1}, \ldots, x_D) \in \{0,1\}^{D-1}$ s.t. $f(x_1, \ldots, x_{t-1}, 0, x_{t+1}, \ldots, x_D) \neq f(x_1, \ldots, x_{t-1}, 1, x_{t+1}, \ldots, x_D)$, otherwise t is a constant entry. d_e is the number of intrinsic entries, called the intrinsic dimensionality (also known as effective dimensionality or active dimensionality) of f.*

The definition is straightforward, only the values at intrinsic entries of a vector x may affect the value of $f(x)$ while constant entries do not. We then introduce the used LSH. For a vector $y \in Y = \mathbb{R}^d$, we apply a hash function defined as $LSH(y) = g(y) = \mathrm{sign}(Ay)$, where $A \in \mathbb{R}^{D \times d}$ is a random matrix with independent entries sampled according to $\mathcal{N}(0,1)$ and $\mathrm{sign}(\cdot)$ denotes the sign function, i.e., mapping positive numbers to 1 and negative numbers to 0. The above mapping $\mathrm{sign}(Ay)$ is named random hyperplane based hash function [6] and is proved to has the property of similarity preservation for cosine similarity [10]. It differs from the standard hash function in that the points close to each other has a higher probability to be hashed into the same bucket. Given Definition 1 and LSH, the following theorem shows that high dimensional discrete problems with intrinsic dimensionality can be solved via LSH.

Theorem 1. *Assume we are given a function $f \colon \{0,1\}^D \to \mathbb{R}$ with intrinsic dimensionality d_e and a random matrix $A \in \mathbb{R}^{D \times d}$ with independent entries sampled according to $\mathcal{N}(0,1)$ and $d \geq d_e$. Then, with probability 1, for any $x \in \mathbb{R}^D$ there exists a $y \in \mathbb{R}^d$ s.t. $f(x) = f(\mathrm{sign}(Ay))$, where $\mathrm{sign}(\cdot)$ projects positive numbers to 1 and negative ones to 0.*

Proof. Since we have defined the intrinsic entries, then for any x', if x' has equivalent values to x at all intrinsic entries, then we have $f(x) = f(x')$. That is to say, if there exists a y that $\mathrm{sign}(Ay)$ has equivalent values to x at all intrinsic entries, then $f(\mathrm{sign}(Ay)) = f(x)$. Suppose the number of intrinsic dimension is d_e and we only consider the intrinsic dimension, the above statement is equivalent to: for a random matrix A', there exists a y such that $\mathrm{sign}(A'y') = x'$, where $A' \in \mathbb{R}^{d_e \times d}$, $y' \in \mathbb{R}^{d \times 1}$ and $x' \in \mathbb{R}^{d_e \times 1}$ are A, y and x with only intrinsic dimension respectively. To ensure that the equation $\mathrm{sign}(A'y') = x$ has solutions, A' should have rank d_e. It remains to show that, with probability 1, the random matrix A' has rank d_e, which is similar to [30].   □

LSH-BO. Theorem 1 states that for any vector x in X, with probability 1, there exists a corresponding y that satisfies $f(x) = g(y)$. Further, if there exists an optimal point x^* of f, we can find a solution y^* in low dimensional space Y such that $x^* = \mathrm{sign}(Ay^*)$. This observation motivates our LSH-BO in which we apply LSH to generate another search space Y that is low dimensional and continuous, and construct a mapping from Y to X. We can use the standard Bayesian optimization method to find the optimal point of $g(\boldsymbol{y})$ and embed it back to X as the final solution. The algorithm is shown in Algorithm 1.

Algorithm 1. Locality Sensitive Hashing based Bayesian Optimization (LSH-BO)

Input:
    Objective function f;
    acquisition function $\texttt{acq}(\cdot)$;
    The upper bound of intrinsic dimensionality d.

Procedure:
  1: Sample a random matrix $\boldsymbol{A} \in \mathbb{R}^{D \times d}$ with $\boldsymbol{A}_{i,j} \sim \mathcal{N}(0,1)$.
  2: Define the function $g(\boldsymbol{y}) = f(\texttt{sign}(\boldsymbol{Ay}))$.
  3: Sample initial points $Y_0 \in Y$ and let $D_0 = \{(\boldsymbol{y}, g(\boldsymbol{y})) \mid \boldsymbol{y} \in Y_0\}$.
  4: Construct a GP model.
  5: **for** $t = 1$ to N **do**
  6:    Find $\boldsymbol{y}_{t+1}$ by optimizing the acquisition function $\boldsymbol{y}_{t+1} = \arg\max_{\boldsymbol{y} \in Y} \texttt{acq}(\boldsymbol{y})$.
  7:    $D_{t+1} = D_t \cup \{\boldsymbol{y}_{t+1}, g(\boldsymbol{y}_{t+1})\}$, and update the posterior distribution with D_{t+1}.
  8: **end for**
  9: $\boldsymbol{y}^* = \arg\max_{i=1,\dots,N} g(\boldsymbol{y}_i)$.
10: **return** $\boldsymbol{x}^* = \texttt{sign}(\boldsymbol{Ay}^*)$.

It is worth noting that, the design of this mapping is motivated from random hyperplane based hash function [6] that real vectors can be converted to discrete vectors with pairwise distance preservation. Specifically, we treat the discrete input vectors as hash buckets with 0–1 encoding and continuous vectors as the input of hash function. Though both LSH-BO and LSH make conversions between continuous and discrete variables, they focus on different situations. LSH is mainly for dimensionality reduction, while $g(\boldsymbol{y})$ in LSH-BO maps vectors from low dimensional continuous space into high dimensional discrete space. LSH-BO itself aims to turn high dimensional discrete optimization problem into low dimensional continuous one to effectively use standard BO to handle it.

Generally speaking, LSH-BO is simple to implement yet can avoid the difficulties in both high-dimensional and discrete optimization problems after turning the search space into low dimensional and continuous one.

Choice of Kernels. This section discusses the choice of kernels that determines the smoothness of functions sampled from the GP model. One natural choice is to use the kernels from standard BO, e.g., squared exponential kernel, Matern kernel and so on. We denote these kernels as LSH-LK, representing that the distance is measured in low dimension. They benefit from only constructing GPs in low dimensional space and thus save the computational costs.

Another intuition for using LSH-LK is that, the standard BO kernels have a distance preserving property, which states that two points with similar cosine distance tends to have same values in the original space. Formally, $\Pr(g(\boldsymbol{y_1}) = g(\boldsymbol{y_2})) = (1 - \texttt{angle}(\boldsymbol{y_1}, \boldsymbol{y_2})/\pi)^{d_e}$, where $\texttt{angle}(\cdot)$ presents the angel between two vectors, thus it is feasible to use low dimensional pairwise distance in the kernel to define the smoothness. It matters because the objective function $g(\boldsymbol{y})$ is indeed a compound function, which may complicate the original function $f(\boldsymbol{x})$ with an extra function $\texttt{sign}(\boldsymbol{Ay})$. The above issue may lead the updated GP model to be rather "sharper", i.e., low smoothness, and result in a higher demand for numbers of evaluations to well fit GP and higher computational cost to optimize the acquisition function. However, LSH-LK also has the following drawback. LSH-LK kernels may result in repeated recommendations by the acquisition function because the candidates may behave differently in low dimensional search space but be identical in high dimensional space. This leads to a demand for performing an additional check before evaluation.

Another choice of kernels is to define the pairwise distance in the original space as $k_{HK}(\boldsymbol{y_1}, \boldsymbol{y_2}) = k(\texttt{sign}(\boldsymbol{Ay_1}), \texttt{sign}(\boldsymbol{Ay_2}))$, where $k(\cdot, \cdot)$ refers to any kernel that is available for BO with continuous input. We refer to the notion of "high-dimensional kernel" defined in REMBO [30] which embeds the low dimensional pair of points into high dimensional space. Instead of using the hamming distance and a specific type of squared exponential kernel, we just choose Euclidean distance and expand to any kernel suitable for BO. The motivation is that we only care about the similarity between two points in the high-dimensional space, thus Euclidean distance is enough. We denote these kernels as LSH-HK.

An intuitive benefit for LSH-HK is that the similarity between two points described by the kernel function is the real similarity, so we do not have to consider the repeated recommendation as in LSH-LK. Besides, LSH-HK is more sensitive to subtle differences between original vectors as it directly calculates their distances. However, LSH-HK lacks its matching acquisition functions since the kernels are built over high dimensional discrete space and the existing acquisition functions are designed for low dimensional continuous space, thus they do not take high dimensional space information into consideration.

5   Experiments

This section empirically studies the proposed LSH-BO. First, 4 widely-used synthetic functions with intrinsic dimension are used to verify the proposed method outperforms other compared methods. Then we apply LSH-BO to optimize the binary quadratic programming [1] problem. In this task, its intrinsic dimensionality is not guaranteed. The results show that LSH-BO still outperforms other methods even when the theoretical assumption of intrinsic dimension whether holds or not. Further, we conduct experiments to discuss the impact of hyperparameters, specifically, the choice of kernels, acquisition functions and d.

5.1   Experimental Setup

The proposed method is compared with 5 competitive baselines: SMAC [12], TPE [2], Discrete-BO [17], BOCS [1] and COMBO [21]. We also include two additional baselines BO, named BaseBO, which performs the naive BO approach in optimizing the original discrete search space, and random search, denoted as RANDOM, which indeed is a competitive baseline [3] in high-dimensional sparse space. We apply EI [18] as acquisition function and for the choice of kernels, we apply the Matern kernel, which degenerates to high dimensional kernels used in REMBO after changing the distance measurement. The search boundary of low dimensional solution space is set as $[-3, 3]$ for each dimension. The experiment is conducted on the server with the configurations: AMD EPYC 7742 64-Core processor, 2.25 GHz, 128 GB memory. All experiments are repeated 20 times.

5.2   On Synthetic Functions

In this section we employ 4 standard benchmark problems (minimize the objective function values): (a) Sphere, (b) Zakharov, (c) Sumsquares, and (d) Levy. In particular, each test function is with $d_e = 30$ and $D = 500$, i.e., there are $D - d_e = 470$ constant entries that have no impact on the function value as defined in Definition 1. Besides, the optimization starts with an initial sample size 5 and the fixed budget for Zakharov, Levy, and Sumsquares are 150 while for Sphere it is 100. We compare LSH-BO to 7 competitors, namely SMAC, TPE, Discrete-BO, BOCS, COMBO, BaseBO and RANDOM.

Effectiveness. The results of optimization performance, i.e., effectiveness, are shown in Fig. 1. In Fig. 1(b), the performance of LSH-BO is close to or even worse than others at early iterations, however after iteration 50, it starts to outperform all of its competitors and at iteration 150, it has a better result. The same phenomenon also exists in all other 3 experiments. This is because the use of LSH may bring the extra complexity to original function, and as a consequence the GP model may fail to surrogate the function at the beginning. However, as the number of evaluations grows, this issue alleviates and the performance of LSH-BO starts to exceed other competitors. To draw a conclusion, LSH-BO performs better than all other methods, this shows that our proposed strategy can effectively handle the existing challenges in high dimensional discrete BO.

Hyper-parameter Analysis. For the issue of choice of kernels, we evaluate the performance of LSH-BO on Zakharov with different choices of kernels and d. Specifically, we compare low-dimensional and high-dimensional kernels, denoted as LSH-LK and LSH-HK, that are defined in Sect. 4, the naive BO is also included as a baseline. The results are shown in Fig. 2. We can find that for the problem of Zakharov, no matter what kernel and acquisition function LSH-BO chooses, LSH-BO achieves significantly better solutions compared with the naive BO. Besides, the choice of kernel has little impact on the performance of LSH-BO.

For the issue of upper bound of intrinsic dimensionality, we study the impact of different d on LSH-BO with fixed $D = 500$ and $d_e = 30$. Specifically, we consider three cases: (1) $d \ll d_e$. (2) $d = d_e$. (3) $d > d_e$. Figure 3 shows the results

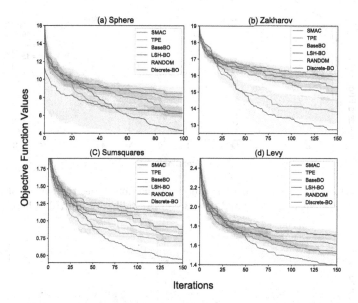

Fig. 1. Performance (the smaller the objective function values the better) on 4 synthetic functions with $d_e = 30$, $d = 30$ and $D = 500$.

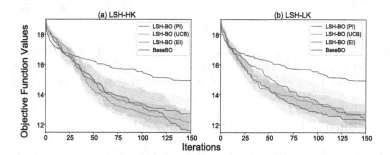

Fig. 2. Performance (the smaller the objective function values the better) on Zakharov with different kernels. (a) and (b) respectively show the performance of LSH-HK and LSH-LK with different acuiquisition functions.

on Zakharov with different $d \in \{15, 30, 40\}$, standing for the above three cases. From Fig. 3 we can find that for case (1), when $d = 15$ and $d_e = 30$, LSH-BO does not work well. This is because the low dimensional search space may not cover an optimal solution. For case (2), when $d = d_e = 30$, it performs better than case (1). Finally, for case (3), when d increases to 40, the performance is slightly better than case (2). The results above generally match our intuition. When addressing high dimensional discrete problems with low intrinsic dimension, we would better conduct an experiment to get an approximate range of intrinsic dimensionality and choose a slightly larger d according to the approximation of d_e.

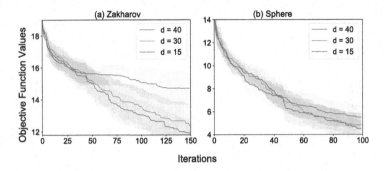

Fig. 3. Performance (the smaller the objective function values the better) of LSH-BO with different d when $D = 500$ and $d_e = 30$ on (a) Zakharov and (b) Sphere.

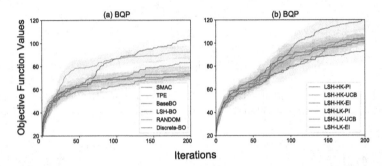

Fig. 4. (a) Performance (the higher the objective function values the better) on BQP with $d = 50$ and $D = 500$. (b) Performance (the higher the objective function values the better) of LSH-BO with different kernels and acquisition functions on BQP.

5.3   On Binary Quadratic Programming Task

The binary quadratic programming (BQP) [11] is pervasive in computer vision, such as in image segmentation [26], BQP is used to find a cut solution to segment a given image into two parts that conform to given constraints. BQP can be formulated as the following optimization problem [1]: $\arg\max_{x \in X} \lambda P(x) + x^T Q x - \lambda \|x\|_1$, where $Q \in \mathbb{R}^{D \times D}$ is a random matrix with entries sampled independently according to $\mathcal{N}(0, 1)$ and then multiplied element-wise by $K \in \mathbb{R}^{D \times D}$, where $K_{i,j} = \exp(-(i - j)/L_c^2)$. The correlation length L_c^2 defines the rate that entries of K decay away from the diagonal. We set $\lambda = 0$ and $L_c^2 = 10$. For BQP, the higher objective function values represent the better performance.

We first present that LSH-BO could deal with BQP problem even when its intrinsic dimension whether holds or not is unknown. We set $D = 10$ and $d = 7$. Apparently by enumerating the total inputs is $2^D = 1024$, we can get the optimal value. We set the evaluation budget as 50 and apply LSH-BO to see whether it can find the optima or not. In 30 repetitions, there are 25 times LSH-BO can find the optimal or suboptimal solution. This empirically verifies that LSH-BO can still work even when the low intrinsic dimensionality assumption may not hold.

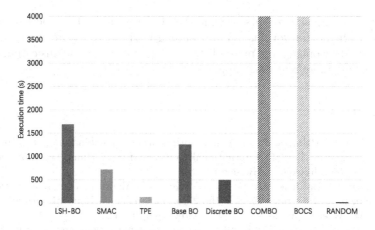

Fig. 5. Wall-clock time (s) on BQP

We further study the performance of LSH-BO in BQP, where we set $D = 500$ and $d = 50$. The results are shown in Fig. 4(a). Besides, the performance of LSH-BO with different choices of kernels (HK, LK) and acquisition functions (PI, UCB, EI) is shown in Fig. 4(b). From Fig. 4(a), we can observe the similar phenomenon as in the synthetic functions experiment. The performance of LSH-BO is close to or even worse than others at the beginning, however at about iteration 100, it is close to TPE and at the end of the optimization LSH-BO achieves a better solution compared to others. Figure 4(b) exhibits the performance when choosing different kernels and acquisition functions in which LSH-LK has the best performance, approximately 20% higher than others.

The execution time of each method is presented in Fig. 5. BOCS and COMBO are shown in striped bars, meaning that they may be infeasible, i.e., cannot accomplish within 10 h. Figure 5 implies that LSH-BO achieves a balance between time efficiency and scalability effectiveness.

This section demonstrates the effectiveness and competitiveness of LSH-BO. However, some limitations still exist. We only set the input dimension D up to 500 dimensions and also lack the discussion of the search boundary in the low dimensional space. LSH-BO is less competitive in low dimensional input space. In this case, direct optimization may work better than transforming the search space given the small evaluation budget of solution points in discrete space.

6 Conclusion

This paper proposes a locality sensitive hashing based Bayesian optimization (LSH-BO) method for high-dimensional discrete functions with intrinsic dimension. Via randomly embedding solutions from intrinsic subspace to original space and discretization, LSH-BO turns high-dimensional discrete optimization problems into low-dimensional continuous ones. Theoretical analysis verifies the existence of optima solution on optimization problem with intrinsic dimension.

And the experimental results present the effectiveness and competitiveness of LSH-BO. The future work includes extending LSH-BO to approximate intrinsic dimension, developing more methods to test the existence of intrinsic dimension, and exploring more real-world applications.

References

1. Baptista, R., Poloczek, M.: Bayesian optimization of combinatorial structures. In: Proceedings of the 35th International Conference on Machine Learning, vol. 80, pp. 471–480. Stockholm, Sweden (2018)
2. Bergstra, J., Bardenet, R., Bengio, Y., Kégl, B.: Algorithms for hyper-parameter optimization. In: Proceedings of the 25th Conference on Neural Information Processing Systems, pp. 2546–2554, Granada, Spain (2011)
3. Bergstra, J., Bengio, Y.: Random search for hyper-parameter optimization. J. Mach. Learn. Res. **13**, 281–305 (2012)
4. Breiman, L.: Random forests. Mach. Learn. **45**(1), 5–32 (2001)
5. Brochu, E., Cora, V.M., de Freitas, N.: A tutorial on Bayesian optimization of expensive cost functions, with application to active user modeling and hierarchical reinforcement learning. CoRR abs/1012.2599 (2010)
6. Charikar, M.: Similarity estimation techniques from rounding algorithms. In: Reif, J.H. (ed.) Proceedings on 34th ACM Symposium on Theory of Computing, pp. 380–388, Montréal, Canada (2002)
7. Cox, D.D., John, S.: A statistical method for global optimization. In: Proceedings of the 1992 International Conference on Systems, Man, and Cybernetics, pp. 1241–1246, Chicago, Illinois (1992)
8. Garnett, R.: Bayesian Optimization. Cambridge University Press, Cambridge (2022)
9. Garrido-Merchán, E.C., Hernández-Lobato, D.: Dealing with categorical and integer-valued variables in Bayesian optimization with gaussian processes. Neurocomputing **380**, 20–35 (2020)
10. Goemans, M.X., Williamson, D.P.: Improved approximation algorithms for maximum cut and satisfiability problems using semidefinite programming. J. ACM **42**(6), 1115–1145 (1995)
11. Huang, H., Pardalos, P.M., Prokopyev, O.A.: Lower bound improvement and forcing rule for quadratic binary programming. Comput. Optim. Appl. **33**(2–3), 187–208 (2006)
12. Hutter, F., Hoos, H.H., Leyton-Brown, K.: Sequential model-based optimization for general algorithm configuration. In: Proceedings of the 5th International Conference on Learning and Intelligent Optimization, vol. 6683, pp. 507–523, Rome, Italy (2011)
13. Hutter, F., Hoos, H.H., Leyton-Brown, K.: An efficient approach for assessing hyperparameter importance. In: Proceedings of the 31th International Conference on Machine Learning, vol. 32, pp. 754–762, Beijing, China (2014)
14. Kandasamy, K., Schneider, J., Poczos, B.: High dimensional Bayesian optimisation and bandits via additive models. In: Proceedings of the 32nd International Conference on Machine Learning, pp. 295–304, Lille, France (2015)
15. Kushner, H.J.: A new method of locating the maximum point of an arbitrary multipeak curve in the presence of noise. J. Basic Eng. **86**(1), 97–106 (1964)

16. Letham, B., Calandra, R., Rai, A., Bakshy, E.: Re-examining linear embeddings for high-dimensional Bayesian optimization. In: Advances in Neural Information Processing Systems 33. virtual (2020)
17. Luong, P., Gupta, S., Nguyen, D., Rana, S., Venkatesh, S.: Bayesian optimization with discrete variables. In: Proceedings of the 32nd Australasian Joint Conference, vol. 11919, pp. 473–484, Adelaide, Australia (2019)
18. Mockus, J., Tiesis, V., Zilinskas, A.: The application of Bayesian methods for seeking the extremum. In: Towards Global Optimization, vol. 2, pp. 117–129. North-Holland (1978)
19. Nayebi, A., Munteanu, A., Poloczek, M.: A framework for Bayesian optimization in embedded subspaces. In: Proceedings of the 36th International Conference on Machine Learning, vol. 97, pp. 4752–4761, Long Beach, California (2019)
20. Negoescu, D.M., Frazier, P.I., Powell, W.B.: The knowledge-gradient algorithm for sequencing experiments in drug discovery. INFORMS J. Comput. **23**(3), 346–363 (2011)
21. Oh, C., Tomczak, J.M., Gavves, E., Welling, M.: Combinatorial Bayesian optimization using the graph cartesian product. In: Wallach, H.M., Larochelle, H., Beygelzimer, A., d'Alché-Buc, F., Fox, E.B., Garnett, R. (eds.) Proceedings of the 32th Conference on Neural Information Processing Systems, pp. 2910–2920, Vancouver, Canada (2019)
22. Qian, H., Hu, Y., Yu, Y.: Derivative-free optimization of high-dimensional nonconvex functions by sequential random embeddings. In: Proceedings of the 25th International Joint Conference on Artificial Intelligence, pp. 1946–1952, New York (2016)
23. Rasmussen, C.E., Williams, C.K.I.: Gaussian Processes for Machine Learning. MIT Press, Cambridge (2006)
24. Rolland, P., Scarlett, J., Bogunovic, I., Cevher, V.: High-dimensional Bayesian optimization via additive models with overlapping groups. In: Proceedings of the 21st International Conference on Artificial Intelligence and Statistics, pp. 298–307, Playa Blanca, Spain (2018)
25. Shahriari, B., Swersky, K., Wang, Z., Adams, R.P., de Freitas, N.: Taking the human out of the loop: a review of Bayesian optimization. Proc. IEEE **104**(1), 148–175 (2016)
26. Shi, J., Malik, J.: Normalized cuts and image segmentation. IEEE Trans. Pattern Anal. Mach. Intell. **22**(8), 888–905 (2000)
27. Snoek, J., Larochelle, H., Adams, R.P.: Practical Bayesian optimization of machine learning algorithms. In: Proceedings of the 26th Conference on Neural Information Processing Systems, pp. 2960–2968, Lake Tahoe, Nevada (2012)
28. Swersky, K., Rubanova, Y., Dohan, D., Murphy, K.: Amortized Bayesian optimization over discrete spaces. In: Proceedings of the 36th Conference on Uncertainty in Artificial Intelligence, vol. 124, pp. 769–778. Virtual (2020)
29. Wan, X., Nguyen, V., Ha, H., Ru, B.X., Lu, C., Osborne, M.A.: Think global and act local: Bayesian optimisation over high-dimensional categorical and mixed search spaces. In: Proceedings of the 38th International Conference on Machine Learning, vol. 139, pp. 10663–10674. Virtual (2021)
30. Wang, Z., Hutter, F., Zoghi, M., Matheson, D., de Freitas, N.: Bayesian optimization in a billion dimensions via random embeddings. J. Artif. Intell. Res. **55**, 361–387 (2016)

Multi-objective Evolutionary Instance Selection for Multi-label Classification

Dingming Liu[1], Haopu Shang[1], Wenjing Hong[2], and Chao Qian[1(✉)]

[1] State Key Laboratory for Novel Software Technology, Nanjing University,
Nanjing 210023, China
{liudm,shanghp,qianc}@lamda.nju.edu.cn
[2] Department of Computer Science and Engineering, Southern University of Science
and Technology, Shenzhen 518055, China
hongwj@sustech.edu.cn

Abstract. Multi-label classification is an important topic in machine learning, where each instance can be classified into more than one category, i.e., have a subset of labels instead of only one. Among existing methods, ML-kNN [25], the direct extension of k-nearest neighbors algorithm to the multi-label scenario, has received much attention due to its conciseness, great interpretability, and good performance. However, ML-kNN usually suffers from a terrible storage cost since all training instances need to be saved in the memory. To address this issue, a natural way is instance selection, intending to save the important instances while deleting the redundant ones. However, previous instance selection methods mainly focus on the single-label scenario, which may have a poor performance when adapted to the multi-label scenario. Recently, few works begin to consider the multi-label scenario, but their performance is limited due to the inapposite modeling. In this paper, we propose to formulate the instance selection problem for ML-kNN as a natural bi-objective optimization problem that considers the accuracy and the number of retained instances simultaneously, and adapt NSGA-II to solve it. Experiments on six real-world data sets show that our proposed method can achieve both not worse prediction accuracy and significantly better compression ratio, compared with state-of-the-art methods.

Keywords: Multi-label classification · ML-kNN · Instance selection · Multi-objective optimization · Multi-objective evolutionary algorithm

1 Introduction

Multi-label classification concerns an important class of classification problems where each instance may belong to multiple categories simultaneously, i.e., have several different labels. For example, an image may be associated with several predefined topics such as "Mountain", "Tree", "Water", etc. [4]. This situation is

C. Qian—This work was supported by the National Science Foundation of China (62022039, 62106098).

© The Author(s), under exclusive license to Springer Nature Switzerland AG 2022

S. Khanna et al. (Eds.): PRICAI 2022, LNCS 13629, pp. 548–561, 2022.
https://doi.org/10.1007/978-3-031-20862-1_40

different from the traditional single-label classification (i.e., multi-class) where each instance can be classified into only one category (i.e., one label), and it is more challenging. In the past decade, multi-label classification has been extensively studied [26]. Among existing methods, the Multi-Label k-Nearest Neighbor (ML-kNN) algorithm [25] has received much attention due to its conciseness, great interpretability and good performance.

Despite its potential, ML-kNN has an open issue to be addressed, that is, all training instances need to be saved in the memory. With the ever-growing of big data in the real world, this issue would hinder the use of ML-kNN on more computing platforms, especially those with limited memory, such as smartphones and embedded systems. To address this issue, a natural way is instance selection that only requires a small number of instances [17]. It has been widely reported that instance selection contributes in reducing memory consumption for single-label classification problems [17]. Thus, it is natural to ask whether instance selection still works well when applied to ML-kNN.

However, the instance selection for ML-kNN has been rarely addressed in the literature. To the best of our knowledge, there are only two works [1,10] in this direction. Although they show some potential of instance selection in context of multi-label classification scenarios, they both handle the problem in a single-objective manner, i.e., the instances are selected with the only purpose to maximize the accuracy [1], or to optimize with respect to a weighted sum of the classifier accuracy and the compression ratio [10]. This might be inappropriate as both classifier accuracy and compression ratio are important but conflicting objectives in practice, and it is unrealistic to overlook either of them. If more instances are removed, a decrease in the accuracy of the classifier built on the retained instances is usually inevitable. Hence, it is impossible that a single solution is optimal in terms of both accuracy and compression ratio. Besides, as the accuracy and compression ratio are of different physical meanings, summing them up does not really provide meaningful information and might cause difficulties in determining the appropriate values of weights.

In this paper, we propose to employ Multi-Objective Evolutionary Algorithms (MOEAs) to solve the instance selection problem for ML-kNN. Specifically, we formulate the instance selection problem for ML-kNN as a bi-objective optimization problem that considers the accuracy and the compression ratio as two separate objectives. The two objectives are conflict with each other, and they are typically non-differentiable. To address these issues, the well-known Nondominated Sorting Genetic Algorithm II (NSGA-II) [7] that possesses the strong capability of tackling multi-objective black-box optimization problems [27] is employed and adapted to the bi-objective instance selection for ML-kNN, leading to the Multi-Objective Evolutionary Instance Selection algorithm for Multi-Label classification (MOEIS-ML). To the best of our knowledge, MOEIS-ML is the first multi-objective evolutionary instance selection algorithm for ML-kNN that can provide a set of different compromise solutions between accuracy and compression ratio in a single simulation run. In this way, MOEIS-ML could offer more options to the end-user, thus providing more flexibility than the single-objective approaches. Experiments on six real-world data sets further show that our proposed algorithm can achieve both not worse prediction accuracy and significantly better compression ratio, compared with state-of-the-art methods.

The remainder of this paper is organized as follows. Section 2 introduces some preliminaries and reviews the related work. Section 3 presents the bi-objective problem formulation and the proposed MOEIS-ML. The experimental results and discussions are provided in Sect. 4. Section 5 concludes this paper and discusses some promising future work.

2   Preliminaries and Related Work

2.1   Multi-label k Nearest Neighbor Algorithm

ML-kNN [25] is a direct extension of the popular kNN [5,14] to dealing with multi-label classification problems, which aims to predict the label set of an unseen instance based on statistical information gained from the label sets of its neighboring training instances with known label sets.

More formally, let $\mathcal{X} = \mathbf{R}^d$ denote the d-dimensional instance space and let $\mathcal{Y} = \{y_1, y_2, \cdots, y_q\}$ be the label set of q possible labels. Given a training set $TR = \{(x_i, Y_i) | 1 \leq i \leq n\}$, $x_i \in \mathcal{X}$, $Y_i \subseteq \mathcal{Y}$, the task of multi-label classification is to find a multi-label classifier $h : \mathcal{X} \rightarrow 2^{\mathcal{Y}}$ such that the classifier is able to accurately predict the label set for any unseen instance $x \in \mathcal{X}$. To accomplish this task, ML-kNN conducts as follows.

Several notations are first introduced. For an unseen instance x, let $N_k(x)$ represent the set of its k nearest neighbors identified in the training set TR. Let $I[\cdot]$ denote the indicator function, i.e., if $\cdot$ is true, $I[\cdot]$ is set to 1; else, $I[\cdot]$ is set to 0. The number of instances in $N_k(x)$ with label y_j is counted as $C_j = \sum_{(x', Y') \in N_k(x)} I[y_j \in Y']$. Define H_j as the event that x has label y_j, then the prior probability that H_j holds is represented as $P(H_j)$, and that H_j does not hold is represented as $P(\neg H_j)$. The posterior probability that H_j holds under the condition that x has exactly r neighbors with label y_j is denoted as $P(H_j | C_j = r)$, and the posterior probability that H_j does not holds under that condition is denoted as $P(\neg H_j | C_j = r)$. Accordingly, let $P(C_j = r | H_j)$ and $P(C_j = r | \neg H_j)$ represent the likelihood that x has exactly r neighbors with label y_j when H_j holds and when H_j doesn't hold, respectively. Based on these notations, the Maximum A Posterior (MAP) rule is utilized to make predictions by reasoning with the labeling information embodied in the neighbors. Specifically, the predicted label set for an unseen instance x is determined as follows:

$$Y = \{y_j | P(H_j | C_j = r) > P(\neg H_j | C_j = r), 1 \leq j \leq q\}. \tag{1}$$

Based on Bayes Theorem, we have $P(H_j | C_j = r) - P(\neg H_j | C_j = r)$ equals to $(P(C_j = r | H_j) P(H_j) - P(C_j = r | \neg H_j) P(\neg H_j)) / P(C_j = r)$. Then, it suffices to estimate the prior probabilities as well as likelihoods for making predictions.

ML-kNN fulfills the above estimation task via a frequency counting strategy. First, the prior probabilities are estimated by counting the number of training instances associated with each label, i.e. $P(H_j) = (s + \sum_{i=1}^{n} I[y_j \in Y_i])/(2s + n)$, $P(\neg H_j) = 1 - P(H_j), 1 \le j \le q$, where s is a smoothing parameter controlling the effect of the uniform prior to the estimation and is commonly set to 1 for Laplace smoothing. Second, the likelihoods are estimated as follows. Given an integer $r \in [0, k]$ and label y_j, let $\kappa_j[r]$ denote the number of training instances that not only have label y_j itself, but also have exactly r neighbors with label y_j, i.e., $\kappa_j[r] = \sum_{i=1}^{n} I[y_j \in Y_i] \cdot I[\delta_j(\boldsymbol{x}_i) = r]$; and let $\tilde{\kappa}_j[r]$ denote the number of training instances that do not have label y_j itself, but have exactly r neighbors with label y_j, i.e., $\tilde{\kappa}_j[r] = \sum_{i=1}^{n} I[y_j \notin Y_i] \cdot I[\delta_j(\boldsymbol{x}_i) = r]$; where $\delta_j(\boldsymbol{x}_i) = \sum_{(\boldsymbol{x}', Y') \in N_k(\boldsymbol{x}_i)} I[y_j \in Y']$. Then, based on the two frequency arrays κ_j and $\tilde{\kappa}_j$, the likelihoods can be estimated as follows: $P(C_j = r | H_j) = (s + \kappa_j[r])/(s(k + 1) + \sum_{r=0}^{k} \kappa_j[r])$, $P(C_j = r | \neg H_j) = (s + \tilde{\kappa}_j[r])/(s(k+1) + \sum_{r=0}^{k} \tilde{\kappa}_j[r])$, where $1 \le j \le q$. Thereafter, by combining the estimated prior probabilities and estimated likelihoods, the predicted label set can be obtained accordingly.

2.2 Instance Selection for ML-kNN

The basic idea of instance selection is to select a subset of the training set instead of directly using the entire training set, thus reducing the memory consumption. In the past decades, the effectiveness of instance selection has been demonstrated in a wide range of applications such as intrusion detection [2] and active learning [9]. In particular, instance selection for kNN has been widely reported to greatly reduce memory consumption while still performing well for single-label classification problems [17]. To name a few, the Edited Nearest Neighbor (ENN) [22] discards an instance in the training set when its class is different from the majority class of its k nearest neighbors, which achieves better accuracy on most data sets; the Local Set-based Smoother (LSSm) selector [5] proposes a concept named the local set, which indicates the set of instances included in the largest hypersphere centered on a specific instance, to help remove less important instances and has been shown to achieve better performance compared with a number of state-of-the-art methods.

In contrast with the extensive studies on instance selection for single-label classification mentioned above, instance selection for multi-label classification has been rarely studied. To the best of our knowledge, there are only two works reported in this direction. One is the LSSm using Hamming Distance (LSSm-HD) [1] which extends LSSm to the multi-label scenario, and the other is the Cooperative Co-evolutionary Instance Selection for Multi-Label classification (CCISML) algorithm [10]. Although LSSm-HD inherits the good performance of LSSm, it also carries over its dependence on the assumption of the correlation between the local set concept and the instance importance, which limits its scope of application. Besides, as LSSm-HD does not explicitly consider the compression ratio in the instance selection, the compression ratio of the subset found by LSSm-HD might be unstable. The CCISML algorithm formulates the instance selection for multi-label classification as a single-objective optimization problem by summing up the accuracy and the compression ratio, and then employs an

Evolutionary Algorithm (EA) [3] to solve it. In this way, this work does not rely on assumptions about instance importance. However, CCISML still treats the instance selection problem for ML-kNN as a single-objective optimization problem. Such an approach, as presented in Sect. 1, might be inappropriate due to the conflicting nature between classifier accuracy and compression ratio.

3   Multi-objective Instance Selection for ML-kNN

In this paper, we propose to formulate the instance selection for ML-kNN as a multi-objective optimization problem and solve it with MOEAs. The multi-objective problem formulation and the proposed MOEIS-ML are presented below.

3.1   Multi-objective Problem Formulation

Let $\mathcal{X} = \mathbf{R}^d$ denote the d-dimensional instance space and let $\mathcal{Y} = \{y_1, y_2, \cdots, y_q\}$ be the label set of q possible labels. Given a training set $TR = \{(\boldsymbol{x}_i, Y_i)|1 \leq i \leq n\}$, $\boldsymbol{x}_i \in \mathcal{X}$, $Y_i \subseteq \mathcal{Y}$, and a test set TE, the task of instance selection for multi-label classification is to find a small subset $S \subseteq TR$ such that the classifier $h_S : \mathcal{X} \rightarrow 2^{\mathcal{Y}}$ learned from S is able to accurately predict the label set for any unseen instance in TE.

A solution of instance selection for multi-label classification can be naturally represented by a binary vector $\boldsymbol{z} = (z_1, \ldots, z_n)$, where element z_i indicates whether the i-th instance in TR will be retained in the selected subset S. That is, if $z_i = 1$, the i-th instance is retained in S; otherwise, the i-th instance is removed. Given a seleted instance subset, the ML-kNN, as presented in Sect. 2.1, is used as the base classifier. More formally, the instance selection problem for ML-kNN can be formulated as

$$\max_{S \subseteq TR} (1 - HammingLoss_{TE}(S), CompressionRatio(S)), \qquad (2)$$

where the two objectives are described in the following.

The first objective, i.e., $HammingLoss$, is with respect to the classifier accuracy, which is a commonly-used metric in the literature of multi-label classification [23] and can be computed as

$$HammingLoss_{TE}(S) = \frac{1}{|TE|} \sum_{(\boldsymbol{x},Y) \in TE} \frac{1}{q} \Delta(h_S(\boldsymbol{x}), Y), \qquad (3)$$

where $\Delta(\cdot, \cdot)$ indicates the Hamming distance between the two binary vectors representing two subsets of $\mathcal{Y}$.

The second objective, i.e., $CompressionRatio$, is with respect to the data compression ratio, which measures the compression effect of the instance selection algorithm. It is computed as

$$CompressionRatio(S) = 1 - \frac{|S|}{|TR|}. \qquad (4)$$

Generally, the above two objectives are often conflict with each other, and the improvement of one objective may lead to the deterioration of the other. Thus, there exists no single optimal solution that optimizes both objectives simultaneously. Instead, we aim to find the best trade-off solutions, which is well-known as the Pareto-optimal solutions [7], so that decision-makers can make choices from this set of solutions based on their actual needs.

3.2 MOEIS-ML Algorithm

In the past decades, EAs have emerged as an effective approach to multi-objective optimization problems and numerous MOEAs have been proposed [16,21]. Among these MOEAs, NSGA-II [7] has shown superior performance on not only benchmark problems [27], but also real-world applications [6,15,24]. For this reason, NSGA-II is adapted to tackle the multi-objective instance selection problem for ML-kNN, leading to the MOEIS-ML algorithm.

The framework of MOEIS-ML is presented in Algorithm 1. It starts from initializing a set of diverse solutions. During the initialization, unlike conventional MOEAs that generate solutions completely at random (which as shown in Fig. 1 fails to generate a set of diverse solutions), the following population initialization method is employed to enhance population diversity. Recall that given a training set TR with n instances, each individual is represented as a binary vector z with length n. By adjusting the number of non-zero elements in z, a set of individuals with different compression ratios can be easily obtained, and thus a population with better diversity can be obtained accordingly. Specifically, the probability that each element in an individual takes a value of 1 is set differently for different individuals. Concretely, when initializing a new individual, a probability p_{init} is first randomly selected from the set $\{0.1, 0.2, \ldots, 0.9\}$ and then each element of this individual is set to 1 with probability p_{init}. A set of N individuals is generated and constitutes the initial population P.

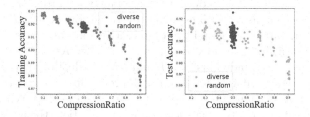

Fig. 1. Examination of population initialization on the data set *scene*.

After the population initialization, the algorithm performs the optimization by conducting offspring generation and environmental selection iteratively until some stopping criterion is fulfilled (usually when a certain predefined number of evaluation times is reached), and the population finally obtained is the outcome of the algorithm. For the offspring generation, the classic one-point crossover is

---

Algorithm 1: MOEIS-ML

Input: Training set TR, population size N, maximum fitness evaluation times $maxFE$

Output: A set of solutions with different trade-offs between accuracy and the compression ratio

1 Initialize a population P with N diverse individuals, each of which corresponds to an instance subset of TR;

2 Evaluate the accuracy and compression ratio of each individual in P;

3 Sort individuals in P using the non-dominated sorting and crowding distance;

4 $i = N$;

5 **while** $i < maxFE$ **do**

6 $\quad$ $Q = \emptyset$;

7 $\quad$ **while** $|Q| \leq N$ **do**

8 $\quad\quad$ Select two parents using the tournament selection;

9 $\quad\quad$ Generate two new individuals by conducting one-point crossover and the modified bit-wise mutation on parents, and add them to Q

10 $\quad$ **end**

11 $\quad$ Evaluate the accuracy and compression ratio of each individual in Q;

12 $\quad$ $P = P \cup Q$;

13 $\quad$ Select the top N individuals from P using the non-dominated sorting and crowding distance, and save them as P;

14 $\quad$ $i = i + N$

15 **end**

16 **return** P

---

first employed and then the bit-wise mutation with a slight modification to further promote population diversity takes place on the newly generated individuals. For space considerations, we refrain from providing the detailed information of the one-point crossover, but direct interested readers to [11]. The modified bit-wise mutation works as follows: consistent with that of the population initialization, the main idea is to diversify the compression ratios of new solutions, which can be accomplished with negligible overhead. Before describing the modified bit-wise mutation, we would like to have a look at how the original bit-wise mutation performs in the context of instance selection. Assuming that the number of 1-bits in a given individual z is l, and a new individual z' is generated by applying the original bit-wise mutation with probability p to z, the expectation of the number of 1-bits in z' is $l(1-p)+(n-l)p = l+(n-2l)p$. With this expectation, by repeatedly performing such mutation operation, the number of 1-bits for the population is likely to aggregate to $n/2$, which might be detrimental to population diversity. Thus, to enhance the diversity, we make each individual have the same opportunity to increase or decrease the number of 1-bits. Concretely, we first set two variants of bit-wise mutation, one is 0-mutation that only allows 0 to flip to 1 and the other is 1-mutation that only allows 1 to flip to 0, and each individual has a $1/2$ probability to employ 0-mutation or 1-mutation. In this way, the number of 1-bits in an individual will not aggregate to some specific area, thus contributing to more diverse individuals. For the environmental selection, as that done in NSGA-II, the non-dominated sorting and the crowding distance-based selection are employed to sort and update the population.

During the above search process, each time a new individual is generated, a fitness evaluation is performed. As a multi-objective optimization problem, the fitness of an individual needs to be assigned according to mutliple objectives, i.e., *HammingLoss* and *CompressionRatio*. The objective *CompressionRatio* can be natually computed as that shown in Eq. 4, while the objective *HammingLoss* cannot for the fact that the test set is unavailable during the optmization. Fortunately, since the training and test sets are usually assumed to be identically distributed, the training set can be used for estimation. On the other hand, another issue in computing *HammingLoss* is the high computational overhead in identifying neighbors throughout the whole iterative search process. To reduce this overhead, instead of identifying neighbors for each individual separately, we construct a global nearest neighbor table for all individuals to query. Specifically, given an instance x, all instances in TR are sorted by the ascending order of their distances from x, and saved as a new list A_x. Then, given an individual z to be evaluated and assumming its corresponding selected instance subset is S, the first k instances in A_x that are involved in S are identified as the neighbors for x. Thus, the objective *HammingLoss* is estimated on the training set on the assist of the global nearest neighbor table. Note that this table is released at the end of the optimization, so there is no additional memory overhead when the obtained solutions are used.

With all the above components, the algorithm searches and terminates until some stopping criterion is fulfilled (usually when a certain predefined number of evaluation times is reached), and the population finally obtained is the outcome of the algorithm.

4   Experimental Studies

Experimental studies have been carried to evaluate the efficacy of our proposed approach. The proposed MOEIS-ML is compared with three state-of-the-art instance selection approaches for ML-kNN to evaluate from two aspects. One is to evaluate whether the multi-objective MOEIS-ML is able to provide some advantage over the single-objective approaches. The other is to compare MOEIS-ML with the state-of-the-art approaches in terms of solution quality.

4.1   Experimental Setup

In the experiments, six real-world data sets from the Mulan multi-label data sets[1] are employed to examine the performance of the proposed algorithm. They are selected from different application domains and with different number of instances. The details of the data sets are described in Table 1.

---

[1] http://mulan.sourceforge.net/datasets-mlc.html.

Table 1. Data set description

Name	Domain	#Instances	#Features	#Labels
emotions	Music	593	72	6
genbase	Biology	662	1185	27
enron	Text	1702	1001	53
scene	Images	2407	294	6
yeast	Biology	2417	103	14
bibtex	Text	7395	1836	159

Three state-of-the-art instance selection approaches for ML-kNN are examined. Two of them are the two only works in the literature for instance selection for ML-kNN, i.e., LSSm-HD [1] and CCISML [10]. The third one is an extension of a classic approach for instance selection for single-label classification, namely ENN [22], to multi-label scenarios, and it is denoted as ENN-HD in the experiments. Specifically, ENN-HD is extended from ENN by introducing the Hamming distance to measure the neighbor relationship, as that done in LSSm-HD. For LSSm-HD and ENN-HD, the parameter θ is set to 0.14 as recommended in the original paper of LSSm-HD [1]. For the EA-based algorithms, i.e., CCISML [10] and our MOEIS-ML, the population or subpopulation size is set to 100, and the maxmimum fitness evaluation times is set to 50,000. The tournament size is 2 and the probabilities of applying crossover and mutation are 1.0 for MOEIS-ML. The algorithms are run 10 times independently and similar results are obtained.

4.2 Results and Discussions

Figure 2 illustrates the solutions obtained by the examined algorithms in the objective space. For the EA-based algorithms (CCISML and MOEIS-ML), the nondominated solutions obtained on training sets in the first run are presented, as well as their corresponding results when examined on test sets. The solutions obtained by LSSm-HD and ENN-HD are together illustrated in the figures. From the figures, it can be clearly observed that compared with the three single-objective approaches, MOEIS-ML achieves a set of solutions that provide a variety of trade-offs between accuracy and compression ratio. Moreover, MOEIS-ML always manages to find better or very similar solutions compared with the compared algorithms. Specifically, when compared with ENN-HD and LSSm-HD, MOEIS-ML consistently generates better solutions that provides both better compression ratio and better prediction accuracy; as ENN-HD and LSSm-HD do not explicitly consider the compression ratio in the instance selection, the compression ratio the subset found by them is unstable and for this reason, no feasible solution is found for ENN-HD when it is applied to the data set *bibtex*; when compared with CCISML, MOEIS-ML obtains better or very similar solutions.

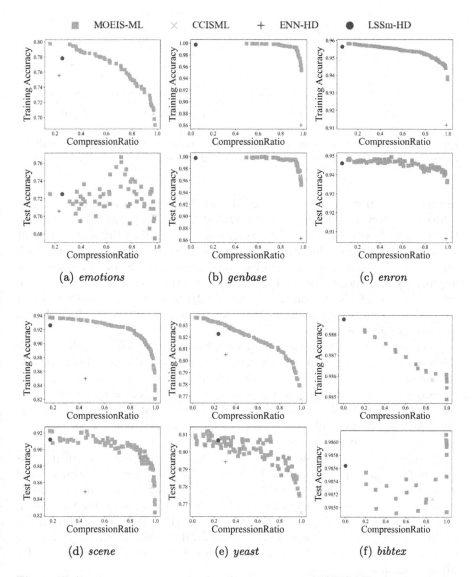

Fig. 2. Illustration comparisons in the objective space. MOEIS-ML always achieves better or very similar solutions when compared with the other examined algorithms.

Furthermore, it would be interesting to check whether a diverse set of solutions can be satisfactorily obtained if the single-objective approaches are carried out multiple times. The ENN-HD and LSSm-HD are examined in this experiments and CCISML is omitted for its high computational overhead. They are examined by changing the threshold θ from 0.00 to 0.30 to generate a set of solutions. Figure 3 illustrates the results obtained by running ENN-HD and LSSm-HD multiple times when applied to the two data sets *scene* and *yeast*. The results

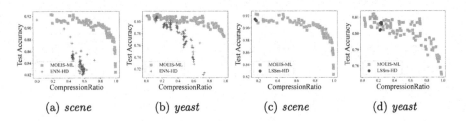

| (a) *scene* | (b) *yeast* | (c) *scene* | (d) *yeast* |

Fig. 3. Illustration comparisons when carrying out single-objective approaches multiple times. MOEIS-ML still performs better in such scenarios.

further demonstrate the advantages of MOEIS-ML in generating a set of diverse solutions, especially when compared with LSSm-HD. First, the results indicate that even if the single-objective approaches are run multiple times, it is difficult to ensure that diverse solutions will be generated in different runs. Second, such unsatisfactory results imply difficulties in setting parameters for single-objective approaches when dealing with the essentially multi-objective instance selection problem for ML-kNN. In constrast, MOEIS-ML provides many additional and competitive solutions, enabling an end-user to conveniently make their choices to meet specific demands.

To compare the algorithms in a quantitative way, the solutions obtained by the examined algorithms in terms of accuracy and compression ratio are further presented in Table 2. The results of MOEIS-ML are sorted by compression ratio in descending order. Consistant with the figures, the advantage of MOEIS-ML compared with the other examined algorithms lies in that it not only simultaneously provides many additional choices to a practitioner, but also achieves not worse accuracy and significantly better compression ratio.

Despite these advantages, the results show the overfitting problem (e.g., as observed in Fig. 2f) to be aware of when using MOEIS-ML, which is also an issue with most optimization-based methods. Specifically, since the algorithm needs to estimate the fitness of solutions based on the training set during the search, its performance largely relies on the precision of the estimation. Although the training and test sets are theoretically identically distributed, they are practically difficult to achieve this. Thus, the setting of the training set is important for MOEIS-ML and its counterparts.

Table 2. Comparison results in terms of test accuracy and compression ratio. For MOEIS-ML, as a set of solutions with different trade-offs are obtained, for space consideration, we select several representative solutions that dominate as many as or are very similar to the solutions obtained by other examined algorithms. The values are shown in %. (For the data set *bibtex*, ENN-HD with $\theta = 0.14$ gets a set whose size is less than 10 so its result is marked with "$\sim$".)

	emotions		genbase		enron	
	Accuracy	Compression	Accuracy	Compression	Accuracy	Compression
Basic	72.50	0.00	99.72	0.00	94.64	0.00
LSSm-HD	72.50	25.52	99.78	4.20	94.60	6.21
ENN-HD	70.56	23.08	86.29	97.98	90.64	98.50
CCISML	70.00	97.00	96.79	97.31	93.64	99.28
MOEIS-ML	67.50	98.12	95.30	98.32	94.78	11.43
	73.06	95.68	96.68	97.48	94.26	95.30
	73.89	82.55	99.94	66.39	94.05	97.78
	72.50	16.14	99.89	49.75	93.68	99.35
	scene		yeast		bibtex	
	Accuracy	Compression	Accuracy	Compression	Accuracy	Compression
Basic	91.36	0.00	80.93	0.00	98.56	0.00
LSSm-HD	91.22	17.68	80.67	23.72	98.56	0.08
ENN-HD	84.85	44.74	79.43	30.57	$\sim$	$\sim$
CCISML	85.48	97.32	76.51	99.45	98.51	85.98
MOEIS-ML	82.37	99.54	77.48	98.25	98.49	99.85
	87.55	98.06	80.67	71.54	98.58	99.80
	92.05	41.37	80.73	45.66	98.54	89.18
	92.25	17.54	80.93	2.44	98.55	20.26

5   Conclusion and Future Work

In this paper, we propose a multi-objective evolutionary optimization approach for instance selection for multi-label classification. We first formulate the instance selection for ML-kNN as a bi-objective optimization problem to consider both accuracy and compression ratio. Then, we propose the MOEIS-ML algorithm by adapting the well-known NSGA-II to solve the resultant bi-objective optimization problem. Experimental studies on six real-world data sets show that compared with the state-of-the-art instance selection algorithms for ML-kNN, MOEIS-ML not only simultaneously provides a set of diverse solutions, but also achieves not worse accuracy and significantly better compression ratio.

There are several important directions for future work. First, it is worthy to extend MOEIS-ML to involve more objectives, such as subset accuracy and ranking loss, to fulfill the comprehensive optimization expectation in practice [23]. Second, it would be interesting to combine MOEIS-ML with more sophisticated search operators. For example, with the ever increasing number of instances, the problem tends to be a large-scale multi-objective optimization problem [12,13], and enhancing its scalability would be worthy of studies. Finally, MOEAs have shown good performance both theoretically and empirically for solving diverse subset selection problems, e.g., sparse regression [20], ensemble pruning [19], unsupervised feature selection [8], and result diversification [18]. Thus, an interesting future work is to perform theoretical analysis of MOEIS-ML.

References

1. Arnaiz-González, Á., Díez-Pastor, J., Diez, J.J.R., García-Osorio, C.: Local sets for multi-label instance selection. Appl. Soft Comput. **68**, 651–666 (2018)
2. Ashfaq, R.A.R., He, Y., Chen, D.: Toward an efficient fuzziness based instance selection methodology for intrusion detection system. Int. J. Mach. Learn. Cybern. **8**(6), 1767–1776 (2017)
3. Bäck, T.: Evolutionary Algorithms in Theory and Practice: Evolution Strategies, Evolutionary Programming. Oxford University Press, Genetic Algorithms (1996)
4. Boutell, M.R., Luo, J., Shen, X., Brown, C.M.: Learning multi-label scene classification. Patt. Recogn. **37**(9), 1757–1771 (2004)
5. Brighton, H., Mellish, C.: On the consistency of information filters for lazy learning algorithms. In: Proceedings of the 3rd Principles of Data Mining and Knowledge Discovery (PKDD 1999), Prague, Czech Republic, pp. 283–288 (1999)
6. Cai, X., Wang, P., Du, L., Cui, Z., Zhang, W., Chen, J.: Multi-objective three-dimensional dv-hop localization algorithm with NSGA-II. IEEE Sens. J. **19**(21), 10003–10015 (2019)
7. Deb, K., Agrawal, S., Pratap, A., Meyarivan, T.: A fast and elitist multiobjective genetic algorithm: NSGA-II. IEEE Trans. Evolut. Comput. **6**(2), 182–197 (2002)
8. Feng, C., Qian, C., Tang, K.: Unsupervised feature selection by Pareto optimization. In: Proceedings of the 33rd AAAI Conference on Artificial Intelligence (AAAI 2019), Honolulu, HI, pp. 3534–3541 (2019)
9. Fu, Y., Zhu, X., Li, B.: A survey on instance selection for active learning. Knowl. Inf. Syst. **35**(2), 249–283 (2013)
10. García-Pedrajas, N., García, G.C.: Cooperative coevolutionary instance selection for multilabel problems. Knowl.-Based Syst. **234**, 107569 (2021)
11. Holland, J.H.: Adaptation in Natural and Artificial Systems: An Introductory Analysis with Applications to Biology, Control, and Artificial Intelligence. MIT Press, Cambridge (1992)
12. Hong, W., Tang, K., Zhou, A., Ishibuchi, H., Yao, X.: A scalable indicator-based evolutionary algorithm for large-scale multiobjective optimization. IEEE Trans. Evolut. Comput. **23**(3), 525–537 (2019)
13. Hong, W., Yang, P., Tang, K.: Evolutionary computation for large-scale multi-objective optimization: a decade of progresses. Int. J. Autom. Comput. **18**(2), 155–169 (2021)
14. Liu, Y., Chen, Z., Fu, A.W., Wong, R.C., Dai, G.: Optimal location query based on k nearest neighbours. Front. Comput. Sci. **15**(2), 152606 (2021)
15. Lu, Z., et al.: NSGA-Net: neural architecture search using multi-objective genetic algorithm (extended abstract). In: Proceedings of the 29th International Joint Conference on Artificial Intelligence (IJCAI 2020), Yokohama, Japan, pp. 4750–4754 (2020)
16. Mukhopadhyay, A., Maulik, U., Bandyopadhyay, S., Coello, C.A.C.: A survey of multiobjective evolutionary algorithms for data mining: Part I. IEEE Trans. Evolut. Comput. **18**(1), 4–19 (2014)

17. Olvera-López, J.A., Carrasco-Ochoa, J.A., Trinidad, J.F.M., Kittler, J.: A review of instance selection methods. Artif. Intell. Rev. **34**(2), 133–143 (2010)
18. Qian, C., Liu, D., Zhou, Z.: Result diversification by multi-objective evolutionary algorithms with theoretical guarantees. Artif. Intell. **309**, 103737 (2022)
19. Qian, C., Yu, Y., Zhou, Z.: Pareto ensemble pruning. In: Proceedings of the 29th AAAI Conference on Artificial Intelligence (AAAI 2015), Austin, TX, pp. 2935–2941 (2015)
20. Qian, C., Yu, Y., Zhou, Z.: Subset selection by Pareto optimization. In: Advances in Neural Information Processing Systems 28 (NIPS 2015), Montreal, Canada, pp. 1774–1782 (2015)
21. Qu, B., Zhu, Y., Jiao, Y.C., Wu, M.Y., Suganthan, P.N., Liang, J.J.: A survey on multi-objective evolutionary algorithms for the solution of the environmental/economic dispatch problems. Swarm Evolut. Comput. **38**, 1–11 (2018)
22. Wilson, D.L.: Asymptotic properties of nearest neighbor rules using edited data. IEEE Trans. Syst. Man Cybern. **2**(3), 408–421 (1972)
23. Wu, X., Zhou, Z.: A unified view of multi-label performance measures. In: Proceedings of the 34th International Conference on Machine Learning (ICML 2017), Sydney, Australia, pp. 3780–3788 (2017)
24. Wu, Y., He, Y., Qian, C., Zhou, Z.: Multi-objective evolutionary ensemble pruning guided by margin distribution. In: Proceedings of the 17th International Conference on Parallel Problem Solving from Nature (PPSN 2022), Dortmund, Germany, pp. 427–441 (2022)
25. Zhang, M., Zhou, Z.: ML-KNN: a lazy learning approach to multi-label learning. Patt. Recogn. **40**(7), 2038–2048 (2007)
26. Zhang, M., Zhou, Z.: A review on multi-label learning algorithms. IEEE Trans. Knowl. Data Eng. **26**(8), 1819–1837 (2014)
27. Zhou, A., Qu, B., Li, H., Zhao, S., Suganthan, P.N., Zhang, Q.: Multiobjective evolutionary algorithms: a survey of the state of the art. Swarm Evolut. Comput. **1**(1), 32–49 (2011)

An Investigation of Adaptive Operator Selection in Solving Complex Vehicle Routing Problem

Jiyuan Pei[1], Yi Mei[2] , Jialin Liu[1]([✉]) , and Xin Yao[1]

[1] Department of Computer Science and Engineering, Southern University of Science and Technology (SUSTech), Shenzhen 518055, China
peijy2020@mail.sustech.edu.cn, {liujl,xiny}@sustech.edu.cn
[2] School of Engineering and Computer Science, Victoria University of Wellington, Wellington 6012, New Zealand
yi.mei@ecs.vuw.ac.nz

Abstract. Search operators play an important role in meta-heuristics. There are typically a variety of search operators available for solving a problem, and the selection and order of using the operators can greatly affect the algorithm performance. Adaptive operator selection (AOS) has been proposed to select operators during optimisation dynamically and adaptively. However, most existing studies focus on real-value optimisation problems, while combinatorial optimisation problems, especially complex routing problems, are seldom considered. Motivated by the effectiveness of AOS on real-value optimisation problems and the urgent need of efficiency in solving real routing problems, this paper investigates AOS in complex routing problems obtained from real-world scenarios, the multi-depot multi-disposal-facility multi-trip capacitated vehicle routing problems (M3CVRPs). Specifically, the stateless AOS, arguable the most classic, intuitive and commonly used category of AOS approaches, is integrated into the region-focused local search (RFLS), the state-of-the-art algorithm for solving M3CVRPs. Unexpectedly and yet within understanding, experimental results show that the original RFLS performs better than the RFLS embedded with stateless AOS approaches. To determine the causes, a novel neighbourhood analysis is conducted to investigate the characteristics of M3CVRP and the factors that affect the performance of the AOS. Experimental results indicate that the momentum assumption of stateless AOS, good operators in history will also work well in current stage, is not satisfied within most of the time during the optimisation of the complex problem, leading to the unstable performance of operators and the failure of stateless AOS.

This work was supported by the National Natural Science Foundation of China (Grant No. 61906083), the Shenzhen Science and Technology Program (Grant No. KQTD2016112514355531), the Shenzhen Fundamental Research Program (Grant No. JCYJ20190809121403553), the Guangdong Provincial Key Laboratory (Grant No. 2020B121201001), and Marsden Fund of New Zealand Government (VUW1614).

© The Author(s), under exclusive license to Springer Nature Switzerland AG 2022
S. Khanna et al. (Eds.): PRICAI 2022, LNCS 13629, pp. 562–573, 2022.
https://doi.org/10.1007/978-3-031-20862-1_41

Keywords: Adaptive operator selection · Vehicle routing problem ·
Neighbourhood analysis · Local search · Meta-heuristics

1   Introduction

Meta-heuristics in generate-and-test style have shown their effectiveness in optimising real-world problems, such as vehicle scheduling [13,15,22] and engineering problems [16]. In those algorithms, new solutions are sequentially generated
by search operators based on incumbent solutions. Then, those new solutions
are tested and good ones will be accepted as new incumbents. Search operators, like crossover and mutation operators in evolutionary algorithm and neighbourhood relation operators in local search algorithm, play an essential role in
meta-heuristics and significantly affect their effectiveness and efficiency. When
tackling a real-world problem, novel search operators are often designed with
domain knowledge according to the problem's characteristics and cooperate with
classic search operators. A well-known example is vehicle scheduling [5]. Besides
the classic *swap*, *insert* and *2-opt* operators, diverse problem-specific operators,
such as region-focused mutation and crossover operators [13], that integrate the
consideration of limited route swap region in real life, have also been proposed.
Consequently, to improve the efficiency of applying operators, adaptive operator
selection (AOS) strategies that dynamically select operators according to their
performance have been studied for $(1+\lambda)$-evolutionary algorithm [11], genetic
algorithms [17], differential evolution [10,18,19], memetic algorithms [3,12,14].

AOS has achieved great success on real-value optimisation problems [10,19,
21,25] and benchmark combinatorial optimisation problems, such as OneMax [2,
8,11,20], quadratic assignment problem [12,23] and knapsack problem [20]. In
particular, even a simple stateless AOS approach that selects the operator based
on purely the history of its performance regardless of the search state can achieve
promising results. The stateless AOS approach also has other advantages, such as
it is intuitive, simple to design and implement, and requires no extra computation
resource for training the predictor, which is particularly suitable for solving
large-scale real-world optimisation problems. However, in real-world scenarios,
there are much more complex combinatorial optimisation problems with many
complex constraints and a rugged fitness landscape. The effectiveness of AOS on
more complex combinatorial optimisation problems has been seldom studied.

In this paper, we aim to answer the following research questions. (i) Whether
the successful stateless AOS approaches can also work well for complex combinatorial optimisation problems? (ii) Whether the complexity of the problem affect
the effectiveness of AOS? (iii) Which factors could affect the effectiveness of AOS
in solving combinatorial optimisation problems?

To answer these questions, we conduct empirical experiments and analyses
as a preliminary study. Specifically, we consider the multi-depot multi-disposal-
facility multi-trip capacitated vehicle routing problem (M3CVRP) [13], which
is a very complex and challenging combinatorial optimisation problem with
many important real-world applications such as logistics. We consider a recent

---

Algorithm 1. RFLS-AOS.

Require: Solution S, stopping criteria SC_1 and SC_2
1: $S' \leftarrow S$
2: **while** stopping criterion SC_1 not met **do**
3:      **while** stopping criterion SC_2 not met **do**
4:          $ope \leftarrow OSR$
5:          Apply ope with corresponding parameter to S'
6:          $r \leftarrow CA$ ▷ Detailed in Eq. (4)
7:          Update selection probability with reward r
8:      **end while**
9:      Apply RMPS with parameters ρ_3 and α to S'
10: **end while**
11: **return** S'

---

and state-of-the-art heuristic optimisation algorithm for M3CVRP, the region-focused local search (RFLS) [13], and investigate the behaviours of the most commonly used stateless AOS approaches in the algorithm for solving M3CVRP.

Experimental results on a real-world instance together with 6 re-sampled instances show that RFLS performs better than the modified RFLS, in which stateless AOS approaches are embedded. There is a high probability that operators that performed well in the recent past will not perform as well afterwards, especially when it becomes increasingly hard to improve an existing solution in the later stage of optimisation. The momentum assumption of stateless AOS approaches, operators that performed well in the past will also own a good performance in the later stage, is not satisfied in such complex routing problems. We suggest that it is a major factor in the unpromising performance of stateless AOS approaches. At last, we discuss the feature of tested AOS approaches and the potential improvement of AOS on complex routing problems.

The rest of this paper is organised as follows. Section 2 reviews the existing work on AOS and briefly describes the RFLS and M3CVRP considered in this work. The proposed neighbourhood analysis method and the framework of embedding classic AOS approaches into RFLS are described in Sect. 3. Section 4 presents the experiment setup and discusses the results. Section 5 concludes.

2   Background

This section first introduces the stateless AOS approaches, the focus of this study, and then describes the M3CVRP and RFLS [13] studied in this paper.

2.1   Stateless Adaptive Operator Selection

The study of AOS dates back to 1989 [6]. Generally, AOS consists of two parts: the *credit assignment* (CA), i.e., evaluation of operators' performance, and the *operator selection rule* (OSR), i.e., selection of operators based on the credits.

Fitness improvement is a commonly used CA in most literature [4,9,24]. State-less OSRs assume a momentum assumption that operators with good historical performance are likely to own high searching ability and therefore select high historical performance operators. Differing from state-based OSRs which extract features of search state and train learners to map states to operator selection, expensive feature extraction and training are not required in stateless OSRs. Therefore, stateless OSRs are manageable in large-scale problems.

Probability matching (PM), adaptive pursuit (AP) and dynamic multi-armed bandit (D-MAB) are three classic and commonly used OSR approaches in literature [3,7,14,19]. Various novel approaches have also been proposed [2,18].

Probability matching (PM) is a classic selection strategy in machine learning that assigns the selection probability of each candidate as its reward probability. PM in the AOS context is demonstrated as Eq. (1), in which P_i and r_i are the selection probability and the immediate reward of operator i, respectively. K is the total number of operators, P_{min} is the pre-defined lower bound of selection probability, Q_i represents the discounted cumulative reward of operator i and α is a pre-defined parameter for balancing exploration and exploitation.

$$P_i = P_{min} + (1 - K \cdot P_{min})\frac{Q_i}{\sum_{j=1}^{K} Q_j}, \text{ where } Q_i = \alpha r_i + (1 - \alpha)Q_i. \quad (1)$$

Adaptive pursuit (AP) [24] is developed from PM with an extra pre-defined parameter β, as in Eq. (2). It allocates more resource to candidates with better performance, which makes it more sensitive to environmental changes than PM.

$$P_i = \begin{cases} \beta(1 - (K - 1)P_{min}) + (1 - \beta)P_i, & \text{if } i = \arg\max_j Q_j \\ \beta P_{min} + (1 - \beta)P_i, & \text{otherwise.} \end{cases} \quad (2)$$

UCB1 [1] is well-known multi-armed bandit (MAB) algorithm. In UCB1, the estimated reward $\hat{p}_i$ and the number of applications n_i of each operator i are recorded, so that resources will be allocated to rarely selected operators for exploration and the ones with high performance for exploitation. Specifically, the operator with the maximal value of $\hat{p}_i + \sqrt{\frac{2\log\sum_k n_k}{n_i}}$ will be selected. The study of [4] formed AOS as the dynamic case of MAB and developed D-MAB based on UCB1 as an OSR. The detailed process of D-MAB is demonstrated in Eq. (3) with pre-defined parameters λ and θ. Only the chosen operator i will be updated at each iteration. In D-MAB, UCB1 is used for decision making and Page-Hinkley (PH) test is embedded to detect the abrupt changes in operators' performance. The PH test will be triggered $(M_i - m_i > \lambda)$ by the abrupt changes and all the recorded values $(n_i, \hat{p}_i, m_i, M_i)$ are reset for better agility.

$$\hat{p}_i = \frac{n_i \hat{p}_i + r_i}{n_i + 1}, \quad m_i = m_i + (\hat{p}_i - r_i + \theta), \quad M_i = \max(M_i, m_i). \quad (3)$$

2.2 M3CVRP

The multi-depot, multi-disposal-facility, multi-trip capacitated vehicle routing problem (M3CVRP) is a complex combinatorial optimisation problem [13]. Different from classic CVRPs, there are multiple depots and facilities. A solution of M3CVRP is a set of routes which serves all the tasks. Each route can be represented by a sequence of task points served by a vehicle. Each task point has a specific amount of demand. When a vehicle serves a task, it will collect its demand. Each vehicle is limited by a capacity value. No vehicle is allowed to collect demands that exceed the capacity. A vehicle is allowed to clear its load at a facility at any time and continue serving. Each vehicle must finish the work within a given time limit and return to the depot from where it departs. In M3CVRP, there are multiple depots and facilities, which significantly enlarge the search space, as well as the optimisation difficulty, which makes it a benchmark for studying AOS with problems of higher complexity. More details of M3CVRP and a real-world M3CVRP instance of thousands of tasks can be found in [13].

2.3   Region-Focused Local Search

We consider a state-of-the-art algorithm for solving M3CVRP, region-focused local search (RFLS). Based on the classic local search framework, RFLS involves three novel search operators: *region-focused single-point swap* (RFSPS), *region-focused segment swap* (RFSS) and *relaxed multi-point swap* (RMPS) [13]. Combined with another three classic search operators, *insertion*, *swap* and *2-opt*, a total number of 6 search operators are used. It makes RFLS a good case for studying AOS. Details of RFLS can be found in [13].

3   Methodology and Experiment Design

To answer our research questions, two sets of experiments are designed. To verify the effectiveness of AOS in the context of a complex combinatorial optimisation problem, in the first set of experiments, we incorporate the AOS into RFLS for solving M3CVRP and compare it to the original RFLS on several M3CVRP instances. In the second set of experiments, we investigate the progress of RFLS and analyse the relationship among the best operators in subsequent iterations to understand the factors that affect the performance of the AOS.

3.1   Experiment 1: AOS in RFLS

We embed the classic stateless AOS approaches into RFLS, denoted as RFLS-AOS. Algorithm 1 shows the overall framework of RFLS-AOS. In line 4 of Algorithm 1, the OSR is applied to select the estimated best operator *ope* from the five local operators (swap, insertion, 2-opt, PRFSP and RFSS). Then, *ope* is used to update the solution S'. In line 6, the reward r is defined as the normalised fitness improvement and calculated as follows:

$$r = \frac{2\tau_t}{\max \Phi_t + \max(\max \Phi_{t-1}, \max \Phi_t)}, \tag{4}$$

where τ_t is the fitness improvement at iteration t (set as 0 if the new solution has lower fitness), and Φ_t is the sliding window (with size l) of fitness improvements, i.e., $\Phi_t = \{\tau_{t-l+1}, \tau_{t-l+2}, \ldots, \tau_t\}$. Compared with linear normalisation, the described method has a better ability to avoid false triggering of the PH test when a sudden singular large fitness improvement leaves the sliding window.

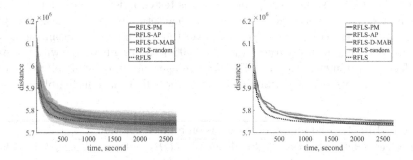

Fig. 1. Total distance of solutions over optimisation time, averaged over 30 trials.

In the experiments, the three classic stateless selecting approaches described in Sect. 2.1, PM, AP and D-MAB, are implemented as OSR, and the resulting algorithms are referred to as RFLS-PM, RFLS-AP, RFLS-D-MAB, respectively. We also implement random selection for comparison, denoted as RFLS-random.

3.2 Experiment 2: Neighbourhood Analysis

We design a neighbourhood analysis method, as demonstrated in Algorithm 2, to analyse the performance of operators on a solution. For a given solution, a set of neighbour solutions are sampled by each operator independently, as shown in lines 7–14, referred to as *neighbourhood sampling*. The best operator to a solution is defined as the one that achieves the largest average fitness improvement in neighbourhood sampling. Then the solution is replaced by its best neighbour and the sampling is repeated, where a new best operator will be found. After repeating a predefined number of times, a sequence of best operators is generated.

We record the sequence of best operators, denoted as M, and the average fitness improvement value matrix of each operator at each iteration, denoted as $\bar{T}$. Stability operators' performance can be measured based on M and $\bar{T}$. The more successive repeated items are in M, the more stable the choice of the best operator is. At each iteration t, a high improvement of the best operator M_t in $t+1$, recorded in $\bar{T}$, implies that the performance of M_t is stable.

4   Results and Analysis

The first part of this section presents the performance of RFLS-AOS in solving M3CVRP. In the second part, the results of neighbourhood analysis and discussion of factors that affect the performance are presented.

4.1   Effectiveness of AOS in RFLS for M3CVRP

In the first set of experiments, we test the RFLS-AOS on the real-world M3CVRP instance given in [13]. The parameter setting of RFLS-AOS is identical to [13], while the parameters of AOS are set as follows. In PM and AP, $\alpha = 0.3, \beta = 0.3, P_{min} = 0.5$. In D-MAB, θ and λ are set to 0.1 and 0.5, respectively. For each instance, each approach was tested independently for 30 times. Figure 1 shows the convergence curves (average total distance of the 30 independent runs) of the compared algorithms over the search process. From the figure, we can see that in the earlier stage (0–1000s) the origin RFLS without AOS performs a distinct advantage. For the average quality of final solutions, only RFLS-AP shows better performance, while the difference is negligible.

Algorithm 2. Neighbourhood analysis on a given solution.

Require: Solution s, a set of K search operators $OPE = \{ope_1, \ldots, ope_K\}$, predefined parameters m and n, a problem instance I and an evaluator E
1: $M \leftarrow$ empty vector with size m
2: $x \leftarrow s$
3: $\bar{T} \leftarrow m \times K$ empty matrix
4: $dist(x) \leftarrow$ evaluate x with given evaluator E and instance I
5: **for** $j \leftarrow 1$ to m **do**
6:    $neighbours \leftarrow \emptyset$
7:    **for** $k \leftarrow 1$ to K **do**
8:       **for** $t \leftarrow 1$ to n **do**
9:          $y_{j,t}^k \leftarrow$ apply ope_k on x
10:         add $y_{j,t}^k$ to $neighbours$
11:         $dist(y_{j,t}^k) \leftarrow$ evaluate $y_{j,t}^k$ with given evaluator E and instance I
12:       **end for**
13:       $\bar{T}_{j,k} \leftarrow \frac{\sum_{t=1}^{n} \max\{0, dist(x) - dist(y_{j,t}^k)\}}{n}$
14:    **end for**
15:    $ope_j^* \leftarrow \arg\max_{k \in \{1,\ldots,K\}} \{ \frac{\sum_{t=1}^{n} \max\{0, dist(x) - dist(y_{j,t}^k)\}}{n} \}$
16:    $M_j \leftarrow ope_j^*$
17:    $x \leftarrow \arg\min_{y_{j,t}^k \in neighbours} \{dist(y_{j,t}^k)\}$
18:    $dist(x) \leftarrow \min_{y_{j,t}^k \in neighbours} \{dist(y_{j,t}^k)\}$
19: **end for**
20: **return** $M, \bar{T}$

Solutions' quality, i.e. total distance, of 30 runs of each RFLS-AOS implementation at each time point are tested by the Wilcoxon rank sum test with origin RFLS and RFLS-AOS, respectively. Compared with RFLS, RFLS-random and RFLS-D-MAB are significantly worse the most of time. Other approaches perform inferiorly in the earlier stage (0–600 s). Compared with RFLS-random, only RFLS-AP find final solutions which are significantly better. Solutions' quality of RFLS-PM and RFLS-D-MAB, respectively, has no significant difference with RFLS-random for about 80% of the time during optimisation.

In summary, we find out that none of the stateless AOS approaches managed to achieve better performance than the original version for solving the real-world complex problem, M3CVRP. This is different from the previous success of AOS on benchmark problems. In other words, we have shown that AOS is not always effective, and can fail for complex combinatorial optimisation problems. The Sophisticated design of AOS is still required to achieve promising performance.

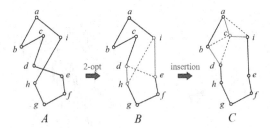

Fig. 2. Example of the case that the best operator of a given route A is different to its best neighbour B. For A, the best operator is 2-opt which eliminates the cross $(d\text{-}e|h\text{-}i)$ and forms route B. However, for B the best operator is insertion which moves c to its best position, i.e. between a and i, and find B's best neighbour C.

4.2   Further Analysis on Neighbours

Stateless AOS approaches are designed based on the momentum assumption. However, in VRP, there are situations where the momentum will vanish. Figure 2 demonstrates an example that the best operators on solutions that are generated in succession, i.e. neighbours, are considerably different. We consider three classic operators, 2-opt (reverse a section in a route), insertion (move an item in a route into another position) and swap (swap the positions of a pair of points) and aim to find the shortest route, i.e., solution in this context. The best operator of the given route A is 2-opt, which reverses the section $d\text{-}e\text{-}f\text{-}g\text{-}h\text{-}i$ to $d\text{-}h\text{-}g\text{-}f\text{-}e\text{-}i$, so that the unnecessary travelling distance introduced by the cross is eliminated. By applying 2-opt, the best neighbour of A, B is found. In the generate-and-test style, B will replace A as the new incumbent, in other words, A is the solution in history and B is the current one. However, the performance of 2-opt drops rapidly after replacement, because all crosses are eliminated and there is no more significant improvement can be achieved by 2-opt in B. The new best operator will be insertion, which inserts c to the best position (between $a\text{-}i$) and forms the best neighbour of B, indexed as C. In such a situation, reasonably it is hard for stateless AOS approaches to make the correct decision, as the momentum assumption is not satisfied. To the best of our knowledge, in literature, there is no study considering verifying the existence of the situation, and the performance of stateless AOS in such situations.

To investigate the existence of the above case occurring in solving M3CVRP with RFLS and the consequent impact, we conduct an experimental study on the real-world instance introduced in Sect. 2.2, together with 6 re-sampled instances based on it. The 6 instances are generated by re-sampling the task points, with sampling rates as 90%, 80% and 70% respectively, from the origin real-world instance with 3000 task points, marked as 2700-1, 2700-2, 2400-1, 2500-2, 2100-1 and 2100-2, where the former number (2700, 2400, 2100) represents the number of task points in the instance. All 7 instances are analysed as the following method.

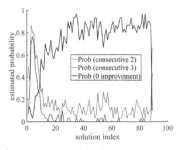 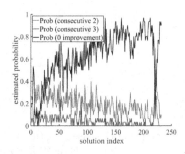

Fig. 3. Neighbourhood analysis on original instance (left) and instance 2400-1 (right). Red line demonstrates the frequency that the previous solution (recorded solution x) has the same best operator with the next solution (the best neighbour of x), i.e. $ope_1^* = ope_2^*$, marked as $Prob$(consecutive 2). Blue line indicates the estimated probability that $ope_1^* = ope_2^* = ope_3^*$, marked as $Prob$(consecutive 3). Black lines indicate the estimated probability that the best operator of previous solution (recorded solution x) is not able to achieve any improvement on the next solution (the best neighbour of x), i.e., $\bar{T}_{1,k} \leq 0$ where k is the index of ope_1^*, marked as $Prob$(0 improvement). (Color figure online)

Firstly RFLS is applied for solving and all accepted solutions are recorded for each instance. Each accepted solution represents a searching stage, therefore characteristics of operators in all stages of optimisation can be better analysed. Recorded solutions are indexed by the order that they are found. Larger index solutions are found in later stages of optimisation. Then each recorded solution is analysed for 30 independent repeats with the neighbourhood analysis method introduced in 3.2. n and m are set to 100 and 3. Analysis results of the original instance and re-sampled instance 2400-1 are demonstrated in Fig. 3. Results indicate that (i) values of $Prob$(consecutive 2) and $Prob$(consecutive 3) are considerably too low (around 15% and 3%) and of $Prob$(0 improvement) are too high (around 80%) for satisfying the momentum assumption, (ii) larger index solution is likely to perform lower $Prob$(consecutive 2) and $Prob$(consecutive 3), while the $Prob$(0 improvement) is higher. Normally in the later stage of optimisation, the solution quality is higher and the difficulty of finding a better solution is also higher. We suggest that there may exist a strong positive correlation between the difficulty of solution improving and operator selection momentum vanishing.

We observe that there are sudden changes of the 3 values in larger indexes, like solution indexed as 89 in original instance and 221 in 2400-1. Detailed experiment information shows that they are caused by that SC_2 is met and RMPS is triggered to apply. RMPS is designed for jumping out from a local optimum with a large step size of change. After applying RMPS, if the new solution is accepted, usually the difficulty of finding a better solution will reduce temporarily because of the escaping from the last local optimum. Therefore the 3 values will perform a rapid change. This is consistent with the above conclusion.

Table 1. Estimated probability of the top 70% solutions that own the largest index.

	Origin	2700-1	2700-2	2400-1	2400-2	2100-1	2100-2
Prob (consecutive 2)	0.1180	0.1974	0.2720	0.1732	0.1815	0.1376	0.2432
Prob (consecutive 3)	0.0132	0.0419	0.0732	0.0368	0.0266	0.0238	0.0551
Prob (0 improvement)	0.8360	0.6585	0.6832	0.7319	0.6751	0.8093	0.5594

Table 1 lists the 3 values on the top 70% solutions that owns the largest index, for example, solutions indexed in range 27–89 in original instance. The above discussion is consistent in the experiment of all instances. This may be the one major factor of stateless AOS performing inferiorly embedding in RFLS on solving M3CVRP.

5 Conclusion

AOS approaches are developed to dynamically and adaptively select the optimal operator to generate new solutions. Arguably the most classic, intuitive and commonly used category of AOS approaches, stateless AOS is studied in many works as the first step. However, in literature, complex combinatorial optimisations, especially the VRPs with real-world characteristics are seldom considered. In this paper, we investigate stateless AOS on M3CVRP, a real-world VRP with multiple constraints and depots. The assumption of stateless AOS, an operator that performs well recently has a high potential at the current stage, is verified with a novel neighbourhood analysis approach in this paper. Experimental results in large-scale M3CVRP instances indicate that the performance of operators is considerably unstable and the aforementioned assumption is not satisfied in most cases, while in literature it is assumed as satisfied without test [3,4,8,19,24]. This explains the poor performance of embedding AOS into RFLS for solving M3CVRP. The proposed analysis approach can be referred to in the study of stateless AOS on related problems. For a better exploration of the characteristics of such complex combinatorial optimisation, more related problems and optimisation algorithms will be studied in our future work.

We also observe that removing the highest reputation operator from the candidate list may be a potential way when the reputation is verified as misguiding. State-based AOS approaches, which train machine learning models that map the state features into operator selection, is worth considering if extra computation resource on training is handled. In literature, most studies focus on calculating the fitness landscape as the state feature, which is relatively expensive due to the sampling needed. The effectiveness of state feature extraction is the key point. Information about the solution itself, such as topology structure, should be concerned more rather than the fitness values of itself and its neighbours.

References

1. Auer, P., Cesa-Bianchi, N., Fischer, P.: Finite-time analysis of the multiarmed bandit problem. Mach. Learn. **47**(2), 235–256 (2002)
2. Candan, C., Goeffon, A., Lardeux, F., Saubion, F.: A dynamic island model for adaptive operator selection. In: Proceedings of the 14th Annual Conference on Genetic and Evolutionary Computation, pp. 1253–1260 (2012)
3. Consoli, P., Yao, X.: Diversity-driven selection of multiple crossover operators for the capacitated arc routing problem. In: Blum, C., Ochoa, G. (eds.) EvoCOP 2014. LNCS, vol. 8600, pp. 97–108. Springer, Heidelberg (2014). https://doi.org/10.1007/978-3-662-44320-0_9
4. DaCosta, L., Fialho, A., Schoenauer, M., Sebag, M.: Adaptive operator selection with dynamic multi-armed bandits. In: Proceedings of the 10th Annual Conference on Genetic and Evolutionary Computation, pp. 913–920 (2008)
5. Dantzig, G.B., Ramser, J.H.: The truck dispatching problem. Manage. Sci. **6**(1), 80–91 (1959)
6. Davis, L.: Adapting operator probabilities in genetic algorithms. In: Proceedings of the 3rd International Conference on Genetic Algorithms, pp. 61–69. Morgan Kaufmann Publishers Inc., San Francisco, CA, USA (1989)
7. Epitropakis, M.G., Caraffini, F., Neri, F., Burke, E.K.: A separability prototype for automatic memes with adaptive operator selection. In: 2014 IEEE Symposium on Foundations of Computational Intelligence (FOCI), pp. 70–77. IEEE (2014)
8. Fialho, Á., Da Costa, L., Schoenauer, M., Sebag, M.: Extreme value based adaptive operator selection. In: Rudolph, G., Jansen, T., Beume, N., Lucas, S., Poloni, C. (eds.) PPSN 2008. LNCS, vol. 5199, pp. 175–184. Springer, Heidelberg (2008). https://doi.org/10.1007/978-3-540-87700-4_18
9. Fialho, A., Da Costa, L., Schoenauer, M., Sebag, M.: Analyzing bandit-based adaptive operator selection mechanisms. Ann. Math. Artif. Intell. **60**(1), 25–64 (2010)
10. Fialho, Á., Ros, R., Schoenauer, M., Sebag, M.: Comparison-based adaptive strategy selection with bandits in differential evolution. In: Schaefer, R., Cotta, C., Kołodziej, J., Rudolph, G. (eds.) PPSN 2010. LNCS, vol. 6238, pp. 194–203. Springer, Heidelberg (2010). https://doi.org/10.1007/978-3-642-15844-5_20
11. Fialho, A., Schoenauer, M., Sebag, M.: Toward comparison-based adaptive operator selection. In: Proceedings of the 12th Annual Conference on Genetic and Evolutionary Computation, pp. 767–774. GECCO 2010. Association for Computing Machinery, New York, NY, USA (2010)
12. Handoko, S.D., Nguyen, D.T., Yuan, Z., Lau, H.C.: Reinforcement learning for adaptive operator selection in memetic search applied to quadratic assignment problem. In: Proceedings of the Companion Publication of the 2014 Annual Conference on Genetic and Evolutionary Computation, pp. 193–194 (2014)
13. Lan, W., Ye, Z., Ruan, P., Liu, J., Yang, P., Yao, X.: Region-focused memetic algorithms with smart initialization for real-world large-scale waste collection problems. IEEE Trans. Evol. Comput. **26**(4), 704–718 (2021)

14. Li, K., Fialho, A., Kwong, S., Zhang, Q.: Adaptive operator selection with bandits for a multiobjective evolutionary algorithm based on decomposition. IEEE Trans. Evolut. Comput. **18**(1), 114–130 (2013)
15. Liu, J., Tang, K., Yao, X.: Robust optimization in uncertain capacitated arc routing problems: progresses and perspectives. IEEE Comput. Intell. Mag. **16**(1), 63–82 (2021)
16. Liu, J., Zhang, Q., Pei, J., Tong, H., Feng, X., Wu, F.: fSDE: efficient evolutionary optimisation for many-objective aero-engine calibration. Complex Intell. Syst. 1–17 (2021). https://doi.org/10.1007/s40747-021-00374-1
17. Maturana, J., Saubion, F.: A compass to guide genetic algorithms. In: Rudolph, G., Jansen, T., Beume, N., Lucas, S., Poloni, C. (eds.) PPSN 2008. LNCS, vol. 5199, pp. 256–265. Springer, Heidelberg (2008). https://doi.org/10.1007/978-3-540-87700-4_26
18. Sallam, K.M., Elsayed, S.M., Sarker, R.A., Essam, D.L.: Landscape-based adaptive operator selection mechanism for differential evolution. Inf. Sci. **418**, 383–404 (2017)
19. Sharma, M., López-Ibáñez, M., Kazakov, D.: Performance assessment of recursive probability matching for adaptive operator selection in differential evolution. In: Auger, A., Fonseca, C.M., Lourenço, N., Machado, P., Paquete, L., Whitley, D. (eds.) PPSN 2018. LNCS, vol. 11102, pp. 321–333. Springer, Cham (2018). https://doi.org/10.1007/978-3-319-99259-4_26
20. Alcaraz, J.A.S., Ochoa, G., Carpio, M., Puga, H.: Evolvability metrics in adaptive operator selection. In: Proceedings of the 2014 Annual Conference on Genetic and Evolutionary Computation, pp. 1327–1334 (2014)
21. Tan, Z., Li, K., Wang, Y.: Differential evolution with adaptive mutation strategy based on fitness landscape analysis. Inf. Sci. **549**, 142–163 (2021)
22. Tang, K., Wang, J., Li, X., Yao, X.: A scalable approach to capacitated arc routing problems based on hierarchical decomposition. IEEE Trans. Cybern. **47**(11), 3928–3940 (2017)
23. Teng, T.-H., Handoko, S.D., Lau, H.C.: Self-organizing neural network for adaptive operator selection in evolutionary search. In: Festa, P., Sellmann, M., Vanschoren, J. (eds.) LION 2016. LNCS, vol. 10079, pp. 187–202. Springer, Cham (2016). https://doi.org/10.1007/978-3-319-50349-3_13
24. Thierens, D.: An adaptive pursuit strategy for allocating operator probabilities. In: Proceedings of the 7th Annual Conference on Genetic and Evolutionary Computation, pp. 1539–1546 (2005)
25. Zhang, H., Sun, J., Xu, Z.: Learning to mutate for differential evolution. In: 2021 IEEE Congress on Evolutionary Computation (CEC), pp. 1–8 (2021). https://doi.org/10.1109/CEC45853.2021.9504990

Evolutionary Automated Feature Engineering

Guanghui Zhu$^{(\boxtimes)}$, Shen Jiang, Xu Guo, Chunfeng Yuan, and Yihua Huang

State Key Laboratory for Novel Software Technology,
Nanjing University, Nanjing, China
{zgh,cfyuan,yhuang}@nju.edu.cn, {jiangshen,guoxu}@smail.nju.edu.cn

Abstract. Effective feature engineering serves as a prerequisite for many machine learning tasks. Feature engineering, which usually uses a series of mathematical functions to transform the features, aims to find valuable new features that can reflect the insight aspect of data. Traditional feature engineering is a labor-intensive and time-consuming task, which depends on expert domain knowledge and requires iterative manner with trial and error. In recent years, many automated feature engineering (AutoFE) methods have been proposed. These methods automatically transform the original features to a set of new features to improve the performance of the machine learning model. However, existing methods either suffer from computational bottleneck, or do not support high-order transformations and various feature types. In this paper, we propose EAAFE, to the best of our knowledge, the first evolutionary algorithm-based automated feature engineering method. We first formalize the AutoFE problem as a search problem of the optimal feature transformation sequence. Then, we leverage roulette wheel selection, subsequence-exchange-based DNA crossover, and ϵ-greedy-based DNA mutation to achieve evolution. Despite its simplicity, EAAFE is flexible and effective, which can not only support feature transformations for both numerical and categorical features, but also support high-order feature transformations. Extensive experimental results on public datasets demonstrate that EAAFE outperforms the existing AutoFE methods in both effectiveness and efficiency.

Keywords: Automated feature engineering · Evolutionary algorithm

1 Introduction

In many practical machine learning (ML) tasks, the quality of features often directly determines the upper bound of ML algorithms. Feature engineering, which aims to extract valuable features from raw data, serves as a prerequisite for ML tasks. However, feature engineering is a labor-intensive task, which depends on extensive domain knowledge and requires an iterative manner with trial-and -error. Although several ML methods such as deep neural networks can automatically generate high-level representations from raw data, but these

© The Author(s), under exclusive license to Springer Nature Switzerland AG 2022
S. Khanna et al. (Eds.): PRICAI 2022, LNCS 13629, pp. 574–586, 2022.
https://doi.org/10.1007/978-3-031-20862-1_42

high-level features are generally uninterpretable [1]. Because of this, feature engineering is viewed as the most creative and time-consuming stage of ML tasks.

Recently, automated feature engineering (AutoFE) that generates useful features without any human intervention has attracted more and more attention. The core of AutoFE is to search for the best-suited transformations (e.g., unary and binary arithmetic operators) for raw features. The *expansion-reduction* methods [10,15] apply all possible transformations to each feature and select the features based on the improvement in model performance. Due to the composition of feature transformation, such a brute-force method leads to exponential growth in the space of constructed features. TransGraph [13] leverages a hierarchical graph structure to represent the feature transformation space. However, the feature explosion problem also exists, especially in the bottom layer of the transformation graph because each transformation will act on all features. To eliminate the feature explosion problem, LFE [20] employ meta-learning to recommend promising transformations for each feature. However, it does not support the composition of transformations (i.e., high-order transformations). Recently, NFS [2] utilizes reinforcement learning to search a transformation sequence for each feature and achieves the state-of-the-art (SOTA) performance. Nevertheless, the computation efficiency of NFS is low because it needs to train an recurrent neural network (RNN) controller for each feature. Moreover, NFS cannot support feature transformations for categorical features.

Inspired by the success of evolutionary neural architecture search (NAS) [22, 23], in this paper, we propose EAAFE[1] to the best of our knowledge, the first evolutionary algorithm-based automated feature engineering method. We first formalize the feature engineering problem as a search problem of feature transformation sequences. Then, we leverage the *roulette wheel selection* [6] assisted evolutionary algorithm to find the optimal feature transformation sequence for each raw feature. Specifically, we concatenate the feature transformation sequences of all features together and view the concatenated sequence as an individual in the population. The DNA of each individual consists of the encoding of all feature transformation operations. The encoding space is constrained by the feature type (i.e., categorical or numerical). The fitness of individual is determined by the performance of the underlying machine learning model that is trained with the raw and constructed features.

During the evolutionary process, we further propose a subsequence-exchange-based DNA crossover method. For each selected DNA pair, we randomly choose two crossover points in the transformation sequence of each feature, and then exchange the subsequences between these crossover points. After the DNA crossover, we propose a ϵ-greedy-based DNA mutation method. Each transformation operation in the DNA is mutated with a probability ϵ.

Our main contributions are summarized as follows:

- We propose an evolutionary AutoFE framework called EAAFE to automatically search for the optimal transformation sequence for each raw feature.

---

[1] EAAFE is available at https://github.com/PasaLab/EAAFE.

In the evolutionary process, we propose a subsequence-exchange-based DNA crossover method and a ϵ-greedy-based DNA mutation method.
- Despite its simplicity, the proposed evolutionary approach is flexible and effective, which can not only support feature transformation for both numerical and categorical features, but also support high-order feature transformations.
- Extensive experimental results on benchmark classification and regression tasks reveal that EAAFE outperforms other existing AutoFE methods in terms of effectiveness and efficiency.

2   Related Work

2.1   Automated Feature Engineering

A basic approach for automated feature engineering is the *expansion-selection* approach. It predefines a series of feature transformations and applies them to raw features for constructing new features, then combines the constructed features and raw features as candidate features. With a feature selection step, only a subset of candidate features is preserved. The *expansion-selection* approach suffers from combinatorial explosion problem. The representative method based on *expansion-selection* is Deep Feature Synthesis [10]. One Button Machine [15] adopts similar approach to relational databases.

Another basic approach is the *performance-guided* method. After new features are constructed, their performances on the machine learning model are evaluated and only promising features will be preserved. Such an approach needs to explicitly expand the feature space and thus suffers from extensive evaluation overhead. FEADIS [5] adds constructed features greedily relying on a combination of random feature generation and feature selection. ExploreKit [11] employs a feature selection method based on machine learning to rank the newly constructed features and greedily evaluate the most promising ones.

To explore the search space more efficiently, *transformation-graph* based approaches are proposed, which describe feature transformations as a hierarchical graph structure. Each node represents a feature set and each edge represents a transformation. Automated feature engineering can be achieved by iteratively constructing the graph and designing efficient algorithms to explore it. Cognito [14] recommends a series of transformations based on a greedy heuristic tree search. The method in [13] utilizes Q-learning to explore the feature transformation tree. LAFEM [19] formalizes feature engineering as a heterogeneous transformation graph and adopts deep reinforcement learning to achieve AutoFE. Although these methods construct more efficient search space, they also suffer from the feature explosion problem and low search efficiency.

Recently, LFE [20] proposes a meta-learning based method that learns from past feature engineering experiences to recommend promising transformations. DIFER [27] performs AutoFE in a continuous vector space and propose a differentiable search method. NFS [2] utilizes an RNN controller trained by reinforcement learning to transform each raw feature through a series of transformation operations. NFS can capture potentially valuable high-order transformations and achieve the SOTA performance. However, it suffers from slow convergence and low search efficiency, because it needs to train an RNN controller for each raw feature.

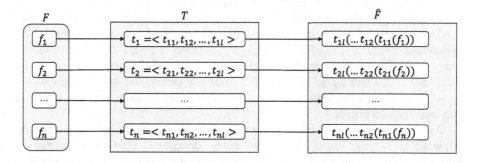

Fig. 1. Feature transformation sequences.

Similar to NFS, the proposed approach EAAFE, models AutoFE as finding the optimal feature transformation sequence for each raw feature. Different from NFS, EAAFE employs a simple and flexible evolutionary algorithm and can achieve better performance in terms of effectiveness and efficiency.

2.2 Evolutionary Algorithm

Evolutionary algorithm (EA) is a kind of random search algorithm that simulates natural selection and evolution processes of creatures. It streamlines the complex evolutionary process and abstracts a set of mathematical models. EA uses an encoding method to represent complex phenomena, and implements heuristic search for complex search spaces according to simplified genetic processes [7]. Traditional evolutionary algorithms first construct a population via randomly initialized individuals, then evaluate each individual to get the fitness, and finally perform mutations to generate a new population [4]. As a result, EA can find the global optimal solution with a high probability [7]. Recently, EA has been successfully adopted to the machine learning pipeline construction [21] and neural architecture search [22,23].

In this paper, we consider encoding constraints during the evolution process [3,17], leading to different search spaces for different feature types. we also propose novel DNA crossover and mutation methods in the context of AutoFE.

3 The Proposed Approach

3.1 Problem Formulation

Given a dataset $\mathcal{D} = \langle F, \mathbf{y} \rangle$ containing raw features $F = \{f_1, f_2, \cdots, f_n\}$ and a target vector $\mathbf{y}$, let $V_M^E(F, \mathbf{y})$ denote the performance of a machine learning model M trained with F and measured by an evaluation metric E. The feature transformation operations mainly contain unary (e.g., *log* and *square*) and binary operations (e.g., *sum* and *multiply*). The transformation performs on more features can be constructed by nesting multiple binary transformations.

The feature set F can be further divided into a categorical feature set F_c and a numerical feature set F_n. Different feature types correspond to different transformation operations. Consequently, we define five types of feature transformation operations, i.e., $T = \{T_c, T_{cc}, T_n, T_{nn}, T_{cn}\}$, where T_n and T_{nn} denote sets of unary and binary transformations performed on numerical features, respectively. T_c and T_{cc} are similar to T_n and T_{nn}, but are performed on categorical features. T_{cn} denotes the aggregate transformation operations between categorical and numerical features.

As shown in Fig. 1, each raw feature f_i corresponds to a transformation sequence $t_i = \langle t_{i1}, \cdots, t_{ij}, \cdots t_{il} \rangle$, where t_{ij} denotes the j-th transformation function in the sequence and l denotes the length of the transformation sequence. Let $T = \{t_1, t_2, \cdots, t_n\}$ denotes the set of feature transformation sequences of all features, which transforms the raw feature set F to $\hat{F}$. We take the union set of F and $\hat{F}$, i.e., $F \cup \hat{F}$, as the newly constructed feature set. As a result, the goal of automated feature engineering is to search for the optimal T which can maximize the performance of the given ML model. Formally as

$$\arg\max_{T} V_M^E(F \cup \hat{F}, \mathbf{y}), \quad \hat{F} = T(F).$$

In practice, the lengths of transformation sequences for different raw features may be required to be different. To support variable sequence lengths, we define a terminate operation, which indicates the early-stopping of the feature transformation sequence. Transformations after it will be ignored. The terminate operation also enables our approach to automatically find the proper length of the transformation sequence.

3.2 Constrained DNA Encoding

During the evolutionary process, we take the concatenated transformation sequence T as an individual in the population, the transformation sequence t_i as a chromosome, and elements in t_i as genes. The DNA of each individual can be viewed as the encoding of all operations in T. The encoding space is represented by non-overlapping integer intervals. Since a binary transformation operator takes two features as input, we convert it to a set of unary transformations. In addition to the operation itself, each converted unary transformation has a feature index attached to it. For example, we can convert the binary transformation *sum* to a set of unary transformations $\{sum(f_1), \cdots, sum(f_i), \cdots, sum(f_n)\}$.

Moreover, different feature types (i.e., categorical or numerical) correspond to different encoding spaces. Let $\mathcal{S}_n$ denote the encoding space of numerical features, which is determined by the feature transformation sets T_n and T_{nn}.

$$\mathcal{S}_n = \{0, \ldots, |T_n|\} \bigcup \{|T_n| + 1, \ldots, |T_n| + |T_{nn}| * |F_n|\}, \qquad (1)$$

where $|\mathcal{T}_n|$ and $|F_n|$ denote the number of transformations and the number of numerical features, respectively. $\mathcal{S}_n$ is the combination of the encoding spaces for the unary and binary transformations. Similarly, let $\mathcal{S}_c$ denote the encoding space of categorical features, which is determined by the feature transformation sets $\mathcal{T}_c$, $\mathcal{T}_{cc}$, and $\mathcal{T}_{cn}$. Thus, $\mathcal{S}_c$ is expressed as:

$$\mathcal{S}_c = \{-|\mathcal{T}_c|, \ldots, 0\} \bigcup \{-|\mathcal{T}_c| - |\mathcal{T}_{cc}| * |F_c| - |\mathcal{T}_{cn}| * |F_n|, \ldots, -|\mathcal{T}_c| - 1\}. \quad (2)$$

In Eq. 1 and Eq. 2, the number 0 indicates the encoding of the terminate operation. And the transformations for numerical features and categorical features are encoded by positive integers and negative integers, respectively. Moreover, $\mathcal{S}_n$ and $\mathcal{S}_c$ are not overlapped.

3.3 Evolutionary Search Algorithm

In this subsection, we introduce the evolutionary search algorithm for automated feature engineering in EAAFE.

In the beginning, we randomly initialize the population according to the encoding space constrained by the feature type. Suppose that the initial population contains p individuals. Then, we perform evolution iteratively. Each evolution is composed of four steps: calculation of DAN fitness, roulette wheel selection, DNA crossover, and DNA mutation.

Calculation of DNA Fitness. The fitness reflects the adaptability of an individual. For an individual T, its fitness is determined by the performance of given ML model $V_M^E(F \cup \hat{F}, \mathbf{y})$, where $\hat{F}$ is constructed by transforming the raw feature set F with T. The evaluation metric E can be F1-score or mean squared error. And the underlying ML model M is set to random forest by default in our experiments. We also evaluate the generalization of EAAFE through different underlying models in Sect. 4.5. Moreover, since the transformation processes of different raw features are independent with each other, we can transform different features in parallel, which can alleviate the combinatorial explosion problem and further improve the efficiency.

Roulette Wheel Selection. [6] To balance the exploration (i.e., population diversity) and exploitation (e.g., higher fitness), we leverage the roulette wheel selection evolutionary algorithm to select N individuals from current population according to the fitness. The core of roulette wheel selection is that the probability of an individual to be selected is proportional to its fitness.

Specifically, let $p(x_i)$ indicate the probability of the individual x_i being selected into the next-generation population. There is

$$p(x_i) = \frac{f(x_i)}{\sum_{j=1}^{m} f(x_j)}, \quad (3)$$

where $f(x_i)$ denotes the fitness of the individual x_i and m is the size of current population. Then, we calculate the cumulative probability of each individual, denoted by $q(x_i)$, i.e.,

$$q(x_i) = \sum_{j=1}^{i} p(x_j). \tag{4}$$

Next, we randomly generate an array A of size m, where each element lies in $(0,1)$. The array A is sorted in ascending order. If $q(x_i) > A[i]$, then x_i will be selected. Otherwise, $q(x_{i+1})$ will be compared with $A[i+1]$ until one individual is selected. Then, we randomly generate an array once again, and the above process is repeated until N individuals are selected.

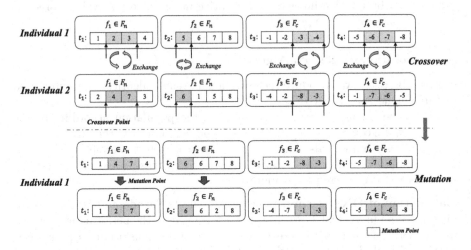

Fig. 2. Crossover and mutation in the evolutionary process.

Subsequence-Exchange-Based DNA Crossover. As shown in Fig. 2, the DNA of an individual is composed of n chromosomes. Each chromosome corresponds to a transformation sequence of a raw feature. In the DNA crossover process, we first randomly select two crossover points in each chromosome. Then, we exchange the subsequences between the crossover points.

ϵ-greedy-Based DNA Mutation. The crossover operation can retain outstanding genes. However, to avoid falling into the local optima, we need to further perform DNA mutation to increase the diversity of population. Every gene (i.e., transformation operation) in the DNA can mutate with a certain probability ϵ. Once a mutation occurs, the selected gene will be replaced by another transformation randomly selected from the same encoding space. We continuously perform crossover and mutation until a new population is generated.

The above-mentioned evolution process is repeated until the predefined number of iterations or the time limit is reached.

4 Experiments

We conduct extensive experiments to evaluate the following aspects: (1) the effectiveness of EAAFE; (2) the efficiency of EAAFE; (3) the effectiveness of the high-order transformation; (4) the generalization performance of EAAFE.

4.1 Experiment Setup

As the SOTA method NFS [2], we use 23 public datasets from OpenML[2], UCI repository[3], and Kaggle[4]. There are 13 classification (C) datasets and 10 regression (R) datasets that have various numbers of features (5 to 57) and instances (500 to 30000). we utilize *Random Forest* as the underlying ML model in all

Table 1. Comparison between EAAFE and other existing AutoFE methods[†]. The best results are marked by bold. F1-Score is reported for classification tasks and 1-(Relative Absolute Error) is reported for regression tasks. "Inst." and "Feat." indicate the number of instances and the number of features, respectively.

Dataset	Source	C\R	Inst.\Feat.	Base	Random	DFS[†]	AutoFeat[†]	NFS[†]	EAAFE
Bikeshare DC	Kaggle	R	10886\11	0.816	0.844	0.821	0.85	0.975	**0.981**
Housing Boston	UCIrvine	R	506\13	0.434	0.445	0.341	0.469	0.501	**0.701**
Airfoil	UCIrvine	R	1503\5	0.496	0.573	0.435	0.596	0.616	**0.81**
OpenML 586	OpenML	R	1000\25	0.662	0.651	0.65	0.728	0.74	**0.792**
OpenML 589	OpenML	R	1000\25	0.644	0.642	0.636	0.686	0.714	**0.757**
OpenML 607	OpenML	R	1000\50	0.634	0.629	0.639	0.67	0.687	**0.734**
OpenML 616	OpenML	R	500\50	0.573	0.571	0.572	0.603	0.592	**0.726**
OpenML 618	OpenML	R	1000\50	0.627	0.617	0.634	0.632	0.64	**0.754**
OpenML 620	OpenML	R	1000\25	0.633	0.618	0.626	0.687	0.675	**0.739**
OpenML 637	OpenML	R	1000\25	0.514	0.527	0.519	0.576	0.569	**0.619**
PimaIndian	UCIrvine	C	768\8	0.756	0.757	0.75	0.763	0.784	**0.802**
SpectF	UCIrvine	C	267\44	0.775	0.828	0.791	0.816	0.85	**0.94**
German credit	UCIrvine	C	1001\24	0.741	0.755	0.749	0.76	0.782	**0.803**
Ionosphere	UCIrvine	C	351\34	0.923	0.934	0.918	0.912	0.952	**0.986**
Credit default	UCIrvine	C	30000\25	0.804	0.806	0.806	0.806	0.805	**0.815**
Messidorfeatures	UCIrvine	C	1150\19	0.658	0.688	0.672	0.736	0.746	**0.797**
Wine quality red	UCIrvine	C	999\12	0.532	0.564	0.548	0.524	0.584	**0.611**
Wine quality white	UCIrvine	C	4900\12	0.494	0.493	0.488	0.502	0.515	**0.524**
SpamBase	UCIrvine	C	4601\57	0.91	0.924	0.91	0.924	0.93	**0.984**
Credit-a	UCIrvine	C	690\6	0.838	0.845	0.819	0.839	0.865	**0.883**
Fertility	UCIrvine	C	100\9	0.853	0.83	0.75	0.79	0.87	**0.91**
Hepatitis	UCIrvine	C	155\6	0.786	0.83	0.826	0.768	0.877	**0.923**
Megawatt1	UCIrvine	C	253\37	0.889	0.897	0.877	0.889	0.913	**0.953**

---

[2] https://www.openml.org/.
[3] https://archive.ics.uci.edu/.
[4] https://www.kaggle.com/.

other experiments except for Sect. 4.5. For evaluation metrics, we use *1-(relative absolute error)* [24] for regression tasks, and *F1-score* for classification tasks. The 5-fold cross validation using random stratified sampling is employed and the average result of 30 runs is reported.

In the evolutionary process, we set the total number of evolution iterations to 5000, the population size to 48, and the mutation probability to 0.1. The length of the transformation sequence for each raw feature is set to 5 for all experiments except the one to verify the effectiveness of high-order transformation. Without loss of generality, we utilize 12 feature transformation operations which cover five types of transformations defined as follows: 1) unary transformations for numerical features: *sqrt*, *minmaxsacler*, *log*, *reciprocal*; 2) binary transformations for numerical features: *add*, *sub*, *mul*, *div*; 3) unary transformation for categorical features: *count*; 4) binary transformations for category features: *cat2cat_count* and *cat2cat_unique*; 5) binary transformation for categorical and numerical features: *cat2num_mean*. Other feature transformation operations can also be flexibly integrated into EAAFE.

Table 2. Comparison between EAAFE and NFS. The number of evaluations is limited to 5000. The best results are marked by bold.

Dataset	Base	NFS	EAAFE	Dataset	Base	NFS	EAAFE
Bikeshare DC	0.816	0.969	**0.98**	German credit	0.741	0.767	**0.803**
Housing boston	0.434	0.478	**0.525**	Ionosphere	0.923	0.949	**0.971**
Airfoil	0.496	0.606	**0.673**	Credit default	0.804	0.808	**0.815**
OpenML 586	0.662	0.662	**0.732**	Messidorfeatures	0.658	0.727	**0.791**
OpenML 589	0.644	0.648	**0.672**	Wine quality red	0.532	0.569	**0.604**
OpenML 607	0.634	0.638	**0.723**	Wine quality white	0.494	0.508	**0.522**
OpenML 616	0.573	0.581	**0.714**	SpamBase	0.91	0.927	**0.98**
OpenML 618	0.627	0.627	**0.748**	Credit-a	0.838	0.861	**0.883**
OpenML 620	0.633	0.633	**0.714**	Fertility	0.853	0.87	**0.91**
OpenML 637	0.514	0.542	**0.601**	Hepatitis	0.786	0.858	**0.923**
PimaIndian	0.756	0.768	**0.802**	Megawatt1	0.889	0.905	**0.945**
SpectF	0.775	0.828	**0.925**				

4.2 Effectiveness of EAAFE

To verify the effectiveness of EAAFE, we compared it with following methods:

- **Base**, which directly uses raw datasets for evaluation.
- **Random**, which generates feature transformation sequences randomly according to the proposed encoding space.
- **DFS** [10]: a well-known *expansion-reduction* method.

- **AutoFeat** [8], a popular Python library for AutoFE and feature selection.
- **NFS** [2], which utilizes the RNN-based controller trained by reinforcement learning to find transformation operations. NFS can achieve better performance than other existing approaches (e.g., TransGraph [13]).

The results of baselines are obtained using open-sourced codes. The experimental settings of these methods, such as the order of transformed features and the evaluation metrics are same as EAAFE for fair comparison. From Table 1, we can see that EAAFE achieves the best performance in all datasets. AutoFeat, NFS and EAAFE achieve average improvements of 4.0%, 8.0% and 17.9% over Base, and average improvements of 2.1%, 5.9% and 15.6% over Random, respectively. The experimental results demonstrate the importance of feature engineering, and the effectiveness of automated feature engineering. Compared with other AutoFE methods, EAAFE is more effective and achieves an average improvement of 10% and 28.2% over Base on regression tasks and classification tasks, respectively. The classification tasks benefit more from the feature engineering. Moreover, EAAFE can achieve highly competitive performance even on relatively larger datasets such as *Credit Default* (with size 30000×25) and *Bikeshare DC* (with size 10886×11).

4.3 Efficiency of EAAFE

The main bottleneck of automated feature engineering methods is the evaluation process which needs to train the ML model from sketch. Moreover, in practice, the computational resource is always limited. In this experiment, in order to verify the efficiency of EAAFE, we limit the total number of evaluations to 5000, and compare EAAFE with NFS .

From Table 2, we can see that EAAFE consistently outperforms NFS and achieves an average improvement of 13% over NFS in the case of limited evaluation budget. Moreover, on most datasets, EAAFE achieves comparable results, but NFS obtains even inferior results compare to the results in Table 1, which can also demonstrate the efficiency and effectiveness of EAAFE.

4.4 Effectiveness of the High-Order Transformation

In order to verify the effectiveness of the high-order transformation, we change the length of transformation sequence from 1 to 6, and report the relative improvements of EAAFE over Base on *Housing Boston, Airfoil, OpenML 586* and *OpenML 616*. We omit other datasets, since the experimental results are similar.

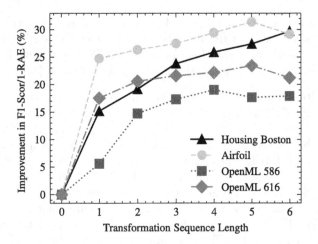

Fig. 3. Improvements of EAAFE over Base with different lengths of feature transformation sequences.

Figure 3 illustrates that the performance of EAAFE increases stably with longer sequence length, but when the sequence length is higher than 5, the performance degrades. Thus, overly complex features will not necessarily bring performance improvement. Moreover, the search space also exponentially increases with the increasing of transformation sequence length, leading to low search efficiency. Therefore, considering both performance and efficiency, we choose 5 as the length of the feature transformation sequence in other experiments.

4.5   Generalization Performance of EAAFE

In the previous experiments, we only use *Random Forest* as the underlying ML model to evaluate EAAFE. In order to verify whether EAAFE can generalize to other frequently-used machine learning models, we further utilize *Lasso Regression* [26], *Linear SVR* [25], and *LightGBM* [12] for regression tasks, and *Logistic Regression* [9], *Linear SVC* [16], and *LightGBM* [12] for classification tasks. Due to lack of space, we omit detailed results and only report the average improvements of EAAFE over all datasets on these models.

Table 3 shows the average improvements of EAAFE on different ML models, which can demonstrate the generalization performance of EAAFE. In conclusion, EAAFE can adapt to various tasks and machine learning models, which is an essential advantage for real-world applications.

Table 3. Average improvements of EAAFE on different ML models.

	Algorithm	Average improvement
Classification	Logistic regression	9.65%
	LinearSVC	26%
	LgbmClassifier	10%
Regression	Lasso regression	14.7%
	LinearSVR	22.1%
	LgbmRegressor	13.8%

5 Conclusion and Future Work

In this paper, we propose an effective and efficient automated feature engineering framework, named EAAFE. We first formalize the AutoFE problem as a search problem of the optimal feature transformation sequence. Then we construct an expressive search space by encoding different types of feature transformations to different sub-spaces, and propose an effective evolutionary algorithm to explore the constrained search space. Moreover, we design novel roulette wheel selection, subsequence-exchange-based crossover, and ϵ-greedy-based mutation strategies for the evolution. Despite its simplicity, EAAFE is flexible and effective, which can support not only both numerical and categorical features, but also high-order feature transformations. Extensive experimental results on public datasets demonstrate that EAAFE consistently outperforms other state-of-the-art AutoFE methods in both effectiveness and efficiency.

In the future, we plan to extend EAAFE to support more feature types and transformation operations. In addition, we intend to employ Ray [18] to parallelize EAAFE for higher efficiency.

Acknowledgment. This work was supported in part by the National Natural Science Foundation of China (No. 62102177 and No. U1811461), the Natural Science Foundation of Jiangsu Province (No. BK20210181), the Key R&D Program of Jiangsu Province (No. BE2021729), and the Collaborative Innovation Center of Novel Software Technology and Industrialization, Jiangsu, China.

References

1. Bengio, Y., Courville, A., Vincent, P.: Representation learning: a review and new perspectives. IEEE Trans. Patt. Anal. Mach. Intell. **35**(8), 1798–1828 (2013)
2. Chen, X., Qiao, B., Zhang, W., Wu, W., Zhang, X.: Neural feature search: a neural architecture for automated feature engineering. In: 2019 IEEE International Conference on Data Mining (ICDM) (2019)
3. Coello, C.A.C.: Theoretical and numerical constraint-handling techniques used with evolutionary algorithms: a survey of the state of the art. Comput. Methods Appl. Mech. Eng. **191**(11–12), 1245–1287 (2002)
4. Deb, K., Anand, A., Joshi, D.: A computationally efficient evolutionary algorithm for real-parameter optimization. Evol. Comput. **10**(4), 371–395 (2002)

5. Dor, O., Reich, Y.: Strengthening learning algorithms by feature discovery. Inf. Sci. **189**, 176–190 (2012)
6. Goldberg, D.E.: Genetic algorithms. Pearson Education India (2006)
7. Holland, J.H., et al.: Adaptation in Natural and Artificial Systems: An Introductory Analysis with Applications to Biology, Control, and Artificial Intelligence. MIT press, Cambridge (1992)
8. Horn, F., Pack, R., Rieger, M.: The autofeat python library for automated feature engineering and selection. arXiv preprint arXiv:1901.07329 (2019)
9. Hosmer Jr, D.W., Lemeshow, S., Sturdivant, R.X.: Applied logistic regression, vol. 398. John Wiley & Sons (2013)
10. Kanter, J.M., Veeramachaneni, K.: Deep feature synthesis: towards automating data science endeavors, pp. 1–10 (2015)
11. Katz, G., Shin, E.C.R., Song, D.: ExploreKit: automatic feature generation and selection, pp. 979–984 (2016)
12. Ke, G., et al.: LightGBM: a highly efficient gradient boosting decision tree. In: Advances in Neural Information Processing Systems, pp. 3146–3154 (2017)
13. Khurana, U., Samulowitz, H., Turaga, D.S.: Feature engineering for predictive modeling using reinforcement learning, pp. 3407–3414 (2018)
14. Khurana, U., Turaga, D.S., Samulowitz, H., Parthasrathy, S.: Cognito: automated feature engineering for supervised learning, pp. 1304–1307 (2016)
15. Lam, H.T., Thiebaut, J., Sinn, M., Chen, B., Mai, T., Alkan, O.: One button machine for automating feature engineering in relational databases. arXiv: Databases (2017)
16. Luts, J., Ojeda, F., De Plas, R.V., De Moor, B., Van Huffel, S., Suykens, J.A.K.: A tutorial on support vector machine-based methods for classification problems in chemometrics. Anal. Chim. Acta **665**(2), 129–145 (2010)
17. Michalewicz, Z., Schoenauer, M.: Evolutionary algorithms for constrained parameter optimization problems. Evol. Comput. **4**(1), 1–32 (1996)
18. Moritz, P., et al.: Ray: a distributed framework for emerging AI applications, pp. 561–577 (2018)
19. Sutton, R.S., Barto, A.G.: Reinforcement Learning: An Introduction. MIT press (2018)
20. Nargesian, F., Samulowitz, H., Khurana, U., Khalil, E.B., Turaga, D.S.: Learning feature engineering for classification, pp. 2529–2535 (2017)
21. Olson, R.S., Moore, J.H.: TPOT: a tree-based pipeline optimization tool for automating machine learning, pp. 66–74 (2016)
22. Real, E., Aggarwal, A., Huang, Y., Le, Q.V.: Regularized evolution for image classifier architecture search. In: Proceedings of the AAAI Conference on Artificial Intelligence, vol. 33, pp. 4780–4789 (2019)
23. Real, E., et al.: Large-scale evolution of image classifiers. In: Proceedings of the 34th International Conference on Machine Learning, pp. 2902–2911 (2017)
24. Shcherbakov, M.V., Brebels, A., Shcherbakova, N.L., Tyukov, A.P., Kamaev, V.A.: A survey of forecast error measures. World Appl. Sci. J. **24**(24), 171–176 (2013)
25. Smola, A.J., Scholkopf, B.: A tutorial on support vector regression. Stat. Comput. **14**(3), 199–222 (2004)
26. Tibshirani, R.: Regression shrinkage and selection via the lasso. J. Royal Stat. Soc.: Ser. B (Methodol.) **58**(1), 267–288 (1996)
27. Zhu, G., Xu, Z., Yuan, C., Huang, Y.: DIFER: differentiable automated feature engineering. In: First Conference on Automated Machine Learning (Main Track) (2022)

Author Index

Printed in the United States
by Baker & Taylor Publisher Services

Printed in the United States
by Baker & Taylor Publisher Services